Consumer Behavior and Marketing Strategy

Consumer Behavior and Marketing Strategy

THIRD EDITION

J. Paul Peter
University of Wisconsin, Madison

Jerry C. Olson
Pennsylvania State University

IRWIN
Homewood, IL 60430
Boston, MA 02116

The first edition of this book was published under the title
Consumer Behavior: Marketing Strategy Perspectives

Senior sponsoring editor: *Stephen M. Patterson*
Developmental editor: *Andy Winston*
Marketing manager: *Scott J. Timian*
Project editor: *Karen Murphy*
Production manager: *Irene H. Sotiroff*
Designer: *Mercedes Santos*
Art coordinator: *Mark Malloy*
Photo research coordinator: *Patricia A. Seefelt*
Compositor: *Better Graphics, Inc.*
Typeface: *10/12 Janson*
Printer: *R. R. Donnelley & Sons Company*

Library of Congress Cataloging-in-Publication Data

Peter, J. Paul.
Consumer behavior and marketing strategy / J. Paul Peter, Jerry C. Olson. – 3rd ed.
p. cm. – (The Irwin series in marketing)
Includes bibliographical references and indexes.
ISBN 0-256-10567-7
1. Consumer behavior. 2. Marketing. I. Olson, Jerry C. (Jerry Corrie), 1944– . II. Title. III. Series.
HF5415.3.P468 1993
658.8'342 – dc20 92-20169

Printed in the United States of America
1 2 3 4 5 6 7 8 9 0 D O C 9 8 7 6 5 4 3 2

ROSE AND ANGIE
BECKY, MATT, AND SETH

THE IRWIN SERIES IN MARKETING

Consulting Editor Gilbert A. Churchill, Jr.
University of Wisconsin – Madison

Alreck & Settle
The Survey Research Handbook
Second Edition

Belch & Belch
Introduction to Advertising and Promotion
Second Edition

Berkowitz, Kerin, Hartley, & Rudelius
Marketing
Third Edition

Bernhardt & Kinnear
Cases in Marketing Management
Fifth Edition

Bingham & Raffield
Business to Business Marketing Management
First Edition

Bovee & Arens
Contemporary Advertising
Fourth Edition

Boyd & Walker
Marketing Management: A Strategic Approach
First Edition

Boyd, Westfall, & Stasch
Marketing Research: Text and Cases
Seventh Edition

Burstiner
Basic Retailing
Second Edition

Cadotte
The Market Place: A Strategic Marketing Simulation
First Edition

Cateora
International Marketing
Eighth Edition

Churchill, Ford, & Walker
Sales Force Management
Fourth Edition

Cole
Consumer and Commercial Credit Management
Ninth Edition

Cravens
Strategic Marketing
Third Edition

Cravens & Lamb
Strategic Marketing Management Cases
Fourth Edition

Crawford
New Products Management
Third Edition

Dillon, Madden, & Firtle
Essentials of Marketing Research
First Edition

Dillon, Madden, & Firtle
Marketing Research in a Marketing Environment
Second Edition

Engel, Warshaw, & Kinnear
Promotional Strategy
Seventh Edition

Faria, Nulsen, & Roussos
Compete
Fourth Edition

Futrell
ABC's of Selling
Third Edition

Futrell
Fundamentals of Selling
Fourth Edition

Hawkins, Best, & Coney
Consumer Behavior
Fifth Edition

Kurtz & Dodge
Professional Selling
Sixth Edition

Lambert & Stock
Strategic Logistics Management
Third Edition

Lehmann & Winer
Analysis for Marketing Planning
Second Edition

Lehmann
Marketing Research and Analysis
Fourth Edition

Levy & Weitz
Retailing Management
First Edition

Mason, Mayer, & Wilkinson
Modern Retailing
Sixth Edition

Mason, Mayer, & Ezell
Retailing
Fourth Edition

Mason & Perrault
The Marketing Game
Second Edition

McCarthy & Perrault
Basic Marketing: A Global-Managerial Approach
Eleventh Edition

McCarthy & Perrault
Essentials of Marketing
Fifth Edition

Peter & Olson
Consumer Behavior and Marketing Strategy
Third Edition

Peter & Donnelly
A Preface to Marketing Management
Fifth Edition

Peter & Donnelly
Marketing Management: Knowledge and Skills
Third Edition

Quelch & Farris
Cases in Advertising and Promotion Management
Third Edition

Quelch, Dolan, & Kosnik
Marketing Management: Text and Cases
First Edition

Smith & Quelch
Ethics in Marketing Management
First Edition

Stanton, Spiro, & Buskirk
Management of a Sales Force
Eighth Edition

Thompson & Stappenbeck
The Marketing Strategy Game
First Edition

Walker, Boyd, & Larreche
Marketing Strategy: Planning and Implementation
First Edition

Weitz, Castleberry, & Tanner
Selling: Building Partnerships
First Edition

PREFACE

Consumer Behavior and Marketing Strategy, third edition, is designed for both undergraduate and graduate courses that focus on consumer behavior theory and research and their use in development marketing strategies.

These courses are typically taught to junior- or senior-level undergraduates at four-year schools, sophomores at two-year schools, and second-year MBA students. Most of these students will have taken a general introductory course in marketing principles, and many will have some background in the social sciences.

The major purpose of the text is to give students the knowledge and skills necessary to perform detailed consumer analyses that could be used for understanding markets and developing effective marketing strategies.

WHY WE WROTE THIS BOOK

Having researched and taught in the area for many years, we saw a need for a text with a more integrative, strategic marketing approach to consumer behavior. Although writing a textbook is never easy, we undertook the task to resolve several specific problems we saw in the existing consumer behavior texts.

- **A consumer behavior text should be more than just a review of the consumer behavior literature.** The history of consumer behavior certainly can be a fascinating topic but we believe that a focus on *marketing strategies* is more appropriate, particularly when the consumer behavior course is taught within a marketing curriculum. Experience has taught us that the strategic approach is more valuable for undergraduates and master's students training for jobs in marketing management.

- **A consumer behavior course should be well integrated into the marketing curriculum.** Although the consumer behavior course is typically housed in marketing departments, it often stands alone as a course in applied or cognitive psychology. Many consumer behavior texts do not make it clear how the psychological and behavioral concepts can be used to develop and evaluate marketing strategies. The application and implications of the material are often unclear. We find, however, that today's marketing and business students want courses more relevant for the types of marketing decisions managers must make.

- **A consumer behavior text should show how the topics fit together and can be used by a manager to develop marketing strategies.** Too often students leave a consumer behavior course with little knowledge of the way topics fit together and how the information can be used. We wanted to present an *integrated view of consumer analysis*, rather than the fragmented knowledge of separate theories and concepts often found in other texts.

Why This Text Differs from Traditional Consumer Behavior Books

To prepare a text that would meet our objectives and overcome the problems described above, we had to make several changes from traditional texts.

- First, we deemphasized or omitted dated consumer behavior topics and research that have little to do with developing marketing strategies.
- Second, we included topics and research from other areas that are not covered in traditional consumer behavior texts but have useful implications for developing marketing strategy.
- Third, we created some new ideas and frameworks that we felt would be useful for educating future marketing managers.

The Wheel of Consumer Analysis

- Fourth, we developed a simple model that encompasses the major elements of consumer analysis and can be used to integrate the field. This model, shown on the previous page, includes four major interacting elements that must be considered in any consumer analysis: **affect and cognition, behavior,** the **environment,** and **marketing strategy.** We believe the Wheel of Consumer Analysis is a powerful tool for analyzing consumer behavior. It can be used as a conceptual tool for understanding consumers and for guiding the development of marketing strategies.

Text Organization

The text is organized around the Wheel of Consumer Analysis.

- **Section One** provides an overview of the Wheel of Consumer Analysis and explains how each of the four elements influences the other elements in a dynamic, reciprocal manner.
- **Section Two**, devoted to *affect and cognition*, provides a current view of consumers' internal psychological processes and their relevance for marketing strategy development.
- **Section Three** discusses *behavior* and provides a detailed treatment of the overt actions of consumers and how these actions influence and are influenced by marketing strategies.
- **Section Four** is devoted to the *environment* and analyzes stimuli external to consumers that influence how they think, feel, and act.
- **Section Five** discusses *marketing strategies* by which marketing stimuli (such as products, advertisements, stores, and price information) are created and placed in consumer environments in order to influence consumer affect, cognitions, and behaviors.

Special Features of the Text

This book contains a variety of pedagogical aids to enhance student learning and facilitate the application of consumer behavior concepts to marketing practice:

- **Introductory scenarios.** Each chapter begins with an interesting example that discusses a real-world situation involving some aspect of consumer behavior. Then, each chapter ends with a **"Back to . . ."** section that summarizes how the chapter material relates to the opening example. This clearly shows students how the chapter concepts are relevant for marketing strategy decisions. This feature has been very successful in generating student interest and increasing understanding of the chapter material.

- **Examples.** Reviewers have applauded the inclusion of many examples of marketing strategies used by actual companies. These examples demonstrate how consumer behavior concepts are used by marketers. Also, they increase student interest in the material.
- **Highlights.** Each chapter contains longer examples called Highlights that show the relevance of consumer behavior concepts and give students real-life examples of marketing strategies. All Highlights are referenced in the text but are self-contained for individual study.
- **Key terms and concepts.** We include a list of key terms and concepts and the page on which they are discussed at the end of each chapter to facilitate study of the material. These terms and concepts are also boldfaced within the chapter text.
- **Marketing Strategy in Action.** Each chapter concludes with a minicase that focuses on consumer analysis issues facing real companies. These short cases are included to help integrate consumer behavior information into the marketing strategy development process. The discussion questions accompanying the minicases can be used for written assignments or to stimulate in-class discussion.
- **Review and discussion questions.** Each chapter contains a series of review and discussion questions that emphasize the understanding and application of chapter material to strategic marketing issues. These can be used for written assignments, in-class discussions, essay exam questions, or for student self-study.
- **Annotated additional reading.** For students who wish to study specific topics covered in a chapter more deeply, we selected readings, articles, books, and other materials appropriate for them. The readings are briefly annotated to help direct students to appropriate sources. Chapters also contain selected **footnotes** for the most current and useful references and additional sources of information.
- **Glossary.** The text contains a glossary of key consumer behavior terms. Many of these definitions were previously prepared by the authors for the American Marketing Association's *Dictionary of Marketing Terms.*

Changes in the Third Edition

We made a number of changes and improvements in the third edition without changing the key features that give *Consumer Behavior and Marketing Strategy* its unique character. For instance, we retained the Wheel of Consumer Analysis, the up-to-date conceptual coverage, the clear writing style, and the many current, real-world examples.

Changes in this edition are the result of research interviews with faculty and students as well as suggestions from knowledgeable reviewers. These changes include:

- **New chapter on culture.** Recognizing the increased importance of understanding cultural factors for developing international marketing strategies, we have written a separate new chapter on the topic. This chapter offers a state-of-the-art approach to understanding cultural and cross-cultural analysis.
- **Major revision of the environment section.** Comments from adopters and reviewers of the second edition suggested that the text could be improved by increasing the coverage of topics in the environmental section of the text. We added a signficant amount of new material to all of the chapters in this section.
- **Other chapter revisions.** We revised all of the chapters to reflect recent developments in consumer research. Several of the chapters were substantially revised to accommodate topics receiving increased research attention. We continued to simplify presentation of chapter material where possible.
- **New material.** We included a number of new introductory vignettes, highlights, and cases dealing with marketing problems faced by well-known companies.
- **Updating.** We continue to believe that only recent research of high quality should be integrated into our text and taught to students. Thus, we carefully updated many examples and references to maintain our emphasis on current ideas and concepts.

Instructional Aids

The text package contains two major instructional aids. These include:

- **Instructor's Manual.** We have carefully revised the Instructor's Manual to reflect the changes in this edition. The Manual contains a variety of useful information and suggestions for teaching each of the chapters in the text, plus transparency masters, notes for the Marketing Strategy in Action cases, and information for designing several types of term projects.
- **Manual of Tests and CompuTest.** The revised Manual of Tests consists of 2,000 multiple-choice and short-answer questions. "Rationales" for the answers to some of the more difficult application questions have been included. The Manual of Tests has been thoroughly reviewed to ensure a reliable, high-quality teaching tool for the instructor. In addition, CompuTest offers the instructor the option of constructing a computer-generated test from the questions in the Manual of Tests.

Acknowledgments

We are indebted to many people who contributed to the development of the current and previous editions of this book. First, we thank our students for *their* contribution to *our* education. Second, we thank Gilbert A. Churchill, Jr., Irwin Consulting Editor, Steve Patterson, Sponsoring Editor, and Eleanore Snow and Andy Winston, Irwin Developmental Editors, for their encouragement, constructive criticism, and patience throughout the preparation of these editions. Finally, we thank the reviewers of this text for the time, effort, and insights they offered. They include:

M. Wayne Alexander
Moorhead State University

Delores Barsellotti
California State Polytechnic University—Pomona

Mickey Belch
San Diego State University

Russell Belk
University of Utah

Ray Burke
University of Pennsylvania

James Cagley
The University of Tulsa

Louis M. Capella
Mississippi State University

Ellen Day
University of Georgia

Mike Etzel
University of Notre Dame

Andrew M. Forman
Hoestra University

Bill Gaidis
Marquette University

Meryl Gardner
New York University

Peter L. Gillett
University of Central Florida

Kenneth A. Heischmidt
Southeast Missouri State University

Robert M. Isotalo
Lakehead University

Walter Nord
University of South Florida

William S. Piper
The University of Southern Mississippi—Gulf Park

David W. Schumann
University of Tennessee

Shirley M. Stretch
California State University, Los Angeles

Cathie H. Tinney
University of Texas of the Permian Basin

Gail Tom
California State University

J. Dennis White
Florida State University

Arch Woodside
Tulane University

Tommy Whittler
University of Kentucky

In addition to the reviewers named above, we also found feedback from individual users of the first and second editions—both professors and students—to be invaluable in helping us shape this third edition to meet your needs and interests. We would appreciate your comments and suggestions on the third edition.

J. Paul Peter

Jerry C. Olson

Contents in Brief

Contents

SECTION 1

A Perspective on Consumer Behavior

1

SECTION 2

AFFECT AND COGNITION AND MARKETING STRATEGY

41

A Perspective on Consumer Behavior

1

SECTION

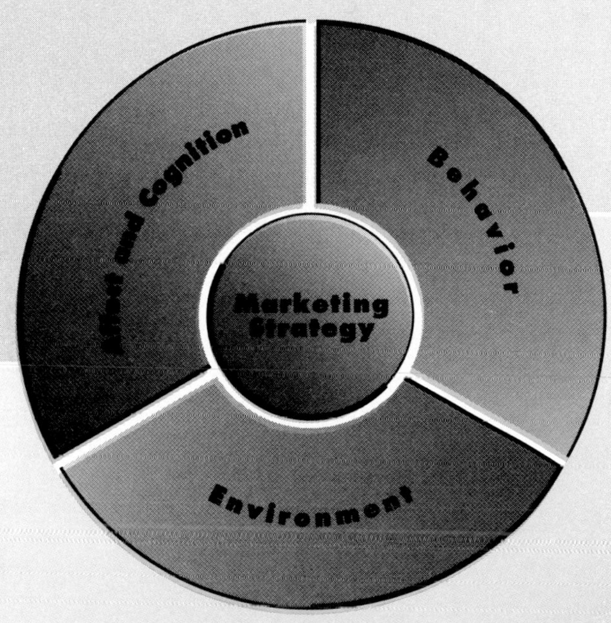

Introduction to Consumer Behavior and Marketing Strategy

CHAPTER 1

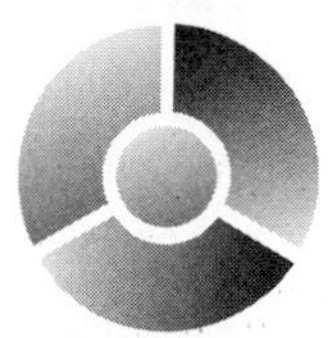

STAYING CLOSE TO CUSTOMERS: LESSONS FROM "THE DEAD"

In the 1990s, U.S. companies have increasingly realized that satisfying consumers with quality products and offering superior customer service is the foundation for success in the highly competitive business world. Maybe these companies should take some lessons from the rock 'n' roll group the Grateful Dead, which may be one of the sharpest business operations in popular music.

Although the group has an image of being zonked-out hippies from the 1960s, it has survived and prospered for nearly 30 years by staying close to its customers and offering services that few other bands would even consider. For example, the band realized in the early 1980s that some fans, especially those in their 30s and 40s who have jobs and families, can't wait in line for tickets. To make sure those people get a chance to see the band, the Dead started selling some tickets—typically 20 to 40 percent of a show—by mail. The band also set up recorded telephone messages to tell mail-order fans about the shows.

Another customer service arose when the band realized many fans—known as Deadheads—want to record concerts. No other rock 'n' roll band would even think of letting fans tape shows for fear of hurting record sales. But the Dead ropes off a portion of the

floor at every show so about 200 "tapeheads" with special tickets can set up recorders. "It doesn't hurt our record sales," says guitarist Bob Weir, 43. "Every time we approach a song (in concert) it is different. The tapeheads want copies of them all." And the tapeheads, naturally, keep buying tickets to the band's concerts.

The Dead keeps its 140-song repertoire fresh by almost never playing a song the same way twice, and shows change every night. A different show each night encourages fans to buy tickets for all shows in a city. The band's shows last three to three-and-a-half hours versus two hours or less for many headliners. Yet the Grateful Dead keeps ticket prices at or just below other performers.

Despite the band's less-than-saintly image, the Dead can offer tips on community relations. Several years ago when "Touch of Grey" became the Dead's first top 10 hit, the scene outside the show went from wild to crazy. Hawkers selling T-shirts and jewelry took over parking lots. Neighborhoods were overrun. The number of arrests got more attention than the music.

The Dead responded in what critics would have to agree was a remarkable way. Weir and others made radio ads urging people not to come unless they had tickets. Security guards were encouraged to make it hard to sell anything outside shows. Local police officials were briefed by tour manager Cameron Sears about what to expect and how to deal with Dead fans. The band did these things for three reasons: to gain some control over the crowds, to cut down unauthorized merchandise sales, and to improve relations with the cities where it plays.

Source: Mark Memmott, "Sales, Service and Rock 'n' Roll," *USA Today,* March 22, 1991, pp. 1B, 2B.

Do you think the Grateful Dead understands its customers and has a profitable marketing strategy? Marketers have long argued that the marketing concept is the appropriate philosophy for conducting business. Simply stated, the **marketing concept** suggests an organization should satisfy consumer needs and wants in order to make profits. To implement the marketing concept, organizations must understand their customers and stay close to them to provide products and services that consumers will purchase and use appropriately.

For many years, the marketing concept was not fully understood or implemented properly by U.S. firms. Often, even firms that accepted the marketing concept in principle did not recognize that the marketing concept required the organization to change its existing practices dramatically. In general, these firms viewed implementing the marketing concept as a marketing task rather than something in which the entire organization had to be involved. While these companies did marketing and consumer research, this research was seldom used as the basis for designing not just the marketing strategy but also the entire organizational strategy.

Today, many of the most successful companies in the world have become so by designing their entire organizations to serve consumers and stay close to them.[1] These companies are committed to developing quality products and services and selling them at a price that gives consumers high value. In these companies, the marketing department and also design, engineering, production, human resources, finance, and other departments are focused on doing their jobs in ways that enhance the value of products to consumers. Some firms have found they can actually increase product quality and reduce costs at the same time, and they encourage employees throughout the company to seek ways to do so. Other firms first determine what consumers want and how much they are willing to pay for a product and then design, produce, and market the best quality product they can for the price consumers are willing to pay. Figure 1.1 discusses four companies that owe their survival and success to focusing on customers.

Companies are making changes to serve consumers better for three major reasons. First, the dramatic success of Japanese companies, such as Toyota and Sony, that focus on providing consumers value-laden products has spurred other companies to also do so. During the 1960s and 1970s, many U.S. companies could sell almost anything they could produce. Consumers accepted the level of quality of goods and services produced by U.S. companies as being as good as could be expected. However, as American consumers discovered the superior quality and lower prices of many Japanese products, they began to realize that many American products offered inferior value, and they shifted to purchasing foreign-made goods. Many U.S. companies had to redesign their organizations to serve consumers in order to survive and compete not only in U.S. but also in world markets.

The second major reason for the shift to focusing on consumers is the dramatic increase in the quality of consumer and marketing research. In the past, companies often did not have detailed information on the actual purchasers and users of their products. While they did research to investigate new product concepts and to try to understand consumers, often this research was not continuous and did not identify the firm's actual customers. Today, computer technology and scanner and other data sources have made it possible for companies to know personally who their customers are and the effects on them of marketing strategy and changes in it. Both manufacturers and retailers can

FIGURE 1.1
Getting Close and Staying Close to Customers

A number of leading U.S. companies owe their success and profitability to designing the organization to stay close to customers. Below are a few examples.

Harley-Davidson, Inc.

By the early 1980s, Japanese motorcycle manufacturers dominated the U.S. market. The Japanese bikes were more sophisticated, of better quality, and cheaper than Harleys. Harley-Davidson was days away from filing for bankruptcy by the end of 1985. However, it got refinanced and continued to work hard to improve the quality of its motorcycles through bettering the design, getting employees more committed to quality, working with dealers, and interacting continuously with consumers to get feedback on its products and ideas for improvements. By 1990, Harley-Davidson dominated the superheavyweight motorcycle market with a market share of over 62 percent.

Monroe Auto Equipment

In the past decade, nine companies from Japan and Europe stormed the U.S. market for shock absorbers and struts—under-the-body parts that give cars a smooth ride. Monroe Auto Equipment recognized that to survive in this mature market, it had to increase the quality of its products and reduce costs. Since 1986, productivity in its 36 plants increased 26 percent, annual sales increased 70 percent to $900 million, and profits increased 20 percent. In the $1.5 billion-a-year market, Monroe sells more than half of all the replacement shocks and close to one third of those put on new cars. Monroe learned how to build better quality products by studying Japanese methods and focused on having zero defects, which satisfies both organizational and consumer buyers.

Nike

While there are many strong competitors in the sports shoe market, Nike is at the top. In 1990, sales jumped 31 percent to $2.2 billion, about $75 million higher than archrival Reebok International. Nike's profits were $243 million compared to $177 million for Reebok. The company sells over 800 models for use in about 25 sports. It makes three lines of basketball shoes, each expressing what Nike calls a different attitude. The Air Jordan (retail price $125) is for consumers who want to follow in the footsteps of the Chicago Bulls superstar. The Flight (up to $115) is for players who value the lightest Nikes, while the Force (up to $150) incorporates the latest designs, such as a custom air bladder, for consumers who want a snug fit. The company updates its shoes at least every six months to tempt new customers to lace on new pairs before last year's wear out. By carefully segmenting the market, coming out with frequent innovations and style changes, and continually researching to develop the most effective and stylish athletic shoes, Nike offers quality products that consumers want.

Wal-Mart

Sam Walton, founder of Wal-Mart, has a simple idea on how to be a successful retailer: be an agent for consumers, find out what they want, and sell it to them for the lowest possible price. To do so effectively, Wal-Mart has developed a corporate culture focused on consumers. The company has a sophisticated computerized warehouse and inventory system that carefully tracks sales and communicates sales data with manufacturers to ensure stores remain well stocked with high-demand merchandise. Wal-Mart bargains hard with manufacturers to get the lowest possible price and keeps overhead low, in fact, the lowest in the industry. Wal-Mart stays close to customers. Is it any wonder that in 1991 it became the No. 1 retailer in the United States with sales of over $32 billion?

Sources: John Kekis, "Business Rev Charges Harley after Long Slump," *Wisconsin State Journal,* June 1, 1991, p. 6B; Erik Calonius, "Smart Moves by Quality Champs," *Fortune,* 1991, pp. 24–28; Bill Saporito, "Is Wal-Mart Unstoppable?" *Fortune,* May 6, 1991, pp. 50–59.

HIGHLIGHT 1.1

MAILING LIST OF CONSUMERS

Companies today can buy or rent a variety of mailing lists to focus their marketing efforts on individual consumers. These mailing lists include the names and addresses of consumers who have performed particular behaviors that might indicate they would be interested in the company's products. For example, some of the lists available for sale include:

- 26,912 Southern California investors who own at least $100,000 worth of "jumbo" certificates of deposit.
- 95,293 people who visited the Basketball Hall of Fame and bought a souvenir at the novelty shop.
- 140,426 grandparents who bought Johnson & Johnson child-development toys.
- 323,050 users of Wordstar, a computer software program.
- 356,330 contributors to the Democratic National Committee.
- 861,345 owners of Apple II computers. A separate list of 253,448 women who bought Apple products.
- 2.4 million people who ordered by phone using a credit card.
- 11 million people who recently moved.
- 15 million families with children.
- 30 million mail-order shoppers.

Source: Robert S. Boyd, "Nearly Everyone's on Somebody's List," *Wisconsin State Journal*, July 8, 1990, p. 4B.

now carefully track consumer reactions to new products and services and evaluate marketing strategies better than ever before. Thus, companies are now better able to actually implement the marketing concept. Highlight 1.1 offers several examples of mailing lists companies can buy that offer information about consumers.

A third reason for the increased emphasis on consumers is the development of consumer behavior research. Both the number and sophistication of theories, concepts, and models to describe and understand consumer behavior has grown dramatically in recent years. While there is not a consensus on which theories or approaches are best, marketers do have a greater variety of useful ideas for understanding consumers than they did in the past.

In sum, many successful companies have recognized the importance of consumers and have sophisticated approaches and detailed data from which to develop organizational and marketing strategies. All of this should convince you that the consumer behavior course you are about to take is an important part of your business education. In the remainder of this chapter, we will discuss the nature of consumer behavior and the parties involved in studying and analyzing

HIGHLIGHT 1.2

Staying Close to Customers—For a Long Time!

Some analysts argue that brand names are becoming less important to consumers. However, some companies have been able to stay close to their customers and keep their brands on top for many years. Here is a list of some brands that have been sales leaders for many decades.

Category	Leading Brand in 1923	Current Rank
Cameras	Kodak	No. 1
Canned fruit	Del Monte	No. 1
Chewing gum	Wrigley's	No. 1
Crackers	Nabisco	No. 1
Razors	Gillette	No. 1
Soft drinks	Coca-Cola	No. 1
Soap	Ivory	No. 1
Soup	Campbell	No. 1
Toothpaste	Colgate	No. 2

Source: Mark Landler, Zachary Schiller, and Lois Therrien, "What's in a Name?: Less and Less," *Business Week*, July 8, 1991, pp. 66–67.

it. We will also investigate some relationships between consumer behavior and marketing strategy and the value of this course for a successful career. While this text focuses on consumer behavior and marketing strategy, it should not be forgotten that employees in every business function should be involved in serving consumers. Highlight 1.2 lists some companies that have stayed close to their customers for many years.

What Is Consumer Behavior?

The American Marketing Association defines **consumer behavior** as "the dynamic interaction of affect and cognition, behavior, and environmental events by which human beings conduct the exchange aspects of their lives."[2] There are at least three important ideas in this definition: (1) consumer behavior is dynamic; (2) it involves interactions between affect and cognitions, behaviors, and environmental events; and (3) it involves exchanges.

The interaction of affect and cognition, behavior, and environment determines exchanges.

Consumer Behavior Is Dynamic

First, the definition emphasizes that consumer behavior is *dynamic*. This means individual consumers, consumer groups, and society at large are constantly changing and evolving across time. This has important implications for the study of consumer behavior as well as for developing marketing strategies. In terms of studying consumer behavior, one implication is that generalizations about consumer behavior are usually limited to specific time periods, products, and individuals or groups. Thus, students of consumer behavior must be careful not to overgeneralize theories and research findings.

In terms of developing marketing strategies, the dynamic nature of consumer behavior implies that one should not expect the same marketing strategy to work all of the time, across all products, markets, and industries. While this may seem obvious, many companies have failed to recognize the need to adapt their strategies in different markets. For example, Philip Morris failed to make 7UP a leading brand although it used strategies that had been successful in other industries.

Further, a strategy that is successful at one point may fail miserably at another point. For example, the American automobile industry was very successful in selling automobiles of relatively low quality—until American consumers learned about the superior quality and value of Japanese cars. This has resulted in American manufacturers working hard to improve the quality of their offerings. As health-conscious consumers learned about the cholesterol problems associated with palm or coconut oil, Kellogg's adapted its marketing strategy by removing these oils from its Cracklin' Oat Bran. In sum, it is the

Nonprofit organizations also use marketing strategies to achieve their objectives.

dynamic nature of consumer behavior that makes marketing strategy development such an exciting, yet challenging, task.

Consumer Behavior Involves Interactions

A second important point emphasized in the definition of consumer behavior is that it involves *interactions* between affect and cognitions, behaviors, and environmental events. This means that to understand consumers and develop superior marketing strategies, we must understand what they think (cognitions) and feel (affect), what they do (behaviors), and the things and places (environmental events) that influence and are influenced by what consumers think, feel, and do. We believe it is shortsighted to analyze only the effects of an environmental event on affect, cognitions, or behaviors, as is commonly done in basic research. Instead, whether we are evaluating a single consumer, a target market, or an entire society, analysis of all three elements is useful for understanding and developing marketing strategies.

Consumer Behavior Involves Exchanges

A final point emphasized in the definition of consumer behavior is that it involves *exchanges* between human beings. This makes the definition of consumer behavior consistent with current definitions of marketing that also emphasize exchange. In fact, the role of marketing is to create exchanges with consumers by formulating and implementing marketing strategies.

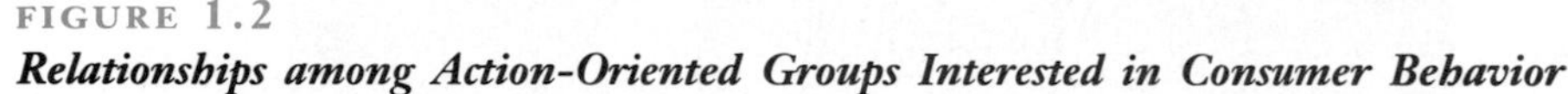

FIGURE 1.2
Relationships among Action-Oriented Groups Interested in Consumer Behavior

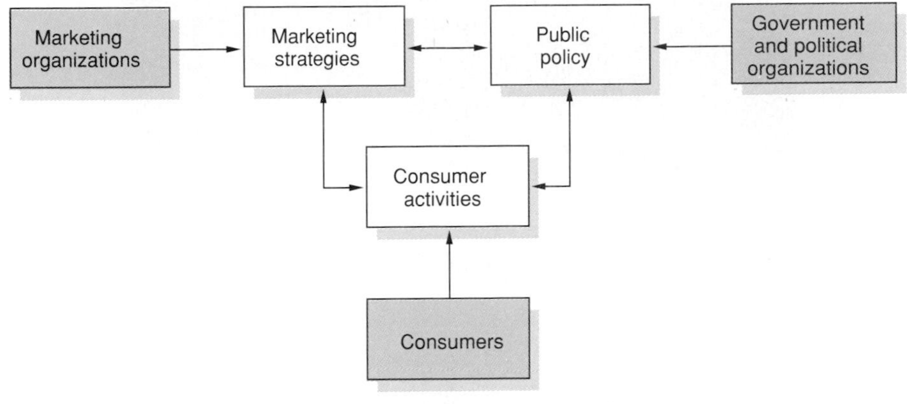

Who Is Interested in Consumer Behavior?

Two broad groups are interested in consumer behavior – a basic research group and an action-oriented group. The basic research group is mainly composed of academic researchers interested in studying consumer behavior as a way of developing a unique body of knowledge about this aspect of human behavior. These researchers have backgrounds in anthropology, sociology, psychology, economics, and marketing, as well as other fields. The majority of published work on consumer behavior is basic research and this work forms the foundation for our text. However, the major thrust of our book is applying this research to the problem of developing successful marketing strategies.

As shown in Figure 1.2, the action-oriented group can be divided into three constituencies: (1) marketing organizations, (2) government and political organizations, and (3) consumers. Each of these is interested in consumer behavior not just for the sake of knowledge, but for using this knowledge to influence the other constituencies. The first of these is marketing organizations. These include not only what are conventionally thought of as business firms, but also other organizations such as hospitals, museums, law firms, and universities. Thus, marketing organizations include all groups that have a market offering and are seeking exchanges with consumers. While the primary focus of our text is on relationships between marketing strategy and consumers from the perspective of business firms, the ideas we present can also be applied to other marketing organizations, such as the American Cancer Society or your college or university.

Toyota has had a number of market successes by staying close to its customers.

The second group in Figure 1.2 comprises various government and political organizations. These include government agencies such as the Federal Trade Commission and the Food and Drug Administration. The major concern of these organizations is monitoring and regulating exchanges between marketing organizations and consumers. This is accomplished through the development of public policy, which affects marketing strategies and consumer activities. Political constituencies include activists such as Ralph Nader or the members of Students Against Drunk Driving. While these relationships are not the major concern of our text, they are considered, particulary in Chapter 21.

The third group in Figure 1.2 includes both individual consumers and organizational buyers who exchange resources for various goods and services. Their interest in consumer behavior is primarily to make exchanges that help

FIGURE 1.3

Examples of Consumer Issues Involved in Developing Marketing Strategy

Strategy Element	Consumer Issues
Segmentation	Which consumers are the prime prospects for our product? What consumer characteristics should we use to segment the market for our product?
Product	What products do consumers use now? What benefits do consumers want from this product?
Promotion	What promotion appeal would influence consumers to purchase and use our product? What advertising claims would be most effective for our product?
Pricing	How important is price to consumers in various target markets? What effects will a price change have on purchase behavior?
Distribution	Where do consumers buy this product? Would a different distribution system change consumers' purchasing behavior?

them achieve their goals. Although the major concern of our text is with ultimate consumers, the logic presented here can be applied in organizational markets, and several examples of organizational buyer behavior are discussed later in the text.

What Is the Relationship Between Consumer Behavior and Marketing Strategy?

From the viewpoint of marketing organizations, a **marketing strategy** is a plan designed to influence exchanges to achieve organizational objectives. Typically, a marketing strategy is intended to increase the probability or frequency of consumer behaviors, such as frequenting particular stores or purchasing particular products. This is accomplished by developing and presenting marketing mixes directed at selected target markets. A marketing mix consists of product, promotion, distribution, and pricing elements.

In Figure 1.3 we present some consumer behavior issues involved in developing various aspects of marketing strategy. Issues such as these can be addressed through formal marketing research, informal discussions with consumers, or intuition and thinking about the relationships between consumer behavior and marketing strategy.

HIGHLIGHT 1.3

Tips for Being a Successful Marketer

Know Your Customers

Consumer-goods companies are using high-tech techniques to find out who their customers are—and aren't. By linking that knowledge with data about ads and coupons, they can fine-tune their marketing.

Make What They Want

In an age of diversity, products must be tailored to individual tastes. So where once there were just Oreos, now there are Fudge Covered Oreos, Oreo Double Stufs, and Oreo Big Stufs, too.

Use Targeted and New Media

Companies aiming for micromarkets are advertising on cable TV and in magazines to reach special audiences. And they're putting their messages on walls in high school lunchrooms, on videocassettes, and even on blood pressure monitors.

Use Nonmedia

Marketers are sponsoring sports, festivals, and other events to reach local or ethnic markets. Latino events such as Carnaval Miami are hot. So are sports ranging from golf to hydroplane racing.

Reach Customers in the Store

Consumers make most buying decisions while they're shopping. So marketers are putting ads on supermarket loudspeakers, shopping carts, and in-store monitors.

Sharpen Your Promotions

Couponing and price promotions are expensive and often harmful to a brand's image. Thanks to better data, some companies are using fewer, more effective promotions. One promising approach: Aiming coupons at a competitor's customers.

Work with Retailers

Consumer-goods manufacturers must learn to "micromarket" to the retail trade, too. Some are linking their computers to the retailers', and some are tailoring their marketing and promotions to an individual retailer's needs.

Source: Zachary Schiller, "Stalking the New Consumer," *Business Week,* August 28, 1989, p. 54.

Figure 1.3 shows that understanding consumers is a critical element in developing marketing strategies. Very few—if any—strategy decisions do not involve consideration of consumer behavior. For example, analysis of the competition requires an understanding of what consumers think and feel about competitive brands, which consumers buy these brands and why, and in what situations consumers purchase and use competitive products. In sum, the more you learn about consumers (and approaches to analyzing them), the better your chances for developing successful marketing strategies. Highlight 1.3 offers some tips for developing marketing strategies.

Pepsi tries to stay close to its customers by using celebrities, such as Ray Charles, and coupons.

Finally, it should be clear that marketing strategies, particularly as developed and implemented by successful corporations, have a powerful force on consumers and society at large. We believe that marketing strategies not only adapt to consumers, but also change what consumers think and feel about themselves, about various market offerings, and about the appropriate situations for product purchase and use. This does not mean marketing is unethical or an inappropriate activity. However, the power of marketing and the ability of marketing research and consumer analysis to gain insight into consumer behavior should not be discounted or misused.

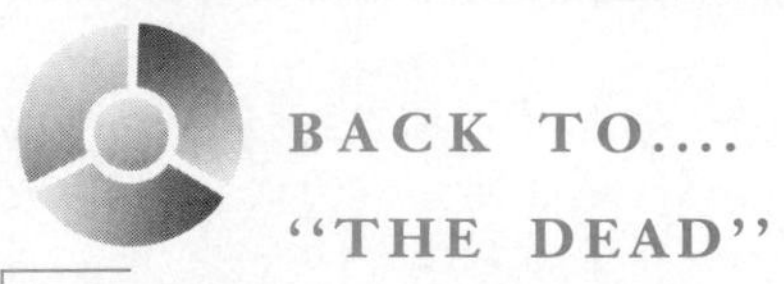

BACK TO.... "THE DEAD"

Regardless of whether you like Grateful Dead's music or approve of the band's behavior, it should be clear that the Dead understands its customers and has generated a profitable long-term marketing strategy. By offering tickets by mail, by allowing concerts to be recorded, by changing shows nightly, by offering extra-long concerts at competitive prices, and by trying to keep control over crowd problems, the band has attracted concertgoers for nearly 30 years. Some of its songs, such as "Truckin'," "Uncle John's Band," and "Touch of Grey," are staples on classic-rock radio stations. Some longtime fans have seen the band hundreds of times and are extremely loyal customers. For example, Stephen Brown, 36, says he's collected 1,800 tape recordings of the Dead and has seen 300 of the band's concerts.

In terms of sales and profits, in 1990 the Grateful Dead sold $29 million worth of tickets to 63 North American shows, fourth among rock stars for that year. In a more recent tour, four shows at the 18,000-seat Capital Centre in Landover, Maryland, were sold out in 90 minutes. Many of these fans were 18 to 25 years old, but about 25 percent were substantially older. The four Capital Centre shows generated revenue of $1.6 million. A rough rule of thumb is that 15 percent ($240,000) of that gross goes to promoters. By the time the Dead pays for renting the Capital Centre and other local costs, the band's share of revenues is about 50 percent, or $800,000. Apparently, the Grateful Dead understands that profitable marketing strategies depend on "staying close to customers."

Summary

In this chapter, we argued that consumer behavior is an important topic in business education because achieving marketing objectives depends on knowing, serving, and influencing consumers. We discussed the nature of consumer behavior and the various groups interested in the topic. We also discussed the relationships between consumer behavior and marketing strategy. We hope that after reading this chapter you can now appreciate the relevance and importance of a consumer behavior course for your business education. We also hope you will learn something about yourself by considering how the analytic framework and information in our text applies to you as a potential marketing manager, a consumer, and a human being.

Key Terms and Concepts

Marketing Concept *4*

Consumer Behavior *8*

Marketing Strategy *13*

Review and Discussion Questions

1. Why is consumer behavior an important course in business education?
2. Do you think marketing is a powerful force in society? Why or why not?
3. What is the role of consumer analysis in developing marketing strategies?
4. Offer three examples of situations in which a marketing strategy influenced your purchase behavior. Why did each succeed over competitive strategies?
5. Using Figure 1.3 as a takeoff point, discuss other questions and decisions in marketing strategy that could be affected by your study of consumer behavior.
6. Select a market segment of which you are *not* a member and, with other students in the class, discuss the kinds of information you would need to develop a strategy aimed at that segment.
7. Using a campus organization of interest (i.e., student government, professional fraternity, political interest group), discuss how a better understanding of the consumer behavior of students could help the organization improve its influence strategies.

Notes

1. The popular business literature has many articles on the importance of organizations staying close to consumers. For examples, see Terence P. Pare, "Banks Discover the Consumer," *Fortune*, February 12, 1990, pp. 96–104; Stephen Phillips, et al., "King Customer," *Business Week*, pp. 88–94; Patricia Sellers, "What Customers Really Want," *Fortune*, June 4, 1990, pp. 58–68; Frank Rose, "Now Quality Means Service Too," *Fortune*, April 22, 1991, pp. 97–108.
2. Peter D. Bennett, *Dictionary of Marketing Terms* (Chicago: American Marketing Association, 1989), p. 40.

MARKETING STRATEGY IN ACTION

Toyota

Of all the slogans kicked around Toyota, the key one is *kaizen*, which means "continuous improvement" in Japanese. While many other companies strive for dramatic breakthrough, Toyota keeps doing lots of little things better and better. Consider the subcompact Tercel, the smallest Toyota sold in the United States. While this model contributes only modestly to profits, Toyota made the 1991 Tercel faster, roomier, and quieter than its predecessor—with less weight, equally good mileage, and remarkably, the same under-$8,000 price for the basic four-door sedan. It's $100 cheaper than GM's new Saturn and as much as $1,600 less than other competing models.

One consultant calls Toyota's strategy "rapid inch-up": Take enough tiny steps and soon you outdistance the competition. By introducing six all-new vehicles within 14 months, Toyota grabbed a crushing 43 percent share of car sales in Japan. In the 1990 model year, it sold more than 1 million cars and trucks in the United States and is pressing to move up from its No. 4 position in the U.S. market; it is the No. 3 automaker in the world market. The company has the highest operating margins in the world auto industry and is so rich it makes more money on financial investments than it does on operations. It has over $22 billion in cash and could buy both Ford Motor Co. and Chrysler Corp. with nearly $5 billion to spare.

The company simply is tops in quality, production, and efficiency. From its factories pour a wide range of cars, built with unequaled precision. Toyota turns out luxury sedans with Mercedes-Benz-like quality using *one sixth* the labor Mercedes does. The company originated just-in-time production and remains its leading practitioner. It has close relationships with its suppliers and rigid engineering specifications for the products it purchases.

Toyota pioneered quality circles, which involve workers in discussions of ways to improve their tasks and avoid what it calls the three D's: the dangerous, dirty, and demanding aspects of factory work. The company is investing $770 million to improve worker housing, add dining halls, and

Additional Reading

For insightful discussions of the role of consumers in developing marketing strategies, see:

Day, George S. *Market Driven Strategies: Processes for Creating Value.* New York: Free Press, 1990.

Donnelly, James H., Jr. *Close to the Customer.* Homewood, Ill.: Business One Irwin, 1992.

Levitt, Theodore. *The Marketing Imagination.* New York: Free Press, 1983.

Peters, Thomas J., and Nancy K. Austin. *A Passion for Excellence.* New York: Random House, 1985.

Peters, Thomas J., and Robert H. Waterman, Jr. *In Search of Excellence.* New York: Harper & Row, 1982.

Ries, Al, and Jack Trout. *Bottom-Up Marketing.* New York: McGraw-Hill, 1989.

build new recreational facilities. On the assembly line, quality is not defined as zero defects but as another Toyota slogan has it, "building the very best and giving the customer what she/he wants." Because each worker serves as the customer for the process just before hers/his, she/he, becomes a quality-control inspector. If a piece isn't installed properly when it reaches him, he won't accept it.

Toyota's engineering system allows it to take a new car design from concept to showroom in less than four years versus more than five years for U.S. companies and seven years for Mercedes. This cuts costs, allows quicker correction of mistakes, and keeps Toyota better abreast of market trends. Gains from speed feed on themselves. Toyota can get its advanced engineering and design done sooner because, as one manager puts it, "we are closer to the customer and thus have a shorter concept time." New products are appointed to a chief engineer who has complete responsibility and authority for the product from design and manufacturing through marketing and has direct contacts with both dealers and consumers. New-model bosses for U.S. companies seldom have such control and almost never have direct contact with dealers or consumers.

In Toyota's manufacturing system, parts and cars don't get built until orders come from dealers requesting them. In placing orders, dealers essentially reserve a portion of factory capacity. The system is so effective that rather than wait several months for a new car, the customer can get a built-to-order car in a week to 10 days.

Toyota is the best carmaker in the world because it stays close to its customers. "We have learned that universal mass production is not enough," said the head of Toyota's Tokyo Design Center. "In the 21st century, you personalize things more to make them more reflective of individual needs." The winners will be those who target narrow customer niches most successfully with specific models.

Discussion Questions

1. In what ways is Toyota's new-product development system designed to serve customers?
2. In what ways is Toyota's manufacturing system designed to serve customers?
3. How does Toyota personalize its cars and trucks to meet individual consumer needs?
4. In its price range, how do you think the Toyota Tercel stacks up against the competition?

Source: Alex Taylor III, "Why Toyota Keeps Getting Better and Better and Better," *Fortune,* November 19, 1990, pp. 66–77.

A Framework for Consumer Analysis

CHAPTER 2

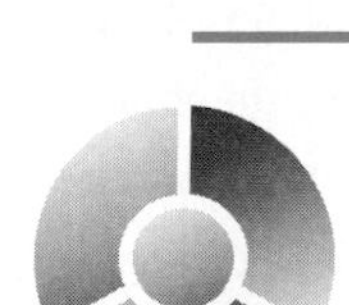

BUYING A SMITH & WESSON

Barbara Linton is 37, divorced, and the mother of two daughters, Joanne and Jenny, ages 7 and 9. She is a successful doctor and makes over $90,000 annually. She lives in her own home in a Chicago suburb with her children, who go to private schools.

Recently, a number of robberies and burglaries have occurred close to her neighborhood. One of her friends was attacked in a mall parking lot and robbed. Barbara is concerned about her safety and that of her children and is considering buying a gun for home protection. However, she is also worried about the safety of having a loaded gun in her home with the kids around.

Barbara's uncle owns a gun store and shooting club in her hometown near Minneapolis. She decides that on her next trip home she will visit him at the store and evaluate further the pros and cons of getting a gun.

After the 10 o'clock news report on another robbery in her area, Barbara decides to take the kids and fly home to see her family the following weekend. While there, she goes to see her uncle at his shop.

"Hi, Uncle Al," she greets him. "How is the gun business?"

Uncle Al replies that the gun business is doing fine. He says the shooting club is also doing well and has lots of new members.

Barbara explains that she is thinking about buying a gun because of all the crime recently in her area. She also explains her concerns with the safety of having a gun around the house.

Uncle Al tells her he does not want to try to influence her decision. He believes people have to decide for themselves whether owning a gun is right for them. However, if they do choose to buy one, they need to learn how to load and fire it safely and effectively. He also says a gun lock that can be put on the trigger housing can be used to avoid problems with the children.

Barbara decides to buy a gun for her home. She asks her uncle to recommend the best model for her needs.

Uncle Al tells her he thinks a revolver is much simpler to operate and safer to handle than an automatic. He recommends a Smith & Wesson Model 66 stainless-steel revolver with a four-inch barrel and black rubber Pachmeyer grips for better handling. While the Model 66 handles .357 caliber ammunition, .38 Special cartridges can also be used in it. He recommends using the .38s at first because they produce less recoil when fired, but stepping up to the .357s when her skills develop because they have more stopping power.

Barbara and her uncle walk over to the shooting range with his Model 66. He explains how to load the revolver and how to shoot it in both single and double action. He also shows her a trigger lock and how to put it on the gun. Barbara loads the gun and tries it out at the range. She is surprised how easy it is to shoot and hit a silhouette target at 25 feet. She thinks the gun looks and feels good and would be right for her needs.

Her uncle cannot sell her one because she is no longer a resident of that state, so she purchases a Model 66 when she returns to Chicago. She also buys rubber grips, two boxes of .38 Special cartridges, a Kolpin gun case, and a trigger lock for the gun. She joins an upscale shooting club to improve her skills and meet other people who face the same problems she does. She feels safer in her home.

What factors are involved in the purchases made by Barbara Linton? Many theories, models, and concepts have been borrowed from other fields as well as developed by marketing researchers in attempts to understand consumer behavior. In many cases, these ideas overlap and even compete with each other as useful descriptions of consumers. To date, no one approach is fully accepted; nor is it likely that a single, grand theory of consumer behavior can be devised that all researchers would agree on.

For these reasons, neither this chapter nor the text itself should be viewed as a theory of consumer behavior. Rather, it is a *framework* for studying, analyzing, and understanding consumers to help you develop successful marketing strategies.

This chapter introduces the general framework on which our text is organized. It is divided into two major parts. In the first section, we introduce three of the major elements of our framework: affect and cognition, behavior, and the environment. We then discuss the nature of the relationships among these elements.

In the second part of the chapter, we discuss the fourth element of our framework: marketing strategy. In addition, we discuss several levels of consumer analysis.

Consumer Behavior: A Conceptual Framework

Figure 2.1 presents three of the four major elements of consumer analysis: (1) affect and cognition, (2) behavior, and (3) the environment. In the following section, we provide an overview of these elements and the special relationships among them.

Affect and Cognition

In this text, **affect and cognition** refer to two types of internal, psychological responses that consumers may have to environmental stimuli and events. In simple language, *affect* concerns *feelings*, while *cognition* involves *thinking*.

Affective responses vary in evaluation—positive or negative, favorable or unfavorable—and in intensity or level of bodily arousal. For instance, affect includes relatively intense *emotions* such as love or anger, less strong *feeling states* such as satisfaction or frustration, diffuse *moods* such as relaxation or boredom, and rather mild overall *evaluations* such as "I like McDonald's french fries" or "I dislike BIC pens."

Cognition refers to the mental processes and knowledge structures involved in people's responses to the environment. For instance, it includes knowledge that people have acquired from their experiences and have stored in their memories. Cognition also includes the psychological processes associated with paying attention to and understanding aspects of the environment, remembering past events, forming evaluations, and making purchase choice decisions. While many aspects of cognition are conscious thinking processes, other cognitive processes are unconscious and essentially automatic.

FIGURE 2.1

Three Elements of Consumer Analysis

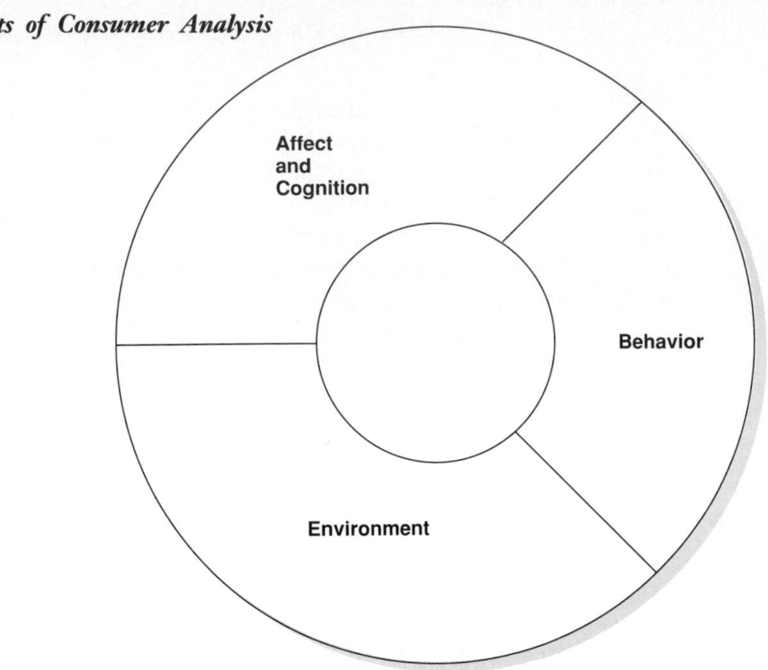

Some marketing strategies encourage considerable cognitive activity.

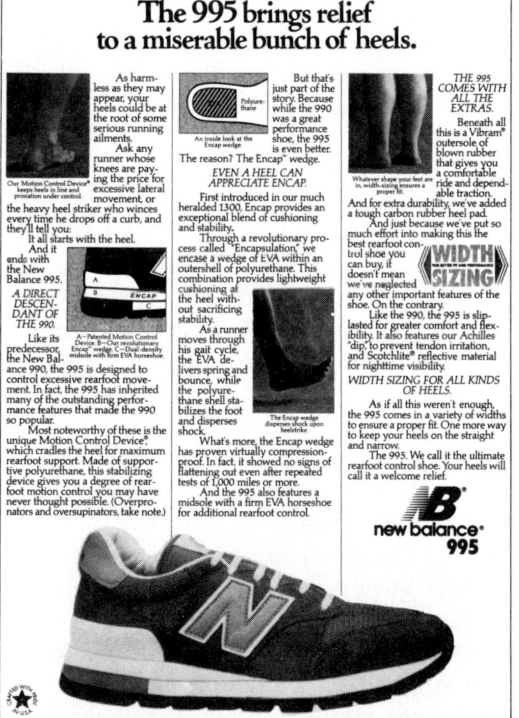

HIGHLIGHT 2.1

Some Basic Questions about Consumer Affect and Cognition

Although many competing theories and ideas about consumer affect and cognitions have been proposed, no single theory completely describes the workings of the consumer's mind. However, carefully studying and thinking about the information in Section 2 of this text should help you develop informed answers to questions about affect and cognition such as:

1. How do consumers interpret information about marketing stimuli such as products, stores, and advertising?
2. How do consumers choose from among alternative product classes, products, and brands?
3. How do consumers form evaluations of products and brands?
4. How does memory affect consumer decision making?
5. How do affect and cognition influence behavior and environments?
6. How do behavior and environments influence affect and cognition?
7. How do consumers interpret the benefits of marketing offerings?
8. Why are consumers more interested or involved in some products or brands than others?
9. How do marketing strategies influence consumers' affective and cognitive responses?
10. How do affective and cognitive responses influence each other?

Section 2 of this text is devoted to a discussion of consumer affect and cognition. Highlight 2.1 offers a sample of the types of questions Section 2 is designed to answer.

Behavior

In this text, **behavior** refers to the overt acts or actions of consumers that can be directly observed. Examples of behaviors include watching a television commercial, visiting a store, or buying a product. Thus, while affect and cognition is concerned with what consumers *feel* and *think*, behavior deals with what consumers actually *do*. Despite the importance of behavior for marketing strategy development, little consumer research has been conducted on it. Section 3 of this text is devoted to a discussion of consumer overt behavior. Highlight 2.2 offers a sample of the types of questions Section 3 is designed to answer. Overall, this section is designed to encourage the analysis of overt behavior in developing marketing strategies.

Learning to use a complex product may be a long-term process.

HIGHLIGHT 2.2

SOME BASIC QUESTIONS ABOUT CONSUMER BEHAVIORS

Although little attention has been given to studying the overt behavior of consumers, many behavior influence techniques seem to be commonly used by marketing practitioners. Carefully studying and thinking about the information in Section 2 of the text should help you develop informed answers to questions about behavior such as:

1. How do behavior approaches differ from affective and cognitive approaches to studying consumer behavior?
2. What is classical conditioning, and how is it used by marketers to influence consumer behavior?
3. What is operant conditioning, and how is it used by marketers to influence consumer behavior?
4. What is vicarious learning, and how is it used by marketers to influence consumer behavior?
5. What consumer behaviors are of interest to marketing management?
6. How much control does marketing have over consumers' behavior?
7. How do affect and cognition and environments affect behavior?
8. How does behavior influence affect and cognition and environments?
9. How can behavior theory be used by marketing managers?
10. Does the frequency and quality of consumer behavior vary by individuals, products, and situations?

Store environments influence consumers.

Environment

In this text, **environment** refers to the complex of physical and social stimuli in the external world of consumers. It includes the things, places, and other people that influence consumers' affect and cognition and their behaviors. Section 4 of this text is devoted to a discussion of the environment. Highlight 2.3 offers a sample of the types of questions Section 4 is designed to answer.

Important parts of the environment are the physical and social stimuli created by marketers to influence consumers. These include such things as products, advertisements, verbal statements by salespeople, price tags, signs, and stores. These are critical for an understanding of consumer behavior, and we will give them special attention as the fourth element of our model, to be discussed later in the chapter.

Relationships among Model Elements

Perhaps the major difference between our model and other approaches to describing consumer behavior involves causality. In general, most approaches are concerned with one-way cause-and-effect relationships. For instance, some cognitive researchers focus only on the causal impact of cognitive factors on behavior, whereas some behavior-oriented researchers focus only on the causal impact of the environment on behavior.

While such one-way causal approaches have value, they may lead consumer researchers and marketing strategists to overlook other interrelationships

HIGHLIGHT 2.3

Some Basic Questions about Consumer Environments

Environmental psychology seeks to extend knowledge about the relationships between environmental stimuli and human behavior. In consumer research, the major environmental factors examined have been concerned with the impact of various societal aspects. Carefully studying and thinking about the information in Section 4 of the text should help you develop informed answers to questions about the environment such as:

1. In what physical environments do consumer behaviors occur?
2. How do environments affect consumers' affect and cognitions and behavior?
3. How do consumer affect and cognition and behavior affect the environment?
4. What effect does culture have on consumers?
5. What effect does subculture have on consumers?
6. What effect does social class have on consumers?
7. What effect do reference groups have on consumers?
8. What effect do families have on consumers?
9. In what ways do consumers influence each other concerning marketing offerings?
10. How powerful are interpersonal influences on consumer behavior?

among affect and cognition, behavior, and environments. To overcome this problem, we believe it is useful to view the relationships among these elements as a continuous set of interactions, called **reciprocal determinism.** *Reciprocal* refers to a mutual action between factors, and *determinism* indicates the effects caused by these factors. Thus, reciprocal determinism means each element in the model both causes the other elements and, in turn, is caused by them, usually in a continuous fashion, over a period of time.

Bandura illustrates reciprocal determinism as follows:

> Television-viewing behavior provides an everyday example. Personal preferences influence when and which programs, from among the available alternatives, individuals choose to watch on television. Although the potential televised environment is identical for all viewers, the actual televised environment that impinges on given individuals depends on what they select to watch. Through their viewing behavior, they partly shape the nature of the future televised environment. Because production costs and commercial requirements also determine what people are shown, the options provided in the televised environment partly shape the viewer's preferences. Here, all three factors—viewer preferences, viewing behavior, and televised offerings—reciprocally affect each other.[1]

FIGURE 2.2
What Affects What in TV Viewing

1. Do consumer preferences for TV shows impact which shows consumers view? If so, affect and cognition influence behavior.
2. Do consumer preferences and perceptions affect what TV programs are produced and shown? If so, affect and cognition influence the environment.
3. Do consumer viewing behaviors influence consumer preferences for watching the same show again? If so, behavior alters affect and cognitions.
4. Do consumer viewing behaviors influence what shows remain and what shows are canceled? If so, behavior influences the environment.
5. Does the availability of various TV shows influence consumer preferences for them? If so, the environment modifies affect and cognitions.
6. Does the availability of various TV shows influence consumer viewing behavior? If so, the environment influences behavior.

In this example, personal preference involves affect and cognition; TV viewing is behavior; and TV shows and their availability are parts of the television environment. Figure 2.2 presents a series of six questions, based on this example, that illustrate six possible one-way relationships among affect, cognition, behaviors, and environments. If the answer to all six questions is yes — and we believe that yes is the appropriate answer — it should be clear that each element in the model affects and is affected by the other elements; i.e., they are reciprocally determined. Thus, simple one-way cause-and-effect relationships are incapable of providing a complete explanation of even simple events. There are always a variety of causal interactions involved.

Four important points can be made about reciprocal determinism and the relationships among the elements in the model. First, any comprehensive analysis of consumer behavior must *consider all three elements.* Descriptions of consumer behavior in terms of only one or two of the elements are incomplete. For example, to assume that affect and cognitions cause behavior and to ignore the influence of the environment underestimates the dynamic nature of consumer behavior and may lead to a less effective marketing strategy.

Second, it is important to recognize that any of the three elements may be the *starting point* for consumer analysis. In the example above, the analysis began with consumer preferences; we could have begun with television viewing behavior or with the television programming environment. However, because marketers are usually interested in influencing behaviors, consumer analysis often should begin with a focus on behavior.

Third, the model is *dynamic;* it views consumer behavior as a process of continuous change. While we may offer a good description of consumers in terms of these elements at a particular time, any or all of these elements can change. Thus, the results of consumer research often become quickly outdated. For this reason, we have chosen not to emphasize specific research findings that are more than a few years old. The results of much of that work, even if valid in its day, may have little relevance in today's market.

Fourth, the model can be usefully applied at several *levels of analysis.* That is, it can be used to describe the relationships and changes among affect and cognition, behaviors, and environments for a single consumer, for a group of consumers (such as a particular target market), or for society in general. In sum, we believe it is a general model that can be fruitfully applied to an unlimited number of marketing problems

Marketing Strategy

The fourth element in our framework is **marketing strategy.** As noted earlier, marketing strategies are part of the environment and consist of a variety of physical and social stimuli. These stimuli include products and services, promotional materials (advertisements), places for exchange (retail stores), and price information (price tags attached to products). Implementing marketing strategies involves placing these marketing stimuli in consumers' environments in order to influence their affect, cognition and behaviors.

To highlight its importance in this text, we represent marketing strategy as a separate element in our framework, as shown in Figure 2.3. Marketing strategy can influence each of the other elements—affect and cognition, behavior, and the environment—and, in turn, can be influenced by each of these factors. For example, placing a service station sign next to an interstate highway changes the *landscape* (the environment) and may change consumer *intentions* (a cognition) to stop for gas with the result of *stopping and purchasing* from the station (behavior). The success of using the sign may lead to placing more signs along highways, thus changing other environments, cognitions, and behaviors. Eventually, research may show that many consumers dislike (affect) having too many signs cluttering the landscape and a new strategy may have to be developed. In other words, marketing strategies interact reciprocally with affect and cognition, behaviors, and environments across time. Marketing strategies may change the other elements and be changed by them.

Of course, not every consumer is equally likely to be influenced by a particular marketing strategy. For example, young married couples without children are less likely to be heavy consumers of Mattel toys than are parents of small children. Therefore, marketers are encouraged to segment markets on the basis of the probability that various consumers will purchase, use, and continue to repurchase their products. Also, marketers have a social responsibility to consumers that needs to be carefully considered in designing marketing strategies.

Section Five of this text is devoted to a discussion of marketing strategy. Highlight 2.4 offers a sample of the types of questions Section 5 is designed to answer.

FIGURE 2.3
The Wheel of Consumer Analysis

Levels of Consumer Analysis

While the focus of our text is on understanding consumer behavior in general, the wheel of consumer analysis is flexible and can aid in understanding consumers and developing marketing strategies at many levels. For example, it can be applied to the analysis of different societies, industries, market segments, or individual consumers. It can be used fruitfully by both marketing strategists and public policy officials to understand the dynamics of consumer behavior. Below, we briefly discuss how the Wheel of Consumer Analysis can be applied at several different levels.

Societies

Changes in what a society believes and how its members behave can be analyzed with the wheel of consumer analysis. For example, a recent change in our society involves greater concern with health and fitness. How did this change occur? Surely, consumers were always concerned with living long, happy lives. A growing body of medical research indicated people could be healthier and live

HIGHLIGHT 2.4

Some Basic Questions about Marketing Strategy and Consumers

Consumers are the focal point in developing successful marketing strategies. According to the principle of reciprocal determinism, marketing strategies both influence and are influenced by consumers' affect and cognitions, behaviors, and environments. Carefully studying and thinking about the information in Section 5 of the text should help you develop informed answers to questions about marketing strategies such as:

1. What are some effective ways to segment markets?
2. How can products be effectively positioned?
3. What are the relationships between product strategies and consumers?
4. What are the relationships between promotion strategies and consumers?
5. What are the relationships between channels of distribution and consumers?
6. What are the relationships between pricing strategies and consumers?
7. What consumer variables affect the success of a marketing strategy?
8. How can a firm develop brand-loyal consumers?
9. What is the role of consumer satisfaction in developing successful market offerings?
10. What obligations do marketers have to consumers and society at large?

longer if they ate properly and exercised regularly. This research may have changed attitudes of some consumers about their eating and exercise habits. As these consumers, particularly on the West Coast, changed their attitudes and began living more healthy lifestyles, many other consumers copied these beliefs and behavior patterns. In addition, healthy, well-shaped people are considered more attractive in our society. This belief may have accelerated the health and fitness movement. Also, because a variety of health-related industries, such as health foods, exercise equipment, and sports apparel, developed and promoted eating right and exercising regularly, consumers were more exposed to the idea and effects of an active lifestyle.

Of course, not everyone in society has changed his or her lifestyle, and some who did reverted to less healthy habits. However, from the brief discussion above, it should be clear that there were changes in the environment (medical research reports), cognitions and affect (beliefs about how to live longer and healthier), behavior (eating healthier foods and exercising), and marketing strat-

Our society's emphasis on health and fitness can be accounted for by the wheel of consumer analysis.

egies (development and promotion of health food, equipment, and apparel products) that interacted to create this change in society in general. The Wheel of Consumer Analysis can account for these changes in our society but also could be applied to other societies to help understand their structures and practices.

Industries

The Wheel of Consumer Analysis can be used to analyze the relationships of a company and its competitors with consumers in specific industries. For example, consider the effects of health concerns on the beer industry. Lite beer from Miller took advantage of the health movement and created the market for reduced-calorie beer. Miller Brewing Co. became the light-beer market leader by being the first to offer a product that was more consistent with a change occurring in society, and it also, through developing and marketing the product, helped accelerate the change. Thus, a change in consumer beliefs and behavior concerning calorie intake influenced a marketing strategy to introduce and market a low-calorie beer. In turn, this marketing strategy helped reinforce and spread the change in consumer beliefs and behaviors. The success of the product influenced competitors to also offer light beers, further changing demand for this product category.

However, another change in this industry is the concern with responsible drinking, which decreases demand for alcohol products in general. This change has led to the development and marketing of nonalcohol beers and, for many consumers, abstinence from any alcoholic beverages. Consumer groups, such as Mothers Against Drunk Driving and Students Against Drunk Driving, have also influenced many members of society to reduce their alcohol consumption. While being drunk and boisterous at one time was considered acceptable behavior, many consumers no longer find it so. Similarly, smoking was at one time considered a sign of maturity and being cool, whereas today fewer and fewer public places tolerate smoking.

At the industry level, changes in consumer cognitions, affect, and behavior can threaten existing products but also offer opportunities to develop products more consistent with new values and behaviors. Successful marketing strategies depend on analyzing consumer/product relationships not only for the company's products, but also those of competitors, and creating an advantage over competitive offerings.

Market Segments

The Wheel of Consumer Analysis can be used to analyze segments of consumers who have some similarity in cognitions, affect, behaviors, and environments. Successful firms in an industry usually divide the total market into segments and try to appeal most strongly to one or more of them. For example, the emphasis on health encouraged many consumers to become involved in sports. However, there were not always specific shoes designed to play each sport effectively. Today, consumers can find many varieties and styles of shoes for running, bicycling, soccer, basketball, and other sports. These shoes vary in design, features, and price ranges to appeal to groups of consumers that are similar in some ways.

Reebok, for example, developed its Blacktop shoe for young basketball players on urban outdoor courts. The shoe is a few ounces heavier than competitors, moderately priced, and designed for performance on asphalt and concrete. The shoe looks good, so it appeals to the 80 percent of consumers who buy athletic shoes solely for fashion, but it also is tough enough to stand up to rugged outdoor play. The shoe was sold out in many stores in its first two months and was expected to sell over 2.2 million pairs in its first year, a smashing marketing success.[2] Thus, by understanding the wants and prefer-

The food industry has developed and marketed new products to respond to consumers' demand for faster food preparation.

ences (cognitions and affect) of urban youths (target market) for a good-looking, moderately-priced, long-wearing shoe, promoted for regular guys who play basketball (behavior) on outdoor courts (environment), Reebok developed a successful marketing strategy.

Individual Consumers

Finally, the Wheel of Consumer Analysis can be used to analyze the consumption history, a single purchase, or some aspect of a purchase for a specific consumer. For example, to understand Barbara Linton's purchase of a Smith & Wesson handgun, we need to consider her cognitions, affect, behavior, and environments.

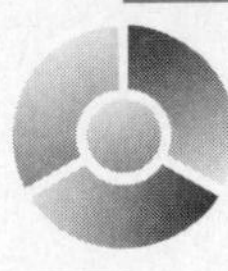

BACK TO....
BUYING A SMITH & WESSON

This case provides a simple description of the purchase of a gun and accessories. We hope it is written in such a manner that you can easily understand the sequence of events. However, imagine how difficult it would be to try to describe these events by considering *only* cognitive and affective *or* behavioral *or* environmental factors.

Cognitive and affective factors such as Barbara's concern for her family's safety, her information processing and decision making to buy a gun, and her feelings of greater safety, are useful—but they alone could not explain what Barbara did and the environmental factors that influenced these thoughts and actions. Her overt behaviors, such as visiting her uncle, trying the gun, and purchasing the gun and equipment, are also helpful—but are incomplete for capturing the meaning of these behaviors and the contexts in which these actions occurred. Environmental factors such as the news reports on crimes, the proximity of the crimes to her neighborhood, the information from her uncle, the look and feel of the gun, the feedback from the environment from her shots hitting the target, the time lapses and place changes between the events described are

Summary

In this chapter, we presented our overall framework for the analysis of consumer behavior. We also described a general approach to developing marketing strategies intended to influence consumers' affect and cognitions, behaviors, and environments. We believe this conceptual framework can help you understand many of the complexities of consumer behavior. However, other concepts related to consumer behavior must be considered. Later in this text, we will present many of these concepts and discuss how they can be used to develop, select, and evaluate marketing strategies.

necessary for understanding the case—but are quite sterile when discussed independently of Barbara's cognitive, affective, and behavioral events.

Thus, even for a simple description of a consumer purchase, all three elements—affect and cognition, behavior, and environment—work together to provide efficient, useful knowledge of consumer behavior. All three are also necessary for academic attempts to understand consumers and for managerial attempts to develop successful marketing strategies. Analysis of all three elements is superior to any one or two of the elements taken in isolation.

Finally, all three elements of the wheel are needed to understand not just a gun purchase by an individual consumer, but also society's views and uses of guns, the gun industry, and various target markets for guns. All three elements are needed to analyze questions concerning the pros and cons of gun ownership in various societies, the relationships among gun buyers and various gun manufacturers and retailers in the industry, and relationships among the target markets for guns and various brands and models. Whether one is developing a marketing strategy to sell guns or legislation to stop the sale of guns, analysis of consumer cognitions and affect, behaviors, and environments is required for effective action.

Key Terms and Concepts

Affect *23*
Cognition *23*
Behavior *25*
Environment *27*
Reciprocal Determinism *28*
Marketing Strategy *30*

Review and Discussion Questions

1. How is the concept of reciprocal determinism different from the idea of one-way causal relationships?
2. Explain the relationship between the environment and marketing strategy.

3. Return to Figure 2.2 and investigate the six relationships between the model elements for TV viewing. Are some of these relationships weaker than others in this example?
4. Relate each of the four points the text makes about the use of the model to the impact these issues would have on marketing strategy.
5. The text indicates that analysis could begin with affect and cognitions, behaviors, or environment. Why not begin with marketing strategy?
6. Offer three examples of changes in a marketing strategy that led to changes in your affect and cognitions and behaviors.

NOTES

1. Albert Bandura, "The Self System in Reciprocal Determinism," *American Psychologist*, April 1978, p. 346. Also see Albert Bandura, *Social Foundations of Thought and Action: A Social Cognitive Theory* (Englewood Cliffs, NJ: Prentice-Hall, 1986).
2. See Keith H. Hammonds, "The 'Blacktop' Is Paving Reebok's Road to Recovery," *Business Week*, August 12, 1991, p. 27.

ADDITIONAL READING

For further discussion of reciprocal determinism, see:

Bandura, Albert. *Social Learning Theory*. Englewood Cliffs, N.J.: Prentice-Hall, 1977.

________. "Temporal Dynamics and Decomposition of Reciprocal Determinism: A Reply to Phillips and Orton." *Psychological Review*, April 1983, pp. 166–170.

________. "Human Agency in Social Cognitive Theory." *American Psychologist*, September 1989, pp. 1175–84.

Phillips, D.C. and Rob Orton. "The New Causal Principle of Cognitive Learning Theory: Perspectives on Bandura's Reciprocal Determinism." *Psychological Review;* April 1983, pp. 158–65.

For discussions of consumer behavior that include several elements of our model, see:

Mowen, John C. "Beyond Consumer Decision Making." *Journal of Consumer Marketing*. Winter 1988, pp. 15–25.

Punj, Girish H., and David W. Stewart. "An Interaction Framework of Consumer Decision Making." *Journal of Consumer Research*, September 1983, pp. 181–96.

MARKETING STRATEGY IN ACTION

Suzuki Motor Co.

Suzuki Motor Co. entered the U.S. automobile market in November 1985 with a single model, the Samurai. The Samurai is a cross between a jeep and an economy car and was initially promoted as a fun car for the youth market. In one ad, for example, four witty and attractive people in a Samurai are shown playfully negotiating a test track. The ad ends with a "brake" test, that is, the driver says, "Let's break for lunch."

Suzuki sold 47,732 Samurais in 1986 and sales jumped to 81,349 in 1987. Apparently, the car was successfully filling the niche left by American Motors Corp.'s removal of the Jeep CJ5 a few years earlier. However, in December 1987 and January 1988, sales of the Samurai had declined a total of 16.6 percent from this period a year earlier. Auto market analysts blamed the decrease on increases in insurance rates. Apparently, insurance companies had concluded the Samurai was prone to accidents and expensive to repair.

Questions about the Samurai's safety continued to mount. In February 1988, the Center for Auto Safety, a Washington, D.C.-based consumer group, filed a petition with the National Highway Traffic Safety Administration, charging the Samurai's high center of gravity made it unstable on the road. The center said it had evidence of 11 accidents in which Samurais had rolled over, causing three deaths and leaving eight other people injured.

Suzuki reacted to this by changing its advertising messages. The new ads, shot almost entirely in black and white, featured laudatory quotes from car enthusiast magazines. For example, the following quote was used from *Off-Road* magazine: "We gave the Samurai good points for maneuverability, engine performance, and chassis balance." The ads helped: sales of the Samurai in May 1988 were 6,074 units.

In June 1988, Consumers Union published an article in its *Consumer Reports* magazine stating the Samurai had a "dangerous propensity" to roll over when its driver attempted to make a sharp turn. Consumers Union charged that the vehicle was too tall for its small wheelbase and called for the immediate recall of all 160,000 Samurais on U.S. roads and reimbursement to their owners. Sales of the Samurai dropped to 2,199 units in June 1988, compared with 7,479 in June 1987.

At this point, Suzuki took some extraordinary marketing measures to try to stop the sales plunge of its car. First, it offered dealers $2,000 incentives on each Samurai. The company didn't require dealers to cut the Samurai's price with the incentive, but many dealers immediately lopped off 25 percent from the base price of $7,995. Second, the company boosted its advertising budget by $1.5 million per week to try to counter consumer fears raised by the tests. Third, some dealers began offering free $1 million life insurance policies for Samurai buyers. The policy lasted for one year after purchase and covered only the death of the driver in a rollover accident. As one dealer put it: "We can't run enough ads to convince the public that our cars are safe. But with the insurance we can draw attention by saying we're willing to pay $1 million to back up the Samurai's safety." Fourth, Suzuki hinted that it might sue the critics of its car.

By August 1988, sales of the Samurai had rebounded sharply. In fact, in August, a two-month inventory was wiped out as Suzuki sold 12,208 Samurais, the best month it had had since entering the U.S market. Suzuki also announced it was introducing two new models in the U.S. market.

Discussion Questions

1. Describe and evaluate Suzuki's marketing strategy in terms of its reactions to changes in consumer affect and cognitions, behaviors, and environmental factors.
2. Do you think there are ethical problems with Suzuki's responses to criticism of its Samurai?

Source: "Suzuki Takes Extraordinary Measures to Halt Sales Plunge of the Samurai Model," *The Wall Street Journal,* July 11, 1988; "Suzuki Reverses Ad Strategy to Combat Claims that Samurai Vehicle Isn't Safe," *The Wall Street Journal,* March 3, 1988, "Suzuki Samurai's Sales Have Plunged Since Consumers Union Called It Unsafe," *The Wall Street Journal,* July 7, 1988: "Suzuki Vehemently Defends Its Samurai," *Capitol Times,* June 10, 1988; and "Sudden Deceleration," *American Way,* January 1989, pp. 20-23.

Affect and Cognition and Marketing Strategy

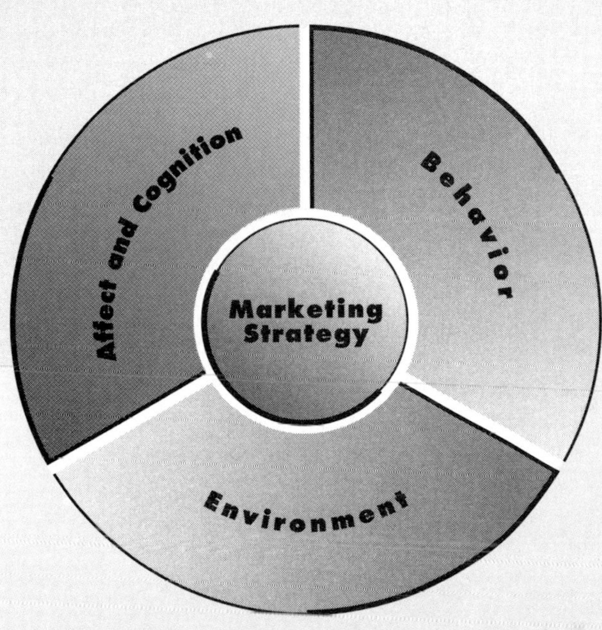

Introduction to Affect and Cognition

CHAPTER 3

"EVERYDAY" AFFECT AND COGNITION: THE BRUCE MACKLIN STORY

As do millions of other consumers, Bruce Macklin makes a weekly trip to a local supermarket to buy groceries. On this sunny Saturday morning, Bruce has driven to the Giant supermarket with his three-year-old daughter, Angela. As he walks through the front doors of the store, Bruce enters one of the most complex information environments a consumer can face.

A supermarket is loaded with information. The average American grocery store stocks some 10,000 items, but some very large stores may carry as many as 20,000. Large supermarkets offer many alternatives in each product category. For instance, one large store offers 18 brands of mustard in a variety of sizes. Moreover, most product packages contain lots of information. The average package of breakfast cereal, for example, contains some 250 individual pieces of information!

Despite this complexity, Bruce (like most of us) feels no particular uneasiness or anxiety about grocery shopping. Neither is he particularly excited, for this is familiar territory. During the next 50 minutes (the average time consumers spend in the store on a major shopping trip), Bruce will process a great deal of information. He will make numerous decisions during the time it takes to fill his

grocery cart. Most of his choices will be made easily and quickly, seemingly with little effort. Some choices, though, will involve noticeable cognition (thinking) and may require a few seconds. And a few of his choices may require substantial cognitive processing and several seconds, perhaps even minutes. How does Bruce Macklin move through this complex informational environment so easily, buying dozens, perhaps hundreds, of products? The affective and cognitive processes that make this possible are the subject of this chapter.

This apparently simple, everyday example of shopping for groceries actually involves rather complex interactions between various aspects of the supermarket environment, marketing strategies, Bruce Macklin's behaviors, and his affective and cognitive systems. In this chapter, we begin our examination of the affect and cognition portion of the Wheel of Consumer Analysis. We will describe consumers' affective and cognitive systems, present a cognitive processing model of consumer decision making, and discuss the knowledge structures that consumers learn and store in memory. Our goal is to understand consumers' affective responses to their experiences, their cognitive interpretations of those experiences, and how these responses influence consumers' interpretations of new experiences and choice of behaviors to achieve their consumption goals.

Components of the Wheel of Consumer Analysis

In Chapter 2, you learned that consumer behavior situations such as Bruce Macklin's grocery shopping trip can be analyzed in terms of four elements—behavior, environment, marketing strategies, and the internal factors of affect and cognition. We organized these four factors into a model called the Wheel of Consumer Analysis (see Figure 3.1). Because these factors interact and influence each other in a continuous, reciprocal manner, no factor can be fully understood in isolation. Therefore, we begin our analysis of affect and cognition by first analyzing Bruce Macklin's shopping trip in terms of the four elements in the wheel model.

FIGURE 3.1
The Wheel of Consumer Analysis

ENVIRONMENT

What is the supermarket environment like? Well, on a Saturday morning, the market is likely to be *busy*, with many people *crowding* the aisles. The store is likely to be somewhat *noisy*. Because Bruce is shopping with Angela, her *chattering* adds to the commotion. These social aspects of the environment will influence Bruce's affect and cognitions and his overt behavior. The store *layout*, the *width* of the aisles, the special sale *signs* on the shelves, the product *displays* at the ends of the aisles and elsewhere in the store, the *lighting*, and other physical aspects of the supermarket environment may also have an effect. Other environmental factors such as the *temperature*, background *music* playing, and the *wobbly wheel* on his shopping cart may have important effects on Bruce's affect, cognitions, and behaviors.

BEHAVIOR

What kinds of behaviors occur in this situation? Bruce is engaged in a large number of behaviors, including *walking* down the aisles, *looking* at products on

Grocery shopping involves interactions between consumer's affective and cognitive systems, their behaviors, and the store environment.

the shelves, *picking up* and *examining* packages, *talking* to Angela and a friend he met in the store, *steering* the wobbly cart, and so on. While many of these behaviors may not seem to be of much interest to a marketing manager, some behaviors have important influences on Bruce's affect and cognitions and his eventual purchases. For example, unless Bruce *walks* down the aisle containing breakfast cereals, he cannot *notice* and *buy* a package of Kellogg's Raisin Squares. Typically, marketers are most concerned about purchase behavior. In the supermarket environment, this means *picking up* a package, *placing* it in the cart, and *paying* for it at the checkout counter.

Marketing Strategies

Much of the in-store environment Bruce experiences is due to marketing strategy decisions made by the retailer and the manufacturers whose products are carried by the store. In fact, a grocery store is a very good place to observe marketing strategies in action. The huge number of products sold in such stores requires an equally large number of marketing strategies. For instance, a firm's *distribution* strategy (place products only in upscale stores) determines whether that product is even present in a particular store. A variety of *pricing* strategies (reduced price on Oreo cookies) and *promotion* strategies (free samples of cheese) are evident in a supermarket environment. *Package designs* (easy-opening milk containers) and specific *product characteristics* (low-calorie frozen entrées) are also marketing strategies. Finally, specific environmental details such as *point-of-purchase displays* (a stack of Pepsi six-packs near the store entrance) are important aspects of marketing strategy. All of these marketing strategies are environmental stimuli that are meant to influence consumers' affect and cognitions and their behaviors.

Affect and Cognition

Bruce's affective and cognitive systems were active in the supermarket environment. Indeed, consumers' affective and cognitive systems are active in every environment, but only some of this internal activity is conscious, while a great deal of activity may occur without much awareness. For instance, Bruce may *feel a bit angry* about getting a cart with a wobbly wheel. He also *pays attention* to certain aspects of the store environment and *ignores* other parts. Some products capture his *attention* while others do not. He *interprets* a large amount of information in the store environment—from aisle signs to brand names to price tags to nutrition labels. In addition, he *evaluates* some of the products in terms of meeting his needs and those of his family. He *remembers* what products he still has on hand at home and what he has run out of and needs to replace. He *makes choices* from among some of the 10,000 to 20,000 items available in the store. In addition, he *makes decisions* about other specific behaviors. Should he go down aisle 3 or skip it this week? Should he stock up on canned peaches or buy just one can? Should he give Angela a cookie for being good? Should he take the wobbly cart back and get another one? Should he pay with cash or by check?

In sum, Bruce's grocery purchasing behavior on this particular Saturday morning is a complex function of his social and physical environment, the marketing strategies intended to influence him, his own behaviors, and the processes of his affective and cognitive systems. Each factor interacts with and reciprocally influences the others.

About 45 minutes after entering the Giant supermarket, Bruce emerges with five bags of groceries containing 48 different products. Given our analysis of his shopping trip, we might be somewhat surprised to find that he has a smile on his face and does not feel at all tired. In fact, he is already looking forward to his tennis match. How did Bruce's affective and cognitive systems accomplish so much so quickly, with such apparent ease? How do we all perform similar cognitive feats while shopping?

Two Modes of Psychological Response

In understanding consumers, it is useful to distinguish between two modes of psychological response that people may have to their environment—*affect* and *cognition.* These two types of internal responses are produced by the affective and cognitive systems, respectively. The two systems are richly interconnected and each one influences and is influenced by the other.[1]

Affect

In distinguishing affect from cognition, it is useful to think of affective states as something that people *are* (I *am* happy, he *is* in a bad mood, Joe *likes* Mazda cars).[2] In contrast, one *has* cognitions (someone *believes* that Diet Pepsi is not fattening, Susan *knows* the grocery store is down the street). Consumers feel affect; they possess cognitions.

Our affective system reacts to the stimuli we encounter by producing various forms of affective responses.[3] For our purposes in this book, we identify four broad types of **affect** that consumers can experience: emotions, specific feelings, moods, and evaluations. Figure 3.2 shows how these types of affective responses are related and presents examples of each. Each type of affective response can be positive or negative, pro or con. Also, the four affective responses vary in their level of arousal and in the intensity with which they are experienced by consumers.[4] For instance, the stronger affective responses such as emotions and specific feelings usually involve the arousal or activation of various physiological systems in the body such as the cardiovascular system (increases in heart rate and blood pressure), glandular responses (sweating, dry mouth, crying, rushes of adrenaline), and visceral feelings of arousal (excitement or nervous butterflies in the stomach). Moods, on the other hand, are rather diffuse affective states (relaxed or bored), usually accompanied by moderate to low levels of arousal.[5] In contrast, most product evaluations (I like Crest toothpaste) involve relatively low levels of arousal and activation and few bodily feelings.

It is important to understand the basic characteristics of the affective system.[6] First, the affective system is *largely reactive.* That is, the affective system responds, usually immediately and automatically, to the stimuli a person encounters. The response could be any of the affective, feeling-type states shown in Figure 3.2. Because of its immediate and automatic response to stimuli, the affective system can have strong effects on people's cognitive systems and their behaviors. For instance, most people have favorite colors, and their immediate affective responses to the color of car or item of clothing can influence their cognitions (beliefs) about the product.

FIGURE 3.2
Types of Affective Responses

Type of Affective Response	Level of Physiological Arousal	Intensity or Strength of Feeling	Examples of Positive and Negative Affect
Emotions	Higher arousal and activation ↑	Stronger ↑	• Joy, love • Fear, guilt, anger
Specific feelings			• Warmth, appreciation, satisfaction • Disgust, sadness
Moods	↓	↓	• Alert, relaxed, calm • Blue, listless, bored
Evaluations	Lower arousal and activation	Weaker	• Like, good, favorable • Dislike, bad, unfavorable

A second point is that people have *little direct control* over their affective systems or the emotional responses they produce. For instance, if you are insulted by a rude sales clerk, your affective system is likely to immediately respond with feelings or emotions such as frustration or anger. Although you cannot directly control your emotional response, you could decide to leave the situation and thereby indirectly influence your affective state by changing your environment. For instance, the number of other people in a store and the level of crowding can influence consumers' affective responses.[7] Consumers who react to a very crowded clothing shop with negative feelings of discomfort, frustration, or even anger may leave that environment to shop somewhere else. Interestingly, these same consumers might consider an even more crowded bar or pub to be desirable and respond with positive affective feelings and emotions to that environment. These examples show that the type of affective response depends partially on how the cognitive system interprets the environment.

The affective system can *respond to virtually any type of stimulus*, including physical objects in the external environment (a Pioneer stereo system) or social situations (a conversation with a salesperson in an electronic shop). But consumers' affective systems can also respond to their own personal behaviors in various situations (playing your stereo system at a party). And finally, consumer's affective systems can respond to thoughts produced by their cognitive systems (thinking about your stereo system).

Another important characteristic is that affective responses are *represented physically* in the body. Consider the affective feelings of excitement and arousal (butterflies in the stomach) that many consumers experience when making a very important purchase, such as buying a new car or a first house. These bodily reactions can be powerful internal stimuli for the person experiencing them.

Moreover, people's muscle movements often reflect their affective states (facial expressions such as smiling or frowning, fists clenched in anger, alert or bored body positions). These responses can be important cues in interpersonal communication. For instance, many successful salespeople are skilled at reading the body language of their prospects, and they are able to adapt the sales presentation to the apparent affective responses of their potential customers.

Finally, it is important to recognize that most affective responses are learned, although some very basic affective responses (such as liking sweet tastes or reacting negatively to loud, sudden noises) seem to have an innate, biological basis. Consumers acquire many of their affective responses through their early experiences as very young children (these socialization processes are discussed in Chapter 15). Consumers also acquire affective responses through classical conditioning processes, some of which may be part of a marketing strategy (these learning processes are discussed in detail in Chapter 9).[8]

Cognition

A major function of the human cognitive system is to interpret, make sense of, and understand significant aspects of people's experiences in their environment. To do so, the cognitive system creates symbolic or cognitive representations that stand for the meaning of these elements. **Cognitive representations** are the subjective meanings that reflect each person's personal interpretation of the stimuli in question.[9]

Our cognitive systems are capable of interpreting and forming cognitive representations of virtually any environmental stimulus we encounter, as well as our own behaviors ("Why did I buy that record?"). These representations include the deeper, symbolic meanings of products and behaviors (see Highlight 3.1).[10] In addition, we can form cognitive representations of our own affective states ("Do I really like this sweater?" or "Am I in a bad mood or just tired?").[11] And we can interpret the meaning of other cognitive representations ("What does it mean that Hill's Department Store has 'Everyday Low Prices?'"). Although many cognitive representations are in the form of verbal language (words), it is usually assumed that other forms of meaning representation are possible. Figure 3.3 lists some of the cognitive representations or meanings that consumers' cognitive systems may create.

The other important function of our cognitive systems is to use (think about) these cognitive representations or meanings to carry out cognitive tasks such as identifying goals and objectives, developing and evaluating alternative actions to meet those goals, choosing a course of action, and carrying out the behaviors. Stated simply, our cognitive system is designed to understand our environment and effectively guide our behaviors in that environment.

To most people, cognition means thinking, or perhaps mental processes. Human beings have evolved highly sophisticated cognitive systems by which they engage in the so-called higher mental processes of understanding, learning,

The American bald eagle is used to convey symbolic meanings about products and services.

remembering, evaluating, deciding, and planning (see Highlight 3.2). Some researchers treat cognition as the particular symbolic representations or meanings (or particular thoughts) that a person constructs to stand for some stimulus. In this book, we use the term **cognition** in a broad sense to refer both to mental processes and to the thoughts and meanings they produce.

An important aspect of cognition is that consumers often are unaware of their cognitive processes—much of cognition is not conscious. However, consumers frequently are aware of the meanings (see Figure 3.3) produced by those cognitive processes. Also, the intensity of cognitive activity varies widely across purchase contexts, products, environments, and consumers. Our detailed analysis of cognition does not imply that consumers are always engaged in extensive,

HIGHLIGHT 3.1

Symbolic Meanings

Most marketers recognize that the consumption of many products depends on their symbolic meanings as well as their functional utility. In fact, the symbolic qualities of products and services can be the key determinants of product evaluation and purchase. Take food, for example.

Some foods symbolize age and sex differences. Milk and soft mushy foods are appropriate for babies or the elderly. Boys are supposed to prefer chunky peanut butter, while girls like smooth. Hamburgers are a youth food, especially appropriate for teenagers, whereas foods such as steak or lamb are appropriate for more sophisticated adults.

Certain foods are symbols of social status. Ordinary American foods such as hot dogs and potato chips symbolize ordinary American values. More exotic and expensive foods, such as lobster or caviar, symbolize high status and sophisticated palates. Drinking wine with meals connotes higher status in America, but probably not in France or Italy where wine is ordinary and expected at most meals.

Eating away from the home also connotes symbolic meaning. For instance, eating outdoors (in the backyard, on the deck, at the beach) symbolizes freedom from conventions, a return to nature, and a return to more primitive ways of cooking (open fire) and eating (with fingers). The symbolic meaning of going out to eat in a restaurant depends very much on the type of restaurant. Truck stops, outdoor cafes, bars, and cafeteria restaurants possess very different symbolic meanings. Fast-food restaurants symbolize youth and unpretentious values. Going to "nice" restaurants involves rituals of dressing up and having "good" manners that help create special, festive meanings and contribute to the symbolic meanings of the experience.

The method of food preparation also has symbolic meanings. Very elaborate cooking procedures (haute cuisine) signify the rarified, sophisticated tastes of people who can appreciate such fare. Raw foods tend to symbolize primitive, animal meanings. However, a few foods that are served uncooked have higher status meanings—caviar, sushi (raw fish and rice), steak tartare (raw ground beef)—perhaps because they symbolize mature, refined, aesthetic tastes.

Sources: Sidney J. Levy, "Interpreting Consumer Mythology: A Structural Approach to Consumer Behavior," *Journal of Marketing,* Summer, 1981, pp. 49–61; Michael R. Solomon, "The Role of Products as Social Stimuli: A Symbolic Interactionism Perspective," *Journal of Consumer Research,* December 1983, pp. 319–329.

highly elaborate cognitive processes. In fact, many purchase behaviors probably involve minimal cognitive activity. However, we do assume that most voluntary (nonhabitual) behaviors require at least some amount of cognitive processing.

HIGHLIGHT 3.2

"Higher" Mental Processes

What do we mean by higher mental processes? Consider the following general capabilities of the human cognitive system and the cognitive activities involved in each.

- Understanding—Interpreting specific aspects of one's environment, especially determining the meaning of those environmental features in terms of personal relevance.
- Evaluating—Judging whether an aspect of the environment, or one's own behavior, is good or bad, positive or negative, or favorable or unfavorable.
- Planning—Determining how to achieve a solution to a problem.
- Deciding—Comparing alternative solutions to a problem in terms of their relevant characteristics and selecting the best (or a satisfactory) alternative.
- Thinking—The cognitive activity that occurs during all of the above processes.

Source: Adapted from John R. Anderson, *Cognitive Psychology and Its Implications* (San Francisco: W. H. Freeman, 1985).

FIGURE 3.3

Types of Meanings Created by the Cognitive System

Cognitive representations of physical stimuli
This sweater is made of lambswool.
This car gets 28 miles per gallon.

Cognitive representations of social stimuli
The salesperson was helpful.
My friends think Pizza Hut is the best.

Cognitive representations of affective responses
I love Dove (ice cream) Bars.
I feel guilty about not sending Mom a birthday card.
I feel mildly excited and interested in a new store.

Cognitive representations of symbolic meanings
This car is sexy.
This style of dress is appropriate for older women.
Wearing a Rolex watch means you are successful.

Cognitive representations of sensations
Colors on a box of breakfast cereal.
Sound of a soft-drink can being opened and poured.
Sweet taste of chocolate chip cookies.
Smell of your favorite cologne.
Feel of your favorite pair of jeans.

Cognitive representations of behaviors
I drink a lot of Diet Pepsi.
How to pay with a credit card.

Relationships between Affect and Cognition

Currently, a rather heated debate is raging in psychology and consumer research concerning the relationship between affect and cognition.[12] Some theorists consider affect and cognition to be (at least somewhat) independent, while others argue that affect is largely influenced by the cognitive system.[13] Some degree of separation seems plausible since the affective and cognitive systems involve different parts of the brain. However, we believe it is more important to emphasize that both systems are richly interconnected at a neurophysiological level and that both systems operate continuously as people come into contact with various aspects of their environment.[14] For understanding most consumer behavior situations, we believe it is more useful to consider how the affective and cognitive systems interact with and influence each other rather than analyze whether one is more important or more dominant than the other.

Recently, consumer researchers have become quite interested in documenting some of the interactions between the affective and cognitive systems. Most of this research has focused on the influences of affective states on consumers' cognitions and their overt behaviors. For example, you may have noticed that if you go grocery shopping while in a bad mood, you are less likely to notice attractive (positive, good) things to buy and you might end up spending less money than if you had been in a good mood. Research has also shown that consumers' affective states such as moods and feelings can influence their cognitive responses to advertising.[15]

Less research has been done to determine how cognitions influence the affective system. However, it is well established that people's affective systems are sensitive to their cognitive interpretations of their experiences in particular situations.[16] For instance, if you interpret a salesperson's behaviors as being too pushy, you are likely to have a negative feeling, whereas if your interpretation is that he or she is being helpful, you are likely to have a favorable affective reaction.

Marketing Implications

In sum, both affect and cognition are important aspects of consumer behavior. For instance, a brand image consists of the entire set of meanings associated with a brand.[17] Thus, a brand image includes cognitions (beliefs) about brand attributes, consequences of brand use, and appropriate consumption situations, as well as affective responses such as the feelings and emotions linked to the brand and brand evaluations. Marketers need to understand both modes of consumer response to marketing strategies such as product design, advertisements, and store layouts. For some marketing purposes, consumers' affective responses may be more important; in other situations, cognitions will take precedence.

Affective responses are especially important for so-called feeling products.[18] These include certain foods (donuts, snacks, pizza), beverages (soft drinks, beer,

In 1984, Calvin Klein introduced Obsession using interlocked, nude bodies to convey an image of casual but intense sexuality.

Eternity, introduced in 1989, used images that symbolized commitment and romance, emerging trends in the market at the time.

wine), greeting cards, fragrances, skin-care products, and sports cars. For instance, consider consumers' affective responses to ice cream. Eating ice cream is a highly sensory experience, and the product is associated with affective feelings of happiness, fun, and excitement, even sensual pleasure. Consider the marketing strategies used by Haagen-Dazs company, the American maker of superpremium ice cream noted for its high butterfat content and intense flavors, to support its expansion into Europe.[19] Haagen-Dazs's European ads reflect the sensual, affective nature of ice cream marketing – one British ad portrays a seminude couple feeding ice cream to each other. The product has been extremely successful in England, France, and Germany, where sales grew from $2 million to $30 million in just two years.

Consumers' initial affective responses when they first smell a cologne may be critical to its purchase. To introduce its new scent, Spellbound, Estee Lauder inserted 11 million scent strips in magazines such as *Vanity Fair* and *Vogue*.[20] Once the product is bought, consumers' affective responses to the fragrance are highly influenced by their cognitive interpretation of how other people (in the social environment) react to the scent. Fragrance advertising may try to portray both affective and cognitive responses. For example, Estee Lauder's ads for Spellbound portray attractive models gazing intently into each others' eyes. Apparently, Lauder hopes to communicate the affective and cognitive meanings associated with romance, sensuality, and sexual attraction. (Highlight 3.3 dis-

HIGHLIGHT 3.3

The Return of Romance

The concept of romance gained favor in American society during the late 1980s and early 1990s, as people sought a refuge from the pressures of work and economic crisis. Wedding advertisements in *Bride's* magazine portray much more romantic settings. Sales of romance novels are strong. The rising interest in Victorian furniture and decorations is seen as a nostalgic return to a more romantic time.

Romance is difficult to define, but it surely involves affective states, including emotions, feelings, and moods. Romance is about relationships, fantasy, imagery, nostalgia, and tradition. The affective responses associated with romantic love are quite different from those associated with explicit sexual stimuli. For instance, Calvin Klein introduced Obsession cologne in the mid-1980s and portrayed naked, interlocked bodies in the advertising to create an image of casual but intense sexuality. Klein used completely different advertising imagery to promote Eternity cologne, introduced in 1989. Here the goal was to elicit different types of affective responses—romantic emotions and moods, feelings of commitment and close relationships.

Romance involves both affective and cognitive responses. Romantic love is a whole psychological package that combines cognitive beliefs (about equality of the sexes), ideals (marriage is forever), and expectations (inspiring each other and sharing are the most important aspects of marriage) with various affective responses (feelings of "true love" and the warm "fuzzy" feelings of closeness, warmth, comfort, and mutual respect). Recent advertising has picked up on this trend by showing much more romantic settings and situations for restaurants, vacation locations, and boy/girl situations in general.

Interestingly, the trend toward romance may be spreading around the world. The engagement ring is a new idea in Japan, a very romantic concept indeed.

Source: Adapted from Lea Bayers Rapp, "The Return of Romance," *Marketing Insights,* June 1989, pp. 31–39.

cusses the affective and cognitive aspects of romance.) In the remainder of this chapter, we consider in more detail how the cognitive system operates.

Cognition as Information Processing

It is common for researchers to think of all the stimuli in the external environment as *information.* Thus, information includes various stimuli associated with marketing strategies (a price tag, a coupon, a package, a store window display).

To be effective, marketing information must be processed (taken in and "handled") by consumers' cognitive systems. Researchers have developed **information-processing models** to simplify and explain these complex cognitive activities.[21] From an information-processing perspective, cognition concerns (1) how people interpret information and transform it into knowledge or meaning, and (2) how they use this knowledge to form judgments of objects and events to make decisions about appropriate behaviors.

The simplest information-processing model has just two components—a *memory* that contains interpreted information or knowledge and a *processor* that creates that knowledge and uses it to perform various tasks.[22] Most researchers, however, identify several separate cognitive processes and arrange them in a sequence of steps or stages. Each stage refers to a set of information-handling processes that transform or modify information. Each processing stage receives the transformed output of the preceding stage and, in turn, processes (transforms) the information and passes it on to the next stage for additional processing. Since marketers are especially interested in consumers' purchasing behaviors, they have emphasized how consumers process information about products and brands in deciding which products and brands to buy.[23]

Researchers often express their theories about information processing in the form of a flowchart, which graphically depicts the flow of information through the cognitive system. Figure 3.4 presents a simple information processing model.[24] This model (at least partially) accounts for the flow of information during decision making, beginning with an awareness of the product created by exposure to environmental information (an ad in this case) and ending with purchase behavior. In sum, researchers use information-processing models to break down complex cognitive processes into a series of simple subprocesses that are more easily measured and understood.

Criticisms of Information-Processing Models

The information-processing approach to consumer decision making has been criticized on several grounds.[25] A common objection is that some information-processing models make decision making seem too rational and mechanical. Another problem is that information-processing models tend to ignore the affective system and downplay the influences of the affective system during decision making. In addition, information-processing models usually do not account for consumers' actual experiences when using a product (feelings of enjoyment, fun, satisfaction, or frustration).[26] Another criticism is that some information-processing models focus only on internal, mental factors and give little or no attention to the influences of consumers' own behaviors or environmental factors. A final problem is that most simple information-processing models (like that in Figure 3.4) do not account for the effects of consumers' knowledge stored in memory.[27]

FIGURE 3.4
A Simple Information Processing Model

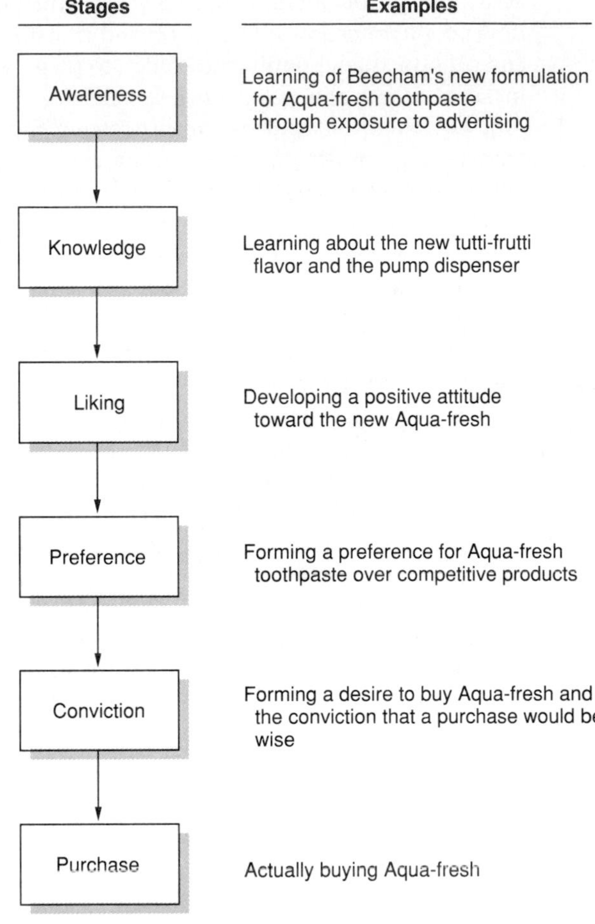

Source: Adapted from Robert J. Lavidge and Gary A. Steiner, "A Model for Predictive Measurements of Advertising Effectiveness," *Journal of Marketing,* vol. 25 (October 1961), pp. 59–62. Published by the American Marketing Association.

Despite these legitimate criticisms, an information-processing approach (with modifications to deal with these problems) remains the best way of understanding cognition. In the next section, we present a more general and flexible model of the cognitive processes that occur in consumer decision making.

FIGURE 3.5
A Cognitive Processing Model of Consumer Decision Making

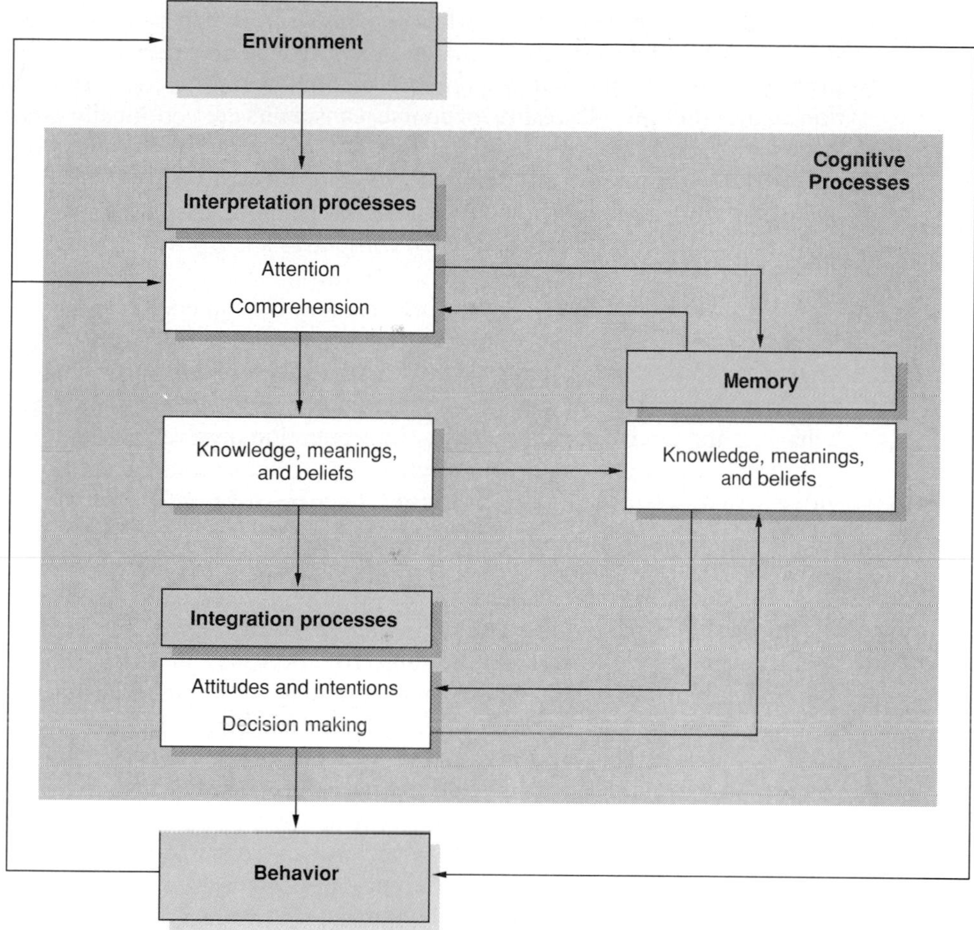

A Cognitive Processing Model of Consumer Decision Making

The model of consumer decision making shown in Figure 3.5 includes two broad cognitive processes – interpretation and integration. This model emphasizes the interaction between these two processes and stored knowledge in memory. Moreover, it can account for the influence of the affective system. We provide only a brief overview of the cognitive processing model here. Subsequent chapters in this section will cover each aspect of the model in detail.

Cognitive processes occur when a consumer is exposed to an external stimulus in the environment (as shown in Figure 3.5) or experiences an internal stimulus such as an affective response. Both types of stimuli constitute information to the consumer. In reality, of course, consumers are continually exposed to information, so cognitive processes, like affective processes, operate continuously. However, when marketers wish to determine the effects of a particular marketing strategy (a new ad or a 25-cents-off coupon), they usually begin their analysis of cognition at the point when consumers are exposed to the marketing stimulus.

When they encounter relevant information, consumers interpret its meaning in terms of their own interests, values, and knowledge. **Interpretation processes** concern how consumers make sense of or determine the meaning of important aspects of the physical and social environment as well as their own behaviors and internal affective states. Interpretation involves two highly related (sub)processes: attention and comprehension. *Attention* concerns how the cognitive system selects stimuli to interpret. *Comprehension* refers to the processes by which the cognitive system creates cognitive representations that stand for the subjective meaning of information. Attention and comprehension are discussed in detail in later chapters.

In this book, we use the terms **knowledge, meanings,** and **beliefs** more or less interchangeably to refer to the subjective, personal meanings produced by comprehension processes. These meanings may be organized and stored in memory as *knowledge structures.* Then, when needed later, parts of this knowledge may be activated (retrieved from memory) for use in other interpretative processes. Knowledge structures are discussed later in this chapter.

Figure 3.5 identifies a second cognitive process, integration. There are two types of **integration processes** that concern how consumers combine and use information. One concerns how different types of knowledge are combined to form *attitudes* or overall evaluative judgments of products and brands ("I like chocolate chip ice cream," or "I don't think Lee jeans are as good as Levi's"). Attitudes may involve both cognitive and affective responses. Integration processes are also used to make decisions or choices about what behaviors to perform. The outcome of a choice between different purchase behaviors is an *intention to buy* ("I intend to buy a new pen this afternoon"). Of course, integration processes can be used to make other behavioral choices besides purchase decisions. For instance, consumers may have to decide when to go on a shopping trip to search for suitable products, whether to pay with a check or credit card, or whether to recommend a brand of potato chips to a friend. Both attitudes and decision-making integration processes are discussed in detail in later chapters.

Reciprocal Interactions between Cognitive Processes and Knowledge

Our model emphasizes the *reciprocal interactions* between cognitive processes and consumers' knowledge stored in memory. As shown in Figure 3.5, interpretation processes create new knowledge, meanings, and beliefs that represent the subjective meaning of environmental information. This knowledge may be stored in long-term, permanent memory. But these interpretation processes had to draw on knowledge in memory to interpret the information in the first place. For instance, American consumers need a great deal of knowledge about vitamins and minerals to fully interpret the many health claims made by U.S. food companies.

Similarly, integration processes may also draw on consumers' knowledge in memory. Integration processes may combine knowledge from memory with new knowledge to make evaluative judgments of products and brands (form attitudes) and make decision choices (form purchase intentions). Since attitudes and intentions are forms of knowledge, they may be stored in memory and retrieved for use later. In sum, consumers' cognitive systems involve continuous, reciprocal interactions between the cognitive processes of interpretation and integration and knowledge stored in memory.

Characteristics of Cognitive Processes

We have identified four important characteristics of cognitive processes: (1) cognition involves interpreting or making sense of important aspects of the environment, (2) the cognitive system creates knowledge that symbolically represents important meanings, (3) interpretation processes create this knowledge and integration processes use it to evaluate objects and make purchase decisions, and (4) the meanings, knowledge, and beliefs in memory influence these cognitive processes and in turn are influenced by their outputs. Next, we discuss four additional characteristics of cognitive processes.

The first of these is **activation,** which refers to the essentially automatic process by which meanings are retrieved from long-term memory and made available for use by cognitive processes.[28] Activated knowledge may be experienced as conscious thoughts, but consumers are not always consciously aware of their activated cognitive representations. Knowledge can be activated in various ways, including exposure to an external stimulus in the environment (seeing the distinctive BMW grille might activate various meanings associated with BMW such as "a rich person's car" or "sporty"). The choice of a brand name can be very important for the marketing success of a product because of the various meanings it activates from memory. Jaguar is a good name for a sports car because it activates symbolic meanings such as speed, agility, exotic, rare, beautiful, powerful, and graceful.[29] Knowledge can also be activated by internal stimuli such as an affective state (a feeling of happiness might activate other

HIGHLIGHT 3.4

AUTOMATIC ACTIVATION OF MEANINGS FROM MEMORY

Awareness of Activation. It is difficult to become aware of our own activation processes. You would have to pay special attention to what happens when you are exposed to an object, for instance, because most activation tends to be automatic and very rapid. Normally, we are not conscious of the activation process that retrieves stored information from memory. The meanings just "come to mind."

("The Family Circus" by Bil Keane. Reprinted with special permission of Cowles Syndicate, Inc.)

positively evaluated knowledge). It is important to note that the same stimulus, whether internal or external, can and often does activate different knowledge in different consumers. The cartoon in Highlight 3.4 illustrates this point.

Knowledge can also be activated merely by being associated with another activated meaning. Because meanings are interconnected in knowledge structures, the activation of one meaning concept may spread to related concepts and activate those meanings. For instance, seeing a package of Jell-O in a store might first activate the Jell-O brand name and then related meanings such as jiggly, tastes sweet, good for a quick dessert, and Bill Cosby likes it. Though this unconscious process of **spreading activation,** parts of a knowledge structure

HIGHLIGHT 3.5

Increasing Automatic Cognitive Processing— Learning to Drive a Car

Practiced subjects can do what seems impossible to both the novice and the theorist. People can achieve dramatic improvements in skills with practice. For instance, consider your experience in learning to drive a car. When you first learned to drive, you probably couldn't drive and talk at the same time. The task of driving seemed difficult and was probably physically and mentally tiring. Today, if you are a skilled driver, you can probably drive in moderate traffic, listen to music on the radio, and carry on a casual conversation with a friend. Could you have done this when you first started driving? Probably then you kept the radio off. If anyone tried to talk to you, you ignored them or told them to shut up. Of course, even today you will probably stop talking if something unfamiliar occurs such as an emergency situation on the road up ahead. At least, we hope you do!

Learning to drive a car illustrates how cognitive processes (and associated behaviors) become increasingly automatic as they are learned through practice. However, even highly automatic skills such as eating seem to require some "capacity." Perhaps you like to munch on something while you study. You might snack on pretzels (as this author does) or eat an apple while you read this chapter. But if you come upon a difficult passage that requires greater thought, you probably will stop chewing or your hand with the pretzel may pause in midair, while you interpret the meaning of what you are reading.

may be activated during interpretation and integration processes, or even daydreaming.[30] Because spreading activation usually occurs unconsciously and automatically, consumers have little control over it. Usually, meanings or thoughts just come to mind during the course of cognitive processing.

Another important characteristic of cognitive processing is its **limited capacity** to deal with knowledge and meanings at a conscious level. The amount of knowledge that can be activated and consciously thought about at one time is quite small. This capacity limit suggests that consumers' conscious cognitive processes during decision making are likely to be fairly simple. However, over time, with practice, most cognitive processes become increasingly automatic and require less and less conscious control.[31] For instance, grocery shopping is familiar, routine, and cognitively easy for most consumers because it involves a great deal of automatic cognitive processing. Highlight 3.5 describes a common example of developing **automatic processing.**

Knowledge Structures

Consumer's knowledge structures are an important influence on cognitive processing. In this section, we identify the types of knowledge, meanings, and beliefs that consumers create. Then we describe how this knowledge can be organized or structured in memory, and we discuss two types of knowledge structures. Finally, we discuss processes of cognitive learning by which consumers acquire knowledge and organize it into knowledge structures.

Types of Knowledge

Our model of cognitive processing assumes that virtually any stimulus to which our cognitive systems attend is interpreted and given some meaning.[32] For instance, consumers interpret the meaning of their physical and social environments, including marketing strategies, as well as their own behaviors, affective responses, and cognitions.

Researchers have distinguished between two broad types of knowledge — declarative and procedural.[33] **Declarative knowledge** refers to the meanings that consumers construct to represent important information they encounter in the environment. This type of knowledge is stored in memory as a proposition. A *proposition* links or connects two or more meaning concepts, such as:

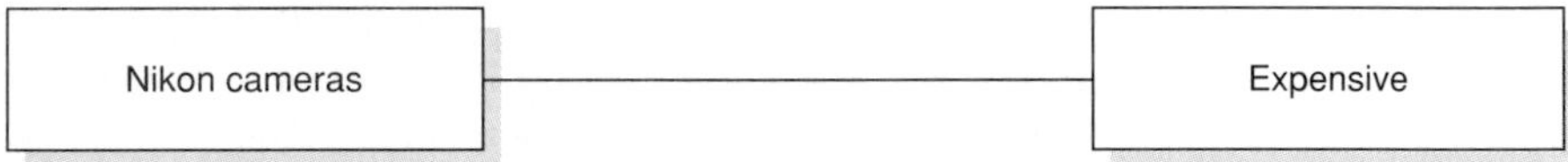

Essentially, any two meanings can be connected by a proposition. For instance, your self may be linked to an affective state ("I feel sad"), a brand may be associated with a consequence of using it (a Snickers bar fills you up), a product category may be connected to a characteristic (foreign cars are well made), or a behavior may be associated with a situation ("I order a pizza every Friday evening"). Many consumer researchers treat such propositions as *beliefs* that vary in their strength or the confidence with which consumers believe the association is true.

It is useful to distinguish between episodic and semantic types of declarative knowledge.[34] *Episodic knowledge* refers to consumers' cognitive representations of specific events that have occurred in thier lives. For instance, "Yesterday I bought a Snickers candy bar from a vending machine" or "My last credit card bill had another mistake" are examples of episodic knowledge.

Semantic knowledge, on the other hand, refers to people's general world knowledge. For instance, the cognitive representations you may have for Snickers candy bars — the peanuts, caramel, and calories it contains; the wrapper design; the aroma or the feel of it in your mouth; and your liking for the taste — are part of your semantic knowledge. Typically, marketers are more interested in consumers' semantic meanings than their episodic meanings, but both types of declarative knowledge can be important in understanding consumer behavior.

Procedural knowledge refers to consumers' cognitive representations of how to do things. Procedural knowledge is represented by the cognitive system as *productions,* a special kind of "if . . . then" proposition. Productions link people's cognitive representations of concepts or events with their cognitive representations of appropriate behaviors ("If the phone rings when you are busy . . . then don't answer it," or "If a salesperson presses you for a quick decision . . . then say no and leave").

Over a lifetime of experiences, consumers learn many productions, most of which are highly specific to particular situations. When activated from memory, these productions operate like rules that directly and automatically influence cognitive processes or overt behaviors. For instance, consider a shopping production that Susan has acquired: "If the price on clothing is reduced by 50 percent or more, then I decide whether I need it." If this procedural knowledge is activated when Susan sees a half-price sign in the jeans section, she would stop to think about whether she needs a new pair of jeans.

Productions are important knowledge structures that have many everyday implications. Consider the procedural knowledge necessary to operate many types of high-tech equipment such as video cameras, videocassette recorders, 35mm cameras, stereo receivers and compact disk players, and microwave ovens. Many consumers believe this equipment has become too complex and difficult to understand.[35] For instance, most people do not know the appropriate productions to make full use of their VCRs. A 1991 survey found that only 3 percent of total TV viewing time went to watch shows that had been recorded in advance using the VCR's programming feature.[36] Instead, most people used their VCRs only to play rented movies. Few consumers can operate all of the features of their high-tech equipment, and few even want these features. Some manufacturers are getting the message. For instance, Philips, the giant Dutch electronic firm, developed a group of easy-to-use clock radios, VCRs, and tape players called "Easy Line."

Both declarative and procedural knowledge are relevant for most of the consumer behavior situations that occur in everyday life. For instance, in the grocery shopping situation described at the beginning of this chapter, various parts of Bruce Macklin's declarative and procedural knowledge were activated in a continuous stream to affect his interpretation and integration processes while he shopped.

Knowledge Structures as Associative Networks

Earlier in this chapter, we mentioned that consumers' cognitive representations or meanings are organized as structures of knowledge. At minimum, this means every unique meaning concept that someone acquires is connected to at least one other concept. Most links are based on some personally meaningful association between the two concepts. For instance, your knowledge that a favorite clothing store is having a sale could be represented as a proposition linking two meaning concepts:

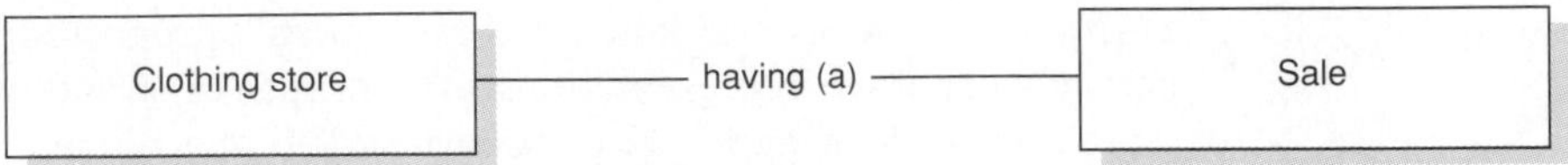

Our cognitive system may combine several propositions to form an **associative network** that links a number of different meanings. Researchers have found it useful to represent consumers' knowledge structures as associate networks.[37] For example, Figure 3.6 presents an associative network for Nike running shoes.

This knowledge structure connects the Nike concept to various types of declarative knowledge, including episodic representations of past events (shopping at Wilson's), general semantic knowledge about the characteristics of Nike shoes (their appearance, weight, and cushioning), a representation of an affec-

This ad is intended to create an associative network of semantic and procedural knowledge about the NordicTrack home exerciser.

GET WEIGHT OFF AND KEEP IT OFF FOR GOOD WITH NORDICTRACK...

America's most efficient, total-body workout.

Diets Alone Don't Work.
When you eat less, your body automatically adjusts its metabolism to a lower level; attempting to maintain a set point between your food intake and activity level. You do lose some weight, but you feel tired, grumpy and hungry. As the body strives to regain its "normal" balance, you give in to the urge to splurge—and gain it all back. Discouraged, you begin the cycle again.

The Secret To Lasting Weight Loss.
It's simple. Eat sensible, nutritious, well-balanced meals. Don't starve. Exercise on your NordicTrack 20 minutes each day. That's it. The highly efficient aerobics of NordicTrack's total-body workout raises your body's metabolism, making it possible for you to get weight off and keep it off for good. NordicTrack burns off calories while toning and firming.

NordicTrack: "The World's Best Aerobic Exerciser."™
Fitness experts agree that cross-country skiing is the world's best aerobic exercise. And NordicTrack's patented design duplicates the smooth, rhythmic, total-body action of cross-country skiing to give you the world's best aerobic workout. Better than walking, running or any other in-home exerciser. With NordicTrack, you'll work more muscle groups and burn more calories in less time than with an exercise bike, hydraulic cylinder rower, treadmill or stairclimber. Up to 1,100 calories per hour, according to fitness experts.

NordicTrack A CML Company *You're worth it!*

Easy To Use; Just 20 Minutes A Day.
NordicTracking is as easy as walking and swinging your arms. As you ski and "pole" against independent upper- and lower-body resistance levels, your body begins to replace fat tissue with muscle tissue which further increases calorie consumption. Your metabolism is raised during the workout and the calorie burning effects continue even two hours after you're finished.

Call today for a 30-day in-home trial!

Call or Write for a
FREE VIDEO
& Brochure
1-800-328-5888 EXT. 215D2
❑ Please send me a free brochure
❑ Also a free video ❑ VHS ❑ BETA
Name ______
Street ______
City ______ State ____ Zip ____
Phone ( ) ______
NordicTrack, Dept. #215D2, 141C Jonathan Blvd. N., Chaska, MN 55318

FIGURE 3.6
An Associative Network of Knowledge

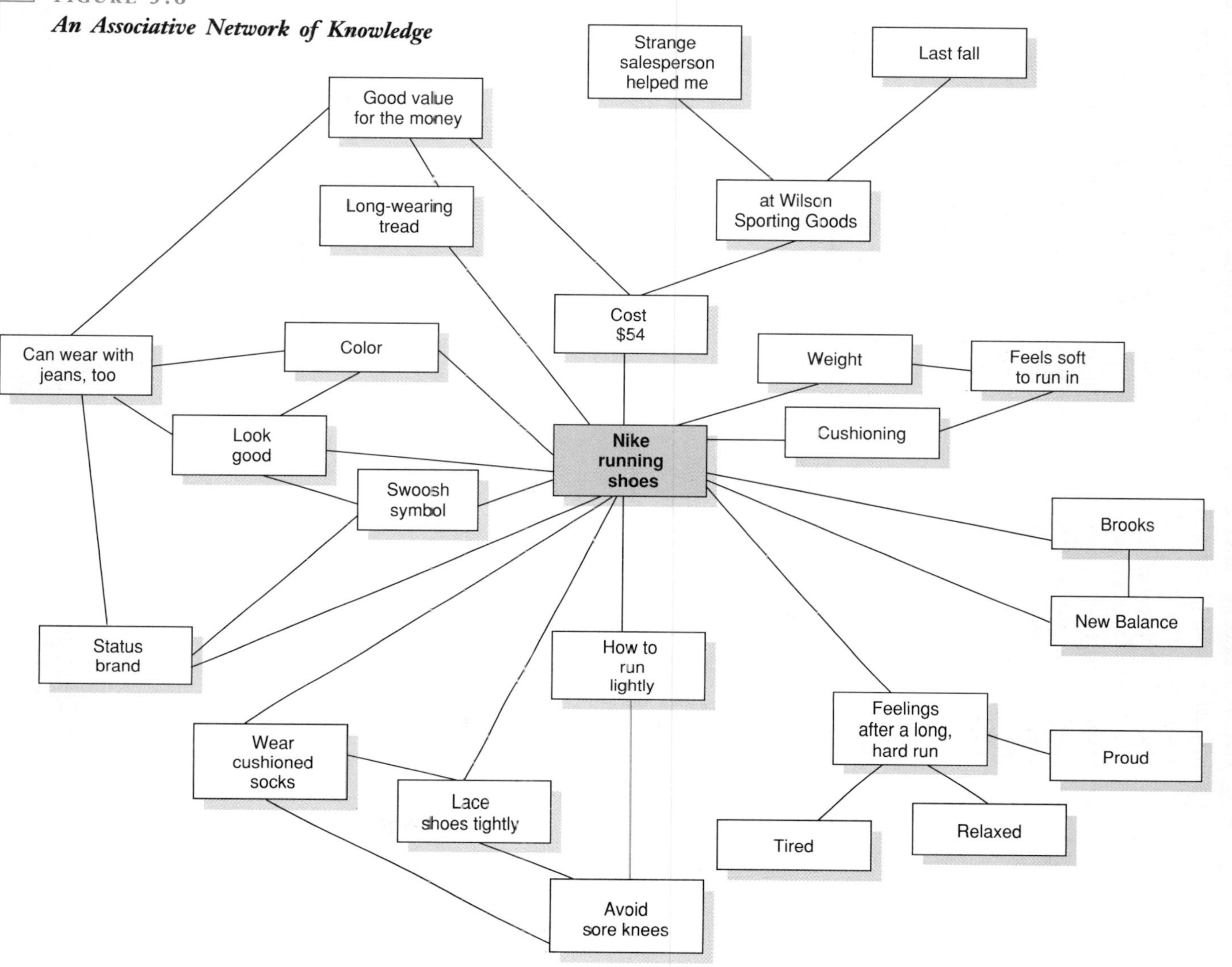

tive state (feelings after a hard run), and the cognitive interpretations of that affective state ("I feel relaxed and proud"). This knowledge structure also contains a production (how to run lightly) and related semantic knowledge about the consequences of doing so (avoid sore knees).

Parts of this knowledge structure could be activated in different circumstances and used in interpretation and integration processes. Some meanings might be activated directly by exposure to a physical stimulus in the environment. For instance, seeing a professional athlete wearing a pair of Nike shoes on TV or noticing the Nike symbol in a billboard advertisement might activate parts of one's knowledge structure for Nike shoes. Or some Nike meanings might be activated by stimuli associated with the pleasant affective responses of satisfaction and relaxation that some people experience after a hard workout. Finally, Nike meanings could be activated indirectly, as "activation energy" spreads from one meaning in the network to other related meanings. Through the activation spreading process, consumers' thoughts can range across many meanings in a knowledge structure.

Types of Knowledge Structures

Broadly speaking, consumers possess two types of knowledge structures—schemas and scripts. Each can be thought of as an associate network of linked meanings, but schemas contain declarative knowledge, while scripts contain procedural knowledge.[38]

A **schema** is an associative network of interrelated meanings that represent a person's declarative knowledge about some concept.[39] For instance, the knowledge structure for Nike running shoes shown in Figure 3.6 is a brand schema. Consumers may have a schema of knowledge for virtually any concept, including product categories (compact disks, fast-food hamburger restaurants), stores (Sears and K mart), particular behaviors (skydiving or shopping in malls), other people (one's best friend, the cute clerk at the 7-Eleven store), and even themselves ("I am shy, intelligent, and funny").

In contrast, **scripts** are associative networks of knowledge that contain procedural knowledge.[40] Scripts represent consumers' knowledge about appropirate behaviors in a situation. When consumers have experience with recurring situations such as eating in a fast-food restaurant, their cognitive systems may create several "if . . . then" productions. These productions represent specific behaviors that are appropriate to perform in response to events commonly experienced in that environment. For instance, consider this ample production for fast-food restaurant situations:

FIGURE 3.7
A Hypothetical Script of Appropriate Procedures for Dining at a "Fancy" Restaurant

- Enter restaurant.
- Give reservation name to mâitre´d.
- Wait to be shown to table.
- Walk to table and sit down.
- Order drinks when waiter asks.
- Select dinner items from menu.
- Order meal when waiter returns.
- Drink drinks and talk until first course arrives.
- Eat soup or salad when it arrives.
- Eat main course when it arrives.
- Order dessert when finished with dinner.
- Eat dessert when it arrives.
- Talk until bill arrives.
- Examine bill for accuracy.
- Give waiter credit card to pay for bill.
- Add tip to credit card form and sign.
- Leave restaurant.

Source: Reprinted with permission from "Scripts in Memory for Text," by Gordon H. Bower, John B. Black, and Terrence J. Turner, which appeared in *Cognitive Psychology,* April 1979, pp. 177–220.

Then, as consumers gain more experience in a situation, their cognitive system may organize several of these productions into a script sequence. For example, consumers who frequently go to auctions may develop a generalized script containing productions about how to register with the auctioneer before the sale, how to bid, when to use particular bidding strategies, how and when to pay for one's purchases, and so on. When activated in an auction environment, this script automatically guides and directs consumers' overt behaviors. Thus, these consumers do not have to make many conscious decisions since most of their relevant behaviors are controlled by the script. Figure 3.7 presents a highly simplified script for eating in a "fancy" restaurant.

Cognitive Learning

How do consumers learn the declarative and procedural knowledge in their schema and script structures? In this text, we distinguish between two broad types of learning – behavioral and cognitive learning. Behavioral learning is discussed in Section 3, cognitive learning is discussed here.

Cognitive learning occurs when people interpret information in the environment and create new knowledge or modify their existing knowledge structures in memory. Basically, consumers come into contact with information about products and services in three ways. Consumers can learn about products or services through *direct personal experience use.* Marketers use a variety of strategies such as in-store trial and free samples to give consumers a direct use experience. Auto dealers encourage consumers to "drive the car around the block." Clothing stores provide changing rooms for customers to try on garments and mirrors to evaluate their appearance. Ice cream parlors offer free sample tastes, and bedding retailers nearly always set up beds so customers can lie down and experience the feel of a mattress before buying.

Cognitive learning can also occur through consumers' *vicarious product experiences.* That is, consumers can acquire knowledge indirectly by observing others using the product. Most vicarious observation probably occurs accidentally when consumers notice other people using a product or service (seeing people using Rollerblades). Marketers can create vicarious product experiences for consumers through marketing strategies such as using in-store demonstrations or paying sports stars to wear certain clothes or shoes. Brands with higher market shares have an advantage over less popular brands because consumers are more likely to observe other people using a best-selling brand. Finally, much cognitive learning occurs when consumers process product-related information from the mass media (news stories, advertising, *Consumer Reports,* etc.) or from personal sources (friends and family).

Processing information about products and services can result in three types or levels of cognitive learning—accretion, tuning, and restructuring.[41] Figure 3.8 illustrates how these three types of cognitive learning can create and modify associative networks of knowledge. Marketers may develop strategies to influence each type of cognitive learning.

Accretion

Most cognitive learning probably occurs by **accretion.** As consumers interpret information about products and services, they add new knowledge, meaning, and beliefs to their existing knowledge structures—"Nike shoes are expensive, Nike shoes have good cushioning" (see Figure 3.8). Much learning research has focused on how people form declarative knowledge through accretion learning. However, more complex types of cognitive learning that involve changes to the *structure* of the associative knowledge network can also occur.

Tuning

As consumers gain experience with a product, knowledge structures tend to become larger and more complex through accretion processes. At some point, consumers may adjust their knowledge structures to make them more accurate and more generalizable. Most knowledge structures undergo minor changes in meaning as consumers continue to process information from the environment. As shown in Figure 3.8, **tuning** can occur when parts of a knowledge structure

FIGURE 3.8
Three Types of Cognitive Learning

Type of cognitive learning

Changes in knowledge structure

Accretion
Consumer begins to acquire knowledge, meanings, and beliefs about Nike shoes. With various experiences, new meanings are connected to the "Nike shoes" concept.

Consumer continues to add new meanings and beliefs to the knowledge structure for Nike shoes.

Tuning
Consumer forms an overall meaning for entire knowledge structure that summarizes all the meanings and beliefs: "Nike shoes are running shoes." Sets of related meanings are combined to form "larger," more abstract meanings.

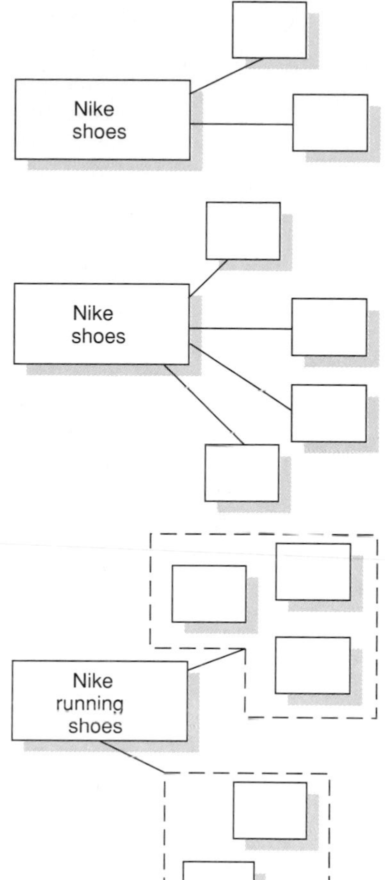

Restructuring
As more experience accumulates, consumer learns that Nike running shoes are highly variable. Not all Nike shoes are suitable for running. A restructuring of knowledge takes place. Separate knowledge structures, each with its own unique set of knowledge, meanings, and beliefs, are organized for the different types of Nike shoes that the consumer perceives.

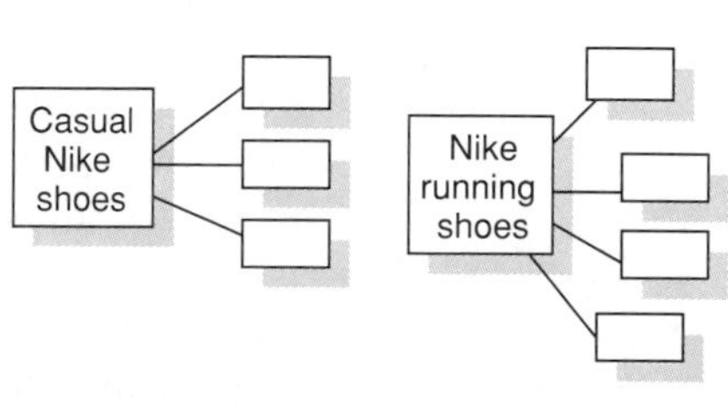

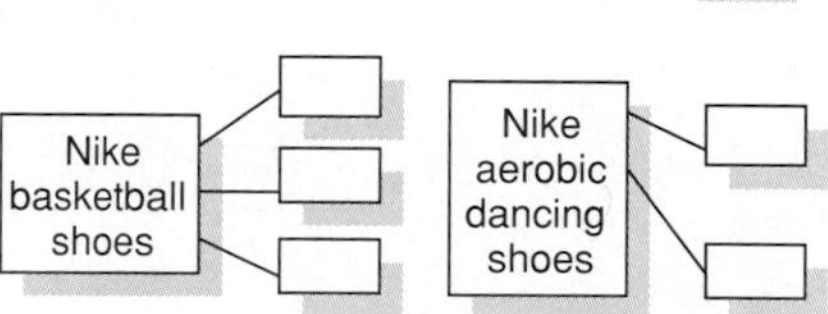

are combined and given a new overall meaning. For instance, several characteristics of a Nike shoe (lacing pattern, insole, reinforced heel) might be interpreted to mean "good support."

Restructuring

Restructuring involves revising the entire associative network of knowledge, which might involve creating entirely new meaning structures and/or reorganizing an old knowledge structure. Accretion, and sometimes tuning, can occur without much cognitive effort or awareness (essentially automatically). In contrast, restructuring usually involves extensive cognitive effort and substantial thinking and reasoning processes. Therefore, restructuring tends to be rare, occurring only when existing knowledge structures become excessively large and cumbersome (and possibly inaccurate). As illustrated in Figure 3.8, this may have happened in the athletic shoe market with the proliferation of specialized shoe models and styles introduced in the 1980s.

Sometimes the introduction of a product that is different from current products can force consumers to restructure their existing product knowledge to accommodate the new product. For instance, many consumers had to restructure their knowledge about cooking techniques when they began using microwave ovens. Changes in consumers' values can also precipitate a restructuring of consumers' product knowledge. For instance, the increasing environmental values of the late 1980s may have led some consumers to restructure their knowledge about disposable diapers and aerosol containers.

Marketing Implications

Many marketing strategies are aimed at accretion learning. Marketers often present simple informational claims about their products (Crest has a tartar control ingredient) and hope that consumers will accurately interpret the information and add this knowledge to their knowledge structures. In other cases, marketers may try to stimulate consumers to tune their knowledge structures (you need special Nike shoes for "cross training"). On rare occasions, marketers may wish to encourage consumers to restructure their knowledge (actually, beef is just as healthy as chicken).

In sum, marketers need to monitor consumers' knowledge structures and manage that knowledge. Marketers need to consider what types of meanings they want consumers to form and provide the appropriate information for consumers to process. The next chapter presents several ideas for analyzing consumers' product knowledge.

BACK TO....

BRUCE MACKLIN

To summarize what we have covered in this chapter and to review the cognitive processing model, let's return to our friend Bruce Macklin doing his weekly grocery shopping. Consider what happened as Bruce walked down the aisle containing breakfast cereal. We have divided this purchase occasion into smaller, discrete events and related each one to the appropriate part of our cognitive processing model. As you work through this example, consider how the various pieces and parts of the model fit together to help explain each event. (You may want to refer to Figure 3.5.)

Environmental/ behavioral event	Cognitive and affective processes
• Bruce noticed a bright orange shelf tag with an arrow and the words "Unadvertised Special."	Exposure to information and initial attention; slightly positive affective response
• The sign reminded him the supply of breakfast cereal at his house is getting low.	Activation of stored knowledge
• He looked at the package more closely.	More attention
• He saw that the product was a Kellogg's cereal, Raisin Squares.	Simple comprehension—interaction with stored knowledge
• He thought to himself that he likes most Kellogg's cereals and that his wife likes raisins.	Activation of additional stored knowledge about affective state
• He picked up a package and read "provides 11 essential vitamins and minerals."	Comprehension—interaction with activated knowledge
• As he turned the package around, he noticed more nutritional information. This "reminded" him of things he knows about nutrition.	Attention and more activated knowledge
• Bruce quickly noticed that Raisin Squares has the standard 25 percent RDA of most vitamins and minerals and it has no added salt. He understood what most of this nutritional information meant.	Attention and comprehension; interaction with activated knowledge

Packaging often includes a great deal of product information that consumers may process.

• Based on this information, Bruce was favorably disposed toward Raisin Squares.	Integration and attitude formation with mildly positive affect
• He then looked at the price on the shelf—$1.99 for 16.5 ounces.	Attention and comprehension
• Bruce considered all this information . . . and decided to buy a package . . . to see whether his wife would like it.	Integration processes Form an intention to buy Purchase goal
• He tossed a package of Raisin Squares into the grocery cart and continued shopping.	Choice behavior
• When Bruce got to the checkout counter, he paid for the Raisin Squares and the other products.	Purchase behavior

Summary

This chapter presents a number of concepts and ideas that will be used in later chapters. In particular, we introduced the important internal factors of affect and cognition and the affective and cognitive systems. We identified four types of affective responses ranging from emotions to specific feelings to moods to evaluations. We also described the cognitive system and the various types of meanings it constructs. We emphasized that these two systems are highly interrelated and the respective outputs of each constitute stimuli that elicit responses from the other. We believe this interactive view is the most useful for understanding consumer behavior.

Next, we presented a model of the cognitive processes involved in consumer decision making. The model has three basic components — knowledge, meanings, and beliefs in memory — and two broad cognitive processes — interpretation and integration. An important feature of this model is the close reciprocal interaction between knowledge structures and the cognitive processes that both create and use this knowledge.

Then we discussed the content and organization of knowledge as associative networks or knowledge structures. We described how meaning concepts are linked together to form propositions and productions that represent declarative knowledge (episodic and semantic knowledge) and procedural knowledge (how to perform behaviors). Then, we described two types of knowledge structures — schemas and scripts — that contain declarative and procedural knowledge, respectively. Schemas and scripts can be activated to guide cognitive processes and influence overt behaviors.

Key Terms and Concepts

Affect *48*
Cognitive Representations *50*
Cognition *51*
Information-Processing Models *57*
Interpretation Processes *60*
Integration Processes *60*
Knowledge, Meanings, and Beliefs *60*
Activation *61*
Spreading Activation *62*
Limited Capacity *63*
Automatic Processing *63*
Declarative Knowledge *64*
Procedural Knowledge *65*
Associative Network *66*
Schema *68*
Scripts *68*
Cognitive Learning *70*
Accretion *70*
Tuning *70*
Restructuring *72*

Review and Discussion Questions

1. Describe the four broad types of affective responses that are produced by the affective system.

2. What is a cognitive representation? Give an example that illustrates the distinction between information (stimuli) and cognitive representations of information.
3. How are the cognitive and affective systems different? How are they interrelated?
4. Consider a product such as an automobile or a perfume. Describe at least three types of subjective meanings that consumers might construct to represent various aspects of the product and ways marketers might try to influence the meaning.
5. What do researchers hope to accomplish by developing information-processing models of consumer cognition? What are some of the problems with these models?
6. For each type of knowledge activation process give an example from personal experience that is related to marketer influence and one that is not marketing related.
7. Compare and contrast declarative and procedural knowledge. Are they related?
8. Give an example of how exposure to a marketing strategy could cause spreading activation within a consumer's associative network of product knowledge.
9. Using a recent purchase as an example, develop a list of (*a*) influence factors; (*b*) reciprocal interactions; (*c*) affective responses; and (*d*) cognitive responses.
10. Describe how each of the cognitive processes in the model of consumer decision making (Figure 3.5) were present in your purchase situation (Question 9).

Notes

1. C. E. Izard, "Emotion-Cognition Relationships and Human Development," in *Emotions, Cognition and Behavior*, ed. C. E. Izard, J. Kagan, and R. B. Zajonc (New York: Cambridge University Press, 1984, pp. 17–37; Rom Harre, David Clarke, and Nicola De Carlo, *Motives and Mechanisms: An Introduction to the Psychology of Action* (London: Methuen, 1985), chap. 2, pp. 20–39; Jaak Panaksepp, "Toward a General Psychobiological Theory of Emotions. With Commentaries," *The Behavioral and Brain Sciences* 5 (1982), pp. 407–67; and Robert Plutchik, *Emotion: A Psychoevoluntionary Synthesis* (New York: Harper & Row, 1980).
2. Rik G. M. Pieters and W. Fred Van Raaij, "Functions and Management of Affect: Applications to Economic Behavior," *Journal of Economic Psychology* 9 (1988), pp. 251–82.
3. Martin L. Hoffman, "Affect, Cognition, and

Motivaton," in *Handbook of Motivation and Cognition,*" ed. R. M. Sorrentino and E. T. Higgins (New York: Guilford Press, 1986), pp. 244–80; and Anthony Ortony and Gerald L. Clore, "Disentangling the Affective Lexicon," *Proceedings of the Third Annual Conference of the Cognitive Science Society*, Berkeley, Calif., 1982.

4. Werner Kroeber-Riel, "Activation Research: Psychobiological Approaches in Consumer Research," *Journal of Consumer Research*, March 1979, pp. 240–50.

5. Meryl Paula Gardner, "Mood States and Consumer Behavior: A Critical Review," *Journal of Consumer Research*, December 1985, pp. 281–300.

6. See Harre et al., *Motives and Mechanisms: An Introduction to the Psychology of Action;* Robert B. Zajonc and Hazel Markus, "Affective and Cognitive Factors in Preferences," *Journal of Consumer Research* 9 (1982), pp. 123–31; Hoffman, "Affect, Cognition, and Motivation," pp. 244–80; Robert B. Zajonc, "On the Primacy of Affect," *American Psychologist* 39 (1984), pp. 117–23; and Richard S. Lazarus, "On the Primacy of Cognition," *American Psychologist* 39 (1984), pp. 124–29.

7. Michael K. Hui and John E. G. Bateson, "Perceived Control and the Effects of Crowding and Consumer Choice on the Service Experience," *Journal of Consumer Research*, September 1991, pp. 174–84.

8. Werner Kroeber-Riel, "Emotional Product Differentiation by Classical Conditioning," in *Advances in Consumer Research*, vol. 11, ed Thomas C. Kinnear (Ann Arbor, Mich.: Association for Consumer Research, 1982).

9. F. C. Bartlett, *Remembering: A Study in Experimental and Social Psychology* (Cambridge, England: Cambridge University Press, 1932); Jerry C. Olson, "Theories of Information Encoding and Storage: Implications for Consumer Research," in *The Effect of Information on Consumer and Market Behavior*, ed. A. A. Mitchell (Chicago: American Marketing Association, 1978), pp. 49–60; and Walter Weimer, "Overview of a Cognitive Conspiracy: Reflections on this Volume," in *Cognition and the Symbolic Process*, ed. W. B. Weimer and D. S. Palermo (New York: John Wiley & Sons, 1974).

10. For example, Sidney J. Levy, "Symbols for Sale," *Harvard Business Review*, July–August 1959, pp. 117–24; David Glen Mick, "Consumer Research and Semiotics: Exploring the Morphology of Signs, Symbols, and Significance," *Journal of Consumer Research*, September 1986, pp. 196–213; and Michael Solomon, "The Role of Products as Social Stimuli: A Symbolic Interactionism Perspective," *Journal of Consumer Research*, December 1983, pp. 319–29.

11. Gordon H. Bower, "Mood and Memory," *American Psychologist* 36 (1981), pp. 129–48.

12. For example, see the exchange between Yehoshua Tsal, "On the Relationship between Cognitive and Affective Processes: A Critique of Zajonc and Markus," *Journal of Consumer Research* 12 (1985), pp. 358–64; Zajonc and Markus, "Affective and Cognitive Factors in Preferences"; and Robert B. Zajonc and Hazel Markus, "Must All Affect Be Mediated by Cognition?" *Journal of Consumer Research* 12 (1985), pp. 363–64.

13. S. S. Tomkins, "Affect Theory," in *Emotion in the Human Face*, ed. P. Ekman (Cambridge, England: Cambridge University Press, 1983); Robert B. Zajonc, "On the Primacy of Affect," *American Psychologist* 39 (1984), pp. 117–23; and Richard S. Lazarus, "On the Primacy of Cognition," *American Psychologist* 39 (1984), pp. 124–29.

14. Lazarus, "On the Primacy of Cognition," pp. 124–29; Pieters and Van Raaij, "Functions and Management of Affect: Applications to Economic Behavior," pp. 251–82; and Richard S. Lazarus, "Cognition and Motivation in Emotion," *American Psychologist*, April 1991, pp. 352–67.

15. For example, see Julie A. Edell and Marian Chapman Burke, "The Power of Feelings in Understanding Advertising Effects," *Journal of*

Consumer Research, December 1987, pp. 421–33; William J. Havlena and Morris B. Holbrook, "The Varieties of Consumption Experience: Comparing Two Typologies of Emotion in Consumer Behavior," *Journal of Consumer Research*, December 1986, pp. 394–404; Morris B. Holbrook and Rajeev Batra, "Assessing the Role of Emotions as Mediators of Consumer Responses to Advertising," *Journal of Consumer Research*, December 1987, pp. 404–20; Rajeev Batra and Douglas M. Stayman, "The Role of Mood in Advertising Effectiveness," *Journal of Consumer Research*, September 1990, pp. 203–14.

16. For example, see Hoffman, "Affect, Cognition, and Motivation," pp. 244–80.

17. Dawn Dobni and George M. Zinkhan, "In Search of Brand Image: A Foundation Analysis," in *Advances in Consumer Research*, vol. 17 (Provo, Utah: Association for Consumer Research, 1990), pp. 110–19; Ernest Dichter, "What's in an Image?" *Journal of Consumer Marketing*, Winter 1985, pp. 75–81.

18. John R. Rossiter, Larry Percy, and Robert J. Donovan, "A Better Advertising Planning Grid," *Journal of Advertising Research*, October–November 1991, pp. 11–21; Brian Ratchford, "New Insights about the FCB Grid," *Journal of Advertising Research*, August–September 1987, pp. 24–38.

19. Mark Maremont, "They're All Screaming for Haagen-Dazs," *Business Week*, October 14, 1991, p. 121.

20. Kathleen Deveny, "As Lauder's Scent Battles Calvin Klein's, Cosmetics Whiz Finds Herself on the Spot," *The Wall Street Journal*, June 27, 1991, pp. B1, B6.

21. Robert Chestnut and Jacob Jacoby, "Consumer Information Processing: Emerging Theory and Findings," in *Consumer and Industrial Buying Behavior*, ed. A. Woodside, J. N. Sheth, and P. D. Bennett (New York: Elsevier-North Holland, 1977), pp. 119–33; and Roy Lachman, Janet Lachman, and Earl Butterfield, *Cognitive Psychology and Information Processing: An Introduction* (Hillsdale, N.J.: Lawrence Erlbaum, 1979).

22. Allan Newell and Herbert A. Simon, *Human Problem Solving* (Englewood Cliffs, N.J.: Prentice Hall, 1972).

23. A complex information-processing model of consumer decision making was developed by John Howard and Jagdish Sheth, *The Theory of Buyer Behavior* (New York: John Wiley & Sons, 1969). More recently Bettman introduced another complex information-processing model—James R. Bettman, *An Information processing Model of Consumer Choice* (Reading, Mass.: Addison-Wesley Publishing, 1979).

24. For example, see William J. McGuire, "The Internal Psychological Factors Influencing Consumer Choice," *Journal of Consumer Research*, March 1976, pp. 302–19; and Ivan L. Preston, "The Association Model of the Advertising Communication Process," *Journal of Advertising* 2 (1982), pp. 3–15.

25. Harold H. Kassarjian, "Consumer Research: Some Recollections and a Commentary," in *Advances in Consumer Research*, vol. 9, ed. Richard J. Lutz (Ann Arbor, Mich.: Association for Consumer Research, 1986), pp. 240–50; and Kent Nakamoto, "Alternatives to Information Processing in Consumer Research: New Perspectives on Old Controversies," *International Journal of Research in Marketing* 4 (1987), pp. 11–27.

26. Morris B. Holbrook and Elizabeth C. Hirschman, "The Experimental Aspects of Consumption: Consumer Fantasies, Feelings, and Fun," *Journal of Consumer Research*, September 1982, pp. 132–40.

27. Olson, "Theories of Information Encoding and Storage," pp. 49–60.

28. Alan M. Collins and Elizabeth F. Loftus, "A Spreading Activation Theory of Semantic Memory," *Psychological Review* 82 (1975), pp. 407–28.

29. Jeffrey F. Durgee and Robert W. Stuart, "Advertising Symbols and Brand Names that Best

Represent Key Product Meanings," *Journal of Advertising*, Summer 1987, pp. 15–24.

30. John R. Anderson, "A Spreading Activation Theory of Memory," *Journal of Verbal Learning and Verbal Behavior* 22 (1983), pp. 261–75; and Collins and Loftus, "A Spreading Activation Theory of Semantic Memory," pp. 407–28.

31. John A. Bargh, "Automatic and Conscious Processing of Social Information," in *Handbook of Social Cognition*, vol. 3, ed. R. S. Wyer and T. K. Srull (Hillsdale, N.J.: Lawrence Erlbaum, 1984), pp. 1–43; and Richard M. Schiffrin and Susan T. Dumais, "The Development of Automatism," in Cognitive Skills and Their Development, ed. John R. Anderson (Hillsdale, N.J.: Lawrence Erlbaum, 1981), pp. 111–40.

32. Wayne A. Wickelgren, "Human Learning and Memory," in *Annual Review of Psychology*, ed. M. R. Rosenzweig and L. W. Porter (Palo Alto, Calif.: Annual Reviews, 1981), pp. 21–52.

33. John R. Anderson, *The Architecture of Cognition* (Cambridge, Mass.: Harvard University Press, 1983); and Terence R. Smith, Andrew A. Mitchell, and Robert Meyer, "A Computational Process Model of Evaluation Based on the Cognitive Structuring of Episodic Knowledge," in *Advances in Consumer Research*, vol. 9, ed. Andrew A. Mitchell (Ann Arbor, Mich.: Association for Consumer Research, 1982), pp. 136–43.

34. Endel Tulving, "Episodic and Semantic Memory," in *Organization of Memory*, ed. Endel Tulving (New York: Academic Press, 1972), pp. 382–404.

35. Donald A. Norman, *The Psychology of Everyday Things* (New York: Basic Books, 1988).

36. Bruce Nussbaum and Robert Neff, "I Can't Work This Thing!" *Business Week*, April 29, 1991, pp. 58–66.

37. Although many types of memory structures have been proposed, most can be reduced to the more general associative network model. See James R. Bettman, "Memory Factors in Consumer Choice: A Review," *Journal of Marketing* 43 (Spring 1979), pp. 37–53; Andrew A. Mitchell, "Models of Memory: Implications for Measuring Knowledge Structures," in *Advances in Consumer Research*, vol. 9, ed. Andrew A. Mitchell (Ann Arbor, Mich.: Association for Consumer Research, 1982), pp. 45–51; and Edward Smith, "Theories of Semantic Memory," in *Handbook of Learning and Cognitive Processes*, vol. 6, ed. W. K. Estes (Hillsdale, N.J.: Lawrence Erlbaum, 1978), pp. 1–56.

38. Merrie Brucks and Andrew Mitchell, "Knowledge Structures, Production Systems and Decision Strategies," in *Advances in Consumer Research*, vol. 8, ed. Kent B. Monroe (Ann Arbor, Mich.: Association for Consumer Research, 1982).

39. Joseph W. Alba and Lynn Hasher, "Is Memory Schematic?" *Psychological Bulletin*, March 1983, pp. 203–31; and Donald E. Rumelhart and Anthony Ortony, "The Representation of Knowledge in Memory," in *Schooling and the Acquisition of Knowledge*, eds. R. C. Anderson, R. J. Spiro, and W. E. Montague (Hillsdale, N.J.: Lawrence Erlbaum, 1977), pp. 99–136.

40. Thomas W. Leigh and Arno J. Rethans, "Experiences with Script Elicitation within Consumer Decision-Making Contexts," in *Advances in Consumer Research*, vol. 10, ed. R. P. Bagozzi and A. M. Tybout (Ann Arbor, Mich.: Association for Consumer Research, 1983), pp. 667–72; and Roger C. Schank and Robert P. Abelson, *Scripts, Plans, Goals and Understanding: An Inquiry into Human Knowledge Structure* (Hillsdale, N.J.: Lawrence Erlbaum, 1977).

41. David E. Rumelhart and Donald A. Norman, "Accretion, Tuning and Restructuring: Three Modes of Learning," in *Semantic Factors in Cognition*, ed. J. W. Cotton and R. L. Klatsky (Hillsdale, N.J.: Lawrence Erlbaum, 1978), pp. 37–53.

Additional Reading

For a discussion of the relationship between affect and cognition, see:

Pieters, Rik G. M., and W. Fred Van Raaij. "Functions and Management of Affect: Applications to Economic Behavior," *Journal of Economic Psychology* 9 (1988), pp. 251–82.

Many examples of how affect can influence consumer behavior are provided in:

Peterson, Robert A.; Wayne D. Hoyer; and William R. Wilson, ed. *The Role of Affect in Consumer Behavior: Emerging Theories and Applications.* Lexington, Mass.: D.C. Heath, 1986.

For a general discussion of the information-processing approach to cognition, see:

Lachman, Roy; Janet Lachman; and Earl Butterfield. *Cognitive Psychology and Information Processing: An Introduction.* Hillsdale, N.J.: Lawrence Erlbaum, 1979, especially chapter 2.

For a current review of information-processing research in consumer behavior, see:

Bettman, James R. and Mita Sujan. "Research in Consumer Information Processing." In *Review of Marketing, 1987*, ed. M. J. Houston, Chicago: American Marketing Association, 1988, pp. 197–235.

For discussions of how information-processing theory can be used to understand consumers and develop marketing strategies, see:

Tybout, Alice M.; Bobby J. Calder; and Brian Sternthal. "Using Information Processing Theory to Design Marketing Strategies." *Journal of Marketing Research*, February 1981.

For a readable discussion of some of the problems with the early information-processing models and suggestions for how they can be improved, see:

Grunert, Klaus. "Research in Consumer Behavior: Beyond Attitudes and Decision Making." *European Research*, August 1988, pp. 172–83.

For an analysis of procedural knowledge and scripts (of salespeople, not consumers), see:

Leigh, Thomas W., and Patrick F. McGraw. "Mapping the Procedural Knowledge of Industrial Sales Personnel: A Script-Theoretic Investigation." *Journal of Marketing*, January 1989, pp. 16–34.

For an analysis of how consumers' knowledge structures change as they acquire more experience and expertise, see:

Alba, Joseph, and J. Wesley Hutchinson. "Dimensions of Consumer Expertise." *Journal of Consumer Research*, March 1987, pp. 411–54.

For a discussion of five types of emotional experiences, see:

Westbrook, Robert A., and Richard L. Oliver. "The Dimensionality of Consumption Emotion Patterns and Consumer Satisfaction." *Journal of Consumer Research*, June 1991, pp. 84–91.

For a discussion of the meanings of music, see:

Scott, Linda M. "Understanding Jingles and Needledrop: A Rhetorical Approach to Music in Advertising." *Journal of Consumer Research*, September 1990, pp. 223–36.

For a discussion of the activation of price knowledge, see:

Herr, Paul M. "Priming Price: Prior Knowledge and Context Effects," *Journal of Consumer Research*, June 1989, pp. 67–75.

MARKETING STRATEGY IN ACTION

Please Don't Squeeze the Charmin!

In 1980, the Proctor & Gamble Co. (P&G) celebrated the 15th anniversary of the "Mr. Whipple" advertising campaign for Charmin bathroom tissue. At the time, it was probably the longest running and most widely recognized national television advertising ever produced. Certainly, it was one of the most effective.

Procter & Gamble purchased the Charmin brand in 1957. At the time, Charmin bathroom tissue (toilet paper to most of us) was sold only in the Midwest and was not the category leader. Under P&G management, however, that was soon to change. Through marketing research, P&G learned consumers considered softness to be of key importance in a bathroom tissue. Unfortunately, the original Charmin was not particularly soft, so P&G set out to improve product quality.

Toilet paper begins as a mixture of 99 percent water and 1 percent wood pulp. Most manufacturers squeeze the solution to extract the water, but tissue made in this way is compacted, "hard," and "rough." By the early 1960s, P&G had developed a new manufacturing technology that used hot air dryers to remove water from the paper. This process significantly improved tissue softness (and also absorption).

The new, softer Charmin was an overwhelming success in its 1966 rollout and increased its share of the midwestern market by 30 percent in two years. As P&G expanded into each new market area, Charmin usually became the leading brand. In fact, Charmin was the no. 1 brand in the United States even before it achieved complete national distribution in 1975.

A key reason for this success, of course, was Charmin's high quality and the distinct product benefit (softness) it provided consumers. But part of Charmin's success must be attributed to its advertising strategy and to the unique television commercials that P&G's agency, Benton & Bowles, developed to communicate the softness benefit. In 1964, they introduced the advertising strategy, "Please Don't Squeeze the Charmin," which remained essentially unchanged over the entire life of the campaign.

Do you remember these ads? In each one, George Whipple, the mild-mannered owner of a grocery store, tried to keep people (usually homemakers) from squeezing the Charmin. He always failed and ended up squeezing the Charmin himself. In this long-running campaign, the Charmin product was portrayed as irresistible due to its special softness, the consumer was shown handling the product (which had previously been thought too sensitive an object to show), and humor was used to defuse a previously taboo subject. Although this strategy initially had a number of detractors, the critics were overcome when a Mr. Whipple test commercial received one of the highest recall scores ever recorded by the company and agency.

At least three characteristics of this advertising strategy made it easy for consumers to understand and remember it, thus accounting for its longevity:

Source: Adapted from "Marketing Classics: Please Don't Squeeze the Charmin," *Marketing Communications,* March 1990, pp. 54–55.

1. Squeezing Charmin is similar to squeezing vegetables, a behavior that most people who buy toilet paper can relate to.
2. Squeezing is a unique method of demonstrating the product's softness.
3. Repeatedly showing the Mr. Whipple character in a variety of similar situations maintained consumers' interest.

Despite these advantages, sustaining the Mr. Whipple campaign over more than two decades was not easy. The agency had to guard against doing the same thing over and over. At the same time, while freshness was desired, the essential elements crucial to the success of the strategy had to be preserved. Thus, all Charmin ads had the same simple plot—women always squeezed the Charmin and Mr. Whipple always tried to stop them (unsuccessfully). Moreover, Mr. Whipple was never able to resist squeezing the Charmin himself, and, much to his chagrin, he was usually caught doing so.

To introduce variety, the details of the ads differed widely. Mr. Whipple was seen in his store, in front of it, in his home, in his neighborhood, in a competitor's store, and even in a rowboat on a lake. He used all manner of devices to catch women squeezing the Charmin, including a Whipple-activated phonograph that admonished women not to squeeze and a giant finger that popped up to identify the offending squeezer. Whipple enlisted a policeman, a store clerk, a parrot, and even a "twin" Whipple to help catch squeezers. And in one series of ads, Mr. Whipple had to contend with the unthinkable—a rival storekeeper who actually encouraged women to squeeze the Charmin.

Was all this advertising effective? Apparently so, given the sales success of Charmin during this period. And, in 1980, research showed Charmin awareness and memorability at or near its highest levels ever.

At least part of the credit for this longevity must go to Dick Wilson, who played George Whipple in over 300 commercials. He managed to keep the Whipple character fresh and believable, despite the whimsical nature of the advertising. In fact, Wilson was so believable as Mr. Whipple that people were startled to run into him at the North Hollywood California grocery where he did his own shopping. Apparently, some people thought they were in the real Mr. Whipple's store.

Did the Mr. Whipple campaign continue forever? Surely not. No marketing strategy can expect to be successful over the very long run. But during the 15-year run described here, none of the more than 50 alternative, non-Whipple campaigns that Benton & Bowles developed tested strong enough to dislodge Mr. Whipple.

Discussion Questions

1. Three reasons were mentioned for why the Mr. Whipple campaign was so long-lived. Explain each of these three reasons in terms of consumers' affective and cognitive reactions to these ads. Why don't the ad campaigns for most other products have such a long life?
2. Discuss how consumers' affective responses to the ads could have influenced their cognitive interpretations of Charmin, and vice versa. How might these affective and cognitive responses have affected consumers' purchase behaviors?
3. Describe how consumers' knowledge about Charmin (and other factors) might have interacted with their interpretation processes when they were exposed to a Mr. Whipple ad. How might consumers' knowledge about Charmin (and other factors) interact with their integration processes in a decision-making situation?
4. Using an associative network model, describe a possible knowledge structure that a consumer might have formed for Charmin. How might this knowledge structure have changed over the period of this advertising campaign?

Consumers' Product Knowledge and Involvement

CHAPTER 4

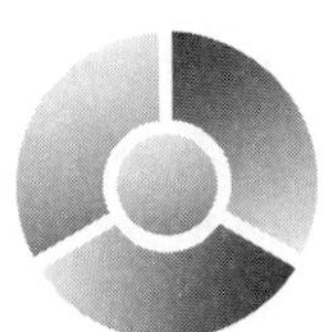

PROCTER & GAMBLE'S REBOUND

It was hard to believe, but in the early 1980s Procter & Gamble's seemingly invincible marketing juggernaut was sputtering. Many of its blockbuster brands had lost market share. Worse, profits plummeted 29 percent in 1985, the biggest decline in 37 years. Although some thought P&G might be in a terminal decline, the "wounded lion" came roaring back. In 1986, P&G scored big market gains in diapers, toothpaste, and detergents—its strongest product categories that together account for about half of its profits.

A key reason for the turnaround was P&G's renewed commitment to developing high quality products. P&G stopped chasing the competition with lackluster, me-too products and returned to its original philosophy of producing items with superior product attributes that deliver important benefits to consumers.

Take disposable diapers, for instance. P&G had created the product category and was the market leader with the Pampers brand. Since 1979, however, Kimberly-Clark had been soaking up market share from P&G. Its brand, Huggies, with a contoured shape and no-leak elastic leg openings was considered by many consumers to be superior to P&G's premium-priced Luvs. And,

at the other end of the market, shoppers had been deserting the mid-priced Pampers for cheaper generic brands. These factors combined to reduce P&G's share of the disposable diaper market from 69 to 47 percent beween 1978 and 1985. Earnings were even worse, with profits falling from $275 million in 1983 to a mere $25 million in 1985.

Then, in late 1985, P&G introduced Blue Ribbon Pampers with an elasticized waist and legs (the leakproof benefits are obvious). This was closely followed by the introduction of Ultra Pampers, a technically sophisticated product containing a special chemical that turns to a gel when wet and holds moisture away from babies' skin. This results in drier babies and less diaper rash. Drier, nonirritated babies are more comfortable and happier and this, in turn, makes parents happier. In addition, Ultra Pampers were also thinner than competitive brands, making them easier for parents to tote around. Although introducing Ultra Pampers wasn't cheap for P&G (the company spent more than $500 million to renovate its manufacturing facilities), the payoff was spectacular. P&G's market share skyrocketed to 61 percent in 1986, while Kimberly-Clark's share slipped 7 points to 28 percent.

The same story played in the toothpaste market. There, too, P&G had an exceptionally strong brand, Crest. In 1979, P&G enjoyed a 19 percent market share lead over rival Colgate-Palmolive, but by 1985, the P&G lead had almost evaporated to less than 2 percent. P&G had become complacent while Colgate and other companies developed new products such as gels and pump dispensers. Finally, P&G responded with its own gels and pump dispensers. But most importantly, P&G introduced new Tartar Control Crest. This was the first toothpaste to use a new cleansing agent, sodium pyrophosphate, that P&G claimed was the most important new toothpaste ingredient since the company first introduced fluoride some 30 years before. Why? Sodium pyrophosphate reduces hard tartar buildup on the teeth, a common problem for adults. The result? P&G's market share rebounded.

Despite P&G's recent successes, its major competitors such as Kimberly-Clark, Colgate-Palmolive, and Lever (detergents) are not giving up. They are continuing to develop new product attributes that provide important consumer benefits. As usual, the ultimate winner in these marketing battles is the consumer.

Source: Adapted from Faye Rice, "The King of Suds Reigns Again," *Fortune,* August 4, 1986, pp. 130-32, and 134.

This description of Procter & Gamble's problems illustrates the importance of product attributes in marketing strategy and the need for marketers to understand what consumers think about product attributes and related concepts. In this chapter, we examine consumers' product knowledge and involvement, two important concepts in the affect and cognition portion of the Wheel of Consumer Analysis. We begin by discussing four levels of product-related knowledge. Then we discuss consumers' knowledge about product attributes, benefits, and values. We show how these three types of meanings can be linked to form a simple associative network of knowledge, called a *means-end chain.* Next, we examine the important concept of consumers' interest or involvement with products and other aspects of their environments. The means-end model is used to help explain consumers' feelings of involvement. We conclude the chapter by discussing how means-end chains can be used to analyze consumers' relationships with products and brands and how marketing strategies can influence consumers' felt involvement.

Levels of Abstraction in Product Knowledge

Consumers can have product knowledge, meanings, and beliefs at different **levels of abstraction.** For instance, consumers may think about a tennis racket at a rather *concrete level* in terms of its physical characteristics—grip material (leather or synthetic), shape (oversize or regular), composition (ceramic or graphite).[1] At a *more abstract level,* consumers could think about the functional performance of the racket—its responsiveness, control, or power. Finally, consumers can think about a tennis racket at a *very abstract level,* in terms of the enjoyment or feelings of accomplishment it provides.

No one level of abstraction captures all the possible meanings of an object, event, or behavior. Each level of meaning is useful for certain purposes, but may not be appropriate for other purposes. Meanings at different levels of abstraction are related hierarchically, in that more abstract meanings subsume less abstract meanings. For instance, the responsiveness of a tennis racket subsumes (incorporates or includes) the materials of its construction, shape of the head, type of strings, and so on. The concept of levels of abstraction is used throughout the text.

As you learned in Chapter 3, meanings (at different levels of abstraction) are formed by comprehension processes, a fundamental aspect of cognition. Categorization theory can help us understand the comprehension process and how consumers make sense of products and brands. **Categorization** can be described as follows:

> The world consists of a virtually infinite number of discriminably different stimuli. One of the most basic functions of all organisms is the cutting up of the environment into classifications [categories] by which nonidentical stimuli can be treated as equivalent.[2]

Consumers interpret aspects of their environment by forming new categories of meaning (cognitive representations). Categorization involves combining separate cognitive concepts into "larger meaning units," or categories, that subsume their individual component meanings.[3] For instance, a consumer might combine automobile meanings of braking, acceleration, and cornering ability to form a more abstract category called handling. Once a meaning category is formed, the cognitive system can respond to each member of that category *as if it were the category concept*, even though the member concepts are not identical. For instance, people can consider various types of bicycles as bikes, an overall category. But people can also think about various (sub)categories of bicycles—racing, mountain, BMX, city bikes—each of which is itself a meaning category made up of separate concepts (different types of racing bikes or mountain bikes). These meaning categories—bikes, mountain bikes, and types of mountain bikes—are at different levels of abstraction and form a hierarchical structure. As a central aspect of comprehension, categorization has many applications and implications for consumer behavior analysis. These are discussed throughout this text.[4]

For now, we focus on how consumers organize the product offerings in a market into categories with distinctive meanings. Figure 4.1 identifies four categories of product knowledge—product class, product form, brand, and model—and gives several examples of these levels.

Consumers' knowledge about *brands* is probably of greatest interest to marketing managers. Most marketing strategies are brand oriented in that they are intended to make consumers aware of a brand, teach people about a brand, or influence consumers to buy a particular brand. Thus, the bulk of marketing research focuses on consumers' knowledge and beliefs about brands. Likewise,

FIGURE 4.1
Types or Levels of Product Knowledge

More Abstract ←→ Less Abstract			
Product Class	Product Form	Brand	Model/Features
Coffee	Ground Instant	Folgers Maxwell House	3-pound can 8-ounce jar
Automobiles	Sedan Sports car Sports sedan	Ford Nissan BMW	Taurus, with air and power steering 300ZX, with air and 5-speed Model 325e, with air and automatic transmission
Pens	Ball point Felt tip	Bic Pilot	$.79 model, regular tip $.99 model, extra-fine tip
Beer	Imported Light Low alcohol	Heineken Miller Lite Sharps	Dark Kegs 12-ounce cans

much of the discussion in this text concerns consumers' brand knowledge. Other categories of knowledge, however, are relevant to marketers.

For many products, the brand level of product knowledge is itself a category that subsumes several models. *Models* of a brand differ in certain product features or attributes (see Figure 4.1 for examples). For instance, Nikon 35mm cameras are available in several different models; Coca-Cola comes in diet, caffeine-free, and flavored versions; and Haagen-Dazs ice cream is sold in multiple flavors. Each model of BMW automobile (including the various 325, 525, and 850 models) varies in size, price, and exterior design and is available with distinctive features and options such as air-conditioning, fancy wheels, automatic braking systems, leather seats, and so on.

Multiple brands that are similar in some important way may be combined to form a broader, more abstract category of meaning called a *product form.* Often, the basis for forming a product-form category is a dominant physical characteristic of the brands, such as freeze-dried, instant, ground, and whole-bean forms of coffee. In some cases, certain product forms become so well established in consumers' minds that marketers can treat them as separate markets (diet soft drinks, sports sedans, and laptop computers may be examples).

The *product class* is the most inclusive level of product knowledge, subsuming several product forms (and all the brands and models within those categories). Concepts at the product-class level have relatively few features in common. For example, about the only feature that defines the product class of coffee is that the various product forms are made from coffee beans. In some cases, marketers might develop strategies to promote the entire product class, which can be effective if one's brand has a high market share. For example, Frito-Lay could promote consumption of salty snacks (potato and flavored chips) in general because it controls as much as 60 or 70 percent of that product-class category.

Marketers need to understand consumers' knowledge at these different levels because consumers often make separate purchase decisions at each level.[5] For instance, a consumer might choose between alternative product classes (buy a television rather than a stereo system), different product forms (purchase a large-screen TV rather than a console type), various brands (buy an RCA rather than Sony), and alternative models (choose a 27-inch RCA TV with stereo speakers rather than a 25-inch RCA set without stereo). In sum, consumers' brand-level knowledge is important, but other levels of product knowledge are also of concern to the marketing manager.

Consumers' Product Knowledge

Consumers can have knowledge about the attributes or characteristics of products, the consequences of using products, and the values that products may help consumers to achieve (see Figure 4.2). Marketers have thought about and analyzed these three types or levels of consumers' product knowledge, as we discuss below.

Products as Bundles of Attributes

As the Procter & Gamble example demonstrates, decisions about product characteristics or attributes are important elements of marketing strategy. Within the limits imposed by production capabilities and financial resources, marketing managers can add new attributes to a product ("Now, Diet 7UP contains 100% NutraSweet"), remove old attributes ("Caffeine-free Diet Pepsi"), or modify existing attributes (in 1985, Coca-Cola managers modified the century-old secret recipe for Coke). Marketers change brand attributes in an attempt to make their products more appealing to consumers. For instance, to give Liquid Tide its cleaning power, chemists at Procter & Gamble created a new molecule and included twice as many active ingredients as competitive brands. The 400,000 hours of research and development time seemed to pay off, as Liquid Tide's initial sales skyrocketed.[6] Highlight 4.1 describes a successful change of product attributes.

Perhaps because they are so interested in the physical characteristics of their products, marketers sometimes act as if consumers think about products and brands as *bundles of attributes.* Even the simplest products have several attributes

FIGURE 4.2
What Is a Product?

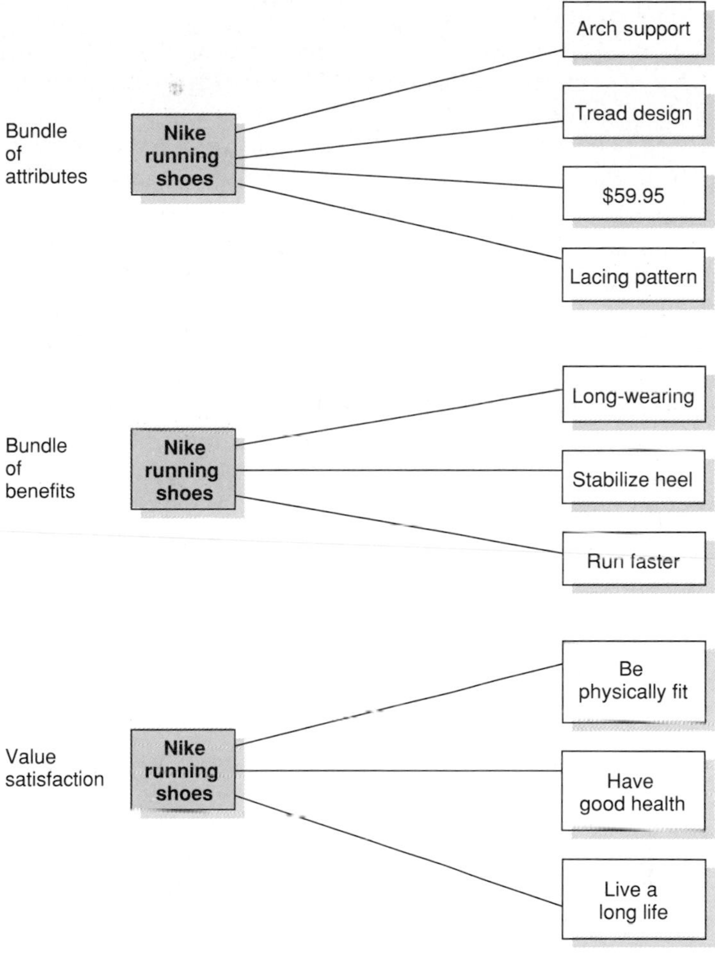

(pencils have varying lead densities, softness of erasers, shapes, and colors). Of course, complex products such as automobiles and stereo receivers have a great many attributes. From a cognitive processing perspective, however, we might wonder if consumers really have knowledge in memory about all of these attributes, and whether consumers actually activate and use this knowledge when thinking about products and brands. This raises important questions about which product attributes are most important to consumers, what those attributes mean to consumers, and how this knowledge is used in cognitive processes such as comprehension and decision making.

HIGHLIGHT 4.1

What's in a Handle?

The old Pyrex measuring cup made by Corning Glass Works was a kitchen classic. The glass cup with its familiar attributes—a simple volume gauge printed in red on one side, the pouring lip, and the nice big handle—was found in as many as 80 percent of American households. Even though the bulky handle made the three sizes (1-, 2-, and 4-cup) difficult to stack, no one complained. In fact, the cups had not changed much since they had been introduced some 50 years before. Why should marketers change the attributes of a product this successful?

The idea for changing the attributes of the Pyrex measuring cup came about by accident when the handle on a test product sagged during heating. This gave designers the idea of an "open" handle that was attached to the cup only at one end. Besides being cheaper to produce, this handle would make the cups stackable, and therefore more convenient to store in a cupboard. Corning also added a second new attribute, making the cup a bit deeper so that foods could be heated in microwave ovens without boiling over. However, the designers kept the familiar red measuring gauge on the side. What was the result of making these simple changes in the attributes of this product? Sales increased 150 percent.

Source: Toni Mack, "What's in a Handle?" *Forbes,* January 25, 1988, p. 87.

Consumers have different levels of knowledge about product attributes.[7] Knowledge about **abstract attributes** represents intangible, subjective characteristics of a product such as the quality or warmth of a blanket or the stylishness or comfort of a car. Consumers' knowledge about **concrete attributes** represents tangible, physical characteristics of a product such as the type of fiber in a blanket or the front-seat legroom in a car.[8] In addition, attribute knowledge may also contain representations of consumers' affective evaluations of each attribute (I dislike the itchiness of wool blankets; I like the layout of the Apple keyboard).

Products as Bundles of Benefits

Some marketers have pointed out that consumers usually tend to think about products and brands in terms of their consequences, not their attributes.[9] *Consequences* are specific outcomes that happen to a consumer when the product is purchased and used or consumed. For instance, a stereo system might work well, require assembly or repairs, or make the user feel proud. A facial cream might cause an allergic reaction or cost too much. Other consumers might think the buyer is either hip or foolish for buying a certain brand of jeans or sneakers.

It is useful to distinguish between two broad types or levels of product consequences — functional and psychosocial. **Functional consequences** are less abstract outcomes of product use that are more tangible and more directly experienced by consumers. For instance, functional consequences include the immediate physiological outcomes of product use (eating a Big Mac satisfies your hunger; drinking a Pepsi eliminates your thirst). Functional consequences also include the physical, tangible, performance outcomes of using or consuming a product — a hair blower dries your hair quickly, a car gets a certain number of miles per gallon, a toaster browns bread evenly, and an ink pen writes smoothly without skipping.

In contrast, *psychological consequences* of product use are less tangible and more personal outcomes, such as how the product makes you feel. For instance, using Nexxus shampoo might make you feel more attractive, wearing Benetton sportswear might make you feel more attractive or stylish, and eating an ice cream cone from Baskin-Robbins might make you feel happy. Consumers also have knowledge about the relatively abstract, intangible *social consequences* of product use ("My friends will like/respect/envy me if I buy a Fischer stereo system"; "My mother will think I am a smart shopper if I buy this jacket on sale"). We use the term **psychosocial consequences** to refer to both types of outcomes.

The subjective, personal meanings of functional and psychosocial consequences are represented by consumers' cognitive systems. Since these consequences are experienced by consumers, they are likely to elicit affective responses such as emotions, feelings, and evaluations. For instance, most consumers would feel a negative affect if a product needed repairs soon after it is bought. Or a consumer might have positive feelings of pride and self-esteem if other people comment favorably on a new dress or sweater. These affective responses may be stored in memory, where they can be activated and used later.

It is important to distinguish between the positive and negative consequences of product purchase and use (perceived benefits and perceived risks, respectively). **Benefits** represent the desirable consequences consumers seek when buying and using products and brands ("I want my stereo system to have excellent sound reproduction," or "I want people to notice me"). The cognitive representations of benefits may also include the positive affects associated with these desirable outcomes (favorable evaluations, positive feelings and emotions).

Because marketers tend to focus on the positive consequences of buying and using products, consumers have been characterized as thinking about products as *bundles of benefits*, not attributes.[10] This idea has led to *benefit segmentation*, the process of dividing consumers into homogeneous subgroups or segments based on their desire for particular product benefits.[11] For example, some consumers of toothpaste are seeking appearance benefits (whiter teeth), while others are more interested in health benefits (preventing tooth decay).

This ad promotes one benefit (a desirable consequence) of using Colgate toothpaste.

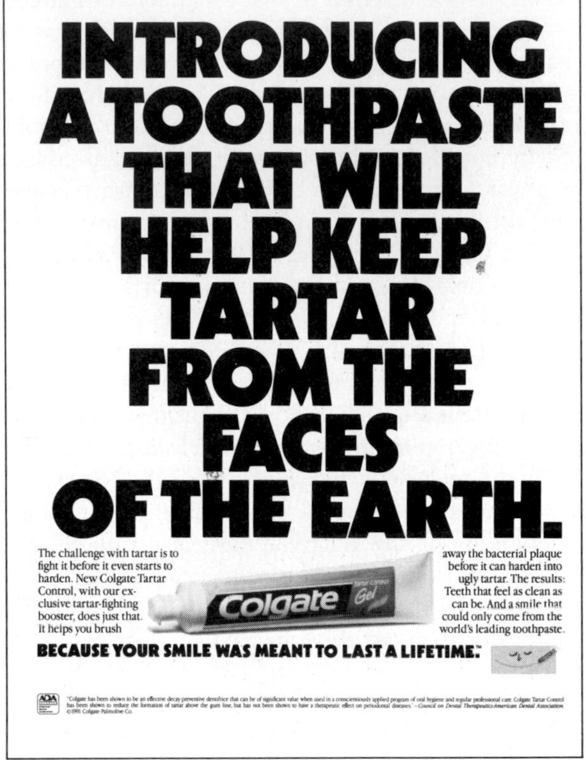

In contrast, **perceived risks** represent the undesirable consequences people seek to avoid when buying and using products. There are several types of perceived risk, corresponding to the various negative consequences that might occur. Many consumers worry about the *physical risks* of product consumption (being harmed by a product). Highlight 4.2 discusses some problems in realistically assessing the physical risks of products. Other types of unpleasant consequences include *financial risk* (paying more than one should), *functional risk* (the product doesn't work as well as it should), and *psychosocial risk* (other people might think negatively of me). Consumers' knowledge about risk also contains representations of the negative affect associated with these unpleasant consequences (unfavorable evaluations, negative feelings and emotions).

Marketers sometimes try to create perceived risk and show how their brand reduces or avoids it. For instance, the advertising campaigns run by American Telephone & Telegraph in the late 1980s were intended to generate fear, anxiety, and perceived risk among business executives by reminding them of the negative consequences of making a bad decision about their phone system (not buying AT&T).[12] In one of these "slice of death" commercials, two young

HIGHLIGHT 4.2

The Perception and Reality of Risk

Many Americans seem to believe consumer products should involve no risk and that attaining zero risk is possible. Yet, as we reduce significant risks in our environments, consumers seem to become ever more anxious about the imagined hazards of modern life. People are confused about perceived risks of products, partly because several of the major "hazards" of recent years turned out to be false alarms or were greatly exaggerated.

The Alar scare of 1989 was an example. A series of news stories (including a televised segment on "60 Minutes") reported a study in which rats developed cancers when fed dosages of Alar (a growth hormone used on apple trees). Estimates of 200 to 900 deaths from cancer per million people created a great deal of publicity and hysteria. People dumped apple juice down the drain, and apple sales plummeted. Some hysterical consumers even called the Environmental Protection Agency to ask if the ground water could be contaminated by discarded apple juice. The original study was discredited when it was found that the rats were fed dosages of Alar over 200,000 times higher than human exposure levels. Studies were redone, and the recomputed risk estimates were found to be minuscule. In fact, because Alar makes apples bond to the tree more strongly, it reduces the need for stronger pesticides and, therefore, might actually reduce the incidence of cancers.

A similar situation occurred in 1990, when Perrier (a French brand of mineral water) was discovered to contain minute amounts of benzene, a known carcinogen. The benzene was a natural ingredient in the carbon dioxide gas that bubbles up in the springs in France. The benzene usually was removed by filters, but an employee had not changed the filter frequently enough. One problem in risk assessment is that our technologies for measuring tiny quantities of harmful compounds in products outstrips our ability to make reasonable judgments about what to do about it. The amount of benzene detected in Perrier was 19 parts per billion. Fifteen years earlier, that level of benzene concentration could not have been detected.

Did this make Perrier dangerous? It all depends on your perceptions of and tolerance for very small risks. The actual risks of developing cancer from drinking Perrier were extremely small. One expert estimated the additional cancer risk from drinking one liter of the "contaminated" Perrier every day for 70 years as somewhere between 1 in 100,000 and 1 in 10 million. This means that if every American drank one liter of Perrier a day every day of their life, the additional number of cancer deaths might be 200 or so per year. Of course, virtually no one consumes that much mineral water. Yet in the emotional climate of 1990, Perrier believed it had to throw away $40 million of essentially harmless product.

Source: Warren T. Brookes, "The Wasteful Pursuit of Zero Risk," *Forbes,* April 30, 1990, pp. 161–72.

This ad illustrates how Volvos reduce the physical risk of driving a car.

executives meet in the washroom, and one confides he is worried about having selected a phone system that has become obsolete. He wonders if he, too, is now obsolete. In sum, consumers' knowledge of the perceived benefit and risk consequences of product use can influence their purchase decisions, a topic we discuss in Chapter 7.

Products as Value Satisfiers

Consumers can also have knowledge about the personal values that products and brands help them achieve (security, achievement, happiness). From a cognitive perspective, **values** are the mental representations of important life goals that consumers are trying to achieve. As knowledge or meanings, values are more abstract than functional or psychosocial consequences. Values represent important and desirable end goals ("What do I want out of life?"), whereas functional and psychosocial consequences represent outcomes at the more tangible level of

This ad attempts to link Bertolli olive oil to important life values.

"What do I want from this product?" Satisfying a value is a consequence in the sense that achieving a basic life goal is an outcome that consumers experience. The experience of value satisfaction tends to be quite subjective and intangible and may involve considerable symbolic meaning as well.

Many value taxonomies have been developed.[13] In one useful scheme, Milton Rokeach identified two types or levels of values—instrumental and terminal.[14] Figure 4.3 lists the instrumental and terminal values he identified among Americans.[15] **Instrumental values** are the cognitive representations of *preferred modes of conduct or behavior* (having a good time, being independent and self-reliant). **Terminal values,** on the other hand, represent *preferred end states of being* (happy, at peace, wealthy). In cognitive terms, instrumental and terminal values are the mental representations of the most basic or fundamental goals, needs, and end states that consumers are trying to acheive in life. Highlight 4.3 describes a dominant value for many American consumers. The cognitive representations of a person's core values are part of his/her *self-schema*—an

FIGURE 4.3

Instrumental and Terminal Values

Instrumental Values (Preferred Modes of Behavior)	Terminal Values (Preferred End States of Being)
Competence	Social harmony
Ambitious (hardworking)	World at peace
Independent (self-reliant)	Equality (brotherhood)
Imaginative (creative)	Freedom (independence)
Capable (competent)	National security
Logical (rational)	Salvation (eternal life)
Courageous	Personal gratification
Compassion	Social recognition
Forgiving (pardon others)	Comfortable life
Helpful (work for others)	Pleasure (enjoyable life)
Cheerful (joyful)	Sense of accomplishment
Loving (affectionate)	Self-actualization
Sociality	Beauty (nature and arts)
Polite (courteous)	Wisdom (understanding)
Obedient (dutiful)	Inner harmony (no conflict)
Clean (neat, tidy)	Self-respect (self-esteem)
Integrity	Sense of accomplishment
Responsible (reliable)	Security
Honest (sincere)	Taking care of family
Self-controlled	Salvation (eternal life)
	Love and affection
	Mature love (sexual and spiritual intimacy)
	True friendship (close companionship)
	Personal contentedness
	Happiness (contentment)

Source: The values are from Milton J. Rokeach, *The Nature of Human Values* (New York: Free Press, 1973). The underlined category labels for groupings of Rokeach's values shown are identified by Donald E. Vinson, J. Michael Munson, and Masao Nakanishi, "An Investigation of the Rokeach Value Survey for Consumer Research Applications," in *Advances in Consumer Research,* vol. 4, ed. W. D. Perreault (Atlanta, Ga.: Association for Consumer Research, 1977), pp. 247–52.

associative network of interrelated knowledge about one's self.[16] Besides values, self-schemas also may include beliefs and feelings about one's body (body image), representations of important life events (episodic memories), and knowledge about one's own behaviors and affective states.[17] In this book, however, we are primarily concerned with the instrumental and terminal values in consumers' self-schemas.

Because they represent important, self-relevant goals, values are associated with strong affective responses. For instance, a person's affective system is likely to produce positive emotions or specific feelings such as joy or pride when an important value such as achievement or self-esteem is satisfied. Sometimes, merely thinking about achieving an important value can produce affective responses. Negative affective responses such as disappointment, frustration, and

HIGHLIGHT 4.3

THE VALUE OF THE ENVIRONMENT

Americans rapidly became "green," environmentally concerned, in the late 1980s. The media both reflected and stimulated these shifts in values. For instance, the network news ran about one environmental story every three nights in 1987, one story every two nights in 1988, and two stories every night in 1989. Most observers believed this wasn't just a fad, but a long-term value trend.

But it isn't easy being green—either for Kermit, the Muppets frog, or for marketers. Faced with rapidly shifting legal, political, and social environments, many American manufacturers frantically relabeled, repackaged, and repositioned their products in an effort to link them to the growing environment values in American society. In 1990, 26 percent of all new products made some environmental claim. But, many of these efforts did not impress American consumers or environmental activists. Nearly half of consumers surveyed in 1990 dismissed environmental claims as "mere gimmickry."

Consider the lowly trash bag. After years of pressure from consumers to make a biodegradable version of its Hefty bag, Mobil did so in June 1989. Each package box proclaimed the bags were biodegradable, which they were, if left exposed to open air and sun. But over 90 percent of trash bags are put into landfills where no light or oxygen exists to begin the degradation process. Less than six months after introduction, the Environmental Defense Fund called for a boycott of the bags, and several state agencies sued Mobil for deceptive advertising. Mobil, in response, removed all environmental claims from the boxes.

In late 1990, McDonald's switched from using polystyrene shell containers for its hamburgers (which it had adopted in the 1970s at the request of environmentalists) to quilted paper wrappers. But not all environmentalists thought this was a good move. In an attempt to make peace with environmental activists, McDonald's agreed to let the Environmental Defense Fund create a plan for recycling and cutting waste. McDonald's planned to institute 42 ideas aimed at cutting solid-waste volume by 80 percent at the 8,500 U.S. McDonald's restaurants.

Some companies, such as S. C. Johnson, avoid making environmental claims about their products. According to a company spokesperson, "As soon as you go out on a limb and claim you're doing something, a consumer group attacks the validity of your claim." In the face of widespread confusion about environmental claims among consumers, companies, and environmentalists, the Federal Trade Commission was asked to develop acceptable definitions for such environmental terms as *recycled* and *biodegradable*.

Source: Jaclyn Fierman, "The Big Green Muddle in Green Marketing," *Fortune*, June 3, 1991, pp. 91–101.

anger may be produced when the satisfaction of desirable values is blocked. In sum, satisfying values usually elicits positive responses, whereas blocking values produces negative reactions. These affective responses may also be cognitively represented and linked to the value representations in memory.

In sum, consumers can have knowledge about product attributes, consequences of product use, and personal values. Most marketing research focuses on one level of product-related knowledge – usually attributes, consequences (benefits), or values. Unfortunately, this gives us only a partial understanding of consumers' product knowledge. In the next section, we describe how consumers can organize these three levels of knowledge to form a simple associative network called a *means-end chain.*[18]

MEANS-END CHAINS OF PRODUCT KNOWLEDGE

Researchers have developed several means-end chain models of consumers' knowledge structures.[19] Despite different terminology, each model includes the three levels of product meaning discussed above – knowledge about attributes, consequences (benefits or risks), and values. Each means-end model proposes that consumers form meaningful associations that link product attributes with consequences and values.

A **means-end chain** is a simple knowledge structure containing interconnected meanings about attributes, consequences, and values.[20] From a means-end chain perspective, the meaning of an attribute is given by the consequences consumers perceive that it leads to – "What is it good for?" or "What does it do for me?" That is, a product attribute is seen as a *means* to an *end.* The end could be either an immediate consequence (a benefit or risk) or a more abstract value.

We can create a more detailed means-end chain by dividing each of the three levels into two:[21]

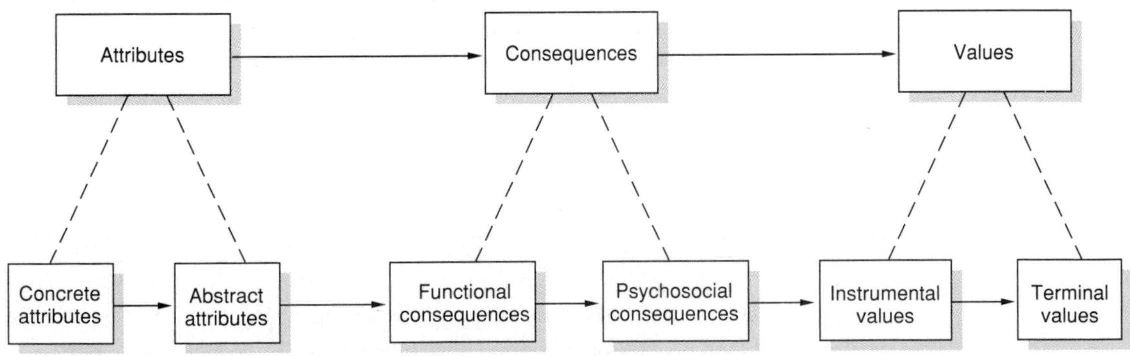

FIGURE 4.4
A Means-End Chain Model of Consumers' Product Knowledge

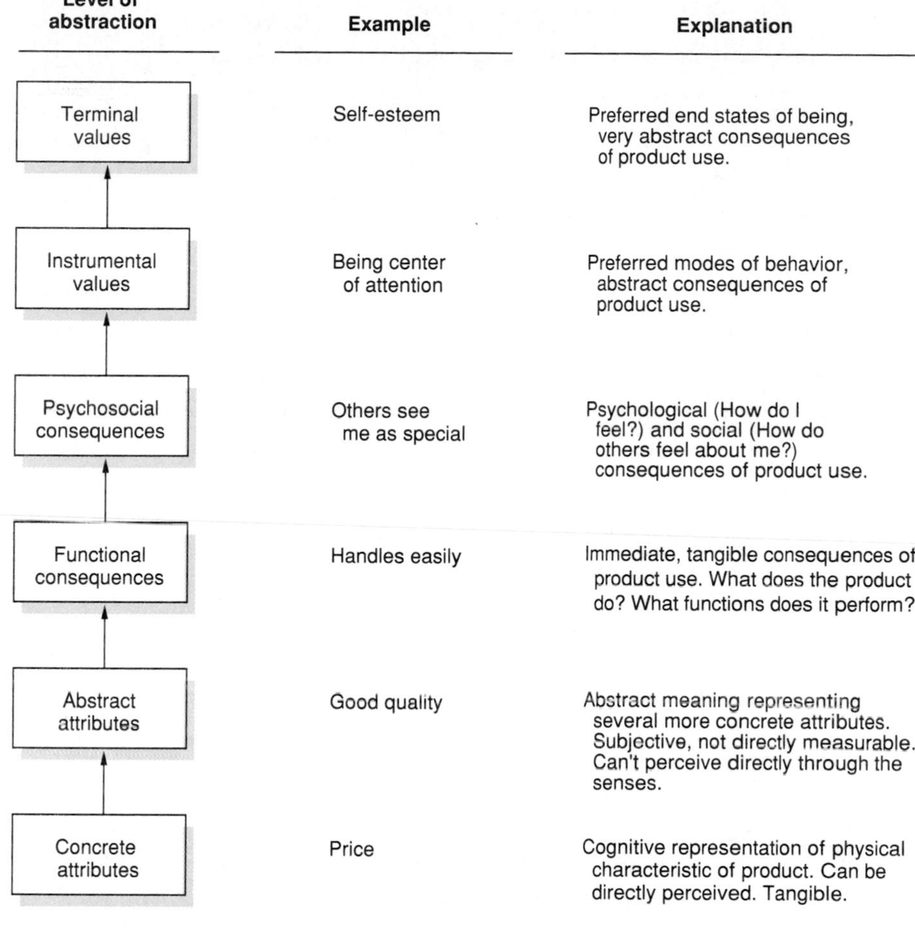

Figure 4.4 defines these six levels of product meaning and gives examples to illustrate them. This more complex means-end chain allows a detailed analysis of consumers' product knowledge. However, some of the differences can be rather fuzzy. For instance, it can be difficult to distinguish between some psychosocial consequences and some instrumental values. Fortunately, making such fine distinctions is seldom necessary, since the simple, three-element means-end structure is sufficient for many marketing purposes.

Because means-end knowledge structures contain the personally relevant meanings consumers create for products and brands, they are unique to each

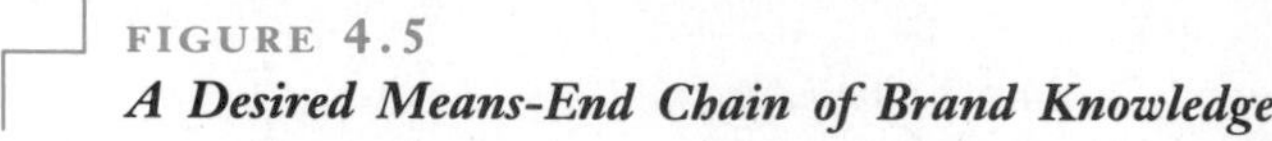

FIGURE 4.5
A Desired Means-End Chain of Brand Knowledge

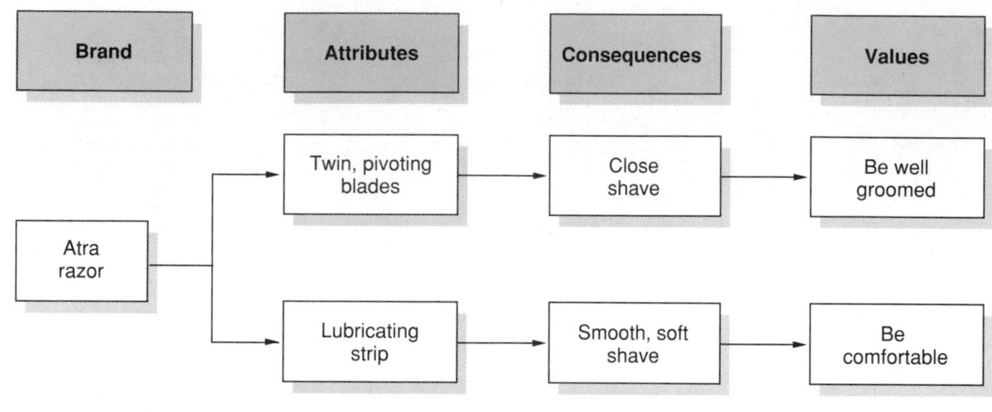

consumer's own background and personal interests. Thus, we should expect different consumers to have different means-end chains for the same product or brand. And we would not be surprised to find that consumers' meanings for a product often are different from those of a marketing manager.

The means-end model is based on the idea that the dominant meaning of a product attribute is determined by the consequences it is perceived to have.[22] Consider the "lubricating strip" that Gillette added to its popular Atra razor.[23] This attribute probably didn't mean much to consumers until they figured out what consequences the strip had for their shaving experiences. Gillette marketers probably hoped consumers would learn a means-end knowledge structure like that diagrammed in Figure 4.5 and their advertising strategy was designed to communicate this extra benefit—a smooth and soft shave—to current and prospective Atra users.

Examples of Means-End Chains

Figure 4.6 presents several means-end chains that represent one consumer's product knowledge for a product class (hair spray), a product form (flavored potato chips), and a brand (Scope mouthwash). This figure illustrates four important points about means-end chains. First, actual means-end chains vary considerably in the meanings they contain. Second, not every means-end chain leads to an instrumental or terminal value. In fact, the end of a means-end chain can be a consequence at any level of abstraction—from a functional consequence ("This toothpaste will give me fresh breath"), to a psychosocial consequence ("My friends will like being close to me"), to an instrumental value ("I will be clean"), to a terminal value ("I will be happy"). In cases where product

FIGURE 4.6
Examples of Means-End Chains

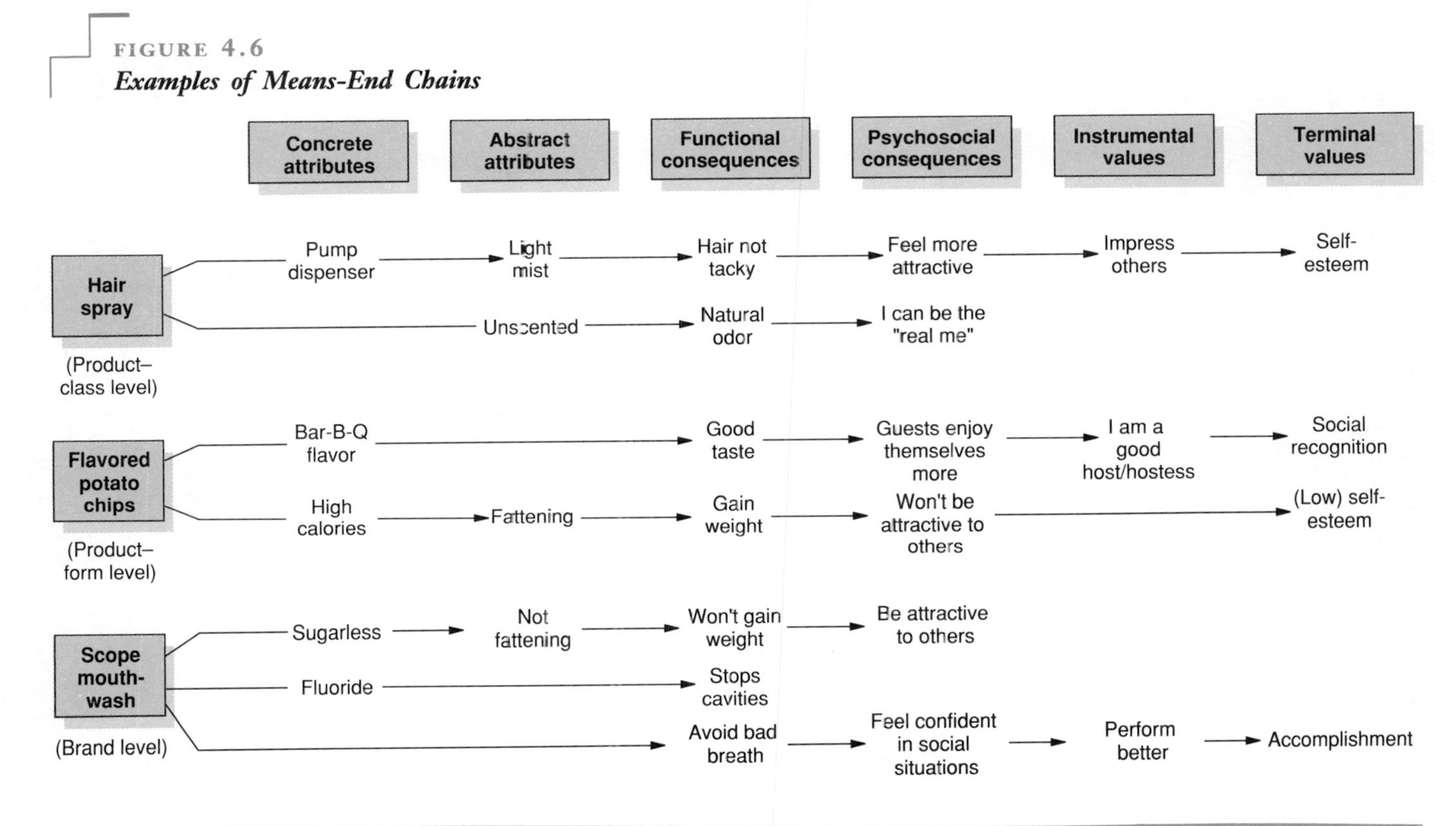

attributes have no connections to consequences, consumers will not know what the attribute is good for, and it will probably have little effect on their behavior. Third, some of the means-end chains in Figure 4.6 are incomplete, with "missing" levels of meanings. This illustrates that the actual product knowledge in consumers' means-end chains does not necessarily contain each of the six levels of product meaning shown in the idealized means-end chain model. Finally, although not shown in Figure 4.6, some product attributes may have multiple means-end chains, which can be conflicting. That is, some attributes can lead to both positive and negative ends. For example, consider the means-end chains that may be associated with price. For a fairly expensive product such as a watch, higher prices may have both positive and negative consequences (perceived benefits and risks).

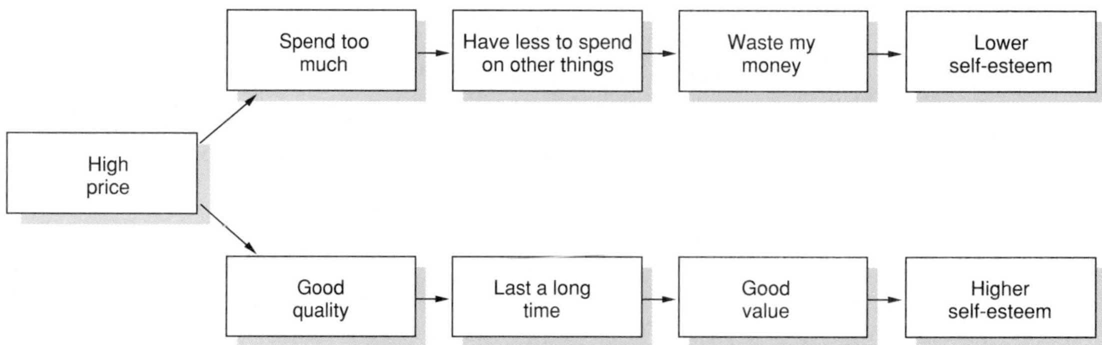

Measuring Means-End Chains

Focus group interviews (talking to 6 to 10 consumers about some topic) have become extremely popular as a way of trying to understand what consumers think about products. But measuring means-end chains is better accomplished by one-on-one, in-depth interviews that can probe deeper into the meanings of attributes and consequences and establish the "whys" of consumers' behaviors.

There are two main steps in measuring consumers' means-end chains. First, one must identify or elicit the product attributes that consumers consider important in choosing products or brands. Figure 4.7 describes three ways of asking consumers to identify the important product characteristics they consider when making a purchase choice. Alternatively, marketing managers may select certain attributes of interest. The second step is to conduct a special type of interview, called *laddering*, in which consumers are encouraged through a series of "why" questions to reveal how the product attributes are connected to higher consequences and/or values.[24] Figure 4.8 shows part of a laddering interview. Marketing managers can use the resulting means-end chain structures to develop marketing strategies.

FIGURE 4.7
Methods of Identifying Key Attributes Considered by Consumers

Direct elicitation

Researcher: "Please tell me what characteristics you usually consider when deciding which brand of ballpoint pen to buy."

Consumer: "Let's see. I think about the *price,* the *color* of the ink, the *fineness* of the tip, and *how the pen feels* in my hand."

Free-sort task

Researcher: "Here are several brands of running shoes. Assume that you are thinking of buying a pair of running shoes. I want you to sort them into groups so that the shoes in each pile are alike in some way important to you and are different from the shoes in the other piles." or . . .

Researcher: "Here are several brands of running shoes. I want you to sort them into groups using any basis you wish."

Researcher: "Now, please describe what each pile means to you. Why are these brands together?"

Consumer: "Well, these shoes are all *high-tech* and *expensive.* These are *cheaper* and have *fewer fancy features.* And these brands are "in between."

Triad task

Researcher: "Here are three brands of running shoes. Assume that you were thinking of buying a pair of running shoes. In what important way are two of these similar and different from the third? Are there any other ways?

Consumer: "Hmmm. Well, these two shoes have *special construction features* to keep your heel stable and solid. This one doesn't. And these two have a *staggered lacing system,* while this one has a traditional lacing pattern."

Marketing Implications

A basic advantage of means end chain models is that they provide a deeper understanding of consumers' product knowledge than methods focusing only on attributes or benefits.[25] For instance, consider the following means-end chain for Liquid Tide laundry detergent:

This hypothetical consumer interprets the chemical attributes of Liquid Tide (special molecules) in terms of the more abstract attribute "cleaning power." Cleaning power, in turn, is seen as providing the functional benefit of "cleaner clothes for the kids," which is seen as helping to achieve the instrumental value of "being a good parent," which finally leads to the terminal value of "feeling good about myself" or "self-esteem."

FIGURE 4.8
An Example of a Laddering Interview

Researcher: "You said that a shoe's lacing pattern is important to you in deciding what brand to buy. Why is that?

Consumer: "A staggered lacing pattern makes the shoe fit more snugly on my foot." [**physical attribute and functional consequence**]

Researcher: "Why is it important that the shoe fit more snugly on your foot?"

Consumer: "Because it gives me better support." [**functional consequence**]

Researcher: "Why is better support important to you?"

Consumer: "So I can run without worrying about injurying my feet." [**psychosocial consequence**]

Researcher: "Why is it important for you not to worry while running?"

Consumer: "So I can relax and enjoy the run." [**psychosocial consequence**]

Researcher: "Why is it important that you can relax and enjoy your run?"

Consumer: "Because it gets rid of tension I have built up at work." [**psychosocial consequence**]

Researcher: "Why is it important for you to get rid of tension from work?"

Consumer: "So when I go back to work in the afternoon, I can perform better." [**instrumental value—high performance**]

Researcher: "Why is it important that you perform better?"

Consumer: "I feel better about myself." [**terminal value—self-esteem**]

Researcher: "Why is it important that you feel better about yourself?"

Consumer: "It just is!" [**the end!**]

By identifying the sequence of connections between product-related meanings at different levels of abstraction, marketers can see more clearly what consumers really mean when they mention an attribute or a consequence such as "cleaning power." Means-end chain analyses also identify the basic ends (values and goals) consumers are seeking when they buy and use certain products and brands, and this gives insights into consumers' purchase motivations. Finally, means-end chains reflect the consumer/product relationship – that is, they show how consumers relate product attributes to important aspects of their self-concepts. In sum, the more complete understanding of consumers' product knowledge provided by means-end analysis helps marketers devise more effective advertising, pricing, distribution, and product strategies.

INVOLVEMENT

Why do consumers seem to care about some products and brands and not others? Why are consumers sometimes highly motivated to seek information

In marketing Liquid Tide, P&G emphasized the abstract attribute of "cleaning power."

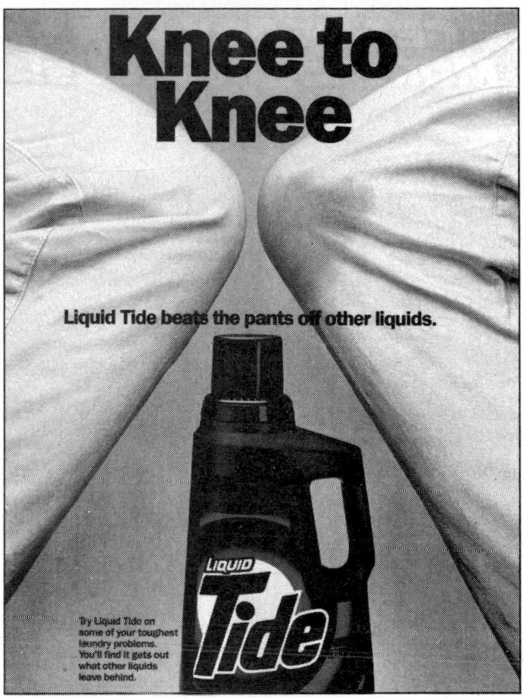

about products, or to buy and use products in certain situations, while other consumers seem to have no interest? Why did some loyal Coke drinkers make such a big fuss when in 1985 Coca-Cola Company managers made a minor change in an inexpensive, simple, and seemingly unimportant soft-drink product (see Highlight 4.4)? These questions concern consumers' involvment, an important concept for understanding consumer behavior.[24]

Over the past 20 years, many different definitions of involvement have been proposed.[26] However, most agree that **involvement** refers to consumers' subjective perception of the personal relevance of an object, activity, or situation.[27] Thus, consumers who perceive that a product is self-relevant are said to be involved and have a personal relationship with it.

We use the term **felt involvement** to emphasize that involvement is a psychological state experienced by consumers in a given situation. For instance, involvement with a product is experienced by a consumer as perceptions of interest and importance along with related affective feelings and general arousal.[29] Such feelings of involvement occur only at certain times and in certain situations. Consumers do not feel involved all the time, even with the most important objects in their lives.

Marketing researchers often have treated involvement as a dichotomy, either high or low, but this is not really appropriate.[30] Consumers' involvement

HIGHLIGHT 4.4

Coca-Cola Learns about Consumer Involvement

In the spring of 1985, the Coca-Cola Company shocked American consumers and other soft-drink manufacturers by announcing the 99-year-old formula for Coke would be changed. The "new" Coke was a bit sweeter, and marketing research showed it was preferred to Pepsi-Cola. The original Coke formula was to be retired to a bank vault and never again produced.

What happened then was the beginning of Coke's lesson in consumer involvement. Outraged U.S. consumers complained bitterly to the Atlanta-based company about the loss of "a great American tradition." In Seattle, a group of strident loyalists calling themselves "Old Coke Drinkers of America" laid plans to file a class-action suit against Coca-Cola. They searched out shop owners, vending-machine owners, and others willing to claim that the company's formula change had cost them business. Then, when June sales didn't pick up as expected, the bottlers also joined in the demand for old Coke's return—and fast.

Although Coca-Cola had spent some $4 million in testing the new formulas, it had missed one important factor. Millions of consumers had a strong *emotional involvement* with the original Coke. They drank it as kids, and still did as adults. Many consumers had a personal attachment to Coke. Says a Coke spokesperson, "We had taken away a little part of them and their past. They [consumers] said, "You have no right to do that. Bring it back.'"

Coca-Cola had learned a costly lesson. Although consumers preferred the new taste in blind taste tests, Coca-Cola did not measure consumers' emotional reactions to removing the original Coke from the marketplace. Coca-Cola learned that a product is more than a production formula; extra meanings such as emotions and strong connections to self-image may also be present.

Source: Adapted from Anne B. Fisher, "Coke's Brand-Loyalty Lesson," *Fortune,* August 5, 1985, pp. 44–46.

actually varies along a continuum from very low (little or no perceived personal relevance), through moderate levels (perceptions of some personal relevance, but not great), to high levels (perceptions of strong personal relevance).

It is important to recognize that people may be involved with other concepts besides products and brands. For instance, consumers may be involved with other *physical objects* such as advertisements. During the 1980s, many consumers became somewhat involved in the ongoing adventures of Frank Bartles and Ed Jaymes, two eccentric characters who appeared in a series of ads for a Gallo wine cooler named Bartles & Jaymes. Of course, consumers may be involved with other *people* — friends, relatives, lovers, perhaps even salespeople. People can also become involved with certain *environments* (their home or backyard, amusement parks, a lake, or the seashore). Some of these may be marketing environments — a clothing store the consumer especially likes, a shopping mall, or a favorite restaurant. Finally, people may be involved with specific *activities* or *behaviors* such as playing tennis, working, windsurfing, or reading. Some consumers become involved with marketing-related activities such as collecting coupons, shopping for new clothes, finding the cheapest price in town, or bargaining with vendors at flea markets.

It is important that marketers clearly identify the focus of consumers' involvement. Marketers need to know exactly what it is that consumers consider to be personally relevant: a product or brand, an object, a behavior, an event, a situation, an environment, or several or all of these together. Since marketers are mostly interested in consumers' involvement with products and brands, this is our main focus in this chapter. In principle, however, marketers can analyze consumers' involvement with virtually anything.

A Means-End Approach to Understanding Involvement

Means-end chains are useful for analyzing consumers' felt involvement because the levels of knowledge represented in means-end chains vary in self-relevance. The attribute levels of product knowledge are not self-relevant per se, while the higher levels of psychosocial consequences and values are more directly related to self.[31]

From a means-end perspective, a consumer's level of felt involvement with a product or brand depends on two factors: (1) the importance and self-relevance of the activated ends and (2) the strength of the means-end connections between the activated product knowledge and self-knowledge. Therefore, consumers who perceive that attributes of a product are associated with important values will experience higher levels of product involvement than consumers who perceive that product attributes lead only to functional consequences. Of course, consumers who perceive that product attributes have no important consequences (basically, they have no means-end chains) will feel little or no involvement with the product.

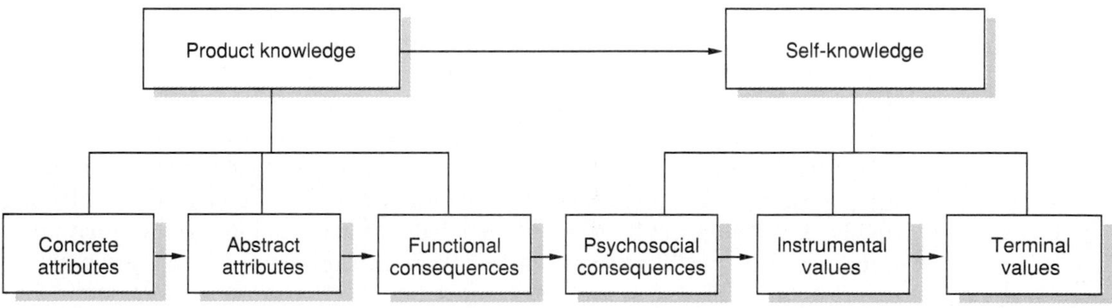

Like any knowledge structure, consumers' means-end chains can be activated from memory and made available for use in cognitive processes (if not activated, the means-end chains remain stored in long-term memory). When activated in a particular situation, these means-end knowledge structures may stimulate the affective system to produce a state of general arousal along with specific emotional, feeling, or evaluation responses.[32] To the extent that more important and more central self-related consequences, values, and goals are activated in a situation, the affective system is likely to produce stronger arousal and more intense affective responses. If less important consequences with little self-relevance are activated, the affective system is likely to produce weak affective responses and little or no arousal. Together, the activated means-end knowledge structures and the associated affective responses are experienced as felt involvement. Although felt involvement can vary from very low or none to very high, most consumers in most situations probably experience moderate to low levels of felt involvement for most products and brands.[33]

Felt Involvement

Felt involvement is a motivational state that energizes and directs consumers' cognitive processes and overt behaviors.[34] For instance, the general arousal and specific affective responses of more involved consumers tend to stimulate more extensive searches for product information while shopping for a product.[35] Moreover, the activated means-end knowledge structures of more involved consumers may influence them to pay more attention to relevant information in the environment.[36]

As shown in Figure 4.9, the level of felt involvement a consumer experiences in a given situation, is determined by two sources — *intrinsic* and *situational self-relevance*.[37] Both sources of self-relevance combine to activate and/or create means-end chains linking product knowledge with self-knowledge. This activated knowledge and the associated affective responses and arousal are experienced by the consumer as felt involvement.

Intrinsic self-relevance refers to the general means-end representations of product/self relationships that consumers have learned from past experience and stored in memory.[38] These knowledge structures may also contain representations of affective responses. Consumers acquire means-end knowledge structures through their experiences as they learn that a product or activity helps them achieve important self-relevant consequences and values. For example, over time, a consumer might come to associate specific attributes of a high quality stereo system (low distortion, remote control) with various favorable consequences of owning and using this product (enjoying the music more, being comfortable and relaxed, impressing friends). As knowledge structures stored in long-term memory, intrinsic self-relevance represents the potential for feeling involved.[39] When this means-end knowledge is activated in a given situation, it influences the overall state of felt involvement experienced by a consumer.

FIGURE 4.9

A Basic Model of Consumer Product Involvement

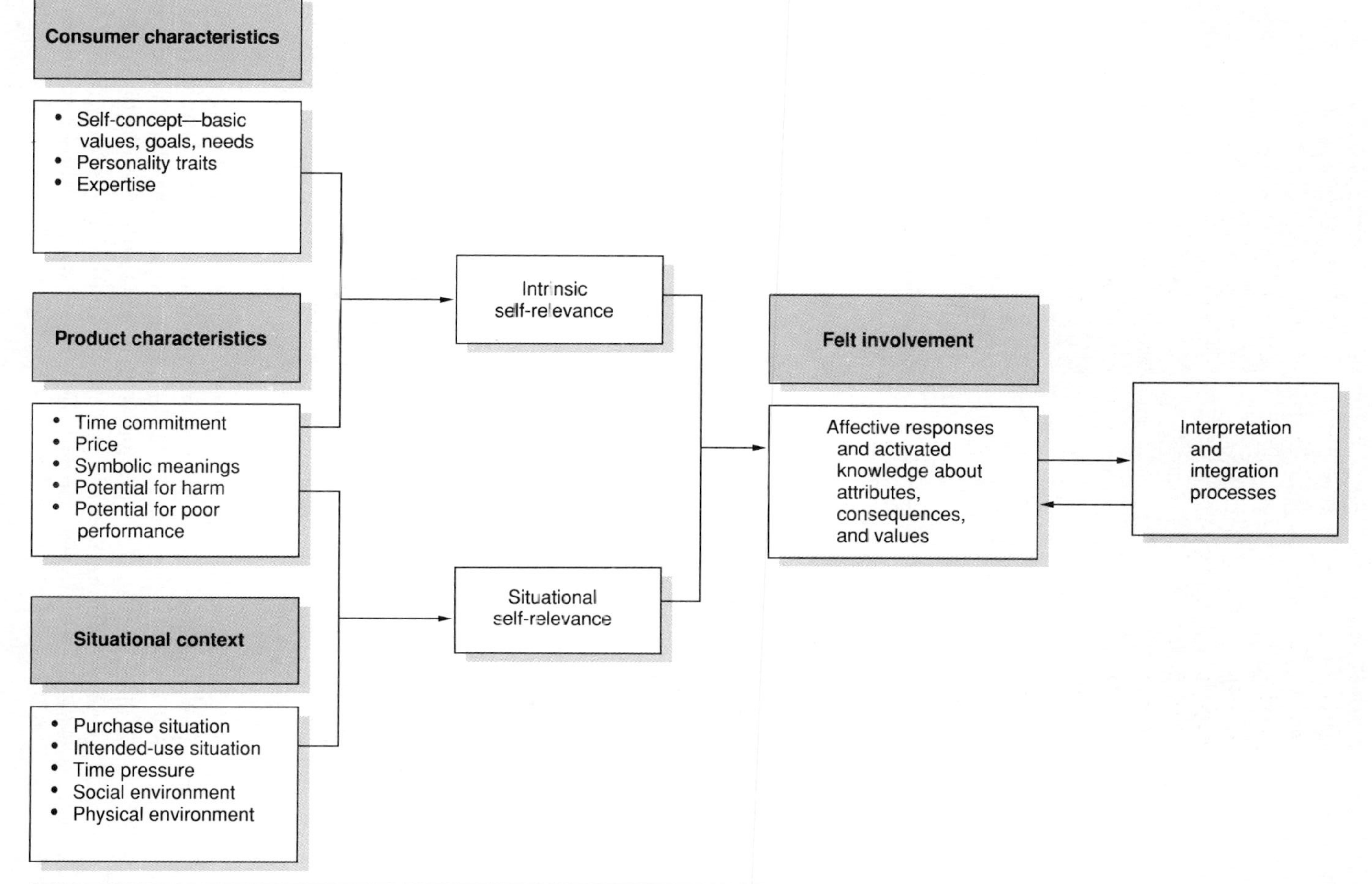

Source: Adapted from Richard L. Celsi and Jerry C. Olson, "The Role of Involvement in Attention and Comprehension Processes," *Journal of Consumer Research,* September 1988, pp. 210–24; and Peter H. Bloch and Marsha L. Richins, "A Theoretical Model for the Study of Product Importance Perceptions," *Journal of Marketing,* Summer 1983, pp. 69–81.

Hobbies and leisure activities, such as working in one's home workshop, have intrinsic self-relevance for many people.

Situational self-relevance refers to temporary feelings of self-relevance due to specific external physical and social stimuli in the environment. If these factors activate self-relevant values, goals, and psychosocial consequences that become linked to the product or activity in question, a state of situational self-relevance is created. The immediate environment and context often have a great impact on the consequences and values that consumers consider self-relevant in that situation. For instance, shopping with other people (friends or relatives) might make us feel more self-conscious and activate self-presentation goals ("I want to appear to be a shrewd shopper") that are not relevant when we go shopping alone. As another example, accidentally noticing a window display in a clothing store might activate self-relevant consequences and values that become linked to the clothing in the display ("That sweater looks nice—it would be good for the party next weekend—people would notice me"). Or the high temperature on a summer day could activate desired consequences (take a break, cool off, relax) that might make buying an ice cream cone or going to a movie (in an air-conditioned theater) seem more self-relevant and involving than otherwise.

As shown in Figure 4.9, a consumers' overall level of felt involvement is always determined by the combination of his or her intrinsic and situational self-relevance. Consider the rather common situation in which a consumer's intrinsic self-relevance for a product is relatively low (the product is not considered to be very important). For instance, most consumers probably do not consider hot water heaters to have strong connections with psychosocial consequences and values. However, when Sam's hot water heater suddenly developed a leak, it quickly became very important that he replace it within a day or two. That is, the negative consequences of showering and washing in cold water were highly self-relevant to Sam. Thus, this situation caused Sam to experience a fairly high level of felt involvement with choosing and buying a new hot water heater. Sam felt this arousal and interest throughout the several hours it took him to find and evaluate a few alternatives and make a purchase decision.

It is very important for marketers to understand the *sources* and *focus* of consumers' felt involvement. Sam, for instance, was involved with *buying* a hot water heater, not with using (consuming) hot water heaters. Sam's means-end chains for hot water heaters did not end in self-relevant consequences and values (his typical ends were functional consequences such as energy efficiency and capacity). Therefore, most of the self-relevant consequences and values that influenced Sam's purchase decision process were activated by the situation of having to replace a broken product quickly. They concerned the consequences of buying a hot water heater—its price, speed of delivery, installation charges, etc. Because some of these factors were connected to important higher-ordered consequences (save money, be comfortable, avoid stress), purchasing the hot water heater had some degree of self-relevance, and Sam experienced some level of felt involvement in this situation.

However, once Sam made the product choice, the situational source of self-relevance (the leaking heater) was no longer present, and Sam's felt involvement quickly faded. Now, whenever Sam thinks about the product (which is seldom), few self-related consequences are activated. Sam's intrinsic self-relevance for hot water heaters is weak.

This is not an isolated or unusual example. In many cases, consumers' felt involvement with buying products and brands is strongly influenced by the immediate environment and situational context. If intrinsic self-relevance is low or moderate for many consumer products, as many researchers suspect, intrinsic sources are likely to have less effect on felt involvement than do situational sources. This gives marketers an opportunity to affect consumers' felt involvement by manipulating aspects of consumers' environments that might function as situational sources of self-relevance.

Marketing Implications

The concepts of means-end chains and involvement have important implications for marketing analysis and developing effective marketing strategies. In this section, we examine how both concepts can be used to analyze the critical consumer/product relationship. Marketers need to understand the connection consumers make between their self-concepts and the products or services the marketer is selling. We also will examine some specific marketing strategies intended to influence intrinsic and situational self-relevance.

Understanding the Key Reasons for Purchase

Marketers can use means-end chain analyses to identify the key attributes and consequences underlying a product purchase decision and to understand the meaning of those concepts to consumers. For instance, consider restaurant decisions. Unlike people in some cultures (France), many Americans do not feel highly involved with food. The fast-food industry's research suggests the three most important factors in many consumers' decisions on where to eat are: (1) time of day, (2) how long the customer wants to spend eating, and (3) price.[40] According to one expert, "We used to eat when the food was ready. Now we eat when we are ready." Speed and convenience are critical consequences.

Rally's, a small restaurant chain of 240 restaurants, has developed marketing strategies to provide these desired consequences. The typical Rally's is small enough to be placed anywhere. A Rally's can be built for about $350,000, compared to more than $1 million for the average McDonald's. Rally's offers no customer seating. Food is ordered at walk-up or drive-through windows and eaten elsewhere. The drive-through line at a Rally's restaurant moves so rapidly that many customers are on their way within 30 seconds! Moreover, they pay only $3 for a cheesburger, french fries, and a large Coke, about 85 cents less than the nearby McDonald's would charge. And the food? Actually, the food itself is not that important for many consumers. As one Rally's customer admitted, "The food is not very good here, but it's cheap, quick, and easy." By understanding what attributes and consequences customers really want, Rally's sales doubled from 1989 to 1990, and profits trebled, while several competitors experienced stagnant growth or decline. For example, annual sales at an average Rally's ran about $1,300 a square foot, compared to $400 at McDonald's.

Understanding the Consumer/Product Relationship

One of the most important concepts in this book concerns consumers' relationships with products and brands. For instance, Highlight 4.5 describes the relationships that many Americans have with their cars. Marketers need to understand the cognitive and affective aspects of these consumer/product relationships.[41] For instance, teenagers who are "into" cars may link the general attributes of cars to important self-relevant consequences (self-respect, envy of peers, freedom). In fact, we believe the customer/product relationship is so important that marketing management's major task is to manage this relationship.[42] Marketing strategies should be designed to create, maintain, and modify meaningful consumer/product relationships. The means-end chain model can be useful in analyzing these consumer/product relationships and in developing strategies to influence them.

There are innumerable examples of the importance of the consumer/product relationship. Consider the huge market for athletic shoes.[43] Americans spent $11.7 billion in 1990 on 393 million pairs of brand-name athletic shoes,

HIGHLIGHT 4.5

Consumers' Relationships with Cars

More than 1 billion automobiles have been sold in this century. Most have been in the United States, where there are two cars for every 3 people, compared to one car for every 3 people in Denmark and one for every 15,000 in China. Car ownership continues to rise worldwide, despite recessions, rising interest rates, and high taxes and gasoline prices. In 1986, for instance, some 11 million new cars entered the crowded U.S. roadways.

Many Americans feel highly involved with their autos, often treating them like pets (stroking, petting, grooming). For some consumers, the product/self relationship reflects a passionate level of intrinsic self-relevance. Such people love their cars and may engage in ritual forms of "worship," such as weekend cleaning and waxing. What self-relevant consequences of owning and driving cars can create such high levels of felt involvement?

Cars provide numerous opportunities for control and mastery—a sence of domination—a desirable value for some consumers. Cars also provide thrills. For instance, a major part of the driving experience involves acceleration, which elicits strong positive affect and arousal responses in many people. For some consumers, these feelings can be intensely pleasurable.

In addition, cars are a powerful means of self-expression for many consumers. For instance, people can acquire expensive, distinctive automobiles to increase their social status. Other consumers can buy a reasonable car to establish or express their rational, serious qualities. Some car owners buy personalized license plates, unique gadgets, and other custom products to embellish their cars and further express their self-relevant values.

Source: Peter Marsh and Peter Collett, "Driving Passion," *Psychology Today,* June 1987, pp. 16–24.

and Nike commanded a $2.2 billion of that market. Nike's revenues soared during the 1980s, based partly on the relationships its marketing strategies created between fashion-conscious youth and the Nike brand. Muggings and even murders have been attributed to the desire of some young people to acquire a trendy pair of athletic shoes. In the face of such events, Nike has been criticized for promoting its expensive basketball shoes to inner-city black and Hispanic youths.

An obvious implication for marketers is to segment consumers in terms of their intrinsic self-relevance for the product category and brands. Figure 4.10 summarizes four different consumer/product/brand relationships. Different strategies would be devised to market the product and brand to these segments. For instance, the marketing strategies appropriate for brand loyalists (maintain product quality and brand image) are quite different from the strategies neces-

FIGURE 4.10

Consumer Segments Defined in Terms of Their Intrinsic Self-Relevance for the Product Category and Brand

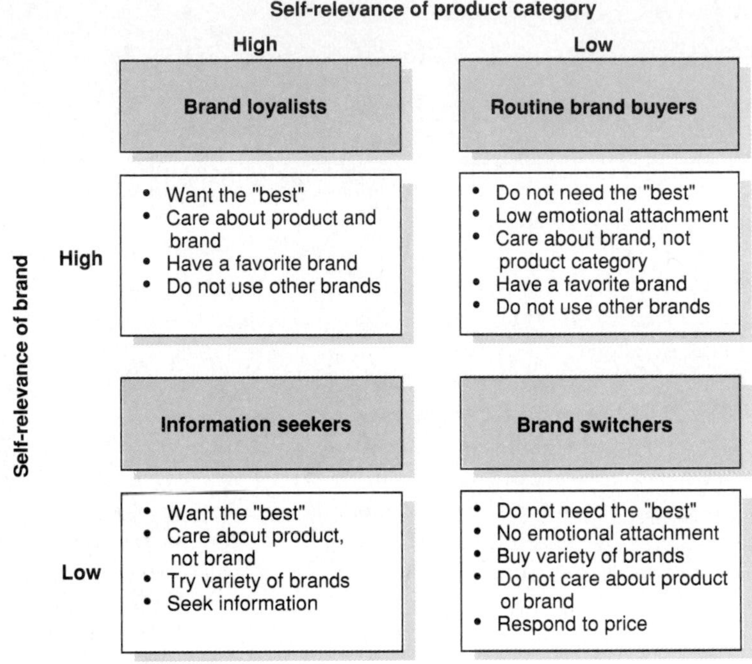

Source: Adapted from Peter Cushing and Melody Douglas-Tate, "The Effect of People/Product Relationships on Advertising Processing," in *Psychological Processes and Advertising Effects,* eds. Linda Alwitt and Andrew A. Mitchell (Hillsdale, N.J.: Lawrence Erlbaum, 1985), pp. 241–59.

sary to appeal to brand switchers (offer price discounts or other promotions to prompt switching). Highlight 4.6 shows that consumers have widely varying levels of brand loyalty across product categories, which also calls for different marketing strategies.

Influencing Intrinsic Self-Relevance

The means-end knowledge structures that make up consumers' intrinsic self-relevance are important for understanding the consumer/product relationship. For instance, the types of ends represented in consumer's means-end chains indicate the level of perceived personal relevance.[44] With this knowledge, marketers can design products with attributes that consumers link to important consequences and values.[45] Then, if consumers can be induced to try the product, they should learn that it produces important consequences (as men-

Some consumers have strong intrinsic self-relevance for their cars. They may spend considerable time "nurturing" and caring for their cars.

tioned at the beginning of this chapter, P&G tried this type of strategy). Finally, advertising strategies should be consistent with the means-end knowledge structures that constitute consumers' intrinsic self-relevance.

Marketers also could try to develop strategies that would strengthen consumers' intrinsic sources of felt involvement with a given product or brand. For

HIGHLIGHT 4.6

Consumers' Relationships with Brands

Faithful or Fickle?
Percentage of users of these products who are loyal to one brand

Product	Loyal to one brand
Cigarettes	71%
Mayonnaise	65%
Toothpaste	61%
Coffee	58%
Headache remedy	56%
Film	56%
Bath soap	53%
Ketchup	51%
Laundry detergent	48%
Beer	48%
Automobile	47%
Perfume/after shave	46%
Pet food	45%
Shampoo	44%
Soft drink	44%
Tuna fish	44%
Gasoline	39%
Underwear	36%
Television	35%
Tires	33%
Blue jeans	33%
Batteries	29%
Athletic shoes	27%
Canned vegetables	25%
Garbage bags	23%

Brand loyalty among consumers is a highly desirable goal for most marketers. Although brand loyalty seems to have eroded considerably over the past 30 years due to increased brand competition and extensive sales promotions (coupons and price reductions), it is not dead. A survey of some 2,000 customers found wide variations in brand loyalty across product classes (people who claimed to buy mostly the same brand).

Source: Ronald Alsop, "Brand Loyalty Is Rarely Blind Loyalty," *The Wall Street Journal,* October 19, 1989, pp. B1, B8.

instance, Mazda once ran a campaign in which Mazda car owners were encouraged to send in pictures of themselves with their cars. Some of these pictures were printed in national magazine ads. This promotion might have increased the intrinsic self-relevance of Mazda cars for their owners.

In the short run, it is difficult to modify consumers' intrinsic sources of felt involvement for a product or brand. Over longer periods though, intrinsic self-relevance probably can be influenced by various marketing strategies, especially advertising.[46] However, this process is likely to be long and the outcome somewhat uncertain because advertising strategies are only one of many influences on consumers' intrinsic sources of felt involvement. For instance, direct product experience also influences the contents and organization of consumers' means-end chains. If the product use experience doesn't measure up to the image created by advertising, consumers probably will not form the desired means-end meanings.

INFLUENCING SITUATIONAL SELF-RELEVANCE

Marketers use many strategies to create, modify, and maintain consumers' situational sources of felt involvement, most commonly in the context of a purchase situation. For example, the semiannual clearance sales on summer or winter clothing most retailers run are sources of situational self-relevance that may temporarily raise consumers' felt involvement with buying such products. Likewise, premiums such as stickers or small toys placed into cereal boxes or candy packages may temporarily increase children's self-relevance and felt involvement with a brand. Finally, special pricing strategies, including the popular rebates on some new car models ("Get $1,000 back if you buy within the next two weeks") may function as situational sources of self-relevance that create, for some consumers, a temorary increase in the felt involvement with buying the brand or model.

A cents-off coupon may be a source of situational self-relevance that increases consumers' felt involvement with a purchase.

Another way to increase the situational self-relevance of a product is to link it to an important cause or value.[47] For instance, in 1983, American Express donated one cent from every purchase made with its card to refurbish the Statue of Liberty. In addition to a total contribution of $1.7 million, American Express Company got lots of publicity and some new card applications. Johnson & Johnson has promoted Shelter Aid, a program that makes donations to shelters for battered women. If you buy enough weiners and bologna, Oscar Mayer will donate bats, uniforms, and scoreboards to children's baseball teams. Finally, as environmental values grew in the early 1990s, many companies tried to show how they were protecting the environment.[48] Obviously, companies hope these strategies will influence consumers to buy and use the brand and learn about its intrinsic self-relevance.

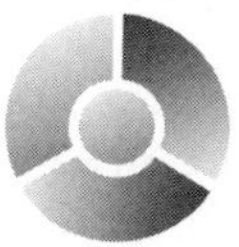

BACK TO.... PROCTER & GAMBLE

Understanding consumers' product knowledge and consumer/product relationships requires that marketers examine the meanings by which consumers represent product attributes and link those to higher-ordered meanings, such as the psychosocial consequences and values in consumers' self-schemas. A major reason for P&G's successes was its ability to develop products with superior product attributes that consumers perceived as linked to important, self-relevant psychosocial consequences and perhaps even values.

Consider the means-end chains consumers might have formed for the P&G products mentioned in the case. For instance, sodium pyrophosphate, the chemical attribute in Tartar Control Crest, removes hard, tartar buildup from teeth. Some consumers might believe this makes their teeth whiter and more attractive, which might give them greater confidence in social situations and, in turn, add to their self-esteem. As another example, Ultra Pam-

pers have a special chemical that soaks up fluids. This keeps the baby drier and more comfortable, reducing diaper rash, which helps parents feel more comfortable and successful as parents and adds to their self-esteem. Companies like P&G should identify and promote the desirable higher-ordered consequences linked to their product attributes (and avoid attributes having negative consequences).

The means-end chain perspective is also useful for understanding consumers' intrinsic self-relevance for products and brands. It is likely that most consumers do not have intense levels of intrinsic self-relevance for any of these P&G products. However, certain market segments of consumers probably believe these products have a moderate degree of intrinsic self-relevance. For example, because couples with a new baby likely perceive the disposable diaper category (and perhaps the Ultra Pampers brand) to have greater intrinsic self-relevance than do other consumers segments, they probably experience higher levels of felt involvement during purchase decision processes. P&G might create special marketing strategies for such segments.

SUMMARY

In this chapter, you learned about consumers' affective and cognitive responses to products. Consumers don't buy products to get attributes; rather, they think about products in terms of their desirable or undesirable consequences—benefits or perceived risks. By relating product attributes to their own personal and self-relevant consequences, values, goals, and needs, consumers form hierarchical knowledge structures called means-end chains. The attributes of some products are strongly linked to important ends (consequences and values), whereas other products are only weakly associated with self-relevant consequences. These are sometimes called high and low involvement products, respectively. Consumers experience involvement as cognitive perceptions of importance and interest and affective feelings of arousal. This felt involvement is jointly determined by intrinsic self-relevance—the means-end representations of personal relevance stored in memory. In addition, situational factors in the environment also influence the content of activated means-end chains and thereby affect the felt involvement consumers experience when choosing which products and brands to buy.

Key Terms and Concepts

Levels of Abstraction *87*
Categorization *88*
Abstract Attributes *92*
Concrete Attributes *92*
Functional Consequences *93*
Psychosocial Consequences *93*
Benefits *93*
Perceived Risks *94*
Values *96*
Instrumental Values *97*
Terminal Values *97*
Means-End Chain *100*
Involvement *107*
Felt Involvement *107*
Intrinsic Self-Relevance *110*
Situational Self-Relevance *112*

Review and Discussion Questions

1. Select a product category and identify examples of product forms, brands, and models. Describe some of the attribute, consequence, and value meanings for each of these levels.

2. Analyze the possible meanings of mouthwash or deodorant in terms of positive (perceived benefits) and negative (perceived risks) consequences of use. Why are both types of meanings important?

3. Relate the fundamental assumptions underlying means-ends chains to your own assessment of the managerial usefulness of means-ends chains.

4. Define the concept of involvement and illustrate it by discussing products that, for you, would fall at each extreme of an involvement continuum.

5. Consider the difference between consequences of possession and the consequences of consumption as the basis for intrinsic self-relevance. What products are relevant to you for each of these reasons? How does that change your purchasing behavior?

6. Do you agree that most products have low to moderate levels of intrinsic self-relevance for most consumers? Why or why not?
7. Prepare a means-ends chain for your choice of a major or an emphasis in marketing as part of your degree program. Label the attributes, consequences, and values that you identify.
8. Using the concept of means-end chains, discuss why different people might shop for athletic shoes at department stores, specialty athletic footwear shops, and discount stores. Why might the same consumer shop these stores on different occasions?
9. Discuss how a marketer of casual clothing for men and women can use consumers' product knowledge (means-end chains) and involvement to understand the consumer/product relationship.
10. Identify three ways that marketers can influence consumers' situational self-relevance and discuss how this will affect consumers' overall level of felt involvement. For what types of products are these strategies most suitable?

NOTES

1. This example is adapted from Roy Lachman, Janet L. Lachman, and Earl C. Butterfield, *Cognitive Psychology and Information Processing* (Hillsdale, N.J.: Lawrence Erlbaum, 1979), p. 108.
2. Eleanor Rosch, Carolyn B. Mervis, Wayne D. Gray, David M. Johnson, and Penny Boyes-Braem, "Basic Objects in Natural Categories," *Cognitive Psychology*, July 1976, pp. 382–439.
3. For examples, see Joseph W. Alba and Amitava Chattopadhyay, "The Effects of Context and Part-Category Cues on the Recall of Competing Brands," *Journal of Marketing Research*, August 1985, pp. 340–49; Mita Sujan and Christine Dekleva, "Product Categorization and Inference Making: Some Implications for Comparative Advertising," *Journal of Consumer Research*, September 1987, pp. 14–54; Mita Sujan and James R. Bettman, "The Effects of Brand Positioning Strategies on Consumers' Brand and Category Perceptions: Some Insights from Schema Research," *Journal of Marketing Research*, November 1989, pp. 454–67.
4. Mita Sujan, "Consumer Knowledge: Effects on Evaluation Strategies Mediating Consumer Judgments," *Journal of Consumer Research*, June 1985, pp. 31–46; Joel Cohen and Kunal Basu, "Alternative Models of Categorization: Toward a Contingent Processing Framework," *Journal of Consumer Research*, March 1987, pp. 455–72; Carolyn B. Mervis, "Category Structure and the Development of Categorization," in *Theoretical Issues in Reading Comprehension*, ed. Rand Spiro et al. (Hillsdale, N.J.: Lawrence Erlbaum, 1980), pp. 279–307.
5. Michael D. Johnson, "The Differential Processing of Product Category and Noncomparable Choice Alternatives," *Journal of Consumer Research*, December 1989, pp. 300–9.
6. Zachary Schiller and Mark N. Varmmos, "Liquid Tide Looks Like Solid Gold," *Business Week*, December 24, 1984, p. 32.
7. For example, Elizabeth C. Hirschman, "Attributes of Attributes and Layers of Meaning," in *Advances in Consumer Research*, vol. 7, ed. Jerry

C. Olson (Ann Arbor, Mich.: Association for Consumer Research, 1980), pp. 7–12.

8. Lyle V. Geistfeld, George B. Sproles, and Susan B. Badenhop, "The Concept and Measurement of a Hierarchy of Product Characteristics," in *Advances in Consumer Research*, vol. 4, ed. H. Keith Hunt (Ann Arbor, Mich.: Association for Consumer Research, 1977), pp. 302–7.

9. Theodore Levitt, "Marketing Myopia," *Harvard Business Review*, July–August 1960, pp. 45–56.

10. Paul E. Green, Yoram Wind, and Arun K. Jain, "Benefit Bundle Analysis," *Journal of Advertising Research*, April 1972, pp. 32–36.

11. Russell I. Haley, "Benefit Segmentation: A Decision-Oriented Research Tool," *Journal of Marketing*, July 1972, pp. 30–35.

12. Lynn Coleman, "Advertisers Put Fear into the Hearts of Their Prospects," *Marketing News*, August 15, 1988, pp. 1–2.

13. For instance, Jonathan Gutman and Donald E. Vinson, "Values Structures and Consumer Behavior," in *Advances in Consumer Research*, vol. 6, ed. William L. Wilkie (Ann Arbor, Mich.: Association for Consumer Research, 1979), pp. 335–39; Janice G. Hanna, "A Typology of Consumer Needs," in *Research in Marketing*, vol. 3. ed. Jagdish N. Sheth (Greenwich, Conn.: JAI Press, 1980), pp. 83–104; and Lynn Kahle, "The Values of Americans: Implications for Consumer Adaptation," in *Personal Values & Consumer Psychology*, ed. Robert E. Pitts, Jr., and Arch G. Woodside (Lexington, Mass.: Lexington Books, 1984), pp. 77–86.

14. Milton J. Rokeach, *The Nature of Human Values* (New York: Free Press, 1973).

15. Apparently Rokeach based these values on his study of the research literature, personal introspection, and interviews with graduate students and a small sample of adults. See Russell A. Jones, John Sensenig, and Richard D. Ashmore, "Systems of Values and Their Multidimensional Representations," *Multivariate Behavioral Research*, 1978, pp. 255–70.

16. Anthony G. Greenwald and Anthony R. Pratkanis, "The Self," in *The Handbook of Social Cognition*, ed. Robert S. Wyer and Thomas K. Srull (Hillsdale, N.J.: Lawrence Erlbaum, 1984), pp. 129–78; and Hazel Markus and Paula Nurius, "Possible Selves," *American Psychologist*, September 1986, pp. 954–69.

17. John F. Kihlstrom and Nancy Cantor, "Mental Representations of the Self," in *Advances in Experimental Social Psychology* 17 (1984), pp. 1–47; Hazel Markus, "Self-Schemata and Processing Information about the Self," *Journal of Personality and Social Psychology* 35 (1977), pp. 63–78; and Hazel Markus and Keith Sentis, "The Self in Social Information Processing," in *Psychological Perspective on the Self*, ed. J. Suls (Hillsdale, N.J.: Lawrence Erlbaum, 1982), pp. 41–70.

18. The basic idea of means-end chains can be traced back at least to Edward C. Tolman, *Purposive Behavior in Animals and Men* (New York: Century, 1932). Among the first to suggest its use in marketing was John A. Howard, *Consumer Behavior Application and Theory* (New York: McGraw-Hill, 1977). More recently Jon Gutman, Tom Reynolds, and Jerry Olson have been active proponents of means-end chain models. For example, see Jonathan Gutman and Thomas J. Reynolds, "An Investigation of the Levels of Cognitive Abstraction Utilized by Consumers in Product Differentiation," in *Attitude Research under the Sun*, ed. John Eighmey (Chicago: American Marketing Association, 1979), pp. 125–50; Jonathan Gutman, "A Means-End Chain Model Based on Consumer Categorization Processes," *Journal of Marketing*, Spring 1982, pp. 60–72; and Jerry C. Olson and Thomas J. Reynolds, "Understanding Consumers' Cognitive Structures: Implications for Marketing Strategy," in *Advertising and Consumer Psychology*, vol. 1, ed. Larry Percy and Arch Woodside (Lexington, Mass.: Lexington Books, 1983), pp. 77–90.

19. Shirley Young and Barbara Feigen, "Using the Benefit Chair for Improved Strategy Formulation," *Journal of Marketing*, July 975, pp. 72–74; James H. Myers and Alan D. Schocker, "The Nature of Product-Related Attributes," in *Research in Marketing*, ed. J. N. Sheth (Greenwich, Conn.: JAI Press, 1981), pp. 211–36; Gutman

and Reynolds, "An Investigation of the Levels of Cognitive Abstraction Utilized by Consumers in Product Differentiation," pp. 128–50; and Joel B. Cohen, "The Structure of Product Attributes: Defining Attribute Dimensions for Planning and Evaluation," in *Analytic Approaches to Product and Marketing Planning*, ed. A. D. Shocker (Cambridge, Mass.: Marketing Science Institute, 1979), pp. 54–86.

20. Jonathan Gutman, "A Means-End Chain Model Based on Consumer Categorization Processes," *Journal of Marketing*, Spring 1982, pp. 60–72; and Jerry C. Olson, "The Theoretical Foundations of Means-End Chains," Paper 174, Working Series in Marketing Research, Penn State University, 1989.

21. Olson and Reynolds, "Understanding Consumer Cognitive Structures," pp. 77–90.

22. For a good example, see Sunil Mehrotra and John Palmer, "Relating Product Features to Perceptions of Quality: Appliances," in *Perceived Quality*, ed. Jacob Jacoby and Jerry Olson (Lexington, Mass.: Lexington Books, 1985), pp. 81–96.

23. Gay Jervey, "Gillette and Bic Spots Taking on Sensitive Subject," *Advertising Age*, March 18, 1985, p. 53.

24. Thomas J. Reynolds and Jonathan Gutman, "Laddering Theory, Method, Analysis, and Interpretation," *Journal of Advertising Research*, February–March 1988, pp. 11–31; Jonathan Gutman, "Exploring the Nature of Linkages between Consequences and Values," *Journal of Business Research*, 22 (1991), pp. 143–148.

25. For a good example, see Jonathan Gutman and Scott D. Alden, "Adolescents' Cognitive Structures of Retail Stores and Fashion Consumption: A Means-End Chain Analysis of Quality," in *Perceived Quality*, ed. Jacob Jacoby and Jerry Olson (Lexington, Mass.: Lexington Books, 1985), pp. 99–114.

26. One of the first and most influential writers about involvement was Herbert E. Krugman. See Herbert E. Krugman, "The Impact of Television Advertising Learning without Involvement," *Public Opinion Quarterly* 29 (1965), pp. 349–56; and Herbert E. Krugman, "The Measurement of Advertising Involvement," *Public Opinion Quarterly*, 30 (1967), pp. 583–96.

27. For instance, see John H. Antil, "Conceptualization and Operationalization of Involvement," in *Advances in Consumer Research*, vol. 11, ed. Thomas C. Kinnear (Ann Arbor, Mich.: Association for Consumer Research, 1984), pp. 203–9; Andrew A. Mitchell, "Involvement: A Potentially Important Mediator of Consumer Behavior," in *Advances in Consumer Research*, vol. 6, ed. William Wilkie (Ann Arbor, Mich.: Association for Consumer Research, 1979), pp. 191–96; or Robert N. Stone, "The Marketing Characteristics of Involvement," in *Advances in Consumer Research*, vol. 11, ed. Thomas C. Kinnear (Ann Arbor, Mich.: Association for Consumer Research, 1984), pp. 210–15.

28. For instance, see Peter N. Bloch, "An Exploration into the Scaling of Consumers' Involvement with a Product Class," in *Advances in Consumer Research*, vol. 8, ed. Kent B. Monroe (Ann Arbor, Mich.: Association for Consumer Research, 1981), pp. 61–65; and Judith Lynne Zaichkowsky, "Measuring the Involvement Construct," *Journal of Consumer Research*, December 1985, pp. 341–52.

29. This section draws on Richard L. Celsi and Jerry C. Olson, "The Role of Involvement in Attention and Comprehension Processes," *Journal of Consumer Research*, September 1988, pp. 210–24.

30. Joel B. Cohen, "Involvement and You: 100 Great Ideas," in *Advances in Consumer Research*, vol. 9, ed. Andrew A. Mitchell (Ann Arbor, Mich.: Association for Consumer Research, 1982), pp. 324–27.

31. Beth A. Walker, and Jerry C. Olson, "Means-End Chains: Connecting Products with Self," *Journal of Business Research*, no. 2 (1991), pp. 111–118.

32. Celsi and Olson, "The Role of Involvement in Attention and Comprehension Processes," pp. 210–24.

33. Harold H. Kassarjian, "Low Involvement—A Second Look," in *Advances in Consumer Research*,

vol. 8, ed. Kent B. Monroe (Ann Arbor, Mich.: Association for Consumer Research, 1981), pp. 31–34.

34. Andrew A. Mitchell, "The Dimensions of Advertising Involvement," in *Advances in Consumer Research*, vol. 8, ed. Kent B. Monroe (Ann Arbor, Mich.: Association for Consumer Research, 1981), pp. 25–30.

35. William L. Moore and Donald R. Lehmann, "Individual Differences in Search Behavior for a Nondurable," *Journal of Consumer Research*, December 1980, pp. 296–307.

36. Celsi and Olson, "The Role of Involvement in Attention and Comprehension Processes," pp. 210–24.

37. See Celsi and Olson, "The Role of Involvement in Attention and Comprehension Processes," pp. 210–24. A similar perspective is provided by Peter H. Bloch and Marsha L. Richins, "A Theoretical Model of the Study of Product Importance Perceptions," *Journal of Marketing*, Summer 1983, pp. 69–81. Some researchers treat these two factors as two forms of involvement — enduring and situational involvement, respectively. For instance, see Michael J. Houston and Michael L. Rothschild, "Conceptual and Methodological Perspectives on Involvement," in *1978 Educators' Proceedings*, ed. S. C. Jain (Chicago: American Marketing Association, 1978), pp. 184–87. We believe it is clearer to treat these factors as sources of (left) involvement.

38. For a similar proposal, see Peter H. Bloch, "Involvement Beyond the Purchase Process: Conceptual Issues and Empirical Investigation," in *Advances in Consumer Research*, vol. 9, ed. Andrew A. Mitchell (Ann Arbor, Mich.: Association for Consumer Research, 1982), pp. 413–17.

39. Some researchers have called this "enduring involvement" — e.g., Houston and Rothschild, "Conceptual and Methodological Perspectives on Involvement," pp. 184–87.

40. John Harris, "I Don't Want Good, I Want Fast," *Forbes*, October 1, 1990, p. 186.

41. Russell W. Belk, "Worldly Possessions: Issues and Criticisms," in *Advances in Consumer Research*, vol. 10, ed. Richard P. Bagozzi and Alice M. Tybout (Ann Arbor, Mich.: Association for Consumer Research, 1983), pp. 514–19; and Terence A. Shimp and Thomas J. Madden, "Consumer-Object Relations: A Conceptual Framework Based Analogously on Sternberg's Triangular Theory of Love," in *Advances in Consumer Research*, vol. 15, ed. Michael J. Houston (Ann Arbor, Mich.: Association for Consumer Research, 1988), pp. 163–68.

42. For a similar idea in an advertising context, see Thomas J. Reynolds and Jonathan Gutman, "Advertising Is Image Management," *Journal of Advertising Research*, February–March 1984, pp. 27–37.

43. Bill Brubaker, "Athletic Shoes: Beyond Big Business," *Washington Post*, March 10, 1991, pp. A1, A18.

44. For a detailed description of the perceived personal relevance (felt involvement) of some consumer researchers, see Donald R. Lehmann, "Pumping Iron III: An Examination of Compulsive Lifting," in *Advances in Consumer Research*, vol. 14, ed. Melanie Wallendorf and Paul Anderson (Ann Arbor, Mich.: Association for Consumer Research, 1987), pp. 129–31; and Debra Scammon, "Breeding, Training and Riding: The Serious Side of Horsing Around," in *Advances in Consumer Research*, vol. 14, ed. Melanie Wallendorf and Paul Anderson (Ann Arbor, Mich.: Association for Consumer Research, 1987), pp. 125–28.

45. Sunil Mehrotra and John Palmer, "Relating Product Features to Perceptions of Quality: Appliances," in *Perceived Quality*, ed. Jacob Jacoby and Jerry C. Olson (Lexington, Mass.: Lexington Books, 1985), pp. 81–96.

46. Grant McCracken, "Advertising: Meaning or Information," in *Advances in Consumer Research*, vol. 14, ed. Melanie Wallendorf and Paul Anderson (Ann Arbor, Mich.: Association for Consumer Research, 1987), pp. 121–24.

47. Joshua Levine, "I Gave at the Supermarket," *Forbes*, December 25, 1989, pp. 138–40.

48. Jaclyn Fierman, "The Big Muddle in Green Marketing," *Fortune*, June 3, 1991, pp. 91–101.

Additional Reading

For a discussion of how young children form product categories, see:

Roedder-John, Deborah, and Mita Sujan. "Age Differences in Product Categorization." *Journal of Consumer Research*, March 1990, pp. 452–60.

For a discussion of the influences of knowledge structures on categorization, see:

Sujan, Mita, and James R. Bettman. "The Effects of Brand Positioning Strategies on Consumers' Brand and Category Perceptions: Some Insights from Schema Research." *Journal of Marketing Research*, November 1989, pp. 454–67.

For examples of using means-end chains to understand consumers' meanings for a product attribute, see:

Gutman, Jonathan, and Scott D. Alden. "Adolescents' Cognitive Structures of Retail Stores and Fashion Consumption: A Means-End Chain Analysis of Quality." In *Perceived Quality: How Consumers View Stores and Merchandise*, ed. Jacob Jacoby and Jerry C. Olson, Lexington, Mass.: Lexington Books, 1985, pp. 99–114.

Zeithaml, Valarie A. "Consumer Perceptions of Price, Quality, and Value: A Means-End Model and Synthesis of Evidence," *Journal of Marketing*, July 1988, pp. 2–22.

For a discussion of how consumers use products to define and establish a self-concept or self-schema, see:

Belk, Russell W. "Possessions and the Extended Self." *Journal of Consumer Research*, September 1988, pp. 139–68.

For a discussion of the role of affective responses in involvement, see:

Zaichkowsky, Judith Lynne. "The Emotional Aspect of Product Involvement." In *Advances in Consumer Research*, vol. 14, ed. Melanie Wallendorf and Paul Anderson. Provo, Utah: Association for Consumer Research, 1987, pp. 17–21.

For a discussion of the widespread prevalence of low involvement in consumer behavior, see:

Kassarjian, Harold H. "Low Involvement: A Second Look." In *Advances in Consumer Research*, vol. 8, ed. Kent B. Monroe. Ann Arbor, Mich.: Association for Consumer Research, 1981, pp. 31–34.

For interesting examples of how involved some consumers can become with a simple product like blue jeans, see:

Solomon, Michael R. "Deep-Seated Materialism: The Case of Levi's 501 Jeans." In *Advances in Consumer Research*, vol. 13, ed. Richard J. Lutz. Ann Arbor, Mich.: Association for Consumer Research, 1986, pp. 619–22.

MARKETING STRATEGY IN ACTION

Nike

By mid-1985, the signs were becoming clear—after years of mystique and spectacular growth, jogging was puffing into middle age. In 1984, for instance, unit sales of running shoes decreased 17 percent, and dollar sales were off by 15 percent. Nike, the market leader in 1983 with a 31 percent market share, sold about $270 million worth of running shoes. By 1984, Nike's share of the running shoe market was down 26 percent. The decline continued so that by 1987 Nike had only an 18.6 percent share of the market for athletic shoes, a market it had dominated just a few years earlier. What happened?

Nike had become successful as a manufacturer of technically sophisticated shoes for the serious runner. Unfortunately, the market for running shoes had peaked. According to the director of the National Sporting Goods Association, "We've probably reached pretty close to the maximum participation in running." The running shoe market was saturated, as nearly everyone who wanted to run had tried it.

Part of the reason was demographic. During the late 1970s and early 1980s, the large baby boomers group filled the primary market for running gear—ages 25 to 40. But in the mid- to late-1980s, fewer people were entering this age group, thus decreasing overall demand. As the leading age of this group pushed toward 40, lacing up the old shoes for another 5-mile run began to seem less adventurous and fun than it had at age 24.

Also, the running shoe market had become highly segmented by the mid-1980s—a sure sign of a mature market. This meant marketers had to pay even closer attention to consumers' needs, goals, and values in order to produce product variations for smaller groups of consumers. And, finally, the industry had begun to engage in sporadic price cutting as companies fought to maintain their market shares.

Another reason for the drop in running concerns consumers' ideas about health. Running develops the legs and cardiovascular system, but little else. Many runners had begun to notice that the rest of their bodies needed conditioning too. Athletically oriented people became increasingly interested in total fitness.

All these changes meant fewer people were taking up running and the millions of joggers who were still on the run were doing fewer laps. This translated into fewer replacement shoes sold by Nike, Converse, New Balance, Brooks, and all the others. As the biggest manufacturer in the business, Nike had the most to lose.

From one perspective, makers of running shoes had enjoyed a long run, especially in the sports equipment market, which is often dominated by short-lived fads. Consider tennis, for example. Sales of tennis rackets peaked in 1976 when an estimated 8.6 million rackets were sold. Despite technological innovations and space-age materials such as kevlar, boron, and graphite, the industry sold only about 3.2 million rackets in 1984. Instead, the big boom in 1984 and 1985 was aerobics gear and home gym equipment.

Some commentators believe Nike didn't react quickly enough to these fundamental changes in the consumer markets. One company that did capitalize on these changes was Reebok International. Its sales shot up from $84 million in 1984 to $307 million the next year, with profits increasing sixfold to $39 million. According to Reebok President Paul Fireman, "We go out to consumers and find out what they want. Other companies don't seem to do that."

It seems that what many consumers wanted in the mid-1980s was fashion. Perhaps this would have been evident by simple observation of consumers' product-use behaviors. It is estimated that between 70 and 80 percent of the shoes designed for basketball and aerobic exericise are actually used for street wear instead of the sports for which they were intended. These products must have been satisfying some fashion needs or ends.

So when Reebok introduced its first soft-leather Freestyle aerobic shoes in 1983, the brilliant colors and soft leather made them an overnight sensation in the United States. In a way, Reebok actually expanded the overall market for athletic shoes, because it attracted women customers from more traditional shoe manufacturers such as Bass and got them to spend $40 on athletic shoes. People began to think of this product class as something more than "just sneakers." Reebok's spectacular popularity continued, and by 1986 Nike had lost the top spot to Reebok.

During 1987 and 1988, Nike worked feverishly (and with some success) to recapture the lead in this expanding and profitable market. In 1987, Nike introduced its Air shoes. This product line was headed by the successful basketball shoe Air Jordan, named after Chicago Bulls basketball star Michael Jordan (noted for his soaring leaps), who wore and promoted the product. Nike spent heavily on TV and print advertising to introduce this innovative product. But perhaps its best strategy was to produce the top-of-the-line models with a transparent "cut-out" in the sole so the consumer could actually see how the air cushioned their impact. In 1988, Nike spent some $34 million on advertising, the highest level yet for the company that once eschewed mass advertising as unnecessary and somewhat demeaning. Of course, Reebok, the once-small competitor, wasn't sitting still: it increased its own advertising spending with a substantial amount channeled to TV.

In response to these changes in consumers, Nike expanded its product line beyond running shoes in the mid-1980s. It began to produce shoes for the aerobic market and other specialty sports activities. Nike introduced a line of walking shoes to appeal to a submarket that had emerged rapidly in the mid-1980s, perhaps as aging baby boomers found running too stressful on their joints.

In 1988, Nike considered introducing a fashion-oriented shoe to compete head-on with archrival Reebok. The new shoe was to be targeted at women, the primary buyers of such shoes, and was to be called IE. It would not carry the Nike name. Prices were targeted between $25 and $40, somewhat below the price for the average Nike shoe. "With the IE, Nike is attempting to penetrate the very market [the fashion market] where it has been weakest historically," said one industry analyst. The independent brand name seemed a good strategy, as it would not give its core customers (serious and would-be athletes) mixed signals about the meaning of the Nike brand.

Discussion Questions

1. Apparently there are two market segments of consumers for many product forms of athletic shoes — those who use the shoes to engage in the designated athletic activity and those who primarily use the shoes for casual wear and seldom engage in the athletic activity.
   a. Discuss the differences between these two segments in means-end chains and especially end goals, needs, and values for running, basketball, aerobics, or tennis shoes.
   b. Draw means-end chains to illustrate your

ideas about how these two segments differ.

c. What types of special difficulties does a marketer face in promoting its products to two segments of consumers who use the product in very different ways?

2. Many manufacturers of athletic shoes promote so-called technological advances such as the "Air sole" or the "Energy Wave." How do consumers make sense of such attributes? Which types of attributes are likely to have a major impact on their purchasing behavior?

3. As the market for athletic shoes has become more segmented, marketers have produced shoes for very specialized purposes. Why? Discuss the special types of means-end chains held by people who buy athletic shoes for very special purposes (walking, tennis, aerobics, etc.). Analyze the source of consumers' felt involvement in these products – intrinsic or situational self-relevance. How can these analyses help understand the consumer/product relationship and help marketers develop more effective marketing strategies?

4. Analyze the changes that have occurred over time in consumers' product/self relationships for running shoes (or some other type of athletic shoe). Consider changes in consumers' affective responses and their product knowledge, as well as their overt behaviors and general environmental factors. How could Nike have kept better track of these changes so that its marketing strategies would have been more effective in the mid-1980s?

Source: Adapted from Marcy Magiera, "Nike Plans Rebound with Fashion Shoe," *Advertising Age,* January 25, 1988, p. 1; Patrick McGeehan, "Wave Action: Converse Goes Toe-to-Toe with Nike High-Performance," *Advertising Age,* February 22, 1988, p. 76; Richard Phalon, "Out of Breath," *Forbes,* October 22, 1984. pp. 39–40; and Lois Therrien and Amy Borrus, "Reeboks: How Far Can a Fad Run?" *Business Week,* February 24, 1986, pp. 89–90.

Attention and Comprehension

5

CHAPTER

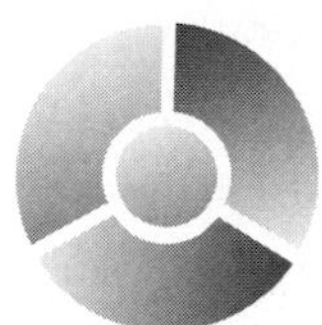

IS ANYBODY WATCHING?

On most Thursday nights during the mid-1980s, approximately 60 million Americans settled down to watch "The Cosby Show," then the nation's top-rated program. Advertisers also liked the show, even though they had to pay $350,000 for each 30-second spot in 1987, up from $270,000 in 1986. But how could marketers know if their ads were reaching the audience they were paying for? Researchers have been trying to measure viewer exposure and attention to TV commercials since at least 1952, when a water commissioner in Toledo, Ohio, noticed that huge drops in the city's water pressure (due to thousands of flushing toilets) coincided with commercial breaks in the popular "I Love Lucy" show.

By the mid-1980s, audience measurement had become a bit more sophisticated. Two rival companies in the United States, A. C. Nielsen and Arbitron, measured TV audiences using the same 20-year-old method. They attached electronic meters to the TV sets of a sample of 1,500 to 2,000 households. The meters measured whether the set was on, which channel was selected, and how long the set was tuned to that channel. But the meters could not tell which, if any, family members watched the program (and presumably the commercials). So Nielsen and Arbitron supplemented the

meter data with another, larger sample of households that recorded which programs each family member watched. The diaries were supposed to be filled in each week and mailed in monthly.

This procedure had obvious problems. For one, the diary data did not reveal whether the purported viewer(s) actually paid attention to the program or the commercials. In addition, the television environment had become so complex by the mid-1980s that filling out diaries describing the TV viewing behavior of an entire family was extremely difficult. Many American homes received multiple TV channels via cable and had multiple TV sets. Adding further complexity were VCRs, which can record shows for later viewing, and remote controls, which made switching between channels easy. Little wonder that few advertisers had much faith in the accuracy of people's diaries. Who could remember which family member watched what program when? A new system was needed that could provide more accurate measures of exposure and attention to television advertising.

Enter AGB Research, the top ratings company in Europe, with a new idea—a people meter. This remote-controlled device had eight buttons that signaled a small monitor box wired to the set. Each family member was assigned a number to push each time he or she started and stopped watching TV. The data were recorded electronically and passed automatically over telephone lines each night to the company, where it was analyzed and given to broadcasters the next day.

Under this competitive threat, the A. C. Nielsen Company quickly developed its own version of a people meter and had installed 2,000 devices by late 1987. Although many questions remained about the validity of the people meter system, one thing was clear—it gave different answers than the old diary system. The people meter measured smaller audiences for many programs, especially popular ones like "The Cosby Show" (which went down

10 percent in this system). Placing ads on these shows was costing advertisers more money to reach a thousand viewers (CPM) than they thought. But a few shows, such as "Miami Vice," seemed to have bigger audiences when measured by people meters (up 11 percent).

People meters were an advance, but even they could not tell if anyone was paying attention to the advertising. Research showed that many people were not. One resourceful researcher mounted a small camera on the sets in about 20 British households to periodically take pictures of the room. He found that approximately equal numbers of viewers were paying close attention, some attention, and no attention at all. The last group included consumers who were sleeping, reading, or kissing instead of watching the commercials.

An even more sophisticated system was tested in 1987–1988 by R. D. Percy & Company, which combined a people meter with a heat sensor that could determine if anyone was in the room. If a viewer left the room and forgot to indicate that on the people meter, the system would ask if anyone was there. If no response was forthcoming, it would record that the set played to an empty room. This system could produce separate ratings for the program and for the commercials. Of course, we would expect that most commercial ratings would be lower than the show's rating.

In 1992, the so-called passive people meter was still on the horizon, and questions remained about whether people would allow such "seeing" devices into their homes (and bedrooms).

Sources: Brian Dumaine, "Who's Gypping Whom in TV Ads?" *Fortune,* July 6, 1987, pp. 78-79; Dennis Kneale, "Using High-Tech Tools to Measure Audience," *The Wall Street Journal,* April 25, 1988, p. 21; Jeffery A. Tachtenberg, "Anybody Home Out There?" *Forbes,* May 19, 1986, pp. 169-70; Jeffery A. Tachtenberg, "Diary of a Failure," *Forbes,* September 19, 1988, pp. 168-70; Howard Scholssberg, "Case of Missing TV Viewers," *Marketing News,* September 17, 1990, pp. 1, 7; and Lynn G. Coleman, "People Meter Rerun," *Marketing News,* September 2, 1991, pp. 1, 44.

This example illustrates the importance to marketers of understanding consumers' exposure to marketing information as well as their attention to and comprehension of that information. The example also illustrates the difficulty in measuring consumers' exposure and attention to TV programs and commercials, given multiple TV sets in households, 10 to 50 channels of TV programming, and remote controls that make frequent channel changing easy. The Wheel of Consumer Analysis provides an overall perspective for understanding exposure attention and comprehension (see Figure 5.1). Consumers' everyday environment contains a great deal of information, large parts of which are created through marketing strategies. For example, marketers modify consumers' environments by creating advertisements and placing them on TV. For the advertisements to be effective, consumers must come in contact with them. Exposure often occurs through consumers' own behaviors—they turn on the TV and switch to a favorite show. Once exposed, consumers must attend to and comprehend the advertisements (affective responses and cognitive interpretations).

FIGURE 5.1
The Wheel of Consumer Analysis

In this chapter, we continue our examination of the affect and cognition portion of the Wheel of Consumer Analysis. We will consider the interpretation process, a key cognitive process in our general model of consumers' cognition shown in Figure 5.2. First, we examine how consumers become exposed to marketing information. Then, we discuss attention processes by which consumers select certain information in the environment to be interpreted. Finally, we examine the comprehension processes by which consumers construct meanings to represent this information, organize them into knowledge structures, and

FIGURE 5.2
Consumers' Cognitive Processes Involved in Interpretation

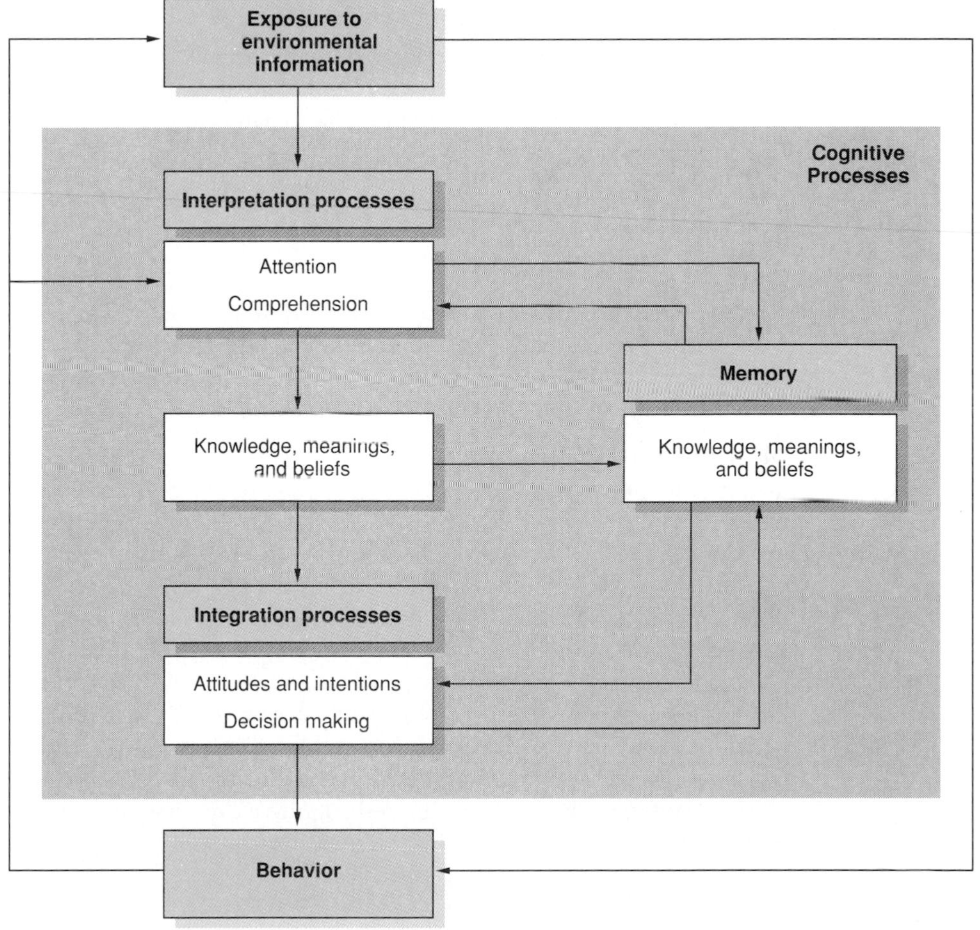

store them in memory. We emphasize the reciprocal interactions between attention and comprehension and stored knowledge, meanings, and beliefs in memory. Throughout the chapter, we discuss the implications of these interpretation processes for developing marketing strategy.

Although we discuss attention and comprehension separately, the boundary between the two processes is not very distinct. Rather, attention shades off into comprehension.[1] As interrelated interpretation processes, attention and comprehension serve the same basic function of the cognitive system — to construct personal, subjective cognitive representations or meanings that make sense of the environment and one's behaviors. This knowledge can then be used in subsequent interpretation and integration processes to guide consumers' behaviors and help them get along in their environment.

Before beginning our analyses, we briefly review four important aspects of the cognitive system that influence interpretation processes.

- Interpretation involves interactions between knowledge in memory and information from the environment. The incoming environmental information activates relevant knowledge in memory, which could be either schema or script knowledge structures.
- The activated knowledge influences the direction and intensity of attention and comprehension processes as well as the specific meanings (interpretations) produced.
- Because their cognitive systems have a limited capacity, consumers can consciously process only small amounts of information at a time. Because some attention and comprehension processes are under the consumers' conscious control, they are subject to these capacity limits.[2]
- Much attention and comprehension processing occurs automatically with little or no conscious awareness.[3] Automatic interpretation processes occur quickly, require little or no cognitive capacity, and are not easily controlled by the consumer. Over time, our cognitive processes must become more automatic, or we would expend all our limited cognitive capacity on a few tasks that never become easier. Fortunately, as we take in new knowledge and become more familiar with using it, that knowledge tends to be activated and used in interpretation processes in increasingly automatic ways. For instance, simple interpretations such as recognizing a familiar product occur automatically and virtually instantly upon exposure, without any conscious awareness of comprehension. Automatic processing has the obvious advantage of keeping our limited cognitive capacity free for unfamiliar interpretation tasks that do require conscious thought.

Exposure to Information

Although not a part of cognition in a strict sense, **exposure** to information is critically important for consumers' interpretation processes. Consumers are exposed to information in the environment, including marketing strategies, primarily through their own behaviors. We can distinguish between two types of exposure to marketing information: purposive or **intentional exposure** and random or **accidental exposure.**

Consumers are exposed to some marketing information due to their own intentional, goal-directed *search behavior*. Consumers search for relevant marketing information to help solve a purchasing problem. Before buying a camera, for instance, a consumer might read product evaluations of 35mm cameras in *Consumer Reports* or photography magazines. Another consumer might ask a friend or a salesperson for advice about which brand of earphones to buy for her Walkman radio.

Most investigations of consumer search behavior have found that levels of intentional exposure to marketing information are rather low. Often, consumers visit only one or a few retail stores, and consult very few salespersons and external sources of information.[4] This limited search may be surprising, until you realize that most consumers already have substantial product-related knowledge, meanings, and beliefs stored in their memories. If they feel confident in their existing knowledge, or if they feel little involvement with the decision (low self-relevance), consumers have little motivation to engage in extensive search behaviors. (We will discuss search behavior again in Chapter 8, in the context of consumer decision making.)

Marketing information is everywhere in the consumer-oriented environments of most industrialized countries. In the United States, for instance, advertisements for products and services are found in magazines and newspapers, on radio and TV, and on bus placards and bus-stop shelters — and they are increasing. Between 1967 and 1982, the total number of ads doubled; and by 1997 that number is expected to double again.[5] Billboards and signs promoting products, services, and retail stores are found along most highways. Stores contain a great deal of marketing information, including signs, point-of-purchase displays, and advertisements, in addition to information on packages. Consumers also receive product information from friends and relatives, from salespersons, and occasionally even from strangers.

Typically, consumers' exposure to these types of marketing information is not the result of intentional search behavior. Instead, most exposures are random or semirandom events that occur as consumers move through their environments and "accidentally" come into contact with marketing information. For instance, browsing ("just looking") in stores is a common source of accidental exposure to marketing information.[6] Consumers may discover new products, sales promotions, or new retail outlets when browsing. Some retailers design their store environments to encourage browsing and maximize the amount of time consumers spend in the store, which increases the likelihood they will be exposed to products and make a purchase.

Consumers are seldom intentionally seeking information about products or services when they watch television, yet they are accidentally exposed to many commercials during an evening. Since consumers probably don't feel very involved with most of the products promoted in these ads, their attention and

Marketers place ads in the environment to maximize the chances of accidental exposure.

comprehension processes are probably not extensive. Even so, increased levels of accidental exposure can have a powerful effect on behaviors. Consider the situation during the Persian Gulf War in early 1991 when viewership of CNN skyrocketed to almost twice previous levels (exposure was up as much as 20 times in some time periods).[7] Advertisers on CNN such as 800 Flowers, a New York-based company that delivers flowers anywhere in the United States, and Sterling/Range Rover received large increases in accidental exposure to their ads, which also increased their business. For example, 800 Flowers' business on Valentine's Day is usually triple a normal day; but in 1991, orders increased 9 or 10 times. In fact, the company couldn't handle all the calls received.

Selective Exposure to Information

As the amount of marketing information in the environment increases, consumers become more adept at avoiding exposure (some consumers intentionally avoid reading product test reports or talking with salespeople). Or consumers do not maintain accidental exposure to marketing information (some people automatically throw away most junk mail unopened). Such behaviors result in **selective exposure** to marketing information. Consider the problem marketers are having with consumers' exposure to TV commercials. In one simple study, college students observed family members watching TV. Only 47 percent of viewers watched all or almost all of the ads that appeared on ABC, NBC, and CBS, and about 10 percent left the room.[8]

Current technology enables consumers to control what ads they see on TV more easily than ever before. Thanks to remote controls for TV sets, viewers can turn off the sound or "dial hop" from one station to another during a commercial break. Consumers who have videocassette recorders can run fast-forward past commercials on taped programs. In advertising circles, these practices are known as *zapping* and *zipping*, respectively. In homes with remote controls, the zapping (tune-out) factor has been estimated at about 10 percent for the average commercial. Some 20 percent of homes contain heavy zappers, who switch channels at the rate of one zap every two minutes. As remote controls become even more popular, the situation is likely to get worse. Advertisers, who pay media rates based on a full audience (currently $100,000 to $300,000 or more for 30 seconds of prime time on a major network), are worried they are not getting their money's worth. One of their strategies to combat zapping is to develop commercials that are so interesting and exciting they won't be zapped. For instance, one study found that Pepsi ads featuring Michael Jackson were zapped by only 1 to 2 percent of the audience.[9]

Marketing Implications

Because of the crucial importance of exposure, marketers should develop specific strategies to enhance the probability that consumers will be exposed to their information and products. There are three ways to do this: facilitate intentional exposure, maximize accidental exposure, and maintain exposure.

In cases where consumers' exposure to marketing information is the result of intentional search, marketers should *facilitate intentional exposure* by making appropriate marketing information available when and where the consumers need it. For instance, to increase sales, International Business Machines Corporation trains its retail salespeople to answer consumers' technical questions on the spot so that they don't have to wait while the salesperson looks up the answer. Consumers' search for information should be made as easy as possible. This requires that marketers anticipate consumers' needs for information and devise strategies to meet them. Some lumber companies cater to the novice do-it-yourself market by providing in-store seminars on various building techniques such as how to build a masonry wall or install a storm door.

Obviously, marketers should try to place their information in environmental settings that maximize *accidential exposure* to the appropriate target groups of consumers. For instance, the average person looks at a parking meter for about 14 seconds as he or she deposits the right change.[10] This is plenty of time to be exposed to an ad for Cambell's Soup Co. or Minolta, which have appeared atop parking meters in Baltimore. Certain types of retail outlets such as convenience stores, ice cream shops, and fast-food restaurants should be placed in locations where accidental exposure is high. High-traffic locations such as malls, busy intersections, and downtown locations are prime spots. Consider the Au Bon Pain cafes, a growing chain selling gourmet sandwiches, freshly squeezed orange juice, and fresh-baked French bread, muffins, and croissants.[11] Using a saturation distribution strategy, Au Bon Pain has packed 16 stores into downtown Boston; some stores are less than 100 yards apart. In fact, five outlets are inside Filene's Department Store. Besides being highly convenient for regular customers, the saturation strategy maximizes the chances of accidental exposure. The thousands of busy commuters leaving Boston's South Station can hardly avoid walking by an Au Bon Pain cafe. Consumer awareness levels in Boston are high, although the company has never advertised. "It's like having an outdoor billboard in every block; the stores themselves are a substitute for ads."

Most media strategies are intended to maximize accidental exposures to a firms' advertisements. Media planners must carefully select a mix of media (magazines, billboards, radio and TV programming) that will maximize the chances that the target segment will be exposed to the company's ads. Solving this very complex problem is crucial to the success of the company's communication strategy because the ads cannot have any impact if no one sees them. Besides inserting ads in the traditional media, companies attempt to increase accidental exposure by placing ads inside taxicabs, in sports stadiums, and on boats, buses, and blimps. Another marketing strategy involves placing several four-color ads (for noncompeting products) on grocery store shopping carts.[12]

HIGHLIGHT 5.1

AD EXPOSURE AT POINT OF PURCHASE

After a long day at work, Lisa stops at the supermarket to pick up dinner. As she wheels the grocery cart down the coffee aisle, an ad for Folger's coffee flashes on the liquid-crystal screen attached to her cart's handle. Seeing the ad reminds Lisa that she needs coffee, and she drops a can of Folger's into her cart.

It's a marketer's dream to show its ads right at the point where consumers make the purchase decision. Thanks to Information Resources, Inc. (IRI), this dream has come true. In April 1988, IRI unveiled a prototype of the Videocart, a standard grocery cart outfitted with a flat, 6-by-8-inch liquid-crystal display mounted on the cart handle. The display is not a TV video. Instead, it shows animated graphics created by a personal computer. The ads and other program material shown on each shopping cart are controlled by an in-store computer. The store receives ads from IRI via satellite and transfers them to the carts via a low-power FM transmitter.

The idea is to show the ads during breaks in an information and entertainment program. But the particular ads seen on each cart are determined by consumers' own behaviors, as they push the cart through the store. Ads are triggered by infrared devices implanted in the aisles. Only two ads are seen per aisle, and they are for products on the shelves in that aisle. The system also can present other useful information such as a store map, recipes, or which checkout counters are open. Local news and weather are automatically triggered when the cart reaches the checkout line. Eventually, shoppers may be able to get instant "electronic coupons" for the advertised products by pushing a button next to the video screen.

John Malac, chairman of IRI, says a supermarket can be equipped for about $95,000. The average supermarket has about 100 carts, and IRI would turn about 75 of them into Videocarts. In early 1991, the Videocart technology was in about 50 stores in 10 major markets. Some 15 companies, including Procter & Gamble, Pepsi, Nabisco, and Ralston Purina, have signed up. They pay about $4 to reach 1,000 consumers, compared to about $7 for a coupon and $10 to $20 for a prime-time commercial on network television. Malac's goal is to be in 5,000 top supermarkets by 1995, representing 40 percent of the $350 billion grocery business.

Early results suggest the advertising actually works: shoppers pushing Videocarts spend about $1 more per visit than those who don't. Every dollar counts when you have 20,000 shoppers per week in the stores that have Videocarts.

Sources: "VideOcart Shopping Cart with Computer Screen Creates New Ad Medium that also Gathers Data," *Marketing News,* May 9, 1988, pp. 1–2; Lois Therrien and Walecia Konrad, "Coming to a Shopping Cart near You: TV Commercials," *Business Week,* May 30, 1988, pp. 61–62; Joshua Levine, "The Ultimate Sell," *Forbes,* May 13, 1991, pp. 108–10; and Scott Hume, "Improved VideOcart Starts Test," *Advertising Age,* November 12, 1990, p. 66.

In 1990, these rolling billboards were in some 13,000 supermarkets. A big advantage of shopping cart ads is the much lower cost compared to the price of TV ads—$.50 per 1,000 exposures compared to about $10 to $20 per 1,000 exposures for network television. Advocates also claim this "reminder advertising" reaches consumers at the critical point when they make a purchase choice (an estimated 65 to 80 percent of brand buying decisions occur in the supermarket). Highlight 5.1 describes another way to expose consumers to marketing information inside the grocery store.

A long-standing strategy to increase accidental exposure to a brand is to get it into the movies, but many companies are trying to get their brands into TV shows for even greater exposure.[13] Sometimes actors mention brand names on TV. Typically, these exposures are not paid for; they are just part of the new realism in television. For instance, on the show "thirtysomething," Hope announced she was going out to buy some Junior Mints. It is illegal for marketers to pay to place a product on TV unless the payment is disclosed, but it is OK to provide products free to be used as props. For instance, a box of Quaker Oats Squares was seen on "Roseanne," and the secretaries on "L.A. Law" use IBM computers. Marketers may hire a company that specializes in placing products in movies and on TV in hope of exposing their brand to millions of viewers.

A company's distribution strategy plays the key role in creating accidental exposure to products. Distribution is to products such as beer, cigarettes, chewing gum, and potato chips, what location is to fast-food restaurants—it's nearly everything. Obviously, if the product is not on the grocery store shelves, at the checkout counter, or in the vending machine, the consumer cannot be exposed at the point of purchase, and sales will suffer.

Maximum exposure at the retail level is not desirable for all products, though. For instance, Burberry all-weather coats (with the distinctive plaid lining) or Bang & Olafson stereo equipment are sold only in a few exclusive, high-quality stores. Exposure is controlled by using a highly selective distribution strategy. In sum, one of the most important functions of a company's distribution strategy is to create the *appropriate level of exposure* to the product.

Other marketing strategies are intended to *maintain exposure* once it has begun. Television advertisements, for instance, must generate enough attention and interest so that the consumer will maintain exposure for 30 seconds rather than zap the ad, turn to a magazine, or leave the room to go to the kitchen for a snack. One tactic is to use distinctive sounds in TV commercials. For example, ads in the "Minds over Money" campaign for Shearson Lehman Brothers incorporated a buzzing, droning background sound that gradually grew louder every second, supposedly to represent the sound of a thought. Apparently the device did help maintain exposure to the ad because consumer awareness of the company increased by 50 percent over a three-year period.[14] As another example, Ikea, the Swedish furniture retailer, encourages browsing by providing lots of real-life furniture settings in its huge stores.[15] Ikea also provides baby-sitting, restaurants, and snack bars that serve Swedish specialties at low prices. A key goal is to maximize the amount of time consumers spend in the store, which maintains their exposure to the products and increases the likelihood they will make a purchase.

Attention Processes

Once consumers are exposed to marketing information, whether accidentally or through their own intentional behaviors, the interpretation processes of attention and comprehension begin. In this section, we discuss attention, levels of attention, and factors affecting attention, and we describe several marketing strategies that can influence consumers' attention.

What does it mean for a consumer to attend to a marketing stimulus such as a newspaper ad, a display in a store, or a clerk's sales pitch? First, **attention** implies selectivity.[16] Attending to certain information involves *selecting* it from a large set of information and ignoring other information. Consider the cognitive processes of shoppers in a crowded, noisy department store. They must selectively attend to conversations with salespersons, attend to certain products and brands, read labels and signs, and so on. At the same time, they must ignore other stimuli in the environment. Selective attention is highly influenced by the goals that are activated in a situation.

Attention also connotes awareness and consciousness. To attend to a stimulus usually means being *conscious* of it. Attention also suggests intensity and arousal.[17] Consumers must be somewhat *alert* and *aroused* to consciously attend to something, and their level of alertness influences how intensively they process the information. If you have ever tried to study when you were very tired, you know about the importance of arousal. If your level of arousal is very low, you might drift off to sleep while trying to read a text chapter (not this one, we hope!). When arousal is low, attention (and comprehension) suffers.

Variations in Attention

Attention processes vary along a continuum from a highly automatic, unconscious level called **preconscious attention** to a controlled, conscious level called **focal attention.**[18] As a consumers' interpretation processes shift from preconscious attention toward focal attention, greater cognitive capacity is needed, and the consumer gradually becomes more conscious of selecting and paying attention to a stimulus. At a focal level, attention is largely controlled by the consumer who decides which stimuli to attend to and comprehend based on what goals are activated. As attention processes reach focal levels, comprehension begins to involve sense-making processes for constructing meaning. Figure 5.3 summarizes these differences in levels of attention.

FIGURE 5.3
Levels of Attention

Preconscious attention	Focal attention
• Uses activated knowledge from long-term memory • No conscious awareness • Automatic processes • Uses little or no cognitive capacity • More likely for familiar, frequently encountered concepts, with well-learned memory representations • More likely for concepts of low to moderate importance or involvement	• Uses activated knowledge from long-term memory • Conscious awareness • Controlled processes • Uses some cognitive capacity • More likely for novel, unusual, infrequently encountered concepts, without well-learned memory representations • More likely for concepts of high importance or involvement

As an example of these levels of attention, consider the shopping cart ads described earlier. How well do they work? ACTMEDIA, a dominant company in the industry, claims cart ads increased sales of advertised brands by an average of 8 percent. But other research has found rather low levels of attention to these ads.[19] For instance, one study interviewed shoppers in stores with the cart ads. Only about 60 percent of these shoppers were aware of *ever* having seen any cart ads. Presumably the other 40 percent of shoppers apparently did not attend to the ads beyond a preconscious level, even though they were exposed to the ads (they had the opportunity to see them). In addition, only 13 percent of the interviewed shoppers were aware of seeing any ads on that particular shopping occasion. Apparently, these consumers processed the ads at relatively low levels of focal attention that produced some memory that an ad had been seen, but not enough to be aware of the brand. Only 7 percent of the interviewed shoppers could name any brands advertised on their cart. Only these few consumers processed the ads at a sufficiently high level of focal attention to comprehend the brand names of the advertised brands and create a strong memory for them. In sum, these results question the effectiveness of shopping cart ads. In the crowded information environment of the supermarket, most consumers do not pay much attention to ads, even those on their grocery cart.

Most researchers assume that consumers' cognitive systems respond to all stimuli that receive some level of attention, whether preconscious or focal. The affective system also responds to attended stimuli. Affective responses can range from simple evaluations (good/bad), to strong feelings (disgust), to emotions (joy or anger). As interpretation processes move toward focal levels of attention, affective responses usually become more intense, and consumers become more conscious of their affective states.

A Videocart can expose consumers to ads at the point of purchase.

Factors Influencing Attention

Many factors can affect consumers' attention to marketing information. In this section, we discuss three particularly important influences — consumers' *general affective state*, consumers' *felt involvement* with the information, and the *prominence* of the information in the environment. We also discuss how marketers can try to influence consumers' attention to marketing information by influencing their felt involvement and by making the information more prominent.

Affective States

Consumers' affective arousal can influence their attention processes. As discussed earlier, low arousal reduces the amount and intensity of attention. In contrast, a state of high affective arousal is thought to narrow consumers' focus of attention and make attention more selective.[20] Some affective states that are responses to specific stimuli or situations are considered part of felt involvement. These are discussed in the next section. Other affective states like moods are diffuse and general and are not related to any particular stimulus. These affective states can also influence attention. For instance, consumers who are in a bad (or good) mood are more likely to notice negative (or positive) aspects of their environment.[21] Another example concerns whether consumers' general affective responses to happy and sad TV programs influence their cognitive reactions to the TV commercials shown on those programs.[22]

A cute baby has high attention value.

Felt Involvement

A state of felt involvement is determined by the means-end chains activated from memory and related affective responses and arousal. Felt involvement is a motivational state that guides the selection of stimuli for focal attention and comprehension.[23] For instance, consumers who experience high felt involvement because of an intense need (Joe desperately needs a new pair of shoes for a wedding in two days) tend to focus their attention on marketing stimuli that are relevant to their needs.

A consumers' felt involvement is determined by a combination of situational and intrinsic self-relevance. Thus, people who find photography to be intrinsically self-relevant are more likely to notice and attend to ads for photo products. Or the felt involvement generated by actively considering the purchase of a new refrigerator influences consumers to notice and attend to ads and sales announcements for refrigerators. On occasion, marketing strategies (contests, sales, price deals) can create a temporary state of felt involvement that influences consumers' attention to stimuli in that situation.

Sometimes, marketers can take advantage of situational sources of self-relevance. For instance, a magazine called *Rx Being Well*, distributed to some 150,000 physicians' offices, bases its marketing strategy on the situational self-relevance of being in a doctor's office. The magazine is promoted to advertisers of health-care products as an ideal medium to "reach consumers when they are most receptive. People in waiting rooms aren't just waiting. They're thinking about their health. . . . You'll be reaching consumers right before they go to drugstores or supermarkets with pharmacies where they'll see, remember, and buy your product."[24]

Environmental Prominence

The stimuli associated with marketing strategies can also influence consumers' attention. However, not every marketing stimulus is equally likely to activate relevant knowledge structures, receive attention, and be comprehended. In general, the most prominent marketing stimuli are most likely to attract attention; hence, marketers usually try to make their stimuli prominent features in the environment. For instance, to capture consumers' attention, some radio and TV commercials are slightly louder than the surrounding program material, and the smells of baking products are exhausted from bakeries onto sidewalks or into malls. Highlight 5.2 describes how large amounts of advertising can influence attention and brand awareness.

Marketing Implications

Marketers have developed many strategies to increase (or maintain) consumers' attention to their marketing information. Basically these strategies involve increasing consumers' felt involvement with the marketing information and/or making the marketing information more prominent in the environment. Influencing felt involvement requires attention to intrinsic and situational self-relevance.

Intrinsic Self-Relevance

In the short run, marketers have little ability to control consumers' intrinsic self-relevance for a product. Therefore, the usual strategy is to deal with consumers' existing intrinsic self-relevance (the relationship between a product and the consumer's self-concept). First, marketers must identify through research (or guess) the product consequences and values that consumers consider most self-relevant. Then, marketers design strategies that will activate those meanings and link them to the product. The felt involvement thus produced should motivate consumers to attend to this information and interpret it further.

For instance, many marketers of antiperspirants have emphasized qualities such as "stops odor" and "stops wetness" — rational and fairly tangible functional consequences of using the product. The marketers of Sure deodorant, however, identified two more self-relevant and emotionally motivating consequences of using their product — social confidence and avoiding embarrassment. They communicated these psychosocial consequences in an ad campaign, "Raise your hand if you're Sure," that showed coatless consumers in social situations raising their arms and not being embarrassed by damp spots on their

HIGHLIGHT 5.2

Attention and Brand Awareness

What is Avia International, Ltd?

a. A small Italian commuter airline

b. An up-and-coming courier service

c. A map exporter specializing in exotic spots

d. None of the above

If you answered "none of the above," you might be among the 4 percent of Americans who know that Avia (ah-VEE-ah) makes sneakers and sports apparel. According to a company vice president, Avia has a big problem: "There's a whole segment of people who are not buying our shoes because they don't know who we are." In contrast, Nike and Reebok are known by more than 70 percent of U.S consumers.

The power of a well-known brand name, supported by strong advertising, is so great (and long-lasting) that 20 of the top 25 leading brands in 1990 were also among the top 25 in 1923. But companies are finding it increasingly difficult to attract the customer's attention and create brand awareness, given the clutter of new products, brands, and advertising in the environment. Thus, approximately 90 percent of new products are pulled from the market within two or three years of their introduction. Most of them failed for lack of name recognition—consumers were just not aware of them.

The risks of creating a new brand are so great that many companies are developing so-called line extensions. Rather than developing a new brand name, marketers are applying their existing, well-known brand name to new products. Bud Light, Diet Coke, and Liquid Tide are but a few well-known examples.

Building name recognition can be very difficult and very expensive, especially for small companies. Market leaders often command budgets up to 10 times greater than smaller companies. For instance, Nike and Reebok spend about $100 million and $70 million, respectively, on annual advertising, compared to Avia's $10 million. Coca-Cola and Pepsi-Cola can afford to spend hundreds of millions of dollars on extensive advertising campaigns. For instance, Coca-Cola spent about $385 million in 1989. However, this was only 4 percent of its total sales of $9 billion, while Royal Crown Cola, a smaller competitor, spent upwards of 40 percent of its total revenues on advertising and promotions.

Other small companies that cannot afford large advertising budgets have used creative marketing strategies to gain exposure for their brands and attract consumers' attention. For example, Nevica, a British manufacturer of high quality ski clothing, lacked the funds to saturate the ad pages of skiing magazines. So it offered freelance photographers free ski gear and a fee for every picture of a Nevica-clad skier that got published in a magazine. Nevica clothes were frequently pictured in the magazines, which increased brand awareness.

Sources: William M. Bulkeley, "It Needn't Always Cost a Bundle to Get Consumers to Notice Unknown Brands," *The Wall Street Journal*, February 14, 1991, pp. B1, B4; Joseph Pereira, "Name of the Game: Brand Awareness," *The Wall Street Journal*, February 14, 1991, pp. B1, B4.

This ad recognizes that Avia aerobic shoes are not widely known to the general public.

By showing that "experts" use Avia shoes, the ad attempts to stimulate inferences that the product is high quality and provides important benefits.

clothing. In a similar example, the marketers of Vaseline Intensive Care lotion identified a consequence that represented the key meaning of many consumers' intrinsic self-relevance with the hand-lotion product category: while brands such as Touch of Sweden discussed their greaseless formula, Vaseline marketers promoted skin restoration. They communicated the implied psychosocial consequence of "looking younger" in ads showing dried-up leaves before and after being rejuvenated with Intensive Care Lotion.[25]

Situational Self-Relevance

All marketing strategies involve creating or modifying aspects of consumers' environments. Some of these environmental stimuli may act as situational sources of self-relevance (a temporary association between a product and important self-relevant consequences). Situational self-relevance generates higher levels of felt involvement and motivation to attend to marketing information.[26] Consider consumers who receive a brochure in the mail describing a $1 million sweepstakes contest sponsored by a magazine publisher. This marketing information might generate affective feelings of excitement and perceptions of interest and personal relevance with the details of the contest. The resulting felt involvement could motivate consumers to maintain exposure and focus their attention on the marketing offer for magazine subscriptions that accompanies the sweepstakes announcement.

Factors Affecting Environmental Prominence

Marketers attempt to influence the prominence of their marketing information by designing bright, colorful, or unusual packages; by developing novel advertising executions; or by setting unique prices (having a sale on small items, all priced at 88 cents). Because they must attract the attention of consumers hurrying by the newsstand, magazine covers often feature photos known to have high attention value – pictures of celebrities, babies, or dogs, or pictures using that old standby, sex (attractive, seductively clothed models).

Vivid pictoral images can attract consumers' attention and help focus it on the product.[27] Nike, for instance, places powerful graphic portrayals of athletes (wearing Nike shoes, of course) on large billboards. Window displays in retail stores attract the attention (and subsequent interest) of consumers who happen to pass by. Tiffany's, the famous New York jeweler, once used a window display showing construction of a giant doll, four times larger than the figures who were working on it. The doll had nothing to do with jewelry: it was intended to attract the attention of shoppers during the Christmas season.[28] Many stores use creative lighting to emphasize selected merchandise and thus attract and focus consumers' attention on their products. Mirrors are used in clothing shops and hair salons to focus consumers' attention on their appearance.

Novel or *unusual* stimuli that don't fit with the consumers' expectations may be "selected" for additional attention (and comprehension processing to figure out what it is). For instance, a British ad agency created a dramatic stimulus to attract attention to the staying qualities of an adhesive called Araldite. The

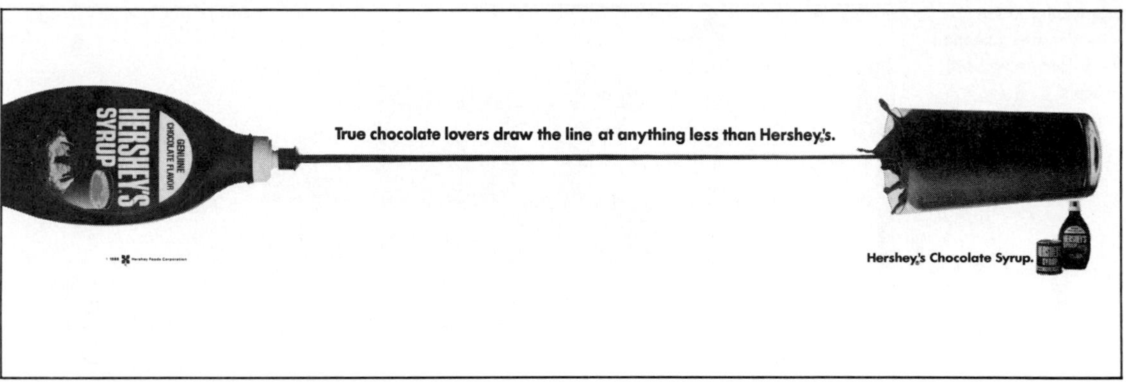

An ad designed with unusual size and shape can attract consumers' attention.

product was used to attach a car to a billboard along a major road into London. The caption read, "It also sticks handles to teapots."[29]

Even a novel placement of a print ad on a page can influence consumers' attention.[30] For instance, Sisley, a manufacturer and retailer of trendy clothing owned by Benetton, has run its print ads in an upside-down position on the back pages of magazines like *Elle* and *Outdoors.* Other marketers have experimented with ads placed sideways, in the center of a page surrounded by editorial content, or spanning the top half of two adjacent pages.

Marketers must be careful in using novel and unusual stimuli over long periods, though, because over time the prominence due to novelty wears off and fails to attract extra attention. For instance, placing a black-and-white ad in a magazine where all the other ads are in color will capture consumers' attention only as long as few other black-and-white ads are present.

The strategy of trying to capture consumers' attention by making stimuli more prominent sometimes backfires. When many marketers are trying very hard to gain attention, consumers may tune most of the stimuli out, giving little thought to any of them. Consider the "miracle-mile strips" of fast-food restaurants, gas stations, and discount stores—each with a large sign—that line highways in many American cities. Individually, each sign is large, bright, colorful, and vivid. Together, the signs are cluttered, and none is particularly prominent in the environment. Consumers find it easy to ignore individual signs, and their attention (and comprehension) levels are likely to be low. Unfortunately, the typical marketing strategy is to make even larger and more garish signs in hope of becoming a slightly more prominent stimulus in the environment. The clutter gets worse, consumers' attention decreases further, and communities become outraged and pass ordinances limiting signs.

Clutter is also relevant for print and television advertising (too many commercials during program breaks). To cut the ad clutter found in most magazines, Whittle Communications limits the number of ads that can be put into its magazines.[31] Whittle has developed more than 40 magazines targeted at

Sign clutter in Las Vegas makes attention (and comprehension) difficult.

rather narrow audiences, including *GO* (Girl's Only) for girls age 11 to 14 and *in View* for college-age women. In fact, some of the magazines have only one advertiser, thus maximizing possibilities of exposure and attention to that company's marketing messages.

Comprehension

Comprehension refers to the interpretation processes by which consumers understand or make sense of their own behaviors and relevant aspects of their environment. In this section, we discuss the comprehension process, variations in comprehension, and the factors that influence comprehension. We conclude by discussing implications for developing marketing strategy.

During comprehension, consumers construct meanings and form knowledge structures that represent salient concepts, objects, behaviors, and events. When consumers' attention is focused on specific environmental stimuli, relevant knowledge structures (schemas and scripts) may be activated from long-term memory. This knowledge provides a framework that guides and directs comprehension processing. Thus, the environmental stimuli are interpreted in terms of one's "old" knowledge that is activated from memory. Through cognitive learning processes (accretion or tuning, sometimes restructuring), these newly constructed meanings are incorporated into existing knowledge structures in memory. Then, in future comprehension episodes, these modified

To comprehend this ad, most consumers will fill in the missing information.

knowledge structures might be activated to influence the interpretation of new information, the reciprocal process continues.

Variations in Comprehension

As shown in Figure 5.4, consumers' comprehension processes can vary in four important ways: (1) comprehension may be automatic or controlled, (2) it may produce more concrete or abstract meanings, (3) it may produce few or many meanings, and (4) it may create weaker or stronger memories.

Automatic Processing

Like attention, simple comprehension processes tend to be *automatic*. For instance, most consumers around the world who see a can of Coca-Cola or a McDonald's restaurant immediately comprehend "Coke" or "McDonald's." We can think of the direct recognition of familiar products as a simple comprehension process in that exposure to a familiar stimulus automatically activates its relevant meanings from memory—perhaps its name and other associated knowledge. Thus, the person "recognizes" the stimulus.

In contrast, comprehending less familiar stimuli usually requires more conscious thought and control. Because consumers do not have well developed knowledge structures for unfamiliar objects and events, they may have to consciously construct the meanings of such information (or else intentionally ignore it). Exposure to completely unfamiliar stimuli is likely to activate knowl-

FIGURE 5.4
Variations in Comprehension

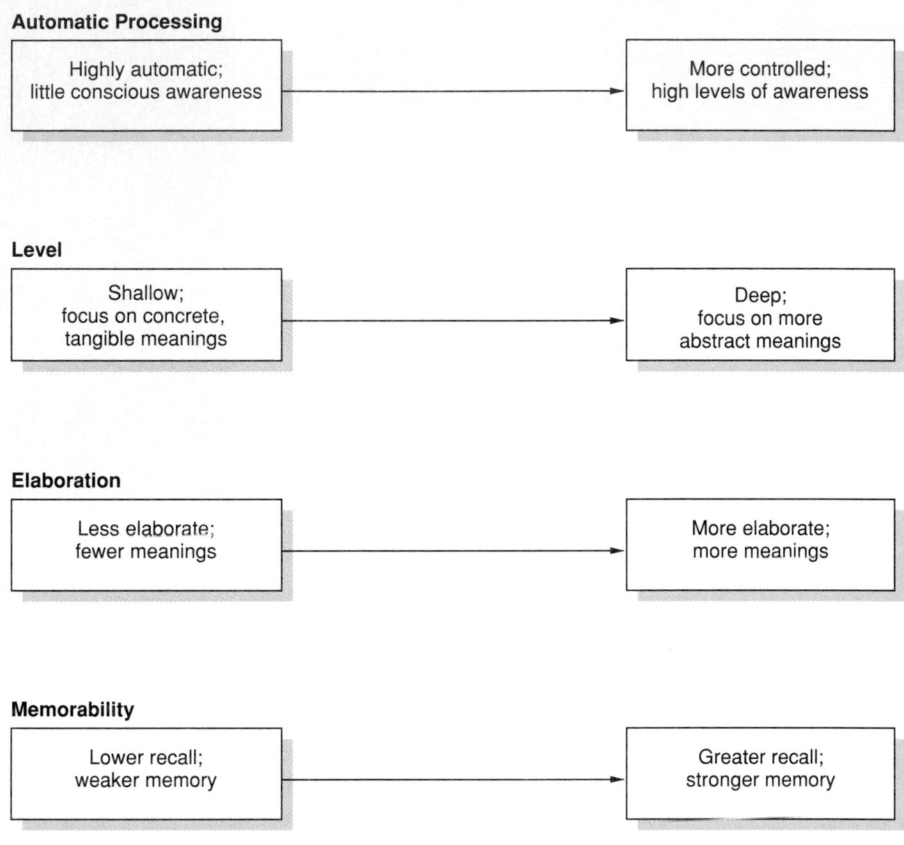

edge structures that are only partially relevant at best. In such cases, comprehension is likely to be highly conscious and controlled and require substantial cognitive capacity. Interpretations may be difficult and uncertain.

Level

The specific meanings that consumers construct to represent products and other marketing information in their environment depend on the **level of comprehension** that occurs during interpretation.[32] Comprehension can vary along a continuum from "shallow" to "deep."[33] *Shallow comprehension* produces meanings at a concrete, tangible level. For example, a consumer could interpret a product in terms of its concrete product attributes (these running shoes are black, size 10, and made of leather and nylon).

Ads that encourage deeper and more elaborate comprehension are likely to be more memorable.

In contrast, *deep comprehension* produces more abstract meanings that represent less tangible, more subjective, and more symbolic concepts. For instance, deep comprehension of product information might create meanings about the functional consequences of product use ("I can run faster in these shoes") or the psychosocial and value consequences ("I feel confident when I wear these shoes"). From a means-end perspective, deeper comprehension processes generate product-related meanings that are more self-relevant, whereas shallow comprehension processes tend to produce meanings about concrete product attributes.

Elaboration

Comprehension processes also vary in their extensiveness or **elaboration.**[34] The degree of elaboration during comprehension determines the amount of knowledge or the number of meanings produced as well as the complexity of the interconnections between those meanings.[35] *Less elaborate* (simpler) *comprehension* produces relatively few meanings and requires little cognitive effort, conscious control, and cognitive capacity. *More elaborate comprehension* requires greater cognitive capacity, effort, and control of the thought processes. More elaborate comprehension produces a greater number of meanings that tend to be organized as more complex knowledge structures (schemas or scripts).

Memorability

Both the level and elaboration of comprehension processes influence consumers' ability to remember the meanings created during comprehension.[36] Deeper comprehension processes create more abstract, more self-relevant meanings that tend to be remembered better (higher levels of recall and recognition) than the more concrete meanings created by shallow comprehension processes. More elaborate comprehension processes create greater numbers of meanings that tend to be interconnected in knowledge structures. Memory is enhanced because the activation of one meaning can spread to other connected meanings and bring them to conscious awareness.[37] In sum, marketing strategies that stimulate consumers to engage in deeper, more elaborate comprehension processes tend to produce meanings and knowledge that consumers remember better.

Inferences During Comprehension

When consumers engage in deep, elaborate comprehension processes they create inferences. **Inferences** are knowledge or beliefs that are not based on explicit information in the environment.[38] That is, inferences are interpretations that always go beyond the information given. For instance, some consumers might infer that a product is of good quality because it is advertised heavily on TV.[39]

Inferences play a large role in the construction of means-end changes.[40] By making inferences during comprehension, consumers can link meanings about the physical attributes of a product with more abstract meanings about its functional consequences and perhaps the psychosocial and value consequences of product use.

Inferences are heavily influenced by consumers' existing knowledge in memory.[41] If activated during comprehension, relevant knowledge provides a basis for forming inferences. For instance, consumers who believe that more expensive brands of chocolates are higher in quality than cheaper brands are likely to infer that Godiva chocolates are high quality when they learn that the chocolates cost up to $20 per pound.[42] As another example, incomplete or missing product information sometimes prompts consumers to form inferences to "fill in the blanks," based on their schemas of knowledge acquired from past experience.[43] For instance, consumers who are highly knowledgeable about clothing styles may be able to infer the country of origin and even the designer of a coat or dress merely by noticing a few details.

Consumers often use tangible, concrete product attributes as *cues* in making inferences about more abstract attributes, consequences, and values. In highly familiar situations, these inferences may be made automatically without much conscious awareness. For instance, some consumers draw inferences about the cleaning power of a powdered laundry detergent from the color of the granules: blue and white seem to connote cleanliness. Or consumers could base inferences about product quality from physical characteristics of the package: the color, shape, and material of cologne bottles are important cues to quality inferences. As another example, Hershey sells a premium-priced candy bar, Golden Almond, wrapped in gold foil, a packaging cue that implies quality to many

HIGHLIGHT 5.3

What's In a Name?

Marketers try to create marketing strategies that enable consumers to comprehend the appropriate meanings for their products. A key aspect of the marketing strategy for a new product is the brand name. Consumers can form inferences about important meanings just from the brand name—and those meanings, of course, should be consistent with the intended brand image. For instance, Ford selected a nonword, *Merkur*, for its imported car. Although the word really doesn't mean anything, it is German-sounding and connotes a high-tech image, just the meanings Ford wanted consumers to infer.

A primary function of a brand name is to differentiate the item from the competition. That is, the name should be different from other names and should help create a distinctive image (a unique network of meanings). The dominant image for most fragrances has been romance, so many of the brand names are quite similar—Cie, Ciara, Cerissa, Chimere, Cachet, and Chanel. Marketers of some fragrances have tried to create more distinctive images by using different types of names like Votre, Charlie, Scoundrel, and Babe.

The brand name should describe or connote the key meaning of the product, if possible. Consider how clearly names such as Pudding Pops frozen snacks, Liquid-Plummer drain cleaner, Head and Shoulders shampoo, Easy-Off oven cleaner, and Seduction cologne convey the product's basic function or key benefit.

Finally, a brand name should be memorable and easy to pronounce. Many believe short names have an advantage here. For instance, the name *Acura* was selected for Honda's luxury car because it was thought to connote precision (as in accuracy), which was Honda's intended meaning. *Acura* also meets other important criteria for a coined word. Because it ends with an "a," it is read as a noun and is obviously the name of something. Also, the word begins and ends with the same letter, making it more memorable. Finally, *Acura* contains three clearly voiced syllables in only five letters, making it easy to pronounce.

In sum, the key consideration in selecting a brand name, whether short or long, is that it conveys a set of distinctive meanings that are consistent with the image intended by the marketing strategy.

Source: Daniel Doeden, "How to Select a Brand Name," *Marketing Communications,* November 1981, pp. 56–61; and Jeffrey A. Trachtenberg, "Name That Brand," *Forbes,* April 8, 1985, pp. 128, 130.

consumers. Finally, as Highlight 5.3 illustrates, even the brand name of a product can serve as a cue for making inferences during comprehension.

Marketers sometimes try to stimulate consumers to form inferences during comprehension. For example, Kellogg's once used an advertising strategy for All-Bran with the headline, "At last, some news about cancer you can live with."

The ads repeated the National Cancer Institute's recommendation for increasing levels of fiber in the diet and then stated "no cereal has more fiber" than All-Bran. Apparently, Kellogg's hoped consumers would make the inference that the product attribute of high fiber leads to the desirable consequence of reduced risk of cancer. Most consumers probably then formed additional inferences that reduced risk of cancer helps to achieve the universal values of long life, health, and happiness. For most consumers, such self-relevant consequences probably elicited favorable affective responses. Highlight 5.4 describes other health-related inferences that have come under government scrutiny.

Factors Influencing Comprehension

Many factors affect the depth and elaboration of comprehension that occurs when consumers interpret marketing information.[44] In this section, we examine three important influences—consumers' existing knowledge in memory, their felt involvement at the time of exposure, and various aspects of the environment during exposure.

Knowledge in Memory

Consumers' *ability to comprehend* marketing information is largely determined by their existing knowledge in memory. The particular knowledge, meanings, and beliefs that are activated in a given comprehension situation determine the level of comprehension that will occur and the comprehended meanings that are produced.

Marketing researchers often discuss consumers' knowledge in terms of **expertise** or familiarity.[45] *Expert consumers* are quite familiar with a product category, product forms, and specific brands. They tend to possess substantial amounts of declarative and procedural knowledge organized in schemas and scripts. When parts of this knowledge are activated, these expert consumers are able to comprehend marketing information at relativley deep, elaborate levels.[46]

In contrast, *novice consumers* have little prior experience or familiarity with the product or brand. They tend to have poorly organized knowledge structures containing relatively few, typically shallow meanings and beliefs. When parts of these knowledge structures are activated during exposure to marketing information, novices are able to comprehend the information only at shallow and nonelaborate levels that produce relatively few concrete meanings. Novices find it difficult, if not impossible, to comprehend at a deep, elaborate level. To do so, they would have to increase their knowledge to the level of an expert.

Marketers need to understand the existing knowledge structures of their target audience in order to develop effective marketing strategies that consumers can comprehend. For instance, the S. C. Johnson Company, manufacturer of Raid and other bug killers, knows that most consumers have limited technical

HIGHLIGHT 5.4

Cholesterol Inferences

In the 1980s, many American consumers became very interested (involved) in the topic of cholesterol. Due to high levels of publicity about research studies, a means-end chain developed that linked the cholesterol attribute to growing values of healthy living styles and good health. Many companies made claims in their advertising and on labels about the low levels of cholesterol in their products. Such claims proliferated on such products as oils, margarines, and many other processed foods. Finally, in 1991, the Food and Drug Administration got tough with many food companies about their cholesterol claims.

Bob Harris, president of a small food-processing company in New Jersey, found himself in trouble with the government. In 1991, he was ordered by the FDA to stop using the labels "no cholesterol" and "lowest in saturated fats" for his oils, cheese substitutes, and corn oil spread. Even worse, he was ordered to stop using the "Heart Beat" trademark for his products, a brand name he had invested over $10 million in developing.

Harris was not alone; many other companies were likely to come under FDA scrutiny, including:

Keebler cookies	Package claimed "no cholesterol" but what about saturated fat?
Procter & Gamble's Duncan Hines cake mixes	Contain no cholesterol, but what about the added ingredients (eggs)?
Kraft Parkay margarine	If claims of "no cholesterol" are made, company must also disclose fat content
Anheuser-Busch Eagle potato chips	Although chips have no cholesterol, they do contain other forms of fat

What was the problem? The FDA thought consumers would make inappropriate and/or incorrect *inferences* about the health qualities of these products, based on the no-cholesterol claim. These products did not contain cholesterol, making the claims technically correct, but many contained high levels of fat, which is not healthy. David Kessler, an FDA commissioner, said the agency would not tolerate "deceptive claims regarding cholesterol on any products that were high in fat." He further accused American companies of "passing off half-truths to health-minded consumers."

Sources: Adapted from Bruce Ingersoll, "FDA Takes on 'No Cholesterol' Claims," *The Wall Street Journal,* May 15, 1991, pp. B1, B10; and Lois Therrien, John Carey, and Joseph Weber, "The Cholesterol Is in the Fire Now," *Business Week,* June 10, 1991, pp. 34–35.

knowledge about how insecticides work. Instead of technical information, "the customer wants to see action."[47] The company's formulation for Raid bug spray allows consumers to immediately comprehend that the product works effectively. It attacks cockroaches' central nervous systems and drives them into a frenzy out onto the kitchen floor, where they race around in circles before they die.

Felt Involvement

Consumers' felt involvement at the time of exposure has a major influence on their *motivation to comprehend* marketing information.[48] Consumers with high intrinsic self-relevance for certain products associate those products with personally relevant consequences and values that are central to their self-concept. The felt involvement experienced when such self-relevant knowledge structures are activated motivates these consumers to process the information in a more conscious, intensive, and controlled manner. For instance, consumers who feel highly involved tend to form deeper, more abstract meanings for the marketing information, creating more elaborate knowledge structures. In contrast, consumers who experience low levels of felt involvement when exposed to marketing information tend to find the information uninteresting and irrelevant. Because of their low motivation to interpret the information, their attention probably will be low and they are likely to produce few meanings (low elaboration) at a relatively shallow, concrete level. Their comprehension processes might produce only a simple, identification response (this is a pair of socks).

Exposure Environment

Various aspects of the exposure situation or environment can affect consumers' *opportunity to comprehend* marketing information. These include factors such as time pressure, consumers' affective states (a good or bad mood), and distractions (noisy, pushing crowds). For instance, consumers who are in a hurry and under a lot of time pressure don't have much opportunity to process marketing information even though they may be motivated to do so (high felt involvement).[49] In this situational environment, they are likely to engage in relatively shallow and nonelaborate comprehension processes. Highlight 5.5 describes attention and comprehension processes in the exposure environments for radio advertising.

Marketers can consider these environmental factors when designing their marketing strategies. Some retailers, for instance, have created a relaxed, slow-paced environment that encourages people to slow down and thoroughly comprehend the information marketers make available. For instance, Ralph Lauren's Polo store in New York City is a special environment of glowing wood, antique furniture, oriental carpets, and warm lighting fixtures that seems to simulate an elegant English manor house. In addition, this environment helps create the desired images for the casually elegant clothing Lauren designs and sells.

Marketing Implications

To develop effective marketing strategies, marketers need to understand consumers' comprehension processes in order to design marketing information that

HIGHLIGHT 5.5

DRIVE TIME

Radio is often treated like the shabby relation to rich television. But radio delivers high exposure rates to targeted audiences, attracts attention by using offbeat ads at appropriate times of the day, and stimulates comprehension and brand awareness. Best of all, radio is cheap compared to alternative media. For example, an ad on network radio costs only about $2.50 per thousand exposures, while the average costs per thousand for magazine ads are about $8, $14 for prime-time TV, and about $23 for newspapers.

Advertisers are beginning to appreciate that radio can reach narrowly targeted audiences better than TV. The most attractive (and most expensive) period for radio advertising is so-called drive time, generally from 6 to 10 A.M. and from 3 to 7 P.M. Ads aired during drive time can achieve high exposure rates because captive commuters have little else to do but listen to the radio, and almost 90 percent of them tune in at least once a week. Moreover, targeting is relatively easy with various stations drawing fairly distinct audiences.

Radio is good for attracting attention because listeners are often in a receptive mood. Burger King, for instance, directs radio spots at drivers who may be only minutes from a Burger King location. Heinz advertises its Ore-Ida french-fried potatoes during evening drive time to target women while they are making dinner plans on their way home from work.

What about comprehension of radio spots? Although people weaned on TV criticize the visual blankness of radio, this might actually be its chief advantage. Listeners have to use their own imaginations to visualize the action, and these self-generated interpretations may be more powerful than the "direct comprehension" of TV ads.

For instance, Motel 6 ran its first radio ads in 1987. With only $1 million to spend, radio was the only choice to reach a national audience. Tom Bodett, the spokesperson for the chain, presented a number of folksy messages that positioned Motel 6 as the low-frills alternative to the swankier competition. "You won't find a treadmill or a weight machine like you might at those big fancy motels," he drawled in one spot aimed at business travelers, "but just take a few laps around the parking lot or down the frontage. . . . Now, you're a lean, mean working machine with a few extra bucks in your pocket."

One reason these radio spots worked so well was that listeners couldn't see Tom Bodett, so they formed their own images of him. In fact, customers of widely differing ages and occupations said Tom was like themselves. This comprehension process created a customer/product relationship based on trust and credibility. Since beginning the radio spots, occupancy levels at Motel 6 were a healthy 76 percent.

Source: Joshua Levine, "Drive Time," *Forbes,* March 19, 1990, pp. 144, 146.

will be interpreted appropriately. This requires a consideration of the characteristics of the target consumers and the environment in which consumers are exposed to the information.[50]

Knowledge and Involvement

To encourage appropriate comprehension processing, marketers should design their messages to fit consumers' ability and motivation to comprehend (their knowledge structures and felt involvement). For instance, marketers of high involvement products such as luxury cars usually want consumers to form self-relevant meanings about their products. Many of the U.S. print ads for Saab, BMW, or Mercedes-Benz contain a great deal of information describing technical attributes and functional aspects of the cars. To comprehend this information at a deep, elaborate level, consumers must have fairly sophisticated knowledge about automobiles and sufficient felt involvement to motivate extensive comprehension processes.

For other types of products, however, marketers may not want consumers to engage in extensive comprehension processes. Sometimes marketers are interested in creating only simple, nonelaborate meanings about their product. For example, simple products (cologne or beer) are promoted largely through *image advertising*, which is not meant to be comprehended deeply or elaborately.[51] Consider the typical advertising for cigarettes or soft drinks. Often these ads contain virtually no written information beyond a brief slogan such as "Come to Marlboro Country" or "Coke Is It." Most consumers probably comprehend such information in a nonelaborate way that produces an overall image and perhaps a general affective reaction, but not detailed means-end chains.[52] Other ads, such as billboards, are reminders mainly intended to activate the brand name and keep it at a high level of "top-of-mind" awareness. In such cases, comprehension might be limited to simple brand recognition.

Remembering

Memory and consumers' ability to recall meanings is important to marketers because consumers often do not make purchase decisions at the time of exposure, attention, and comprehension. Marketers usually want consumers to remember certain key meanings associated with their marketing strategy. Marketers hope consumers will remember the brand name and main attributes and benefits (main copy points) conveyed in their ads. Retailers want consumers to remember their name and location, the types of merchandise they carry, and the dates of the big sale. Despite the millions spent each year on advertising and other marketing strategies, much marketing information is not remembered well. For instance, few advertising slogans are accurately recalled from memory. And, even though some people can remember a slogan, many of them can not associate it with the right brand name.[53] For instance, 60 percent of consumers recognized the slogan, "Never Let Them See You Sweat," but only 4 percent correctly associated it with Dry Idea deodorant. Although 32 percent recognized "Cars that Make Sense," only 4 percent associated it with Hyundai. "America's Business Address" was recognized by 17 percent, but only 3 percent knew it was the slogan for Hilton hotels. Slogans have to be very heavily advertised to be remembered – a high scorer was General Electric's, "We Bring Good Things to Life."

Miscomprehension of Marketing Information

Research shows that a substantial amount of marketing (and other) information is miscomprehended, in that consumers form inaccurate, confused, or inappropriate interpretations. In fact, most (perhaps all) marketing information is probably miscomprehended by at least some consumers.[54] The type of miscomprehension can vary from confusion over similar brand names (see Highlight 5.6) to misinterpreting a product claim by forming an inaccurate means-end chain. It has been estimated that people may miscomprehend an average of 20 to 25 percent of the many different types of information they encounter, including ads, news reports, etc.[55]

Although unethical marketers may intentionally create deceptive or misleading information that will be miscomprehended by consumers, most professional marketers work hard to create marketing information that is understood correctly. For those who don't, the Federal Trade Commission has a program to identify and remove deceptive marketing information and force a company to correct the false beliefs it creates.[56] For instance, in 1991, the Food and Drug Administration demanded that P&G stop using "fresh" on the labels of Citrus Hill orange juice, a processed food.[57]

Exposure Environment

Many aspects of the environment in which exposure to marketing information occurs can influence consumers' comprehension processes. For instance, the type of store can affect how consumers comprehend the product and brands sold there. Thus, for some customers, a brand of jeans purchased in a "high-image store" like Sak's or Bloomingdale's may have a more positive set of meanings than the same brand bought at Sears or K mart. Store characteristics such as size, exterior design, or interior decorations can activate networks of meanings that influence consumers' comprehension of the meanings of products and brands displayed there.

Another aspect of the exposure environment concerns the actual content and format of the marketing information.[58] Some information may be confusing, unclear, and hard to comprehend. For instance, the huge amounts of nutritional information on food product labels and in advertising claims can be difficult for many consumers to comprehend in a meaningful way.[59]

HIGHLIGHT 5.6

CONFUSING BRAND NAMES

Marketers guard their brand names jealously. Establishing a brand name in consumers' minds (making it familiar and meaningful) usually requires a large financial investment. When another manufacturer uses the same brand name or a similar one, companies believe their hard work and creative marketing strategy is being stolen. Lawsuits often result.

For example, Adolph Coors Co., a beer manufacturer in Golden, Colorado, filed a trademark infringement suit against Robert Corr, owner of a small Chicago company, Corr's Natural Beverages, that manufactures an eight-flavor line of "natural sodas."

The two companies reached an out-of-court settlement in which Corr's Natural Beverages agreed to change the name of its product from Corr's to Robert Corr. Corr, who claimed to be happy with the agreement, said, "It is probably better for us not to be associated in consumers' minds with a beer company."

(Photo courtesy R. J. Corr Naturals, Inc.)

Source: Scott Hume, "Of Corr's There's a Happy Ending," *Advertising Age,* June 11, 1984, p. 12.

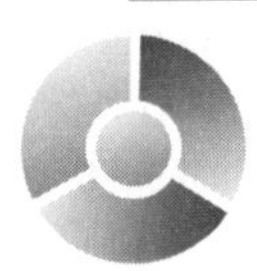

BACK TO....
IS ANYBODY WATCHING?

The opening vignette described some of the difficulties in measuring the audience for television advertising. The sophisticated people meter technology described in the case attempts to measure

exposure to television programs and commercials. However, the people meter does not provide good measures of consumers' *attention* to the ads. Taking pictures every two seconds of people in their living rooms does indicate attention, but obviously isn't practical on a large scale. Finally, the task of measuring consumers' *comprehension* of advertising in a natural viewing environment is even more difficult.

Because of the difficulties in studying consumers' interpretation processes in the real world, most measures of attention and comprehension are produced in small-scale research studies, often using only a few consumers (50 to 150). Many of these are conducted in highly artificial viewing contexts such as a theater setting, where several ads are shown to a group of consumers. Although exposure does not occur in a natural way, marketers can measure the *amount of attention* consumers give to a marketing stimulus and/or the *level and elaboration of comprehension.* Such research can provide useful information to marketers about the relative likelihood of success of alternative marketing strategies. In these artificial settings, marketers can learn which package design or billboard layout attracts the most attention, what inferences consumers make about different price increases, what types of meanings are elicited by different brand names, or how deeply and elaborately consumers comprehend alternative television commercials. By understanding consumers' interpretation processes, marketers are better able to design effective new marketing strategies and modify existing ones.

Summary

In this chapter, we discussed the behavioral process of *exposure,* by which consumers come into contact with marketing information. We also discussed the interrelated cognitive processes of *attention,* by which consumers select some of this marketing information for further processing, and *comprehension*, by which consumers interpret the meaning of this information.

Exposure to marketing information can occur by accident or as a result of an intentional search for information. Once exposure has occurred, the interpretation processes of attention and comprehension begin. For unfamiliar marketing information, these processes are likely to require some conscious thought. However, as consumers become more experienced in interpreting marketing stimuli, attention and comprehension processes require less cognitive capacity and conscious control and become more automatic. Attention varies from preconscious, automatic levels to focal levels where the comprehension begins. Comprehension varies in the depth of meanings produced (from concrete product attributes to abstract consequences and values) and in elaboration (few or many interrelated meanings). Both factors influence the memorability of the meanings created.

Attention and comprehension are strongly influenced by two internal factors — the knowledge structures activated in the exposure situation and the level of consumers' felt involvement. These factors respectively influence consumers' ability and motivation to interpret the information.

In sum, designing and implementing successful marketing strategies — whether price, product, promotion, or distribution strategies — require that marketers consider three issues associated with these three processes:

1. How can I *maximize and/or maintain exposure* of the target segment of consumers to my marketing information?
2. How can I *capture and maintain the attention* of the target consumers?
3. How can I influence the target consumers to *comprehend* my marketing information *at the appropriate level of depth and elaboration?*

Key Terms and Concepts

Exposure *136*	Focal Attention *143*
Intentional Exposure *137*	Comprehension *152*
Accidental Exposure *137*	Level of Comprehension *154*
Selective Exposure *139*	Elaboration *155*
Attention *143*	Inferences *156*
Preconscious Attention *143*	Expertise *158*

Review and Discussion Questions

1. Describe the differences between accidental and intentional exposure to marketing information. Identify a product for which each type of exposure

is most common and discuss implications for developing effective marketing strategies.

2. Give an example of automatic attention and contrast it with an example of controlled attention. What implications does this distinction have for marketing strategy?

3. Give an example of automatic comprehension and contrast it with an example of controlled comprehension. What implications does this distinction have for marketing strategy?

4. Discuss the different types of knowledge and meanings that "shallow and deep" comprehension processes create. Can you relate these differences to different segments of consumers for the same product?

5. Review the differences in the knowledge and meanings that are produced by more and less elaborate comprehension processes. Should marketing activities encourage or discourage elaboration of knowledge and meaning?

6. Describe how consumers' existing knowledge structures and their level of felt involvement might affect (*a*) attention to and (*b*) comprehension of marketing communications regarding prices of branded products.

7. List some factors that could affect the inferences formed during comprehension of ads for packaged foods and for medical services. Give examples of marketing strategies you'd recommend to influence the inferences that consumers form.

8. Consider an example of a marketing strategy you think might result in some consumer miscomprehension. Describe why this miscomprehension occurs. What could marketers (or public policymakers) do to reduce the chances of miscomprehension?

9. Discuss how interpretation processes (attention and comprehension) affect consumers' ability to recall marketing information. Illustrate your points with marketing examples.

10. Identify a recent brand extension and discuss how exposure, attention, and comprehension processes can influence the effectiveness of that brand extension.

NOTES

1. See Anthony A. Greenwald and Clark Leavitt, "Audience Involvement in Advertising Four Levels," *Journal of Consumer Research*, June 1984, pp. 581–92.

2. For example, see William Schneider and Richard M. Shiffrin, "Controlled and Automatic Human Information Processing: I. Detection, Search, and Attention," *Psychological Review*, January 1977, pp. 1–66; and Richard M. Shiffrin and William Schneider, "Controlled and Automatic Human Information Processing: II. Perceptual Learning, Automatic Attending, and a

General Theory," *Psychological Review*, March 1977, pp. 127–90.

3. Daniel Kahneman and Anne Treisman, "Changing Views of Attention and Automaticity," in *Varieties of Attention*, ed. R. Parasuraman and D. R. Davies (New York: Academic Press, 1984), pp. 29–61; and John G. Lynch, Jr. and Thomas K. Snull, "Memory and Attention Factors in Consumer Choice: Concepts and Research Methods," *Journal of Consumer Research*, September 1982, pp. 18–37.

4. Sharon E. Beatty and Scott M. Smith, "External Search Effort: An Investigation across Several Product Categories," *Journal of Consumer Research*, June 1987, pp. 83–95; Peter H. Bloch, Daniel Sherrell, and Nancy M. Ridgway, "Consumer Search: An Extended Framework," *Journal of Consumer Research*, June 1986, pp. 119–26; Joseph W. Newman, "Consumer External Search: Amount and Determinants," in *Consumer and Industrial Buying Behavior*, ed. A. G. Woodside, J. N. Sheth, and P. D. Bennett (New York: Elsevier-North Holland, 1977), pp. 79–94; and Richard R. Olshavsky and Donald H. Granbois, "Consumer Decision Making—Fact or Fiction," *Journal of Consumer Research*, June 1979, pp. 63–70.

5. Leo Bogart, "Executives Fear Ad Overload Will Lower Effectiveness," *Marketing News*, May 25, 1984, pp. 4–5.

6. Peter H. Bloch and Marsha L. Ritchins, "Shopping without Purchase: An Investigation of Consumer Browsing Behavior," in *Advances in Consumer Research*, vol. 10. ed. R. P. Baggozi and A. M. Tybout (Ann Arbor, Mich.: Association for Consumer Research, 1983), pp. 389–93.

7. Joanne Lipman, "CNN Ads Get Extra Mileage during the War," *The Wall Street Journal*, February 27, 1991, pp. B1, B4.

8. Avery Abernethy and Herbert Rotfield, "Zipping through TV Ads Is Old Tradition—But Viewers Are Getting Better at It," *Marketing News*, January 7, 1991, pp. 6, 14.

9. Dennis Kneale, "Zapping of TV Ads Appears Pervasive," *The Wall Street Journal*, April 25, 1988, p. 21.

10. Christine Dugas, "Ad Space Now Has a Whole New Meaning," *Business Week*, July 29, 1985, p. 52.

11. Suzanne Alexander, "Saturating Cities with Stores Can Pay," September 11, 1990, p. B1.

12. This section is adapted from David W. Schumann, Jennifer Gayson, Johanna Ault, Kerri Hargrove, Lois Hollingsworth, Russell Ruelle, and Sharon Seguin, "The Effectiveness of Shopping Cart Signage: Perceptual Measures Tell a Different Story," *Journal of Advertising Research*, February–March 1991, pp. 17–22.

13. Joanne Lipman, "Brand-Name Products Are Popping up in TV Shows," *The Wall Street Journal*, February 19, 1991, pp. B1, B3.

14. Sana Siwolop, "You Can't (Hum) Ignore (Hum) That Ad," *Business Week*, September 21, 1987, p. 56.

15. Bill Saporito, "Ikea's Got 'Em Lining Up," *Fortune*, March 11, 1991, p. 72.

16. Roy Lachman, Janet L. Lachman, and Earl C. Butterfield, *Cognitive Psychology and Information Processing: An Introduction* (Hillsdale, N.J.: Lawrence Erlbaum, 1979).

17. Daniel Kahneman, *Attention and Effort* (Englewood Cliffs, N.J.: Prentice Hall, 1973).

18. Anthony A. Greenwald and Clark Leavitt, "Audience Involvement in Advertising Four Levels," *Journal of Consumer Research*, June 1984, pp. 58–92; and Chris Janiszewski, "The Influence of Nonattended Material on the Processing of Advertising Claims," *Journal of Marketing Research*, August 1990, pp. 263–78.

19. Schumann et al., "The Effectiveness of Shopping Cart Signage."

20. David M. Sanbonmatsu and Frank R. Kardes, "The Effects of Physiological Arousal on Information Processing and Persuasion," *Journal of Consumer Research*, December 1988, pp. 379–85.

21. Meryl Paula Gardner, "Mood States and Consumer Behavior," *Journal of Consumer Research*, December 1985, pp. 281–300; and Noel Murray, Harish Sujan, Edward R. Hirt, and Mita Sujan, "The Effects of Mood on Categorization:

A Cognitive Flexibility Hypothesis," *Journal of Personality and Social Psychology*, September 1990, pp. 411–25.

22. Marvin E. Goldberg and Gerald J. Gorn, "Happy and Sad TV Programs: How They Affect Reactions to Commercials," *Journal of Consumer Research*, December 1987, pp. 387–403.
23. See Richard L. Celsi and Jerry C. Olson, "The Role of Involvement in Attention and Comprehension Processes," *Journal of Consumer Research*, September 1988, pp. 210–24.
24. Adapted from an advertisement in *Advertising Age*, November 4, 1985, p. 69.
25. Both examples were taken from "Intuition, Microstudies, Humanized Research Can Identify Emotions that Motivate Consumers," *Marketing News*, March 19, 1982, p. 11.
26. Celsi and Olson, "The Role of Involvement in Attention and Comprehension Processes."
27. Ann L. McGill and Punam Anand, "The Effect of Vivid Attributes on the Evaluation of Alternatives: The Role of Differential Attention and Cognitive Elaboration," *Journal of Consumer Research*, September 1989, pp. 188–96.
28. "Four More Years: The Marketing Implications," *Marketing News*, January 4, 1985, pp. 1, 50, 52.
29. Brian Davis, "FCO's Run of Bad Luck," *Advertising Age*, June 10, 1985, p. 58.
30. Patricia Winters, "Topsy-Turvy Look Puts a New Spin on Ad Placements," *Advertising Age*, September 12, 1988, p. 4.
31. Cathryn Donohoe, "Whittle Zeroses in on His Target," *Insight*, August 14, 1989, pp. 50–52.
32. Fergus I. M. Craik and Robert S. Lockhart, "Levels of Processing: A Framework for Memory Research," *Journal of Verbal Learning and Verbal Behavior*, 1972, pp. 671–89; and Jerry C. Olson, "Encoding Processes: Levels of Processing and Existing Knowledge Structures," in *Advances in Consumer Research*, vol. 7. ed. J. C. Olson (Ann Arbor, Mich.: Association for Consumer Research, 1980), pp. 154–59.
33. The term *depth* is being used as a metaphor, of course. Depth does not connote any physical dimension of brain storage.
34. John R. Anderson and Lynne M. Reder, "An Elaboration Processing Explanation of Depth of Processing," in *Levels of Processing in Human Memory*, ed. Larry S. Cermak and Fergus I. M. Craik (Hillsdale, N.J.: Lawrence Erlbaum, 1979), pp. 385–404; and Richard E. Petty and John T. Cacioppo, "The Elaboration Likelihood Model of Persuasion," in *Advances in Experimental Social Psychology*, vol. 19. ed. Leonard Berkowitz (New York: Academic Press, 1986), pp. 123–205.
35. Anderson and Reder, "An Elaboration Processing Explanation of Depth of Processing," pp. 385–404.
36. Alain d'Astous and Marc Dubuc, "Retrieval Processes in Consumer Evaluative Judgment Making: The Role of Elaborative Processing," in *Advances in Consumer Research*, vol. 13. ed. Richard J. Lutz (Provo, Utah: Association for Consumer Research, 1986), pp. 132–37; Jerry C. Olson, "Encoding Processes: Levels of Processing and Existing Knowledge Structures," in *Advances in Consumer Research*, vol. 7. ed. J. C. Olson (Ann Arbor, Mich.: Association for Consumer Research, 1980), pp. 154–59; and Douglas M. Stayman and Rajeev Batra, "Encoding and Retrieval of Ad Affect in Memory," *Journal of Consumer Research*, May 1991, pp. 232–39.
37. Kevin Lane Keller, "Memory Factors in Advertising: The Effect of Advertising Retrieval Cues on Brand Evaluations," *Journal of Consumer Research*, December 1987, pp. 316–33; Joan Myers-Levy, "Priming Effects on Product Judgments: A Hemispheric Interpretation," *Journal of Consumer Research*, 16 (June), 1989, pp. 76–86.
38. Gary T. Ford and Ruth Ann Smith, "Inferential Beliefs in Consumer Evaluations: An Assessment of Alternative Processing Strategies," *Journal of Consumer Research*, December 1987, pp. 363–71; Richard J. Harris, "Inference in Information Processing," in *The Psychology of Learning and Motivation*, vol. 15. ed. Gordon A. Bower (New York: Academic Press, 1981), pp.

81–128; and Mita Sujan and Christine Dekleva, "Product Categorization and Inference Making: Some Implications for Comparative Advertising," *Journal of Consumer Research*, December 1987, pp. 372–78.

39. Amna Kirmani, "The Effect of Perceived Advertising Costs on Brand Perceptions," *Journal of Consumer Research*, September 1990, pp. 160–71; Amna Kirmani and Peter Wright, "Money Talks: Perceived Advertising Expense and Expected Product Quality," *Journal of Consumer Research*, December 1989, pp. 344–53.

40. For examples of inferring means-end chains, see Valarie A. Zeithaml, "Consumer Perceptions of Price, Quality, and Value," *Journal of Marketing*, July 1988, pp. 2–22; and Sunil Mehrotra and John Palmer, "Relating Product Features to Perceptions of Quality: Appliances," in *Perceived Quality*, ed. Jacob Jacoby and Jerry C. Olson (Lexington, Mass.: Lexington Books, 1985), pp. 81–96.

41. See Joseph W. Alba and J. Wesley Hutchinson, "Dimensions of Consumer Expertise," *Journal of Consumer Research*, March 1987, pp. 411–54; and Jerry C. Olson, "Inferential Belief Formation in the Cue Utilization Process," in *Advances in Consumer Research*, vol. 5. ed. H. Keith Hunt (Ann Arbor, Mich.: Association for Consumer Research, 1978), pp. 706–13.

42. Carl Obermiller, "When Do Consumers Infer Quality from Price?" in *Advances in Consumer Research*, vol. 15, ed. Michael J. Houston (Provo, Utah: Association for Consumer Research, 1988), pp. 304–10; Jerry C. Olson, "Price as an Informational Cue: Effects on Product Evaluations," in *Consumer and Industrial Buying Behavior*, ed. Arch G. Woodside, Jagdish N. Sheth, and Peter D. Bennett (New York: North Holland, 1977), pp. 267–86; and Zeithaml, "Consumer Perceptions of Price, Quality, and Value," pp. 2–22.

43. Frank R. Kardes, "Spontaneous Inference Processes in Advertising: The Effects of Conclusion Omission and Involvement on Persuasion," *Journal of Consumer Research*, September 1988, pp. 225–33; Richard D. Johnson and Irwin P. Levin, "More than Meets the Eye: The Effect of Missing Information on Purchase Evaluations," *Journal of Consumer Research*, June 1985, pp. 169–77; and Carolyn J. Simmons and John G. Lynch, Jr., "Inference Effects with Inference Making? Effects of Missing Information on Discounting and Use of Presented Information," *Journal of Consumer Research*, March 1991, pp. 477–91.

44. Durairaj Maheswaran and Brian Sternthal, "The Effects of Knowledge, Motivation, and Type of Message on Ad Processing and Product Judgments," *Journal of Consumer Research*, June 1990, pp. 66–73.

45. James R. Bettman and Mita Sujan, "Effects of Framing on Evaluation of Comparable and Noncomparable Alternatives by Expert and Novice Consumers," *Journal of Consumer Research*, September 1987, pp. 141–54; Joseph W. Alba and J. Wesley Hutchinson, "Dimensions of Consumer Expertise," *Journal of Consumer Research*, March 1987, pp. 411–54; Eric J. Johnson and J. Edward Russo, "Product Familiarity and Learning New Information," *Journal of Consumer Research*, June 1984, pp. 542–50; and Larry J. Marks and Jerry C. Olson, "Toward a Cognitive Structure Conceptualization of Product Familiarity," in *Advances in Consumer Research*, vol. 8. ed. Kent B. Monroe (Ann Arbor, Mich.: Association for Consumer Research, 1981), pp. 145–50.

46. Mita Sujan, "Consumer Knowledge: Effects on Evaluation Processes Mediating Consumer Judgments," *Journal of Consumer Research*, June 1985, pp. 31–46.

47. Michael Oneal, "Attack of the Bug Killers," *Business Week*, May 16, 1988, p. 81.

48. Richard E. Petty, John T. Cacioppo, and David Schumann, "Central and Peripheral Routes to Advertising Effectiveness: The Moderating Role of Involvement": *Journal of Consumer Research*, September 1983, pp. 135–44.

49. Peter L. Wright and Barton Weitz, "Time Horizon Effects on Product Evaluation Strategies," *Journal of Marketing Research*, November 1977, pp. 429–43.

50. Christine Moorman, "The Effects of Stimulus and Consumer Characteristics on the Utilization of Nutrition Information," *Journal of Consumer Research*, December 1990, pp. 362–74.

51. Deborah J. MacInnis and Linda L. Price, "The Role of Imagery in Information Processing: Review and Extensions," *Journal of Consumer Research*, March 1987, pp. 473–91.

52. Elizabeth C. Hirschman, "Point of View: Sacred, Secular, and Mediating Consumption Imagery in Television Commercials," *Journal of Marketing Research*, December–January 1991, pp. 38–43.

53. Ronald Alsop, "Marketing: The Slogan's Familiar, But What's the Brand? *The Wall Street Journal*, January 8, 1988, p. B1.

54. Jacob Jacoby and Wayne D. Hoyer, "Viewer Miscomprehension of Televised Communications: Selected Findings," *Journal of Marketing*, Fall 1982, pp. 12–26; and Jacob Jacoby and Wayne D. Hoyer, "The Comprehension/Miscomprehension of Print Communicaton: Selected Findings," *Journal of Consumer Research*, March 1989, pp. 434–43.

55. Some researchers believe these estimates are too high due to problems in measuring miscomprehension. See Gary T. Ford and Richard Yalch, "Viewer Miscomprehension of Televised Communication A Comment," *Journal of Marketing*, Fall 1982, pp. 27–31; and Richard W. Mzerski, "Viewer Miscomprehension Findings Are Measurement Bound," *Journal of Marketing*, Fall 1982, pp. 32–34.

56. Gary T. Ford and John E. Calfee, "Recent Developments in FTC Policy on Deceptions," *Journal of Marketing*, July 1986, pp. 82–103; and Ivan L. Preston and Jef I. Richards, "The Relationship of Miscomprehension to Deceptiveness in FTC Cases," in *Advances in Consumer Research*, vol. 13. ed. Richard J. Lutz (Provo, Utah: Association for Consumer Research, 1986), pp. 138–42.

57. Bruce Ingersoll, "FDA Takes on 'No Cholesterol' Claims," *The Wall Street Journal*, May 15, 1991, pp. B1, B10.

58. Chris Janiszewski, "The Influence of Print Advertisement Organization on Affect toward a Brand Name," *Journal of Consumer Research*, June 1990, pp. 53–65; James M. Munch and Jack L. Swasy, "Rhetorical Question, Summarization Frequency, and Argument Strength Effects on Recall," *Journal of Consumer Research*, June 1988, pp. 69–76; and Thomas J. Olney, Morris B. Holbrook, and Rajeev Batra, "Consumer Responses to Advertising: The Effects of Ad Content, Emotions, and Attitude toward the Ad on Viewing Time," *Journal of Consumer Research*, March 1991, pp. 440–453.

59. Jacob Jacoby, Robert W. Chestnut, and William Silberman, "Consumer Use and Comprehension of Nutrition Information," *Journal of Consumer Research*, September 1977, pp. 119–28; Joyce A. Vermeersch and Helene Swenerton, "Interpretations of Nutrition Claims in Food Advertisements by Low-Income Consumers," *Journal of Nutrition Education*, January–March 1980, pp. 19–25; and Moorman, "The Effects of Stimulus and Consumer Characteristics."

Additional Reading

For a discussion of how various factors affect interpretation processes, see:

MacInnis, Deborah J.; Christine Moorman; and Bernard J. Jaworski. "Enhancing and Measuring Consumers' Motivation, Opportunity, and Ability to Process Brand Information from Ads." *Journal of Marketing*, October 1991, pp. 32–53.

For a discussion of consumers' intentional search for information, see:

Harvey, James W. "Correlates of Search Patterns for an Innovation," in *Advances in Consumer Research*, vol. 13, ed. Richard J. Lutz. Provo, Utah: Association for Consumer Research, 1986, pp. 414–18.

Brucks, Merrie. "The Effects of Product Class Knowledge on Information Search Behavior," *Journal of Consumer Research*, June 1985, pp. 1–16.

For a discussion of the effects of attention in decision making, see:

Schindler, Robert M.; Michael Berbaum; and Donna R. Weinzimer. "How an Attention-Getting Device can Affect Choice among Similar Alternatives." In *Advances in Consumer Research*, vol. 14. ed. Melanie Wallendorf and Paul Anderson, Provo, Utah: Association for Consumer Research, 1987, pp. 505–9.

For a discussion of elaboration in comprehension of advertising, see:

Lord, Kenneth R., and Robert E. Burnkrant. "Television Program Elaboration Effects on Commercial Processing." In *Advances in Consumer Research*, vol. 15. ed. Michael J. Houston, Provo, Utah: Association for Consumer Research, 1988, pp. 213–18.

For a discussion of how involvement affects attention and comprehension processes, see:

Buchholz, Laura M., and Robert E. Smith. "The Role of Consumer Involvement in Determining

MARKETING STRATEGY IN ACTION

Black & Decker

At the end of 1985, Black & Decker was about halfway through the biggest brand name swap in marketing history. The company, once best known for its power tools, bought General Electric's small-appliance business in 1984 for $300 million. Black & Decker had until mid-1987 to bring all of GE's 150 or so appliance products under its own logo.

By renaming the GE appliances, B&D did for its competitors something they could not possibly have accomplished for themselves – eliminated the best-known brand name in the small-appliance business. But these other companies – including Sunbeam, Rival, Hamilton Beach, and Norelco – did not show much gratitude. Sensing confusion in the market and weakness in their competitor, they increased their advertising budgets and introduced new products in an attempt to intercept GE customers before they got to Black & Decker. In return, Black & Decker unleashed a new product blitz of its own and began a $100 million advertising and promotion campaign, the largest ever in the small-appliance industry.

For years, GE had been the best-loved name in the appliance game. It still was in 1985. In one survey, consumers were asked to name small-appliance makers: GE came up a remarkable 92 percent of the time, Sunbeam was a distant second at 41 percent, and Black & Decker was mentioned only 12 percent of the time. In fact, another 1985 survey showed that most consumers didn't know GE had left the game.

Kenneth Homa, vice president for marketing, directed the complex Black & Decker strategy to make GE's name its own. The company broke the changeover process for each product into about 140 steps to be completed over 14 months. According to Black & Decker, the process went so smoothly that it stepped up the timetable to be complete by the end of 1986.

Black & Decker decided to launch each product as if it were new. For some products, it made alterations ranging from simple changes in color to major redesigns. For instance, GE's under-the-cabinet Spacemaker products – including a coffee maker, a toaster oven, and a can opener – were

Cognitive Response to Broadcast Advertising." *Journal of Advertising*, 20 (1991), pp. 4–17.

For a discussion of how consumers react to brand extensions, see:

Park, C. Whan; Sandra Milberg; and Robert Lawson. "Evaluation of Brand Extensions: The Role of Product Feature Similarity and Brand Concept Consistency." *Journal of Consumer Research*, September 1991, pp. 185–93.

For a discussion of how men and women vary in their interpretation processes, see:

Meyers-Levy, Joan, and Durairaj Maheswaran. "Exploring Differences in Males and Females' Processing Strategies." *Journal of Consumer Research*, June 1991, pp. 63–70.

For a discussion of measuring miscomprehension of marketing information, see:

Gates, Fliece R., and Wayne D. Hoyer. "Measuring Miscomprehension: A Comparison of Alternate Formats." In *Advances in Consumer Research*, vol. 13, ed. Richard J. Lutz. Provo, Utah: Association for Consumer Research, 1986, pp. 143–46.

remodeled into sleeker units. Black & Decker also doubled the warranty period for every GE product to two years.

One big question for Black & Decker was whether to use its own brand name alongside GE's in the initial promotion and advertising. It decided not to for most appliances. Research had revealed that consumers associated the same qualities with Black & Decker – among them reliability and durability – that they did with GE. So Black & Decker tried to keep consumer confusion to a minimum by making a clean switch – the Black & Decker name for GE. For instance, the popular Spacemaker line was remarketed without a reference to GE. TV commercials emphasized the Spacemaker brand name and ended with the tag line "Now by Black & Decker."

Competitors, of course, did not stand still while the brand-name switch occurred. In particular, Sunbeam wanted consumers to forget both GE and Black & Decker. It increased its 1985 advertising budget to $42 million, four times what had been planned, to take advantage of the confusing situation.

Irons are a very important part (about 25 percent) of Black & Decker's small-appliance business. Thus, the company delayed conversion until it had experience with other lines. Research showed that 40 percent of customers go into a store intending to buy a particular brand of iron (usually GE). Therefore, Black & Decker modified its "clean switch" strategy. It included GE's name next to its own in print ads for irons and in promotional materials in the stores. On TV, however, it was more difficult to explain the switch. So, Black & Decker promoted the irons under its own name in television commercials.

The short-run concerns with the name change were not the only problems Black & Decker had to face. Most appliances are sold to people replacing their worn-out items, rather than to first-time buyers. Therefore, in any given year, only about 10 percent of the small-appliance market turns over. This means most consumers who now own GE products won't buy new ones until after the GE name is long gone from the small-appliance scene. What will they think when they go into the store and find no GE products?

Discussion Questions

1. Describe some typical situations in which consumers would be accidentally and intentionally exposed to information about Black & Decker's new line of appliances. What

implications would the type of exposure have for Black & Decker's approach to making the name switch from GE?

2. Discuss how consumers' prior knowledge about Black & Decker and GE (their corporate images) could have affected consumers' comprehension of the small home appliances now marketed by Black & Decker.
   a. What types of inferences might consumers have drawn when they first became aware that Black & Decker was now selling small home appliances?
   b. How would these inferences change over time as consumers became familiar with Black & Decker's appliances?
3. In what ways might consumers become confused and miscomprehend marketing information from Black & Decker? What could Black & Decker do about it?
4. Analyze the pros and cons of Black & Decker's decision not to mention the GE name in its brand-name changeover. What do you think of the decision to feature the GE name only on electric irons?
5. What types of strategies could Sunbeam (or some other competitor) have used to try to derail Black & Decker's strategy? How could Black & Decker have countered each of these attacks?

Source: Excerpted from Bill Saporito, "Ganging Up on Black & Decker," *Fortune,* December 23, 1985, pp. 63–72.

Attitudes and Intentions

CHAPTER 6

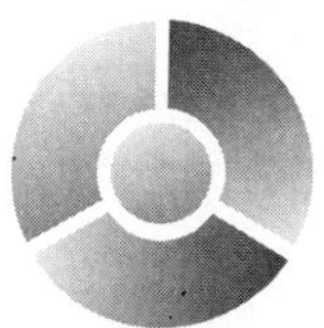

THE TURNAROUND IN JAGUAR OWNERS' ATTITUDES

In the early 1980s, Jaguar was in desperate shape. Sales were falling, especially in the United States. Product quality was terrible, and owners were developing increasingly negative attitudes toward the company, the car, and the dealers. Then, almost at the last minute, Jaguar pulled itself back from the brink of disaster.

The problem with Jaguar was not that the cars were boring or unattractive; to the contrary, few automobile makes had such passionate customers. But in the early 1980s, these passions were mostly negative. Owners (and many nonowners, too) had unfavorable beliefs about product quality and reliability. Jokes about Jaguar abounded, such as "Jaguar will soon begin selling its cars in pairs, so you can have one to drive while the other is in the service shop." J. D. Power, the market research company that regularly measures consumers' attitudes toward automobile makes, did not include Jaguar in its studies because so few owners were willing to even discuss owning the car. Unfortunately, the beliefs and attitudes of Jaguar owners accurately reflected reality—the car and the dealers did have serious problems.

Finally, Jaguar management, factory workers, and dealers set out to save the company. Drastic measures were taken to improve

production quality and dealer service. As these began to work, the company boldly doubled the warranty to two years. Customers' beliefs and attitudes began to change, and sales increased dramatically. To learn firsthand what owners felt about their cars, Jaguar management began to track consumers' attitudes toward the car, dealers, and the company. The J. D. Power research company was hired to interview several hundred buyers each month. Then Power tracked these customers by measuring their attitudes and beliefs after 1, 8, and 18 months.

The early results showed that consumers believed the cars were improved. By mid-1983, Jaguar scored about average among all makes on consumer satisfaction, but attitudes toward dealer service were still poor. So Jaguar again took strong action to improve service, including terminating about 20 percent of its worst dealers. That, combined with the continued improvements in product quality and service, produced the single biggest jump in favorable consumer attitudes ever recorded. By 1985, Jaguar had taken fifth place in the United States in favorable consumer attitudes (overall satisfaction with the car), right behind Honda and ahead of Mazda. In the luxury car market, only Mercedes-Benz was ahead. Of course, not every Jaguar owner had entirely positive beliefs and attitudes, but the turnaround in consumer attitudes toward Jaguar had succeeded.

Source: Adapted from Michael H. Dale, "How We Rebuilt Jaguar in the U.S.," *Fortune*, April 28, 1986, pp. 110–19.

This example illustrates the concept of consumers' attitudes, one of the most important concepts in the study of consumer behavior. Each year, marketing managers, like those at Jaguar, spend millions of dollars researching consumers' attitudes toward products and brands, and many more millions trying to influence those attitudes through advertisements, sales promotions, and other types of persuasion. By influencing consumers' attitudes, marketers hope to influence their purchase behaviors. In this chapter, we examine two types of attitudes—

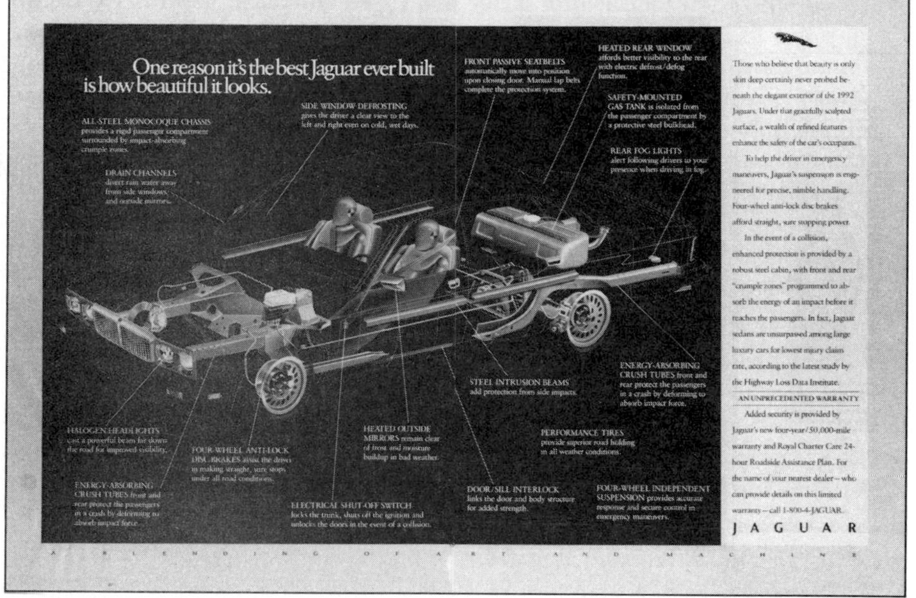

This ad attempts to create an overall evaluation or attitude toward the Jaguar.

attitudes toward objects and attitudes toward behaviors. We begin by defining the concept of attitude and discussing how people's salient beliefs cause attitudes. Then we consider the information integration process by which attitudes toward objects are formed. Next, we discuss the information integration process that forms attitudes toward actions and influences people's intentions to perform behaviors. Finally, we discuss the imperfect relationship between behavioral intentions and actual behaviors. Throughout, we identify implications of these concepts and processes for developing marketing strategies.

What Is an Attitude?

Attitude has been a key concept in psychology for more than a century, and at least 100 definitions and 500 measures of attitude have been proposed.[1] Although the dominant approach to attitudes has changed over the years (see Highlight 6.1), nearly all definitions of attitude have one thing in common: they refer to people's evaluations.[2] We define **attitude** as a person's *overall evaluation of a concept.*[3]

As you learned in Chapter 3, **evaluations** are *affective responses* at relatively low levels of intensity and arousal (refer to Figure 3.2). These evaluations can be created by both the affective and the cognitive systems.[4] The affective system automatically produces affective responses—including emotions, feelings, moods, and evaluations or attitudes—as immediate, direct responses to certain

HIGHLIGHT 6.1

A Brief History of the Study of Attitude

Attitude has been called "the most distinctive and indispensable concept in contemporary American social psychology." And it is one of the most important concepts marketers use to understand consumers. Over the years, researchers have tried a variety of approaches to studying attitudes in an attempt to provide a more complete understanding of behavior.

One of the earliest definitions of attitude was introduced by Thurstone in 1931. He viewed attitude as a fairly simple concept—the amount of *affect* a person has for or against an object. A few years later, Allport proposed a much broader definition: "Attitude is a mental and neural state of *readiness* to *respond*, organized through experience, and exerting a directive and/or dynamic influence on behavior."

Triandis and others combined three response types (thoughts, feelings, and actions) into the *tripartite model of attitude*. In this scheme, attitude was seen as comprising three related components—*cognition* (knowledge about the object), *affect* (positive or negative evaluations of the object), and *conation* (intentions or actual behavior toward the object). Later, Fishbein, like Thurstone, argued that it is most useful to consider attitude as a simple, undimensional concept—the amount of affect a person feels for an object.

Today, most researchers agree that the simple concept of attitude proposed by Thurstone and Fishbein is the most useful. That is, attitude represents a person's favorable or unfavorable feelings toward the object in question. Beliefs (cognition) and intentions to behave (conation) are seen as related to attitude, but are separate cognitive concepts, not part of attitude itself. This is the perspective we take in this book.

Source: Adapted from Martin Fishbein, "An Overview of the Attitude Construct," in *A Look Back, A Look Ahead*, ed. G. B. Hafer (Chicago: American Marketing Association, 1980), pp. 1–19; and Richard J. Lutz, "The Role of Attitude Theory in Marketing," in *Perspectives in Consumer Behavior*, 3rd ed., ed. H. H. Kassarjian and T. S. Robertson (Glenview, Ill.: Scott, Foresman, 1981), pp. 234–35.

stimuli. These favorable or unfavorable affective responses are generated without conscious, cognitive processing of information about the product. Then, through classical conditioning processes, these evaluations may become associated with a product or brand, thus creating an attitude.[5] We discuss this affective, noncognitive learning in Chapter 9.

In this chapter, however, we treat attitudes as evaluations created by the cognitive system. The cognitive processing model of consumer decision making, as shown in Figure 6.1, shows that an overall evaluation is formed when consumers integrate (combine) knowledge, meanings, or beliefs about the attitude concept. The goal of this **integration process** is to analyze the *personal relevance* of the concept and determine whether it is favorable or unfavorable: "What does this concept have to do with me? Is this a good or bad thing for me?

FIGURE 6.1
Consumers' Cognitive Processes Involved in Interpretation

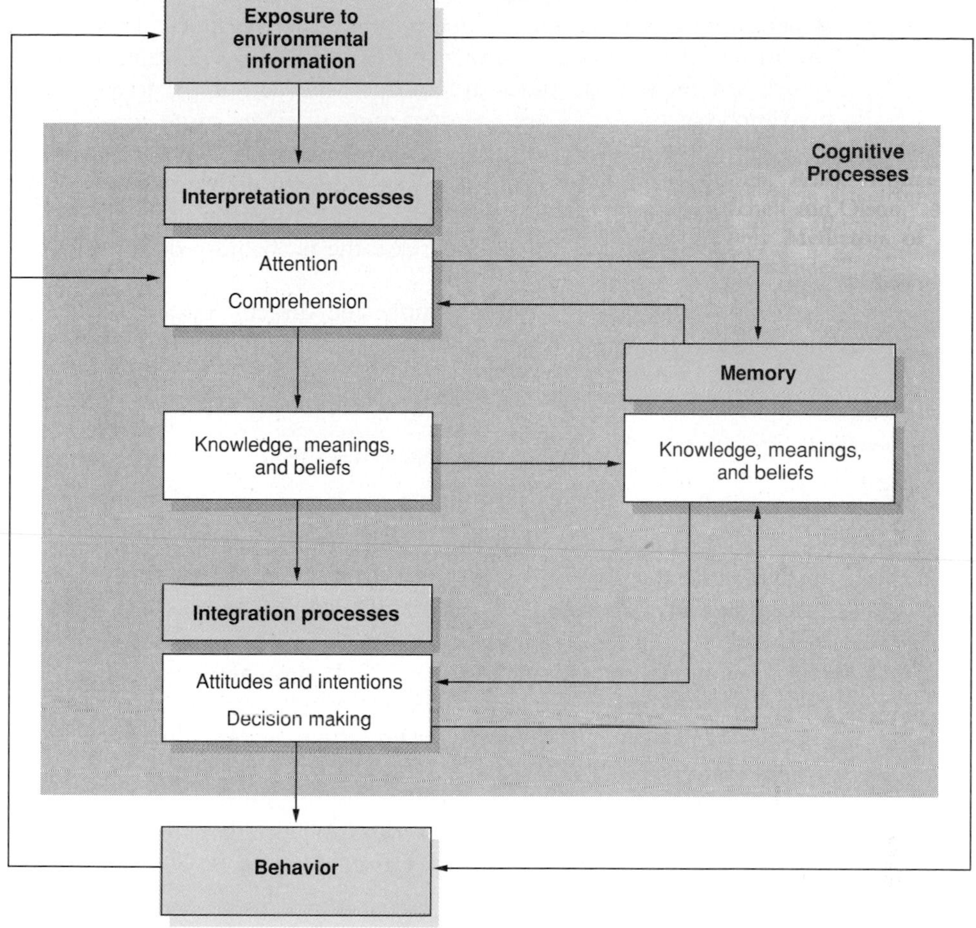

Do I like or dislike this object?" We assume consumers form attitudes toward every concept they process in terms of its personal relevance.

As shown in Figure 6.1, the evaluations produced by the attitude formation process may be stored in memory. Once an attitude has been formed and stored in memory, consumers do not have to engage in another integration process to construct another attitude when they need to evaluate the concept again. Instead, the existing attitude can be activated from memory and used to interpret new information, and the activated attitude can be integrated with other knowledge in decision making (we discuss how attitudes are used in decision processes in the next chapter).[6] For instance, taste tests usually are conducted blind in that tasters are not told what brands they are tasting. This avoids activating brand attitudes that could bias the taste judgments.

Whether a given attitude will affect interpretation or integration processes depends on its **accessibility** in memory or its *probability of activation.*[7] Among the many factors that can influence the accessibility of attitudes are salience (more self-relevant attitudes are more easily activated), frequency of prior activation (attitudes that are activated more often are more accessible), and the strength of the association between a concept and its attitude (puppies tend to activate positive attitudes; zebras usually do not activate an attitude).[8] Some research has examined priming effects—presenting cues to people that partially activate a concept and thereby increase the probability of accessing a related attitude.[9]

Attitudes can be measured simply and directly by asking consumers to evaluate the concept of interest. For instance, marketing researchers might ask consumers to indicate their attitudes toward McDonald's french fries on three evaluative scales:

McDonald's French Fries

Extremely Unfavorable	−3	−2	−1	0	+1	+2	+3	Extremely Favorable
Dislike Very Much	−3	−2	−1	0	+1	+2	+3	Like Very Much
Very Bad	−3	−2	−1	0	+1	+2	+3	Very Good

Consumers' overall attitudes toward McDonald's french fries *(A_o)* are indicated by the average of their ratings across the three evaluative scales. Attitudes can vary from *negative* (ratings of −3, −2, −1) through *neutral* (a rating of 0) to *positive* (ratings of +1, +2, or +3). Also, attitudes are not necessarily intense or extreme. On the contrary, many consumers have essentially neutral evaluations (neither favorable nor unfavorable) toward relatively unimportant, noninvolving concepts. A neutral evaluation is still an attitude, however, although probably a weakly held one. Highlight 6.2 describes the problems of marketing brands toward which consumers hold weak attitudes.

Attitudes toward What?

Consumers' attitudes are always toward some concept. We can distinguish between two broad types of concepts—objects and behaviors. Consumers can have *attitudes toward various physical and social objects (A_o)* including products, brands, models, stores, people (salesperson at the camera store), as well as aspects of marketing strategy (a rebate from General Motors; an ad for Wrigley's chewing gum). Consumers also can have attitudes toward imaginary objects such as concepts and ideas (capitalism, a fair price for gasoline). Also, consumers can have *attitudes toward their own behaviors or actions (A_{act})* including their past actions (Why did I buy that sweater?) and future behaviors (going to the mall this afternoon).

HIGHLIGHT 6.2

MARKETING "MIDDLE" BRANDS

At one time, it was a blessing to be in the middle of a market. Brands that were midpriced and had middle-of-the road attributes appealed to the mass market and often enjoyed great success. But by the late 1980s, many consumers did not have strong, positive attitudes toward brands that are "just OK." Thus, many middle brands, such as Sears Roebuck & Co., Holiday Inn, Smirnoff, J. C. Penney Company, and others, found it difficult to retain existing customers and acquire new ones.

The mass market for many products seemed to have fragmented into a large consumer segment that wanted lower prices (and presumably would accept somewhat lower quality) and another group that wanted top quality and was willing to pay extra for it. Many companies found it increasingly difficult to market an average brand toward which consumers had only lukewarm attitudes. According to one industry analyst, "There seems to be no future for products [and brands] that everyone likes a little."

By 1990, many upscale retail stores such as Neiman-Marcus Co., Nordstrom, and Macy's were thriving along with discount outlets such as Wal-Mart and K mart, while Sears floundered in the middle. Sears and Penney's saw many of their once-loyal customers defect to upscale retailers or the discount stores, and both retailers scrambled in the late 1980s to create and convey images a step up from ordinary. But success was difficult. One industry analyst claimed, "Sears doesn't stand for anything anymore."

This same phenomenon has occurred in other markets as consumers moved away from OK brands with only moderately positive attitudes to brands that generate more excitement and stronger attitudes. Consider the problems of Smirnoff vodka, a middle brand selling for a moderate $6 to $9 a bottle. Although Smirnoff was still the no. 1 brand in the United States in 1990, sales of the higher-priced, imported brands such as Stolichnaya, Finlandia, and Absolut had gained more than 20 percent in 1989, while sales of Smirnoff were flat. In response, Smirnoff tried to enhance its image and create more positive consumer attitudes by raising prices and running ads with a more upscale look.

As another example, sales of upscale ice cream brands such as Haagen-Dazs and Ben and Jerry's increased along with those of private store brands. In contrast, sales rates for the middle brands have been stagnant. Thus, middle brands such as Sealtest tried such marketing strategies as adding a cellophane flap to retard formation of ice crystals and modernizing the package graphics, while maintaining the price at about $3 per half-gallon. Sealtest hoped to convey higher value to the consumer and increase brand attitudes.

Source: Kathleen Deveny, "Middle-Price Brands Come under Seige," *The Wall Street Journal,* April 2, 1990, pp. B1, B6.

Levels of Attitude Concepts

Consumers can have distinct attitudes to many variations of essentially the same concept. Figure 6.2 shows several attitude concepts that vary in their *level of specificity*, even though all concepts are in the same product domain. For instance, Rich has a moderately positive attitude toward fast-food restaurants in general, but he has a highly favorable attitude toward one product form (hamburger restaurants). However, his attitude toward McDonald's, a specific brand of hamburger restaurant, is only slightly favorable (he likes Wendy's better). Finally, his attitude toward a particular "model" – the McDonald's on the corner of Grant and Main – is somewhat negative (he had an unpleasant meal there).

FIGURE 6.2
Variations in Level of Specificity of Attitude Concept

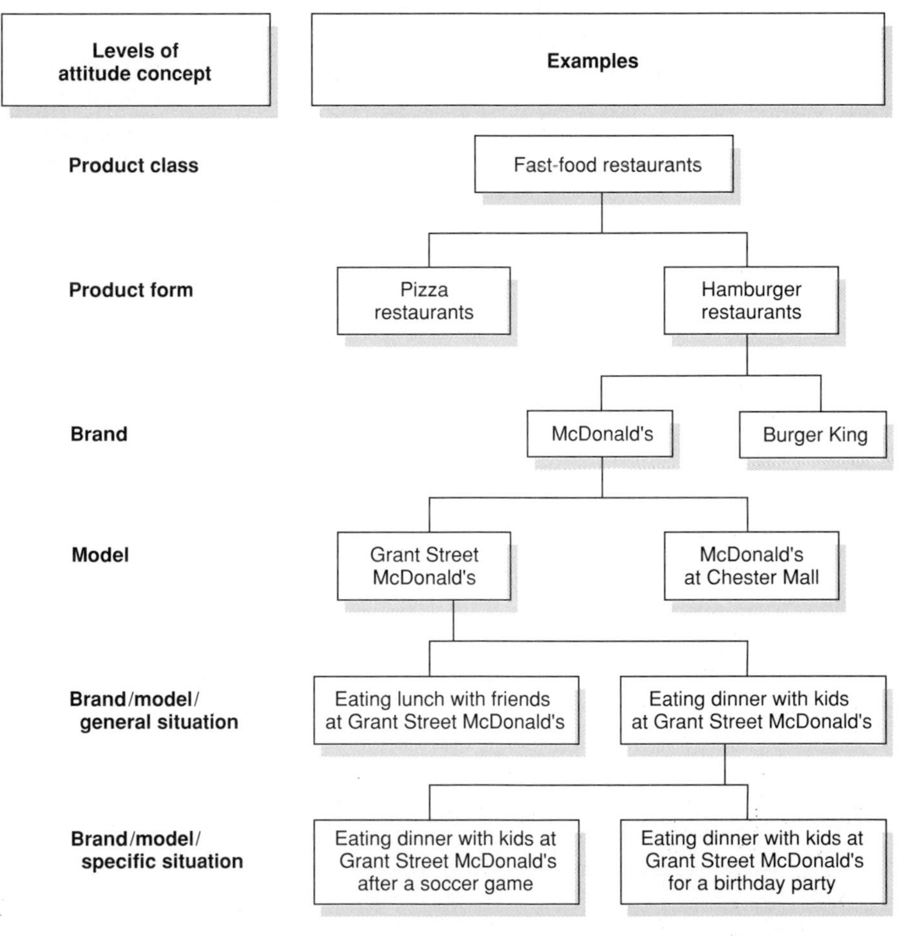

Note that some attitude concepts are defined in terms of a particular behavioral and situational context (eating dinner with his children at the Grant Street McDonald's after a soccer game), whereas other concepts are more general (McDonald's restaurants). Consumers could have different attitudes toward these concepts, and the attitudes might not be consistent with each other. Rich has an unfavorable attitude toward eating lunch with his friends at the Grant Street McDonald's (he'd rather go to a full-service restaurant); however, he has a somewhat favorable attitude toward eating dinner there with his kids (it's easy and fast). Note that although the same McDonald's "object" is present in each of these concepts, Rich's attitudes are toward the *combination* of the object and situation, which is quite a different concept than the object alone.[10]

Because consumers are likely to have different attitudes toward different attitude concepts, *marketers must precisely identify the attitude concept at the level of specificity most relevant to the marketing problem of interest.*

Marketing Implications

Marketers are highly interested in market share, a measure of purchasing behavior indicating the proportion of total sales in a product category (or product form) received by a brand. But marketers also need to attend to consumers' brand attitudes.

Brand Equity

Brand attitude is a critically important aspect of brand equity. Brand equity concerns the *value* of the brand to the marketer and to the consumer.[11] From the marketer's perspective, brand equity implies greater profits, more cash flow, and greater market share. For instance, Marriott estimated that adding its name to Fairfield Inn increased occupancy rates by 15 percent (a tangible indicator of the value of the Marriott brand). In England, Hitachi and G.E. once co-owned a factory that made identical televisions for both companies.[12] The only differences were the brand name on the set and a $75 greater price for the Hitachi, reflecting the equity value of the Hitachi brand.

From the consumer's perspective, **brand equity** involves a strong, *positive brand attitude* (favorable evaluation of the brand) based on *consistent meanings and beliefs* which are *accessible* in memory (easily activated).[13] These three factors create a *strong, favorable consumer-brand relationship*, a very important asset for a company and the basis for brand equity. Highlight 6.3 presents more about the concept of brand equity.

Basically, marketers can get brand equity in three ways: they can build it, borrow it, or buy it.[14] Companies can *build brand equity* by insuring the brand actually does deliver salient consequences and by consistently advertising these important consequences. Consider the considerable brand equity built up over time by Campbell's soup, Green Giant vegetables, Mercedes-Benz automobiles, and NutraSweet artificial sweetener. Anheuser-Busch created the Eagle brand

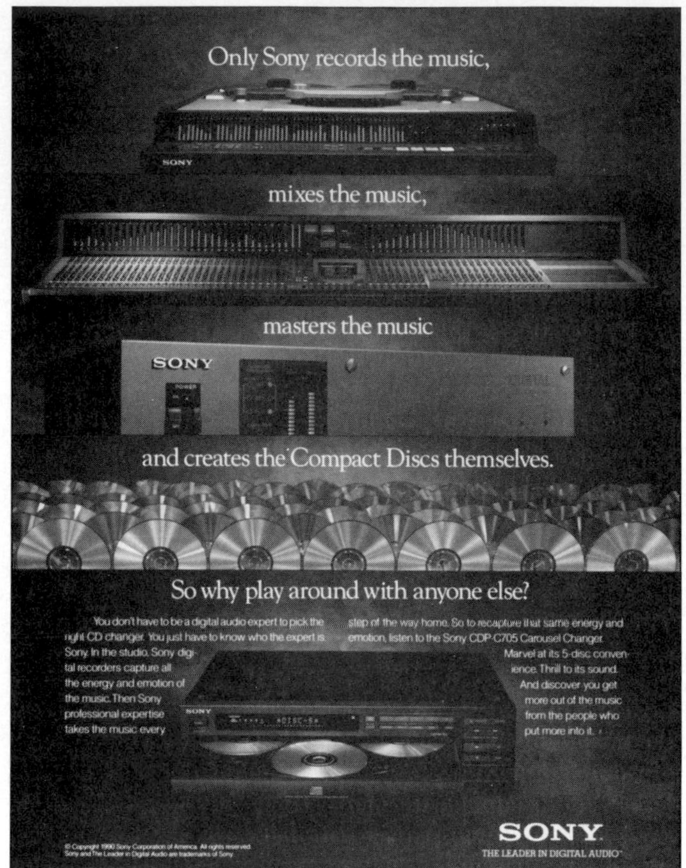

This ad attempts to create brand equity for Sony home stereo equipment by emphasizing the competence of the Sony company.

of snack foods (including honey roasted peanuts) and invested heavily in creating positive consumer attitudes (and brand equity).

Companies can *borrow brand equity* by extending a positive brand name to other products. For example, the Coca-Cola line now includes Coca-Cola Classic, Coke, Diet Coke, Caffeine-Free Coke, Cherry Coke, and others. Tide no longer refers to only one type of detergent; the brand name has been extended to other products, and presumably some of Tide's original equity has been passed along, too. Consumer researchers are busy trying to determine how brand equity is transferred by brand-name extensions.[15] Some research shows the success of a brand extension depends on the key meanings consumers associate with a brand name and whether those meanings are consistent or appropriate for the other product.[16] Finally, a company can *buy brand equity* by purchasing brands that already have equity. For instance, the mergers and leveraged buyouts of the 1980s were partially motivated by the desire to buy brands with strong equity. Thus, when Grand Metropolitan bought Pillsbury and Philip Morris bought Kraft, they acquired the equity of all their brands.

HIGHLIGHT 6.3

BRAND EQUITY AND BRAND ATTITUDES

The important concept of brand equity concerns the *value* of the brand. From a means-end perspective, equity is based on the degree to which consumers value the consequences the brand delivers. A key aspect of equity is substitutability. For instance, Susan and Julie are next-door neighbors who both buy Parkay margarine. Both women received an advertisement and coupon for Promise margarine. On their next shopping trips, Julie bought a pound of Promise, but Susan bought a pound of Parkay. Their different behaviors were determined by their beliefs and attitudes, and their perceptions of brand equity. Julie believed Promise was essentially the same as Parkay, so she switched brands when offered the small inducement of the coupon. Susan, however, believed Parkay was the superior product, and she intended to buy it no matter what.

People like Susan are a marketer's dream because they create brand equity. If a brand has high equity, it is less vulnerable to competition. Consumers are less willing to accept substitutes for a brand with high equity because they want the consequences they believe the brand uniquely provides. Thus, marketers have to spend less money promoting brands with strong equity. This, in turn, makes high equity brands more profitable.

Source: Gretchen Morgenson, "The Trend Is Not Their Friend," *Forbes*, September 16, 1991, pp. 114–19; and William Moran and Kenneth Longman, "Boosting Profit Potential," *Marketing Insights*, Summer 1991, pp. 24–32.

Attitude Tracking Studies

Because many marketing strategies are intended to influence consumers' attitudes toward a brand, marketers can use measures of consumers' attitudes to indicate the success of those strategies. For instance, many companies regularly conduct large-scale attitude surveys, called *tracking studies*, to monitor consumers' brand attitudes over time. As these studies identify trends in consumer attitudes, marketers can adjust their marketing strategies, as Jaguar did in the opening example.

One company that failed to track consumers' increasingly unfavorable attitudes was Howard Johnson's, one of the original restaurant chains in the United States. During the highway building boom in the 1950s and 1960s, HoJo's was known as a clean place with nice washrooms, predictable and wholesome food, and ice cream the kids would like. Consumers' attitudes were positive, and Howard Johnson's prospered. But over the next 20 years, HoJo's did not monitor customers' attitudes well; nor did it respond effectively to the strategies of competitors that were passing them by. For instance, Howard Johnson's used informal gauges of consumer attitudes, such as comment cards left on restaurant tables. Competitors such as Marriott, Denny's and McDonald's ran sophisticated market tests that told them what customers liked and didn't like. Finally, after a long decline, Marriott bought out the once-powerful chain of Howard Johnson's restaurants.[17]

Attitudes toward Objects

In this section, we examine the information integration process by which consumers form **attitudes toward objects (A_o),** including products or brands. As shown in Figure 6.1, during the integration process, consumers combine some of their knowledge, meanings, and beliefs about a product or brand to form an overall evaluation. These considered beliefs may be formed by interpretation processes or activated from memory.

Salient Beliefs

Through their varied experiences, consumers acquire many beliefs about products, brands, and other objects in their environments. As an example, Figure 6.3 presents some of the beliefs one consumer has about Crest toothpaste. These beliefs constitute an associative network of linked meanings stored in memory. Because peoples cognitive capacity is limited, only a few of these beliefs can be activated and consciously considered at once. The activated beliefs (highlighted in Figure 6.3) are called **salient beliefs.** Only the salient beliefs about an object (those that are activated at a particular time and in a specific context) cause or create a person's attitude toward that object.[18] Thus, one key to understanding consumers' attitudes is to identify and understand the underlying set of salient beliefs.

In principle, consumers can have salient beliefs about any type and level of meaning associated with a product. For instance, consumers with complete means-end chains of product knowledge could activate beliefs about the product's attributes, its functional consequences, or the values achieved through using it. In addition, beliefs about other types of product-related meanings such as country of origin could be activated.[19] Salient beliefs could include tactile, olfactory, and visual images as well as cognitive representations of the emotions and moods associated with using the product. If activated, any of these beliefs could influence a consumer's attitude toward a product.

Many factors influence which beliefs about an object will be *activated* in a situation and thus become salient and determinant of A_o. They include prominent stimuli in the immediate environment (point-of-purchase displays, advertisements, package information), recent events, consumers' moods and emotional states, and consumers' values and goals activated in the situation.[20] For instance, noticing a price-reduction sign for bath soap may make price beliefs salient and therefore influential on A_o.

FIGURE 6.3

Relationship between Salient Beliefs about an Object and Attitude toward the Object

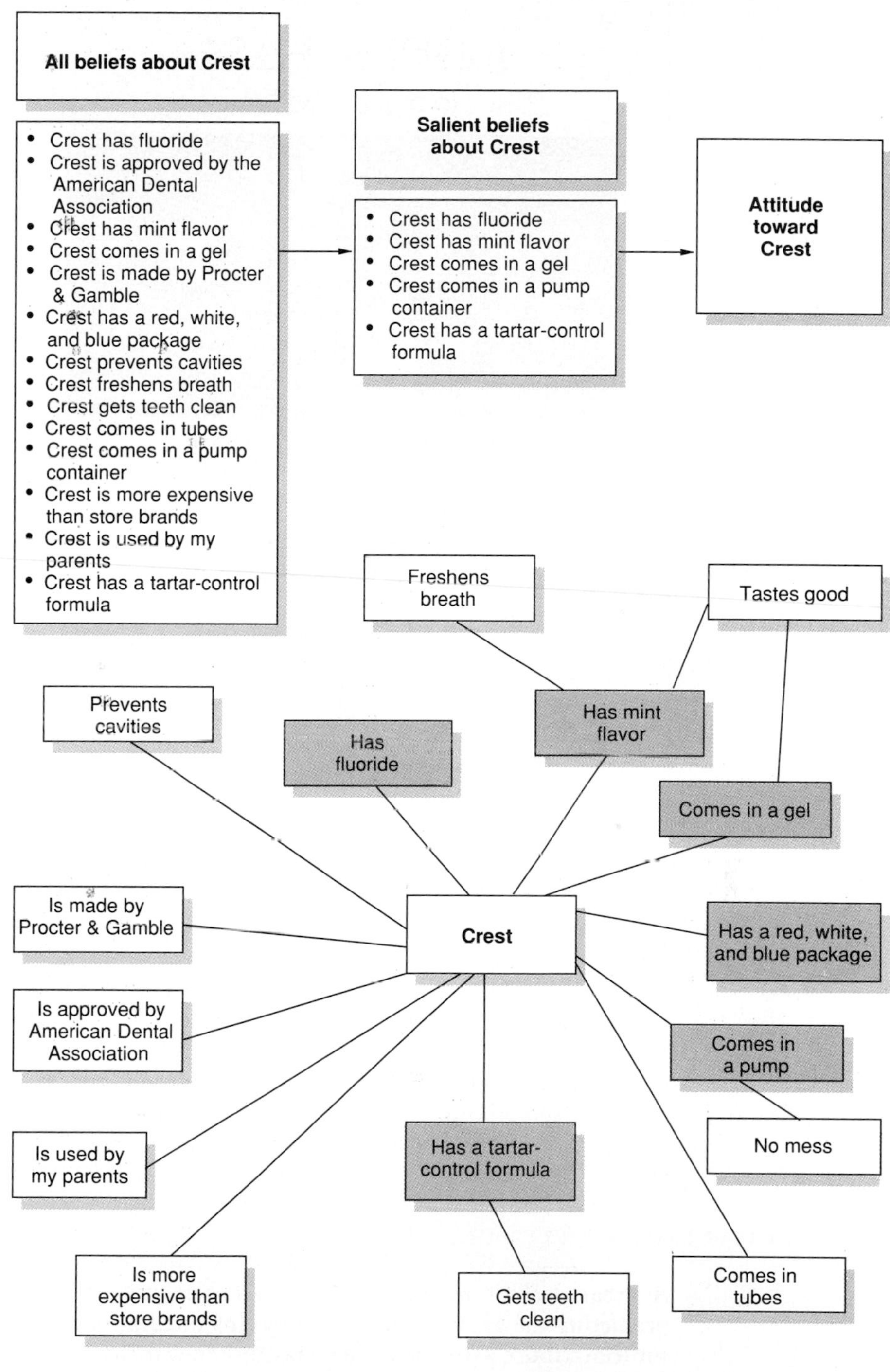

This ad is intended to create salient beliefs about product attributes and related benefits.

Marketers may find that consumers' salient beliefs vary over time or situations for some products. That is, different sets of salient beliefs about a product may be activated in different situations or at different times.[21] For instance, consumers who have just returned from the dentist are more likely to activate beliefs about tooth decay and cavities when thinking about which brand of toothpaste to buy. Variations in the set of salient beliefs over time and situations can produce changes in consumer attitudes depending on the situation, context, time, consumer's mood, and so forth. Consumers have more stable attitudes toward objects that have a stable set of salient beliefs. Normally, though, the amount of variation in salient beliefs and attitudes is not great for most objects.

The Multiattribute Attitude Model

A great deal of marketing research has focused on developing models for predicting the attitudes produced by this integration process. These are called **multiattribute attitude models** because they focus on consumers' beliefs about multiple product or brand attributes.[22] Of these, Martin Fishbein's model has been most influential in marketing.

The key proposition in Fishbein's theory is that *the evaluations of salient beliefs cause overall attitude.* Simply stated, people tend to like objects that are associated with "good" characteristics and dislike objects they believe have "bad" attributes. In Fishbein's multiattribute model, overall attitude toward an object is a function of two factors: the *strengths* of the salient beliefs associated with the object and the *evaluations* of those beliefs.[23] Formally, the model proposes that:

$$A_o = \sum_{i=1}^{n} b_i e_i$$

where

A_o = Attitude toward the object
b_i = The strength of the belief that the object has attribute i
e_i = The evaluation of attribute i
n = The number of salient beliefs about the object

This multiattribute attitude model accounts for the integration process by which product knowledge (the evaluations and strengths of salient beliefs) are combined to form an overall evaluation or attitude. The model, however, does not claim that consumers actually add up the products of belief strength and evaluation when forming attitudes toward objects. Rather, this and similar models attempt to predict the attitude outcome of the integration process; they are not meant to describe the actual cognitive operations by which knowledge is integrated. In this book, we consider the multiattribute model to be a useful tool for investigating attitude formation and predicting attitudes.

Model Components

The two major elements of Fishbein's multiattribute model are the *strengths* and *evaluations* of the salient beliefs. Figure 6.4 illustrates how these components are combined to form attitudes toward two brands of soft drinks. This consumer has salient beliefs about three attributes for each brand. These beliefs vary in content, strength, and evaluation. The Fishbein model predicts that this consumer has a more favorable attitude toward 7UP than toward Diet Pepsi.

Belief strength (b_i) is the perceived probability of association between an object and its relevant attributes. Belief strength is measured by having consumers rate this probability of association for each of their salient beliefs, as shown here:

"How likely is it that 7UP has no caffeine?"

Extremely Unlikely 1 2 3 4 5 6 7 8 9 10 Extremely Likely

"How likely is it that 7UP is made from all natural ingredients?"

Extremely Unlikely 1 2 3 4 5 6 7 8 9 10 Extremely Likely

FIGURE 6.4
An Example of the Multiattribute Attitude Model

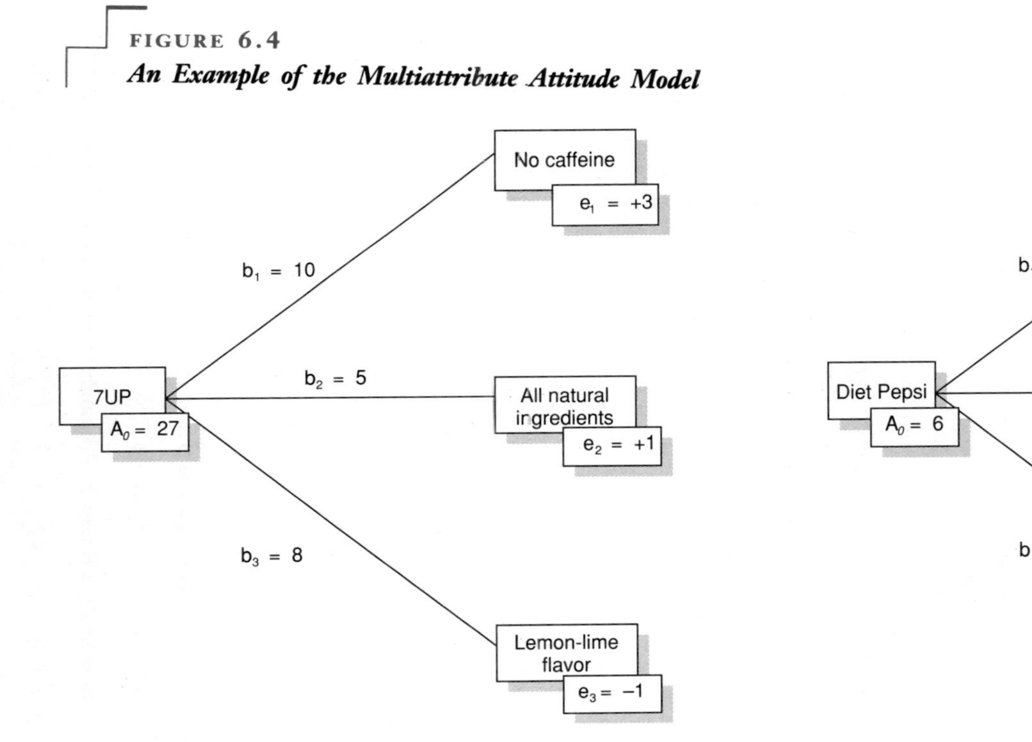

$$\text{Attitude}_{7UP} = \sum_{i=1}^{3} b_i e_i$$

$$A_o = (10)(3) + (5)(1) + (8)(-1)$$

$$A_o = 30 + 5 - 8$$

$$A_o = 27$$

$$\text{Attitude}_{DP} = \sum_{i=1}^{3} b_i e_i$$

$$A_o = (7)(2) + (6)(-3) + (10)(1)$$

$$A_o = 14 - 18 + 10$$

$$A_o = 6$$

Consumers who are quite certain that 7UP has no caffeine would indicate a very strong belief strength, perhaps 9 or 10. Consumers who have only a moderately strong belief that 7UP is made from only natural ingredients might rate their belief strength as 5 or 6.

The strength of consumers' product or brand beliefs is affected by their past experiences with the object. Beliefs about product attributes or consequences tend to be stronger when based on actual use of the product. Beliefs that were formed indirectly from mass advertising or conversations with a salesperson tend to be weaker. For instance, consumers are more likely to form a strong belief that "7UP tastes good" if they actually drink a 7UP and experience its taste directly than if they read a product claim in an advertisement. Because they are stronger (and more likely to be activated), beliefs based on direct experience tend to have a greater impact on A_o.[24] Marketers, therefore, try to induce potential customers to actually use their product. They may distribute free samples; sell small, less-expensive trial sizes; offer cents-off coupons; or have a no-obligation trial policy.

Fishbein argued that the typical number of salient beliefs about an attitude object is not likely to exceed seven to nine.[25] Given consumers' limited capacities for interpreting and integrating information, we might expect even fewer salient beliefs for many objects. In fact, when consumers have little knowledge about low-involvement products, their brand attitudes might be based on very few salient beliefs, perhaps only one or two. In contrast, their attitudes toward products or brands that are more self-relevant might be based on more salient beliefs.

Associated with each salient belief is a **belief evaluation** (e_i) that reflects how favorably the consumer perceives that attribute. Marketers measure the e_i component by having consumers indicate their evaluation of (favorability toward) each salient belief, as shown below.

"7UP has no caffeine."

Very Bad −3 −2 −1 0 +1 +2 +3 Very Good

"7UP has all natural ingredients."

Very Bad −3 −2 −1 0 +1 +2 +3 Very Good

As shown in Figure 6.4, the evaluations of the salient beliefs influence the overall A_o in proportion to the strength of each belief (b_i). Thus, strong beliefs about positive attributes have greater effects on A_o than do weak beliefs about equally positive attributes. Likewise, negative e_is reduce the favorability of A_o in proportion to their b_i "weights."

As you learned in Chapter 4, beliefs may be linked to form means-end chains of product knowledge. Figure 6.5 presents means-end chains for three attributes of 7UP. Note that the evaluation of each product attribute is ultimately derived from the evaluation of the end consequence in its means-end chain. As shown in Figure 6.5 the evaluation of the end "flows down" the

FIGURE 6.5
The Means-End Chain Basis for Attribute Evaluations

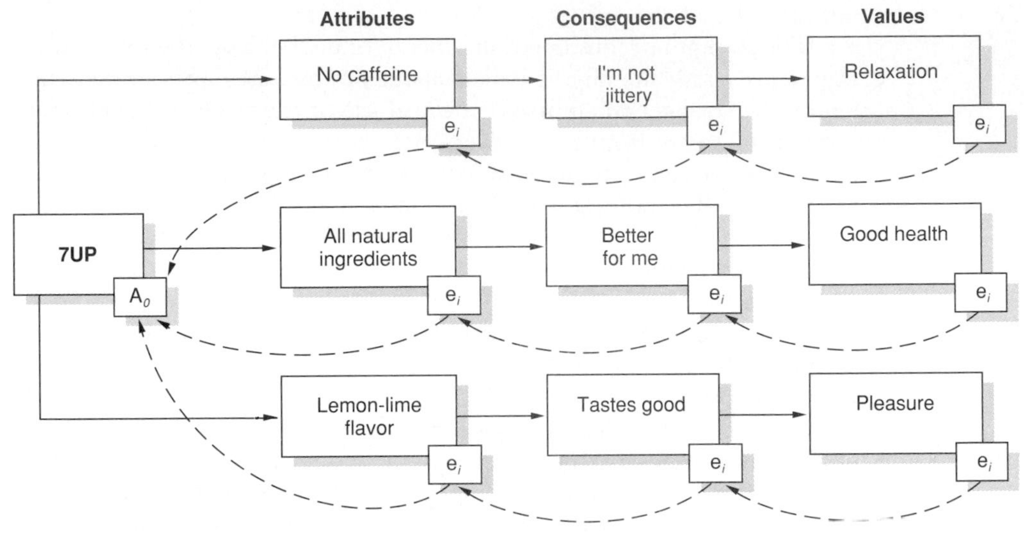

means-end chain to determine the evaluations of the less abstract consequences and attributes.[26] For instance, a person who positively evaluates the end "relaxation," an instrumental value, would tend to positively evaluate the functional consequence "I'm not jittery." In turn, the product attribute "no caffeine," which is perceived to lead to relaxation and not being jittery, would have a positive evaluation. These evaluations would then influence the overall attitude, A_o, toward 7UP.

Consumers' evaluations of salient attributes are not necessarily fixed over time or constant across different situations.[27] For instance, consumers may change their minds about how good or bad an attribute is as they learn more about its higher-order consequences. Situational factors can also change the e_i components. In a different situation, some consumers may want to be stimulated (when getting up in the morning or working late at night to finish a project). If so, the now-negative evaluation of the end value "relaxation" would flow down the means-end chain and create a *negative* evaluation of the "no caffeine" attribute—which, in turn, would contribute to a less positive overall attitude toward 7UP (for that situation). In this situation, the consumer might have a more positive attitude toward Diet Pepsi, which does contain caffeine. This is yet another example of how the physical and social environment can influence consumers' affect and cognitions.

Marketing Implications

Marketers have been using multiattribute models to explore consumer behavior since the late 1960s. These models became popular because they have an intuitive appeal to researchers and managers and are relatively easy to use in research.[28] Not all of these models accurately reflect the basic Fishbein model, but most are adaptations of it. We will discuss a few of the many applications of these models below.

Understanding Your Customers

The multiattribute attitude model is useful for identifying which attributes are the most important (or most salient) to consumers. For instance, airline passengers love to complain about the lousy food served on planes.[29] Yet in a 1988 survey, only 40 percent of passengers rated good food and beverage service as important, while other attributes were mentioned as important much more frequently. These included convenient schedules (over 90 percent), fast check-in (about 80 percent), comfortable seats (about 80 percent), and good on-time performance (about 85 percent). Perhaps airlines use such data to justify not improving the quality of the food they serve (airlines spend only about $4.25 per passenger on food). The relative importance of different attributes is likely to vary across market segments. For instance, three segments of the airline market—light travelers (1 or 2 trips per year), moderate travelers (3 to 9 trips per year), and frequent travelers (10 or more trips per year)—evaluated some attributes differently. For instance, light travelers had greater concerns about safety and efficient baggage handling, while frequent travelers were more concerned with convenient schedules and the frequent-flier program.

Diagnosis of Marketing Strategies

Although multiattribute models were developed to predict overall attitudes, marketers often use them to diagnose marketing strategies. By examining the salient beliefs that underlie attitudes toward various brands, marketers can learn how their strategies are performing and make adjustments to improve their effectiveness. For instance, in the suddenly value conscious 1990s, marketers found that many consumers were more concerned with the quality and value of products relative to their prices.[30] It became fashionable once again to get a bargain, spend one's money wisely, and not overpay for quality. Many companies adjusted their strategies in light of these beliefs. Consider the motto of Wal-Mart, the world's largest retailer, "The low price on the brands you trust." Southwest Airlines combined low fares with friendly but bare-bones service to enhance consumers' value beliefs and overall attitudes. Taco Bell reduced its operating costs enough to price several items on the menu under $1 and create stronger beliefs about the value provided by the fast-food restaurant. Highlight 6.4 presents another example of marketing strategies directed at consumers' beliefs about value.

HIGHLIGHT 6.4

My Value Is Bigger Than Your Value

In focus groups conducted in 1989 and 1990, marketers at MasterCard International recognized changes in consumers' beliefs about the importance of quality, value, and thrift. For instance, an ad showing a yuppie buying a diamond for herself with a Gold Mastercard was rejected by nearly all participants, although the ad had elicited favorable attitudes only 18 months earlier.

Based on this and other information, MasterCard changed its marketing strategy. During the latter 1980s, its theme had been "Master the Possibilities," a theme that focused on self-indulgence and buying all the things one wanted. The ads for the 1990s were much more utilitarian, describing such things as how MasterCard can access cash machines at convenient times. For example, the company ran a holiday promotion in 1991, called "Master Values," that offered cardholders a 10 to 25 percent discount for purchases made at stores such as K mart and the Dress Barn.

Sears markets its competitive Discover card using a similar "no-frills" approach including no annual fee and a 1 percent rebate on charges made with the card. Launched in 1986, the Discover card gained $19 billion in business by 1990.

All this was serious competition for American Express, which charged annual fees from $55 and up for its card. AmEx continued to use its established marketing strategy based largely on prestige and status. Its immediate response to the Visa challenge was to offer more upscale frills with the prestige Gold Card including free travel checks by phone or earning points good for a free tennis lesson from Ivan Lendl. Do you think these marketing strategies would be successful?

Source: Christopher Power, "Card Wars: My Value Is Bigger Than Your Value," *Business Week,* November 11, 1991, p. 138.

Understanding Situational Influences

Marketers also can use the multiattribute attitude model to examine the influence of situations. The relative salience of beliefs about certain product attributes may be greatly influenced by the situations in which the product is used. Situations vary in many ways, including time of day, consumer mood, environmental setting, weather, and hundreds of other variables. These situational characteristics affect which beliefs are activated from memory and influence attitudes toward the brands that might be purchased for use in those situations. For instance, one study of snack products found that beliefs about economy and taste were most important for three common snacking occasions – for everyday desserts, for watching TV in the evening, and for kids' lunches.[31] However, when buying snacks for a children's party, beliefs about nutrition and convenience were most important. Such differences in salient beliefs can lead to different brand attitudes in these various situations.

This situational context in which the product is used can have a significant influence on brand attitude.

Attitude-Change Strategies

The multiattribute model is a useful guide for devising strategies to change consumers' attitudes. Basically, a marketer has four possible **attitude change strategies:** (1) add a new salient belief about the attitude object—ideally, one with a positive e_i; (2) increase the strength of an existing positive belief; (3) increase the evaluation of a strongly held belief; or (4) make an existing belief more salient.

Adding a new salient belief to the existing beliefs that consumers have about a product or brand is probably the most common attitude-change strategy.[32] This strategy may require a physical change in the product. Hasbro Inc. is the biggest and perhaps the most successful toy marketer in the United States.[33] Its goal is to achieve 70 percent of revenues from existing products. One of Hasbro's marketing strengths is its ability to manage old products effectively, which

By adding a new salient belief about "extra fiber," Gerber hopes to create more favorable attitudes toward their product.

involves adding new attributes and creating new salient beliefs for old products. In 1989, for example, Hasbro discovered that many children were becoming bored with G.I. Joe figures (attitudes were becoming less favorable), and sales were dropping. In response, Hasbro redesigned 80 percent of the line by removing old attributes such as combat fatigues and adding new attributes such as space suits, jet packs, and combat helicopters. Kids loved the new look and sales jumped back quickly. When Hasbro acquired the languishing Tonka brand of toy trucks and other vehicles, it considered adding a salient attribute to the Tonka brand – a lifetime guarantee – to increase consumers' attitudes.

Marketers can also try to change attitudes by *changing the strength of already salient beliefs.*[34] They can attempt to increase the strength of beliefs about positive attributes and consequences; or they can decrease the strength of beliefs about negative attributes and consequences. Consider the $10 million promotion campaign developed in 1985 by the Beef Industry Council to develop more favorable attitudes toward beef. Beef consumption had fallen steadily from a high of 94 pounds per capita in 1976 to about 75 pounds in 1985. At the same

This ad attempts to change the strength of consumer beliefs that beef is not as healthful as other meats such as chicken.

time, consumption of chicken rose from 43 to 70 pounds per capita. Consumers' attitudes also changed dramatically as the percentage of people who said they were meat lovers dropped from 22 percent in 1983 to only 10 percent in 1985. To weaken consumers' negative beliefs that beef is fattening and has high levels of cholesterol, TV and print ads claimed that three ounces of trimmed sirloin has about the same calories and cholesterol as three ounces of chicken breast. To strengthen consumers' beliefs that beef is healthful, charts displayed at many supermarket meat counters showed that the calorie and cholesterol levels for a cut of beef compared favorably with the dietary standards recommended by the American Heart Association.[35]

Also, marketers can try to change consumers' attitudes by *changing the evaluative aspect of an existing, strongly held belief* about a salient attribute. This requires constructing a new means-end chain by linking a more positive, higher-ordered consequence to that attribute. Cereal manufacturers such as Kellogg's have tried to enhance consumers' attitudes by linking the food attribute fiber to cancer prevention.

Consider how evaluations of beliefs about food attributes have changed (in the United States, at least) as their means-end meanings have changed.[36] Attributes such as butterfat and egg yolks once were evaluated highly because they gave foods a rich, satisfying taste. But by the late 1980s, they were becoming negative attributes, while attributes once seen as rather undesirable such as low fat (skim) milk were becoming more highly valued. For instance, Sealtest tried to link nonfat characteristics of "Sealtest Free" ice cream to important values such as health and fitness. Likewise, Kraft tried to link the key attributes of its fat-free line of salad dressings and mayonnaise (egg whites, skim milk, cellulose gel, and various gums) to important health consequences and values (lower risk of heart disease and longer life).

The final strategy for changing consumers' attitudes is to *make an existing favorable belief more salient*, usually by convincing consumers that the attribute is more self-relevant than it seemed. This strategy is similar to the previous one, in that it attempts to link the attribute to valued consequences and values. Creating such means-end chains increases both the salience of consumers' beliefs about the attribute as well as the evaluations (e_i) of those beliefs. For example, the marketing strategies of sun-care lotion manufacturers such as Bain de Soleil and Hawaiian Tropic emphasized the perceived risks of not using their products with a sunscreen attribute.[37] By linking the sunscreen attribute to important ends such as avoiding skin cancer and premature wrinkling, they sought to make the sunscreen attribute more salient (more self-relevant) for consumers. Such means-end chains should make sunscreen beliefs more likely to be activated and considered during decision making.

Attitudes toward Behavior

Consumers' attitudes have been studied intensively, but marketers tend to be more concerned about consumers' overt *behavior*, especially their purchase behavior. Thus, it is not surprising that a great deal of research has tried to establish the relationship between attitudes and behavior.[38] Based on the idea of consistency, attitudes toward an object (A_o) are usually expected to be related to behaviors toward the object. For instance, "most market researchers believe, and operate under the assumption, that the more favorable a person's attitude toward a given product (or brand), the more likely the person is to buy or use that product (or brand)."[39]

Thus, a marketing researcher might measure the attitudes of consumers toward Pizza Hut and use this to predict whether each person will purchase a pizza at Pizza Hut within the next month. If this approach seems reasonable, you may be surprised to learn that consumers' attitudes toward objects often are not good predictors of their specific behaviors regarding those objects. In fact, with a few notable exceptions, most research has found rather weak relationships between A_o and *specific* single behaviors.[40]

FIGURE 6.6

Relationships among Beliefs, Attitude, and Behaviors Regarding a Specific Object

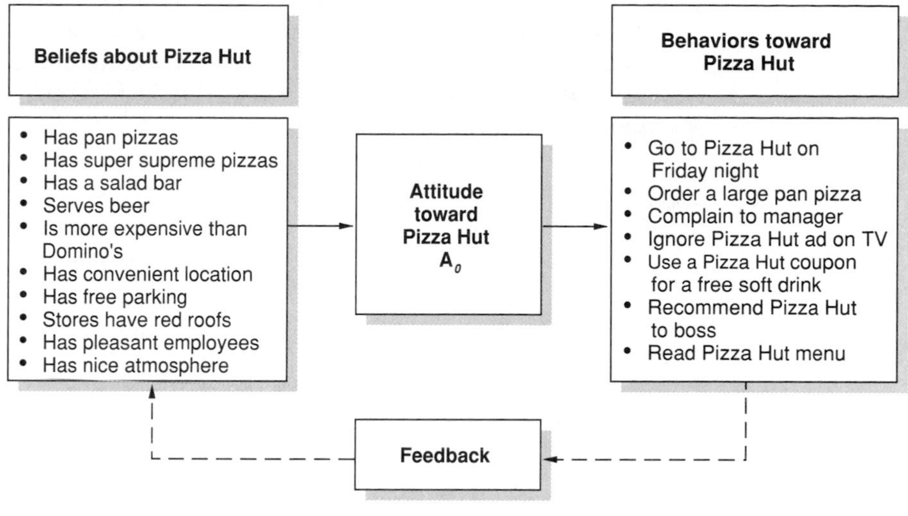

One of the problems with relating A_o to individual behaviors is illustrated in Figure 6.6. This figure presents the relationships among a consumer's beliefs, attitude, and behaviors concerning a particular object—Pizza Hut. First, note that Judy, our consumer, has a *single overall attitude* toward Pizza Hut (in her case, a favorable A_o), which is based on her salient beliefs about Pizza Hut. Second, note that Judy *can engage in many different behaviors* regarding Pizza Hut. For instance, she might go to Pizza Hut on Friday night and order a pizza, ignore a Pizza Hut ad on television, use a Pizza Hut coupon for a free soft drink, or recommend Pizza Hut to her boss. However, none of these specific behaviors is necessarily consistent with or strongly related to her overall A_o, although some of them might be.

This does not mean consumers' attitudes are irrelevant to their behaviors. As shown in Figure 6.6, Judy's overall attitude (A_o) is related to the overall pattern of her behaviors (all of her behaviors regarding Pizza Hut taken together). However, her overall attitude has no direct relationship with any single behavior.

Although this proposition may seem strange, there are many examples of its validity. Consider that many consumers probably have positive attitudes toward Porsche cars, Rolex watches, and vacation homes, but most do not buy these products. Because favorable attitudes toward these products can be expressed in many different behaviors, it is difficult to predict which specific behavior will be performed. Consider three consumers who have generally favorable attitudes toward Porsches. One consumer may read ads and test reports about Porsches.

Another consumer may go to showrooms to look at Porsches. A third consumer may just daydream about owning a Porsche. In sum, having a generally favorable (or unfavorable) attitude toward a product does not mean the consumer will perform every possible favorable (or unfavorable) behavior regarding that product. Marketers need a model that identifies the attitudinal factors that influence specific behaviors; such a model is available in Fishbein's theory of reasoned action.

THE THEORY OF REASONED ACTION

Fishbein recognized that people's attitudes toward an object may not be strongly or systematically related to their specific behaviors.[41] Rather, the immediate determinant of whether or not consumers will engage in a particular behavior is their *intention* to engage in that behavior. Fishbein modified and extended his multiattribute attitude model to relate consumers' beliefs and attitudes to their behavioral intentions. The entire model is presented in Figure 6.7.

The model is called a **theory of reasoned action** because it assumes consumers *consciously consider* the consequences of the alternative behaviors under consideration and choose the one that leads to the most desirable consequences.[42] The outcome of this reasoned choice process is an intention to engage in the selected behavior. This behavioral intention is the single best predictor of their actual behavior. In sum, the theory of reasoned action proposes that any reasonably complex, *voluntary* behavior (such as buying a pair of shoes) is determined by the person's *intention* to perform that behavior. The theory of reasoned action is not relevant for extremely simple or involuntary behaviors such as automatic eye blinking, turning your head at the sound of the telephone, or sneezing.

Formally, the theory of reasoned action can be presented as follows:

$$B \sim BI = A_{act}(w_1) + SN\,(w_2)$$

where

B = a specific behavior
BI = consumer's intention to engage in that behavior
A_{act} = consumer's attitude toward engaging in that behavior
SN = subjective norm regarding whether other people want the consumer to engage in that behavior
w_1 and w_2 = weights that reflect the relative influence of the A_{act} and SN components on BI

According to this theory, people tend to perform behaviors that are evaluated favorably and that are popular with other people. They tend to refrain from behaviors that are regarded unfavorably and that are unpopular with others.

FIGURE 6.7

The Theory of Reasoned Action

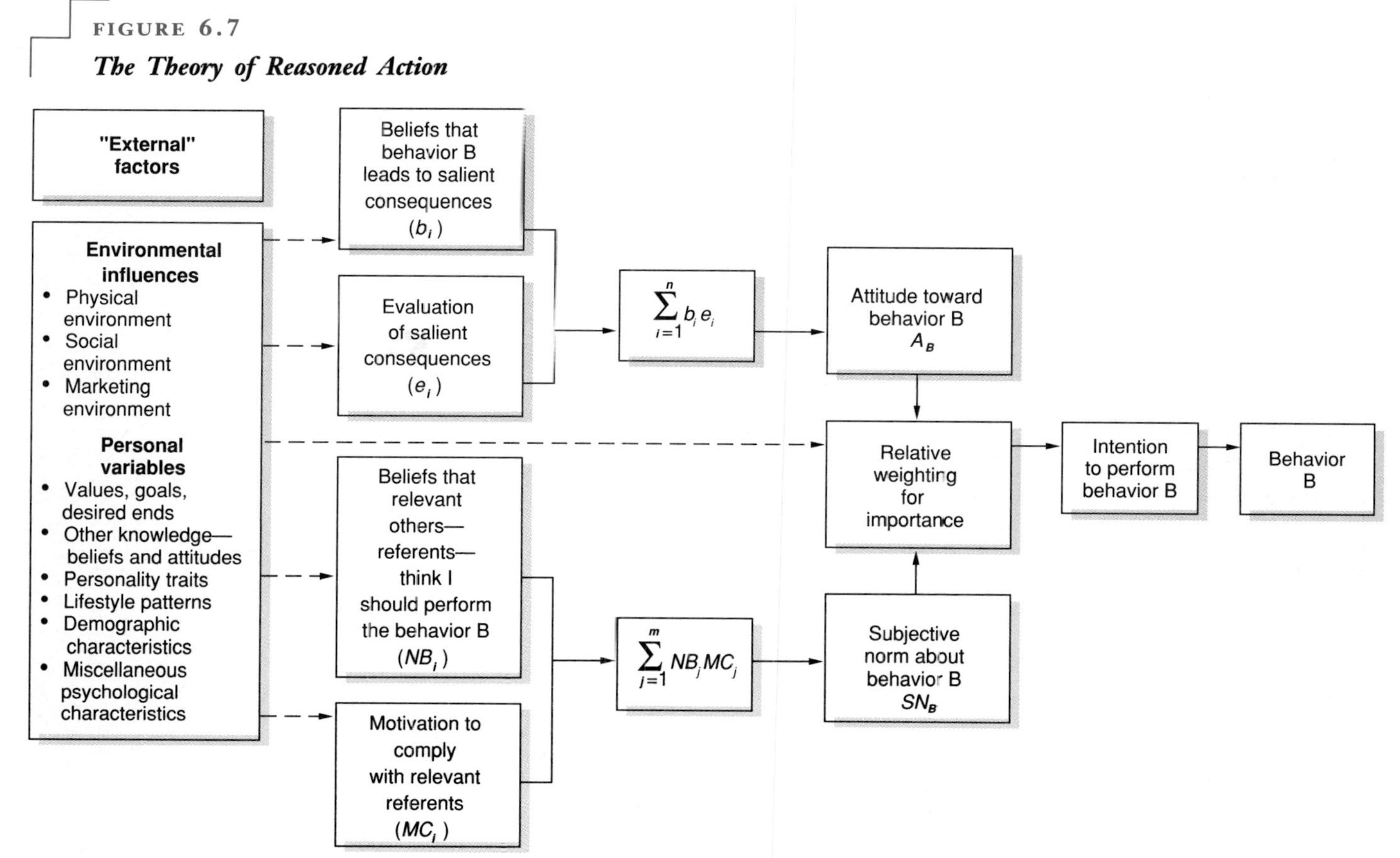

Source: Adapted from Martin Fishbein, "An Overview of the Attitude Construct," in *A Look Back, A Look Ahead,* ed. G. B. Hafer (Chicago: American Marketing Association, 1980), p. 8

Model Components

In this section, we describe and discuss each component of the theory of reasoned action, beginning with behavior.[43] Note that all the components of the model are defined in terms of a specific behavior, *B*.

Behaviors are specific actions directed at some target object (driving to the store, buying a swimsuit, looking for a lost Bic pen). Behaviors always occur in a situational context or environment and at a particular time (at home right now, in the grocery store this afternoon, or at an unspecified location in your town next week).[44] Marketers need to be clear about these aspects of the behavior of interest because the components of the theory of reasoned action must be defined and measured in terms of these specific features.

Basically, a **behavioral intention** is a proposition connecting self and a future action: "I intend to go shopping this Saturday." One can think of an intention as a *plan* to engage in a specified behavior in order to reach a goal.[45] Behavioral intentions are created through a choice/decision process in which beliefs about two types of consequences—A_{act} and SN—are considered and integrated to evaluate alternative behaviors and select among them. Behavioral intentions vary in strength, which can be measured by having consumers rate the probability that they will perform the behavior of interest, as shown below:

"All things considered, how likely are you to use newspaper coupons when buying groceries this week or next?"

Extremely Unlikely 1 2 3 4 5 6 7 8 9 10 Extremely Likely

As shown in Figure 6.7, the strengths and evaluations of a consumer's salient beliefs about the *functional consequences* of an action are combined ($\sum_{i=1}^{n} b_i e_i$) to form an **attitude toward the behavior or action (A_{act}).** A_{act} reflects the consumer's overall evaluation of performing the behavior. Marketers measure the strengths and evaluations of the salient beliefs about the consequences of a behavior in the same way that they measure beliefs about product attributes.

A_{act} is quite different from A_o. Although both attitudes are based on an underlying set of salient beliefs, the beliefs are about rather different concepts. For instance, consider the following salient beliefs about "Chevrolet" (an object) and "buying a new Chevrolet this year" (a specific action involving the object).

Chevrolet *(A_o)*	**Buying a new Chevrolet this year *(A_{act})***
Moderately priced (+)	Gives me a mode of transportation (+)
Ordinary (−)	Will put me in financial difficulty (−)
Well built (+)	Will lead to high upkeep costs (−)
Dependable (+)	Will cost more now than later (−)
Easily serviced (+)	Will lead to high insurance rates (−)

HIGHLIGHT 6.5

INCREASING A_{act} AND BEHAVIORAL INTENTIONS

Marketers of credit cards have a difficult marketing task to influence specific consumer behaviors. First, they have to get consumers to *accept* the cards; then they have to get consumers to *carry* and *use* the cards. According to the *Nilson Report*, a credit-card newsletter, the average cardholder carries about 7.5 pieces of plastic. Issuers can't make money on cards that aren't used – thus, they need strategies to make A_{act} and *BI* more positive.

Over the years, marketers have tried such inducements as free flight insurance when air travel is charged on an American Express card and discounts on merchandise that most consumers probably wouldn't buy anyway. Neither of these promotions was evaluated very highly, and card usage was not affected very much.

Then, in the mid-1980s, some credit-card marketers finally got serious and began giving away cold, hard cash as an incentive. If you used their card to charge lodging expenses, you could get a 10 percent cash refund. That's what the Bank of New York (TBNY) offered holders of its Visa and MasterCard credit cards. Consumers had to book (in advance) at least $150 worth of hotel expenses and send in a claim with a copy of the credit-card receipt.

Will this marketing strategy work? Well, note that TBNY's strategy adds a belief about a new consequence (getting money back) to the behavior they want consumers to perform more often – using the TBNY credit card. Of course, nearly everyone has a positive evaluation for receiving "free" money. Therefore, we would expect most consumers' attitudes toward using the TBNY card to become more favorable. This, in turn, should increase their intentions to use the card.

By 1990, more credit-card issuers, such as the Sears Discover card, offered cash rebates to consumers for using their card.

Source: Adapted from Mary Kuntz, "Credit Cards as Good as Gold," *Forbes,* November 4, 1985, pp. 234–36.

Note that these salient beliefs have quite different evaluations. Thus, we should not be surprised to find that some consumers like Chevrolet in general (A_o), but have negative attitudes toward buying a Chevrolet this year (A_{act}).

It is possible for marketing strategies to have a differential impact on A_o and A_{act}. For instance, one study found that information about the store where a new product was sold affected consumers' attitudes toward purchasing the product (A_{act}), but it did not influence their attitudes toward the product itself (A_o).[46] Marketers, therefore, must be careful to determine whether they are concerned with consumers' attitudes toward the object in general or some action regarding the object (such as buying it). Only attitudes toward behaviors are likely to be strongly related to specific behavioral intentions (see Highlight 6.5).

In addition, marketers must carefully identify the level of specificity most appropriate for the marketing problem. Attitudes at one level of specificity are not always consistently related to attitudes at other levels. For instance, Rick and Linda very much like to go shopping (a general behavior), yet they dislike shopping on Saturdays when the malls are crowded (a more specific behavior).

The **subjective or social norm *(SN)*** component reflects consumers' perceptions of what they think other people want them to do. Consumers' salient *normative beliefs* (NB_j) regarding "doing what other people want me to do" and their *motivation to comply* with the expectations of these other people (MC_j) are combined $(\sum_{j=1}^{m} NB_j\, MC_j)$ to form *SN*. Along with A_{act}, *SN* affects consumers' behavioral intentions *(BI)*.[47]

Measuring the strength of normative beliefs is similar to the belief-strength measures discussed earlier.

"Members of my family are in favor of my using coupons."

Extremely Unlikely 1 2 3 4 5 6 7 Extremely Likely

Motivation to comply is measured by asking consumers to rate how much they want to conform to other people's desires.

"Generally, how much do you want to do what your family wants you to?"

Not at All −3 −2 −1 0 +1 +2 +3 Very Much

The theory of reasoned action proposes that A_{act} and *SN* combine to affect behavioral intentions *(BI)*, and that their relative influence varies from situation to situation. During the information integration process that creates *BI*, A_{act} and *SN* may be weighed differently (see Figure 6.7).[48] Some behaviors are primarily affected by the *SN* factor. For instance, intentions to wear a certain style of clothing to a party or to work are likely to be influenced more strongly by *SN* and the normative beliefs regarding conformity than beliefs about the general consequences of wearing those clothes (A_{act}).[49] For other behaviors, normative influences are minimal, and consumers' intentions are largely determined by A_{act}. For instance, consumers' intentions to purchase Contac cold remedy are more likely to be affected by their salient beliefs about the functional consequences of using Contac and the resulting attitude toward buying it than by what other people expect them to do.

Marketing Implications

The situational context in which behavior occurs can have powerful influences on consumers' behavioral intentions. Consider a consumer named Brian, a 26-year-old assistant brand manager for General Foods. Last week, Brian had to decide whether to buy imported or domestic beer in two different situations. In the first situation, Brian was planning to drink a few beers at home over the weekend while watching sports on TV. In the other context, he was having a beer after work in a plush bar with a group of his co-workers. The different sets of product-related and social beliefs activated in the two situations created different A_{act} and SN components. In the private at-home situation, Brian's product beliefs and A_{act} had the dominant effect on his intentions (he bought an inexpensive domestic beer). In the highly social bar situation, his normative beliefs and SN had the greater impact on his intentions (he bought an expensive imported beer).

To develop effective strategies, it is important to determine whether the A_{act} or SN component has the major influence on behavioral intentions (and thus on behavior). If the primary reason for a behavior (shopping, searching for information, buying a particular brand) is normative (you think others want you to), marketers need to emphasize that the relevant normative influences (friends, family, co-workers) are in favor of the behavior. Often this is done by portraying social influence situations in advertising. On the other hand, if intentions are largely influenced by A_{act} factors, the marketing strategy should attempt to create a set of salient beliefs about the positive consequences of the behavior, perhaps by demonstrating those outcomes in an advertisement. In sum, the theory of reasoned action identifies the types of cognitive and affective factors that underlie a consumer's intention to perform a specific behavior.

Although intentions determine most voluntary behaviors, measures of consumers' intentions may not be perfect indicators of the actual intentions that determine the behavior. In the following section, we discuss the problems of using intention measures to predict actual behaviors.

Intentions and Behaviors

Predicting consumers' future behaviors, especially their purchase behavior (sales, to marketers), is a critically important aspect of forecasting and marketing planning. According to the theory of reasoned action, predicting consumers' purchase behaviors is a matter of measuring their intentions to buy just before they make a purchase. In almost all cases, however, this would be impractical. When planning strategies, marketers need predictions of consumers' purchase and use behaviors weeks, months, or sometimes years in advance.

Unfortunately, predictions of specific behaviors based on intentions measured well before the behavior occurs may not be very accurate. For instance, one survey found that only about 60 percent of people who intended to buy a car actually did so within a year.[50] And of those who claimed they did not intend to buy a car, 17 percent ended up buying one. Similar examples could be cited for other product categories (many with even worse accuracy). This does not mean the theory of reasoned action is wrong in identifying intentions as an immediate influence on behavior. Rather, failures to predict the behavior of interest often lie with *how* and *when* intentions are measured.

FIGURE 6.8

Factors that Reduce or Weaken the Relationship between Measured Behavioral Intentions and Observed Behavior

Factor	Examples
Intervening time	As the time between measurement of intentions and observation of behavior increases, more factors can occur that act to modify or change the original intention, so that it no longer corresponds to the observed behavior.
Different levels of specificity	The measured intention should be specified at the same level as the observed behavior, otherwise the relationship between them will be weakened. Suppose we measured Judy's intentions to wear jeans to class (in general). But we observed her behavior on a day when she made a class presentation and didn't think jeans were appropriate in that specific situation.
Unforeseen environmental event	Sam fully intended to buy Frito's chips this afternoon, but the store was sold out. Sam could not carry out the original intention and had to form a new intention on the spot to buy Ripple chips.
Unforeseen situational context	Sometimes the situational context the consumer had in mind when the intentions were measured was different from the situation at the time of behavior. In general, Peter has a negative intention to buy Andre champagne. However, when he had to prepare a holiday punch calling for eight bottles of champagne, Peter formed a positive intention to buy the inexpensive Andre brand.
Degree of voluntary control	Some behaviors are not under complete volitional control. Thus, intentions may not predict the observed behavior very accurately. For instance, Becky intended to go shopping on Saturday when she hoped to be recovered from a bout with the flu, but she was still sick and couldn't go.
Stability of intentions	Some intentions are quite stable. They are based on a well-developed structure of salient beliefs for A_{act} and *SN*. Other intentions are not stable, as they are founded on only a few weakly held beliefs that may be easily changed.
New information	Consumers may receive new information about the salient consequences of their behavior, which leads to changes in their beliefs and attitudes toward the act and/or in the subjective norm. These changes, in turn, change the intention. The original intention is no longer relevant to the behavior and does not predict the eventual behavior accurately.

Figure 6.8 lists several factors that can weaken the relationship between measured behavioral intentions and the observed behaviors of interest. In situations where few of these factors operate, measured intentions should predict behavior quite well.

To accurately predict behaviors, marketers should measure consumers' intentions at the same level of abstraction and specificity as the action, target, and time components of the behavior. Situation context also should be specified, when it is important.

In a broad sense, *time* is the major factor that reduces the predictive accuracy of measured intentions. Intentions, like other cognitive factors, can and do change over time. The longer the intervening time period, the more unanticipated circumstances (such as exposure to the marketing strategies of competitive companies) can occur and change consumers' original purchase intentions. Thus, marketers must expect lower levels of predictive accuracy when intentions are measured long before the behavior occurs. However, unanticipated events can also occur during very short periods. An appliance manufacturer once asked consumers entering an appliance store what brand they intended to buy. Of those who specified a brand, only 20 percent came out with it.[51] Apparently, events occurred in the store to change these consumers' beliefs, attitudes, intentions, and behavior.

Despite their less-than-perfect accuracy, measures of purchase intentions are often the best way to predict future purchase behavior. For instance, every three months, United Air Lines conducts a passenger survey measuring intentions to travel by air during the next three months. Obviously, many events in the ensuing time period can change consumers' beliefs, A_{act} and *SN* about taking a personal or business trip by airplane. To the extent that these unanticipated factors occur, the measured intentions will give less accurate predictions of future airline travel.

Certain behaviors cannot be accurately predicted from beliefs, attitudes, and intentions.[52] Obvious examples include nonvoluntary behaviors such as sneezing or getting sick. It is also difficult to predict purchase behaviors when the alternatives (brands) are very similar and the person has positive attitudes toward several of them. Finally, behaviors about which consumers have little knowledge and low levels of felt involvement are virtually impossible to predict because consumers have very few beliefs in memory on which to base attitudes and intentions. In such cases, consumers' measured intentions were probably created to answer the marketing researcher's question—such intentions are likely to be unstable and poor predictors of eventual, actual behavior. In sum, before relying on measures of attitude and intentions to predict future behavior, marketers need to determine whether consumers can reasonably be expected to have well-formed beliefs, attitudes, and intentions toward those behaviors.

BACK TO.... *JAGUAR*

The Jaguar example illustrates how consumer attitudes can be used to help develop and evaluate marketing strategies. Measures of A_o (attitudes toward Jaguar) and the related salient beliefs can be useful as diagnostic indicators of consumers' overall feelings about the company and its products. Such data can identify problem areas needing attention. For instance, the problems facing Jaguar were reflected by negative consumer beliefs and attitudes. The underlying beliefs, especially the negative beliefs about poor product quality and shoddy dealer service, suggested actions the company could take to increase the favorability of consumers' attitudes toward Jaguar cars.

Measures of beliefs and attitudes can also be used to gauge the success of marketing strategies in solving a problem. For example, Jaguar commissioned a three-year study to track changes in consumers' beliefs and attitudes toward the car and its dealers. Also, marketers could segment consumers in terms of their attitudes and beliefs.

It is important to recognize that this example dealt primarily with A_o. To predict specific behaviors of consumers (Jaguar owners or potential owners), the company would have had to measure consumers' A_{act} and *SN* concerning the behavior of interest, as well as their behavioral intentions.

SUMMARY

We began this chapter by defining attitude as a consumer's overall evaluation of an object. We discussed how attitude objects varied in levels of abstraction and specificity. We then discussed consumers' attitudes toward objects, A_o, and described Fishbein's multiattribute model of how salient beliefs create A_o. We also discussed the theory of reasoned action that identifies consumers' attitudes toward performing behaviors (A_{act}) and social influences *(SN)* as the basis for behavioral intentions *(BI)*. Finally, we considered the problems of using measures of behavioral intentions to predict actual behaviors. Throughout, we discussed implications for marketers. In this chapter, we identified consumers' activated knowledge, in the form of beliefs, as the basic factor underlying their attitudes, subjective norms, and intentions—and ultimately, their behaviors. Moreover, we showed that these activated salient beliefs, and the resulting attitudes and intentions, are sensitive to situational factors in the environment, including marketing strategies. This provides another example of how cognition, environment, and behavior interact in a continuous, reciprocal process to create new behaviors, new cognitions (beliefs, attitudes and intentions), and new environments.

Key Terms and Concepts

Review and Discussion Questions

1. Define *attitude* and identify the two main ways that consumers can acquire attitudes.
2. How are salient beliefs different from other beliefs? How can marketers attempt to influence belief salience?
3. Discuss the integration process of forming an attitude according to Fishbein's multiattribute attitude model?
4. Consider a product category in which you make regular purchases (such as toothpaste or shampoo). How have your belief strengths and evaluations, and brand attitudes, changed over time?
5. Using an example, describe the key differences between A_o and A_{act}. Under what circumstances would marketers be most interested in each type of attitude?

6. Describe the theory of reasoned action and discuss the two main factors that are integrated to form a behavioral intention. Describe one marketing strategy implication for each factor.

7. Use the example of Jaguar to distinguish between the multiattribute attitude model and the theory of reasoned action. How could each model contribute to the development of a more effective marketing strategy for Jaguar?

8. Discuss the problems in measuring behavioral intentions to (*a*) buy a new car; (*b*) buy a soda from a vending machine; and (*c*) save $250 per month toward the eventual purchase of a house. What factors could occur in each situation to make the measured intentions a poor predictor of actual behavior?

9. How could marketers improve their predictions of behaviors in the situations described in Question 8? Consider improvements in measurements as well as alternate research or forecasting techniques.

10. Negative attitudes present a special challenge for marketing strategy. Consider how what you know about attitudes and intentions could help you to address consumers who have a brand relationship described as "Don't like our brand and buy a competitor's brand."

NOTES

1. Martin Fishbein and Icek Ajzen, *Belief, Attitude, Intention and Behavior: An Introduction to Theory and Research* (Reading, Mass.: Addison-Wesley, 1975), p. 2.

2. Martin Fishbein, "Attitude, Attitude Change, and Behavior: A Theoretical Overview," in *Attitude Research Bridges the Atlantic*, ed. Phillip Levine (Chicago: American Marketing Association, 1975), pp. 3–16.

3. Many authors have defined attitudes in this way, including Russell H. Fazio, "How Do Attitudes Guide Behavior?" in *Handbook of Motivation and Cognition: Foundations of Social Behavior*, ed. R. M. Sorrentino and E. T. Higgins (New York: Guiford Press, 1986), pp. 204–43.

4. Fishbein and Ajzen, *Belief, Attitude, Intention and Behavior*, Andrew A. Mitchell and Jerry C. Olson, "Are Product Attributes the Only Mediator of Advertising Effects on Brand Attitude?" *Journal of Marketing Research*, August 1981, pp. 318-32; Richard E. Petty and John T. Cacioppo, "Central and Peripheral Routes to Advertising Effectiveness: The Moderating Role of Involvement," *Journal of Consumer Research*, September 1983, pp. 135–46; and Danny L. Moore and J. Wesley Hutchinson, "The Influence of Affective Reactions to Advertising: Direct and Indirect Mechanisms of Attitude Change," in *Psychological Processes and Advertising Effects: Theory, Research, and Application*, ed. L. F. Alwitt and A. A. Mitchell (Hillsdale, N.J.: Lawrence Erlbaum, 1985), pp. 65–87.

5. For an excellent overview, see Elenora W. Stuart, Terence A. Shimp, and Randall W. Engle, "Classical Conditioning of Consumer Attitudes: Four Experiments in an Advertising Context," *Journal of Consumer Research*, December 1987, pp. 334–49; also see Chris T. Allen and Thomas J. Madden, "A Closer Look at Classical Conditioning," *Journal of Consumer Research*, December 1985, pp. 301–15; and Terence A. Shimp, Elnora W. Stuart, and Randall W. Engle, "A Program of Classical Condi-

tioning Experiments Testing Variations in the Conditioned Stimulus and Context," *Journal of Consumer Research*, June 1991, pp. 1–12.

6. Alain d'Astous and Marc Dubuc, "Retrieval Processes in Consumer Evaluative Judgment Making: The Role of Elaborative Processing," in *Advances in Consumer Research*, vol. 13, ed. Richard J. Lutz (Provo, Utah: Association for Consumer Research, 1986), pp. 132–37; and Paul W. Miniard, Thomas J. Page, April Atwood, and Randall L. Ross, "Representing Attitude Structure Issues and Evidence," in *Advances in Consumer Research*, vol. 13, ed. Richard J. Lutz (Provo, Utah: Association for Consumer Research, 1986), pp. 72–76.
7. Russell H. Fazio, Martha C. Powell, and Carol J. Williams, "The Role of Attitude Accessibility in the Attitude-to-Behavior Process," *Journal of Consumer Research*, December 1989, pp. 280–88; and Ida E. Berger and Andrew A. Mitchell, "The Effect of Advertising on Attitude Accessibility, Attitude Confidence, and the Attitude-Behavior Relationship," *Journal of Consumer Research*, December 1989, pp. 269–79.
8. Peter H. Farquhar, "Managing Brand Equity," *Marketing Research*, September 1989, pp. 24–33.
9. For instance, see Joan Myers-Levy, "Priming Effects on Product Judgments: A Hemispheric Interpretation," *Journal of Consumer Research*, June 1989, pp. 76–86.
10. Kenneth E. Miller and James L. Ginter, "An Investigation of Situational Variation in Brand Choice Behavior and Attitude," *Journal of Marketing Research*, February 1979, pp. 111–23.
11. Farquhar, "Managing Brand Equity."
12. Norman C. Berry, "Revitalizing Brands," *Journal of Consumer Marketing*, Summer 1988, pp. 15–20.
13. Farquhar, "Managing Brand Equity."
14. Ibid.
15. David M. Boush and Barbara Loken, "A Process-Tracing Study of Brand Extension Evaluation," *Journal of Marketing Research*, February 1991, pp. 16–28.
16. C. Whan Park, Sandra Milberg, and Robert Lawson, "Evaluation of Brand Extensions: The Role of Product Feature Similarity and Brand Concept Consistency," *Journal of Consumer Research*, September 1991, pp. 185–93.
17. This example is adapted from John Merwin, "The Sad Case of the Dwindling Orange Roofs," *Forbes*, December 30, 1985, pp. 75–79.
18. Fishbein and Ajzen, *Belief, Attitude, Intention, and Behavior;* Mitchell and Olson, "Are Product Attributes the Only Mediators of Advertising Effects on Brand Attitude?"
19. Susan B. Hester and Mary Yuen, "The influence of Country of Origin on Consumer Attitudes and Buying Behavior in the United States and Canada," in *Advances in Consumer Research*, vol. 14, ed. Melanie Wallendorf and Paul Anderson (Provo, Utah: Association for Consumer Research, 1987), pp. 538–42; and Sung-Tai Hong and Robert S. Wyer, "Determinants of Product Evaluation: Effects of the Time Interval between Knowledge of a Product's Country of Origin and Information about its Specific Attributes," *Journal of Consumer Research*, December 1990, pp. 277–88.
20. William B. Dodds, Kent B. Monroe, and Dhruv Grewal, "Effects of Price, Brand, and Store Information on Buyer's Product Evaluations," *Journal of Marketing Research*, August 1991, pp. 307–19; Meryl P. Gardner, "Advertising Effects on Attributes Recalled and Criteria Used for Brand Evaluations," *Journal of Consumer Research*, December 1983, pp. 310–18; and Richard Paul Hinkle, "Medals from Wine Competitions Win Sales," *Advertising Age*, January 31, 1985, p. 31.
21. Kenneth E. Miller and James L. Ginter, "An Investigation of Situational Variation in Brand Choice Behavior and Attitude," *Journal of Marketing Research*, February 1979, pp. 111–23.
22. See William L. Wilkie and Edgar A. Pessemier, "Issues in Marketing's Use of Multiattribute Attitude Models," *Journal of Marketing Research*, November 1973, pp. 428–41. However, relatively little work has investigated the integration process itself—see Joel B. Cohen, Paul W. Min-

iard, and Peter R. Dickson, "Information Integration: An Information Processing Perspective," in *Advances in Consumer Research*, vol. 11, ed. Thomas C. Kinnear (Ann Arbor, Mich.: Association for Consumer Research, 1980), pp. 161–70. Another influential model, particularly in the early days of marketing research on attitudes, was developed by Milton J. Rosenberg, "Cognitive Structure and Attitudinal Affect," *Journal of Abnormal and Social Psychology*, November 1956, pp. 367–72. Although different terminology is used, the structure of Rosenberg's model is quite similar to Fishbein's.

23. Fishbein and Ajzen. *Belief, Attitude, Intention and Behavior.*

24. See Phillip A. Dover and Jerry C. Olson, "Dynamic Changes in an Expectancy-Value Attitude Model as a Function of Multiple Exposures to Product Information," in *Contemporary Marketing Thought*, ed. B. A. Greenberg and D. N. Dellenger (Chicago: American Marketing Association, 1977), pp. 455–59; Robert E. Smith and William R. Swinyard, "Information Response Models: An Integrated Approach," *Journal of Marketing*, Winter 1982, pp. 81–93; and Russell H. Fazio and Mark P. Zanna, "Attitudinal Qualities Relating to the Strength of the Attitude-Behavior Relationship," *Journal of Experimental Social Psychology*, vol. 14, 1987, pp. 398–408.

25. Fishbein and Ajzen, *Belief, Attitude, Intention and Behavior.*

26. Richard J. Lutz, "The Role of Attitude Theory in Marketing," in *Perspectives in Consumer Behavior*, ed. H. H. Kassarjian and T. S. Robertson (Glenview, Ill.: Scott, Foresman, 1981), pp. 233–50; an early discussion of this idea was provided by James M. Carmen, "Values and Consumption Patterns: A Closed Loop," in *Advances in Consumer Research*, vol. 5, ed. H. Keith Hunt (Ann Arbor, Mich.: Association for Consumer Research, 1978), pp. 403–07; and Jonathan Gutman, "Exploring the Nature of Linkages between Consequences and Values," *Journal of Business Research* (1991), pp. 143–48.

27. Jerry C. Olson and Phillip A. Dover, "Attitude Maturation: Changes in Related Belief Structures over Time," in *Advances in Consumer Research*, vol. 5, ed. H. Keith Hunt (Ann Arbor, Mich.: Association for Consumer Research, 1978), pp. 333–42.

28. Richard J. Lutz and James R. Bettman, "Multiattribute Models in Marketing: A Bicentennial Review," in *Consumer and Industrial Buying Behavior*, ed. A. G. Woodside, J. N. Sheth, and P. D. Bennett (New York: Elsevier-North Holland Publishing, 1977), pp. 137–50.

29. Monci Jo Williams, "Why is Airline Food So Terrible?" *Fortune*, December 19, 1988, pp. 169–72.

30. Christopher Power, Walecia Konrad, Alice Z. Cuneo, and James B. Treece, "Value Marketing: Quality, Service, and Fair Pricing Are the Keys to Selling in the '90s," *Business Week*, November 11, 1991, pp. 132–40.

31. John B. Palmer and Russ H. Crupnick, "New Dimensions Added to Conjoint Analysis," *Marketing News*, January 3, 1986, p. 62.

32. Richard J. Lutz, "Changing Brand Attitudes through Modification of Cognitive Structure," *Journal of Consumer Research*, March 1975, pp. 49–59; and Andrew A. Mitchell, "The Effect of Verbal and Visual Components of Advertisements on Brand Attitudes and Attitude toward the Advertisement," *Journal of Consumer Research*, June 1986, pp. 12–24.

33. Keith H. Hammonds, " 'Has-Beens' Have Been Very Good to Hasbro," *Business Week*, August 5, 1991, pp. 76–77.

34. Sanford Grossbart, Jim Gill, and Russ Laczniak, "Influence of Brand Commitment and Claim Strategy on Consumer Attitudes," in *Advances in Consumer Research*, vol. 14, ed. Melanie Wallendorf and Paul Anderson (Provo, Utah: Association for Consumer Research, 1987), pp. 510–13.

35. This example is adapted from Edward C. Baig, "Trying to Make Beef Appetizing Again," *Fortune*, November 25, 1985, p. 64.

36. Frank Rose, "If It Feels Good, It Must Be Bad," *Fortune*, October 21, 1991, pp. 91–108.

37. Kathleen Deveny, "Seeking Sunnier Sales, Lotion Makers Play on Fears, Target Teens and

Men," *The Wall Street Journal*, May 24, 1991, pp. B1, B3.

38. See, for example, James Jaccard and Grant Wood, "An Idiothetic Analysis of Attitude-Behavior Models," in *Advances in Consumer Research*, vol. 13, ed. Richard J. Lutz (Provo, Utah: Association for Consumer Research, 1986), pp. 600–5.

39. Martin Fishbein, "An Overview of the Attitude Construct," in *A Look Back, A Look Ahead*," ed. G. B. Hafer (Chicago: American Marketing Association, 1980), p. 3.

40. See Icek Ajzen and Martin Fishbein, "Attitude-Behavior Relations: A Theoretical Analysis and Review of Empirical Research," *Psychological Bulletin*, September 1977, pp. 888–918; and Alan W. Wicker, "Attitudes versus Action: The Relationship of Verbal and Overt Behavioral Responses to Attitude Objects," *Journal of Social Issues* 25 (1969), pp. 41–78, among others.

41. See Fishbein, "An Overview of the Attitude Construct," pp. 1–19; and Fishbein and Ajzen, *Belief, Attitude, Intentions and Behavior*.

42. Icek Ajzen and Martin Fishbein, *Understanding Attitudes and Predicting Social Behavior* (Englewood Cliffs, N.J.: Prentice Hall, 1980); and Fishbein and Ajzen, *Belief, Attitude, Intention and Behavior*. Note that this notion is consistent with our means-end chain conceptualization of consumers' product knowledge.

43. For a detailed exposition, see Terence A. Shimp and Alican Kavas, "The Theory of Reasoned Action Applied to Coupon Usage," *Journal of Consumer Research*, December 1984, pp. 795–809.

44. Ajzen and Fishbein, "Attitude-Behavior Relations: A Theoretical Analysis and Review of Empiral Research," pp. 888–918.

45. Richard P. Baggozzi and Paul R. Warshaw, "Trying to Consume," *Journal of Consumer Research*, September 1990, pp. 127–40.

46. Barbara Loken, "Effects of Uniquely Purchase Information on Attitudes toward Objects and Attitudes toward Behaviors," in *Advances in Consumer Research*, vol. 10, ed. R. P. Bagozzi and A. M. Tybout (Ann Arbor, Mich.: Association for Consumer Research, 1983), pp. 88–93.

47. Some researchers have argued that the strong distinction between A_{act} and *SN* may not be justified. See articles by Paul W. Miniard and Joel B. Cohen, "Isolating Attitudinal and Normative Influences in Behavioral Intentions Models," *Journal of Marketing Research*, February 1979, pp. 102–10; and Paul W. Miniard and Joel B. Cohen, "An Examination of the Fishbein-Ajzen Behavioral Intentions Model's Concepts and Measures," *Journal of Experimental Social Psychology* 17 (1981), pp. 309–39. Also see Ryan (1982) in the Additional Reading section at the end of the chapter. Alternatively, the underlying salient beliefs for both A_{act} and *SN* could be considered as one set of activated beliefs that are combined to form a single, global A_{act}. One version of such a model was proposed by Paul W. Miniard and Joel B. Cohen, "Modeling Personal and Normative Influences on Behavior," *Journal of Consumer Research*, September 1983, pp. 169–80. For simplicity, however, we will follow the separate approach advocated by the theory of reasoned action.

48. Pat McIntyre, Mark A. Barnett, Richard Harris, James Shanteau, John Skowronski, and Michael Klassen, "Psychological Factors Influencing Decisions to Donate Organs," in *Advances in Consumer Research*, vol. 14, ed. Melanie Wallendorf and Paul Anderson (Provo, Utah: Association for Consumer Research, 1987), pp. 331–34.

49. William O. Bearden and Randall L. Rose, "Attention to Social Comparison Information: An Individual Difference Factor Affecting Consumer Conformity," *Journal of Consumer Research*, March 1990, pp. 461–71.

50. Cited in Kenneth A. Longman, "Promises, Promises," in *Attitude Research on the Rocks*, ed. L. Adler and L. Crespi (Chicago: American Marketing Association, 1968), pp. 28–37.

51. Longman, "Promises, Promises," pp. 28–37.

52. For an interesting discussion of this issue, see Gordon R. Foxall, "Consumers' Intentions and Behavior: A Note on Research and a Challenge to Researchers," *Journal of Market Research Society* 26 (1985), pp. 231–41.

Additional Reading

For a thorough review of alternative approaches to attitudes, including a discussion of measuring attitudes and intentions, see:

Petty, Richard E., and John T. Cacioppo. *Attitudes and Persuasion: Classic and Contemporary Approaches.* Dubuque, Iowa: William C. Brown, 1981.

For a discussion of conscious and unconscious processes of attitude formation, see:

Janiszewski, Chris. "Preconscious Processing Effects: The Independence of Attitude Formation and Conscious Thought." *Journal of Consumer Research,* September 1988, pp. 199–209.

For a practical application of multiattribute attitude models, see:

Belch, George E., and Michael A. Belch. "The Application of an Expectancy-Value Operationalization of Functional Theory to Examine Attitudes of Boycotters and Nonboycotters of a Consumer Product." In *Advances in Consumer Research,* vol. 14, ed. M. Wallendorf and P. Anderson, Provo, Utah: Association for Consumer Research, 1987, pp. 232–36.

For a discussion of the integration process in attitude formation, see:

Kahn, Barbara E., and Robert J. Meyer. "Consumer Multiattribute Judgments under Attribute-Weight Uncertainty." *Journal of Consumer Research,* March 1991, pp. 508–22.

Minard, Paul W., Sunil Bhatla, and Randall L. Rose. "On the Formation and Relationship of Ad and Brand Attitudes: An Experimental and Causal Analysis." *Journal of Marketing Research,* August 1990, pp. 290–303.

For a discussion of how product knowledge (salient beliefs) can affect attitudes, see:

Sujan, Mita. "Consumer Knowledge: Effects on Evaluation Strategies Mediating Consumer Judgments." *Journal of Consumer Research,* June 1985, pp. 31–46.

For examples of the difficulty of relating attitudes toward objects (A_o) to specific behaviors, see:

Wells, William D. "Attitudes and Behavior: Lessons from the Needham Life Style Study." *Journal of Advertising Research,* February 1985, pp. 40–44.

For a discussion of the different effects of A_{act} and *SN* on behavioral intentions, see:

Ryan, Michael J. "Behavioral Intention Formation: The Interdependency of Attitudinal and Social Influence Variables." *Journal of Consumer Research,* December 1982, pp. 263–78.

For a discussion of the difficulties of relating measures of behavioral intention to actual behaviors, see:

Belk, Russell. "Theoretical Issues in the Intention/Behavior Discrepancy." In *Research in Consumer Behavior,* vol. 1, ed. Jagdish N. Sheth. Greenwich, Conn.: JAI Press, 1985, pp. 1–34.

Jamieson, Linda F., and Frank M. Bass. "Adjusting Stated Intention Measures to Predict Trial Purchase of New Products: A Comparison of Models and Methods." *Journal of Marketing Research,* August 1989, pp. 336–45.

MARKETING STRATEGY IN ACTION

Coca-Cola

The past 15 years or so have seen tumultuous changes in the soft-drink industry. After years of slow growth and little product innovation in the 1970s, the 1980s were full of activity. No company exemplifies these changes more than the Coca-Cola Company.

For most of its 100-year history, Coca-Cola has dominated the soft-drink business, largely through sheer size rather than savvy marketing. But Coke's complacency vanished in 1977 when Pepsi Co's brand, Pepsi Cola, threatened to become the market leader and take over Coke's cherished role as the top brand in food store sales. Since then, Coke has responded with a number of marketing strategies, including some that would have been unthinkable a few years earlier. In the process, the company learned something about American consumers' brand attitudes toward Coke.

In July 1982, Coca-Cola management did the unthinkable: it introduced a diet cola and called it Diet Coke. This was the first time in history that the company had allowed the world's best known trademark to be put on a product other than the flagship Coca-Cola brand. Despite management's doubts, Diet Coke was extremely successful. By 1984, it had become the third best-selling soft drink in the United States, displacing 7UP. Then, in quick succession, Coca-Cola introduced decaffeinated versions of Coke, Diet Coke, and Tab.

But these earlier decisions were soon to be overshadowed by another controversial marketing strategy. In the spring of 1985, Chairman Roberto Goizueta announced introduction of a new Coca-Cola with an improved taste. The 99-year-old secret formula for the original Coke with a secret ingredient (called Merchandise 7X, it was developed by John Styth Pemberton, an Atlanta pharmacist, in a 30-gallon brass kettle in his backyard) was to be locked in a bank vault in Atlanta, never to be used again. The new formula, with ingredient 7X-100, was to replace the old Coca-Cola. Goizueta called the new product "the most significant soft-drink development in the company's history."

Americans got their first taste of the new Coke in late April 1985. In July, less than three months later, the company had reversed its earlier decision. A rather chagrined management announced the old Coke was coming back under the label Coca-Cola Classic. What happened to Coca-Cola was a classic lesson in consumers' brand attitudes. Some critics thought Coca-Cola had made a giant marketing mistake, and some cynics thought the company had planned the whole thing for publicity value. According to Donald Keough, president of Coca-Cola, "The truth is that we are not that dumb and we are not that smart."

Those positive attitudes and beliefs that keep customers buying the same brand over and over again are sometimes called *brand loyalty.* Brand loyalty is an elusive concept. It begins with the customers' positive attitudes and preferences for a brand based on "objective" beliefs about product attributes—the drink is sweeter or more carbonated. The brand name guarantees that the customer will receive the same expected attributes and benefits from each product use. But once a product has been around for a while, it can accumulate "extra" emotionally laden meanings and beliefs. Some brands may become linked to consumers' lifestyles and self-images. For example, many consumers associated Coke with fond memories of days gone by.

Apparently these strong affective beliefs about Coke were activated when Coca-Cola announced the old "friend" was gone forever. Consumers inundated Coca-Cola's Atlanta headquarters with protests. A group of brand loyalists in Seattle threatened to sue the company. And when June sales didn't pick up as expected, the independent bottlers demanded to have the old Coca-Cola back.

Interestingly, the decision to retire the old Coke formula was not a casual one. It had been very carefully researched, and managers thought they had covered every angle. For instance, Coca-Cola spent over $4 million on many different taste tests of the new flavor, involving over 200,000 consumers in some 25 cities. These tests revealed more people liked the new, sweeter flavor than the old (about 55 percent to 45 percent). But apparently this research didn't measure everything. "All the time and money and skill poured into consumer research on the new Coca-Cola could not measure or reveal the deep and abiding emotional attachment to original Coca-Cola," Keough said later.

It is true that understanding consumers' brand loyalties and product attitudes can be difficult. According to John O'Toole, past chairman of Chicago advertising agency Foote, Cone & Belding, one reason is that "you can't get at people's private motivations. In any kind of interview or questionnaire, they want to seem sensible and prudent. They aren't going to tell you how they feel."

A variety of different types of beliefs, not all of them about product attributes, may be salient influences on attitudes. Consumers' attitudes toward the new and old Cokes included more than just their taste and mouth feel—the factors measured in the extensive taste tests. As a company spokesperson said, "We had taken away more than the product Coca-Cola. We had taken away a little part of them and their past. They said, 'You have no right to do that. Bring it back.' " So Coca-Cola did.

Then what happened? When the old Coke returned in the summer of 1985, consumers found six models of Coke on the supermarket shelf—(new) Coke, Coca-Cola Classic, Caffeine-Free Coke, Diet Coke, Caffeine-Free Diet Coke, and Cherry Coke. In 1980, there had been only one brand, Coca-Cola. Some marketing experts thought the company would have a tough time keeping a clear identity for the different brands in consumers' minds. But Roberto Goizueta considered the lineup to be a "megabrand" and a marketing plus.

One advantage of the brand-name proliferation involves the environment of the supermarket shelf. Having six different brand models gives a company a lot more shelf facings, a great advantage in this market. In addition, it may be possible for consumers to have positive attitudes and be loyal to more than one brand in a product class. The phenomenon, known as ***brand-cluster loyalty*** or ***multibrand loyalty***, may be more common than we realize.

Discussion Questions

1. Discuss the concept of brand loyalty in terms of consumers' attitudes (both A_o and A_{act}) and purchase intentions. Do you think it is possible for consumers to be loyal to more than one brand of soft drink?
2. How do you think attitudes (and underlying belief structures) differed between the intensely loyal and the less involved consumers?
3. Is it possible for positive attitudes from one

brand to be transferred to a different, but related, brand, perhaps with the same name? What aspects of attitude theory would help marketers develop strategies to do this?

4. According to Morgan Hunter of Marketing Corporation of America, a Connecticut marketing firm, "It is important not to confuse a stated preference with what consumers actually do when they're in the store. They may not actually buy the brand they say they prefer." Do you agree? Justify your position in terms of the theoretical relationships between consumers' attitudes, purchase intentions, and actual behaviors.

Sources: Anne B. Fisher, "Coke's Brand-Loyalty Lesson," *Fortune,* August 5, 1985, pp. 44–46; Carrie Gottlieb, "Products of the Year," *Fortune,* December 9, 1985, pp. 106–12; and Thomas Moore, "He Put the Kick Back into Coke," *Fortune,* October 26, 1987, pp. 46–56.

Consumer Decision Making

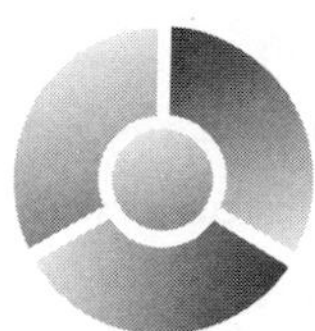

CHAPTER 7

BUYING A SET OF DISHES

In mid-September, Barbara decided to host a dinner party for 10 people on October 17. She immediately called and invited all the guests. But now she had a problem: she didn't have enough dishes to serve 10 people. Actually Barbara had two sets of dishes—Wedgwood stoneware and Lenox china—but several pieces of the stoneware had broken over the years, and she only had seven place settings of the china. Barbara decided she had to buy some new dishes. Given her budget restrictions, Barbara decided to replace the missing pieces of stoneware, as she thought the stoneware would be less expensive than the china.

That Friday, Barbara called several department stores, only to discover that none of them had her pattern in stock. In fact, they said it would take from two to six months to get the dishes, and that Wedgwood would probably discontinue the pattern soon. Barbara decided to order the stoneware and borrow dishes for the party. First, though, she would check with her husband.

Barbara's husband was not very enthusiastic. He thought replacing the stoneware might be more expensive than buying a complete set of new dishes, especially with the sales at the department stores; and he noted that a six-month wait was also a high cost. Besides, their old stoneware was chipped and scratched. But

Barbara argued that at the sale prices, it might be better to replace the missing stoneware or to add three place settings to the china. Barbara developed a complex plan to take all of these factors into consideration. She decided that if finishing her set of china cost $200 or less than the stoneware replacements, she would buy three place settings of china. If a new set of stoneware cost $100 or less than replacing the missing stoneware, she would buy the new set of stoneware dishes. But if these two alternative actions were more expensive, she would order the replacement pieces for her Wedgwood stoneware.

When she called stores to check sale prices, Barbara learned that the sales offered 25 percent off all dishes in stock. She also learned that one store was selling a service for eight of Chinese porcelain for $100. At that price, she could buy two sets (a service for 16) for less than any of her other options would cost. She decided to buy the Chinese porcelain, if she liked it.

On Saturday morning, Barbara's mother-in-law called, and Barbara reviewed the situation with her. Barbara's mother-in-law said to forget the Chinese porcelain because it is too fragile—either bone china or stoneware is much stronger. She also told Barbara about a factory outlet that had a large inventory and very low prices, but she had forgotten the name. Barbara decided to go back to her previous plan, but to check out the factory outlet, too.

Barbara began to visit department stores. She learned from one salesperson that porcelain and bone china are equally strong and both are stronger than stoneware. She also discovered that ordering the replacement Wedgwood would cost several hundred dollars and could take up to 12 months. Barbara saw an Imari stoneware pattern she liked that was on sale and within her budget. She decided to check with the factory outlet to see whether it had the Imari pattern, because she might be able to save a lot of money buying at the

outlet. If the price was low enough, it might be worth the hour and a half round-trip drive.

Barbara found the number of the outlet and called it. She learned it did not have the Imari pattern in stock, and an order would take two months. However, it did have a large number of other patterns. Although the outlet could not quote prices over the phone, Barbara was told that many people drive a considerable distance to shop there. Now, Barbara was in a quandary. She could probably save considerable money by going to the outlet, but it was a long drive and she couldn't go until the weekend. But by then the department store might be sold out of the Imari pattern she liked. And there was a chance that she wouldn't find anything she liked at the outlet. However, the outlet did have a large inventory, so she probably would find an acceptable pattern. Barbara decided to check out the Chinese porcelain and buy it if she liked it. Otherwise, she would drive to the outlet on the weekend and buy something.

On Wednesday, Barbara went to the department store to examine the Chinese porcelain. Although it was pretty, it only came in a delicate flower pattern, which she did not like. She decided to drive to the outlet right away. If it didn't have anything she liked, she could go back to the department store and buy the Imari pattern.

Barbara drove 45 minutes to the outlet. It had a huge inventory at much lower prices than the department store. However, none of the stoneware had the Oriental pattern she wanted. So she telephoned the department store to see whether it still had the Imari pattern. It did, but it didn't have 10 place settings left. Perhaps this disappointment led Barbara to ask once again if the outlet had the Imari pattern. She was surprised to find that it did have the pattern in stock, and even better, it was on sale for 25 percent off the already low price. Unfortunately, the dishes were at the warehouse and couldn't be picked up for 7 to 10 days. Barbara was pleased to find a

complete set of the dishes she liked best at an acceptable price. Her only worry was that the dinner party was exactly 10 days away. She decided to order the Imari dishes and take the chance that they would be there on time. (They were . . . and the dinner party was a great success.)

Source: Adapted from Barbara Hayes-Roth, "Opportunism in Consumer Behavior," in *Advances in Consumer Research,* vol. 9, ed. Andrew A. Mitchell (Ann Arbor, Mich.: Association for Consumer Research, 1982), pp. 132–135.

This example describes a complex decision-making process that includes several decisions. A **decision** involves a choice "between two or more alternative actions [or behaviors]."[1] *Decisions always require choices between different behaviors.* For instance, after examining the products in a vending machine, Joe chose a Snickers candy bar instead of a package of Reese's Pieces. His choice was really between the alternative actions of *buying Snickers* versus *buying Reeses' Pieces.* Jill is trying to decide whether to see a particular movie. Her choice is really between the set of behaviors involved in *attending the movie* versus the behaviors involved in *staying home* (or going bowling, or whatever behavioral alternatives she was considering). In sum, even though marketers often refer to choices between objects (products, brands, or stores), consumers actually are choosing between alternative *behaviors* that concern those objects.

Marketers are particularly interested in consumers' *purchase behaviors,* especially their choices of which brands to buy. Given the marketing orientation of this text, we emphasize consumers' purchase choices ("Should I buy Levi's or Lee jeans?"). It must be recognized, however, that consumers also make many decisions about nonpurchase behaviors. Sometimes these nonpurchase choices can influence consumers' brand purchase decisions (deciding to go for a walk or watch TV may expose consumers to marketing stimuli). Some of these other behaviors are the targets of marketing strategies—"Come down to our store this afternoon for free coffee and donuts." Our analyses of purchase decisions can be generalized to these nonpurchase choices.

As shown in our model of consumer decision making in Figure 7.1, all aspects of affect and cognition are involved in consumer decision making, including the knowledge, meanings, and beliefs activated from memory, and the attention and comprehension processes involved in interpreting new information in the environment.[2] However, the essence of **consumer decision making**

FIGURE 7.1
A Cognitive Processing Model of Consumer Decision Making

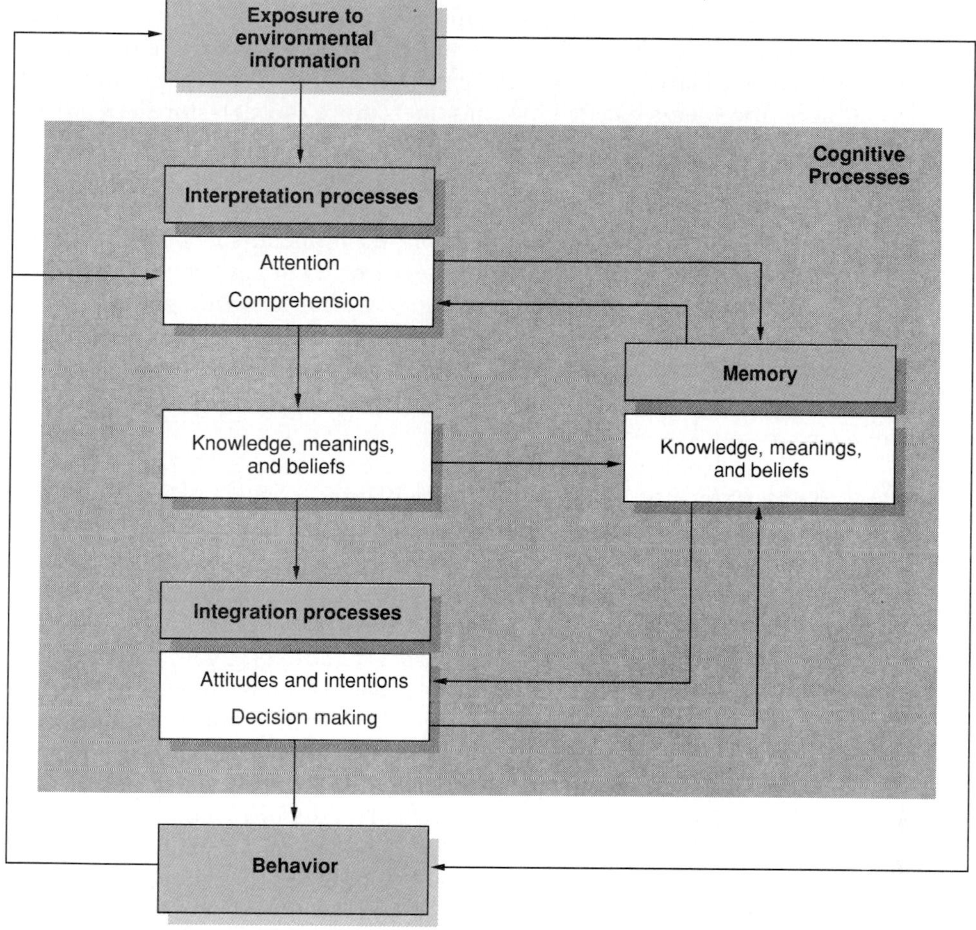

is the *integration process* by which knowledge is combined to *evaluate* two or more alternative behaviors and *select* one.[3] The outcome of this integration process is a **choice,** which is represented cognitively as a *behavioral intention (BI).* As you learned in the previous chapter, a behavioral intention is a *plan* (sometimes called a *decision plan)* to engage in some behavior.

We assume all voluntary behaviors are based on the intentions produced when consumers consciously choose from among alternative actions. However, a conscious decision-making process does not necessarily occur each time such behaviors are performed.[4] Some voluntary behaviors have become habitual. They are based on intentions stored in memory that were produced by a past decision-making process. When activated, these previously formed intentions or decision plans automatically influence behavior; additional decision-making processes may not be necessary. Finally, some behaviors are not voluntary and are affected largely by environmental factors. For instance, product displays and aisle placements dictate how consumers move through stores. Decision making is not relevant in such cases.

In this chapter, we view consumer decision making as a problem-solving process. We begin with a general discussion of this perspective. Then, we identify and describe the key elements in a problem-solving approach. Next, we discuss the problem-solving processes involved in purchase decisions. We identify three levels of problem-solving effort and describe several influences on problem-solving activities. We conclude by identifying several implications of consumer problem solving for marketing strategy.

Decision Making as Problem Solving

In treating consumer decision making as problem solving, we assume consumers have goals (desired consequences or values in a means-end chain) that they seek to achieve or satisfy. A consumer perceives a "problem" because the desired consequences have not been attained ("I am hungry. I need a new, reliable car. I want to lose weight."). Consumers make decisions about which behaviors to perform to achieve their goals and thus "solve the problem." In this sense, then, *consumer decision making is a goal-directed, problem-solving process.*

As the opening example illustrates, consumer problem solving is actually a seamless, continuous flow of reciprocal interactions among environmental factors, cognitive and affective processes, and behavioral actions. Researchers can divide this stream into separate stages and subprocesses to simplify analysis and facilitate understanding. Figure 7.2 presents a generic model of **problem solving** that identifies five basic stages or processes. The first stage involves *problem recognition.* In the opening example, Barbara's plan to host a dinner party made her aware of a problem — she needed a set of dishes or 10 people. The next stage of the problem-solving process involves *searching for alternative solutions.*[5] (Barbara called and visited stores, talked to salespeople, and discussed the purchase with her mother-in-law.) At the next stage, *alternatives are evaluated* and the most desirable action is *chosen.* (Barbara evaluated dishes as she found them during her search. In the end, she decided — formed a behavioral intention — to buy the Imari pattern at the factory outlet.) In the next stage, *purchase,* the choice/intention is carried out. (Barbara ordered the dishes and then returned a few days later to pay for them and pick them up.) Finally, the purchased product is *used,* and the consumer may *reevaluate* the wisdom of the decision. (Apparently

FIGURE 7.2
A Generic Model of Consumer Problem Solving

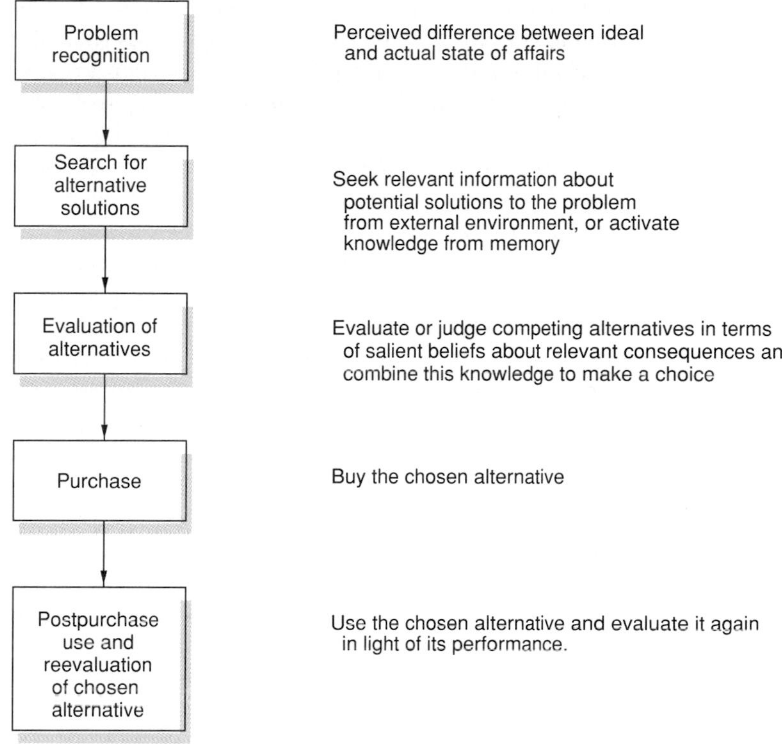

Source: There are many sources for this general model. See James Engel and Roger D. Blackwell, *Consumer Behavior,* 4th ed. (Hinsdale, Ill.: Dryden Press, 1982).

Barbara was quite satisfied with the dishes and with her problem-solving process.)

This basic model identifies several important activities involved in problem solving—activating the initial motivation to engage in problem solving, searching for information relevant to the problem, evaluating alternative actions, and choosing an action. However, for several reasons, the generic model often cannot account for actual problem-solving processes such as those in the opening example.

One reason is that *actual consumer problem-solving seldom proceeds in the linear sequence* portrayed in the generic model. For instance, Barbara evaluated alternative dishes as soon as she found them; she did not wait until all alternatives had been found.

Second, as emphasized in our Wheel of Consumer Analysis (refer to Figure 2.3), *actual problem-solving processes involve multiple, reciprocal interactions among consumers' cognitive processes, their behaviors, and aspects of the physical and social environment.*[6] Reciprocal interactions occurred throughout Barbara's problem-solving process. For instance, her cognitions (beliefs) changed as a function of environmental factors her behaviors led her to: first her mother-in-law said Chinese porcelain is fragile, but later a salesperson said it is quite strong. These complex interactions are not easily handled by the generic model.

Third, *most problem-solving processes actually involve multiple problems and multiple decisions.* Consider the number of separate decisions Barbara made during the two weeks of her problem-solving process: Should I go to the department store? Should I drive to the factory outlet? When should I go? Should I get the Chinese porcelain? Actual problem-solving processes usually involve several choices that produce multiple behavioral intentions. Each intention is a step in an overall decision plan. A decision plan, in turn, produces a sequence of purposive behaviors that consumers perform to achieve their desired consequences, values, and goals (go to the department store, find the dishes section, look at Chinese porcelain). The generic model implies that consumer problem solving involves one decision, typically brand choice, which is seldom the case.

Our cognitive processing model of consumer decision making, shown in Figure 7.1, is flexible enough to account for the nonlinear flow; for the reciprocal interactions among behaviors, environments, and cognitions; and for the multiple decisions that occur in actual consumer problem-solving episodes. Moreover, it can incorporate the important problem-solving stages of problem recognition, search for information, and evaluation of alternatives. Before using this model to analyze actual consumer decisions, however, we must discuss the special concepts or elements involved in problem solving.

Elements of Problem Solving

In this section, we describe three basic elements of problem solving: problem representation, integration processes, and decision plans. Later, we discuss how they operate in consumer decision making.

Problem Representation

When faced with a choice, consumers form cognitive representations of various aspects of the decision problem. This **problem representation** may include (1) an end goal, (2) a set of subgoals organized into a goal hierarchy, (3) relevant product knowledge, and (4) a set of simple rules or heuristics by which consumers search for, evaluate, and integrate this knowledge to make a choice. A problem representation serves as a *decision frame*—a perspective, or frame of

This ad links the product/service to a positive end goal.

reference through which the decision maker views the problem and the alternatives to be evaluated.[7]

Often, consumers' initial problem representations are not clear or well developed (Barbara's wasn't). Neither are they fixed. In fact, the elements of a problem representation often change during the decision-making process, as was true in the opening example. Marketers sometimes try to influence how consumers represent or frame a purchase choice.[8] For instance, consumers might be portrayed in advertisements as representing and then trying to solve a purchase problem in a particular way. Salespeople also try to influence consumers' problem representations by suggesting end goals (buy life insurance to insure your children's college educations), imparting product knowledge (this special flash eliminates red eyes in the pictures), or suggesting choice rules (the more expensive coat is of higher quality).

The basic consequences, needs, or values that consumers want to achieve or satisfy are called **end goals.** They provide the focus for the entire problem-solving process. Some end goals represent more concrete, tangible consequences; other end goals are more abstract. For instance, a purchase decision to replace a bulb for a flashlight probably involves the simple end goal of obtaining a bulb that lights up — a simple functional consequence. Other product choices involve more abstract end goals such as desired psychosocial consequences of a product — some consumers want to serve a wine that indicates their good taste to their guests. Finally, end goals such as instrumental and terminal values are even more abstract and general—consumers might choose a car that makes them happy or enhances their self-esteem. End goals also vary in evaluation. Some consumer decisions are oriented toward positive, desirable end goals, while others are focused on negative end goals—aversive consequences the consumer wishes to avoid.

Some end goals (e.g., being happy) are so general and broad that they cannot be directly acted on by consumers. For instance, most consumers cannot specify the decision plan of specific actions that will yield the best brand of calculator or avoid a "lemon" of a car. When consumers try to solve problems involving abstract end goals, they break down the general goal into several more specific subgoals. The end goal and its subgoals are a **goal hierarchy.** Forming a goal hierarchy is analogous to decomposing a complex problem into a series of simpler subproblems, each of which can be dealt with separately. For instance, buying a new car requires at least one trip to a showroom, creating the subproblems of which dealer(s) to visit and when to go shopping. The consumer can solve the overall problem by solving the simpler subproblems, in order.

Consumers' **relevant knowledge** in memory about the choice domain is an important element in problem solving.[9] Some knowledge may be acquired by interpreting information encountered in the environment during the problem-solving process. For instance, in the opening example, Barbara learned a lot about porcelain, factory locations, and price ranges for dishes. Other relevant knowledge may be activated from memory for use in integration processes.[10] The relevance of knowledge is determined by its means-end linkages to the currently active end goal. Parts of the activated knowledge may be combined in the integration processes by which consumers evaluate alternative behaviors (form A_{act}) and choose among them (form *BI*). Two types of knowledge are particularly important in problem solving—choice alternatives and choice criteria.

The alternative behaviors that consumers consider in the problem-solving process are called **choice alternatives.** For purchase decisions, the choice alternatives are the different product classes, product forms, brands, or models the consumer considers buying. For other types of decisions, the choice alternatives might be different stores to visit, times of the day or week to go shopping, or methods of payment (cash, check, or credit card). Given their limited time, energy, and cognitive capacity, consumers seldom consider every possible choice alternative. Usually, only a subset of all possible alternatives—called the **consideration set**—is evaluated.

Figure 7.3 illustrates how a manageable consideration set of brands can be constructed during the problem-solving process.[11] Some of the brands in the consideration set may be activated directly from memory—this group is called the *evoked set.*[12] For highly familiar decisions, consumers may not consider any brands beyond those in the evoked set. If consumers are confident they already know the important choice alternatives, they are not likely to search for additional ones. In other decisions, choice alternatives may be found through

Wal-Mart's low-price strategy plus strict cost controls have been a major factor in the chain's continuing success.
Chapter 19

Courtesy Wal-Mart

Sometimes it is possible to reach new market segments with an established product by promoting new uses.
Chapter 16

Courtesy Pillsbury Co.

Sometimes it takes just a slight twist to make a product seem new and exciting.
Chapter 18

Courtesy Claritas Corporation

Viable markets can be relatively constant, such as geographical segments . . .

. . . or relatively transient, such as the market of recent college graduates.
Chapter 16

Courtesy Toyota Motor Sales, U.S.A.

Courtesy Gucci Timepieces

Ads for luxury products often evoke a strong mood . . .

. . . while athletic equipment is often marketed with an emphasis on the emotion the consumer wants to achieve.
Chapter 18

Courtesy Champion U.S.A.

FIGURE 7.3
Forming a Consideration Set of Brand Choice Alternatives

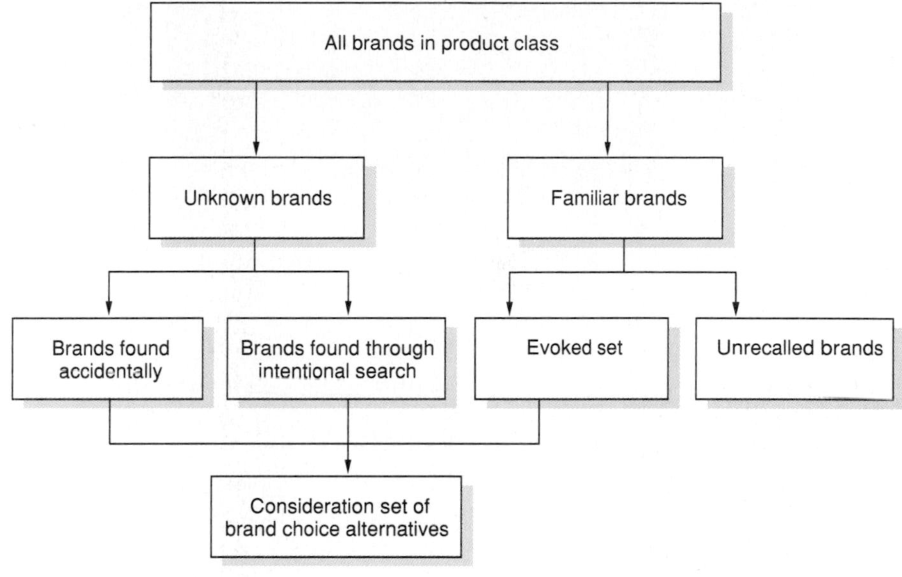

intentional search activities such as reading *Consumer Reports*, talking to knowledgeable friends, or finding brands while shopping.[13] Finally, consumers may learn of still other choice alternatives through accidental exposures to information in the environment, such as overhearing a conversation about a new brand, new store, or sale. In the opening case, Barbara learned about the factory outlet from her mother-in-law, essentially by accident. However the choice alternatives are generated, they form a *consideration set* of possible purchase options to be evaluated in the decision-making process.

To be successful, a brand must be included in the consideration sets of at least some consumers. Marketers, therefore, develop strategies to increase the likelihood that a brand will be activated from consumers' memories and included in their evoked sets of choice alternatives. The activation potential of a brand, sometimes called its *top-of-mind awareness*, is influenced by many factors. One is the amount of past purchase and use experience consumers have had with the brand. Consumers are much more likely to think of (activate) brands that they have used before. For this reason, popular brands with higher market shares have a distinct advantage. Because they are used by more consumers, these brands are more likely to be activated in evoked sets and included in more consumers' consideration sets.[14] This increases the brands' probability of purchase, which, in turn, increases its activation potential, and so on. In contrast, unfamiliar and low-market-share brands are at a disadvantage as they are much

A simple ad to increase top-of-mind awareness and introduce the brand into consumers' evoked sets.

less likely to be included in consumers' evoked sets and thereby be considered as choice alternatives.

One marketing strategy to increase the activation potential of a brand is the repetitive and costly advertising campaigns devised by marketers of cigarettes, beer, soft drinks, and toothpaste (among others).[15] The heavy expenditures may be worth it, because brands with high top-of-mind awareness are more likely to be included in the evoked set of choice alternatives that "come to mind" during problem-solving processes.

Finally, a company's distribution strategy can influence whether a brand is in the consideration sets. Consider food products, where an estimated 65 percent of decisions are made in the store. A key marketing strategy for such products is making sure the product is on the shelf. This enhances the likelihood that consumers will encounter the brand at the time of the decision, which increases its chances of entering consumers' consideration sets.

As we described in Chapter 6, consumers' evaluations of the choice alternatives in the consideration set are based on their beliefs about the consequences of buying those products or brands. The specific consequences that are used to evaluate and choose among choice alternatives are called **choice criteria.** Virtually any type of product-related consequence can become a choice criterion in a brand-choice decision, including salient beliefs about functional consequences

This ad emphasizes a key choice criterion for most purchasers of snack products—taste.

(product performance), psychosocial consequences (admiration of friends), or value consequences (a sense of achievement or self-esteem).[16] Consumers probably have beliefs stored in memory about some of the relevant consequences of at least some of the choice alternatives in the consideration set. If additional knowledge is desired, consumers may form the subgoal of obtaining information about those choice alternatives. Achieving this subgoal may require intentional search behaviors such as visiting stores, reading *Consumer Reports*, and talking with knowledgeable friends. Information search may be motivated by consumers' uncertainty about appropriate choice criteria and/or choice alternatives.[17] In the opening case, Barbara engaged in a substantial amount of intentional search to identify possible choice alternatives and form beliefs about appropriate choice criteria.

The probability that product knowledge is activated and used in the evaluation process is highly influenced by the means-end relevance of that knowledge to the goal or subgoal being considered.[18] For instance, if the dominant end goal is self-esteem, then beliefs about product consequences that are perceived as helping to achieve self-esteem are most likely to be used as choice criteria. Differences in the purchase context such as buying a sweater for yourself versus buying one as a gift may activate different end goals (being perceived as stylish versus being perceived as generous). These end goals, in turn, may activate different choice criteria (fashionable design versus looks like it cost a lot).

As we discussed in earlier chapters, marketers often place prominent stimuli in the immediate decision environment to activate certain choice criteria from consumers' memories. For instance, special price tags activate beliefs about price consequences (saving money). Prominent labels on food packages, such as "sugar-free" or "low sodium," enhance the likelihood that the consequences associated with those attributes are used as choice criteria. Finally, salespeople often emphasize certain product benefits in their sales pitches, which increases the likelihood that beliefs about those consequences are used as choice criteria.

Not every activated belief about product or brand consequences is necessarily used as a choice criterion. Only *discriminant consequences*—consequences that are perceived to differ across choice alternatives—can be used as choice criteria.[19] Beliefs about common or very similar consequences of the choice alternatives do not discriminate between alternative actions. To present an obvious example, if all the soft drinks in a vending machine contain caffeine, the consequences of caffeine (stimulation—"I get a lift") cannot be used as a choice criterion for deciding which brand to buy. However, if a different set of choice alternatives (brands that vary in caffeine content) is being considered, caffeine content might be a choice criterion. This is an important point. The choice criteria that are relevant (activated) for a decision depend, in part, on the particular set of choice alternatives under consideration.[20]

Consumers' choice criteria also vary in evaluation. Some choice criteria are perceived as positive, desirable consequences and elicit positive affective responses. Other choice criteria, such as price, may be thought about in negative terms, as unpleasant consequences or perceived risks to be avoided.[21] To avoid rejection, marketers may try to reduce perceived risk by assuring consumers of product quality or by offering warranties and guarantees (see Highlight 7.1).[22] Choice alternatives perceived to have negative consequences tend to be rejected, unless they also have several positive consequences. For example, during the 1980s, many Americans acquired a negative choice criterion for soft drinks—caffeine content. The popularity of this choice criterion was influenced by basic changes in societal values about health and by 7UP's no-caffeine marketing strategy launched in 1982—"Never had it, never will." Eventually, other soft-drink manufacturers responded to consumers' increasing use of this negative choice criterion by introducing their own brands of caffeine-free soft drinks.[23] Consumers who perceive that a choice involves both positive and negative consequences may be motivated to search for information to resolve the conflict between benefits and the risks of the decision.[24]

HIGHLIGHT 7.1

Marketing Strategies Directed at the Negative Consequences of Price

Shopping by mail from catalogs is perceived by many consumers as a risky undertaking. Direct-mail marketers, therefore, try to reduce this risk by giving consumers various guarantees. A common strategy is to offer consumers their "money back with no questions asked." Thus, no financial loss can be incurred (other than postage expenses).

The Performance Bicycle Shop, a mail-order company selling high quality bicycle components, has a somewhat unusual price strategy to give consumers confidence that they are getting the best deal, a powerful desired consequence for many consumers. This pricing strategy has the added advantage of building shopping loyalty toward the catalog company.

Performance Price Protection Guarantee

We at Performance work hard to provide you with the best values in the cycling market combined with excellent service and the best guarantee you can get on the cycling products you purchase—The "Performance 100% Guarantee."

Occasionally, another company may offer a special sale price on an item which is lower than our current catalog price. The Performance Price Protection Guarantee allows you to buy now from one source the cycling products you want, with the assurance that you received the best value.

This is how the Performance Price Protection Guarantee works: If there is a current nationally advertised special price on the same item you want and you are shopping by telephone, just tell the operator when you are ordering the price and the source where the special is printed. If ordering by mail, send a copy of the ad with your order. This becomes your new Performance Price. That is all there is to it, no more inconvenience of filling out multiple orders or paying multiple shipping charges. And of course, rather than having a limited or no guarantee on these items, you will have bought with the confidence of the "Performance 100% Guarantee"—if any item does not meet your expectations, just send it back for a complete refund, exchange or credit—your choice. You cannot get a better guarantee on the cycling products you buy. Combined with the Performance Price Protection Guarantee, you can shop in complete confidence that you're getting the best value for your money.

(Courtesy Performance Bicycle Shop)

Integration Processes

The integration processes involved in problem solving perform two essential tasks: the choice alternatives must be evaluated in terms of the choice criteria,

Marketers may try to reduce the perceived risk of purchase by offering warranties to protect consumers against unpleasant consequences.

and then one of the alternatives must be chosen.[25] Two types of integration procedures have been proposed to account for these evaluation and choice processes: formal integration strategies and simpler procedures called *heuristics*.

Figure 7.4 presents several formal models of the integration processes involved in evaluating and choosing among choice alternatives. The key distinction is between compensatory and noncompensatory strategies.

Compensatory integration processes combine all the salient beliefs about the consequences of the choice alternatives to form an overall evaluation or attitude (A_{act}) toward each behavioral alternative. The multiattribute attitude model $(A_{act} = \Sigma\, b_i e_i)$ is a compensatory model, so-called because a negative consequence (expensive) can be compensated for or balanced by a positive consequence (high status). It is important to recognize that consumers do not necessarily integrate large numbers of beliefs in their evaluation processes. In fact, given their limited cognitive capacity, the number of choice criteria con-

FIGURE 7.4
Formal Models of Consumer Integration Processes

Process	Description
Compensatory processes	
Multiattribute model	A perceived weakness or negative evaluation on one criterion can be compensated for by a positive evaluation on another criterion. Separate evaluations for each choice criterion are combined (added or averaged) to form overall evaluation of each alternative. Then highest-rated alternative is chosen.
Noncompensatory processes	
Conjunctive	Consumer establishes a minimum acceptable level for each choice criterion. Accept an alternative only if every criterion equals or exceeds the minimum cutoff level.
Disjunctive	Consumer establishes acceptable standards for each criterion. A product is acceptable if it exceeds the minimum level on at least one criterion.
Lexicographic	Consumer ranks choice criteria from most to least important. Choose the best alternative on the most important criterion. If tie occurs, select best alternative on second most important criterion, and so on.
Elimination by aspects	Consumer establishes minimum cutoffs for each choice criterion. Select one criterion and eliminate all alternatives that do not exceed the cutoff level. Continue eliminating alternatives until one alternative remains. Choose it.
Combination processes	Mix of compensatory and noncompensatory processes, combined or "constructed" on the spot to adapt to environmental factors.

Source: Adapted from James R. Bettman, *An Information Processing Theory of Consumer Choice,* © 1979, Addison-Wesley Publishing Co., Inc. Reading, Massachusetts. Reprinted with permission of the publisher.

sumers can consider at one time may be quite restricted, perhaps as few as one or two. Although the multiattribute attitude model accounts for how the choice alternatives are evaluated, it does not specify how the consumer chooses which behavior to perform. Most marketers assume consumers select the alternative with the most positive A_{act}. Other *choice rules* are possible, however. For instance, consumers might choose the first alternative they find with a positive A_{act}.

Several types of **noncompensatory integration processes** are also described in Figure 7.4. They are noncompensatory because the salient beliefs about the positive and negative consequences of the choice alternatives do not balance or compensate for each other. For example, applying the *conjunctive* choice rule requires that an alternative be rejected if any *one* of its consequences does not surpass a minimum threshold level of acceptability. Thus, Edie might reject a particular model of Reebok aerobic shoe if it had one negative consequence (too expensive), even though it had several other positive consequences (good support, comfortable, stylish colors). As another example, applying a *lexicographic* integration strategy might require a consideration of only one choice criterion, which makes a compensatory process impossible. Tina might evaluate a pair of dress shoes favorably and buy them because they were superior to the other alternatives on the most important consequence (the color matched her outfit exactly), while other, even unfavorable consequences were not considered (not durable and slightly uncomfortable).

Research suggests consumers do not seem to follow any single rule or strategy in evaluating and choosing from among alternatives.[26] For one thing, they probably do not have sufficient cognitive capacity to simultaneously integrate several beliefs about many alternatives. Compensatory integration processes are especially likely to exceed cognitive capacity limits.[27] Moreover, many problem-solving tasks do not involve a single choice to which a single integration rule could be applied. Instead, consumers make multiple choices in most purchase situations (choices of information sources to examine, stores to visit, product forms or brands to buy, methods of payment). Each choice is a separate subproblem that requires separate integration processes.

Rather than a single integration strategy, consumers are likely to use a combination of processes in many problem-solving situations.[28] A noncompensatory strategy might be used to quickly reduce the choice alternatives to a manageable number by rejecting those that lack one or two key criteria (a conjunctive strategy). For example, Bill might reject all restaurants that do not have a salad bar. Then the remaining brands in his consideration set (perhaps only two or three restaurants) could be evaluated on several choice criteria (price level, variety, atmosphere) using a more strenuous compensatory strategy.

Another issue is: Do consumers have complete integration rules stored in memory ready to be activated and applied to the relevant product beliefs? Current research suggests instead that most integration processes are *constructed* at the time they are needed, to fit the current situation. This suggests that rather than following fixed strategies, consumers' integration processes are relatively simple, very flexible, and easily adapted to varying decision situations.[29] These simple integration "rules" are called heuristics.

Basically, **heuristics** are simple "if . . . , then . . ." productions that connect an event with an appropriate action. Because they are applied to only a few bits and pieces of knowledge at a time, heuristics are highly adaptive to specific environmental situations and are not likely to exceed cognitive capacity limits.[30] Heuristics may be stored in memory like miniature scripts that are applied fairly

An attempt to create a search heuristic: Shop at True-Value hardware stores.

automatically to information encountered in the environment. Or they may be constructed on the spot in response to the immediate environment.

Figure 7.5 presents examples of three types of heuristics that are particularly important in problem-solving. *Search heuristics* are simple procedures for seeking information relevant to a goal. Some consumers have a simple search rule for buying any small durable product such as a radio or a kitchen appliance – read the product tests in *Consumer Reports*. *Evaluation heuristics* are procedures for evaluating and weighting beliefs in terms of the current goal being addressed in the problem-solving process. Dieting consumers may have a heuristic that identifies the most important choice criteria for food – low calories and the resulting consequence of losing weight. *Choice heuristics* are simple procedures for comparing evaluations of alternative actions in order to choose one. A simple choice heuristic is to select the alternative you bought last time, if it was satisfactory.

Decision Plans

The process of identifying, evaluating, and choosing among alternatives during problem solving produces a **decision plan** made up of one or more behavioral intentions. Decision plans vary in their specificity and complexity.[31] Specific

FIGURE 7.5

Examples of Consumer Heuristics

Search heuristics	Examples
Store selection	If you are buying stereo equipment, always go to Sam's Hi-Fi.
Sources of information	If you want to know which alternatives are worth searching for, read the test reports in *Consumer Reports*.
Source credibility	If a magazine accepts advertisements from the tested products, don't believe its product tests.

Evaluation heuristics	Examples
Key criteria	If comparing processed foods, examine sodium content.
Negative criteria	If a salient consequence is negative (high sodium content), give this choice criterion extra weight in the integration process.
Significant differences	If alternatives are similar on a salient consequence (all low sodium), ignore that choice criterion.

Choice heuristics	Examples
For familiar, frequently purchased products:	If choosing among familiar products, . . .
Works best	Choose the product that you think works best—that provides the best level of performance on the most relevant functional consequences.
Affect referral	Choose the alternative you like the best over all (select the alternative with most favorable attitude).
Bought last	Select the alternative you used last, if it was satisfactory.
Important person	Choose the alternative that some "important" person (spouse, child, friend) likes.
Price-based rule	Buy the least-expensive alternative (or buy the most expensive, depending on your beliefs about the relationship of price to product quality).
Promotion rule	Choose an alternative for which you have a coupon or can get at a price reduction (seasonal sale, promotional rebate, special price reduction).
For new, unfamiliar products:	If choosing among unfamiliar products . . .
Wait and see	Don't buy any software until someone you know has used it for at least a month and recommends it. Don't buy a new car (computer, etc.) until the second model year.
Expert consultant	Find an expert or more knowledgeable person, have them evaluate the alternatives in terms of your goals, then buy the alternative the expert selects.

Source: Reprinted with permission from "An Examination of Consumer Decision Making for a Common Repeat Purchase Product," by Wayne D. Hoyer, in the *Journal of Consumer Research,* December 1984, pp. 822–29.

decision plans concern intentions to perform particular behaviors in highly defined situations: "This afternoon Jim intends to go to Penney's and buy a blue cotton sweater to go with his new slacks." Other decision plans involve rather general intentions: "Paula intends to shop for a new car sometime soon." Some decision plans contain a simple intention to perform a single behavior: "Andy intends to buy a large-size tube of Aim toothpaste." In contrast, more complex decision plans involve a set of intentions to perform a series of behaviors: "Val intends to go to Bloomingdale's and Macy's, browse through their sportswear departments, and look for a lightweight jacket."

Having a decision plan increases the likelihood that the intended behaviors will be performed. However, as we discussed in Chapter 6, behavioral intentions are not always carried out. For instance, a purchase intention may be blocked or modified if environmental circumstances make it difficult for the decision plan to be accomplished. Perhaps the problem-solving process will recycle, and a new decision plan might be developed: "Andy found that the store was sold out of large-sized tubes of Aim, so he decided to buy two medium-sized tubes." Sometimes unanticipated events identify additional choice alternatives or change consumers' beliefs about appropriate choice criteria; this could lead to a revised decision plan: "While reading the paper, Val learned that Saks was having a 25 percent-off sale on lightweight jackets, so she decided to shop there first instead of Bloomingdale's."

Problem-Solving Processes in Purchase Decisions

The amount of cognitive and behavioral effort consumers put into their problem-solving processes is highly variable. Problem-solving effort varies from virtually none (a decision plan is activated from memory and is carried out automatically) to very extensive. For convenience, marketers have divided this continuum into three levels of problem-solving activity: extensive, limited, and routine or habitual.[32] Figure 7.6 identifies these three levels and summarizes the major ways in which they differ.

Relatively few consumer choice problems require **extensive decision making.** Extensive decision making usually involves a substantial amount of search behavior required to identify choice alternatives and learn the appropriate choice criteria with which to evaluate them. Extensive decision making also involves multiple choice decisions and substantial cognitive and behavioral effort. Finally, it is likely to take rather long periods – such as Barbara's decision to buy new dishes in the opening example or purchasing your first stereo system.

Many consumers' choice problems require **limited decision making.** The amount of problem-solving effort in limited decision making ranges from low to moderate. Compared to extensive decision making, limited decision making involves less search for information. Fewer choice alternatives are considered, and less integration processing is required. Choices involving limited decision

FIGURE 7.6
Levels of Problem-Solving Effort

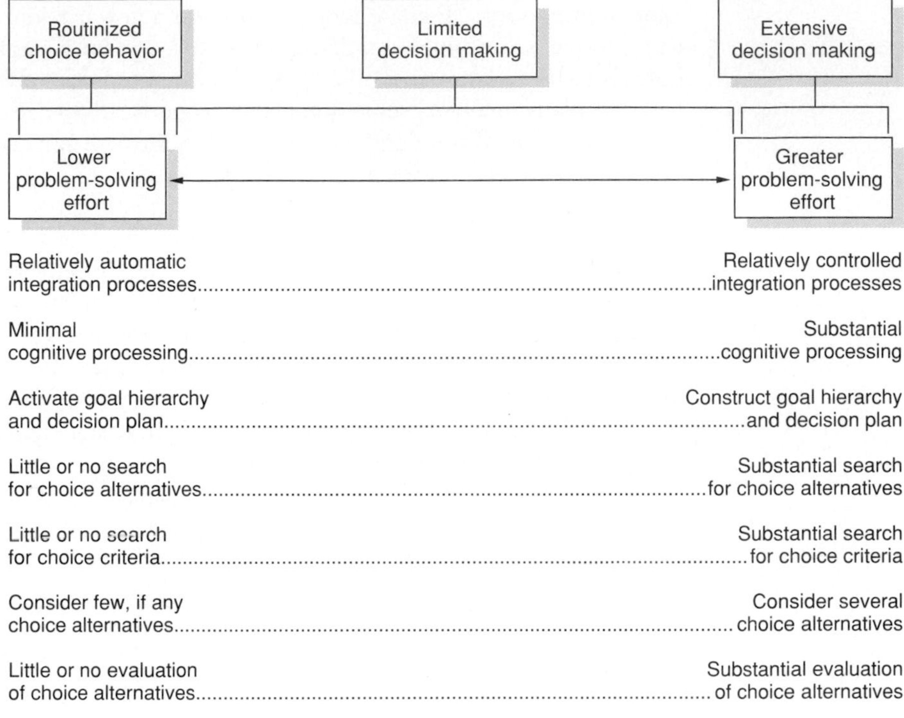

making usually are carried out fairly quickly, with moderate levels of cognitive and behavioral effort.

For still other problems, consumers' choice behavior is habitual or routine. **Routinized choice behavior** — such as buying another Pepsi from the vending machine down the hall or purchasing a package of gum at the checkout counter — occurs relatively automatically with little or no apparent cognitive processing. Compared to the other levels, routinized choice behavior requires very little cognitive capacity or conscious control. Basically, a previously learned decision plan is activated from memory and is carried out relatively automatically to produce the purchase behavior.

The amount of effort consumers exert in problem solving tends to decrease over time as they learn more about a product and gain experience in making decisions. With repeated decisions, product and brand knowledge becomes organized into means-end structures and becomes more clearly related to consumers' goals. Consumers also learn new productions and heuristics, which become organized into scripts or decision plans stored in memory.[33] When activated, these heuristics and decision scripts automatically affect purchase-

HIGHLIGHT 7.2

Routinized Choice Behavior

In one study, 120 consumers were observed shopping and buying laundry detergent in three chain grocery stores. An observer stationed in the detergent aisle coded shoppers' activities as they moved down the aisle and picked out the detergent they wanted. The results showed that for most consumers, laundry detergent choice behavior was quite routinized.

Most consumers examined very few packages of detergent. In fact, 72 percent of the consumers looked at only one package, and only 11 percent looked at more than two. An even lower number of packages were physicially picked up—83 percent of the consumers picked up only one package, and only 4 percent picked up more than two. Obviously, most of these consumers were not engaged in much in-store problem-solving activity for this product. In fact, hardly any across-brand or within-brand comparisons were made; the vast majority of consumers made none. Finally, consumers took an average of 13 seconds after they entered the aisle to make their detergent choice. Given that the detergent section spans an entire aisle and that several seconds were required to walk to the appropriate area, it is obvious the typical consumer is making an extremely quick choice that involves minimal cognitive and behavioral effort.

The majority of consumers in this study were engaged in routinized choice behavior. They were merely carrying out a simple decision plan: for example, find the large size of Tide and buy it. Are most other grocery store products purchased in such an automatic way? What other types of products might be purchased in a habitual manner?

Source: Adapted from "An Examination of Consumer Decision Making for a Common Repeat Purchase Product," by Wayne D. Hoyer, In the *Journal of Consumer Research*, December 1984, pp. 822–29.

related behaviors. Running down to the convenience store for a loaf of bread or stopping to fill up the car's tank at a favorite gas station are well-developed decision plans that require little cognitive effort. In summary, consumers develop increasingly routinized, automatic problem-solving processes as they gain experience making various purchase decisions (see Highlight 7.2).

Influences on Consumers' Problem-Solving Activities

The level of consumers' problem-solving effort in making brand purchase decisions is influenced by environmental factors as well as the cognitive (knowledge) and affective responses activated during the problem-solving process. We discuss three aspects of this activated knowledge and affect that have direct effects on problem solving: (1) consumers' goals; (2) their knowledge about choice alternative and choice criteria, as well as heuristics for using this knowledge; and (3) their level of felt involvement. Following the discussion of these affective and cognitive factors, we examine several environmental influences on consumer problem solving.

Effects of End Goals

The particular end goals consumers are striving to achieve have a powerful effect on the problem-solving process. Figure 7.7 presents five broad end goals that lead to quite different problem-solving processes. For instance, consumers who have an *optimizing* end goal are likely to expend substantial effort searching for the best possible alternative. In contrast, consumers with a *satisficing/maintenance* end goal are likely to engage in minimal search behavior. In yet other decisions, consumers may have conflicting end goals that must be resolved in the problem-solving process.

In general, marketers have relatively little direct influence over consumers' abstract end goals, such as basic values. However, marketers can try to influence less abstract end goals, such as desired functional or psychosocial consequences, through promotional strategies. Perhaps the major implication for marketers is

FIGURE 7.7

Types of Purchase End Goals and Related Problem-Solving Processes

Dominant end goal	Basic purchase motivation	Examples
Optimize satisfaction	Seek maximum positive consequences	Buy dinner at the best restaurant in town
Prevention	Avoid potential unpleasant consequences	Buy rust-proofing for a new car
Resolve conflict	Seek satisfactory balance of positive and negative consequences	Buy a moderately expensive car of very good quality
Escape	Reduce or escape from current aversive circumstances	Buy a shampoo to get rid of dandruff
Maintenance (satisfice)	Maintain satisfaction of basic need with minimal effort	Buy bread at the nearest convenience store

Source: Adapted from Geraldine Fennell, "Motivation Research Revisted," *Journal of Advertising Research,* June 1975, pp. 23–28; and J. Paul Peter and Lawrence X. Tarpey, Sr., "A Comparative Analysis of Three Consumer Decision Strategies," *Journal of Consumer Research,* June 1975, pp. 29–37.

to identify the dominant goals in consumers' problem representations and design product and promotion strategies that link product attributes to those goals.[34]

Effects of Goal Hierarchies

Consumers' goal hierarchies for a problem have a powerful influence on problem-solving processes. If consumers have a well-defined goal hierarchy stored in memory, it may be activated and the associated decision plan carried out automatically.[35] Even if a complete decision plan is not available, a general goal hierarchy provides a useful structure for developing an effective decision plan, without a great deal of problem-solving effort. In contrast, consumers who have very little past experience will not have well developed goal hierarchies. Their problem solving is likely to proceed haltingly, by trial and error. Consider first-time buyers of relatively important products such as stereos, sports equipment, cars, and houses. These consumers must construct a goal hierarchy (a series of

This ad links Marriott room service with a prevention end goal: Avoid unpleasant consequences of being late for a business meeting.

You can't be late for
your business appointments,
and neither can we.

At Marriott, if your breakfast doesn't show up on time, it won't show up on your bill. That's because we take our business just as seriously as you take yours. And our business is service. This commitment is what makes Marriott the business traveler's first choice. See for yourself. Call **1-800-228-9290** or your Travel Professional.

SERVICE. THE ULTIMATE LUXURY.

subgoals that seem related to the end goal) and develop a decision plan to achieve each subgoal (as Barbara had to do in the opening example). In these types of decisions, marketers are likely to find confused or frustrated consumers, who use general "strategies" such as wandering around various stores in a mall, hoping to accidentally run into something that will satisfy their end goal (see Highlight 7.3).

Effects of Felt Involvement and Knowledge

Consumers' problem-solving processes are greatly affected by the amount of product knowledge they have acquired through their past experiences, and by their level of felt involvement with the product and/or the choice process. The activated knowledge about goals, choice alternatives and choice criteria, and heuristics affects consumers' ability to create an effective decision plan. Consumers' felt involvement with the product or decision affects their motivation to engage in the problem-solving process. Figure 7.8 summarizes how different combinations of product knowledge and involvement affect specific elements of consumers' problem representations and the overall problem-solving process. Marketers should determine the levels of knowledge and involvement of their target customers and develop strategies consistent with the types of problem solving described in Figure 7.8.

Environmental Effects

Environmental factors can affect consumer decision making by interrupting or disrupting the ongoing flow of the problem-solving process. Four types of disruptive events, or **interrupts,** have been identified.[36] First, interrupts can occur when *unexpected information* (inconsistent with established knowledge structures) is encountered in the environment. For instance, carrying out a decision plan or script may be interrupted when you unexpectedly find that aspects of the physical or social environment have changed—a store has been remodeled and departments have been moved around, a rejected brand now has a new attribute, or your friends now favor a different night spot. These environmental interrupts may cause the consumer to take conscious control of the problem-solving process, identify a new end goal, develop a new goal hierarchy, and construct a different decision plan.

Second, *prominent environmental stimuli* can interrupt a problem-solving process. Many marketing strategies are intended to interrupt consumers' ongoing problem solving. For instance, a large in-store display for Oreo cookies, "as advertised" shelf tags, or the announcement of a sales promotion ("Attention K mart shoppers. In aisle 3B we are offering . . .") may interrupt an ongoing problem-solving process as well as activate new knowledge or goals from memory.

Third, *affective states*, such as moods (feeling bored) and physiological "events" (feeling hungry, sleepy, or thirsty) can interrupt an ongoing problem-

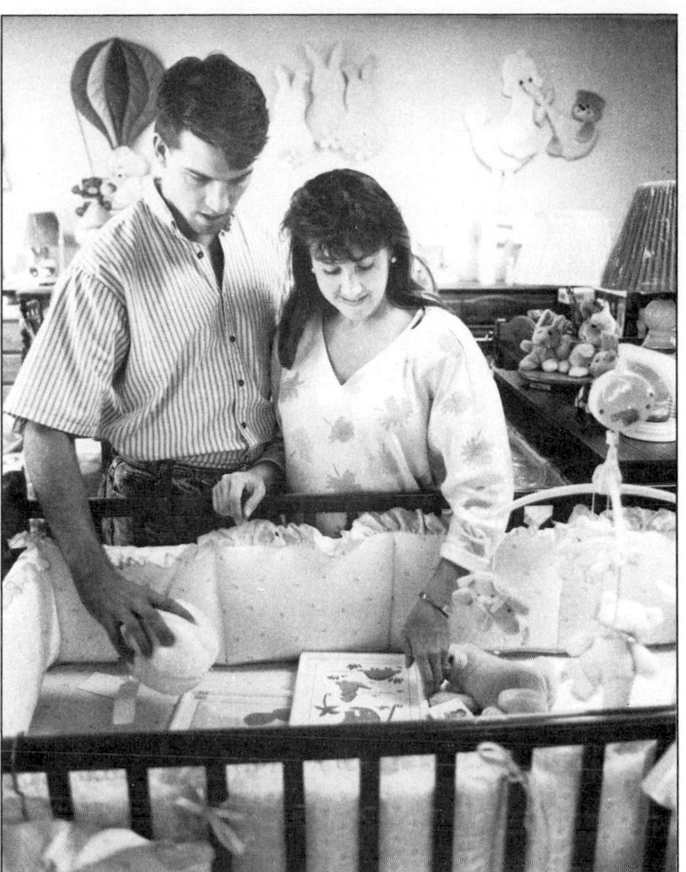

Browsing is often for pleasure rather than directed to the goal of an immediate purchase.

HIGHLIGHT 7.3

Browsing as Search and Entertainment

Sometimes consumers browse as a vague search plan. But frequently, browsing consumers have no specific decision plan in mind. They are shopping for other reasons—recreation, stimulation from store environments, social contact, escape from home or work, or even exercise. In other words, some consumers get satisfaction from shopping/browsing, apart from solving a purchase problem. Browsing, thus, can be both a form of leisure and a problem-solving strategy.

One reason for browsing without a specific decision plan in mind is that the consumer feels involved with a particular product class or form and likes to associate with it. Consumers who are very interested in music may enjoy browsing in record shops. Some consumers are involved with a particular store or set of stores in a mall or a shopping area in town. Perhaps the atmosphere of these stores is exciting and stimulating, and this provides part of the attraction. In sum, browsing can and usually does serve multiple goals, needs, and values for different consumers.

Retail stores need to pay attention to browsers because they can have a major impact on the success of the store. The retailer may have a serious problem if browsers crowd the store and keep serious customers away. Discouraging browsers is relatively easy—just have a salesperson follow the browser around the store asking if he or she can be helped. Some clothing stores seem to do this effectively. But driving browsers away can be risky. Many browsers become buyers later. If a particular store creates a negative reaction, the browser may make a purchase in a different store.

Some retailers seem to have trouble dealing with browsers. Consider auto dealers. Many people feel uncomfortable going into auto showrooms to browse, partly because of the aggressive salespeople who descend upon them. One strategy has been to set up regional auto shows in the shopping mall, where consumers feel more comfortable browsing without having to deal with an enthusiastic salesperson.

Another retailing strategy is to develop a store environment that stimulates impulse buying. In-store promotions, displays, and special signs can help convert a browser to a buyer.

Finally, browsers seem likely to relay information to other consumers. Thus, browsers are doubly important. Not only might they buy something themselves, but they are more likely to spread word-of-mouth information to less well-informed consumers.

Source: Adapted from Peter H. Bloch and Marsha L. Richins, "Shopping without Purchase: An Investigation of Consumer Browsing Behavior," in *Advances in Consumer Research,* vol. 10, ed. R. P. Bagozzi and A. M. Tybout (Ann Arbor, Mich.: Association for Consumer Research, 1983), pp. 389–93.

solving process.[37] For instance, feeling tired during a shopping trip might activate new goals and start a different problem-solving process (find a comfortable place to sit down and have a soda pop or cup of coffee). Getting into a bad mood can terminate a problem-solving process.

Fourth, *conflicts* that arise during the course of purchase decision making can interrupt the problem-solving process. *Goal conflict* occurs when consumers recognize the presence of incompatible goals.[38] Goal conflict may occur when consumers discover that alternatives cannot be found to satisfy incompatible goals. For instance, Susan may experience an *approach-approach conflict* in choosing between a new camera and a new stereo receiver, because each product leads to a desirable goal (creativity and relaxation, respectively), but neither product provides both goals. *Avoidance-avoidance conflicts* occur when consumers choose between two alternatives with different negative consequences. For instance, Sam is trying to decide whether to buy a new suit. He doesn't want to be embarrassed by his old suit, but he doesn't want to spend money on a new one,

FIGURE 7.8

Effects of Felt Involvement and Product Knowledge on Consumers' Problem-Solving Processes

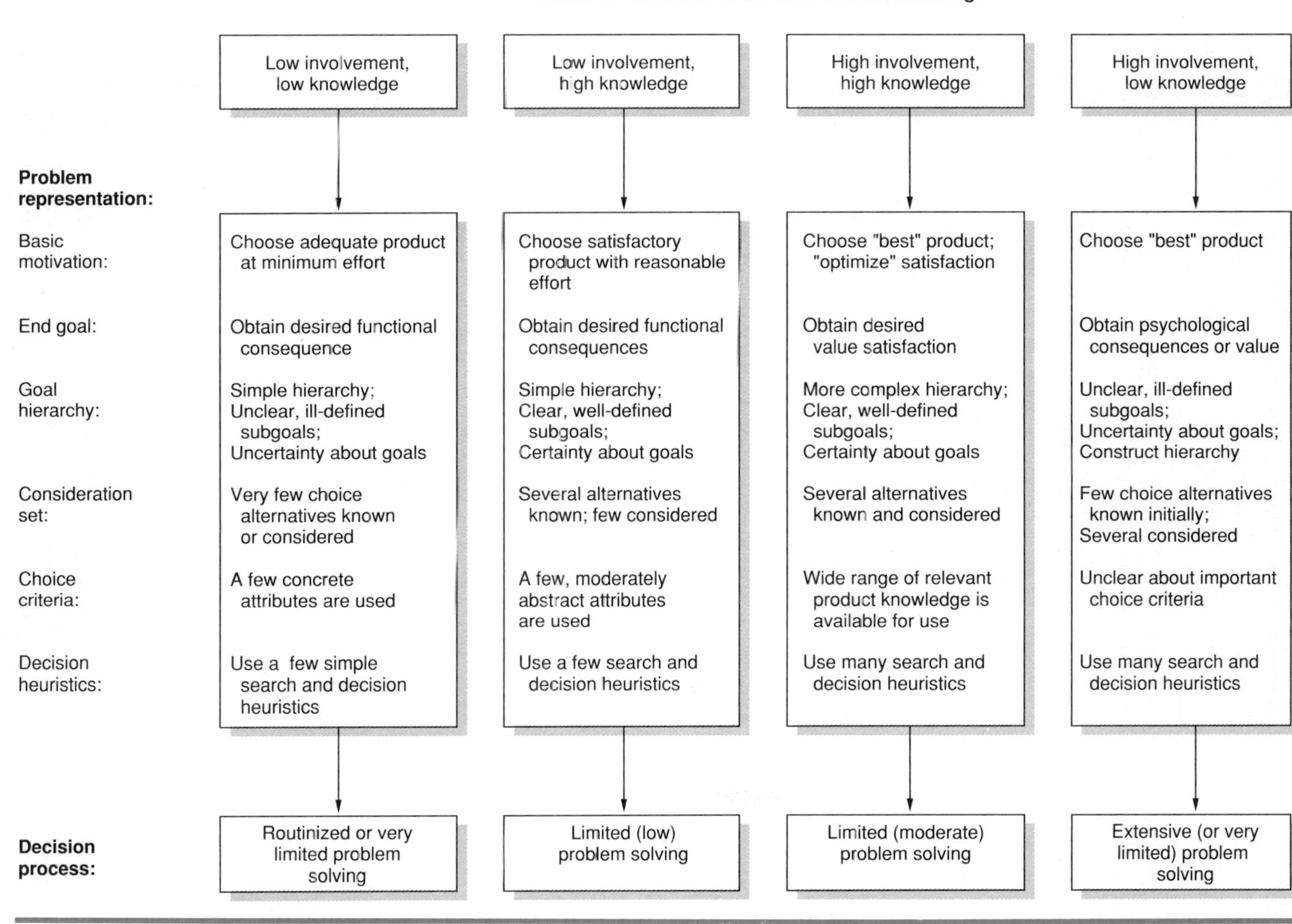

either. Finally, *approach-avoidance conflicts* occur when consumers consider both the positive and negative consequences of a purchase or action. For instance, Paul is trying to decide about a new personal cassette player that is on sale for a very low price (positive outcome), but he is afraid the quality may be low (negative outcome).

Fifth, the effects of *interrupts* on consumers' problem-solving processes depend on how consumers interpret (comprehend) the interrupting event. In general, consumers tend to resume an interrupted problem-solving task, especially if it is important or involving.[39] In other cases, however, an interrupting event can change the problem-solving process. For instance, an interrupt might activate new end goals that require a new problem-solving process. Interrupt events (such as learning about a new product attribute) might activate knowledge structures that suggest new decision criteria. In other cases, a choice heuristic might be activated by the interrupt (a friend recommends a brand, and you decide to take her advice). Finally, an especially strong interrupt, such as losing your job, might block the current problem-solving process (choosing a new car), and the process might not resume again. In sum, the effects of interrupts depend on how they are interpreted by the consumer. For instance, is your hunger severe enough to stop shopping for a new suit, or can you skip lunch today? Does this new brand of styling mousse seem worth trying, or should you ignore it? Do you care that your friend thinks these shoes are ridiculous?

Implications for Marketing Strategy

To develop effective marketing strategies, marketers need to know the type of problem-solving processes their customers use to make purchase decisions. As shown in Figure 7.8, these processes can vary widely. Marketers that target several consumer segments each with different problem-solving processes may have to develop multiple strategies to influence the different decision outcomes. In the following section, we consider some general implications for marketing strategies for routinized choice behavior and limited and extensive decision making.

Routinized Choice Behavior

Much consumer choice behavior is routinized. When consumers think they know all they need to know about a product category, they are not motivated to search for new information. Their choice behavior is based on a learned decision plan. In such cases, the appropriate market strategy depends on the strength of the brand's position in the market.

Marketers of established brands with substantial market shares must maintain their brand in the evoked sets of a significant segment of consumers. Because consumers in this situation engage in little or no search, marketers have minimal opportunities to interject their brand into consumers' consideration sets during problem solving. Thus, it is important that a brand be included in the choice alternatives activated at the beginning of the problem-solving process. In general, the more automatic the choice behavior becomes, the more difficult it is for marketers to interrupt and influence the choice.

Marketers of new brands or brands with a low market share must somehow interrupt consumers' automatic problem-solving processes. They may develop strategies of producing prominent environmental stimuli such as large or unusual store displays, create strong package graphics that stand out on the shelf, give away free samples, or run sales promotions (buy one, get one free).[40] Such strategies are intended to catch consumers' attention and interrupt their routine choice behavior. The goal is to jolt consumers into a more conscious and controlled level of limited decision making that includes the new brand in the consideration set.

Finally, marketers of leading brands such as Doritos snack chips, Snickers candy bars, Budweiser beer, and IBM computers may *want* consumers to follow a routine choice process. Because these brands already have a high market share, they are in the evoked sets of most buyers. It is important for these marketers to avoid marketing-related environmental interrupts such as stockouts, which could jolt consumers into a limited decision-making process and lead them to try a competitor's brand. One critical aspect of the overall marketing strategy for such brands is an efficient distribution system to keep the brands fully stocked and available (in a prominent shelf/display position) whenever consumers are in a choice situation. Frito-Lay, manufacturer of Fritos, Ruffles potato chips, and many other snack products, has developed a superb distribution system partly for this reason. Highlight 7.4 gives several examples of how marketers of industrial products attempt to make their buyers' decision-making processes more routine.

Limited Decision Making

The majority of consumer decisions involve limited problem-solving effort. Because most consumers already have a lot of information about the product from previous experiences, the basic marketing strategy here is to make additional pieces of information available to consumers when and where they need them. Advertisements to increase top-of-mind awareness may help get a brand into the evoked set of choice alternatives at the beginning of the decision process. This is important because most consumers are not likely to search extensively for other alternatives. Moreover, it is critical that the brand is perceived to possess the few key choice criteria used in the evaluation process. Advertisements that capture the attention of the consumer and communicate favorable beliefs about salient attributes and consequences of the brand may be able to create that knowledge. Finally, because consumers are giving some conscious thought to the decision, successful interrupts are not as difficult as they are with routinized problem solving. Marketers may try to design a store environment that stimulates impulsive purchases, a type of limited decision making.[41]

HIGHLIGHT 7.4

Routinizing Consumers' Decision Processes

The basic purpose of marketing is to create and keep customers. The key to keeping customers, of course, is to keep them satisfied. One way industrial-goods companies are keeping their corporate customers satisfied is by routinizing their decision-making processes.

Companies as diverse as Inland Steel, Eastman Kodak, and First Boston Bank have placed computer terminals connected to the main corporate computer system on their customers' desks, free. The network is called a *channel system* because it enables customers to simplify the channel of distribution by ordering supplies instantly and directly from the supplying company. Buyers can thus better manage their expensive inventories. Basically, these systems solve many customer problems. Although the systems are vastly expensive and very tricky to implement successfully, many companies are making the investment because such systems "destroy your customers' interest in competitors' products."

In 1974, American Hospital Supply (AHS) installed one of the pioneer systems in the stockrooms of large hospitals. Instead of having to order from salespeople making regular rounds, purchasing agents and stock clerks could use the terminals to order routine supplies easily and quickly (and directly from AHS). As with most channel systems, customers tend to buy more from the supplier of the system and less from competitors. By making its customers' decision-making process more routine, the marketing company makes it easier than ever to buy from it.

Kodak developed a system called Technet that is targeted at the owners of minilabs (storefront film developers) and takes routinization to an extreme. Based on an IBM PC, the system does everything but feed the night watchdog. It automatically monitors print quality, offers advice on pricing, and keeps track of sales and complaints. The system also detects when paper and chemicals are running low and automatically reorders from Kodak. To get Technet, the lab must agree to use Kodak paper and chemicals exclusively and to let Kodak monitor its adherence to quality guidelines.

These channel systems and other computerized strategies may be only the early steps toward a time when many (perhaps most) marketing transactions are conducted electronically.

Source: Adapted from Peter Petre, "How to Keep Customers Happy Captives," *Fortune,* September 2, 1985, pp. 42–46.

Extensive Decision Making

Compared to more common routinized choices and limited decision making, relatively few consumer decisions involve extensive problem solving. However, when consumers do engage in extensive decision making, marketers must

The purchase of expensive items, such as televisions, often involves an information-filled process of extensive decision making.

recognize and satisfy their special needs for information. In extensive decision-making situations where their knowledge is low, consumers need information about everything—including which end goals are important, how to organize goal hierarchies, which choice alternatives are relevant, what choice criteria are appropriate, and so on. Marketers should strive to make the necessary information available, in a format and at a level that consumers can understand and use in the problem-solving process.[42]

Because consumers intentionally seek product information during extensive decision making, interrupting their problem-solving processes with a brand promotion is relatively easy. Informational displays at the point of purchase—for instance, displays of mattresses that are cut apart to show construction details—or presentations by salespersons can be effective sources of information. Complex sales materials such as brochures and product specifications may be effective, along with high-information advertisements. Consumers in extensive problem-solving situations will attend to relevant information, and they are motivated to comprehend it. Marketers may take advantage of the information receptivity of consumers by offering free samples, coupons, or easy trial (take it home and try it for a couple of days) to help consumers gain knowledge about their brand.

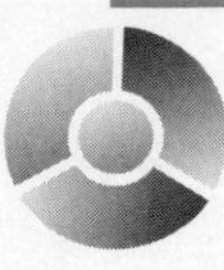

BACK TO....
BUYING A SET OF DISHES

In this chapter, we examined a number of concepts that can help us understand Barbara's problem-solving process. Her decision to buy dishes involved fairly extensive problem-solving activities, including a substantial amount of search behavior and quite a bit of cognitive activity in evaluating alternative actions. As you review her decisions, note that her choice alternatives and choice criteria were greatly influenced by the information she came across in the environment, as she had relatively little knowledge about dishes stored in memory. Her goal hierarchy and decision plan were constructed through trial and error during the problem-solving process. This example shows the importance of the continuous, reciprocal interactions among affect and cognition, behavior, environment, and marketing strategy. Many limited decision-making processes are also like this, although less complex. In contrast, habitual choice behavior involves little or no problem solving. Because the decisions were made in the past and stored in memory, purchase behaviors are generated automatically when the decision plan is activated. Thus, environmental factors have less chance to interrupt and influence the purchase process.

SUMMARY

In this chapter, we examined consumers' decision-making processes as they choose between alternative behaviors. Our primary focus was on purchase choices of products and brands. We treated decision making as a problem-solving process in which the consumer's cognitive representation of the problem is a key to understanding the process. Problem representation involves end goals, a goal hierarchy, activated product knowledge, and choice rules and heuristics. For many consumer decisions, the problem representation involves several interrelated subproblems, each with its own set of subgoals, organized as a goal hierarchy. Consumers use simple decision rules called heuristics for finding, evaluating, and integrating beliefs about the alternatives relevant for each subgoal in a goal hierarchy. The entire set of decisions produces a series of behavioral intentions or a decision plan.

We also saw that consumers' problem-solving processes vary widely. Some purchase choices require very extensive problem-solving efforts, while other purchases are made virtually automatically in a highly routinized manner. Many purchases involve limited decision making that falls somewhere between these two extremes. We described how consumers' end goals, goal hierarchies, product knowledge, and felt involvement affect the problem-solving process. And we discussed how various aspects of the decision environment affect the problem-solving process. We concluded by drawing implications of these concepts for marketing strategy.

Key Terms and Concepts

Decision *222*
Consumer Decision Making *222*
Choice *223*
Problem Solving *224*
Problem Representation *226*
End Goals *227*
Goal Hierarchy *228*
Relevant Knowledge *228*
Choice Alternatives *228*
Consideration Set *228*
Choice Criteria *230*
Compensatory Integration Processes *234*
Noncompensatory Integration Processes *236*
Heuristics *236*
Decision Plan *237*
Extensive Decision Making *239*
Limited Decision Making *239*
Routinized Choice Behavior *240*
Interrupts *244*

Review and Discussion Questions

1. Discuss what it means to say that decision choices are always between alternative behaviors. Illustrate your answer with an example.
2. Describe the problem-solving approach to consumer decision making, and discuss why is it a useful perspective.

3. Identify three ways that choice alternatives can enter the consideration set. Describe a marketing strategy that could be used to get your brand into consumers' consideration sets for each situation. Why do products or brands not in the consideration set have a low probability of being purchased?

4. Describe the components of a problem representation. Is it possible for marketers to influence the consumers' problem representations?

5. Give an example of how two different "frames" for the same purchase decision could lead to different problem-solving processes. Can you relate these differences to consumer/product relationships discussed earlier?

6. Think of a purchase decision from your own experience in which you had a well-developed goal hierarchy. Describe how it affected your problem-solving processes. Then select a decision in which you did not have a well-developed goal hierarchy and describe how it affected your problem-solving processes.

7. Assume the role of a product manager (product management team) for a product about which you (and others in the discussion) have a fairly high level of product knowledge. Consider how each of the formal integration processes would result in different responses to your product and how you could adjust marketing strategy to deal with these differences.

8. Give at least two examples of how a marketing manager could use the various types of interrupts discussed in this chapter to increase the likelihood of purchase of his or her product.

9. Discuss how consumers' felt involvement and their activated product knowledge affect the problem-solving processes during purchase decisions for products like new automobiles, an oil change, cold remedies, and health insurance.

10. Relate the examples of decision heuristics shown in Figure 7.5 to the concept of felt involvement. When are these heuristics likely to be useful to the consumer? Under what conditions might they be dysfunctional?

NOTES

1. Flemming Hansen, "Psychological Theories of Consumer Choice," *Journal of Consumer Research*, December 1976, pp. 117–42.

2. It is important to recognize that consumer decision making is actually a *seamless continuous flow of cognitive processes and behavioral actions.* Researchers "divide" this flow into separate stages and subprocesses for convenience in trying to research and understand the entire process and for helping to develop market strategies.

3. Joel B. Cohen, Paul W. Miniard, and Peter Dickson, "Information Integration: An information Processing Perspective," in *Advances in Consumer Research*, vol. 7, ed. Jerry C. Olson

(Ann Arbor, Mich.: Association for Consumer Research, 1980), pp. 161–70; and Jerry C. Olson. "Theories of information Encoding and Storage: Implications for Consumer Behavior," in *The Effect of Information on Consumer and Market Behavior*, ed. Andrew A. Mitchell (Chicago: American Marketing Association, 1978), pp. 49–60.

4. Richard W. Olshavsky and Donald H. Granbois, "Consumer Decision Making—Fact or Fiction?" *Journal of Consumer Research*, September 1979, pp. 93–100.

5. Peter H. Bloch, Daniel L. Sherrell, and Nancy M. Ridgway, "Consumer Search: An Extended Framework," *Journal of Consumer Research*, June 1986, pp. 119–26.

6. A similar notion is presented by Girish N. Punj and David W. Stewart, "An Interaction Framework of Consumer Decision Making," *Journal of Consumer Research*, September 1983, pp. 181–96.

7. Daniel Kahneman and Amos Tyersky, "Choices, Values, and Frames," *American Psychologist* 39 (1984), pp. 341–50; Christopher P. Puto, "The Framing of Buying Decisions," *Journal of Consumer Research*, December 1987, pp. 301–15; and William J. Qualls and Christopher P. Puto, "Organizational Climate and Decision Framing: An Integrated Approach to Analyzing Industrial Buying Decisions," *Journal of Marketing Research*, May 1989, pp. 179–92.

8. James R. Bettman and Mita Sujan, "Effects of Framing on Evaluation of Comparable and Noncomparable Alternatives by Experts and Novice Consumers," *Journal of Consumer Research*, September 1987, pp. 141–54; Joshua L. Wiener, James W. Gentry, and Ronald K. Miller, "The Framing of the Insurance Purchase Decision," in *Advances in Consumer Research*, vol. 13, ed. Richard J. Lutz (Provo, Utah: Association for Consumer Research, 1986), pp. 257–62; and Peter Wright and Peter D. Rip, "Product Class Advertising effects on First-Time Buyers' Decision Strategies," *Journal of Consumer Research*, September 1980, pp. 176–88.

9. Lawrence A. Crosby and James R. Taylor, "Effects of Consumer Information and Education in Cognition and Choice," *Journal of Consumer Research*, June 1981, pp. 43–56; John G. Lynch and Thomas K. Srull, "Memory and Attentional Factors in Consumer Choice: Concepts and Research Methods," *Journal of Consumer Research*, June 1982, pp. 18–37; and Gabriel Biehal and Dipankar Chakravarti, "Consumers' Use of Memory and External Information in Choice: Macro and Micro Perspectives," *Journal of Consumer Research*, March 1986, pp. 382–405.

10. Gabriel Biehal and Dipankar Chakravarti, "Information Accessibility as a Moderator of Consumer Choice," *Journal of Consumer Research*, June 1983, pp. 1–14; and Valerie S. Folkes, "The Availability Heuristic and Perceived Risk," *Journal of Consumer Research*, June 1988, pp. 13–23.

11. David B. Klenosky and Arno J. Rethans. "The Formation of Consumer Choice Sets: A Longitudinal Investigation at the Product Class Level," in *Advances in Consumer Research*, vol. 15, ed. Michael J. Houston (Provo, Utah: Association for Consumer Research, 1988), pp. 13–18; John R. Hauser and Birger Wernerfelt, "An Evaluation Cost Model of Consideration Set," *Journal of Consumer Research*, March 1990, pp. 393–408; and John H. Roberts and James M. Lattin, "Development and Testing of a Model of Consideration Set Composition," *Journal of Marketing Research*, November 1991, pp. 429–40.

12. John Howard and Jagdish N. Sheth, "The Theory of Buyer Behavior (New York: John Wiley & Sons, 1969); and Prakash Nedungadi, "Recall and Consumer Consideration Sets: Influencing Choice without Altering Brand Evaluations," *Journal of Consumer Research*, December 1990, pp. 263–76.

13. Sharon E. Beatty and Scott M. Smith, "External Search Effort: An Investigation across Several Product Categories," *Journal of Consumer Research*, June 1987, pp. 83–95.

14. Wayne D. Hoyer and Steven P. Brown, "Effects of Brand Awareness on Choice for a Common, Repeat-Purchase Product," *Journal of Consumer Research*, September 1990, pp. 141–48.

15. William Baker, J. Wesley Hutchinson, Danny Moore, and Prakash Nedungadi, "Brand Familiarity and Advertising: Effects on the Evoked Set and Brand Preference," in *Advances in Consumer Research*, vol. 13, ed. Richard J. Lutz (Provo, Utah: Association for Consumer Research, 1986), pp. 637–42.

16. Kristian E. Moller and Pirjo Karppinen, "Role of Motives and Attributes in Consumer Motion Picture Choice," *Journal of Economic Psychology* 4 (1983), pp. 239–62.

17. Joel E. Urbany, Peter R. Dickson, and William L. Wilkie, "Buyer Uncertainty and Information Search," *Journal of Consumer Research*, September 1989, pp. 208–15.

18. Klaus G. Grunert, "Cognitive Determinants of Attribute Information Usage," *Journal of Economic Psychology* 7 (1986), pp. 95–124; and C. Whan Park and Daniel C. Smith, "Product-Level Choice: A Top-Down or Bottom-Up Process?" *Journal of Consumer Research*, December 1989, pp. 289–99.

19. Mark I. Alpert, "Unresolved Issues in Identification of Determinant Attributes," in *Advances in Consumer Research*, vol. 7, ed. Jerry C. Olson (Ann Arbor, Mich.: Association for Consumer Research, 1980), pp. 83–88.

20. John U. Farley, Jerrold Katz, and Donald R. Lehmann, "Impact of Different Comparison Sets on Evaluation of a New Subcompact Car Brand," *Journal of Consumer Research*, September 1978, pp. 138–42; Srinivasan Ratneshwar, Allan D. Shocker, and David W. Steward, "Toward Understanding the Attraction Effect: The Implications of Product Stimulus Meaningfulness and Familiarity," *Journal of Consumer Research*, March 1987, pp. 520–33; Merrie Brucks and Paul H. Schurr, "The Effects of Bargainable Attributes and Attribute Range Knowledge on Consumer Choice Processes," *Journal of Consumer Research*, March 1990, pp. 409–19; Kim P. Corfman, "Comparability and Comparison Levels Used in Choices among Consumer Products," *Journal of Marketing Research*, August 1991, pp. 368–74; Noreen M. Klein and Manjit S. Yadav, "Context Effects on Effort and Accuracy in Choice: An Enquiry into Adaptive Decision Making," *Journal of Consumer Research*, March 1989, pp. 411–21; and Rashi Glazer, Barbara E. Kahn, and William L. Moore, "The Influence of External Constraints on Brand Choice: The Lone Alternative Effect," *Journal of Consumer Research*, June 1991, pp. 119–27.

21. Valerie S. Folkes, "The Availability Heuristic and Perceived Risk," *Journal of Consumer Research*, June 1988, pp. 13–23.

22. John W. Vann, "A Conditional Probability View of the Role of Product Warranties in Reducing Perceived Financial Risk," in *Advances in Consumer Research*, vol. 14, ed. Melanie Wallendorf and Paul Anderson (Provo, Utah: Association for Consumer Research, 1987), pp. 421–25.

23. Scott Hume, "Seven-Up Stands Up to Cola's Challenge," *Advertising Age*, May 20, 1985, pp. 4, 92.

24. Narasimhan Srinivasan and Brian T. Ratchford, "An Empirical Test of a Model of External Search for Automobiles," *Journal of Consumer Research*, September 1991, pp. 233–42; and Keith B. Murray, "A Test of Services Marketing Theory: Consumer Information Acquisition Activities," *Journal of Marketing*, January 1991, pp. 10–25.

25. Robert S. Billings and Lisa L. Scherer, "The Effects of Response Mode and Importance on Decision-Making Strategies: Judgment versus Choice," *Organizational Behavior and Human Decision-Processes* 41 (1988), pp. 1–19; and Peter Wright, "Consumer Choice Strategies: Simplifying versus Optimizing," *Journal of Marketing Research*, February 1975, pp. 60–67.

26. James R. Bettman and C. Whan Park, "Effects of Prior Knowledge and Experience and Phase of the Choice Process on Consumer Decision Processes: A Protocol Analysis," *Journal of Consumer Research*, December 1980, pp. 234–48; Cohen, Miniard, and Dickson, "Information Integration: An Information Processing Perspective," pp. 161–70; Wayne D. Hoyer, "An Examination of Consumer Decision Making for a Common Repeat Purchase Product," *Journal of*

Consumer Research, December 1984, pp. 822–29; and David J. Curry, Michael B. Menasco, and James W. Van Ark, "Multiattribute Dyadic Choice: Models and Tests," *Journal of Marketing Research*, August 1991, pp. 259–67.

27. James R. Bettman, *An Information Processing Theory of Consumer Choice* (Reading, Mass.: Addison-Wesley, 1979); Denis A. Lussier and Richard W. Olshavsky, "Task Complexity and Contingent Processing in Brand Choice," *Journal of Consumer Research*, September 1979, pp. 154–65; and Merrie Brucks and Andrew A. Mitchell, "Knowledge Structures, Production Systems and Decision Strategies," in *Advances in Consumer Research*, vol. 8, ed. Kent B. Monroe (Ann Arbor, Mich.: Association for Consumer Research, 1981).

28. Bettman and Park, "Effects of Prior Knowledge," pp. 234–48; and Hoyer, "An Examination of Consumer Decision Making for a Common Repeat Purchase Product," pp. 822–29.

29. James R. Bettman, "Presidential Address: Processes of Adaptivity in Decision Making," in *Advances in Consumer Research*, vol. 15, ed. Michael J. Houston (Provo, Utah: Association for Consumer Research, 1988), pp. 1–4; Surjit Chabra and Richard W. Olshavsky, "Some Evidence for Additional Types of Choice Strategies," in *Advances in Consumer Research*, vol. 13, ed. Richard J. Lutz (Provo, Utah: Association for Consumer Research, 1986), pp. 12–16; Wayne D. Hoyer, "Variations in Choice Strategies across Decision Contexts: An Examination of Contingent Factors," in *Advances in Consumer Research*, vol. 13, ed. Richard J. Lutz (Provo, Utah: Association for Consumer Research, 1986), pp. 32–36; James R. Bettman and Michel A. Zins, "Constructive Processes in Consumer Choice," *Journal of Consumer Research*, September 1977, pp. 75–85; and Bettman and Park, "Effects of Prior Knowledge," pp. 234–48.

30. Hoyer, "Examination of Consumer Decision Making," pp. 822–29; John Payne, "Task Complexity and Contingent Processing in Decision Making," *Organizational Behavior and Human Performance* 16 (1976), pp. 366–87; and David Grether and Louis Wilde, "An Analysis of Conjunctive Choice: Theory and Experiments," *Journal of Consumer Research*, March 1984, pp. 373–85.

31. C. Whan Park and Richard J. Lutz, "Decision Plans and Consumer Choice Dynamics," *Journal of Marketing Research*, February 1982, pp. 108–15.

32. This terminology is borrowed from John Howard, *Consumer Behavior: Applications of Theory* (New York: McGraw-Hill, 1979).

33. Robert J. Meyer, "The Learning of Multiattribute Judgment Policies," *Journal of Consumer Research*, September 1987, pp. 155–73.

34. James H. Myers, "Attribute Deficiency Segmentation: Measuring Unmet Wants," in *Advances in Consumer Research*, vol. 15, ed. Michael J. Houston (Provo, Utah: Association for Consumer Research, 1988), pp. 108–13.

35. Lawrence W. Barsalou and J. Wesley Hutchinson, "Schema-Based Planning of Events in Consumer Contexts," in *Advances in Consumer Research*, vol. 14, ed. Melanie Wallendorf and Paul Anderson (Provo, Utah: Association for Consumer Research, 1987), pp. 114–18.

36. This section was adapted from Bettman, *An Information Processing Theory of Consumer Choice.*

37. Ronald P. Hill and Meryl P. Gardner, "The Buying Process: Effects Of and On Consumer Mood States," in *Advances in Consumer Research*, vol. 14, ed. Melanie Wallendorf and Paul Anderson (Provo, Utah: Association for Consumer Research, 1987), pp. 408–10.

38. Hansen, "Psychological Theories of Consumer Choice," pp. 117–42; and Bettman, *An Information Processing Theory of Consumer Choice.*

39. George A. Miller, Eugene Galanter, and Karl H. Pribram, *Plans and the Structure of Behavior* (New York: Henry Holt, 1960).

40. Robert M. Schlinder, Michael Berbaum, and Donna R. Weinzimer, "How an Attention Getting Device Can Affect Choice among Similar

Alternatives," in *Advances in Consumer Research*, vol. 14, ed. Melanie Wallendorf and Paul Anderson (Provo, Utah: Association for Consumer Research, 1987), pp. 505–09.

41. Dennis W. Rook, "The Buying Impulse," *Journal of Consumer Research*, September 1987, pp. 189–99.

42. Kevin Lane Keller and Richard Staelin, "Effects of Quality and Quantity of Information on Decision Effectiveness," *Journal of Consumer Research*, September 1987, pp. 200–13.

Additional Reading

For a discussion of consumer decision making, see:

Ursic, Michael. "Consumer Decision Making—Fact or Fiction? Comment." *Journal of Consumer Research*, December 1980, pp. 331–33.

Olshavsky, Richard W., and Donald H. Granbois. "Rejoinder." *Journal of Consumer Research*, December 1980, pp. 333–34.

For a discussion of the problem-solving process, see:

Cox, Anthony; Donald Granbois; and John Summers. "Planning, Search, Certainty and Satisfaction among Durables Buyers: A Longitudinal Study." In *Advances in Consumer Research*, vol. 10, ed. Richard P. Bagozzi and Alice T. Tybout. Ann Arbor, Mich.: Association for Consumer Research, 1983, pp. 394–99.

For a discussion of impulse purchasing and affective response, see:

Gardner, Meryl Paula, and Dennis W. Rook. "Effects of Impulse Purchases on Consumers' Affective States." In *Advances in Consumer Research*, vol. 15, ed. Michael J. Houston. Provo, Utah: Association for Consumer Research, 1988, pp. 127–30.

For a discussion of how decision plans are modified during decision making, see:

Iyer, Easwar S., and Sucheta S. Ahlawat. "Deviations from a Shopping Plan: When and Why Do Consumers Not Buy Items as Planned." In *Advances in Consumer Research*, vol. 14, ed. Melanie Wallendorf and Paul Anderson. Provo, Utah: Association for Consumer Research, 1987, pp. 246–50.

For a discussion of inferential beliefs in consumer decision making, see:

Dick, Alan, Dipankar Chakravarti, and Gabriel Biehal. "Memory-Based Inferences During Consumer Choice." *Journal of Consumer Research*, June 1990, pp. 82–93.

For a discussion of how to measure the cognitive processes that occur during decision making, see:

Biehal, Gabriel, and Dipankar Chakravarti. "The Effects of Concurrent Verbalization on Choice Processing." *Journal of Marketing Research*, February 1989, pp. 84–96.

For a discussion of how marketing managers (in contrast to consumers) use information to make strategy decisions, see:

Perkins, W. Steven, and Ram C. Rao. "The Role of Experience in Information Use and Decision Making by Marketing Managers." *Journal of Marketing Research*, February 1990, pp. 1–10.

For a discussion of an unusual decision (whether or not to shoplift), see:

Cox, Dena, Anthony D. Cox and George P. Moschis. "When Consumer Behavior Goes Bad: An Investigation of Adolescent Shoplifting." *Journal of Consumer Research*, September 1990, pp. 149–59.

For a discussion of desire, willpower, and self-control in consumer problem solving, see:

Hoch, Stephen J., and George F. Lowenstein. "Time-Inconsistent Preferences and Consumer Self-Control." *Journal of Consumer Research*, March 1991, pp. 492–507.

For a discussion of choices of products as gifts to oneself, see:

Mick, David Glen, and Michelle Demoss. "Self-Gifts: Phenomenological Insights from Four Contexts." *Journal of Consumer Research*, December 1990, pp. 322–32.

For a discussion of how consumers make choices among very different choice alternatives, see:

Johnson, Michael D. "The Differential Processing of Product Category and Noncomparable Choice Alternatives." *Journal of Consumer Research*, December 1989, pp. 300–9.

MARKETING STRATEGY IN ACTION

HALLMARK GREETING CARDS

It is one of the least likely businesses ever invented. However, Hallmark and its main competitors—American Greetings and Gibson Greetings, plus an assortment of so-called alternative card companies—make a very good living selling sentiment to American consumers. In fact, greeting cards are one of the most profitable things that can be made with paper and ink.

Pansies always stand for thoughts—
At least that's what folks say,
So this just comes to show my thoughts
Are there with you today.

Since 1941, Hallmark has sold 22 million of this simple card. In 1985, the card cost an estimated 7 cents to manufacture and retailed for about 40 cents. Assuming a 100 percent markup at retail, Hallmark received about 20 cents at wholesale, for almost a 200 percent profit. With these financial numbers, Hallmark has grown at a compounded rate of 17 percent each year for more than 80 years. In 1985, annual revenues approached $2 billion. Although nearly 50 percent of Hallmark's revenues come from ancillary products such as gift wrap, stuffed animals, and paper plates, greeting cards are still the most profitable line.

The costs of a card reflect not so much the paper or even the artwork, but the organized distribution system. Hallmark produces more than 11 million cards per day, which are sent to some 37,000 outlets, most independently owned. The company has invested millions of dollars in computers to keep track of the product. "We know which card is four rows up and five rows over, and how long it's been there," says a company representative. Reorders are shipped from two enormous automated warehouses, based on the past sales of each card. Because 90 percent of the cards are replaced with new designs each year, records must be constantly updated. Currently, Hallmark has some 32,000 card types to keep track of.

Hallmark didn't invent the commercial greeting card. Well-to-do Americans exchanged expensive Christmas cards with friends as long ago as the 1870s. This genteel custom was popularized by two marketing-oriented men—Jacob Sapirstein for American Greetings and Joyce Hall for Hallmark. Between them, they persuaded consumers to buy graduation cards, wedding cards, sympathy cards, and cards for many other occasions.

The card business in the United States is treacherous, highly competitive, and huge. In

1988, American consumers spent about $3.7 billion on cards (not including postage!). So popular are the products, that about 50 percent of all mail between U.S. households is greeting cards.

The market is expected to grow even larger. A forecast by Packaged Facts of New York predicted a $5.2 billion market by 1991, the increase largely due to higher sales for alternative cards. Alternative cards are loosely defined as any card with a fresh approach to the market. For instance, there are cards intended for such diverse groups as stepgrandparents, recent divorcees, stressed-out working parents, and gays. In addition to the traditional birthday, graduation, and Mother's Day cards, cards are being produced for specific occasions such as getting a new job or getting fired from your old one, making up after a romantic tiff, and going on a diet.

There are three main companies in the United States. Hallmark has about 40 percent of the market, American Greetings has 30 to 35 percent, and Gibson Greetings has 10 percent. Hallmark is in the nerve-racking position of being the front-runner in a race where the pace of change has been accelerating. Moreover, "alternative" cards (risque or goofy) are becoming a serious threat, accounting for about 17 percent of the market. For instance, Recycled Paper Products, with sales of $100 million in whimsical animal cards, has been growing at a rate of 30 percent a year. Several small companies are thriving by making cards for niche markets that Hallmark leaves alone—such as cards for gays.

"The big segment of the market is what we deal in," says Irvine Hockaday, president of Hallmark. However, in 1982, Hallmark introduced a "Lite" line of cards ("A third less serious than regular greeding cards"). More recently, it introduced cards to compete with the alternative lines. While not exactly salacious—"I'd like to tell you how much I love you. Have you got all night?"—these cards are not what you'd send to Aunt Tillie.

What is the allure of greeting cards for American consumers? No other society sends so many cards per capita, although the practice is common in Great Britain, where there is a large market. What goals or ends do greeting cards satisfy for the person who sends them? They certainly are not a convenience. "It takes more time to drive down to the store and pick out a card than to write a letter," says a sociology professor. What's wrong with a handwritten note, a telephone call, or a personal visit?

In 1986 to 1987, Hallmark changed its overall marketing strategy to emphasize *image.* This strategy recognized the importance of consumers' store choice in the overall problem-solving processes of selecting a greeting card. Hallmark had a particular interest in store choice since most of its greeting cards are sold in "Hallmark stores" that sell only (or mostly) Hallmark products such as cards, wrapping paper, party goods, toys, and knickknacks. Although most of these stores are privately owned, many are identified as "Hallmark stores" in the store name—e.g., Linda's Hallmark. With this type of distribution system, consumers must first decide to go to a Hallmark store in order to buy a Hallmark card.

To remind consumers where they should go to buy Hallmark cards, the company added a new phrase, ". . . go to Hallmark," after their familiar slogan, "When you care enough to send the very best. . . . " Hallmark also created ads for newspapers and Sunday supplements that listed all the local Hallmark retailers and their addresses. American Greetings, whose cards are widely distributed in grocery, department, and discount stores, countered with its own retailer-oriented campaign, "You never have to go out of your way to find American Greetings, because we're in the kinds of stores you shop every day." The battle to influence consumers' store choice was on.

Discussion Questions

1. What are evaluative criteria for greetings cards, and what are their dominant overall end goals? How do these factors differ by market segment?
2. It has been estimated that approximately 80 percent of all greeting cards sold in the United States are purchased by women. Do you think there are major differences in the decision-making processes of men and women? What are the implications of these differences for marketing strategies?
3. Contrast the problem representations of heavy users of cards (12 or more cards per year, exclusive of Christmas cards) from light users (4 or fewer cards per year) in terms of end goals, goal hierarchy, product-related knowledge, and felt involvement.
4. How do Hallmark cards get into consumers' consideration sets? Analyze the role of the store choice decision in this process. (Hint: How does store choice fit into the overall goal hierarchy for the card decision?) Do you think some consumers might become store loyal?
5. What heuristics might consumers develop to simplify their problem-solving processes for buying greeting cards? How could marketers introduce interrupts to affect this process?

Sources: "Greeting Card Industry Targets New Segments with Offbeat Alternatives," *Marketing News,* January 18, 1988, pp. 19, 22; Robert McGough, "Pansies Are Green," *Forbes,* February 10, 1986, pp. 888–92; and Sara E. Stern, "Card Rivals Deal Ads: Convenience vs. New Lines," *Advertising Age,* July 27, 1987, p. 28.

SECTION 3

BEHAVIOR AND MARKETING STRATEGY

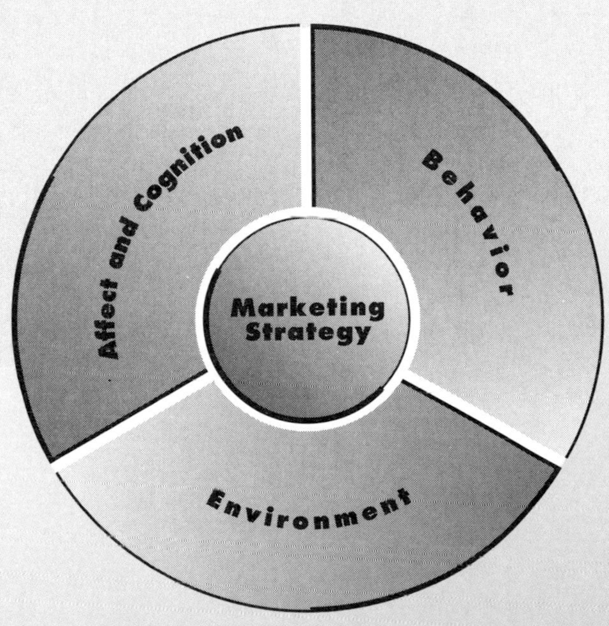

Introduction to Behavior

CHAPTER

WHAT WERE THESE MARKETERS TRYING TO DO?

Ralston-Purina ran a promotion for six of its children's cereals that was aimed at adults. Inside 11 million boxes of cereal with names like Freakies and Ghostbusters, Ralston-Purina included tiny models of sports cars. Ten of the boxes contained a scale-model red Corvette that could be redeemed for the real thing—a $29,000 Chevrolet Corvette.

Citicorp offered gifts tied to the amount charged on its credit cards. For $500 charged on its Visa card, consumers got free golf balls or a travel clock; for $8,000 in charges, they received a round-trip airline ticket for anywhere in the United States.

General Mills inserted a single $1 bill into every 20th box of its Cheerios cereal. The promotion involved giving away $1 million.

Pepsi-Cola offered chances to win cash and prizes in its "Count the Wins" baseball game. Numbers were printed inside specially marked cans and caps. If the number matched the total number of wins by the Milwaukee Brewers on specific dates, the holder qualified for drawings for $10,000 and $30,000. In addition, there were a number of instant prizes including $1,000, two tickets to a Brewers game, and two-liter bottles of any Pepsi product.

American TV of Madison, Wisconsin, offered 100 pounds of beefsteak to those who purchased specially marked items. Some items with prices as low as $69 still qualified for the steak bonus.

What were these marketers trying to do? The previous section presented an in-depth analysis of consumer cognitive and affective processes. The major focus of that section was an attempt to understand the internal psychology or mental aspects of consumer behavior. The focus changes in this section. Our concern here is with attempting to understand overt consumer behavior; i.e., behavior that can be directly observed and measured. We will focus on what consumers *do* rather than on what they *think* and *feel*, and we will delineate some processes by which this behavior can be changed to achieve marketing objectives.

In this chapter, we first compare *cognitive* and *behavior* approaches in terms of some differences in positions and assumptions, research approaches and practices, and views of marketing. We do this so that you can appreciate the differences between the approaches and can understand why there are so few attempts to integrate them. We maintain that both cognitive and behavior approaches have value for the study of consumer behavior and for achieving marketing management objectives. We view attempts to keep the perspectives separated as counterproductive and as a detriment to consumer behavior inquiry. While cognitive and behavior perspectives may not be fully reconcilable, useful information and procedures can be gleaned from each.

After we review the differences in perspectives, we discuss two areas of consumer research that have recognized the value of behavior approaches. These areas are sales promotion and social marketing. The chapter concludes with a discussion of some common misconceptions about behavior approaches.

In Chapter 9, classical and operant conditioning are explained and illustrated with a variety of marketing examples. We then turn to vicarious learning and its value for marketing (Chapter 10). These two chapters provide an overview of the major technology employed in applied behavior analysis. In Chapter 11, the last chapter of this section, we develop a model of overt consumer behavior and a management model for systematically influencing these behaviors.

Cognitive versus Behavior Views

Cognitive approaches, including some aspects of affect, dominate the field of consumer behavior and much of the thinking in marketing. Although behavior approaches have been an important part of psychology for many years, they are relatively new to consumer research and often are not well understood or appreciated. For this reason, we think it is important to give a detailed account of the differences between the two approaches.

There are many types of cognitive theories and assumptions and a variety of behavior positions. For example, some cognitive approaches attempt to apply cognitive theories in explaining overt behavior. Others are concerned only with explaining the mind and mental processes. Some behaviorists view cognitive events as covert behavior to be analyzed in the same way as overt behavior. Other behaviorists see cognitive events as little more than words that may be useful for communication purposes but useless as scientific explanations. It is unlikely that any discussion of differences between cognitive and behavior perspectives would be accepted by all advocates of either position, but we will attempt to offer representative accounts of them.

The **behavior approach** is based on a current view called "applied behavior analysis." The **cognitive view** is based on current research on topics such as information processing and cognitive science. You will soon see why the two perspectives have been antagonists: they often involve quite different views of the world, with conflicting positions and assumptions, approaches to research, and beliefs about what counts as scientifically important. Most important for our purposes, these approaches often have different implications for designing marketing strategies and consumer research.

Positions and Assumptions

Figure 8.1 provides an overview of some of the major differences in positions and assumptions between the two approaches. While the behavior and cognitive approaches have similar philosophical roots, each has selected different routes to seeking knowledge about humans. The behavior view typically prefers observing behavior that can be measured somewhat directly. The cognitive view allows for theoretical or mental variables that are measured indirectly through such means as verbal reports.

We believe both approaches have value, but neither one alone can provide a complete set of guidelines for developing marketing strategy. Neither approach has escaped severe criticism in the literature on the philosophy of science, and the history of science demonstrates clearly that there are many useful approaches to seeking knowledge.[1] Thus, we believe marketing and consumer researchers would be well advised to use whatever means are available to gain knowledge and not attempt to force themselves into one or the other mold. In

FIGURE 8.1
A Comparison of Positions and Assumptions

Positions and Assumptions	Behavior Approaches	Cognitive Approaches
View of concepts	Observational, physical	Theoretical, mental
Role of the environment	Predominant controlling variable	One influence among many others
Role of cognitive factors	Merely mediators	Predominant controlling variables
View of freedom	All behavior is controlled by environmental factors	Humans are autonomous, independent centers of action

fact, attempts to follow only one set of values have resulted in the schism between the behavior and cognitive views.

A critical difference between the two perspectives concerns the cause or causes of behavior. Many behaviorists argue the *environment* controls behavior, while many cognitivists insist *individuals* control their own behavior through the mental processes involved in cognitive processing and decision making. This demonstrates why the two perspectives are not fully reconcilable. For many behaviorists, even if cognitive events are viewed as affecting behavior, the environment still causes the cognitive events. Thus, the environment is the cause and controller of behavior. However, many cognitivists believe consumers are independent decision makers who consciously choose their behavior.

The assumption that much consumer behavior is controlled by the environment is one many people refuse to accept. All of us like to view ourselves as decision makers who control the environment rather than seeing the environment as controlling us. Yet consider the following example: Almost every adult in our society purchases and uses deodorant. In fact, it is socially unacceptable *not* to use it. The social environment conditions this behavior, for its performance is rewarded with social acceptance, and lack of performance is often punished with social sanctions. Are we really free to choose whether or not to use deodorant, given the consequences? Isn't this "choice" determined by environmental contingencies? In any event, you can see that the consequences of a behavior have an important influence on whether or not the behavior is performed.

Research Approaches and Stages

Figure 8.2 presents a comparison of typical approaches and stages in the research process from the two points of view. Behavior approaches often take

FIGURE 8.2
A Comparison of Research Approaches and Stages

Research Approaches

Research Dimensions	Behavior Approaches	Cognitive Approaches
Research objectives	Change behavior	Test theory
Object of study	Overt behavior; functional relationships	Mind: mental structures and processes
Basic data	Observation	Verbal reports
Criteria for successful research	Socially significant amount of behavior change	Logical relationships and statistical significance
Typical research setting	Natural	Laboratory

Research Stages

Behavior Approaches	Cognitive Approaches
1. Identify behavior problem	Find/develop cognitive theory
2. Measure current frequency of behavior problem and environmental conditions	Determine hypotheses
3. Design intervention	Develop measures/manipulations
4. Determine intervention setting/subjects	Sample subjects
5. Implement intervention	Collect data
6. Remeasure target behavior	Analyze data
7. Determine amount of behavior change	Draw inference about internal psychology

the *prediction and control of behavior* to be the fundamental goal of research; cognitive approaches are often concerned with *explanation* and *theory testing.* Typically, behavior approaches suggest that data be collected through observation; cognitive research often employs verbal reports obtained through questionnaires.

A major difference between the two is in the starting point for conducting research. Applied behavior analysis often starts with a behavior problem, such as littering, and then attempts to change this behavior. Cognitive research often starts with a theory and attempts to design research to test it. For example, the dominant approach to consumer research involves attempts to test cognitive theories in a marketing context. While there are some similarities at a number of research stages, the criteria by which research is judged is quite different. Behavior research is usually considered successful if a sufficient amount of behavior is changed; cognitive research is generally considered successful if a logical, statistically significant relationship is supported.[2]

Both research approaches can provide valuable information for designing marketing strategies. For example, cognitive research employing verbal reports could be very useful for investigating differences in consumer perceptions of Gates versus Saranac ski gloves. Behavior research could be very useful for investigating the impact of various sales promotion tools, such as a $20 factory rebate on Head skis.

Views of Marketing

Figure 8.3 offers a comparison of how users of each approach tend to view the field of marketing. From a behavior perspective, marketing can be viewed as a *technology* that seeks solutions to practical problems. From a cognitive perspective, marketing is often viewed as a *science* that seeks explanations. Behavior approaches offer basic principles of behavior as a guide to marketing planning and strategy. Cognitive approaches often depend on the marketing concept as a guide to strategy development.

Using the marketing concept, those supporting the cognitive approach might offer the following view: Because the marketing concept suggests marketing action should be based on an attempt to satisfy needs at a profit, two cognitive assumptions underlie it. First, it is assumed consumers have something called "needs," which they attempt to satisfy through purchase and consumption. Second, it is assumed consumers are somewhat autonomous and rational and are decision makers whose preferences and purchases are largely personally controlled. This view also recognizes that marketing strategies attempt to change consumer affect and cognitions, such as beliefs and attitudes, but usually denies that marketing can *create* consumer needs and wants or even modify them very much. Similarly, the question of whether marketing is very effective at changing consumer behavior is seldom addressed by cognitivists.

In contrast, many behaviorists would tend to offer a different account of marketing activity. Marketing may be seen as an attempt to achieve organizational objectives by predicting and influencing consumer behavior. These objectives typically involve increases in profits and/or market share, both of which are usually achieved by increasing sales. Two primary methods of increasing sales are: (1) influencing current buyers to buy more of the product, and (2) maintaining current buyers while influencing nonbuyers to become buyers. Both of these involve changing consumer purchase behavior. Many behaviorists would argue that marketing strategies are often effective at changing and maintaining consumer behavior—and that a variety of current marketing tactics are quite consistent with behavioral principles. Some behaviorists might even suggest that marketing executives typically pay little attention to consumer needs in developing new products,[3] and that discussions of topics such as pricing, advertising, and personal selling in marketing texts are far more concerned with tactics for making profitable sales than with satisfying consumer needs.

FIGURE 8.3
A Comparison of Views of Marketing

Marketing Issues	Behavior Approaches	Cognitive Approaches
Status of the field	Technology	Science
Role of marketing	Modify and control consumer behavior to achieve organizational objective	Satisfy needs of consumers at a profit
Guide to marketing planning	Behavior principles	Marketing concept
Role of marketing/ consumer research	Investigate strategies for predicting and controlling consumer behavior	Describe internal psychology of consumers
View of marketing effectiveness	Recognize the effectiveness of marketing in changing behavior	Often overlook the effectiveness of marketing

In summary, the two approaches differ considerably when applied to marketing and consumer behavior. Which approach is "true" or "right" is not an important question. What is important is which approach or combination of approaches is most *useful* in various stages of solving marketing problems and developing marketing strategies.

We believe a combination of both approaches is superior to either one taken separately. For example, if consideration of consumer needs is helpful in the development of successful new products, and if operant conditioning is helpful in increasing market share for the product, there is no reason to ignore one or the other approach. Highlight 8.1 illustrates a successful marketing strategy that used both approaches.

Influencing Overt Consumer Behavior

Although consumer researchers have not developed a large body of research based on the behavior approach, behavioral principles form the foundation for work in several areas. The first of these is sales promotion, an area of increasing interest by academic consumer researchers and marketing practitioners. A second area deals with social marketing issues. Although much of the research in this area is outside of the traditional consumer behavior literature, the behavior approach is commonly used to develop strategies to influence socially desirable consumer behaviors.

HIGHLIGHT 8.1

Lifetime Cable Network

Many marketing practitioners are very effective at using a combination of cognitive and behavioral approaches. For example, Lifetime Cable Network conducted cognitive research on why viewers were not watching its programs. A finding of this research was that one in five viewers erroneously thought Lifetime was a religious network.

The network set three behavioral objectives: (1) to get more people to "sample" Lifetime's new programming; (2) to get those who may look at Lifetime now to watch a wider variety of programs; and (3) to get people to *keep* watching.

The strategy used to accomplish these objectives featured a "Chance of a Lifetime" game. The game required viewers to match symbols from a game card with symbols shown on the air. The game cards were sent to viewers with their cable bills or could be obtained in *TV Guide* or through requests during on-air promotion. The game was easy to understand and play, lasted long enough to keep people watching, and spread winning symbols over the entire programming day. The $400,000 worth of prizes included stereo systems, personal computers, romantic get-away weekends for two, and many other prizes with universal appeal. There was a game each week for eight weeks, and 200 prizes per week were awarded. A "second chance" drawing offered the grand prize of a $25,000 tour of Europe.

This strategy greatly increased viewer interest and cable system support. For example, on a single day, nearly 1,100 subscribers sent in entries. Tens of thousands of entries for the "second chance" contest were received before the main contest even finished. Thus, by analyzing cognitions to identify the problem and by devising a unique behavioral intervention to solve the problem, a successful marketing strategy was developed.

Source: Based on "Behind the Lifetime Sweeps," *Promotion Hotline,* Ogilvy & Mather Promotions, May 1985, pp. 1–2.

Sales Promotion

One area of consumer research that has recognized the value of a behavior approach is sales promotion. Leading experts define **sales promotion** as "an action-focused marketing event whose purpose is to have a direct impact on the behavior of a firm's customers."[4] Two points are noteworthy in this definition.

First, the firm's customers may be channel members, such as retailers, in which case the promotion is called a trade promotion. **Trade promotions,** such as advertising or display allowances, are used by companies to push products through the channel to consumers. Alternatively, the firm's customers may be

HIGHLIGHT 8.2

Trends in Sales Promotion Expenditures

Although advertising remains an important promotion tool, sales promotion expenditures have grown rapidly in recent years. For example:

- Combined consumer and trade promotion spending as a percentage of advertising/promotion budgets grew from 58 percent in 1976 to 65 percent in 1987 to 69.4 percent in 1990.
- Manufacturers distributed 75 billion coupons in 1977 and more than 300 billion in 1990.
- More than $1.1 billion was spent on media space to carry coupons in 1990 compared with $979 million in 1989.

Many reasons have been offered for the increase in the use of consuumer promotions including that advertising is becoming less effective, consumers are more price sensitive, and the sales effects of promotions are easier to measure than those of advertising. Perhaps one additional reason is that promotions focus directly on changing consumer behavior, a major goal of marketing.

Sources: The comparative statistics are taken from Robert C. Blattberg and Scott A. Neslin, *Sales Promotion: Concepts, Methods, and Strategies* (Englewood Cliffs, N.J.: Prentice Hall, Inc., 1990), p. 15; Carrie Goerne, "Marketers Using More Coupons to Fight Recession," *Marketing News,* October 29, 1991, p. 6; and Cyndee Miller, "Trade Promotion Spending in 1990 Hits Record Level," *Marketing News,* October 29, 1991, p. 6.

final consumers, in which case the promotions are called **consumer promotions.** Consumer promotions, such as coupons and free samples, are used by manufacturers and retailers to pull consumers to purchase products and visit retail outlets. In one recent year, overall expenditures on promotion were divided 44.3 percent on trade promotions, 30.6 percent on advertising, and 25.1 percent on consumer promotions. As shown in Highlight 8.2, the importance of sales promotion has grown considerably in recent years.

Second, the emphasis on affecting the behavior of customers clearly positions this definition with the behavior approach taken in this section of our text. Many consumer promotions contain little information designed to change consumer cognitions about the product. Rather, most consumer promotions are designed to influence the probability of purchase or other desired behaviors without necessarily changing prepurchase consumer attitudes about a brand. If the promotion is for a new brand, then purchase and use may lead to favorable postpurchase attitudes and future purchases. If purchase is for an existing brand, consumers with a neutral or slightly positive attitude may use the promotion to reduce purchase risk and try it. For consumers who already purchase a brand, a promotion may be an added incentive to remain loyal.

The primary concern of this text is with consumer promotions and their influence on consumer behavior. There are many types of consumer promotions. The list below covers the majority of them.[5]

1. *Sampling.* Consumers are offered regular or trial sizes of the product either free or at a nominal price. For example, Hershey Foods handed out 750,000 candy bars on 170 college campuses.
2. *Price deals.* Consumers are given discounts from the product's regular price. For example, Coke and Pepsi are frequently available at discounted prices.
3. *Bonus packs.* Bonus packs consist of additional amounts of the product that a company gives to buyers of the product. For example, Gillette Atra occasionally adds a few extra blades to its blade packs without increasing the price.
4. *Rebates and refunds.* Consumers, either at purchase or by mail, are given cash reimbursements for purchasing products. For example, consumers are often offered rebates for purchasing Chrysler or Ford automobiles.
5. *Sweepstakes and contests.* Consumers are offered chances to win cash and/or prizes either through chance selection or games of skill. For example, Marriott Hotels teamed up with Hertz Rent-A-Car in a scratch-card sweepstakes that offered over $90 million in prizes.
6. *Premiums.* A premium is a reward or gift that comes from purchasing a product. For example, Procter & Gamble offered a free package of Diaperene baby washcloths with the purchase of any size Pampers.
7. *Coupons.* Consumers are offered cents-off or added-value incentives for purchasing specific products. For example, Lenscrafters offered newspaper coupons for $20 off on the purchase of contact lenses from its stores.

These basic types of consumer promotions are often used in combination to increase the probability of desired behaviors. For example, P&G offered a $1-off coupon plus a premium coupon for a free Duncan Hines cake mix for purchasing any size Folgers coffee. Recently, many consumer promotions have featured coupons plus a promise to make donations to specific charities for every coupon or refund certificate redeemed. For example, Hartz Mountain offered a $1 coupon on its flea and tick repellent plus a 50-cent donation to the Better Health for Pets Program.

Consumer promotions can be used to influence behavior in a variety of ways. Below we discuss four aspects of behavior that promotions are designed to affect.

Purchase Probability

Most consumer promotions are designed to increase the probability that consumers will purchase a particular brand or combination of products. However, a firm may have any of a number of subgoals it hopes to achieve when running a

Do you think rebates change consumer behavior?

promotion. For a new product, the primary goal may be to get consumers to try a product. For example, Hershey offered a free package of Reese's Crunchy peanut butter cups with the purchase of any other Reese's candy product to attempt to induce trial of the new product. Kellogg's offered a coupon for an 18-ounce box of its popular corn flakes with the purchase of its new Kellogg's Mini Buns. Also, some car dealers offer special discounts for first-time buyers.

A second subgoal of consumer promotions may be to position a brand or company in the minds of consumers to encourage them to purchase and continue to purchase the company's brand. In this case, the promotion is designed to maintain or change consumer affect, cognitions, and behaviors. One way of doing so is to use frequent promotions to obtain a competitive price on a brand that is positioned as a high priced, high quality product. In this way, the lower price has less chance of leading consumers to believe the product is of lower quality than competitive brands. For example, Kellogg's frequently offers coupons and premiums on its market-leading cereals.

Another use of promotion for positioning purposes is to offer to make contributions to charity for each coupon or refund certificate redeemed by consumers. This tactic may increase consumer perceptions of the societal commitment of firms. Consumers who are socially and ecologically concerned may then switch to purchasing these companies' brands. In addition to the Hartz

Mountain example noted above, many other companies also use this type of promotion. Post Alpha Bits offered a 50-cent coupon and promised to make an unspecified donation to Hospitals for Children for each coupon redeemed. Chef Boyardee Pizza Mix offered a 20-cent coupon and promised to make a 25-cent donation to Adam Walsh Resource Centers for each coupon redeemed. Krunchers Potato Chips offered a 25-cent coupon and promised to make a contribution to the Better Homes Foundation. Procter & Gamble offered a 50-cent refund for a number of its soap products and promised a $1 contribution to Keep America Beautiful, Inc., for each refund certificate redeemed.

A third subgoal of consumer promotions is to obtain a brand switch. Consumer promotions may obtain brand switches by making the purchase of a brand more attractive than purchasing the usual brand at full price.

A final goal of consumer promotions is to develop brand loyalty. Because some consumers tend to purchase products based on coupons and other deals, frequent deals on particular brands may keep them relatively loyal in terms of purchasing the firm's brands. Companies, such as Kellogg's and P&G, that have broad product lines and a number of top-selling products, frequently offer a variety of forms of consumer promotions for their products. Even deal-prone consumers who have preferred brands may remain loyal through a long succession of coupons and other deals.

Purchase Quantity

A number of consumer promotions are designed not only to influence purchase of a brand but also to influence that number of units purchased or size of units purchased. For example, Quaker Oats offered a 70-cent coupon for purchasing two bottles of Gatorade. Best Foods offered a $1 coupon for purchasing two 18-ounce or larger jars of Skippy peanut butter. P&G offered $2, $5, and $8 refunds for purchasing one, two, or three gallons of Tide, Cheer, Era, or Solo liquid laundry detergent. A free Mennen Speed Stick deodorant was offered with the purchase of two at the regular price. Such promotions may increase the amount of a company's product that consumers purchase and may increase brand loyalty. However, consumers who already are loyal to particular brands may simply stock up on them during a promotion and wait until the next promotion to purchase again. Some consumers prefer to purchase products only when they can get a deal on them. U.S. car manufacturers have unintentionally conditioned many consumers to wait for rebates rather than buy a car without one.

Purchase Timing

Consumer promotions can also be used to influence the time at which consumers purchase. For example, special discounts can be offered to encourage consumers to eat at particular restaurants on nights when business is slow. Pizza Hut often offers discounts and special family prices for Monday or Tuesday nights. Other retail stores have special sales on specific dates to encourage

Some promotions are intended to influence the purchase quantity.

purchases at that time. Services, such as airlines and telephone companies, offer special rates to encourage consumers to use them at specific times and dates to even out demand. One trend in the use of coupons shortens the redemption period to encourage consumers to purchase sooner. Finally, most sweepstakes and contests are of relatively short duration to encourage consumers to enter the contest by purchasing the product promptly.

Purchase Location

Consumer promotions can also be used to influence the location or vendor of particular products. Retail stores and retail chains offer their own coupons, contests, and other deals to encourage consumers to shop at their outlets. For example, one grocery chain offered $20 worth of beef if a consumer was selected at a specific store and was found to have a beef product in his or her shopping cart. Some retail chains, such as Wal Mart, have a standing offer to meet any other store's price on a product if the Wal Mart price is higher. Such promotions and tactics can build store traffic and encourage store loyalty as discussed in Highlight 8.3.

HIGHLIGHT 8.3

Amoco's Big Summer Fill-Up

Amoco Oil Company ran a promotion designed to build store loyalty to Amoco filling stations. The promotion required consumers to fill up (a minimum of eight gallons) at an Amoco station 10 times and to get a promotion card punched by an attendant. This all had to be done within a specified three-month period. After 10 fill-ups, consumers could mail the card to the "Amoco Fill-Up" address and receive coupons for $1 off on their next five fill-ups.

Consider the possible outcomes of this promotion. If consumers complied with all of the requirements and used the five coupons, then they made 15 trips to an Amoco station and made 15 purchases of eight gallons or more. This is a considerable amount of behavior and sales to generate for the company for a relatively small $5 reward. In addition, since Amoco gas is more expensive than gas at discount stations, the consumer may not have saved money. If a consumer averaged buying 10 gallons at a time and paid 5 cents more a gallon for Amoco gas, in 15 trips, he or she spent an additional $7.50 to save $5. However, Amoco gas is of excellent quality, may give the consumer savings in better gas mileage, and the consumer's car may run better by using it. Thus, the promotion could get consumers in the habit of going to an Amoco station and lead to loyalty. The superior product could also contribute to this loyalty.

The promotion card also stated that it would take six to eight weeks to receive the coupons. If the consumer continued to use Amoco in the meantime, the company continued to make full-price sales. If the consumer went to other stations in the waiting period, then receipt of the coupons could bring them back to Amoco, giving the company a second chance to develop loyalty.

If consumers did not fill up 10 times in three months, they did not qualify for the promotion. However, in making a point of trying to go to an Amoco station, the consumer might also have developed a loyalty to it. In this case, Amoco developed a loyal customer but did not have to pay the promotion value to do so. Overall, this promotion strategy would appear to be one that was well designed and capable of building long-term loyal customers.

Effectiveness of Sales Promotions

There is little question that promotions effectively influence consumer behavior. However, which promotion tools are generally most effective for achieving particular behavioral changes is not fully understood. However, one study compared four consumer promotion tools—coupons, rebates, sweepstakes, and premiums—for their impact on various consumer purchase behaviors.[6] These behaviors included purchasing a product consumers said they didn't need, purchasing a product they had never tried before, purchasing a different brand

FIGURE 8.4
Promotion Effects on Consumer Behavior

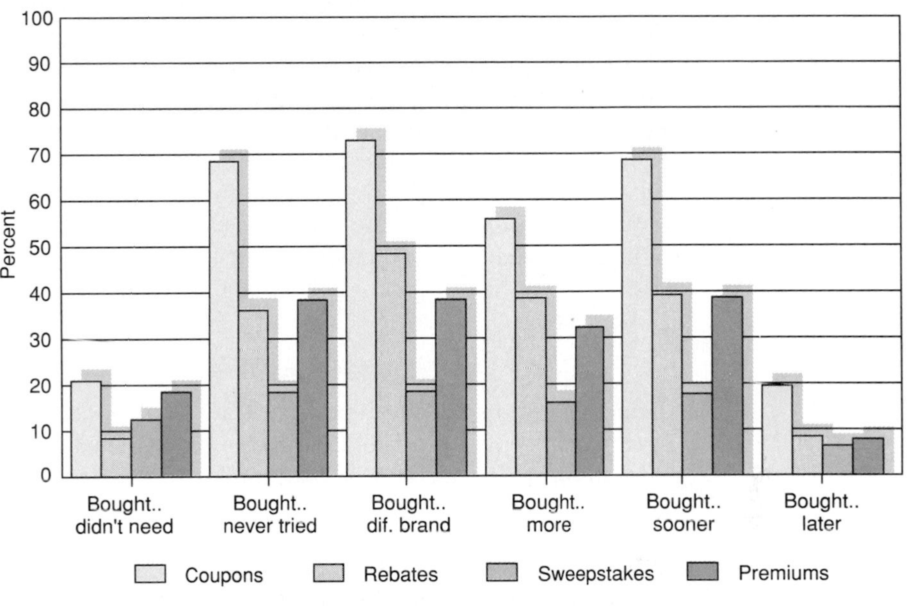

Source: "Study: Some Promotions Change Consumer Behavior," *Marketing News,* October 15, 1990, p. 12.

than they regularly used, purchasing more than usual, purchasing sooner than usual, and purchasing later than usual.

Figure 8.4 presents the results of that study. In general, consumers reported that coupons were the most effective promotions at changing these various behaviors. Over 70 percent of the consumers reported they purchased a product they had never tried before because of a coupon, and more than 75 percent said they purchased a different brand than they regularly use because of a coupon. Of the four promotion tools, coupons are the most commonly available and easiest to use.

Rebates and premiums were both shown to be effective in changing consumer behavior in this study but less so than coupons. The study found that the greater the rebate, the greater effort consumers would expend to obtain it. Finally, while some consumers also reported that sweepstakes influenced them, such promotions were the least effective overall. The study also found that changes in behavior varied by the type of product and characteristics of the consumers. For example, for products such as shampoo, coffee, batteries, toothpaste, and personal appliances, promotions could persuade the majority of consumers to try a different brand. However, for products such as alcoholic beverages, automobiles, motor oil, pet food, and floor coverings, consumers reported that promotions would not persuade them to switch brands. In terms of consumer characteristics, consumers who are more affluent, educated, and older are more likely to participate in consumer promotions, according to this study.

In sum, promotions can change consumer behavior, although there are many contingencies that can influence their effectiveness. Consistent with the behavior approach, it seems likely that the greater the reward, the less effort required to obtain the reward, and the sooner the reward is obtained after the behavior, the more likely the promotion will be influential. However, further research on consumer promotions is needed to better understand the affect and cognitions, behaviors, and environmental factors that influence their effectiveness.

Social Marketing

Social marketing deals with programs and strategies designed to change behavior in ways deemed good for consumers and for society. There is considerable research on such programs, although most of it is in applied behavior analysis

Companies often associate their products with positive societal goals.

literature rather than the traditional consumer behavior literature. This research investigates methods of increasing desired behaviors and decreasing undesired consumer behaviors.

Increasing Desired Behaviors

Many types of behaviors can be increased through the use of behavior approaches. For example, research has shown that various incentives can increase the probability that parents will take their children in for dental and health care. In addition, prompts can be used to increase parental discussion with health-care providers of a child's problems. By providing feedback and chances to win prizes, seat-belt usage can be increased, which could save thousands of lives each year. Small incentives can also increase the use of car pools, which could help save natural resources and reduce air pollution. Providing information to consumers in grocery stores concerning the amount of fat and fiber in products and offering alternatives can influence the purchase of more nutritional foods.

Decreasing Undesired Behaviors

Many types of undesired consumer behaviors also can be decreased through applied behavior analysis. For example, various types of interventions can decrease smoking, drunken and other unsafe driving, dropping out of school, illegal drug use, and teenage pregnancies. While no program has been totally effective, the importance of these problems makes even small changes very valuable for improving individuals' lives and society in general.[7] Greater attention to these problems by consumer researchers might provide better solutions and increase the contribution of consumer research to society.

In sum, we believe applied behavior analysis has been shown to be a useful approach in the areas of sales promotion and social marketing and could be extended to other areas of consumer research. In the chapters that follow, we provide an overview of behavior technology and suggest how it can be used to help formulate successful marketing strategies. However, before concluding this chapter, we investigate several misconceptions about behavior approaches.

Misconceptions about Behavior Approaches

The discussion of sales promotion and social marketing may not have generated strong concern about using behavior approaches to influence consumers. The use of sales promotion tools is well accepted in our society, and improving society through social marketing may not seem ethically problematic. Also, to this point in the text, we have not referred to these approaches as *behavior modification* as this term frequently generates strong negative feelings. However, these reactions frequently occur because of misconceptions about the nature of behavior modification or applied behavior analysis. Because we believe it is important to clarify these issues, we will now investigate three major questions concerning the nature of the approach in general and its application in marketing: (1) Aren't behavior approaches manipulative and unethical? (2) Don't behavior approaches deny that people can think? (3) Why have many consumer researchers avoided behavior approaches?

AREN'T BEHAVIOR APPROACHES MANIPULATIVE AND UNETHICAL?

There is no question that behavior approaches involve changing behavior. They have been criticized as manipulative and unethical because they attempt to change behavior in a systematic way—and they have been found to be very effective in many cases.

The fact that these approaches attempt to change behavior does not make them different from the majority of day-to-day activities in which we all engage. For example, professors attempt to get students to study, and students attempt to get professors to give them good grades; employers attempt to get employees to work hard, and employees attempt to get employers to pay them more money; parents attempt to get their children to behave well, and children attempt to get parents to give them treats; the government attempts to get people to pay taxes and obey laws, while people attempt to get the government to provide municipal services. In fact, very few human interactions are not concerned with one or more individuals attempting to change the behavior of one or more other individuals. Thus, behavior approaches should not be singled out for criticism as manipulative and unethical solely because they involve systematic and effective methods for doing what most of us are attempting to do anyway.

An important ethical question is involved in attempts by marketing managers to get consumers to change or maintain behavior. However, this issue is much larger than questioning the use of behavior technology, for consumer behavior maintenance and change (e.g., brand loyalty and brand switching) are the bases of a competitive, capitalistic system. Firms that survive and prosper in this system are those that are most effective at modifying consumer behavior to purchase and repurchase their products and brands.

It is also true that taking a cognitive approach to marketing and consumer behavior does not avoid questions of manipulation. Cognitive variables are studied in marketing and consumer behavior because they are believed to influence overt behavior. In some cases, cognitive variables are changed in order to change behavior. For example, beliefs and attitudes (and other cognitive variables) are often studied to determine how they are formed and how they can be changed to increase purchase of a particular brand.

In other cases, cognitive variables are studied to develop more efficient marketing strategies to change behavior *without* changing the cognitive variable. For example, needs and benefits sought by consumers are often studied for the purpose of segmenting markets. In these cases, the knowledge gained is used to develop products and marketing stratgies that reach a particular market segment seeking certain benefits or need satisfactions. However, this is of little value unless the firm develops a marketing strategy that effectively changes a sufficient number of these consumers' behaviors so that they actually purchase and repurchase the product.

Similarly, cognitive processes are studied to develop more effective advertising and marketing strategies for reaching the consumer—not as an end in itself, but to increase the probability of purchase and other overt consumer behaviors. Thus, whether attempts are made to change cognitive variables as an intermediate step (such as increasing awareness or knowledge of a product) or cognitive variables are examined to develop other types of marketing strategies (such as market segmentation), the role of cognitive approaches in marketing is still ultimately concerned with efficiently changing or maintaining overt consumer behavior.

In summary, a major concern of human activity in general and of marketing in particular is to change or maintain overt behavior. Society allows this to occur, and in many cases encourages it. Strategy development in marketing is clearly concerned with influencing overt consumer behavior, regardless of whether behavior or cognitive approaches are used. Thus, to argue that behavior approaches are unethical and manipulative—but that societal, marketing, and cognitive approaches to marketing are not—does not seem to be a fair assessment.

Don't Behavior Approaches Deny that People Can Think?

It is commonly believed that behaviorists view people as machines incapable of cognitive activity. While many behaviorists believe behavior is controlled by the environment, few (if any) argue that there is nothing going on in people's brains. The major questions deal with the ability to analyze cognitive variables "scientifically," what causes cognitive processes, and the importance of thinking versus doing.

As we have noted, some behavior approaches emphasize the importance of observation. Historically, behaviorists have been skeptical of the scientific value of cognitive events, because they cannot be observed directly and are generally only inferred from overt behavior. Because they must be inferred, cognitive events are usually not considered to be explanations of behavior. Part of the argument against cognitive approaches, then, is that the variables cannot be observed and measured easily.

Many behaviorists today include self-report measures of cognitive events in their research and find them useful as supplemental, supporting information. However, these behaviorists do not view cognitive information as a substitute for studying overt behavior. In marketing, it has been argued that it would be useful to investigate *what* behaviors consumers perform before we develop cognitive theories designed to explain *why* the behaviors are performed.[8]

Also, as we noted previously, some behaviorists argue that even if cognitive processes do mediate behavior, these processes are developed through interactions with the environment. Interactions with the environment teach the individual which behaviors are rewarded and which are punished, and this becomes part of the individual's conditioning history. While cognitivists might argue that these interactions are stored in memory, behaviorists would say the person is changed through the interaction.

Most behaviorists believe that what people *do* is much more important than what they *think*.[9] They believe that what goes on inside people's heads is of little consequence, because rewards or punishment occur in society only for what people actually do. In this sense, it is unimportant whether consumers need a product, want a product, like a product, plan to purchase a product, or think they would be satisfied with a product, until some overt behavior is performed, such as telling someone else about the product or actually buying it. What goes on in the private world inside one's head makes no difference to society until some overt public behavior is performed. For example, we may like a particular presidential candidate, but only by working for and voting for the candidate do we have any impact. Simply liking the candidate makes no difference in the outcome of the election.

In summary, behaviorists do not argue that people are machines who are incapable of thought or feeling. However, thoughts and feelings are viewed as less operational, as being caused by the environment, and as less important for scientific study than behavior. We believe, however, that historically the major limitation of behavior approaches has been the attempt to exclude cognitive variables from study and to ignore their usefulness; and a major limitation of marketing and consumer research has been to ignore overt behavior.

Why Have Many Consumer Researchers Avoided Behavior Approaches?

There seem to be three reasons behavior approaches have been avoided in much consumer research. First, the field of study of consumer behavior was developed in the early 1960s. At that time, behavior approaches were declining in popularity in psychology while cognitive approaches were becoming more popular. Because consumer researchers have always borrowed concepts and methods from psychology and applied them to marketing problems, the strong cognitive emphasis in marketing may be, in part, a historical accident. Since behavior approaches involve a different world view and different research methods than cognitive approaches, it may have been convenient for consumer analysts to ignore them.

Second, issues of manipulation and ethical concerns may have led researchers to adopt cognitive approaches, which superficially overcome these problems. Similarly, the popularity of the marketing concept and need satisfaction may have constrained research by focusing too narrowly on cognitive variables.

Third, in most academic fields, basic researchers are considered to have higher status than applied researchers. Many consumer researchers may view their work as basic research and may not want to be concerned with application in marketing. One way to appear to be a basic researcher is to avoid studying overt behavior — and to ignore the question of whether the research is useful for specific purposes.

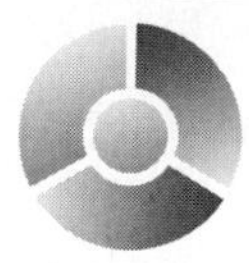

BACK TO.... WHAT WERE THESE MARKETERS TRYING TO DO?

What were these marketers trying to do? Clearly, they were trying to influence consumer behavior by changing the consequences of the behavior. Both Ralston-Purina and General Mills were trying to get consumers to buy their cereals, and Pepsi was trying to get consumers to buy its soft drinks. Note that while consumers would have to do some amount of information processing to purchase these products, the promotions were designed to get them to *buy* the products, not to change their attitudes or beliefs about the products. Perhaps purchase and use would then lead consumers to remember how good the products were or to change their attitudes about the taste or quality of the products. However, such changes in cognitions would likely come after the desired change in purchase and use behavior.

Citicorp was also trying to influence consumer behavior by getting consumers to charge more on its credit cards. American TV was trying to get consumers to come to its retail stores and make purchases, including those with the free steak offer. As with the manufacturers in the discussion above, this credit-card company and this retailer were not trying to change what consumers thought or felt about their services or stores. Rather, they were trying to influence consumer behavior by changing its consequences. Of course, this in turn might change consumer cognitions about these marketers and their products and services.

Further, depending on the success of such promotions, these marketers and their competitors might continue to offer them or come up with new promotion approaches, which are evidenced in the environment. Thus, while the focus of this chapter and section is on behavior, analysis of the reciprocal interactions among affect and cognition, behavior, and the environment is still required for complete understanding of consumer behavior. Finally, after completing this section of the text, you should have new insights into the use of promotions, such as those discussed above.

Summary

This chapter introduced the topic of applied behavior analysis by comparing it with the cognitive approaches that currently dominate marketing and consumer behavior research. Although behavior approaches involve a different world view that requires different methods of research and analysis than those used with the cognitive approach, it is very consistent with the goals and practices of marketing management. Several examples of applied behavior analysis research were reviewed to demonstrate approaches to changing behavior in what are commonly viewed as social marketing settings. The chapter concluded with a discussion of several misconceptions concerning behavior approaches. Marketing strategies that include analyses of affect and cognitions, behaviors, and the environment are superior to strategies that ignore any of these three components.

Key Terms and Concepts

Behavior Approach *267*
Cognitive View *267*
Sales Promotion *272*
Trade Promotion *272*
Consumer Promotion *273*
Social Marketing *280*

Review and Discussion Questions

1. Why have behavior and cognitive approaches not been fully integrated in psychology or consumer research?

2. Explain how behavior and cognitive approaches differ in their views of consumer research.
3. Give examples of purchase decisions where you believe a behavioral view would be sufficient in terms of consumer knowledge needed by the marketing manager.
4. In what kinds of purchase decisions would understanding of consumer cognitive processes be superior to a behavioral view for the marketing manager?
5. Offer three examples of situations where you have attempted to modify someone else's behavior or where someone else has attempted to modify your behavior.
6. Do you think behavior modification is ethical or unethical as a marketing tool? Why?
7. Consider a specific situation, such as dinner at a restaurant. Offer both cognitive and behavioral views of the script you might observe.
8. Presume that you wish to change the response of restaurant patrons. Suggest strategies based on a cognitive view and based on a behavioral view.
9. List conditions that could lead to more emphasis on behavioral approaches in consumer research and marketing strategy development in the future.

NOTES

1. See Paul F. Anderson, "Marketing Scientific Progress, and Scientific Method," *Journal of Marketing*, Fall 1983, pp. 18–31; J. Paul Peter and Jerry C. Olson, "Is Science Marketing?" *Journal of Marketing*, Fall 1983, pp. 111–25; Paul F. Anderson, "On Method in Consumer Research: A Critical Relativist Perspective," *Journal of Consumer Research*, September 1986, pp. 155–73; and Laurel Anderson Hudson and Julie L. Ozanne, "Alternative Ways of Seeking Knowledge in Consumer Research," *Journal of Consumer Research*, March 1988, pp. 508–21.
2. For a discussion of problems with this approach, see Alan G. Sawyer and J. Paul Peter, "The Significance of Statistical Significance Tests in Marketing Research," *Journal of Marketing Research*, May 1983, pp. 122–33.
3. See L. Lawton and A. Parasuraman, "The Impact of the Marketing Concept on New Product Planning," *Journal of Marketing*, Winter 1980, pp. 19–25.
4. Robert C. Blattberg and Scott A. Neslin, *Sales Promotion: Concepts, Methods, and Strategies* (Englewood Cliffs, N.J.: Prentice Hall, 1990), p. 3.
5. J. Paul Peter and James H. Donnelly, Jr., *A Preface to Marketing Management*, 5th ed. (Homewood, Ill.: Richard D. Irwin, Inc., 1990), p. 151.
6. "Study: Some Promotions Change Consumer Behavior," *Marketing News*, October 15, 1990, p. 12.
7. For further discussion and examples of research, see Alan E. Kazdin, *Behavior Modification in Applied Settings*, 4th ed. (Pacific Grove, Calif.: Brooks/Cole Publishing, 1989); Lee Smith, "Getting Junkies to Clean Up," *Fortune*, May 6, 1991, pp. 103–8. Also, see recent issues of the

Journal of Applied Behavior Analysis. For example, the Spring 1991 issue has a series of articles on improving safe driving.

8. J. Paul Peter, "Construct Validity: A Review of Basic Issues and Marketing Practices," *Journal of Marketing Research*, May 1981, pp. 133–45.
9. For insightful discussions of a leading behaviorist's views, see B. F. Skinner, "Whatever Happened to Psychology as the Science of Behavior?" *American Psychologist*, August 1987, pp. 780–86; B. F. Skinner, "The Origins of Cognitive Thought," *American Psychologist*, January 1989, pp. 13–18; and B. F. Skinner, "Can Psychology Be a Science of Mind?" *American Psychologist*, November 1990, pp. 1206–10. The last reference was completed on August 17, 1990, the evening before Dr. Skinner died.

Additional Reading

For discussion and research on sales promotion issues, see:

Campbell, Leland, and William D. Diamond. "Framing and Sales Promotions: The Characteristics of a 'Good Deal'." *Journal of Consumer Marketing*, Fall 1990, pp. 25–31.

Gupta, Sunil. "Impact of Sales Promotions on When, What, and How Much to Buy." *Journal of Marketing Research*, November 1988, pp. 342–55.

Krishna, Aradhna; Imran S. Currim; and Robert W. Shoemaker. "Consumer Perceptions of Promotional Activity." *Journal of Marketing*, April 1991, pp. 4–16.

Lichtenstein, Donald R.; Richard G. Netemeyer; and Scot Burton. "Distinguishing Coupon Proneness from Value Consciousness: An Acquisition-Transaction Utility Theory Perspective." *Journal of Marketing*, July 1990, pp. 54–67.

Neslin, Scott A., and Robert W. Shoemaker. "An Alternative Explanation for Lower Repeat Rates after Promotion Purchases." *Journal of Marketing Research*, May 1989, pp. 205–13.

For examples of empirical research designed to achieve behavioral changes, see:

Berry, Thomas D., and E. Scott Geller. "A Single-Subject Approach to Evaluating Vehicle Safety Belt Reminders: Back to Basics." *Journal of Applied Behavior Analysis*, Spring 1991, pp. 13–22.

Cope, John G.; Linda J. Allred; and Joseph M. Morsell. "Signs as Deterrents of Illegal Parking in Spaces Designated for Individuals with Physical Disabilities." *Journal of Applied Behavior Analysis*, Spring 1991, pp. 59–63.

Finney, Jack W.; Christopher J. Brophy; Patrick C. Friman; Archie S. Golden; Gina S. Richman; and Alexander F. Ross. "Promoting Parent-Provider Interaction during Young Children's Health-Supervision Visits." *Journal of Applied Behavior Analysis*, Summer 1990, pp. 207–13.

Geller, E. Scott, and Gaslen R. Lehman. "The Buckle-Up Promise Card: A Versatile Intervention for Large-Scale Behavior Change." *Journal of Applied Behavior Analysis*, Spring 1991, pp. 91–94.

Van Houwelingen, Jeannet H., and W. Fred Van Raaij. "The Effects of Goal-Setting and Daily Electronic Feedback on In-Home Energy Use." *Journal of Consumer Research*, June 1989, pp. 98–105.

Winnett, Richard A.; John F. Moore; Jana L. Wagner; Lee A. Hite; Michael Leahy; Tamara E. Neubauer; Janet L. Walberg; W. Bruce Walker; David Lombard; E. Scott Geller; and Laurie L. Mundy. "Altering Shoppers' Supermarket Purchases to Fit Nutritional Guidelines: An Interactive Information System." *Journal of Applied Behavior Analysis*, Spring 1991, pp. 95–105.

For an application of behavior modification principles to issues in sales promotion management, see:

Gaidis, William, and James Cross. "Behavior Modification as a Framework for Sales Promotion Management." *Journal of Consumer Marketing*, Spring 1987, pp. 65–74.

For further conceptual discussions of behavior views, see:

Kipnis, David. "Psychology and Behavioral Technology." *American Psychologist,* January 1987, pp. 30–36.

Knouse, Stephen B. "Brand Loyalty and Sequential Learning Theory." *Psychology and Marketing,* Summer 1986, pp. 87–98.

Salafia, W. Ronald. "Behavioral Analysis: Action for Action's Sake." In *Proceedings of the Division of Consumer Psychology,* ed. Linda F. Alwitt. Washington D.C.: American Psychological Association, 1988, pp. 130–34.

Zuriff, G. E. *Behaviorism: A Conceptual Reconstruction.* New York: Columbia University Press, 1985.

MARKETING STRATEGY IN ACTION

CUB FOODS

Leslie Well's recent expedition to the new Cub Foods store in Melrose Park, Illinois, was no ordinary trip to the grocery store. "You go crazy," says Wells, sounding a little shell shocked. Overwhelmed by Cub's vast selection, tables of samples, and discounts as high as 30 percent, Wells spent $76 on groceries – $36 more than she planned. Wells fell prey to what a Cub executive calls "the wow factor" – a shopping frenzy brought on by low prices and clever marketing. That's the reaction Cub's super warehouse stores strive for – and often get.

Cub Foods has been a leader in shaking up the food industry and forcing many conventional supermarkets to lower prices, increase services, or – in some cases – go out of business. With Cub and other super warehouse stores springing up across the country, shopping habits are changing, too. Some shoppers drive 50 miles or more to a Cub store instead of going to the nearest neighborhood supermarket and must bag their own groceries at Cub Foods. Their payoff is that they find almost everything they need under one roof, and most of it is cheaper than at competing supermarkets. Cub's low prices, smart marketing, and sheer size encourage shoppers to spend far more than they do in the average supermarket.

The difference between Cub and most supermarkets is obvious the minute a shopper walks through Cub's doors. The entry aisle, called "power alleys" by some, is lined two stories high with specials, such as bean coffee at $2 a pound and half-price apple juice. Above, the ceiling joists and girders are exposed, giving "the subliminal feeling of all the spaciousness up there. It suggests there's massive buying going on that translates in a shopper's mind that there's tremendous savings going on as well," says Paul Suneson, director of marketing research for Cub's parent, Super Valu Stores Inc., the nation's largest food wholesaler.

Cub's wider-than-usual shopping carts, which are supposed to suggest expansive buying, fit easily through Cub's wide aisles, which channel shoppers toward high-profit impulse foods. The whole store exudes a seductive, horn-of-plenty feeling. Cub customers typically buy in volume and spend $40 to $50 a trip, four times the supermarket average. The average Cub store has sales of $800,000 to $1 million a week, quadruple the volume of conventional stores.

Cub Foods has a simple approach to grocery retailing: low prices, made possible by rigidly controlled costs and high-volume sales; exceptionally high quality for produce and meats — the items people build shopping trips around; and immense variety. It's all packaged in clean stores that are twice as big as most warehouse outlets and four times as big as most supermarkets. A Cub store stocks as many as 25,000 items, double the selection of conventional stores, mixing staples with luxury, ethnic, and hard-to-find foods. This leads to overwhelming displays — 88 kinds of hot dogs and dinner sausages, 12 brands of Mexican food, and fresh meats and produce by the ton.

The store distributes maps to guide shoppers. But without a map or a specific destination, a shopper is subliminally led around by the arrangement of the aisles. The power alley spills into the produce department. From there the aisles lead to highly profitable perimeter departments — meat, fish, bakery, and frozen foods. The deli comes before fresh meat, because Cub wants shoppers to do their impulse buying before their budgets are depleted on essentials.

Overall, Cub's gross margin — the difference between what it pays for its goods and what it sells them for — is 14 percent, six to eight points less than most conventional stores. However, because Cub relies mostly on word-of-mouth advertising, its ad budgets are 25 percent less than those of other chains.

Discussion Questions

1. List at least five marketing tactics Cub Foods employs in its stores to increase the probability of purchases.
2. What accounts for Cub's success in generating such large sales per customer and per store?
3. Given Cub's lower prices, quality merchandise, excellent location, and superior assortment, what reasons can you offer for why many consumers in its trading areas refuse to shop there?

Source: Excerpted from Steve Weiner and Betsy Morris, "Bigger, Shrewder and Cheaper Cub Leads Food Stores into the Future," *The Wall Street Journal,* August 26, 1985, p. 17.

Classical and Operant Conditioning

9

CHAPTER

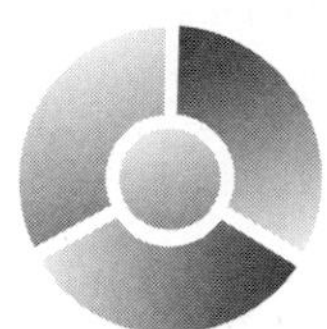

STATE LOTTERY GAMES

Lotteries are legal in 34 states and the District of Columbia. In one recent year, lotteries sold over 20 billion tickets — that's $109 worth for every man, woman, and child in lottery states. Consumers particularly flock to lotteries when the jackpot has grown for a while. In New York, for example, when the Super Lotto drawing reached $90 million, residents formed long lines in the bitter cold of January to buy tickets. Retailers sold 61 million tickets in 10 days — more than 21,000 per minute toward the end. When the Florida Lotto prize reached $106 million, hysteria gripped the state. People who had never dreamed of buying Lotto tickets stood in line with dedicated players, and in the final days before the drawing, retailers sold 44,000 tickets a minute.

On the first day Kentucky started lottery games in 1989, the governor flew to seven cities, each celebrating with bands, prizes, and free tickets. The governor purchased tickets at each stop as the TV cameras rolled. The take for day one of the state lottery was $5 million. The state offered an on-line game, Lotto Kentucky, in which players picked 6 numbers out of 42, and followed up with a second game, Kentucky Cash, in which players picked 3 numbers out of 42. Other lottery games with names like "Tic-Tac-Cash,"

"Break Fort Knox," and "Home for the Holidays" were promoted by Lucky Duck wearing top hat and tails and his "ambassador team" roaming around the state in the Lucky Limo. Additional games included the instant-win type in which players scratch the covering off a card to show winning numbers. These games and all of the hoopla are a long way from the first state lotteries held in New Hampshire, which were simple biannual drawings. The Kentucky lottery games brought in more than $250 million in revenue the first year.

One problem for lotteries is that players often need constant prodding: First-year state lottery sales always boom but then can fall as much as 50 percent in the second year. Instant ticket games have the shortest life span; consumers quit playing in a few months and new games must be constantly introduced to spur sales. In the mid-1980s, lottery officials in Illinois, Ohio, and Pennsylvania were beaming because sales were increasing 30 to 50 percent a year. However, a few years later, growth had skidded to about 3 percent. Now, many lotteries have turned to consumer research including surveys, penetration studies, and focus groups to keep their sales booming. Lottery officials have learned, for instance, that tickets are often impulse items. So they cover convenience stores with banners, place lottery tickets and displays near the cigarettes and candy bars, and use clever TV ads to keep consumers buying.

So what are the chances of winning a lottery? The chances of winning a big jackpot are about 13 million to 1, which is far less than the chances of being killed by lightning at about 400,000 to 1. An award-winning lottery commercial in Michigan took advantage of this knowledge by showing a man in a convenience store saying he would never play the lottery because he'd have a better chance of being struck by lightning. Just then he's hit by a bolt from the blue. Still sizzling, he says, "One ticket, please."

Source: Erik Calonius, "The Big Payoff from Lotteries," *Fortune,* March 25, 1991, pp. 109–14.

Can behavior approaches account for the success of state lottery games? This chapter is concerned with two related processes. The first is called classical conditioning, and the second is called operant conditioning.[1] Many current marketing strategies and tactics are very consistent with conditioning principles, yet only recently has published research on the subject become available in the consumer behavior literature. Perhaps this is because the majority of consumer researchers are cognitively oriented and have not found the area of conditioning to be of much value for investigating cognitive processes. Traditionally, conditioning processes have been primarily concerned with the influence of environmental factors on behavior. But researchers now find that cognitive approaches provide additional insights into these effects. For example, abundant psychological research demonstrates the effectiveness of conditioning processes in changing behavior. Cognitive approaches that attempt to describe the internal mechanisms involved in conditioning processes not only add insight but also help to develop more effective conditioning strategies.

The chapter has two major sections. In the first, the process of classical conditioning is explained and illustrated. In the second section, operant conditioning is explained, some successful applications are described, and examples from marketing practice are given. We treat these two conditioning processes as conceptually distinct, although they overlap in a number of areas.[2]

Classical Conditioning

Many of you have likely heard about Pavlov's experiments in which he conditioned a dog to salivate at the sound of a bell. Pavlov did this by first pairing the sound of a bell with sprays of meat powder for a number of trials. Eventually, he could eliminate the meat powder and the dog would salivate to the sound of the bell alone. Pavlov's research provided the basis for classical conditioning.

In general, **classical conditioning** can be defined as a process by which a previously neutral stimulus (the bell in Pavlov's experiment), by being paired with an unconditioned stimulus (the meat powder), comes to elicit a response (salivation) very similar to the response originally elicited by the unconditioned stimulus. This process is depicted in Figure 9.1, and four points should be noted.

First, classical conditioning can be accomplished not only with unconditioned stimuli but also with previously conditioned stimuli. For example, most of us are previously conditioned to the sound of a doorbell ringing and will look up almost automatically on hearing it. This previously conditioned stimulus has been used in the beginning of Avon TV commercials to attract consumers' attention to the ad itself as well as to Avon's services.

Second, classically conditioned behaviors are controlled by stimuli that occur *before* the behavior. For example, in Pavlov's experiment, the meat powder

FIGURE 9.1
The Process of Classical Conditioning

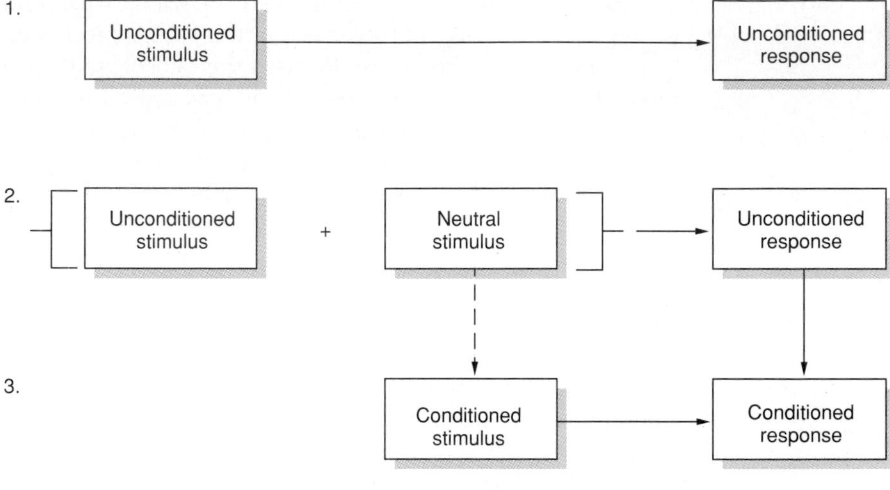

and bell were presented before salivation occurred. Highlight 9.1 presents a discussion of classical conditioning as used by The Coca-Cola Company.

Third, the behaviors influenced by classical conditioning are assumed to be under the control of the autonomic nervous system. This system controls the so-called smooth muscles. Thus, the behaviors are assumed to be involuntary and not under the conscious control of the individual.

Last, and perhaps most important for consumer behavior and marketing strategy, the behaviors called emotions appear to follow the principles of classical conditioning.[3] For example, when a new product for which people have neutral feelings is repeatedly advertised during exciting sports events (such as the Super Bowl), it is possible for the product to eventually generate excitement on its own solely through the repeated pairings with the exciting events. Similarly, an unknown political candidate may come to elicit patriotic feelings in voters simply by having patriotic music constantly playing in the background of his or her political commercials. A number of firms currently use stimuli in commercials and ads that are designed to generate emotions. These firms include Hallmark, AT&T, and Procter & Gamble, makers of Luvs disposable diapers.

Because it can account for many of the responses that environmental stimuli elicit from individuals, classical conditioning has important implications for marketing and consumer behavior. Through it a particular stimulus can come to evoke positive, negative, or neutral feelings. Consequently, classical conditioning can influence an individual to work to obtain, to avoid, or be indifferent to a wide variety of products and services.

HIGHLIGHT 9.1

COCA-COLA TURNS TO PAVLOV . . .

Do television commercials make people behave like Pavlov's dogs? The Coca-Cola Company says the answer is yes. In recent years, the Atlanta soft-drink company has been refining an ad-testing procedure based on the behavioral principles developed by the Russian physiologist. So far, Coca-Cola says, its new testing system has worked remarkably well.

In his classic experiment, Ivan Pavlov discovered he could get dogs to salivate at the ring of a bell by gradually substituting the sound for a spray of meat powder. Coca-Cola says that just as Pavlov's dogs began to associate a new meaning with the bell, advertising is supposed to provide some new image or meaning for a product.

Although the specifics of Coke's test are a secret, the company says it attempts to evaluate how well a commercial conditions a viewer to accept a positive image that can be transferred to the product. During the past three years, Coca-Cola says, ads that scored well in its tests almost always resulted in higher sales of a soft drink.

"We nominate Pavlov as the father of modern advertising," says Joel S. Dubow, communications research manager at Coca-Cola. "Pavlov took a neutral object and, by associating it with a meaningful object, made it a symbol of something else; he imbued it with imagery, he gave it added value. That," says Dubow, "is what we try to do in modern advertising."

Source: *The Wall Street Journal,* January 19, 1984, p. 31.

An ad designed to generate emotion.

Consider product-related stimuli. External stimuli that elicit positive emotions can be paired with the product so that the product itself elicits a positive effect. Behavior may then be triggered that brings the potential consumer into closer contact with the product. "Closer contact" refers to a general relationship between a person's behavior and a given stimulus (e.g., a product). For example, if a product elicits positive affect, an individual exposed to it is more apt to behave positively toward it than if negative emotions are elicited. Attending behavior is also apt to be a function of classically conditioned affect. Stimuli that elicit stronger emotional responses (either positive or negative) are, at least over a considerable range, apt to receive more attention from an individual than stimuli that are affectively neutral. To the degree that attending behavior is necessary for product purchase or other product-related behavior, classical conditioning influences whether consumers come into contact with products.

Similarly, stimuli may produce certain general emotional responses, such as relaxation, excitement, nostalgia, or some other emotion likely to increase the probability of a desired behavior (such as product purchase). Radio and TV ads often use famous broadcasters whose voices have been paired for years with exciting sports events. These voices may elicit excitement as a result of this frequent pairing. Repeated pairings of the voices with the advertised product can result in feelings of excitement associated with the product. For example, Frank Gifford and Don Meredith, formerly of "Monday Night Football," were featured in a series of ads for Planter's peanuts.

Music, sexy voices and bodies, and other stimuli are used in similar ways. For example, magazine ads for Calvin Klein's Obsession perfume featured a naked woman being kissed by three men. Such stimuli may influence behavior without conditioning simply by drawing attention to the ad. Of course, the attention-generating properties of the stimulus itself are apt to have developed through previous conditioning that occurs "naturally" in society.

The use of telephones ringing or sirens in the background of radio and TV ads and the presence of famous celebrities are common examples of how stimuli that are irrelevant to the content of an ad or the function of the product are used to increase attention paid to the ad itself. For example, Michael Jordan was featured in a series of commercials for Gatorade. In this context, one of the major resources that organizations use to market their product is made available through previous classical conditioning of members of society.

Stimuli at or near the point of purchase also serve the goals of marketers through the stimuli's ability to elicit behaviors. Christmas music in a toy department is a good example. Although no data are available to support the point, we suspect that carols are useful in eliciting the emotions labeled the "Christmas spirit." Once these feelings have been elicited, we suspect (and retailers seem to share our suspicions) that people are more apt to purchase a gift for a loved one. In other words, Christmas carols are useful in generating emotions that are compatible with purchasing gifts. Figure 9.2 summarizes many of these examples.

FIGURE 9.2
Some Marketing Tactics Consistent with Classical Conditioning Principles

Conditioning Responses to New Stimuli

Unconditioned or Previously Conditioned Stimulus	Conditioned Stimulus	Examples
Exciting event	A product or theme song	New product advertised during the Super Bowl
Patriotic events or music	A product or person	Patriotic music as background in political commercial

Use of Familiar Stimuli to Elicit Responses

Conditioned Stimulus	Conditioned Response(s)	Examples
Popular music	Relaxation, excitement, "good will"	Christmas music in retail stores
Familiar voices	Excitement, attention	Famous sportscaster or movie star narrating a commercial
Sexy voices, bodies	Excitement, attention, arousal	Special K cereal commercials and many others
Familiar cues	Excitement, attention, anxiety	Sirens sounding, telephones or doorbells ringing in commercials
Familiar social cues	Feelings of friendship and love	Television ads depicting calls from family or close friends

There are several generalizations concerning classical conditioning as a marketing tool. First, the concept of classical conditioning directs attention to the presentation of stimuli that, due to previous conditioning, elicit certain feelings in the potential consumer. Sometimes (as with Christmas music) these stimuli trigger emotions that are apt to increase the probability of certain desired behaviors (or reduce the probability of undesired responses). Second, in many cases, marketers may find it useful to actually condition responses to stimuli. When promoting political candidates, for example, it may be desirable to repeatedly pair the candidate with the American flag to condition the feelings elicited by the flag to the candidate. After a while, the candidate alone may stimulate the same feelings in voters as the flag does. In fact, research on classical conditioning, as well as advertising research, supports the idea that repetition increases the strength of the association between stimuli.[4]

Conditioning nostalgic feelings to a product.

Consumer Research on Classical Conditioning

Several studies in the marketing/consumer behavior literature demonstrate classical conditioning effects. The best known of these was conducted by Gorn; it was the first demonstration of these effects in a marketing context.[5] This study investigated the effects of the music used in advertising on consumer choices. The first study identified one musical selection that was liked and one that was disliked by consumers. It also identified two colors of pens that had neutral evaluations (light blue and beige). This created four conditions: (1) liked music, light blue pen; (2) liked music, beige pen; (3) disliked music, light blue pen; (4) disliked music, beige pen. After looking at an ad for one of the pens while hearing a tape of one of the types of music, subjects were allowed to select and keep one of the pens.

If classical conditioning were occurring, then subjects should select the advertised pen when it was paired with the liked music. Similarly, they should select the other pen when the advertised pen was paired with the disliked music. Figure 9.3 shows the results of this experiment. Clearly, the vast majority of

FIGURE 9.3
Liked versus Disliked Music and Pen Choices

	Pen Choice	
	Advertised Pen	**Nonadvertised Pen**
Liked Music	79%	21%
Disliked Music	30%	70%

Source: Adapted from Gerald J. Gorn, "The Effects of Music in Advertising on Choice Behavior: A Classical Conditioning Approach," *Journal of Marketing* 46 (Winter 1982), pp. 94–101. Published by the American Marketing Association.

FIGURE 9.4
Information versus Music and Pen Choices

	Decision-Making Situation	**Nondecision-Making Situation**
Advertised with Information	71%	29%
Advertised with Music	37%	63%

Source: Adapted from Gerald J. Gorn, "The Effects of Music in Advertising on Choice Behavior: A Classical Conditioning Approach," *Journal of Marketing* 46 (Winter 1982), pp. 94–101. Published by the American Marketing Association.

subjects appear to have been influenced by the pairing of the unconditioned stimulus (liked and disliked music) with the neutral stimulus (light blue and beige pens) resulting in predicted choice behaviors (pen selection).

A second experiment by Gorn compared pen selections after exposure to advertisements that contained either product information or music. Subjects were either in a decision-making or a nondecision-making situation. It was hypothesized that product information would influence pen choice in the decision-making situation, but that music would influence pen choice in the nondecision-making situation. Figure 9.4 presents the results of this experiment. Clearly, the majority of subjects appear to be classically conditioned in the nondecision-making situation but less so in the decision-making situation. These differences might be explained in terms of involvement—the nondecision-making task may be less involving for subjects. In fact, some researchers have suggested that classical conditioning may be most useful in low-involvement situations:

> Consumer involvement is low when the products have only minor quality differences from one another. . . . This is especially the case in saturated markets with mature products. It is exactly in these markets that product differentiation by means of emotional conditioning is the preferred strategy of influencing consumers.[6]

Because a variety of markets meet these conditions, classical conditioning should be a useful strategy for low-involvement purchases. However, classical conditioning principles can also be used in high-involvement situations such as the purchase of a car (see Highlight 9.2).

Another study of classical conditioning investigated the effects of a credit card on the amount of money consumers reported they would be willing to spend on specific items.[7] These items included dresses, tents, sweaters, lamps, electric typewriters, and chess sets. In a simulated buying task, consumers

Credit card stimuli influence consumer behavior.

HIGHLIGHT 9.2

Can Automobile Purchases Be Classically Conditioned?

Research by the Young & Rubicam advertising agency found that awareness of Mercury automobiles was low among the target audience of people aged 24 to 44. The research also found an almost fervent loyalty of this audience to music from the 1960s.

A series of ads known as the "Big Chill" campaign was developed. The first TV spot from this campaign was called "Reunion" and was aired in 1984. The story line of this commercial was a college reunion set to the song "Ain't No Mountain High Enough."

Research conducted after the ad was aired showed the target audience was reading a variety of positive things into the commercial. The audience recalled all kinds of wonderful moments from college days and attributed those moments to Mercury. Mercury's market share climbed from 4.3 percent in 1983 to 5.1 percent in 1985.

Apparently, by featuring the Mercury cars and brand name with well liked music and scenes from a college reunion, awareness of Mercury increased and feelings of nostalgia were produced. More importantly, positive affect was associated with the brand, and purchase behavior was elicited. This example can certainly be interpreted as a successful application of classical conditioning.

Source: Based on "Emotions Sell More Than Perfume; It Sells Cars, Too," *Marketing News* 19, no. 24 (November 22, 1985), p. 4. Published by the American Marketing Association.

consistently reported they would spend more in the "credit-card present" condition. This research suggests credit cards and related stimuli may become associated with spending, partly through classical conditioning.[8]

Recent consumer research on classical conditioning has focused more on conditioning of attitudes rather than behavior, where attitudes are measured as cognitive variables. Some of the studies argue that consumers must be aware of the relationships between the unconditioned and conditioned stimulus for attitudes to be conditioned. Others have focused on developing research to disprove conditioning and have demanded much more stringent research criteria for accepting conditioning explanations than for more popular cognitive theories. However, the authors of one program of research on classical conditioning state, "There are enough demonstrations in our literature to accept *the fact* of classical conditioning of consumers' attitudes toward consumption objects."[9]

In sum, classical conditioning may account for a wide variety of consumer responses. It is commonly used in advertising and in-store promotion, although it may be used by marketing practitioners only on an intuitive basis. Further research in this area could be useful not only for marketing practitioners but also for understanding conditioning effects on information processing, attitude formation and change, and, most importantly, overt consumer behavior.

Operant Conditioning

Operant conditioning differs from classical conditioning in at least two important ways. First, whereas classical conditioning is concerned with involuntary responses, operant conditioning deals with behaviors that are usually assumed to be under the conscious control of the individual. By "conscious control," behaviorists mean under the control of the skeletal nervous system that governs the "striped" muscles; they are not stating that behaviors are under the control of cognitions. Second, while classically conditioned behaviors are *elicited* by stimuli that occur *before* the response, operant behaviors are *emitted* because of consequences that occur *after* the behavior.

In any given situation, at any given time, there is a certain probability that an individual will emit a particular behavior. If all of the possible behaviors are arranged in descending order of probability of occurrence, the result is a **response hierarchy.** Operant conditioning has occurred when the probability that an individual will emit a behavior is altered by changing the events or consequences that follow that behavior.

Some events or consequences increase the frequency with which a given behavior is likely to be repeated. For example, if a reward, such as a cash rebate, is given at the time of purchase, it may increase the probability that a shopper will purchase in the same store in the future. In this case, because the reward increases the probability of the behavior being repeated, it is called **positive reinforcement.** Positive reinforcement is likely the most common type of consequence used by marketers to influence consumer behavior. In general, the greater the amount of the reward and the sooner it is received after the behavior, the more likely it is that the behavior will be reinforced and consumers will perform similar behaviors in the future. For example, a $1 coupon for Tropicana orange juice would likely increase the probability of purchasing more than a 50-cent coupon and lead to future purchases of this product. Similarly, if the coupon is redeemable at the time of purchase, it would likely be more effective than a mail-in coupon for which the consumer has to wait for the reward.

The frequency of consumer behavior can also be increased by removing aversive stimuli. This is called **negative reinforcement.** For example, if a consumer, through purchasing a product, gets a salesperson to quit pressuring him or her, the consumer may be negatively reinforced. That is, by performing

FIGURE 9.5
Operant Conditioning Methods

Operation Performed After Behavior	Name	Effect
Presents positive consequences	Positive reinforcement	Increases the probability of behavior
Removes aversive consequences	Negative reinforcement	Increases the probability of behavior
Neutral consequences occur	Extinction	Decreases the probability of behavior
Presents aversive consequences	Punishment	Decreases the probability of behavior

the behavior of purchasing, the aversive stimuli (the actions of the pushy salesperson) are removed. In the future, when confronted with pushy salespeople, operant conditioning would predict the consumer would be more likely to purchase again.

Sometimes operant techniques are used to decrease the probability of a response. If the environment is arranged so that a particular response results in neutral consequences, over a period of time that response will diminish in frequency. This process is referred to as **extinction.** For example, at one time, the A&P grocery chain was the largest retailer in the world. However, one of the mistakes it made was to overstock its own brands (which had higher profit margins) and understock nationally branded merchandise. Consumers who were loyal to a number of nationally branded products often could not obtain them at an A&P store. Eventually, many consumers quit shopping at A&P, partially because they could not obtain their favorite brands. Thus, A&P inadvertently used extinction on its own customers.

If a response is followed by a noxious or aversive event, the frequency of the response is also likely to decrease. The term **punishment** is usually used to describe this process.[10] For example, suppose you went to a clothing store and the salespeople were rude to you. Wouldn't this decrease the chances of you going back there? Punishment is often confused with negative reinforcement, but they are distinctly different concepts. Figure 9.5 presents a summary of the four methods of operant conditioning.

There are a number of other important ideas about operant conditioning. We discuss three—reinforcement schedules, shaping, and discriminative stimuli—that have major implications for designing marketing strategies to influence consumers' behavior.

Reinforcement Schedules

A number of different **reinforcement schedules** can be employed. For example, it is possible to arrange conditions so a positive reinforcer is administered after every desired behavior. This is called a **continuous schedule.** Marketers usually try to keep the quality of their products and services constant so that they will be continuously reinforcing every time they are purchased, but this is difficult. For example, frequent product recalls for automobiles indicate a failure to maintain product quality. Services such as airlines may not be able to control contingencies, such as bad weather; overbooked, canceled, and late flights; and unfriendly employees, which can make flights not reinforcing. Sporting events, because they may be boring or the home team may get beat, may not be continuously reinforcing for some consumers.

It can also be arranged so that every 2nd, 3rd or 10th, time the behavior is performed, it is reinforced. This is called a **fixed ratio schedule.** Highlight 9.3 illustrates a yogurt chain's use of this schedule to increase purchases.

Similarly, it is possible to have a reinforcer follow a desired behavior *on an average* of one half, one third, one fourth, etc. of the time the behavior occurs, but not necessarily every second time or third time, etc. This is called a **variable ratio schedule.** The various state lotteries are examples of prizes being awarded on variable ratio schedules.

The variable ratio schedules are of particular interest, because they produce high rates of behavior that are reasonably resistant to extinction. Gambling devices are good examples. Slot machines are very effective in producing high rates of response, even under conditions that often result in substantial financial

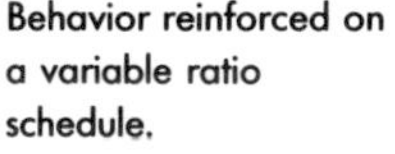
Behavior reinforced on a variable ratio schedule.

HIGHLIGHT 9.3

Developing Loyalty to Yogurt Express Using a Fixed Ratio Schedule

1	2	3	4	5	6

Yogurt Express *Lucky 13 Card*

"One little taste is all it takes"

One punch for each ***Yogurt Express*** visit. 12 punches entitles you to a free LUCKY 13 ounce Super Yogurt Cup. This offer good at any ***Yogurt Express*** in the Madison area.

Name ____________________

Address ____________________

7	8	9	10	11	12

Yogurt Express uses a fixed ratio schedule to try to create loyalty to its stores and yogurt products in Madison, Wisconsin. As shown on the "Lucky 13 Card," it offers a free 13 ounce yogurt cup after 12 visits and purchases. On each visit, the individual or family might make multiple purchases. Also, the cost of a free cup to Yogurt Express is much less than the price charged to consumers. Thus, Yogurt Express may influence considerable consumer behavior for a low-cost, infrequent reward.

The card has to be punched at the store to receive credit for a visit, so consumers will likely carry this card in their purses, wallets, or cars. Seeing the card in these places might remind consumers how good the treats are at Yogurt Express and increase the probability of them returning and buying more yogurt.

losses. This property of the ratio schedule is particularly important for marketers because it suggests that a great deal of desired behavior can be developed and maintained with relatively small, infrequent rewards. Deslauriers and Evertt found that by giving a free token for riding a bus on a variable ratio schedule, the same amount of bus riding could be obtained as when rewards were given on a continuous schedule.[11] Thus, for approximately one third the cost of the continuous schedule, the same amount of behavior was sustained.[12]

HIGHLIGHT 9.4

Using Variable Ratio Schedules to Increase Pepsi Purchases

PepsiCo ran its "Unlock the Great Taste and Win" sweepstakes in 1991. The grand prizes in the contest were two Lamborghini sports cars with an estimated retail value of $215,000 each. Other prizes included Kawaski jet skis, compact vending machines, vacations, and sterling silver key chains.

Although consumers could receive two game chances without purchase by writing the company, most game chances were distributed through purchase of Pepsi and Mountain Dew products. Here's how it worked. With purchases of multipacks, that is, 12-, 20-, or 24-can packages, consumers had a chance of receiving a free, inexpensive key chain. Behind the key-chain package was notification of any major prize won. However, only one out of two multipacks contained the key chain and chance of winning. Thus, on average, consumers would have to purchase two multipacks to get a chance at the major prizes. PepsiCo used a variable ratio schedule to allocate prize chances to increase the probability that consumers would purchase several multipacks.

Some bottle caps on 2-liter, 3-liter, and 16-ounce nonreturnable bottles also contained chances to win but no key chain. Also, the odds of winning were better when consumers bought the more expensive multipacks. For example, the odds of winning the grand prizes from a multipack purchase were 1 in 18,444,000, while the odds of winning the grand prizes from a bottle purchase were 1 in 113,118,597. In addition, only by purchasing multipacks could consumers win the sterling silver key chains valued at $50; the bottle purchases allowed winning only a brass key chain valued at $10. All prizes were awarded on a variable ratio schedule.

Overall, variable ratio schedules were used to allocate the chances to win prizes as well as the prizes. By offering the chances to win and the inexpensive key chain on a variable ratio schedule, the probability of consumers making more than one purchase were likely increased. Also, the cost of the key chains is only half what it would be if every multipack contained one. Offering major prizes on a variable ratio schedule is likely the only way expensive products can be used as reinforcers for purchase of inexpensive products and still be profitable.

Numerous other examples of the use of the variable ratio schedule can be found in marketing practices. In addition to state lotteries, common examples include sweepstakes, contests, and door prizes, in which individuals must behave in a certain way to be eligible for a prize. Highlight 9.4 discusses the use of variable ratio schedules for selling Pepsi and Mountain Dew products.

SHAPING

Another operant conditioning concept that has important implications for marketing and consumer behavior is **shaping.** Shaping is important because—given consumers' existing response hierarchies—the probability that they will make a particular desired response may be very small. In general, shaping involves a process of arranging conditions that change the probabilities of certain behaviors *not as ends in themselves, but to increase the probabilities of other behaviors.* Usually, shaping involves the positive reinforcement of successive approximations of the desired behavior or of behaviors that must be performed before the desired response can be emitted.

Many firms employ marketing activities that are roughly analogous to shaping. For example, loss leaders and other special deals are used to reward individuals for coming to a store. Once customers are in the store, the probability that they will make other desired responses (such as purchasing full-priced items) is much greater than when they are not in the store. Shopping centers or auto dealers that hold carnivals in their parking lots may be viewed as attempting to shape behavior, because consumers are more likely to come in and purchase when they are already in the parking lot than when they are at home. Similarly, free trial periods may be employed to make it more likely the user will have contact with the product so that he or she can experience the product's reinforcing properties. Real estate companies that offer free trips to look over resort property are employing a shaping tactic, as are casinos that offer free trips to gamblers. In both cases, moving people to the place of purchase or place of gambling increases the probability of these behaviors being performed.

Shaping is not confined to a one-step process but can be used to influence several stages in a purchase sequence. For example, suppose a car dealer wants to shape an automobile purchase. Free coffee and donuts are offered to anyone who comes to the dealership. Five dollars cash is offered to any licensed driver who will test-drive a car. A $500 rebate is offered to anyone who purchases a car. This example demonstrates not only how operant principles can be used in a multistep process, but also how they can be used in a high-involvement purchase situation.

DISCRIMINATIVE STIMULI

It is important to distinguish between the reinforcement and discriminative functions played by stimuli in the operant model. In our treatment of classical conditioning, we noted that a stimulus can act as a reinforcer or can function to trigger certain emotions or other behaviors. So far in this section, the focus has been on the reinforcing function. However, the *mere presence or absence of certain stimuli* can serve to change the probabilities of behavior. These are called **discriminative stimuli.**

Discriminative stimuli are often said to "set the occasion" for behaviors. This means discriminative stimuli can be presented before a behavior and can influence whether the behavior occurs. In fact, discriminative stimuli are a major concept by which operant conditioners account for the effects of prebehavior events on changing behavior. (As you recall, reinforcers and other consequences always occur *after* the behavior.) For example, suppose Pizza Hut runs an ad that offers a free quart of Pepsi with every large pizza purchased. This offer may increase the probability of purchasing a large pizza from Pizza Hut. However, the offer itself is not a reinforcer since it is offered *before* the behavior. Rather, the offer is a discriminative stimulus.

Many marketing stimuli are discriminative. Store signs ("50 percent off sale") and store logos (Wal-Mart's sign, K mart's big red "K") or distinctive brand marks (the Nike swoosh, the Levi's tag, the Polo insignia) are examples of discriminative stimuli. Previous experiences have perhaps taught consumers that purchase behavior will be rewarded when the distinctive symbol is present and will not be rewarded when the symbol is absent. For example, many consumers purchase Ralph Lauren shirts, jackets, and shorts that have the embroidered polo player symbol displayed on them and avoid other Ralph Lauren apparel that does not have this symbol. A number of competitors have tried to copy the polo player symbol because of its power as a discriminative stimulus. Clearly, much of marketing strategy involves developing effective discriminative stimuli that increase certain behaviors as well as selecting appropriate reinforcers. Figure 9.6 summarizes a number of marketing tactics consistent with operant conditioning principles.

Consumer Research on Operant Conditioning

While there is considerable research employing operant conditioning procedures in consumer-related contexts, most of it is not reported in the traditional literature on marketing or consumer behavior. However, one exception investigated the effects of positive reinforcement on jewelry store customers.[13] In this study, jewelry store charge-account customers were divided into three groups. One group received a telephone call thanking them for being customers; a second group received a telephone call thanking them and informing them of a special sale; the third group was a control group and received no telephone calls. This study reported a 27 percent increase in sales during the test month over the same month of the previous year. This figure was considered impressive because year-to-date sales were down 25 percent. Seventy percent of the increase came from the "thank-you only" group; the remaining 30 percent of the increase came from the "thank-you and sale-notification" group. Purchases made by customers in the control group were unchanged. The authors suggested that positive reinforcement resulted in sustained increases in purchases for every month but one in the remainder of the year.

FIGURE 9.6
Some Marketing Tactics Consistent with Operant Conditioning Principles

A. Continuous Reinforcement

Desired Behavior	Reward Given Following Behavior
Product purchase	Trading stamps, cash bonus or rebate, prizes, coupons

B. Partial Reinforcement

Desired Behavior	Reward Given Following Behavior
Product purchase	Prize for every second, third, etc. purchase Prize to some fraction of people who purchase

C. Shaping

Approximation of Response	Consequence Following Approximation	Final Response Desired
Opening a charge account	Prizes, etc. for opening account	Expenditure of funds
Trip to point of purchase	Loss leaders, entertainment, or event at the shopping center	Purchase of products
Entry into store	Door prize	Purchase of products
Product trial	Free product and/or some bonus for using	Purchase of products

D. Discriminative Stimuli

Desired Behavior	Reward Signal	Examples
Entry into store	Store signs	50 percent off sale
	Store logos	K mart's big red "K," McDonald's golden arches
Brand purchase	Distinctive brandmarks	Levi's tag, Ralph Lauren polo player

As we have noted, extensive treatment of operant conditioning in marketing and social marketing contexts exists outside of the traditional marketing and consumer behavior literature. Most of this research deals with changing such behaviors as energy conservation, smoking, littering, charitable contributions, and other socially relevant actions.

One interesting example of the use of this technology by a profit-oriented firm concerns the use of punishment by charging phone customers for local

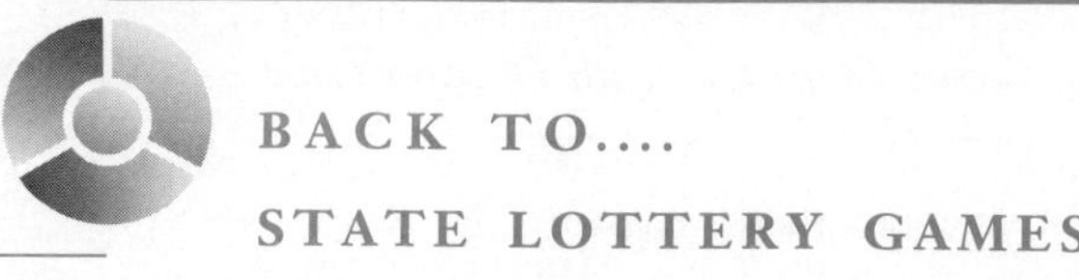

BACK TO.... STATE LOTTERY GAMES

As discussed in this chapter, behavior approaches, particularly operant conditioning, offer a number of insights into the success of state lottery games. First, the fact that more consumers buy lottery tickets when the jackpot is large is consistent with the idea that the greater the reinforcement, the higher the probability of behavior.

Second, although lotteries started out as biannual events, lottery officials soon recognized that more frequent games and instant-winning scratch cards could increase overall lottery revenue. This is consistent with the idea that the sooner the reinforcement after the behavior, the more likely the behavior is to occur and be repeated.

Third, the prizes in the state lottery games are given on a variable ratio schedule, a powerful one for influencing and maintaining behavior. Even though the odds of winning are very small, some players continue to buy tickets for every game. Critics of lotteries state that poorer people buy the most tickets, spend a larger fraction of their income on the games than do others, and may spend money needed for food for their children on them.

directory assistance.[14] Directory assistance is an expensive, labor-intensive service. This study reported the effects of charging 20 cents per local directory-assistance call for more than three calls in a given period. Long-distance directory-assistance calls were not charged. Local directory-assistance calls dropped dramatically through the use of a response-cost punishment. The fact that long-distance directory assistance did not change supports the conclusion that the response cost and not some other factor led to the change in phone customers' behavior. Other types of punishment include voiding car warranties if owners do not perform required maintenance.

Fourth, the fact that lottery purchase behavior decreases after the first year of a lottery is consistent with the concept of extinction. That is, the behavior of consumers who repeatedly buy lottery tickets and consistently fail to win anything decreases and may terminate in the absence of any reinforcement. Thus, lottery games that offer a number of prizes can reinforce more players. Even occasional, relatively small amounts of cash won can keep consumers playing over a number of years or a lifetime. Some critics argue that lottery games encourage consumers to become compulsive gamblers.

In sum, behavior approaches can account for the success of state lotteries. However, cognitive, affective, and environmental theories also do so, and they add insights into the processes involved. For example, cognitive approaches might explain why consumers quit playing instant-cash games after a few weeks. Perhaps consumers purchased some tickets, didn't win, and extinction occurred. However, after a few weeks, consumers may have seen or heard of some winners and may believe most of the big prizes have already been won. Thus, they think their chances of winning are not as good as when the game first started, so they quit buying. Overall, the combination of cognitive, affective, behavior, and environmental theories offers the best account of the success of state lotteries and consumer behavior in general.

SUMMARY

This chapter has provided an overview of classical and operant conditioning processes and has illustrated their use in marketing practice. While research in consumer behavior is in its infancy in these areas, the study of these processes in conjunction with cognitive approaches can increase the effectiveness of marketing strategies as well as our understanding of consumer behavior.

Key Terms and Concepts

Review and Discussion Questions

1. Describe classical conditioning and identify three responses in your own behaviors that are the result of classical conditioning.
2. Under what conditions would the use of classical conditioning be likely to produce positive results as part of marketing strategy?
3. What are the major differences between classical and operant conditioning?
4. Describe operant conditioning and identify three responses in your own behaviors that are the result of operant conditioning.
5. Review each of the four types of manipulations of consequences that can be used to change the probabilities of a behavior under operant conditioning. Give marketing examples for each.
6. Why are variable ratio reinforcement schedules of greater interest to marketing managers than other types of reinforcement schedules?
7. Define "shaping" and tell why it is an essential part of many marketing conditioning strategies.
8. Examine the marketing strategies used to sell fast-food hamburgers and automobiles. Identify specific examples of classical conditioning, operant conditioning, shaping, and discriminative stimuli for each product type.

Notes

1. We will use these terms throughout the chapter because they are common in the consumer behavior literature. However, behaviorists refer to classical conditioning as "respondent conditioning." Operant conditioning can also be called "instrumental conditioning."
2. Much of the material in this chapter is based on

Walter R. Nord and J. Paul Peter, "A Behavior Modification Perspective on Marketing," *Journal of Marketing*, Spring 1980, pp. 36–47; and J. Paul Peter and Walter R. Nord, "A Clarification and Extension of Operant Conditioning Principles in Marketing," *Journal of Marketing*, Summer 1982, pp. 102–7.

3. Behaviorists do not consider emotions or feelings as cognitive events but rather as behaviors. For example, if someone is observed yelling and screaming and throwing books at a classmate, behaviorists would have no problem describing the person as angry. However, the idea that the person is angry is determined through observation of the behaviors. Alternatively, measures of the person's blood pressure or other physiological measures could be used. However, the behaviors of yelling, screaming, and throwing are the problems to be analyzed and changed; the idea that there is an internal feeling called anger is believed to be impossible to prove or study scientifically by behaviorists. Today, many behaviorists find self-report measures of cognitive events useful for providing supportive evidence in an analysis and for diagnostic purposes. However, self-reports alone of mental states and events are still considered less valuable than measures of observed behaviors.

4. For recent discussion and more cognitively oriented interpretations of this type of conditioning, see Terence A. Shimp, "Neo-Pavlovian Conditioning and Its Implications for Consumer Theory and Research," in *Handbook of Consumer Research and Theory*, ed. T. Robertson and H. Kassarjian (Englewood Cliffs, N.J.: Prentice Hall, 1991), pp. 162–87; and Robert A. Rescorla, "Pavlovian Conditioning: It's Not What You Think," *American Psychologist*, March 1988, pp. 151–60.

5. Gerald J. Gorn, "The Effects of Music in Advertising on Choice Behavior: A Classical Conditioning Approach," *Journal of Marketing*, Winter 1982, pp. 94–101.

6. Werner Kroeber-Riel, "Emotional Product Differentiation by Classical Conditioning," in *Advances in Consumer Research*, vol. 11, ed. Thomas C. Kinnear (Provo, Utah: Association for Consumer Research, 1984), pp. 538–43.

7. Richard A. Feinberg, "Classical Conditioning of Credit Cards: Credit Cards May Facilitate Spending," in *Proceedings of the American Psychological Association, Division of Consumer Psychology*, ed. Michael B. Mazis (Washington, D.C.: American Psychological Association, 1982), pp. 28–30; also see Richard A. Feinberg, "Credit Cards as Spending Facilitating Stimuli: A Conditioning Interpretation," *Journal of Consumer Research*, December 1986, pp. 348–56.

8. For additional discussion and empirical research on classical conditioning, see Francis K. McSweeney and Calvin Bierley, "Recent Developments in Classical Conditioning," *Journal of Consumer Research*, December 1985, pp. 310–15; Calvin Bierley, Francis McSweeney, and Renee Vannieuwkerk, "Classical Conditioning of Preferences for Stimuli," *Journal of Consumer Research*, December 1985, pp. 316–23; M. Carole Macklin, "Classical Conditioning Effects in Product/Character Pairings Presented to Children," in *Advances in Consumer Research*, vol. 13, ed. Richard J. Lutz (Provo, Utah: Association for Consumer Research, 1985), pp. 198–203; Larry G. Gresham and Terence A. Shimp, "Attitude toward the Advertisement and Brand Attitudes: A Classical Conditioning Perspective," *Journal of Advertising*, 1985, pp. 10–17; Elnora W. Stuart, Terence A. Shimp, and Randall W. Engle, "Classical Conditioning of Consumer Attitudes: Four Experiments in an Advertising Context," *Journal of Consumer Research*, December 1987, pp. 334–49; and Chris T. Allen and Chris A. Janiszewski, "Assessing the Role of Contingency Awareness in Attitudinal Conditioning with Implications for Advertising Research," *Journal of Marketing Research*, February 1989, pp. 30–43.

9. Terence A. Shimp, Elnora W. Stuart, and Randall W. Engle, "A Program of Classical Conditioning Experiments Testing Variations in Conditioned Stimulus and Context," *Journal of Consumer Research*, June 1991, pp. 1–12.

10. There are also a number of other possibilities,

such as punishment by the removal of a positive consequence. For complete descriptions of these processes, see Arthur W. Staats, *Social Behaviorism* (Chicago: Dorsey Press, 1975).

11. B. C. Deslauriers and P. B. Everett, "The Effects of Intermittent and Continuous Token Reinforcement on Bus Ridership," *Journal of Applied Psychology*, August 1977, pp. 369–75.

12. There are a number of other possible reinforcement schedules. However, we will limit our attention to continuous and ratio schedules. Also, we will not deal with the consequences that the different schedules have on the pattern, rate, and maintenance of behavior. For a detailed treatment of these effects, see W. K. Honig, *Operant Behavior: Areas of Research and Application* (New York: Appleton-Century-Crofts, 1966).

13. J. Ronald Carey, Stephen H. Clicque, Barbara A. Leighton, and Frank Milton, "A Test of Positive Reinforcement of Customers," *Journal of Marketing*, October 1976, pp. 98–100.

14. A. J. McSweeney, "Effects of Response Cost on the Behavior of a Million Persons: Charging for Directory Assistance in Cincinnati," *Journal of Applied Behavioral Analysis*, Spring 1978, pp. 47–51.

Additional Reading

For several consumer behavior works dealing with issues in conditioning and behaviorism, see:

Foxall, Gordon R. *Consumer Psychology in Behavioural Perspective.* London: Routledge, 1990.

________. "Radical Behaviorism and Consumer Research: Theoretical Promise and Empirical Problems." *International Journal of Research in Marketing* 4 (1987), pp. 111–29.

________. "Theoretical Progress in Consumer Psychology: The Contribution of a Behavioral Analysis of Choice," *Journal of Economic Psychology* 7 (1986), pp. 393–414.

Kahn, Barbara E., Manohar U. Kalwani, and Donald G. Morrison. "Measuring Variety-Seeking and Reinforcement Behaviors Using Panel Data." *Journal of Marketing Research*, May 1986, pp. 89–100.

Kassarjian, H. H. "Presidential Address, 1977: Anthropomorphism and Parsimony." In *Advances in Consumer Research*, vol. 5, ed. H. K. Hunt. Chicago: Association for Consumer Research, 1978, pp. xiii–xiv.

Rothschild, Michael L., and William C. Gaidis. "Behavioral Learning Theory: Its Relevance to Marketing and Promotions." *Journal of Marketing*, Spring 1981, pp. 70–78.

For an excellent summary of recent developments in behavior modification, see:

Kazdin, Alan E. *Behavior Modification in Applied Settings.* 4th ed. Pacific Grove, Calif.: Brooks/Cole Publishing, 1989.

For two of the most influential books ever written on behaviorism, see:

Skinner, B. F. *Science and Human Behavior.* New York: Macmillan, 1953.

Skinner, B. F. *Contingencies of Reinforcement: A Theoretical Analysis.* New York: Appleton-Century-Crofts, 1969.

MARKETING STRATEGY IN ACTION

Tupperware

The Dodge van crunches to a stop in the gravel driveway of a red-brick, three-bedroom house. Nancy Schmidt, 41, grabs two large imitation-leather bags packed with a rainbow of plastic bread boxes, cracker crispers, tumblers, and salt and pepper shakers, and marches up to the doorbell. Awaiting her are seven women and their children. The husbands are bowling.

"Hi, ladies," says Schmidt, unpacking her bags on a bridge table in the living room. "Let me show you what I've got here today from Tupperware."

Schmidt hauls out her newest items, the cheese serving tray and the pink and blue picture frames, while pushing the mixing bowls and food containers that are the most reliable sellers. At the end of two hours, Schmidt will have written up some $300 in sales.

Tupperware says 22 million American women went to parties just like this in 1986. Typically sales are about $200, although a big group can spend as much as $800. The salesperson earns a 25 percent commission, and top salespeople average $50,000 a year in salary, plus a company van with a mobile phone to drive to each party.

Tupperware is a strong brand name associated with good quality. Although its prices are 40 percent higher than those of competitors like Eagle Affiliates and Rubbermaid, Tupperware retains two thirds of the $1 billion U.S. plastic food container market. Both Eagle and Rubbermaid, however, sell directly to hardware stores and supermarkets and do not have in-home parties.

Discussion Questions

1. What accounts for the overall success of Tupperware?
2. Offer at least five recommendations for Tupperware salespeople that come from the operant conditioning principles discussed in this chapter.
3. What opportunities are there for Tupperware to increase its sales and profits?

Source: Excerpted from Kerry Hannon, "Party Animal," *Forbes,* November 16, 1987, pp. 262–68.

Vicarious Learning

CHAPTER

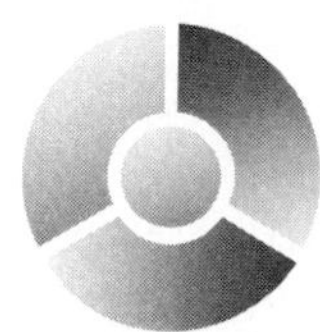

NINTENDO

In the early 1980s, Atari Inc. sold video games like Pong, a video Ping-Pong game, and rapidly ballooned to a company with $2 billion in annual sales. However, children rapidly became bored with the games, and Atari declined as fast as it grew. Nobody thought there was much future for video games; nobody, that is, except Kyoto, the Japanese company that markets Nintendo games.

Nintendo's first major success was Super Mario Brothers, a full-color video game in which players manipulate Italian plumbers through a variety of fantasy worlds. Players face a number of different control-manipulation challenges to keep Mario or his brother, Luigi, moving through the worlds to ultimately save the princess. This game remains the best-seller with sales of over 39 million copies. Mario has become an international cult icon, and a poll of U.S. children revealed he was more popular than Mickey Mouse.

Nintendo has over 200 games that include challenges from baseball to medieval warfare and sell for about $50. Unlike video game marketers in the early 1980s, Nintendo produces quality products, repairs damaged games, and has a customer hot line for users who have problems. One in every four U.S. families has the Nintendo Entertainment System, a phone-book-size gray plastic console that retails for $99 and connects to the back of a TV. Most

kids know how to hook up the system if their parents have problems doing so.

Not all the players are children. Thirty-four percent of them are adults who play both the children's games and adult games such as Concentration, Jeopardy, and Wheel of Fortune. In 1989, Nintendo introduced Game Boy, a hand-held machine that incorporates its own liquid-crystal screen and uses $20 game cartridges. Games, such as Jeopardy and Tetris, designed for adults can be played on this machine. Tetris is a highly addictive, puzzle-like game, the object of which is to prevent falling shapes from filling the screen in a disorderly pile. To score points, the player must maneuver the shapes into neat rows that vanish once complete. Nintendo plans to avoid pornographic games available on the Japanese black market.

The company also introduced a 16-bit graphics system in 1990 to compete with NEC's TurboGrafx-16. However, NEC has only about 10 percent of the market while Nintendo has 80 percent. Sega, which markets the Genesis system, is the other major competitor in the industry.

Whether electronic games will continue to be popular or fade like Atari is a question that will soon be answered. Nintendo, which means "leave it to heaven," hopes marketing innovations such as a $2 million traveling Nintendo show featuring new games, accessories, live entertainment, game counselors offering tips and strategies, and a 200-seat competition arena will keep the product moving. Also, developments in computers, laser disks, high-definition TV screens, and games using human actors rather than cartoons may keep the games exciting. For example, one planned innovation is to have video games in which the viewer manipulates his or her own image, in effect becoming simultaneously director and star.

Source: Based on Susan Moffat, "Can Nintendo Keep Winning?" *Fortune,* November 1990, pp. 131–36; Cleveland Horton, "Nintendo Wired for $95M Push," *Advertising Age,* January 15, 1990, p. 48; Paul M. Barrett, "Nintendo's Latest Novelty Is a Price-Fixing Settlement," *The Wall Street Journal,* April 11, 1991, pp. B1, B2.

Just how do consumers learn to play Nintendo, anyway? This chapter is concerned with vicarious learning or modeling influences on consumer behavior. While vicarious learning has been used successfully in psychological work for many years, it has been almost ignored in published consumer and marketing research. Nonetheless, there are a variety of examples of its use in marketing strategy. In fact, we discuss several real-world marketing examples and suggest that vicarious learning offers a useful approach to develop marketing strategy and consumer education programs. We use the terms *vicarious learning, modeling, observational learning,* and *imitative learning* interchangeably in this chapter, although other writers sometimes draw distinctions between these terms.

Vicarious learning is a deceptively simple idea. Basically, it refers to people changing their behavior because they observed the behavior of others and its consequences. In general, people tend to imitate the behavior of others when they see that it leads to positive consequences, and they avoid performing the behavior of others when they see that it leads to negative consequences. While vicarious learning was developed as part of the behavior approach, a number of attempts have been made to describe the cognitive processes by which it works. We will briefly review these cognitive accounts at the end of the chapter.

We begin our discussion of vicarious learning by focusing on its most common form, called "overt modeling." **Overt modeling** requires that consumers actually observe the model in person; examples include a salesperson demonstrating a product (*live modeling*), or TV commercials or in-store videotapes (*symbolic modeling*).

The modeling process is depicted in Figure 10.1. As an example, many commercials for cosmetics and grooming aids show the model using the product and then being complimented or sought after by a member of the opposite sex. Clairol commercials frequently show a woman with dull, drab hair (and an equivalent social life) being admired and dated by a handsome, well-dressed man after she uses Clairol products. Thus, the modeled behavior (use of the product) is shown to have reinforcing consequences (attention from men).

Uses of Modeling

There are three major uses of modeling in marketing. First, modeling can be used to help observers *acquire one or more new response patterns* that did not previously exist in their behavioral repertoires. Second, modeling can be used *to decrease or inhibit undesired behaviors.* Third, there is *response facilitation*, whereby the behavior of others "serves merely as discriminative stimuli for the observer in facilitating the occurrence of previously learned responses."[1]

Developing New Responses

Modeling can be used to develop new responses that were not previously in the consumer's behavioral repertoire. Consider, for example, the videocassette ma-

FIGURE 10.1
The Modeling Process

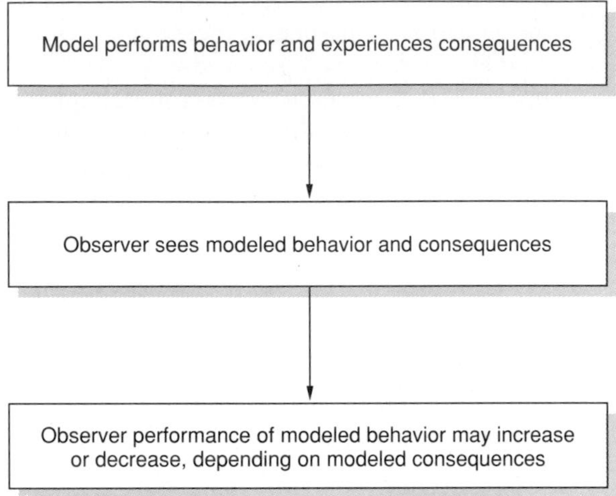

chines used in a variety of department and other stores to demonstrate use of a product. Sears has long used this method to demonstrate the appropriate and safe use of its chain saws. The appropriate use of Berkeley fishing equipment and Olt duck calls are also demonstrated in this way. New behaviors are also frequently modeled in TV commercials. For example, insurance is traditionally purchased from an agent either at the agent's office or in the consumer's home, not in retail stores. A modeling strategy was used by Sears when it began in-store sales of Allstate insurance. Basically, the TV commercial shows a family coming to the Sears store and dropping off its old insurance policy for comparisons with Allstate rates. After a pleasant shopping trip, the family returns and is told that Allstate can provide a better deal, thus modeling the positive consequences of the new behavior. Similarly, Arm & Hammer baking soda ads showed new uses of the product as a carpet and refrigerator freshener and portrayed the models being complimented on the freshness of their homes. WD-40 lubricant ads also model new uses of the product.

These examples offer several generalizations about the use of modeling to develop new consumer behaviors.[2] First, modeling can be used to develop behaviors that enable potential consumers to use products appropriately. Demonstrating ways to use a product may make purchase more probable, particularly if the models appear to experience positive consequences from using the product. Moreover, repurchase, or influencing one's friends, may become more probable if the consumer has learned to use the product appropriately by watching someone else. This type of modeling is commonly used by those selling technically complex industrial and consumer products.

Overt modeling—demonstrating new behaviors.

Second, models may be very helpful in developing the desired purchasing behaviors. Suppose, for example, a firm has a product that is technically superior to those of the firm's competitors. It may be important to teach potential consumers to ask questions about such technical advantages at the point of purchase. Advertisements could show individuals doing just this or behaving in other ways that appear to give the product a differential advantage.

Third, it is often necessary (particularly at early stages in the purchase process) to find ways to increase the degree to which potential customers attend to information in ads and other messages about a product. This can be facilitated by applying findings from recent research on factors that influence the attention observers pay to models. For example, attending behavior is influenced by such factors as incentive conditions, the characteristics of the observers, the characteristics of the model, and the characteristics of the modeling cues themselves. These are discussed in more detail later in the chapter.

Advertising practitioners seem to be sensitive to these factors. Many ads reflect their creators' accurate awareness of salient characteristics of the target audience, of the models in the ad, and of the behaviors exhibited by the model.

Many ads show the models receiving positive social or other reinforcement from the purchase or use of the product. Finally, modeling can also be beneficial for consumers because it can help them to develop effective behaviors in the marketplace and to avoid costly errors resulting from poor product purchases or inappropriate uses of the product.

Inhibiting Undesired Responses

Modeling can also be used to decrease the probability of undesired behaviors. Because of the ethical and practical problems involved in using punishment to affect consumer behavior, we have given little attention to ways of reducing the frequency of undesired responses. Such problems are far less prevalent when aversive consequences are administered to models rather than to actual consumers, however. Thus, vicarious learning may be one of the few approaches that can be used to reduce the frequency of unwanted elements in the behavioral repertoire of a potential or present consumer.

It is well known from the modeling literature that, under appropriate conditions, observers who see a model experience aversive outcomes following a particular act will reduce their tendency to exhibit that behavior. Similarly, vicarious learning can employ extinction to reduce the frequency of behavior.

Consider the following examples. Hefty bags are frequently advertised on TV using a modeling approach. Various family members are shown taking out the trash in "bargain bags." Of course, the bargain bag breaks and garbage is spewed all over the driveway. This is a very annoying experience! The frustrated family member is then told about Hefty bags, uses them successfully, and is socially reinforced for doing so. Head and Shoulders shampoo commercials show people initially being found attractive by members of the opposite sex but then being rejected when the models scratch their heads, indicating they may have dandruff. Following the use of the advertised product, the model is shown being happily greeted by an attractive member of the opposite sex.

A common use of this type of modeling is in public service advertising. Many behaviors considered socially undesirable can be modeled and shown to have aversive consequences. These behaviors include littering, smoking, driving drunk, using drugs, overeating, wasting energy, and polluting. One commercial, for example, showed a drunken driver being caught, taken to court, and given a considerable fine and jail sentence for his behavior.

Response Facilitation

In addition to developing new behaviors and inhibiting undesired ones, modeling can be used to facilitate the occurrence of desired behaviors that are currently in the consumer's repertoire. Modeling has been used extensively in advertising not only to illustrate the uses of a product but also to show what types of people use it and in what settings. Because many of these uses involve behaviors already in the observer's response hierarchy, the model's function is merely to *facilitate these responses* by depicting positive consequences for using the product appropriately. For example, Nyquil ads show adult cold sufferers using the product before going to bed and then sleeping comfortably. This technique also appears frequently in advertising for high-status products. Such ads do not demonstrate any new behaviors, but show the positive consequences of using the product. A series of Lowenbrau ads stressing the use of this beer for very special occasions is a good example.

It is also possible to influence emotional behavior through a vicarious learning approach. Bandura noted that many emotional behaviors can be acquired through observations of others, as well as through direct classical conditioning:

> Vicarious emotional conditioning results from observing others experience positive or negative emotional effects in conjunction with particular stimulus events. Both direct and vicarious conditioning processes are governed by the same basic principles of associative learning, but they differ in the force of the emotional arousal. In the direct prototype, the learner himself is the recipient of pain- or pleasure-producing stimulation, whereas in vicarious forms somebody else experiences the reinforcing stimulation and his affective expressions, in turn, serve as the arousal stimuli for the observer.[3]

Modeling an appropriate occasion for product usage.

FIGURE 10.2

Some Applications of Modeling Principles in Marketing

Modeling Employed	Desired Response
Instructor, expert, salesperson using product (in ads or at point of purchase)	Use product in correct, technically competent way
Models in ads asking questions at point of purchase	Ask questions at point of purchase that highlight product advantages
Models in ads receiving positive reinforcement for product purchase or use	Try product; increase product purchase and use
Models in ads receiving no reinforcement or receiving punishment for performing undesired behaviors	Extinction or decrease of undesired behaviors
Individual or group (similar to target) using product in novel, enjoyable way	Use product in new ways

Source: Reprinted from Walter R. Nord and J. Paul Peter, "A Behavior Modification Perspective on Marketing," *Journal of Marketing* 44 (Spring 1980), p. 43. Published by the American Marketing Association.

To the degree that positive emotions toward a product are desired, vicarious emotional conditioning may also be useful for the design of effective advertisements. Figure 10.2 offers a summary of some applications of modeling principles in marketing.

Covert and Verbal Modeling

Up to this point, we have been discussing the most commonly studied and used type of vicarious learning, overt modeling. Two other types of modeling should be mentioned: covert and verbal modeling.

Covert Modeling

In **covert modeling,** no actual behaviors or consequences are shown or demonstrated. Rather, subjects are told to imagine observing a model behaving in various situations and receiving particular consequences.[4] For example, covert modeling could be used in radio commercials as follows. The commercial could tell listeners to imagine that Joe Smith, a burly construction worker, just got off work. It's July, it's hot and humid, and Joe has just worked for 12 hours pouring concrete. He's driving home; he's tired and thirsty. His mouth is parched and his throat is dry. Imagine how good that first, cold, frosty mug of Oscar's root beer is going to taste!

Covert modeling has received less research attention than overt modeling, but a review of the literature suggests the following generalizations:

1. Covert modeling can be as effective as overt modeling in modifying behavior.
2. The parameters that affect overt modeling should have similar affects on covert modeling.
3. Covert modeling can be tested and shown to be effective.
4. Covert modeling can be made more effective if alternative consequences of the model's behavior are described.[5]

While we are aware of no consumer or marketing research on covert modeling, we believe it is a potentially useful marketing tool and should be investigated.

Verbal Modeling

In **verbal modeling,** behaviors are not demonstrated, and people are not asked to imagine a model performing a behavior. Instead, people are *told* how others similar to themselves behaved in a particular situation. This procedure thus sets a social norm that may influence behavior. One study, for example, investigated the effects of verbal modeling on contributions to charity.[6] People were contacted door to door for donations to the United Way Drive. One condition in the experiment manipulated the percentage of households the solicitor said had

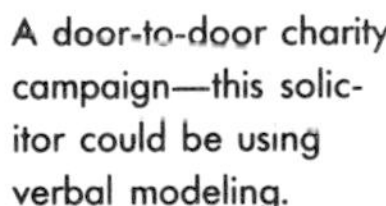
A door-to-door charity campaign—this solicitor could be using verbal modeling.

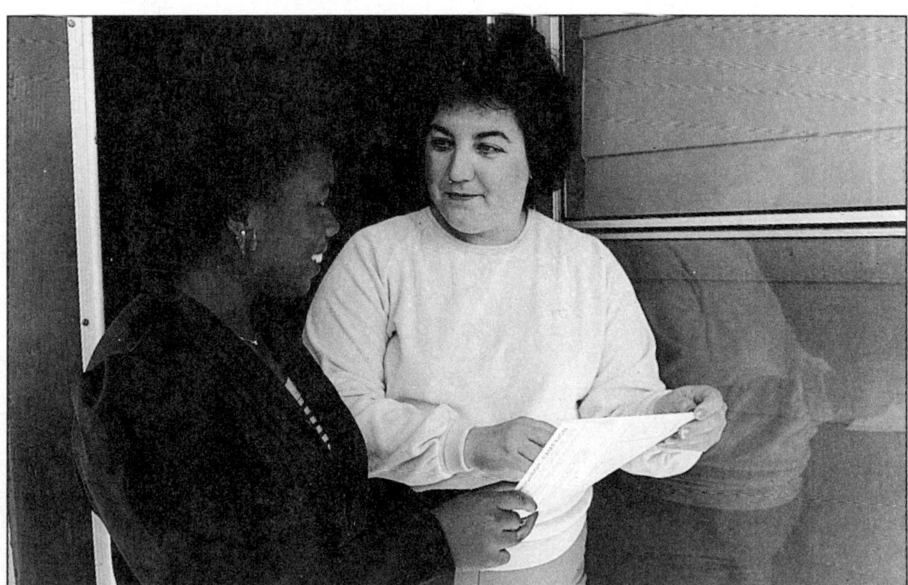

FIGURE 10.3

A Comparison of Three Types of Modeling

Type	Description	Example	Useful Media
Overt modeling (live and symbolic)	Consumer observes modeled behavior and consequences	Allstate Insurance commercials demonstrating new method of purchasing insurance	Television, personal selling, in-store video machines
Covert modeling	Consumer is told to imagine a model (or self) performing behavior and consequences	Airline or travel agency commercial during cold, northern winter inviting consumers to "Imagine you're on the warm sunny beaches of Florida."	Radio, personal selling, possibly print advertising
Verbal modeling	Consumer is given a description of how others similar to him-/herself (or aspirational groups) behave in purchase/use situation	United Way solicitor reporting on gift-giving behavior of neighbors	Personal selling, radio, direct mail, possibly other print advertising

already contributed to the drive: "More than (three fourths/one fourth) of the households that I've contacted in this area have contributed so far." People who were told that three fourths of their neighbors had contributed usually donated more. Verbal modeling also outperformed several other strategies, such as the amount people were told others had given, social responsibility arguments, and arguments for helping less fortunate people. It was concluded that verbal modeling was an effective means of eliciting behavior.

Again, as with covert modeling, little is known about verbal modeling in other consumer behavior contexts. However, the procedure is quite convenient to administer, because actual models need not be present.

Verbal modeling is easily employed in personal selling situations. For example, salespeople sometimes inform potential buyers that people like themselves have purchased a particular product, brand, or model. This may be an effective tactic, but it would be unethical for the salesperson to lie or to use the tactic to induce customers to buy only the most expensive products.

Figure 10.3 summarizes overt, covert, and verbal modeling and suggests appropriate media in which these types of modeling could be used. Investigations of the effectiveness of these procedures using different media and approaches could add considerable insight into effective modeling processes and development of marketing strategies.

Why Does Modeling Work?

In this section, we investigate two related issues. First, we discuss some of the factors that affect how well a particular modeling attempt works. Second, we examine several explanations of why modeling is effective. The fact that there is no consensus on the cognitive processes that mediate modeling influences suggests the need for further inquiry into this area.

Factors Influencing Modeling Effectiveness

There is no question that watching a model perform a behavior often increases the likelihood that the observer will also perform the behavior. It is well established in the psychological literature that in many situations, modeling is effective in changing behavior, as illustrated in Highlight 10.1. However, certain factors have been found to increase the likelihood that vicarious learning will occur. These factors can be divided into three groups: (1) model and modeled behavior characteristics, (2) observer characteristics, and (3) characteristics of modeled consequences.

Model and modeled behavior characteristics

Several personal characteristics of observed models influence the probability that an observer will imitate the modeled behavior.[7] Models who are found to be attractive may be sought out, while less attractive models may be ignored. Models who are perceived to be credible and successful exert greater influence than those who are not. In addition, high-status and competent models are more influential in determining modeling success.

Observers are also influenced by the manner in which the modeled behavior is performed. If the sequence of the modeled behavior is detailed very carefully and vividly, modeling effects tend to increase. The rate of learning also depends on the salience and complexity of the modeled behaviors. Interestingly, models who display a bit of apprehension and difficulty and yet complete the task are more effective than models displaying no struggle or difficulty. A reason for this has been suggested by Manz and Sims:

> It appears that an observer can identify more with a model who struggles and overcomes the difficulties of a threatening task than a model who apparently has no problem. A model who is seen as possessing substantially greater abilities may not be considered a reasonable reference point for the observer. However, experts who display little difficulty in completing a task (e.g., professional athletes) may serve as ideals to be emulated in nonthreatening situations.[8]

HIGHLIGHT 10.1

Modeling Effects in Apes and Humans

Until recently, many zoos always removed newborn primates from their mothers and families. But when these primates grew up, they made lousy parents, sometimes beating and fatally injuring their own babies. Researchers determined the social isolation was the leading cause of the abuse, and they had to alter the primate's environment if the animals were to thrive. They made sure biological mothers reared infants in more spacious group settings, exposed them to play with infants and peers, and introduced older mothers to help with the caretaking. They found that inexperienced and even abusive mothers, once given examples of good mothering (modeling) and a chance to play with infants, became competent parents. Today, as few as 2 percent of primate mothers abuse or neglect their babies, compared to about 75 percent in the 1970s.

A similar program was tested for human mothers by University of Rochester researchers. Nurses developed friendships with new mothers by regularly visiting them in their homes. The nurses showed new mothers how to play and talk to a child, much as the older primates had modeled mothering skills. Attempts were made to get new mothers jobs and obtain benefits to reduce tension in the home. In the end, 4 percent of the low-income teen mothers who received the nurse visits neglected or abused their children compared with 19 percent of those mothers who did not receive the visits. The nurses also succeeded in teaching parents who had been abused as children how to trust in their abilities as nurturing parents.

One important difference was found between the effects of modeling on abusive humans and animals, however. The animals apparently learned much more quickly. Just two days of contact with newborn infants made primate females more likely to hug and feed their own infants. By contrast, the only programs effective for humans required intensive, long-lasting intervention. Apparently, in some cases, humans could become more human by modeling the behavior of primates.

Source: Based on Art Levine, "The Biological Roots of Good Mothering," *U.S. News & World Report,* February 25, 1991, p. 61.

Another factor that influences the effectiveness of models is the perceived similarity of the model to the observer. This finding supports the common practice of using models similar to persons in the target market in commercials and of attempts to increase similarities between customers and salespersons when hiring and assigning sales personnel. Many advertisers take advantage of these characteristics in developing commercials. These characteristics may also influence whether modeling aids in the diffusion of new products, an issue discussed in Highlight 10.2.

Modeling the types of people who use and enjoy a new bath soap.

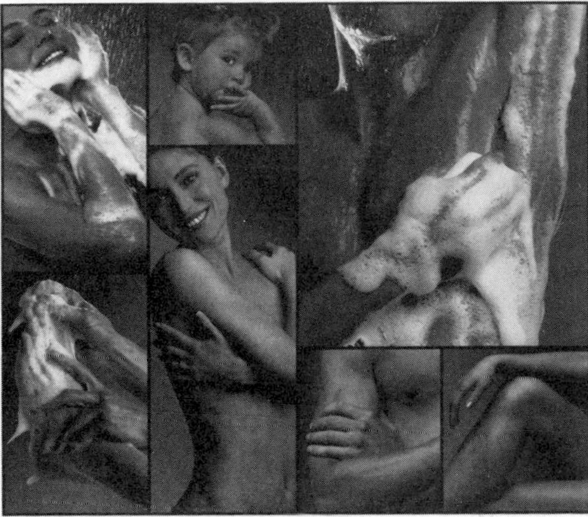

Characteristics of observers

Any number of individual difference variables in observers could be expected to mediate successful modeling. For example, individual differences in cognitive processing as well as in physical ability to perform a modeled behavior may affect the process. In covert modeling, people apparently differ in their ability to imagine modeled behavior. Bandura suggests that in many cases, observers who are dependent, lack confidence and self-esteem, and have been frequently rewarded for imitative behavior are especially prone to adopt the behavior of successful models.[9] However, perceptive and confident people readily emulate idealized models who demonstrate highly useful behaviors.

Perhaps most important is the value the observer places on the consequences of the modeled behavior. For example, if consumers value the social approval obtained by a model in a Grecian Formula (hair coloring) commercial, they are more likely to purchase and use the product.

HIGHLIGHT 10.2

Diffusion of Innovations: A Modeling Process?

Modeling plays a prime role in spreading new ideas, products, and social practices within a society, or from one society to another. Successful diffusion of innovations follows a common pattern: (1) new products and behaviors are introduced by prominent examples, (2) the product/behavior is adopted at a rapidly accelerating rate, and (3) adoption then either stabilizes or declines, depending on the product/behavior's functional role. The general pattern of diffusion is similar, but the mode of transmission, the speed and extent of adoption, and the life span of innovations varies for different products and forms of behavior.

Modeling affects adoption of innovations in several different ways. It instructs people in new styles of behavior through social, pictorial, or verbal displays. Some observers are initially reluctant to buy new products or embark on new undertakings that involve risks until they see the advantages gained by earlier adopters. Modeled benefits accelerate diffusion by weakening the restraints of more cautious, later adopters. As acceptance spreads, the new gains further social support. Models not only exemplify and legitimize innovations, they also serve as advocates for products by encouraging others to adopt them.

Source: Adapted from Albert Bandura, *Social Learning Theory* (Englewood Cliffs, N.J.: Prentice Hall, 1977), pp. 50–51.

Characteristics of modeled consequences

Just as operant conditioning places importance on the consequences of behavior, so does vicarious learning. Of course, in vicarious learning, the observer does not experience the consequences directly. Thus, a major advantage of vicarious learning for consumers is that they can learn effective purchase and use behavior while avoiding negative consequences.

Research has demonstrated that positively reinforcing a model's behavior is a key factor in facilitating vicarious learning. In terms of consumer behavior, much fruitful research could be done on identifying appropriate reinforcers for various types of products. Currently, however, little is known about what types of positive consequences would be most effective to model. Similarly, for modeling applications that seek to decrease undesired behaviors, the most effective types of negative consequences to model in commercials are unknown. While it has been demonstrated that modeling is useful in deterring smoking,[10] reducing drinking,[11] reducing uncooperative behavior of children,[12] and reduc-

HIGHLIGHT 10.3

Marketing by Modeling on Videocassettes

Soloflex Inc., makers of a $495 home exercise machine, provide an impressive example of using modeling on videocassettes as a marketing tool. Jerry Wilson, Soloflex's founder and president, couldn't get sales personnel in sporting-goods stores to model the use of his machine properly, so he took it out of retail distribution and started selling it directly to the public.

Then, after purchasing a videocassette recorder for his family, he realized this was the perfect way to market his product. He spent $150,000 to produce a 22-minute demonstration on videotape and began offering it free in magazine and television ads. Each video cost the company about $6.50 for materials, dubbing, packaging, and postage.

After six years in business, the firm was reported to have sold 100,000 units. It had mailed out more than 60,000 free videotapes. Up to 40 percent of those who requested the demonstration videotape eventually bought a Soloflex—an astounding sales-conversion percentage compared with only 10 percent conversion of those who did not have a videocassette recorder and were sent only a brochure. Thus, it would appear that modeling the appropriate use of this product on videocassette and the consequences (the well-shaped bodies of the models) was an effective marketing strategy.

Source: Based on Stan Rapp and Tom Collins, "Voluminous Video Enlivens Today's Media Market," *Adweek*, November 17, 1986, p. 43.

ing energy consumption,[13] many other areas of consumer behavior are unexplored. Highlight 10.3 presents an example of one successful use of modeling in a business venture.

Theories of Modeling

As we noted earlier, there is no question in the psychological literature that modeling is an effective procedure. As with many phenomena, however, there is considerable disagreement about *why* it works. From a behavior perspective, operant conditioners view modeling as a discriminative stimulus that may change the probability of the modeled behavior. Of course, operant conditioners do not attempt to describe the cognitive processes required for successful modeling. However, several limited attempts have been made to describe these processes, which we discuss below.

One cognitive theory that has been suggested as an explanation for modeling is **expectancy theory.**[14] This theory suggests that models influence observer behavior by influencing expectations. These expectations are of two types: self-efficacy and outcome expectations. *Self-efficacy expectations* deal with the observers' convictions that they can successfully perform the behavior that produces the outcome. In other words, after seeing a model perform the behavior, observers' confidence in their own ability increases. For example, the confidence young children have in their ability to use money to make a purchase may increase when they see other children buying their own toys.

Outcome expectations refer to observers' assessments of whether they will receive the same consequences the model receives. In other words, modeling provides information that helps observers form expectations about the outcomes of performing the modeled behavior. For example, if a child sees a peer being complimented for using money correctly, it may increase the child's expectation of receiving a compliment for performing this behavior well.

A third way of describing modeling effects is a cognitive processing approach called **category accessibility.**[15] This suggests the process of viewing a model's behavior involves the activation of an interpretive schema. Once the schema is activated, the information in it becomes more accessible for subsequent use. If the schema incorporates (or is closely related to) information that helps specify behavior, that information becomes more accessible as well, thus making it more likely to influence overt behavior. Modeled consequences are considered less important with this approach than with others.

The most-detailed and best-documented account of modeling is provided by Albert Bandura in his **social learning theory.**[16] This approach recognizes four subprocesses that intervene in modeling. These four, shown in Figure 10.4, include attentional, retentional, production, and motivational subprocesses. We briefly describe each of these before concluding the chapter.

Attentional processes refer to the ways in which observers attend to and extract information about the major features of the modeled behavior. The characteristics of the model and the modeled behavior, as described earlier, affect this process, as do other attention-getting tactics such as the use of novelty and contrast.

Retention processes refer to the representation of observed models and behavior in memory. Observers cannot be influenced much by modeled behavior if they do not remember it. Retention processes include both visual and verbal representation systems. Visual imagery is particularly important in early periods of human development; most of the cognitive processes that regulate behavior are thought to be verbal.

The third process, *production*, involves converting symbolic representations into appropriate behavior. A modeled behavior is reproduced by organizing responses in accordance with the modeled pattern. This process requires cognitive organization of the response, initiating the response, monitoring performance, and refinement on the basis of feedback.

FIGURE 10.4
A Social Learning Description of the Modeling Process

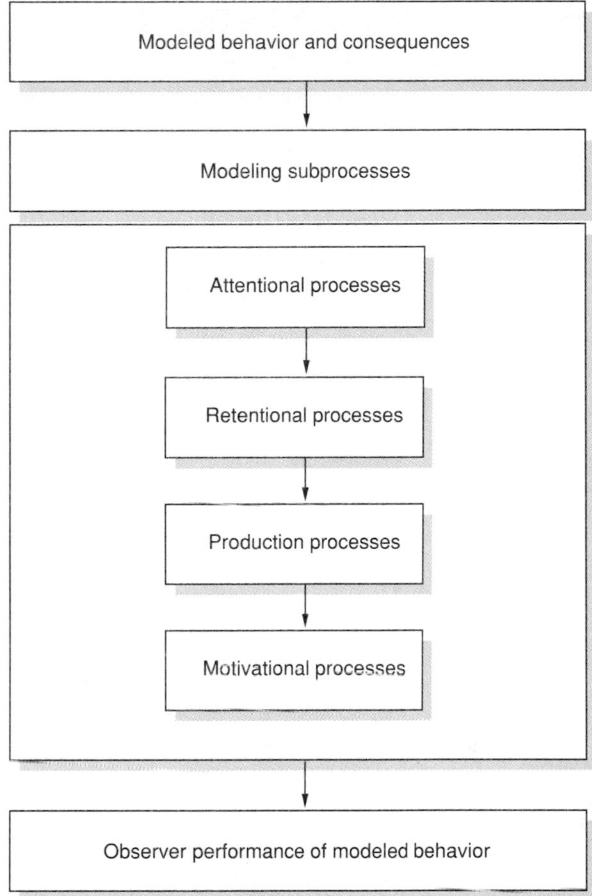

Finally, *motivational process* refers to the factors by which consequences of modeled behaviors are judged to be rewarding or unrewarding. If consumers value the outcomes of modeled behavior, they are more likely to perform the behavior. External reinforcers, vicarious reinforcers, and self-reinforcers can increase the probability of modeled responses.

BACK TO.... NINTENDO

There are many ways consumers learn how to play Nintendo. The most common is by observing the actions of other effective players and the consequences of those actions. Children often play Nintendo together and learn from the better players. In many Nintendo games, a player cannot figure out where various rewards are in the game. For example, in the Super Mario Brothers game, unless a player sees another player locate the mushrooms that give Mario extra strength and lives, it is unlikely they will be found rapidly. Thus, one way consumers learn how to play well is through live modeling. The game counselors in Nintendo's traveling show can perform the same function. Both friends and game counselors may also use verbal modeling, explaining how they play a particular game and the consequences of playing the way they do.

A second way is through symbolic modeling. Consumers can buy books and a magazine, *Nintendo Power*, that illustrate and describe effective moves and strategies. Thus, as with many behaviors, modeling plays an important role in learning.

Nintendo gave $3 million to the Massachusetts Institute of Technology for studies on how children learn. One of the important learning effects studied is called "flow." Flow is the rapt state a child enters when playing an exciting game. If educational tools could be developed that are as effective as Nintendo games at creating flow, many educational problems likely could be overcome.

Summary

This chapter provided an overview of vicarious learning or modeling processes that can be used to develop new responses, inhibit undesired responses, and facilitate previously learned responses. Several factors that increase the effectiveness of modeling were also discussed, as were some theories of how modeling works. While a consensus has not been reached on *why* it works, it is well established that modeling is an effective procedure. Modeling is currently employed in marketing, yet there is little research on the topic in the traditional marketing or consumer-behavior literature. This area represents an excellent opportunity for increasing the effectiveness of current marketing strategies and for integrating affect and cognition, behavior, and the environment.

Key Terms and Concepts

Overt Modeling *319*
Covert Modeling *324*
Verbal Modeling *325*
Expectancy Theory *332*
Category Accessibility *332*
Social Learning Theory *332*

Review and Discussion Questions

1. Describe the steps necessary for behavior change in the modeling process.
2. What are the three major uses of modeling in marketing strategy?

3. Why might a marketing organization use symbolic rather than live overt modeling? Give examples to illustrate your points.
4. How are covert and verbal modeling different from overt modeling? How are they similar?
5. Give examples, not already discussed in the text, in which you have observed marketing strategies that use each of the types of modeling.
6. In what situations would you recommend that a marketing manager use vicarious learning in advertisements?
7. How could modeling be used to facilitate the introduction of the newest models of lightweight portable personal computers?
8. Explain the process of vicarious learning from both behavioral and cognitive perspectives. Which view is more useful for the marketing manager?

Notes

1. Albert Bandura, *Principles of Behavior Modification* (New York: Holt, Rinehart & Winston, 1969), p. 120. This is a classic reference in the psychological literature.
2. This discussion of the three major types of modeling influences is based on Walter R. Nord and J. Paul Peter, "A Behavior Modification Perspective on Marketing", *Journal of Marketing*, Spring 1980, pp. 40–41.
3. Bandura, *Principles of Behavior Modification*, p. 167.
4. See Joseph R. Cautela, "The Present Status of Covert Modeling," *Journal of Behavior Therapy and Experimental Psychiatry*, December 1976, pp. 323–26.
5. Cautela, "Present Status," pp. 323–26.
6. Viola Catt and Peter L. Benson, "Effect of Verbal Modeling on Contributions to Charity," *Journal of Applied Psychology*, February 1977, pp. 81–85.
7. See Charles C. Manz and Henry P. Sims, "Vicarious Learning: The Influence of Modeling on Organizational Behavior," *Academy of Management Review*, January 1981, pp. 105–13. For discussions of model characteristics in advertising, see Michael J. Baker and Gilbert A. Churchill, Jr., "The Impact of Physically Attractive Models on Advertising Evaluations," *Journal of Marketing Research*, November 1977, pp. 538–55; "Models Clothing Speaks to Ad Market: Study," *Marketing News*, November 22, 1985, p. 16; and Lynn R. Kahle and Pamela M. Homer, "Physical Attractiveness of the Celebrity Endorser: A Social Adaptation Perspective," *Journal of Consumer Research*, March 1985, pp. 954–61.
8. Manz and Sims, "Vicarious Learning," p. 107.
9. Albert Bandura, *Social Learning Theory* (Englewood Cliffs, N.J.: Prentice Hall, 1977), p. 89. This book discusses a number of other variables affecting the modeling process.
10. Richard I. Evans, Richard M. Rozelle, Scott E. Maxwell, Betty E. Raines, Charles A. Dill, and Tanya J. Guthrie, "Social Modeling Films to Deter Smoking in Adolescents: Results of a Three-Year Field Investigation," *Journal of Applied Psychology*, August 1981, pp. 399–414.
11. Denise A. DeRicco and John E. Niemann, "*In Vivo* Effects of Peer Modeling on Drinking

Rate," *Journal of Applied Behavioral Analysis*, Spring 1980, pp. 149–52; and Barry D. Caudill and Thomas R. Lipscomb, "Modeling Influences on Alcoholics' Rates of Alcohol Consumption," *Journal of Applied Behavioral Analysis*, Summer 1980, pp. 355–65.

12. Trevor F. Stokes and Suzanne H. Kennedy, "Reducing Child Uncooperative Behavior during Dental Treatment through Modeling and Reinforcement," *Journal of Applied Behavioral Analysis*, Spring 1980, pp. 41–49.

13. Richard A. Winnett, Joseph W. Hatcher, T. Richard Fort, Ingrid N. Lechliter, Susan Q. Love, Anne W. Riley, and James F. Fishback, "The Effects of Videotape Modeling and Daily Feedback on Residential Electricity Conservation, Home Temperature and Humidity, Perceived Comfort and Clothing Worn: Winter and Summer," *Journal of Applied Behavioral Analysis*, Fall 1982, pp. 381–402.

14. See Manz and Sims, "Vicarious Learning," p. 106.

15. William J. Froming and William Chambers, "Modeling: An Analysis in Terms of Category Accessibility," *Journal of Experimental Social Psychology*, September 1983, pp. 403–21.

16. Bandura, *Social Learning Theory*, pp. 24–29; also see Albert Bandura, *Social Foundations of Thought and Action: A Social Cognitive Theory* (Englewood Cliffs, N.J.: Prentice Hall, 1986).

Additional Reading

For an advanced treatment of vicarious learning, see:

Bandura, Albert. *Social Foundations of Thought and Action: A Social Cognitive Theory*. Englewood Cliffs, N.J.: Prentice Hall, 1986, chap. 2.

For an early work examining various views of modeling, see:

Bandura, Albert. *Psychological Modeling: Conflicting Theories*. Chicago: Aldine Publishing, 1971.

For recent empirical research employing modeling, see:

Haring, Thomas G., Craig H. Kennedy, Mary J. Adams, and Valerie Pitts-Conway. "Teaching Generalization of Purchasing Skills across Community Settings to Autistic Youth Using Videotape Modeling," *Journal of Applied Behavior Analysis*, Spring 1987, pp. 89–96.

Winett, Richard A., Kathryn D. Kramer, William B. Walker, Steven W. Malone, and M. K. Lane. "Modifying Food Purchases in Supermarkets with Modeling, Feedback, and Goal Setting Procedures." *Journal of Applied Behavior Analysis*, Spring 1988, pp. 73–80.

MARKETING STRATEGY IN ACTION

Rollerblade Inc.

Minneapolis-based Rollerblade Inc. introduced its first in-line roller skate in 1980. Its founder, Scott Olson, was a hockey player with the Winnipeg Jets' farm teams who envisioned a roller skate with the action of an ice skate that hockey players and skiers could use to train during the off-season. At first, the plan was to use modern materials to construct a model based on an 18th-century design. However, Olson discovered a similar in-line skate already on the market and purchased the patent from the Chicago Roller Skate Company. Olson and his brother, Brennan, perfected the design using a plastic molded ski-type boot atop a blade of polyurethane wheels. Their first sales were to Olson's teammates as well as a few to sporting-goods stores. Thus began the sport of blading.

Although they generally cost twice as much as conventional roller skates, in-line skates, which range in price from $79 for regular models to $399 for racing models—are purchased for two reasons. First, they are faster and therefore more exciting to use than conventional skates. Second, they provide skaters with a better aerobic workout, requiring the use of more muscles. However, it is more difficult to learn how to use in-line skates because they require more balance, and at faster speeds, falls may cause more, and more severe, injuries.

By 1986, wholesale sales of in-line skates had risen to $3.5 million. Recognizing an opportunity to get in on a growing market, a number of companies began producing competitive products in the next several years. First Team Sports Inc., also based in Minneapolis, started manufacturing its Ultra-Wheels brand skates, which included the first in-line skates for children. The Roller Derby Skate Corporation in Litchfield, Illinois, a manufacturer of standard roller skates since 1936, produced an in-line skate with a toe-stopper for those accustomed to conventional skates (Rollerblades had a rubber stopper located on the heel). The ice skate manufacturer Bauer entered the market with a skate that has a leather boot rather than plastic.

Rollerblade Inc.'s sales increased when it expanded its target market. At first, the product was targeted to hockey players who were 95 percent male and were 18 to 25 years old. However, by broadening the target to include 18-to-35-year-old males and females, sales grew considerably.

By 1990, industry wholesale sales of in-line roller skates topped $50 million, almost as big as the conventional roller skate business. Rollerblade Inc. maintained a 66 percent market share; First Team Sports had 22 percent; Bauer had 5 percent; Roller Derby had 3 percent; and other competitors combined had the remaining 4 percent. Rollerblade could have done even better, but it could not fill store orders for several months because it ran out of inventory early in the year.

The fierce competition in the industry involved not only product features but also marketing elements. Companies rushed to sign celebrities to promote their products. For example, First Team Sports signed Wayne Gretzky, the Los Angeles Kings hockey star, and his wife, Janet Jones Gretzky, to a contract to promote its skates. Competitors also moved into new retail markets including discount and department stores. Rollerblade expanded its market by selling to Macy's and Nordstrom.

While the name Rollerblades may become

a generic term for this type of skate, the management of the company will have to work hard to maintain its market lead. "We have been pioneers and continue to maintain an edge," a company spokesperson said. "You only get one shot at pioneering a new sport, and that's exciting."

Discussion Questions

1. What role do you think modeling could have played in the diffusion of this innovation? (See Highlight 10.2.)
2. How could you use live, covert, and verbal modeling to teach a friend how to use Rollerblades?
3. What factors make Wayne and Janet Jones Gretzky good models for Rollerblade's competitor?
4. If you were designing a commercial for Rollerblades to be used for an in-store videotape demonstration, how would you design the commercial to take advantage of your knowledge of modeling?

Source: Based on "Innovator Tries to Protect Its Lead," *New York Times,* August 7, 1990, pp. C1, C6; and Lois Therrian, "Rollerblade Is Skating in Heavier Traffic," *Business Week,* June 24, 1991, pp. 115–16.

Analyzing Consumer Behavior

11

CHAPTER

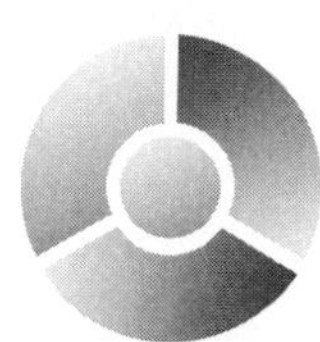

LANDS' END OUTLET STORE

"I have to run over to Walgreen's to pick up Angie's medicine," said Kari Jardine to her husband, Andy. "Do you want to go with me?"

"Sure," Andy responded. "I'd like to pick up some magazines for my flight to New York tomorrow."

On the way, the Jardines chatted about the recent snowfall and how much they enjoyed Christmas and New Year's, although both agreed they were glad the holidays were over. It was nice to get back to a more normal routine without all of the hassle of shopping in crowded malls looking for Christmas gifts.

The snowplows had left large mounds of snow in the parking lot at the strip mall where the drugstore was located. Once in the store, Kari went back to the pharmacy to pick up the prescription, and Andy went to the magazine rack in the front of the store. Andy pulled out $10 from his wallet and purchased copies of *Golf Digest* and *Sports Illustrated* and two Peppermint Patties to munch on the drive home.

As they walked out of Walgreen's, Andy suggested that, rather than going right home, they should take a few minutes to look in Lands' End's Outlet store, two doors down. "I saw a cranberry shawl-collar cardigan sweater in the Lands' End catalog that I liked. Maybe it will be in the store and I could try it on."

"That would be fine with me," replied Kari. "I could look for a new spring coat. I don't have to be at work until noon."

The sweater Andy was interested in was in the store. He tried it on and liked it. He remembered the normal price was $56, but the sale catalog price was $39. The outlet store price was $38.50. He decided to purchase it and saw another sweater he liked. The other sweater was a teal-colored wool cardigan, marked down from $70 to $56. While a little reluctant to purchase the other sweater because it was more expensive and wasn't much different from a green sweater he had received for Christmas, he decided to purchase it, too. After all, he deserved it, and he could return the green sweater to Marshall Field's.

Kari found a three-quarter-length, sand-colored, lightweight parka and was trying it on. "What do you think?" she asked Andy as he walked toward her, sweaters dangling over his arm.

"How much is it?" he asked.

"Let's see. It's $56 marked down from $70," Kari answered. "What did you find?"

After agreeing that the coat and sweaters were good buys, the Jardines went to the checkout counter in the center of the store.

"Did you find everything you need today?" asked the salesclerk.

"Yes, and we're ready to check out," stated Kari.

"Fine," said the salesclerk, checking the price tags and ringing up the merchandise. Well, let's see. The sweaters are an additional 30 percent off today. So that's $11.55 off one and $16.80 off the other.

"See this symbol?" the salesclerk said, pointing to a small black ship's steering wheel stamped on the coat's price tag. "That means it's 60 percent off, which will save you . . . $35.40."

The Jardines looked at each other and smiled. "Wow! You mean we're saving 50 or 60 bucks on this stuff?" shouted Andy, a little too loudly.

"That's right," said the salesclerk handing them their Visa card receipt and the bag of clothes. "We'll have more spring clothes in the next week or two. Be sure to stop back and look for those big markdowns."

Driving home, the Jardines figured out how much they had saved from the normal retail price. The total at retail was $196, and they paid $94.24, which included the 5 percent state sales tax. They felt good about their stop at the Lands' End Outlet. Andy decided to keep the green sweater he had gotten for Christmas since they had gotten such a good deal on the two new sweaters. He enjoys eating his candy bars.

What types of consumer behaviors are performed in this trip to Lands' End Outlet store? At this point in the text, you should have a good understanding of the major aspects of applied behavior analysis. It is now time to tie this perspective more directly to consumer behavior and marketing strategy development. This chapter explains two related models. First, a model of the behaviors involved in a common purchase situation is presented, and alternative marketing strategies used to change these behaviors are discussed. Second, we develop a consumer behavior management model that integrates many of the ideas discussed in this section with traditional marketing approaches.

A Sequential Model of Consumer Behavior

Traditional views of the purchase or adoption process in marketing treat it as a series or chain of cognitive events followed by a single behavior, usually called *adoption* or *purchase.* Consider the models, in Figure 11.1, of the adoption process as it is commonly treated in marketing. These models are consistent with the view that *cognitive variables* (awareness, comprehension, interest, evaluation, conviction, etc.) are the main concern of marketing and the primary controllers of behavior. According to this view, the marketing task is to change these cognitive variables and move consumers through each stage until a purchase is made.

FIGURE 11.1
Traditional Models of the Adoption/Purchase Process

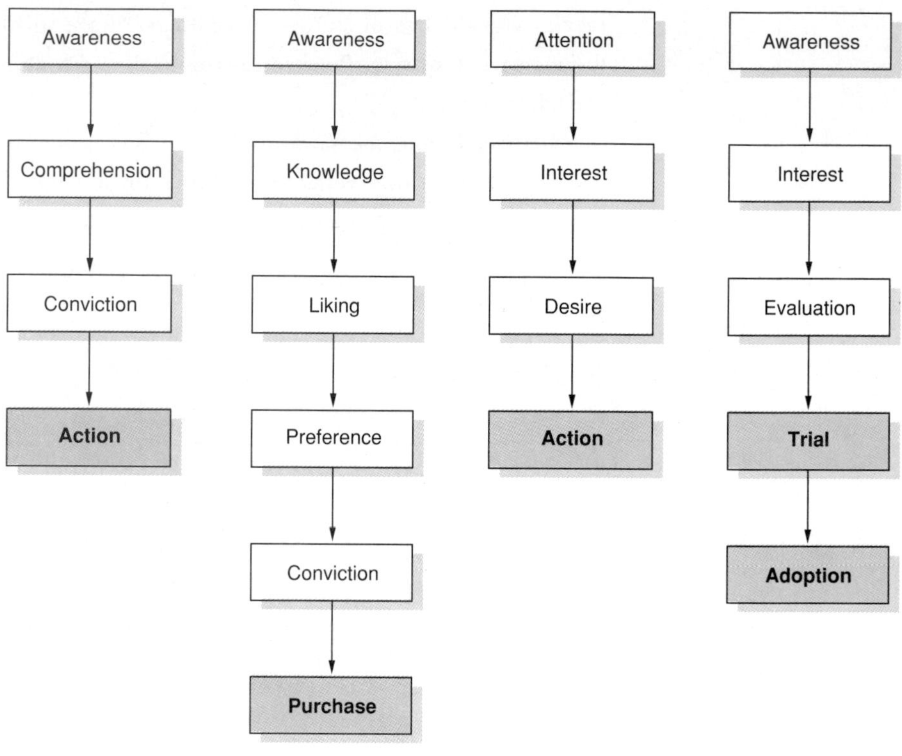

While the models in Figure 11.1 are valuable, adoption or purchase can also be analyzed as a *sequence of behaviors.* From this perspective, marketing managers usually want to increase the frequency of these behaviors, and they design strategies and tactics for doing so. While strategies and tactics to change affective and cognitive processes such as attention or attitude may be useful intermediate steps, they must ultimately change behavior to be profitable for marketers.

Figure 11.2 offers a model of a behavior sequence that occurs in the purchase of many consumer goods. Before discussing each of these stages, several qualifications should be noted. First, while we suggest this is a logical sequence, many other combinations of behavior are also commonly performed by consumers. For example, an unplanned (impulse) purchase of Twix cookie bars could start at the store contact stage. Not every purchase follows the sequence shown in Figure 11.2, and not every purchase requires that all of these

FIGURE 11.2
A Common Behavior Sequence for a Retail Consumer-Goods Purchase

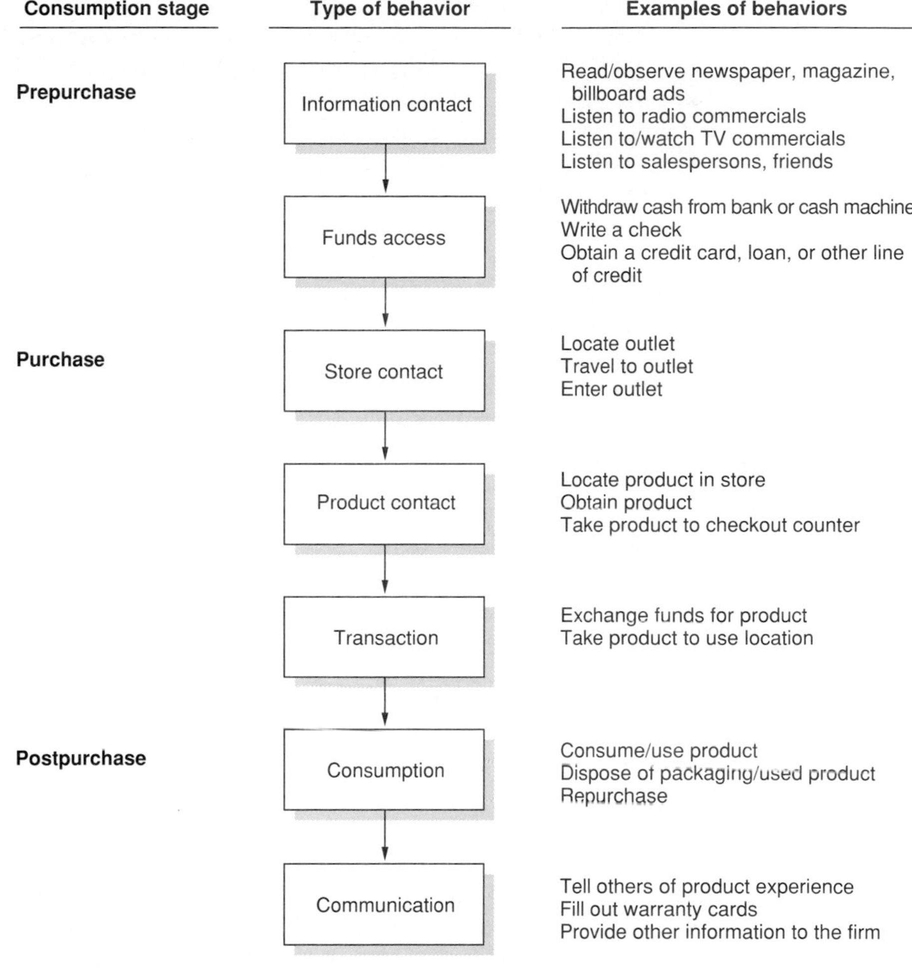

behaviors be performed. However, the model is useful for categorizing a variety of marketing strategies in terms of the behaviors they are designed to influence.

Second, the model in Figure 11.2 is intended to illustrate only one type of behavior sequence for retail purchases; similar models could be developed for other types of purchases, such as mail-order, phone, or catalog-showroom exchanges. Further, the sequences involved with other behaviors of interest to consumer analysis, such as voting, physician care, banking, or consumer education, could also be modeled in much the same way. We believe that any attempt to influence behavior should include an analysis of the behavior sequence that is necessary or desired. Unfortunately, many marketing managers do not consider exactly what behaviors are involved in the actions they are attempting to get consumers to perform.

Third, the time it takes for a consumer to perform these behaviors depends on a variety of factors. Different products, consumers, and situations may affect not only the total time to complete the process but also the time lags between stages. For example, an avid water-skier purchasing a Mastercraft powerboat likely will spend more time per stage, and more time will elapse between stages, than a consumer purchasing a Timex quartz watch.

Fourth, members of the channel of distribution usually vary in their emphasis on encouraging particular behaviors. Retailers may be more concerned with increasing store contact than with purchase of a particular brand; manufacturers are less concerned with the particular store patronized, but attempt to increase brand purchase; credit-card companies may be less concerned with particular store or product contacts so long as their credit card is accepted and used. However, while emphasis may vary, all three of these behaviors are common for a retail exchange, and all three organizations can benefit from the others' efforts. Highlight 11.1 discusses a creative strategy for influencing consumers' purchasing behavior that involves a discount card company and restaurants.

Finally, the seven categories of the consumer behavior chain in Figure 11.2 deserve comment. While we believe these are logical and useful categories of behavior, other labels or breakdowns could also be useful. For instance, this behavior chain could be carefully broken down into individual actions of each muscle in the consumer's body, and research could be conducted at that level. However, given the lack of knowledge concerning overt consumer behavior, the levels in Figure 11.2 are a useful starting point. With these qualifications, we now turn to a discussion of each type of behavior and some marketing strategies currently employed to increase the probability of one or more of them.

Information Contact

A common early stage in the purchase sequence, called **information contact,** occurs when consumers come into contact with information about products, stores, or brands. This stage includes behaviors such as reading or observing newspaper, magazine, and billboard ads; listening to radio commercials; watching TV commercials; and talking to salespeople and friends. At this point, the practical problem for marketers is to increase the probability that consumers will observe and attend to the information, and that this will increase the probability of other behaviors.

Not only do marketers seek to provide consumers with information, but consumers also search for information about products, brands, stores, and prices.[1] Marketing managers for brands with low market shares usually want to increase overall search behavior, because it may increase the probability of switching to the firm's brand.

HIGHLIGHT 11.1

TRANSMEDIA'S EXECUTIVE SAVINGS CARD

Transmedia Network Inc. came up with an innovative strategy to serve consumers profitably with a discount card for restaurant meals. In five years, it attracted 45,000 cardholders, and in 1990, it made $7.5 million in revenues and over $300,000 in net income. The Transmedia Executive Savings Card can be used at over 725 restaurants in parts of New York, New Jersey, Connecticut, and Florida. Here's how it works.

Transmedia offers cash advances to restaurants that in turn give Transmedia twice the cash amount in credits for meals. For example, Transmedia usually offers $5,000 cash for $10,000 in restaurant credits. It then offers its cardholders a 25 percent discount on meals (before tax and tip) eaten at restaurants that honor its cards. Usually, it takes about six months for a group of cardholders to use all the $10,000 credit at a particular restaurant. After giving cardholders the 25 percent discount, Transmedia still gets $7,500 for its initial $5,000 cash advance.

Restaurants deal with Transmedia because they benefit from the quick cash, and the additional business is still profitable and helps fill unused capacity. The cards also are a big help to new restaurants trying to build a clientele.

Consumers use the cards because of the large savings. However, the toughest job for Transmedia was to attract cardholders. Even after advertising and offering free cards, consumers didn't initially sign up; they didn't believe the company could deliver such good deals. To add more cardholders, Transmedia continues to waive the $50 annual fee for at least the first year and offers cardholders $25 cards for their friends. It offers companies free cards for use by employees on expense accounts. In sum, this strategy increases the probability of consumers purchasing meals at specific locations and is profitable for both Transmedia and the restaurants.

Source: Jeffrey A. Tannenbaum, "Issuer of Restaurant Discount Cards Tastes Success," *The Wall Street Journal,* April 23, 1991, p. B2.

High market-share brands may try to discourage external search behaviors, because the behavior may result in a shift to another brand. For example, Heinz has a major share of the market for ketchup and does not want most consumers to search for information concerning different brands. Ads showing Heinz as the thicker, richer ketchup while depicting other brands as thin and unsavory may discourage loyal consumers from searching for an alternative. They may also help attract non-Heinz purchasers by demonstrating the negative consequences of using another brand.

The extent of a consumer's search depends on many factors, such as those listed in Figure 11.3. In general, empirical research has shown that:

FIGURE 11.3

Some Determinants of the Extent of Consumers' Information Search

Market environment
- Number of alternatives
- Complexity of alternatives
- Marketing mix of alternatives
- Stability of alternatives on the market (new alternatives)
- Information available

Situational variables
- Time pressure
- Social pressure (family, peers, boss)
- Financial pressure
- Organizational procedures
- Physical and mental condition
- Ease of access to information sources

Potential payoff/product importance
- Price
- Social visibility
- Perceived risk
- Differences among alternatives
- Number of crucial attributes
- Status of decision-making activity (in family, organization, society)

Knowledge and experience
- Stored knowledge
- Rate of product use
- Previous information
- Previous choices (number and identity)
- Satisfaction

Individual differences
- Training
- Approach to problem solving (compulsiveness, open-mindedness, preplanning, innovativeness)
- Approach to search (enjoyment of shopping, sources of information, etc.)
- Involvement
- Demographics (age, income, education, marital status, household size, social class, occupation)
- Personality/lifestyle variables (self-confidence, etc.)

Conflict and conflict-resolution strategies

Source: Reprinted with permission from "Individual Differences in Search Behavior for a Nondurable," by William L. Moore and Donald R. Lehmann, from the *Journal of Consumer Research,* December 1980, pp. 296–307. For a summary of empirical research on these and other search determinants, see Sharon E. Beatty and Scott M. Smith, "External Search Effort: An Investigation across Several Product Categories," *Journal of Consumer Research,* June 1987, pp. 83–95.

1. Consumers tend to engage in more search when purchasing higher priced, more visible, and more complex products – i.e., products that intrinsically create greater perceived risk.
2. Search is also influenced by individual factors, such as the perceived benefits of search (e.g., enjoyment, self-confidence, role), demographic aspects, and product knowledge already possessed.

FIGURE 11.4
A Comparison of Information Sources

Source	Effort Required	Believability
Internal (stored experiences in memory)	Low	High
Personal (friends, relatives)	Low	High
Marketing (advertising)	Low	Low
Public (*Consumer Reports,* other studies)	High	High
Experiential (examining or testing product)	High	High

3. Search efforts tend to be further influenced by factors in the marketplace (such as store distribution) and by situational factors (such as time pressure impinging on the shopper).[2]

From a public policy standpoint, information search is encouraged to develop more knowledgeable consumers.[3] However, there are differences in the effort required by consumers to obtain information from different sources — and in the believability of the information. For example, Figure 11.4 illustrates five common sources of information and rates them on these two dimensions.

This model predicts that internal sources (stored experiences) and personal sources (friends and relatives) are commonly used because they are easiest to access and most believable. Marketing sources (advertising) would also be commonly used because they are readily available. However, marketing sources are not as believable because advertisers have something to gain from the transaction. Finally, public sources (*Consumer Reports* and other impartial studies) and experiential sources (personally examining or testing the product) are less likely to be used, at least in this early stage, because more effort is required to obtain information from these sources.

Information search could also be broken down into a sequence of basic behaviors. However, the main marketing task is to increase the probability that the target market comes into contact with product, brand, or store information and pays attention to it.

Numerous marketing strategies are directed at bringing about these attentive behaviors. All are remarkably consistent with behavior approaches. For example, media scheduling, message content and layout, color and humor in advertising, and repetition all involve presenting stimuli to increase the probability that potential consumers will attend to relevant cues. In addition, *fear appeals* are used to bring about attentive behaviors and to vicariously stimulate emotions by exposing the observers to possible aversive consequences of certain conditions (inadequate insurance, faulty tires and batteries, the absence of smoke alarms, not flossing regularly).

HIGHLIGHT 11.2

Encouraging Information Contact for Magazine Subscriptions

Including subscription cards in magazines is a useful marketing tactic because the cards are available while the magazine is being read and enjoyed. These cards make it convenient for readers of the magazine (the likely target market for future issues) to renew a subscription or start a new one.

Traditionally, magazine marketers have bound subscription cards to the magazines. One drawback to such "bind-in" cards is that readers often simply ignore them. Because the cards are bound to the issue, readers leaf through the entire magazine without giving the card (or the idea of starting or renewing a subscription) any consideration.

An alternative method of including subscription cards in magazines is to place them between the pages, unbound. These are called "blow-in" cards. When magazines are being read or carried, blow-in cards frequently fall out. Consumers usually pick up on the cards and examine them for at least a moment. In other words, the probability of information contact is increased when blow-in rather than bind-in cards are used. It is not surprising, then, that blow-in cards are more effective than bind-in cards at generating subscription renewals.

Strategies such as contests and prizes bring about attentive behavior and promise rewards for engaging in certain actions that bring the consumer into closer contact with the product or point of purchase. Finally, ads that show models receiving positive reinforcement in the form of social approval and satisfaction for purchasing a product provide stimuli that can move the consumer closer to purchase by stimulating the "buying mood." Highlight 11.2 discusses a strategy for encouraging information contact for magazine subscriptions.

Funds Access

Current views of marketing emphasize exchange as the key concept for understanding the field. However, relatively little attention has been given to *what consumers exchange* in the marketing process. While time and effort costs are involved, money is the primary medium of consumer exchanges. The consumer must access this medium in one form or another before an exchange can occur, engaging in what is known as **funds access.** The primary marketing issues at this stage are (1) the methods used by consumers to pay for particular purchases, and (2) the marketing strategies to increase the probability that the consumers can access funds for purchase.

Consumers can pay for a product offering in a variety of ways. These include cash in pocket; bank withdrawal of cash; writing a check; using credit cards such as Visa, MasterCard, and American Express; opening a store charge account; using debit cards; and drawing on other lines of credit, such as bank loans and GMAC financing. Another issue concerns the *effort* exerted by the consumer to obtain the actual funds that are spent or used to repay loans. Funds obtained from tax refunds, stock sales and dividends, gambling winnings, awards, or regular paychecks may be valued differently by the consumer and spent in different ways. Some retailers encourage the purchase of big-ticket items by offering interest-free loans for a few months while consumers are waiting for their tax refunds.

A variety of other strategies can increase the ability and probability that consumers can access funds for purchases. For example, J.C. Penney offers a small gift to anyone who fills out a Penney's credit-card application. The probability of purchasing at Penney's is increased when a consumer has a credit card, because cash may not always be available. Other strategies include locating cash machines in malls, instituting liberal credit terms and check-cashing policies, and accepting a variety of credit cards. Deferred payment plans and layaway plans that allow the consumer additional time to raise the required funds help stores avoid lost sales. Gift certificates are also used to presell merchandise and to provide some consumers with another source of funds that is restricted for particular purchases.

All of these strategies have a common goal—to increase the probability of an exchange by increasing the probability of accessing funds. The consumer is similar to B. F. Skinner's rat in the box—if the rat cannot reach the bar, it cannot obtain its food; if the potential customer cannot reach financial resources, products cannot be purchased.

Other strategies can be employed to increase certain types of purchases. For example, a store could offer a small discount for using cash to avoid the costs of paying credit-card fees. An analysis of the conditions surrounding particular purchases may lead to other successful tactics. For example, many major home appliances are purchased only when both husband and wife are present, and a necessary condition is that they can obtain funds. One tactic for an appliance store might be to offer a small gift to any couple who comes to the store with checkbook or approved credit card. Thus, the appropriate contingencies are prearranged for an appliance sale. Any number of other tactics (such as offering rebates) could also be used in conjunction with this tactic to further increase the probability of purchase. Highlight 11.3 discusses strategies used by credit-card issuers to encourage consumers to obtain and use their credit cards for funds access.

Funds access can occur in a number of ways.

Store Contact

Although catalog and telephone-order purchases are important, most consumer-goods purchases are still made in retail stores. Thus, a major task of retailers is to get consumers into the store where purchase can occur. **Store contact** includes (1) locating the outlet, (2) traveling to the outlet, and (3) entering the outlet.

The nature of the consumers in their roles as shoppers affects the probability of store contact. Some consumers may enjoy shopping and spend many hours looking in stores. To others, shopping may be drudgery. Some shoppers may be primarily price oriented and favor particular low-price outlets. Others may seek a high level of service or unique products and stores that express their individuality. These differences are important dimensions when designing market segmentation strategies for stores.

Many strategies are designed to increase the probability of store contact. For example, consider the methods used to increase the probability that shoppers will be able to locate a particular outlet. Selecting convenient locations in high-traffic areas with ample parking has been very successful for many retailers, such as 7-Eleven convenience stores and Denny's restaurants.

A major advantage for retailers locating in shopping malls is the increase in consumer's ability to find the outlet as well as the additional shopping traffic created by the presence of the other stores. Yellow Pages, newspaper, and other ads frequently include maps and information numbers to aid shoppers in locating an outlet. Outdoor signs and logos (such as Domino's Pizza's distinctive sign) are well known discriminative stimuli. One recreational vehicle dealer close to Columbus, Ohio, used an interesting modeling approach to aid poten-

HIGHLIGHT 11.3

HEATED COMPETITION IN THE CREDIT-CARD WARS

The credit-card industry is highly competitive and profitable. Banks and other companies offer different card features in hopes of attracting cardholders and getting them to use their cards frequently. Credit-card issuers make money from fees charged to merchants on purchases consumers make, from annual fees charged consumers, and from interest on credit-card balances.

A number of changes have occurred in the credit-card industry as companies vie for market share. Citicorp, the largest issuer of Visa and MasterCards, introduced a program to guarantee its customers the best prices on items they charge. Chemical Bank lowered the interest rate on its cards from a fixed 19.5 percent to a floating rate and offered consumers discounts on phone bills and meals. American Express attacked Visa and MasterCard's over 19 percent interest charges with its Optima card, which has a 16.25 percent rate. Sears offers a 1 percent rebate to consumers on purchases charged on its Discover card. AT&T offered its Universal Visa or MasterCard "free for life" to holders of other companies Visa or MasterCards. The offer included a 10 percent discount on AT&T long-distance phone calls.

Why are credit-card companies competing so fiercely for consumer acceptance? The answer is simple: The cost of money is often far less than half the interest rate being charged on credit cards, making the business very profitable. For example, in one recent year, Citibank made $3.6 billion in credit-card interest and $500 million in card fees! According to one report, Citicorp and Chase Manhattan make about 70 percent of their net profits from credit cards, and other banks often make more than 50 percent of their earnings from them.

Consumers use credit cards because they make funds access simple and convenient. However, if balances are carried over, they can also make funds access very expensive.

Source: Bill Saporito, "Melting Point in the Plastic Wars," *Fortune,* May 20, 1991, pp. 71–78; and Bill Saporito, "Who's Winning the Credit Card War?" *Fortune,* July 2, 1990, pp. 66–72.

tial customers in locating the dealership. The dealer's TV ads consisted of the actual scenery, landmarks, and road signs people would see when traveling to the dealership. Every turn was shown, as were directional signs on the highway, to help potential customers find the outlet.

Other tactics are used to get potential customers to the vicinity of stores or malls. For example, carnivals in mall parking lots, free fashion shows or other mall entertainments, and visits by celebrities such as Santa Claus, the Easter Bunny, Sesame Street characters, and soap-opera actors are used to shape behavior. Further, mall directories and information booths help shoppers find particular stores.

Strategies that facilitate store contacts.

Locating in malls . . .

Ample parking . . .

The presence of the Easter Bunny . . .

Extended store hours.

(Top left: Cynthia Rymer, TSW/Click, Chicago Ltd.; top right: David S. Strickler, TSW/Click, Chicago Ltd.; bottom left; Don Smetzer, TSW/Click, Chicago Ltd.; bottom right: George W. Gardner)

Finally, tactics are used to get the potential customer physically into the store. Frequently advertised sales, sale signs in store windows, door prizes, loss leaders, sounds (such as popular music), and smells (such as fresh popcorn) are commonly employed. A variety of other in-store issues are discussed later in the text, particularly in Chapter 20.

Product Contact

While a major concern of retailers is increasing and maintaining *selective store patronage*, manufacturers are primarily concerned with *selective demand*—purchase of their particular brands and models. Many of the methods employed to accomplish such **product contact** involve **push strategies** such as trade discounts and incentives to enhance the selling effort of retailers. For example, offering retailers a free case of Tide liquid detergent for every 10 cases purchased can be a powerful incentive for retailers to feature liquid Tide in newspaper ads, put it in prominent displays, and even sell it at a lower price while maintaining or increasing profit margins. Many approaches also involve **pull strategies,** such as cents-off coupons to encourage the consumer to purchase the manufacturer's brand.

Cents-off coupons encourage product contact.

This ad creates feelings about a product through classical conditioning.
Chapter 9

Courtesy Nickels Shoes

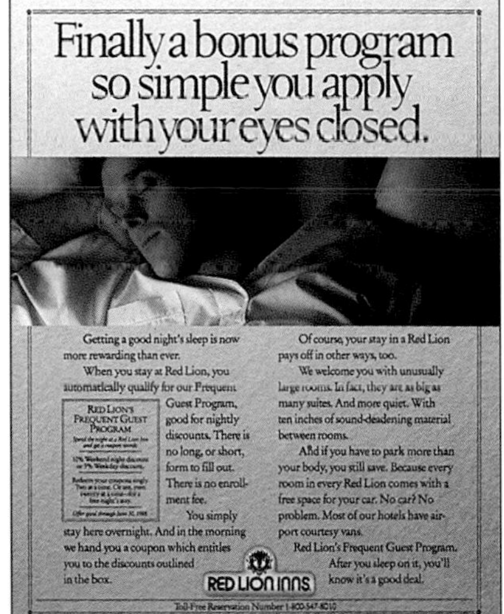

Courtesy Red Lion Inns

Bonus programs can change the behavior of choosy travelers.
Chapter 11

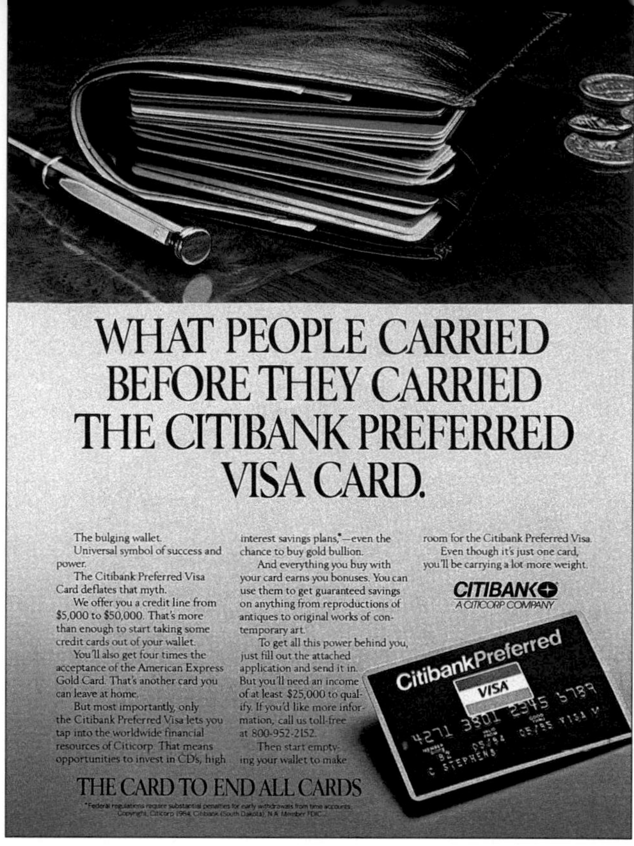

Courtesy Citibank

Research suggests that credit cards and related stimuli may become associated with spending partly because of classical conditioning.
Chapter 9

You want to see everything. Maybe bring something back so you remember it all. Now if you could just find a few nice stores. Ah, there's one. And another. And...

THE CARD.
THE AMERICAN EXPRESS® CARD.
Call 1-800-THE CARD, to apply.

Courtesy American Express

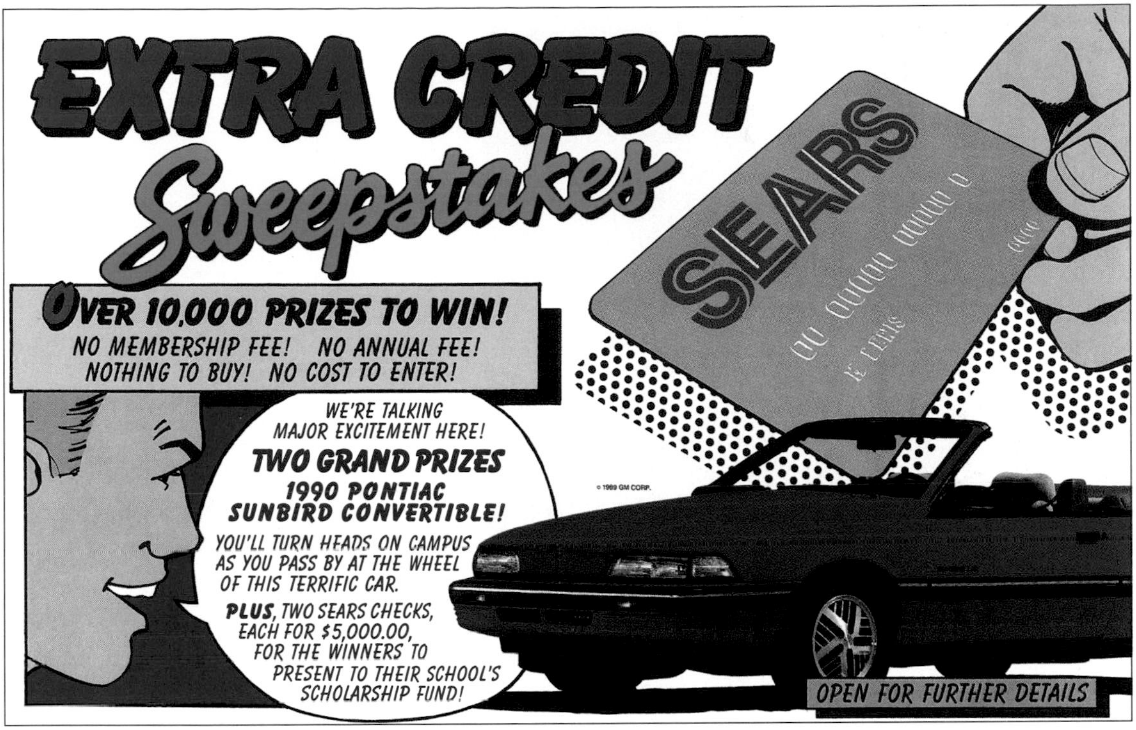
EXTRA CREDIT
Sweepstakes
OVER 10,000 PRIZES TO WIN!
NO MEMBERSHIP FEE! NO ANNUAL FEE!
NOTHING TO BUY! NO COST TO ENTER!
WE'RE TALKING MAJOR EXCITEMENT HERE!
TWO GRAND PRIZES
1990 PONTIAC SUNBIRD CONVERTIBLE!
YOU'LL TURN HEADS ON CAMPUS AS YOU PASS BY AT THE WHEEL OF THIS TERRIFIC CAR.
PLUS, TWO SEARS CHECKS, EACH FOR $5,000.00, FOR THE WINNERS TO PRESENT TO THEIR SCHOOL'S SCHOLARSHIP FUND!
SEARS
© 1989 GM CORP.
OPEN FOR FURTHER DETAILS

Courtesy Sears

Special promotion contests can attract new consumers.
Chapter 8

Post
How to become an expert in choosing a natural, whole grain bran flake.
Make sure you can see the natural high fiber wheat bran in every flake.
Make sure it's made with 100% whole grain wheat and wheat bran.
Make sure it has big, crispy flakes with naturally delicious whole grain taste.
Make sure it has 13 vitamins and minerals.
Make sure it's naturally fat free, cholesterol free with no preservatives.
Make sure it's POST® Bran Flakes.
Post Bran Flakes
Your Natural Choice
MANUFACTURER'S COUPON EXPIRATION DATE 9/30/92
Save 50¢ on any size
Post Bran Flakes
©1992 Kraft General Foods, Inc.

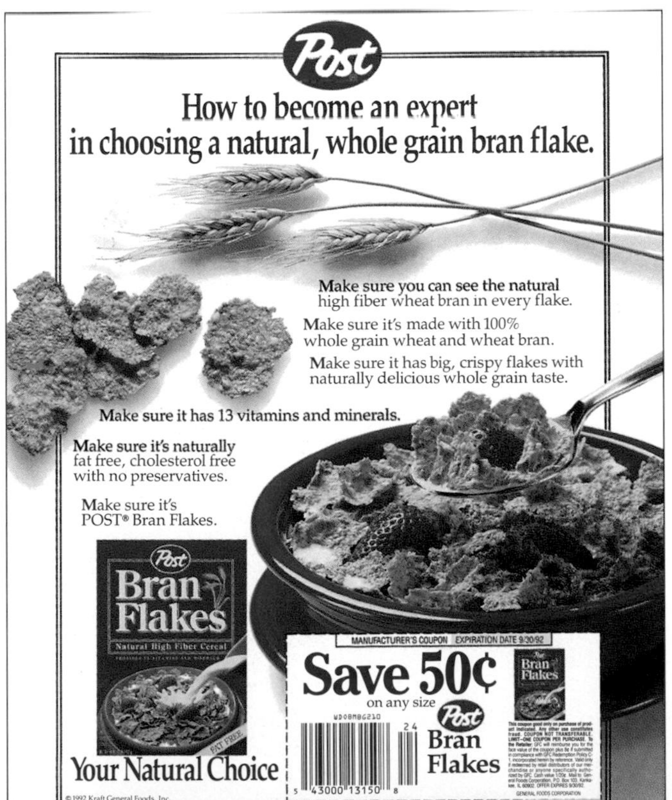

This ad makes the consumer aware of possible choice criteria.
Chapter 7

Courtesy General Mills

Courtesy Russell Athletic

Sometimes a company may find it worthwhile to influence consumers' social behavior unrelated to product purchase.
Chapter 11

Word-of-mouth information can be a potent learning tool.
Chapter 11

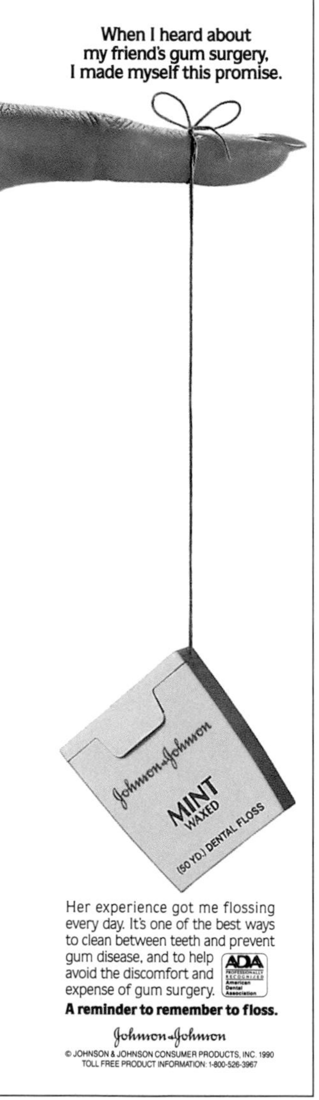

Courtesy Johnson & Johnson

Once potential buyers are in the store, three behaviors are usually necessary for a purchase to occur: (1) locate the product or brand in the store, (2) physically obtain the product or brand, and (3) take the product or brand to the point of exchange (e.g., the checkout counter).

Once consumers are in the store, it is important that products can be located. Store directories, end-of-aisle and other displays, in-store signs, information booths, and helpful store personnel all help consumers move into visual contact with products. While consumers are in the store, their visual contact with the many other available products increases the probability of purchase.

One interesting tactic employed by a major chain involves a variation of "blue-light specials." Blue-light specials were pioneered by K mart. They offer shoppers in the store the opportunity to purchase products at special prices when a blue light is flashing at a particular location. Usually, the sale item is one that is low-priced and sold at its normal location. A variation of this tactic moves the sale merchandise and blue light to a location in the store where high-priced or high-margin items are located. This brings the blue-light shoppers to the vicinity of such products and into visual contact with them – which increases the probability of making these more profitable sales. This has been reported to be very successful.

Physically coming into contact with a product provides an extremely important source of stimuli and possible consequences that influence whether or not a purchase will occur. Attractive, eye-catching packaging and other aspects of product appearance influence the stimuli attended to by the consumer. Trying the product in the store can also affect purchase probabilities.

The behavior of sales personnel can also affect the contingencies at the point of purchase. Sales personnel can positively reinforce certain behaviors, extinguish or punish others, influence the stimuli attended to, and model appropriate product usage. Even negative reinforcement can be employed. For example, consider salespeople who are overly aggressive and use high-pressure tactics. One way for consumers to remove the aversive treatment is to purchase the product – and some consumers do this rather than walk away. Thus, the consumer is negatively reinforced to purchase; and the probability of this response would probably be increased in similar situations in the future. Also, the salesperson is positively reinforced by making the sale using a high-pressure approach. It is likely the salesperson's use of an aggressive selling approach will also increase.

Salespeople can also change the contingencies for purchasing versus not purchasing. For example, one of our associates told us of his experience in selling furniture to ambivalent customers who stated their intention to "go home and think it over." Once the potential buyer leaves the store, the probability of a sale is reduced. Our associate, however, changed the contingencies for leaving. Potential buyers who wanted to think it over were told, "If you buy now, the price is $150. If you go home and come back later, the price will be the original $175." While we are not advocating this specific practice, we do want to stress that salespeople can modify the behavior of potential buyers.

Also, a number of tactics are used to get potential buyers to the checkout or payment location. For example, checkout counters are commonly placed next to the exit and parking vouchers are usually validated at this location. Also, salespeople frequently escort the buyer to the checkout where they may help arrange financing.

Transaction

In a macro sense, *facilitating exchanges* is viewed as the primary objective of marketing. In a micro sense, this involves **transactions** in which consumers' funds are exchanged for products and services. Many marketing strategies involve removing obstacles to transactions. The credit methods discussed earlier are examples. So is the use of express checkout lanes and electronic scanners to decrease the time consumers must wait in line. (Some consumers will leave stores without making a purchase if checkout lines are too long.) Credit-card companies offer prompt purchase approvals to decrease the chances a sale will be missed because of a long wait. American Express, for example, spends $300 million to $400 million annually to ensure prompt service for its 15 million customers. From its Phoenix computer center, the company approves 250,000 credit-card transactions a day from all over the world in an average of five seconds or less.[4]

Because the behavior of checkout personnel has long been recognized as an important influence on purchase, these personnel are often trained to be friendly and efficient. McDonald's personnel frequently offer *prompts* in an attempt to increase the total amount of purchase. Regardless of the food order, prompts for additional food are offered: "Would you like some fresh, hot French fries with that?" or "How about some McDonald's cookies today?" Because these are very low-cost tactics, few incremental sales are required to make them profitable.

The positive reinforcers involved are critical elements in obtaining transactions. Tactics such as rebates, friendly treatment and compliments by store personnel, and contest tickets may increase the probability of purchase and repurchase. The reinforcing properties of the product or service itself are also important. These may involve both functional and psychosocial benefits.

Consumption

While **consumption** or use would seem to be very simple behaviors to delineate, they are not, because of the vast differences in the natures of various products and services. For example, compare typical behaviors involved in the purchase of nondurables such as a burger and fries versus a durable such as an automobile. The burger and fries are likely to be consumed rather quickly and the packaging disposed of properly. Certain strategies can increase the probability that consumption will be rather quick, such as seats in a restaurant that are

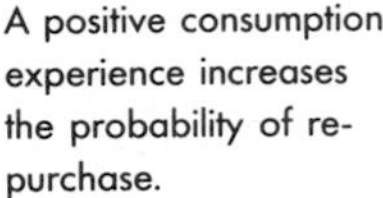

A positive consumption experience increases the probability of repurchase.

comfortable for only a short time. As a result, current customers do not take up space for too long that could be used for new customers. Prompts are often used to encourage proper disposal of packaging, such as "Thank You" signs on refuse containers.

An automobile purchase usually involves several years of consumption or use. In addition, periodic service is required, and additional complementary products such as gas must be purchased. Finally, an automobile may be disposed of in several ways (selling it, junking it, or trading it in on another model). At present, little is known about the process by which consumers dispose of durable goods.

Regardless of the type of product, however, a primary marketing concern is increasing the probability of repurchase. For nondurable package goods, commonly employed tactics include the use of in- or on-package coupons to encourage the consumer to repurchase the same brand. (Many consumers frequently use coupons and take pride in the money they save.) In addition, proof-of-purchase seals have often been used to encourage the consumer to purchase the same brand repeatedly, thereby obtaining enough seals to receive "free" gifts. Gold Medal flour has long used this tactic, and Pampers diapers ran a promotion in which a coupon for a free box of diapers was sent to buyers who mailed in three proof-of-purchase seals.

For durable goods, proper instructions on the care and use of the product may be useful, for they help the consumer receive full product benefits. In addition, high-quality service and maintenance provided by the seller can help to develop long-term client relationships.

Communication

A final set of behaviors that marketers attempt to increase involves **communication.** Marketers want consumers to communicate with two basic audiences. They want consumers to (1) provide the company with marketing information and (2) tell other potential consumers about the product and encourage them to purchase it. Consumers can communicate with the company or other consumers about products, brands, or stores any time, not just at the end of the purchase sequence. We place this behavior here because consumers who have purchased and used a product are likely to be more knowledgeable about it and more influential in telling other consumers about it.

From Consumers to Marketers

Marketers typically want at least three types of information from consumers. First, they want *information about the consumer* to investigate the quality of their marketing strategy and the success of market segmentation. Warranty cards are commonly used for this. These cards commonly ask about consumer demographics, what magazines consumers read, where they obtained information about the product, where they purchased it, and what competing brands they own or have tried. Free gifts are sometimes offered to encourage consumers to return warranty cards—as well as subtle threats that the warranty will be canceled if the card is not filled out and returned promptly.

A second type of information sought from consumers is the *names of other potential buyers* of the product. Some firms and organizations offer awards if the names of several potential buyers are given and a larger award if any of the prospects actually makes a purchase. Finally, marketers also seek consumer information about *defective products.* Money-back or other guarantees that require the consumer to contact the store or company provide this information and also reduce the risk of loss to the consumer. For example, General Mills offers "a prompt adjustment of equal value" if the consumer is dissatisfied with Cheerios.

From Consumers to Consumers

Marketers also want consumers to tell their friends and others about the product. A product that is effective and performs well may encourage this behavior. However, other tactics also can encourage it. Tupperware parties have long been used to take advantage of the fact that consumers respond favorably to information from their friends and to create an environment in which purchase is heavily encouraged. This approach has been so successful that, over the first 25 years of its existence, Tupperware doubled its sales and earnings every 5 years.

Newly opened bars and lounges frequently offer customers free drinks to encourage them not only to return but also to tell others about the place and to bring their friends. Word-of-mouth communication is the primary way such establishments become popular. Health clubs, such as Elaine Powers and Vic

Tanny, often run promotions in which members who bring in new customers get special rates for themselves as well as for their friends. One cable TV company ran a promotion in which any subscriber who got a friend to purchase the service received $10. Such tactics increase not only communication but other behaviors in the purchase sequence as well. Finally, consumers often learn purchase and use behaviors through vicarious learning processes.

A Consumer Behavior Management Model

The preceding part of this chapter outlined a common behavior sequence for retail purchases. A number of examples of current marketing strategies were categorized according to the factors in this model. In this last part of the chapter, we describe a model by which managers can analyze consumer behavior and develop marketing programs to increase the probability of behaviors that are necessary to achieve organizational objectives. This general approach could also be used to develop strategies for decreasing undesired behaviors. We will not emphasize such strategies, however, because of the ethical and practical problems of using punishment or extinction in many marketing management situations.

Two tasks must be performed to use this model. First, given appropriate marketing objectives, the manager must develop a sequential model of the behaviors that are necessary or desired of the consumer. To develop this sequence, we will use our seven-stage model (refer back to Figure 11.2), but other models would have to be developed for other types of purchase/consumption situations.

Second, after the behaviors are delineated, their frequency must be measured to determine baseline data. This step is necessary to identify problem behaviors and to provide a benchmark for comparing the success of the implemented strategy. There are many ways to measure various consumer behaviors; Figure 11.5 provides some examples. These measurement methods are commonly employed in current marketing research, although they are not always used sequentially to assess every behavior stage.

One approach that allows a number of stages in a purchase sequence to be monitored is the **scanner cable method** available from research companies such as Information Resources, Inc., (IRI) and Nielsen Marketing Research USA. Because this approach is very consistent with the requirements of a consumer behavior management model, we will briefly describe how IRI's system works.

IRI's research systems are used by many leading companies including General Foods, Procter & Gamble, General Mills, and Frito-Lay. The systems are designed to predict which products will be successful and which ads work best to sell them. It has been expanded from grocery stores to include drugstores and mass merchandisers. IRI has constructed consumer panels in a number of

FIGURE 11.5
Examples of Methods Used to Measure Consumption Behaviors

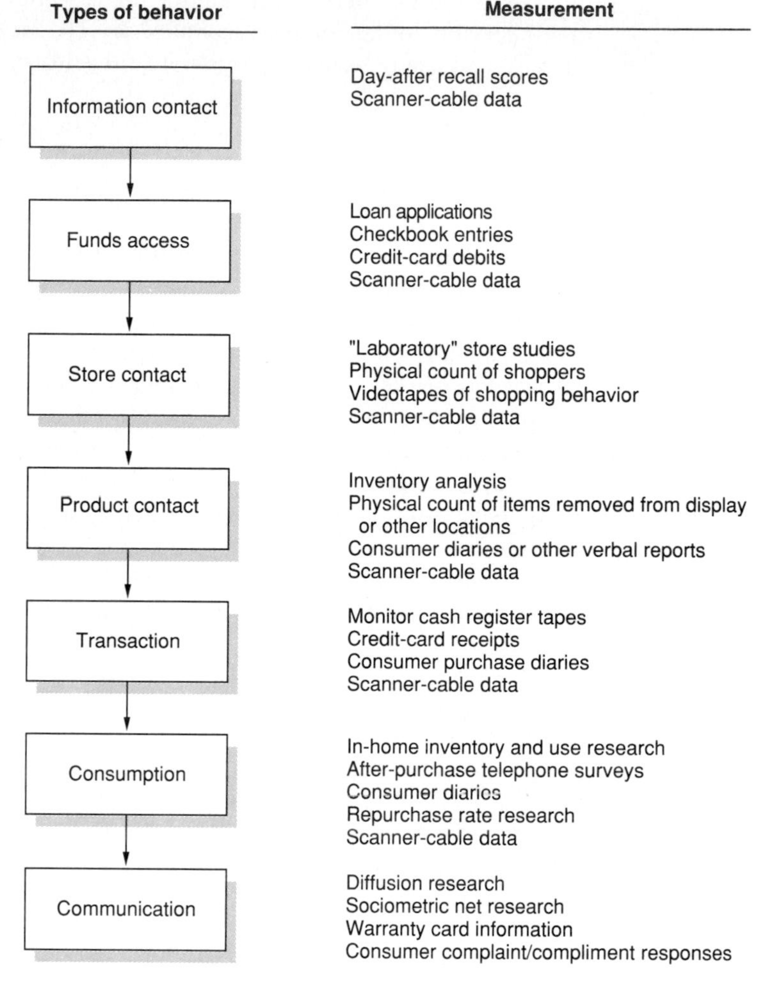

cities and monitors over 60,000 households nationwide. It monitors purchases in 2,700 grocery stores in 66 markets ranging from big cities to small towns.

Panel members provide information about the size of their families, their income, their marital status, how many TVs they own, what types of newspapers and magazines they read, and who does most of the shopping. IRI provides a special bar-coded identification card that shoppers present to the cashier when they pay for products in groceries, drug, and other stores. By passing the card

Consumers use a BehaviorScan coded ID card when shopping in the markets covered by the scanner network.

over the scanner or entering the digits manually into the register, the cashier records everything each shopper has purchased.

One executive for Frito-Lay, which used IRI's services for the introduction of Sun Chips snacks, concluded, "The beauty of scanner data is that we get a complete description of a household from the panel and can match it with purchasing patterns. We know exactly who's out there buying our product and that helps us design marketing and advertising plans accordingly."[5]

A number of behaviors in the purchase sequence can be monitored and influenced using scanner methods. For example, information contact can be influenced since media habits of households are monitored, and commercials can be changed until contact occurs. Funds access can be monitored on the cash register tape by recording prices and the method of payment. Because every purchase in the store is recorded, store contact, product contact, and transaction information is available, as well as the dates and times of these behaviors. As such, the effectiveness of various sales promotions and other marketing strategies on specific consumer behaviors can be determined. Successful promotions can be offered again to encourage store and brand loyalty. Since the time between purchases can be determined, information is also available on consumption and usage rates.

Overall, our discussion is intended to demonstrate that consumer behaviors can be measured quite well using current technology. However, as with any element of marketing strategy, the costs and benefits of extended research on consumer behaviors must be carefully analyzed. While there are substantial benefits, many firms have to use less costly methods. Even simpler, less expensive methods—such as analysis of advertising expenditures and shipping orders in various markets—may provide useful information about consumer behavior.

Given that a sequence of consumer behaviors can be developed and that they can be measured with current and developing technologies, Figure 11.6 offers a model for managing such behaviors. This model, based on ideas in applied behavior analysis, is concerned with the development and maintenance of consumer behavior. It is fully consistent with the objectives of marketing

FIGURE 11.6
A Consumer Behavior Management Model

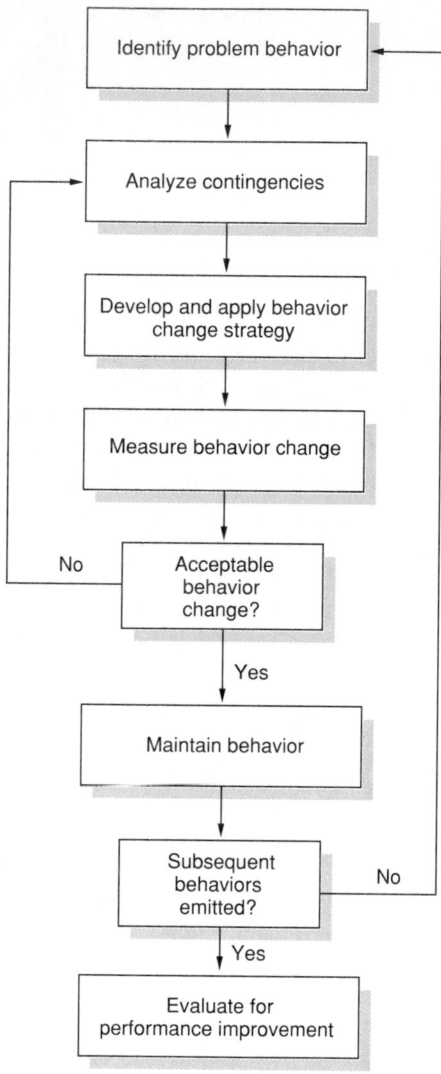

management and common marketing strategies. The model offers a more systematic and efficient approach than many of those used in current marketing practice, however. We now discuss each stage in the **consumer behavior management (CBM) model** shown in Figure 11.6.

Identify Problem Behavior

Each behavior in the purchase/consumption sequence is dependent on many factors. In some cases — such as the promotion of a clearly superior product — information contact may be sufficient to drive the entire behavior chain and result in the successful performance of all of the required behaviors. Even a simple comment about a product by a trusted friend may result in all the required behaviors. In many cases, however, initial consumer behaviors are performed with sufficient frequency and quality to lead to other behaviors — but the other behaviors do not occur. For example, consumers may go to retail stores where the product is carried and may even come into visual contact with the product, but not purchase it. In other cases, information contact may not occur, and thus no additional behaviors are performed.

The problem or **target behavior** is the earliest behavior in the sequence that is not being performed — or is not being performed appropriately or frequently enough to lead to the next behavior. Any behavior in the sequence could be a problem behavior. The problem behavior is identified by examining the differences in behavior frequencies from one stage to the next. For example, consumer research indicated the following:

1. Information contact — 90 percent of the target market has been exposed to two commercials per week in their homes for the past month. Unaided recall scores are 40 percent; 30 percent indicate they like the features of our product.

2. Funds access — 87 percent of the target market purchases a competitive brand at the same price as ours; 67 percent pays with credit cards.

3. Store contact — 96 percent of the target market shops at least once per week in stores where our brand is carried; 40 percent comes into the physical vicinity of our product once per week.

4. Product contact — 30 percent of the target market comes into visual contact with our product; 14 percent picks up the product and inspects it; 2 percent takes our product with them.

5. Transaction — slightly less than 2 percent pays for our product; a few replace it on the shelf.

6. Consumption — most purchasers use the product within two weeks of purchase.

7. Communication — no indication of significant communication with other consumers; 60 percent of warranty cards are returned in three weeks.

What is the problem behavior in this example? It appears that consumers' information contact, funds access, and store contact are all exceptionally good. Even some phases of product contact are good, but few consumers actually take the product with them. Thus, we might conclude the problem behavior is product contact. Potential ways to deal with the problem behavior are discussed below.

Analyze Contingencies

Once the problem behavior is identified, the contingencies or relationships among the behavior and the environment must be analyzed. Among the major contingencies are the efforts of competition and their success in maintaining or changing consumer behavior. Many successful firms attempt to interfere with new-product test marketing (or other marketing efforts) of their competitors to avoid losing market share and to confound competitors' research results. Other contingencies that require analysis are the target market and the marketing mix elements, particularly those elements most closely related to the problem behavior. Figure 11.7 suggests the major marketing mix elements associated with particular problem behaviors. While each element requires analysis, Figure 11.7 suggests useful starting points.

Analyzing contingencies is an extremely important step in the process, because it represents a search for the reasons particular behaviors are not being performed. While some behavior modifiers may focus only on behavior-environment interactions, the assessment of affective and cognitive variables may also contribute valuable information. For example, many new products fail because consumers do not perceive a difference in the new product. Thus, research on consumer perceptions and attitudes can be very useful for investigating the problem and analyzing contingencies.

Returning to the example in which product contact is the problem behavior, analysis of the contingencies might begin with a comparison of our product and package with those of successful competitors. We could interview consumers to investigate their perceptions of and attitudes toward our product. We might directly investigate other contingencies, such as competitive differences in packaging, labeling, instructions for use, colors, and price markings.

Develop and Apply Behavior Change Strategy

Once the problem behavior is delineated and the contingencies surrounding it have been analyzed, a **behavior change strategy** is developed and applied. Such strategies might include any number of the processes we discussed earlier, such as positive reinforcement, negative reinforcement, shaping, classical conditioning, or modeling, among others. Positive reinforcement is generally recommended for increasing behavior because it is both effective and flexible. Of course, as with any approach to marketing strategy, the costs and benefits of various procedures must be carefully assessed.

Returning to our example, suppose the analysis reveals an important difference between our product and those of successful competitors. Their packag-

FIGURE 11.7
Primary Relationships between Consumer Behaviors and Marketing Mix Elements

Consumer Behaviors	Elements			
	Product	Price	Promotion	Place
Information contact			X	
Funds access		X		
Store contact				X
Product contact	X			X
Transaction	X	X	X	X
Consumption	X			
Communication	X	X	X	X

ing gives detailed assembly and use instructions, whereas our package instructions are rather sketchy. We might decide to improve the instructions and also to add pictures of models appropriately assembling and using the product. We could also include a toll-free number consumers can call for additional information or help.

Measure Behavior Change

After implementing the strategy, the target behavior must be remeasured to determine whether the problem has been solved. If the behavior has not changed sufficiently, we must reanalyze the contingencies and develop a new intervention strategy.

How much behavior has to change for the strategy to be successful depends on the marketing objectives, the particular behavior, and the situation. For example, if after implementing the strategy, only 3 percent (instead of 2 percent) of those who inspect the product actually purchase it, this probably would not be considered a successful strategy—and may not even cover the cost of the toll-free number.

If the majority of those who inspect the product now purchase it, however, we might conclude we have successfully solved the behavior problem. In some cases, a very small amount of behavior change may be sufficient for a strategy to be successful. For example, Procter & Gamble increased market share for Crest toothpaste from 35 percent to 41 percent by updating the formula, adding a gel version, and sharply increasing advertising and promotion. While a change in toothpaste market share of 6 percent may not sound impressive, it translated into additional sales of $42 million!

Maintain Behavior

Up to this point, our main focus has been on developing behavior. If the new strategy is successful in developing a sufficient amount of behavior, we must consider methods of maintaining that behavior. Because much consumer behavior is habitual, maintaining behavior is usually much easier and less expensive than developing it. In fact, one of the major reasons new-product introductions are so expensive is the promotional cost of developing the behavior.

Once the behavior is developed, these costs usually can be decreased and behavior can be maintained much more cheaply. As an example, in the most successful cigarette introduction in history, Brown & Williamson gave away free cartons of cigarettes and spent an estimated $150 million to develop use of Barclay cigarettes. Once it obtained an approximately 2 percent market share—and each share point was worth about $125 million to the manufacturer—carton giveaways were eliminated and promotional spending was decreased. Still, much of the market share was maintained.

Often when positive reinforcers are used, their frequency and amount can be decreased without a loss in behavior performance. If continuous schedules of reinforcement were initially employed, it may be possible to switch to ratio schedules and still maintain behavior. Discount coupons of lower value may also be effective; requiring multiunit purchases to receive the same discount may maintain certain behaviors. In fact, encouraging multiunit purchases may not only help develop brand loyalty but also increase usage, because additional units would be readily available in home inventory.

Different organizations may be primarily concerned with maintaining different behaviors in the purchase-consumption chain. Credit-card companies want to maintain card usage or loyalty across a variety of purchase situations; retailers want to maintain store contact or store loyalty; manufacturers want to maintain product contact or brand loyalty. From a behavior viewpoint, these actions are controlled by contingencies in the environment, and loyalty is the degree to which the behaviors are repeated.

Many scholars are critical of viewing loyalty as repeat behavior. They argue that past behavior does not always predict future behavior. While we agree that past behavior is not a perfect predictor, it is still a very good predictor and can be measured more directly than many other variables.

In addition to changing and then maintaining the behavior that was formerly a problem, we must also investigate whether the remaining behaviors are now being performed appropriately and frequently enough to achieve our objectives. If not, we identify the new problem behavior that is blocking the behavior chain—the next one in the sequence that is not being performed appropriately. We then repeat the stages in the consumer behavior management model. This process continues until all of the behaviors are being performed appropriately.

Evaluate for Performance Improvement

Regardless of how successful a particular marketing strategy is, there is always room for improvement. In general, marketing strategies must be monitored for more efficient methods of maintaining behavior as well as increasing it. Any consumer behavior may decrease in frequency because of changes in the environment (such as more powerful or more frequent reinforcement by a competitor). Thus, while the model in Figure 11.6 provides a systematic way to approach marketing strategy development that focuses directly on consumer behavior, it does not replace situational analyses such as careful monitoring and responding to competitive strategies. Of course, this is part of analyzing contingencies in an ongoing marketing program.

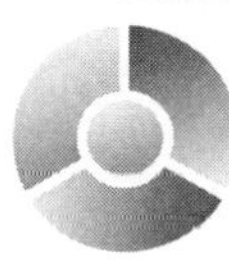

BACK TO.... LANDS' END OUTLET STORE

This case discusses a simple shopping trip and mentions a variety of behaviors. Although the story does not detail every behavior, such as those necessary to get ready to go shopping and drive the car to the strip mall, there is sufficient information so we can understand what occurred. Let's examine Andy Jardine's actions in terms of the types of behaviors discussed in the chapter and evaluate the value of the behavioral sequence model.

Event	Type of Behavior
Offered shopping opportunity	Information contact
Responds verbally to offer	Communication
Drives to drugstore	Store contact
Enters drugstore	Store contact
Locates magazines and candy	Product contact
Obtains products	Product contact
Takes $10 from wallet	Funds access
Exchanges money for products	Transaction
Suggests going to outlet store	Communication
Walks to and enters outlet store	Store contact

Locates and tries on sweaters	Product contact
Discusses Kari's coat	Communication
Takes out Visa card	Funds access
Exchanges funds for products	Transaction
Offered information by salesclerk	Information contact
Purchases sweaters and coat	Transaction
Offered more salesclerk information	Information contact
Takes products home	Transaction
Eats candy bars on the way home	Consumption

From this brief description we get a good idea of what behaviors were performed and consider some marketing strategies to increase desired behaviors. For example, if the Lands' End store had a large sign close to the front door or in the front window that explained the discounts available, perhaps the Jardines would have purchased more products. (The store has such a sign, but it is in the back of the store where consumers may not readily see it.) Thus, the behavioral sequence model helps understand behaviors, isolate them into manageable parts, and allow the analysis of tactics and strategies to increase desired behaviors.

A second point discussed in the chapter is also illustrated in this case. Consumer behaviors do not always follow the exact sequence laid out in Figure 11.2. For example, communication can occur in

SUMMARY

This chapter developed two models that integrated consumer behavior with marketing strategy development. The first model (Figure 11.2) outlined the purchase process as a sequence of behaviors that included information contact, funds access, store contact, product contact, transaction, consumption, and communication. The second model (Figure 11.6) was concerned with a system-

any stage in the process. Also, more than one product is often purchased on a single shopping trip, which can lead to differences from the exact sequence laid out in Figure 11.2.

However, the general model, the categories of behavior listed, and the level of analysis seem useful for understanding the behaviors. In addition, if the probability that the Jardines return to the Lands' End Outlet is increased by receiving the good deals, their behavior has been positively reinforced; the fact that Andy shouted about the savings suggests such reinforcement.

A third point concerns the limitations of the behavior approach for understanding consumer behavior and developing marketing strategies. For one thing, the analysis has not considered what the Jardines were thinking and feeling during this shopping episode. For example, we certainly know more about Andy from the descriptions of what he remembered, what he decided, his reluctance to purchase, his feeling that he deserved the other sweater, and that he felt good about the purchases. In addition, a more detailed description of the major environmental stimuli would allow a deeper understanding of the shopping episode. Thus, while studying overt behavior can provide valuable insights for designing effective marketing strategies, it is also necessary to study consumer's cognitions and affect as well as environmental factors.

atic approach to managing consumer behavior and increasing those behaviors required for successful marketing strategies. The steps in this model include identifying the problem behavior, analyzing contingencies, developing intervention strategies, measuring behavior change, maintaining behavior, and evaluating the program for performance improvement. While the chapter emphasized relationships between behavior and the environment, a number of attempts were made to demonstrate that additional analyses of cognitive and affective variables could improve the effectiveness of the behavior approach.

Key Terms and Concepts

Information Contact *346*
Funds Access *351*
Store Contact *352*
Product Contact *356*
Push Strategies *356*
Pull Strategies *356*
Transactions *358*
Consumption *358*
Communication *360*
Scanner Cable Method *361*
Consumer Behavior Management (CBM) Model *364*
Target Behavior *365*
Behavior Change Strategy *366*

Review and Discussion Questions

1. Describe the differences between traditional cognitive models of the adoption process and the behavior sequence presented in Figure 11.2.
2. What advantages do you see in the use of the behavior sequence model for marketing researchers and for marketing managers?
3. Use the behavior sequence model to describe recent purchases of a product and of a service.
4. Consider the challenges presented by the information search stage of the behavior sequence for each of the following: (*a*) a leading brand, (*b*) a new brand, and (*c*) an existing low-share brand.
5. Give some examples of marketing strategies aimed at addressing the funds access problems of college seniors.
6. Visit several local supermarkets and note evidences you observe of push and pull strategies used to increase product contact for grocery items. Share these observations with other members of your class.
7. List at least three examples of situations in which marketing efforts have been instrumental in changing your consumption or disposal behavior for products you have purchased.
8. Assume the role of a marketing manager for each of the purchases you described in response to Question 3. Which behaviors would you want to change? Using the consumer behavior management model (Figure 11.6), suggest behavior change strategies you might recommend.
9. Use the consumer behavior management model to suggest strategies for decreasing the frequency of post-holiday merchandise returns to a department store.

10. How would the concept of shaping discussed earlier relate to use of the consumer behavior management model?

Notes

1. For example, see Merrie Brucks, "The Effects of Product Class Knowledge on Information Search Behavior," *Journal of Consumer Research*, June 1985, pp. 1–16; and Peter H. Bloch, Daniel L. Sherrell, and Nancy M. Ridgeway, "Consumer Search: An Extended Framework," *Journal of Consumer Research*, June 1986, pp. 119–26.
2. Sharon E. Beatty and Scott M. Smith, "External Search Effort: An Investigation across Several Product Categories," *Journal of Consumer Research*, June 1987, p. 84.
3. For a complete discussion of these issues, see Howard Beales, Michael B. Mazis, Steven Salop, and Richard Staelin, "Consumer Search and Public Policy," *Journal of Consumer Research*, June 1981, pp. 11–22.
4. "American Express Plays Its Trump Card," *Business Week*, October 24, 1983, p. 62; also see "Credit Cards: The U.S. Is Taking Its Time Getting 'Smart,'" *Business Week*, February 9, 1987, pp. 88–89.
5. Susan Caminiti, "What the Scanner Knows About You," *Fortune*, December 3, 1990, pp. 51–52; also see Jeffrey Rothfeder, et al., "How Software is Making Food Sales a Piece of Cake," *Business Week*, July 2, 1990, pp. 54–55; Dom Del Prete, "Advances in Scanner Research Yield Better Data Quicker," *Marketing News*, January 7, 1991, p. 54; Howard Schlossberg, "IRI Expands Sales Tracking to Drugstores, Mass Merchandisers," *Marketing News*, May 27, 1991, pp. 1, 10.

Additional Reading

For further discussion of the role of behavior approaches in everyday life, see:

Baldwin, John D., and Janice I. Baldwin. *Behavior Principles in Everyday Life*, 2nd ed. Englewood Cliffs, N.J.: Prentice Hall, 1986.

For further discussion of the search component of information contact, see:

Brucks, Merrie. "Search Monitor: An Approach for Computer-Controlled Experiments Involving Consumer Information Search." *Journal of Consumer Research*, June 1988, pp. 117–21.

Urbany, Joel E., Peter R. Dickson, and William L. Wilkie. "Buyer Uncertainty and Information Search." *Journal of Consumer Research*, September 1989, pp. 208–15.

For further discussion of a behavior approach to analyzing consumer behavior, see:

Foxall, Gordon. *Consumer Psychology in Behavioral Perspective*. London: Routledge, 1990.

The Environment and Marketing Strategy

SECTION 4

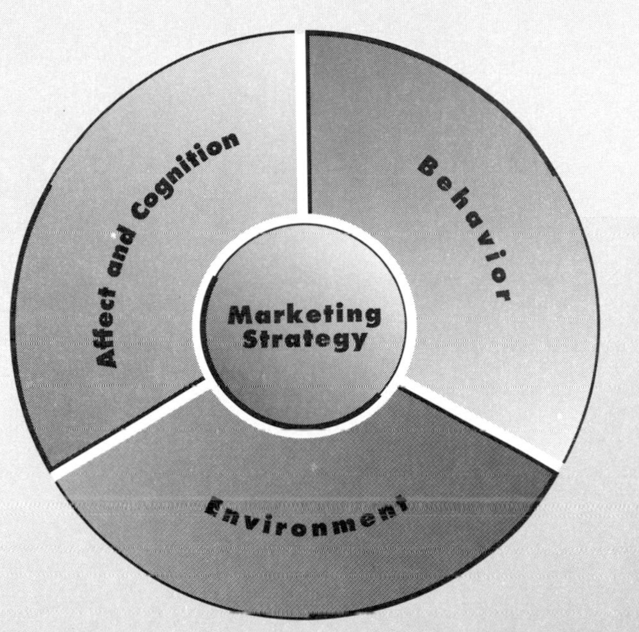

Introduction to the Environment

CHAPTER 12

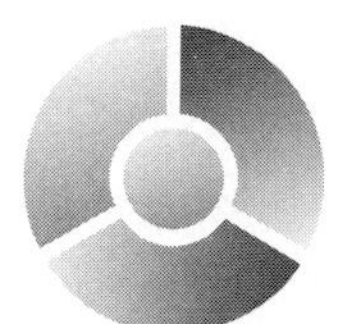

CAESARS BOARDWALK REGENCY

A glimpse of the majestic marble lobby with its Roman statues will lure gamblers off Atlantic City's boardwalk and funnel them through carefully placed lights and open spaces into the casino. Once there, they'll end up betting more and enjoying it—even if they lose. At least that's what interior designer Bob DiLeonardo said would happen when he redesigned Caesars Boardwalk Regency, a 509-room hotel-casino that, with its art deco decor, was only three years old in 1983.

DiLeonardo who owns the 21-employee DiLeonardo's Interiors Inc. in Cranston, Rhode Island, said his mission at Caesars was "to create an environment that relaxes the morality of people." Achieving this is so complex, however, that he enlisted the aid of an "environmental psychologist"—a relatively new breed of psychologist who studies the impact of the environment on behavior. (They're the ones who put uncomfortable seats in fast-food restaurants to cut down on lingering.)

The consultant and DiLeonardo made several changes in the Caesars environment. Lobby windows, for instance, were replaced by sheets of creamy Italian marble so that "people won't be able to relate to time. Once they step inside, they'll be in an adult Disneyland."

DiLeonardo used materials that "enhance" noise for the casino because "noise creates excitement." Lighting for the blackjack tables extended far enough to envelop the player, but not far enough to include spectators, who "may interrupt (the player's) sense of security."

The eight restaurants were done in "vestment colors"—gold, plum, deep reds—to suggest an kinship between gambling and royalty. Restaurants had thick rugs and mohair coverings, meant to impart a "sensuality" and warmth so patrons would "have another brandy," DiLeonardo said.

But the high rollers who get complimentary suites experienced the flip side of environmental psychology. DiLeonardo designed their suites in bold, contrasting colors with lighting so bright and with noise enhanced to such high levels that the occupants would spend more time in the casino areas.

Source: Adapted from Stephen P. Morin, "Interior Designer Sets Out to Make Casino that Relaxes Your Morality," *The Wall Street Journal*, January 10, 1983, p. 21.

This example describes some of the important influences the social and physical environment can have on people's behaviors, cognitions, and affective responses. In this chapter, we provide an overview of these environmental influences. Our goal is to present a framework for thinking about environmental influences on consumers that is useful for creating effective marketing strategies.

We begin by discussing several ways of thinking about the environment. Next, we identify three environments—the social, physical, and marketing environments—and we review the key dimensions of each. Then we discuss the related concept of situations and show how marketers can analyze environmental factors in terms of situations. We conclude the chapter by discussing five marketing-related situations—information, shopping, purchasing, consumption, and disposition situations.

The Environment

As we discussed in Chapter 2, the environment refers to all the physical and social stimuli in the external world of the consumer. We can distinguish between three perspectives on the environment — the complete environment, the functional or perceived environment, and the consensual environment.[1] We focus on the latter two in this text.

The **complete environment** is the total complex of physical and social stimuli in the external world that is potentially available to the consumer. This conception of the environment can never be described in complete detail. However, marketers do analyze how particular aspects of the physical and social environment (the time of day, store location, an ad, or a salesperson's actions) influence consumers' behavioral, affective, and cognitive responses.

The **functional (or perceived) environment** refers to those parts of the complete environment that are attended to and interpreted by a particular consumer on a particular occasion. Each consumer responds to the functional environment (his or her unique sense of the complete environment) and nothing else. For example, a consumer who enters a new supermarket for the first time must interpret this environment and decide what to do.[2] Consumers' knowledge, meanings, goals, and values determine which aspects of the physical and social environment are attended to and comprehended. Because these factors vary considerably, the functional environments perceived by different consumers may be quite different.

The **consensual environment** refers to those parts of the complete environment that are *similarly interpreted* by a group of people with relatively similar cultural and social backgrounds. The consensual environment concerns common or shared interpretations that are broader and more general than the unique features of the functional environment. For example, most American consumers have similar perceptions of shopping malls and use them in similar ways.

Marketers usually are concerned with the consensual environment as interpreted by relatively large groups of consumers or market segments. The idiosyncratic functional environments of individual consumers are seldom of interest. Thus, marketers address such questions as: What do young, affluent Japanese think about American products? What characteristics of discount stores are important for low-income consumers? What does the Christmas holiday season mean to Hispanics?

Although marketers are interested in the consensual environment, the actual cognitions, affect, and behaviors of consumers are influenced by their personal interpretations of the environments they encounter. Fortunately, segments of consumers usually share enough common meaning that a consensual environment can be identified and used as a basis for developing marketing strategies.

HIGHLIGHT 12.1

Macroenvironmental Changes Create Market Opportunities

Until the specter of AIDS raised its deadly shadow, the market for condoms in the United States was slack. But in the mid-1980s, the product received an extraordinary amount of free publicity. The surgeon general and the National Academy of Sciences endorsed it. On the news, in classrooms, and in lectures, people were bluntly urged to use condoms. Around college campuses, lighthearted promotions made condoms a more respectable product. Another aspect of the macroenvironment was the increasing negative publicity about other forms of birth control, including birth control pills and intrauterine devices.

This era also marked major changes in the shopping and purchase environments. In years past, one had to buy condoms from behind pharmacy counters or from vending machines that were usually placed in men's rooms. Now most drugstores and supermarkets display the products openly. Women have become worried enough about safe sex to account for about 50 percent of condom purchases, and many manufacturers have developed promotional campaigns aimed at this large segment.

Before, people seldom talked about such things in public, and most manufacturers never promoted condoms vigorously. Once the only magazines to accept condom ads were the so-called "skin" magazines, but now many magazines carry the ads. By 1986, consumers in Sweden, Finland, and Denmark had seen TV advertising for condoms.

What were the ramifications of these dramatic environmental changes? In the free-wheeling 1970s, few Americans wanted anything to do with condoms, and total sales had shrunk to about $150 million. In 1986, sales grew by 10 percent, and the increase has continued.

Source: Colin Leinster, "The Rubber Barons," *Fortune,* November 24, 1986, pp. 105–18.

Levels of Environments

Like cognition, affect, and behavior, physical and social aspects of the environment can be analyzed at different levels – macro and micro. The *macroenvironment* includes very broad, general factors such as your culture, the climate where you live, the economic conditions in your local community, or the political system of your country. In contrast, the *microenvironment* includes more immediate and more tangible factors: the dirty floor in a store, the hot weather this afternoon, the members of your family, or the person in front of you at the checkout counter pushing a cart piled high with groceries.

HIGHLIGHT 12.2

THE WINDOW-SHOPPING ENVIRONMENT

One of the oldest marketing strategies is still one of the most effective. In cities where walking and window-shopping are still in style (and possible), window displays can have very strong influences on purchasing behavior.

These environmental effects can be clearly seen at the Saks Fifth Avenue store in Manhattan. Saks has 310 feet of prime store frontage along 49th and 50th Streets and the famed Fifth Avenue. Each day at lunchtime, more than 3,000 pedestrians walk by the 31 window displays that Saks changes weekly. These microenvironments attract attention. At Christmastime, the elaborately decorated windows draw crowds five people deep.

The displays in these special information and shopping environments often have incredible impacts on sales. One dramatic window display was credited with selling armloads of heavy velvet and wool fashions for fall in the middle of a July heat wave. Or consider this example: in 1986, the head of Saks' gift division was worried that a forthcoming move from the ground floor to the ninth floor would seriously reduce sales of her crystal and linen merchandise. Saks estimated that sales might drop as much as 15 percent. But an eye-catching window on Fifth Avenue during the first week of the move upstairs produced a 20 percent increase in sales.

Source: Lisa Gubernick, "Through a Glass, Brightly." Reprinted by permission of *Forbes* magazine, August 11, 1986. © Forbes Inc., 1986.

The macroenvironment influences the broad patterns of behavior and the shared cognitions and affective responses of large groups of people. For instance, aggregate purchases of homes and cars are affected by the general state of the economy. Cultural factors influence food preferences of entire populations — chilies are liked in Mexico and herring is popular in Scandinavia. Highlight 12.1 describes how changes in the macroenvironment can create new markets for a product.

Aspects of the macroenvironment are difficult to link to single, particular behaviors. For instance, it is unlikely that consumers' cultural backgrounds or the general economic climate are related to the purchase of a particular brand of toothpaste or television.

In contrast, aspects of the microenvironment can have obvious effects on specific behaviors. For instance, you tend not to linger in a dirty store, you may wait until evening to go shopping during a heat wave, or you might move to another line to speed things up at the checkout station. (See Highlight 12.2 for another example.) Marketers need to determine which level of environmental factors is of interest and design research approaches and marketing strategies suitable for that level.

Analyzing Environmental Influences

Basically, marketers can analyze the effects of the environment in two ways. In the simpler approach, marketers try to determine the direct effects of particular environmental factors on consumers' behaviors and/or cognitive and affective responses. In this approach, marketers identify prominent aspects of the physical and social environment that are of interest (such as a week of especially cold weather, a transit strike, an in-store display for a new product, or a period of high inflation). Then, marketers try to relate these environmental factors to changes in consumers' behavioral, cognitive, and affective responses. An alternative approach is to examine environmental influences within the broader context of situations; this approach is discussed later in the chapter.

Types of Environment

As noted in Chapter 2, we can distinguish three types of environments: the social, physical, and marketing environments. (The marketing environment consists of those aspects of the physical and social environment that are under the direct control of the marketing manager.) Figure 12.1 shows that these three types of environments interact and influence each other as well as influence consumers' overt behaviors, affect, and cognitions.

The Social Environment

Broadly defined, the social environment includes all social interactions between people. Consumers can interact with other people either directly (discuss stereos or clothes with a friend, talk to a salesperson) or vicariously (watch your father negotiate a car price, observe what clothes other people are wearing). Consumers can learn from both types of social interactions.

It is useful to distinguish between macro and micro levels of the social environment. The **macro social environment** includes the many social interactions that occur among very large groups of people, many of which are indirect and vicarious. Researchers have studied three macro social environments: culture, subculture, and social class. These broad social environments have a powerful general influence on the values, beliefs, attitudes, emotions, and behaviors of individual consumers in those groups. Thus, marketers might find that consumers in different social classes have different means-end chains concerning a product and, therefore, are likely to respond differently to marketing strategies. Such differences make macro social environments useful for market segmentation.

FIGURE 12.1
Types of Environments

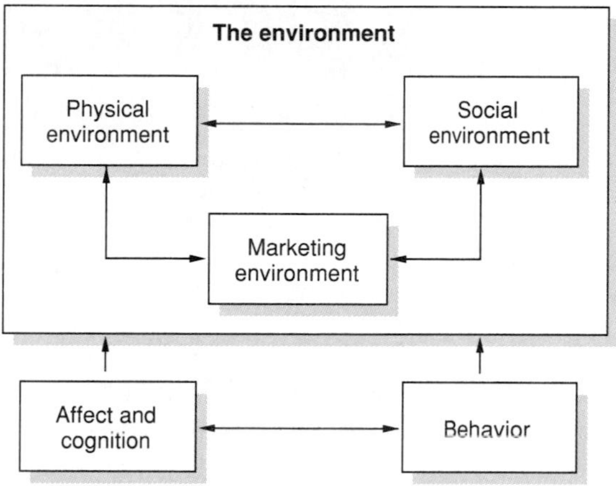

The **micro social environment** includes the typically face-to-face social interactions among smaller groups of people such as families and reference groups. These more direct social interactions tend to have more immediate influences on consumers' knowledge and feelings about products, stores, and ads and on the patterns of their consumption behavior. The influence of families, for instance, can continue for years as some adult consumers purchase the same brands, patronize the same stores, and shop in the same way their parents did.

Most of consumers' perceptions, meanings, values, and behaviors are influenced by macro and micro social environments. For instance, individual consumers learn acceptable and appropriate behaviors and acquire many of their values, beliefs, and attitudes through direct social interactions with their families and reference groups. These concepts are influenced by the macro social environments of culture, subculture, and social class. Figure 12.2 illustrates the flow of social influence from the macroenvironments of culture, subculture, and social class to the micro social environments of reference groups and family and then on to the individual consumer. Although not shown in the figure, some social influence also flows backward from consumers to family and reference groups, which, in turn, exert some influence on the macro social environments.

This hierarchical relationship portrayed in Figure 12.2 has important marketing implications. For instance, different subcultures may reflect the same cultural values in different ways, just as different social classes may respond to subcultural values in different ways. Consider the commonly discussed American cultural value of achievement. In a rural subculture, this value may be

A change in the micro-social environment creates a market opportunity for Wrigley's gum.

evidenced by going to an agricultural college, earning a degree, and becoming an excellent farmer. In an urban or suburban subculture, a person with the same achievement values might go to a law school, earn a degree, and become a successful lawyer. The social class of the individual may influence what type of college or university is selected (a local college or an internationally famous university). Also, these influences will be filtered by a person's reference groups (where a person's friends are going to college) and family (parents' expectations and financial condition).

In sum, while many individuals may share the same cultural values, their methods of trying to achieve them may differ greatly depending on their subculture and social class, as well as a variety of micro social environmental influences such as family and reference groups. We discuss these social influences at length in Chapters 13, 14, and 15.

Finally, Figure 12.2 shows that other social entities are involved in transferring values, meanings, and behaviors from the macro social environment to individual consumers. These include the media, such as TV shows, newspapers,

FIGURE 12.2

Flows of Influence in Social Environment

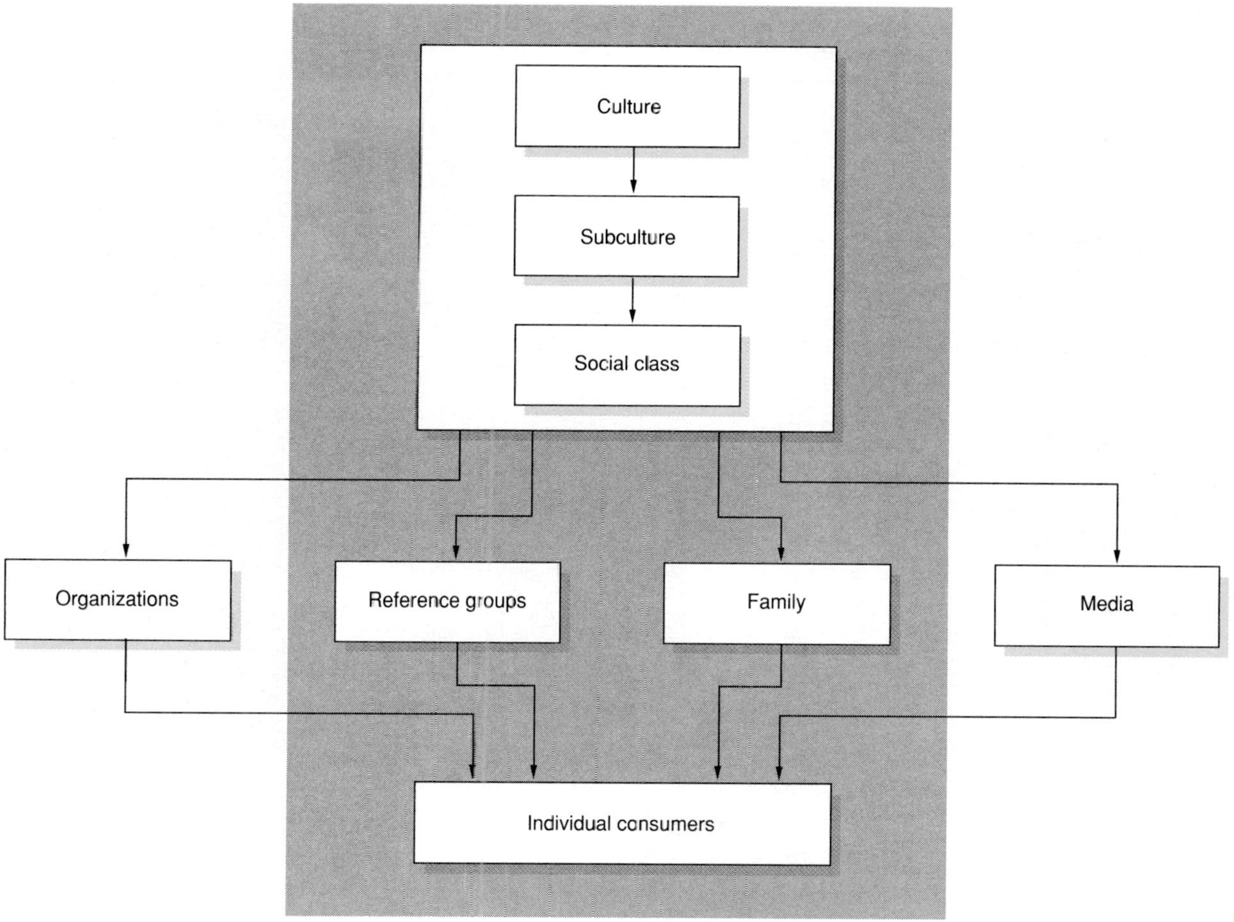

magazines, literature, and music. Other organizations such as churches, police and the courts, educational institutions, and government can have important social influences on consumers. So too can organizations such as business firms that develop marketing strategies to influence individual customers. All of these social entities operate within, and are influenced by, the macro social environment. Thus, as we will see in the next chapters, advertising, product, pricing, and distribution strategies should be consistent with the values and accepted behavior patterns in the macro social environment.

The Physical Environment

The **physical environment** is the collection of nonhuman, physical elements that comprises the field in which consumer behavior occurs.[3] At a basic level, the physical environment can be divided into spatial and nonspatial elements. *Spatial elements* include countries, cities, buildings, stores, the interior design of

Visine reminds consumers of aspects of the physical environment that make the product self-relevant.

rooms, as well as physical objects of all kinds. *Nonspatial elements* include factors such as temperature, humidity, illumination, noise level, and time.

Environmental psychology is the study of how aspects of the physical environment influence affect, cognitions, and behavior.[4] For instance, elements in the physical environment — such as in-store signs, colors, displays, and music — are important in designing retail stores. (We discuss these further in Chapter 21.) However, many other elements in the physical environment also affect consumers' behavior. We will now briefly discuss three of these: time, weather, and lighting.

Time

Time obviously has a great effect on consumer behavior, and researchers have begun to address these influences.[5] For instance, behaviors are influenced by the time of day (stores tend to be more crowded during the lunch hour), the day of the week (Mondays often are slow days for restaurants), the day of the month (sales may drop off just before the last of the month and pick up again after the first), and the season of the year (during the pre-Christmas holiday season, people's shopping behaviors are quite different from other times of the year).

Marketing strategies may vary by the time of the year or special holidays.

As another example of the effects of time, consider that the Daylight Saving Time Coalition once petitioned Congress to increase daylight-saving time by seven weeks per year. Advocates of this change included the management of 7-Eleven convenience stores, who believed more women would stop at its stores on the way home from work if it were still light outside. The company estimated this extra daylight would increase sales by $30 million. Another advocate of this change was the Barbeque Industry Association. Reasoning that people would cook out more if it were light during the dinner hour, this association predicted an increase in sales of charcoal briquettes of 15 percent ($56 million) and 13 percent ($15 million) for starter fluid. Golfers were expected to play 4 million more rounds and buy an additional $7 million worth of clubs and balls, while tennis buffs could get in 9.8 million more hours of outdoor play and spend another $7 million on equipment. Thus, what might seem to be a minor change in time could well have considerable impact on consumer behavior.[6]

Weather

Many firms have recognized that weather influences consumer behavior (see Highlight 12.3). Obviously, earmuffs, gloves, and heavy coats are winter products, and most suntan lotion, air conditioners, and bathing suits are sold during the summer. Some firms are paying even closer attention to the weather, not just for a season but on a daily basis. For example, Campbell Soup Company bases some of its spot radio advertising on weather reports. Whenever a storm is forecast, Campbell's ads urge listeners to stock up on soup before the weather worsens; after the storm hits, the ad copy changes to tell people to relax indoors and warm themselves with soup. While research on the relationships between weather and consumer behavior is in its early stages, the weather is an important influence on affect (such as moods), cognitions, and purchase behavior.[7]

Lighting

Considerable evidence reveals that lighting affects behavior. It has been found that people work better in brighter rooms, but workers find direct overhead lighting unpleasant. In business meetings, people who intend to make themselves heard sit under or near lights, whereas those who intend to be quiet often sit in darker areas. Intimate candlelight may draw people together; bright floodlights can cause people to hurry past a location. Overall, lighting may affect the way people work and interact with others, their overall comfort, and even their mental and physical health.[8]

While it seems likely that lighting could affect consumers' moods, anxiety levels, willingness to shop, and purchase behavior, little research is available on this topic. However, one discussion of lighting in retail stores and malls suggested specialized lighting systems increased sales dramatically. Pillowtex Corporation used tiny spotlights attached to glass shelves, rather than overhead lighting, for illumination in its Dallas World Trade Center showroom. The corporation attributes one third of its $3 million-plus annual sales to this lighting approach.[9]

HIGHLIGHT 12.3

TEMPERATURE AND SALES

The year 1988 will long be remembered in the United States for the searing summer heat that spread over nearly the entire country, accompanied in many places by a prolonged drought. Although the weather wreaked havoc on many of the nation's farmers, it was a blessing for some companies. Sales of products such as water-related toys, fresh cold foods like lettuce and fruit, and bottled water were way up. The Crocodile Mile, a 25-foot plastic water slide that can be used in the backyard, was one of the five hottest selling toys of 1988. Production was completely sold out by July. In a single week during the peak of the hot weather, demand for water sprinklers to soak parched yards (and cool off hot kids) exceeded sales for the previous 12 months combined.

Sales of central air-conditioning hit new monthly records for nearly every month in 1988. But the market for room air conditioners traditionally is even more sensitive to changes in the weather. Just a couple of hot days in summer can send people flooding into stores to buy window units, while a few chilly days in summer can cool down demand just as quickly. Room air conditioner sales jumped by 28 percent in June 1988.

Other behaviors also are affected by hot weather. People tend to cook less at home when it gets really hot. But they don't flock to full-service restaurants because they don't want to get dressed up, either. Instead, they tend to eat things at home that don't require cooking, pushing up sales of fresh fruits and vegetables (for salads). And so it goes, demonstrating that the physical environment can have very large influences on consumers' purchasing and consumption behaviors.

Source: Reprinted from Ted Knutson, "Sales of Some Products Thrive Due to Heat Wave," *Marketing News* 22, no. 19 (September 12, 1988), pp. 2, 12. Published by the American Marketing Association.

THE MARKETING ENVIRONMENT

The **marketing environment** includes all the social and physical stimuli associated with marketing strategies. We learned in Chapter 2 that marketing strategies are part of the consumers' environment. Thus, the many stimuli associated with promotion strategies (a magazine ad, a 25-cents-off coupon), product strategies (a squeeze bottle for Crest toothpaste), pricing strategies (a "sale" sign in a window, a price tag on a sweater), and distribution strategies (the location of a Burger King, a product display in a store) are experienced by consumers as part of their physical environment. Aspects of the social environment may also be part of marketing strategies. For instance, Wal-Mart stations a greeter at the store entrance to smile and welcome customers to the store. Lexus trained its car salespeople to be less aggressive and "pushy." This perspective suggests that marketing is environmental management.[10]

The environmental impacts of marketing and general business strategies on consumers' behaviors can be either indirect or direct. Many business strategies create macro changes in the environment that can influence consumers' behaviors, affect, and cognitions in an indirect manner, perhaps only over the long run. For instance, consider that mergers and acquisitions, legal actions, or lobbying attempts to influence governmental legislation can have a variety of long-term ramifications on consumers. Company mergers may change the level of competition and perhaps reduce (or sometimes increase) the number of alternative products available in the marketplace. The deregulation of the airlines and the breakup of AT&T have had long-range effects on consumers that are still developing.

In contrast, marketing strategies create environmental stimuli that are intended to immediately and directly affect consumers' behaviors, cognitions, and affective responses, although not all are successful. For instance, product strategies create and place tangible products and less tangible services in consumers' environments. Product attributes, packaging, and brand names are all stimuli in the environment that consumers may attend to, interpret, and use in making choice decisions. Promotion decisions create a variety of environmental stimuli, including ads, coupons, and public relations materials. Pricing strategies are experienced by consumers as environmental stimuli in the forms of price tags and shelf labels. And distribution strategies also create environmental stimuli, including store design, store location, in-store displays, and shelf placements. The relations between marketing strategy variables and consumer behavior are discussed in detail in Section Five of the text. For now, we want to emphasize that marketing mix strategies create environmental stimuli in consumers' environments that may influence their cognitions, affective responses, and behaviors.

Situations

Because the social and physical environments contain a huge number of elements, marketers may find it difficult to identify which environmental aspects have the greatest impact on consumers' behaviors, affect, and cognitions. It is often easier to analyze environmental influences in the context of a specific "situation."[11] Researchers have treated situations in two ways — as the objective environment or the subject environment (as perceived by consumers).[12] We prefer the latter approach.

In this book, a situation is not just the raw physical environment (a checkout counter, a storefront, one's living room, the temperature, a landscape), nor is a situation only the objective aspects of the social environment (the number of people in a store, the time of day). *Situations always contain a human actor who is behaving for a purpose in an environment.* Situations occur over a period of time that can be very short (buying a soda in a vending machine), longer (eating lunch), or quite long (buying a house). The consumer's personal goals determine what is included in a situation and also define its beginning, middle, and end. Thus, a **situation** is a *sequence of goal-directed behavioral, affective, and cognitive responses that occur in various environments.* For instance, going to the music store to look for a tape is a shopping situation. Based on the Wheel of Consumer Analysis (see Figure 2.3), a situation is a series of reciprocal interactions among a person's behaviors, affective and cognitive reactions, and environmental factors.

Situations vary in complexity. Some situations occur within a single physical and social environment and involve simple goals, relatively few behaviors, and limited affective and cognitive responses. For instance, buying a stamp at the post office, bargaining with a salesperson over the price of a stereo system, or discussing a spring-break trip with your friends over dinner are examples of relatively simple consumption-related situations.

Other consumer situations are more complex. Complex situations occur in several physical and social environments and may involve multiple, perhaps conflicting, goals and many different behaviors and cognitive and affective responses. Shopping for a new winter coat in several stores or browsing in a flea market on Sunday afternoon are examples of more complex situations.

Many consumer-related situations are common and *recurring*. For instance, American consumers frequently buy gas for their cars, watch TV in the evening, shop for new clothes, rent videos, and go to grocery stores. As their experiences accumulate over time, consumers form clear goals, develop consistent problem representations for these recurring situations, and learn appropriate behaviors. Thereafter, when the problem situation occurs again, appropriate knowledge schemas and scripts may be activated from memory, which influence consumers' behavioral, affective, and cognitive responses in that environment/situation. To the extent that people tend to form approximately the same interpretations for common consumer-related situations, their behaviors will also tend to be similar. When this occurs, marketers can develop marketing strategies that should affect consumers in a target segment in similar ways.

In contrast, consumers may not have clear goals or relevant knowledge when faced with new or unfamiliar situations. They may have to consciously interpret and integrate information to determine their goals, identify salient environmental factors, and choose appropriate behaviors. Marketers should develop strategies to help consumers cope with unfamiliar situations. For instance, life insurance salespeople are trained to help consumers define their goals (college education for children, retirement plans, pay off mortgage) and identify key environmental considerations (current savings, children's ages, time to retirement), before they can demonstrate the self-relevance of life insurance.

Analyzing Situations

A powerful approach to understanding environmental influences is to analyze the situations in which the consumer experiences the environment. This allows marketers to understand the physical, social, and marketing environments in terms of the perspectives of the consumers who experience them.[13]

Despite the advantages of situational analysis, relatively few detailed analyses of situations have been conducted.[14] To analyze a situation, marketers should first determine the major goals of their target customers that define the situation. Then they should identify the key aspects of the social and physical environments in those situations, including marketing strategies that might affect the consumer. Finally, marketers should attempt to understand consumers' affective, cognitive, and behavioral responses to these environmental characteristics. Situational analyses can be conducted at two levels — the personal, idiosyncratic perspective of a single consumer or the more aggregate level of a consensual situation that is defined similarly by many consumers.

Marketers can learn about personal consumption situations by asking consumers to describe the major occasions when they consume the product. A study conducted by one of the authors provides an example of such an analysis. Several candy users were interviewed and asked to describe the major situations when they ate candy. One young woman, a college freshman, identified three major consumption situations which she described as follows:

1. Hungry — in a rush:

    Environment: hectic; many other people around; between classes at the university.

    Goal: satisfy hunger and get energy.

    Affect/cognition: feeling hungry, stressed, and tense.

    Behavior: snack on candy between and during class.

2. Lazy — relaxed.

    Environment: quiet; alone at home in evening.

    Goal: relax so I can concentrate on work.

    Affect/cognition: feeling relaxed and calm, but alert.

    Behavior: snack on candy while reading or studying.

3. Calm — at lunch.

    Environment: calm; alone in kitchen at lunchtime.

    Goal: I need a reward.

    Affect/cognition: happy to be home after hectic class schedule; starting to calm down.

    Behavior: eat candy for dessert.

These three consumption situations are highly personal, defined by the consumer herself in terms of her own goals. The three consumption situations occurred in three different environments, and each situation involved somewhat different affective and cognitive states (goals) and behaviors. Different products might appeal to this consumer when in these situations.

Marketing strategies are seldom based on an analysis of a single consumer. Marketers are interested in identifying *consensual situations* that are experienced in about the same way by large numbers of consumers. If the number of consumers is sufficient, marketers can develop strategies (special products, prices, or advertising campaigns) for specific consumption situations. Consider, for instance, a study of fast-food restaurants that identified four consensual use situations: lunch on a weekday, a snack during a shopping trip, an evening meal when rushed for time, and an evening meal with family when not rushed for time.[15] The authors found that different choice criteria were used in these situations (speed of service was more important at lunch, menu variety was more important in the evening when not rushed). Moreover, certain restaurants (different environments) were considered more appropriate for certain situations. Finally, even if the same fast-food restaurant was patronized in these different situations, consumers' behaviors and affective and cognitive reactions in those situations could be quite different (rushed/not rushed, relaxed/not relaxed).

Generic Consumer Situations

In this section, we consider five *generic consumer situations*—information acquisition, shopping, purchase, consumption, and disposition (see Figure 12.3). These broadly defined situations are generic in the sense that they are relevant for most products. Marketers need to identify consumers' behavioral goals, relevant affect and cognitions, and the key environmental factors in these situations. Based on this analysis, marketers can develop marketing strategies that manipulate the key environmental factors to change, facilitate, or maintain the key behaviors.

Information Acquisition Situations

The **information acquisition situation** includes the environments where consumers acquire information relevant to a problem-solving goal, such as a brand or store choice. An information acquisition situation may contain social factors (word-of-mouth communications from friends, persuasion attempts by a salesperson) and physical stimuli (prominent signs in a store, labels on the product package) that can influence consumers' affect, cognitions, and behaviors. As you learned in Chapter 5, such information may be acquired accidentally, as consumers randomly come across information in their environments, or intentionally, as they consciously seek information relevant to their current goals.

Marketers have considerable control over many aspects of consumers' information environment, especially the advertising, sales promotion, and personal selling elements of the promotion mix. Marketers can place signs in stores and on the front windows of shops, send direct-mail material about their

FIGURE 12.3
Five Generic Consumer Situations

Situations	Generic Behaviors	Specific Behaviors and Environments
Information acquisition	Information contact	Reading a billboard while driving
	Communication	Discussing running shoes with a friend at a track meet
		Watching a TV commercial at home
Shopping	Store contact	Window-shopping in a mall
	Product contact	Browsing through an L. L. Bean catalog in a restaurant
		Comparing brands of shirts in a store
Purchase	Funds access	Obtaining a Visa card at a bank
	Transaction	Going to a checkout counter at Sears
		Calling in an order to Land's End from home
Consumption	Use	Eating a taco at Taco Bell
		Using a refrigerator for 15 years
Disposition	Disposal	Recycling aluminum cans
		Throwing away a hot-dog wrapper at a hockey game

products to consumers, and place ads on TV, in magazines, and on billboards.[16] They can add information to packages and labels or provide salespeople with special information to convey to customers.[17] Other aspects of consumers' information environment are not under marketers' direct control – for example, marketers can try to generate publicity and new articles about their product or encourage consumers to tell other consumers about a product. However, they may not be successful in creating this environmental information.

Two especially important generic behaviors in information acquisition situations are *information contact* and *communication.* Because approximately two thirds of retail purchases are based on decisions made in the store, contact with marketing information in a store can have a significant influence on their behaviors. Various marketing strategies are designed to facilitate information contact. For instance, A & P supermarkets (among others) allow ads on shopping carts.[18] Pepsi-Cola has experimented with putting multicolored ads on paper grocery bags.

Modern technology allows marketers to direct information at precisely defined target groups. In some Giant Foods stores (an East Coast chain), a coupon dispenser connected to the checkout scanner issues different coupons depending on what products a consumer buys. For instance, people buying peanut butter might receive a coupon for bread, or customers who buy Folgers coffee might receive a coupon for Maxwell House. Other marketing strategies are designed to facilitate information contact at the point of purchase. An example is the interactive computer display developed for Clarion Cosmetics. By answering a few simple questions, consumers can receive information about the best cosmetics for their skin color and tone.[19]

Communicating with customers, usually via salespeople, is an important marketing strategy for many companies. For example, Toyota, manufacturer of the Lexus luxury car, intensively trains its salespeople about all aspects of the car.[20] Thus, Lexus salespeople spend an average of 90 minutes presenting a car to each potential customer, much more than the industry average. Service after the sale is extremely important for all auto manufacturers and dealers. Consumers' top complaint with auto service is having to bring the car back because the problem was not fixed properly the first time. Lexus research showed that consumers believed this was largely because of poor communication in that their problem was not adequately explained to the mechanic doing the work. So, when Lexus buyers come to the dealer for service they speak directly to the diagnostic expert who will examine their car. Owners can even stay during the diagnosis to make sure the problem is clearly communicated to the mechanic who will fix the car.

Shopping Situations

The **shopping situation** includes the physical, spacial, and social characteristics of places where consumers shop for products and services. Shopping behavior can occur in a variety of environments, such as boutiques, department and discount stores, malls, pedestrian-only retail areas being developed in many cities, in the home (via catalogs or television home shopping programs), flea markets, auctions, and so on. In retail environments alone, a huge number of physical factors—including store design and layout, lighting and display fixtures, colors, the overall size of the store, and miscellaneous other factors (such as temperature and noise level)—may affect consumers' behavior (the length of time they stay in the store) and their cognitions and affective states (their moods and feelings or their felt involvement with shopping).

Shopping situations also include the merchandise (the particular products and brands) displayed in stores and catalogs. One innovation in car selling is the auto center in which a dealer combines several franchises under one roof. Customers can examine dozens of makes and models on one shopping trip, much like shopping for a new dress or business suit at a large department store.

In addition, the shopping environment includes social factors such as how many salespeople and checkout personnel are in the store, how store personnel act toward customers, the presence of friends and relatives accompanying the consumer, the amount of crowding, and the types of other people found there. All of these aspects of the shopping environment can influence consumers' behaviors, cognitions, and affective responses. For instance, many people dislike going to an auto showroom where they fear being "attacked" by hungry salespeople. At a Lexus dealership, no salespeople are in sight.[21] Instead, consumers are greeted by a receptionist behind a marble desk. Without interruption, they can learn more about the Lexus by studying the "media wall" consisting of videos and print materials. Only on request will the receptionist call a sales representative to talk to the consumer.

Of the many behaviors affected by the shopping environment, two are of particular importance — store contact and product contact. *Store contact* is critical for retailing success, and many marketing strategies are intended to get consumers to come to the store. Giving away a free cassette tape to the first 100 people to show up at an electronics store on a Saturday morning is an example of such a strategy.

Store location is another critical environmental influence on store contact for many types of stores — for example, fast-food restaurants and convenience food stores need to be located in high-traffic locations. (Highlight 12.4 describes an unusual strategy to increase store contact behavior.) Sunglass Hut of America operates about 200 small kiosks selling high quality sunglasses for $35 to $100 (compared to the average price paid for sunglasses in 1987 of about $12).[22] Their location in the well-traveled aisles of shopping centers and malls facilitates store contact. Sunglass Hut's marketing strategy also addresses information acquisition by facilitating communication with the customer. Each hut is staffed with well-trained, highly knowledgeable salespeople who are able to tell customers why they should pay $80 for a pair of sunglasses.

The location of smaller, boutique-type stores (candy, natural foods, gifts) in shopping malls can have a critical effect on store contact behaviors. A very desirable location is close to the entrance of one of the large and glamorous

Consumers can make contact with stores by window-shopping

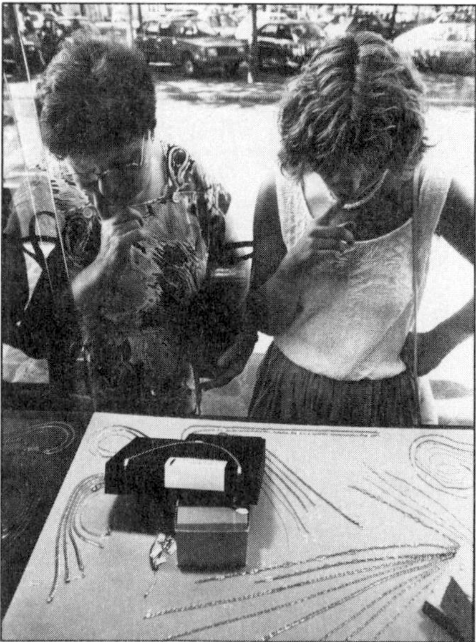

HIGHLIGHT 12.4

MOBILE SHOPPING ENVIRONMENTS

Several companies are experimenting with movable shopping environments. Kentucky Fried Chicken, for example, rolled out a new concept in 1991 – mobile merchandising. KFC built a KFC restaurant in a 42-foot-long trailer. Towed by a truck, the mobile KFC unit can be set up at fairs, outdoor jazz and rock concerts, and amusement parks to pursue customers wherever they go.

Pizza Hut, considered the innovator in the field, has more than 250 mobile kiosks in place, mostly in airports. Taco Bell hopes to increase the number of its outlets to over 10,000 by the end of the decade; a significant proportion will be mobile units. McDonald's is not involved yet, and Dairy Queen is studying the use of carts to sell its products.

Why go to the trouble? One reason is that the fast-food industry has already taken most of the best fixed locations on street corners and in malls. With a mobile unit, if customers don't show up, you move the restaurant to another spot. Another advantage is cost. The mobile units are much less expensive than a fixed site. A Taco Bell cart in an airport runs about $30,000, while the larger KFC truck costs about $200,000, compared to about $1 million for a bricks-and-mortar, fast-food restaurant.

Sometimes these unusual shopping environments create interesting consumer behavior problems. For instance, Pizza Hut discovered that some customers didn't believe the pizzas at the mobile airport kiosk were made fresh on site. So the company redesigned the ovens (changed the purchasing environment) so customers could see the pizzas going into the oven.

Marketers of mobile restaurants must be especially conscious of consumers' consumption environment. In most of these moving restaurants, the range of products available is limited to foods that people can eat on their feet. Therefore, KFC sells only chicken nuggets and sandwiches in its mobile restaurant.

Source: Marj Charlier, "Restaurants Mobilize to Pursue Customers," *The Wall Street Journal,* June 10, 1991, pp. B1, B5.

anchor stores, usually department stores found at the ends or middle of the mall. These anchor stores draw many consumers, and the smaller stores benefit from the traffic flowing past their doors.

The importance of location within the mall was clearly shown during the recession of the early 1990s.[23] When some retailers such as Bonwit Teller and B. Altman filed for bankruptcy, The Mall at Short Hills, an upscale mall in New Jersey, lost two of its four anchor stores. Immediately, the surrounding smaller stores at the mall also began having difficulties. Such changes in a mall shopping environment can initiate a cycle of reciprocal effects on behaviors, affect and cognitions, and the environment. As more stores fail, a mall accumulates more empty, boarded-up stores, the shopping environment further deteriorates, and consumers become concerned and begin staying away.

Product contact is another important behavior affected by environmental characteristics of the shopping situation. Consider how the probability of product contact is reduced in very large stores, or if shoppers are discouraged from lingering in a store by overcrowding (too many other shoppers), or if sales personnel are overly aggressive (driving off some customers). Some stores use restful music, warm color schemes, and low-key salespeople to encourage shoppers to linger in their stores, thus enhancing the probability of product contact. In large self-service stores, signs are hung from the ceiling to identify product locations. To facilitate product contact, Hallmark redesigned its product displays using colored strips to identify different types of greeting cards and help customers find the right card quickly.[24] In sum, retailers try to make the shopping environment attractive, informative, and easy to use.[25]

Another goal of store design is to make the shopping environment more fun and exciting so that consumers will spend more time in the store and be more likely to make contact with the merchandise. When a small chain of clothing stores for young women, called Ups and Downs, redesigned store interiors, it included "kinetically controlled" display racks.[26] This interesting innovation allows customers to revolve an entire carousel of clothes with just a light touch of the hand. These kinetic displays were intended to expose consumers to more of the merchandise and make the shopping experience more fun. Highlight 12.5 describes a similar example of a store environment that makes shopping fun and increases product contact behavior.

Although the retail store environment is important, other types of shopping environments are becoming significant. These include shopping at home by telephone or by mail. Consider the great popularity of TV shopping programs and the continued rise of catalog shopping (mail-order sales are growing at about 10 percent a year in the United States). Obviously, the environment at home is dramatically different from the in-store shopping environment. Other shopping environments are relevant for some products, including garage sales, flea markets and swap meets, auctions, sidewalk sales, and private sales of merchandise by individuals and street vendors. In some cities, you can avoid shopping situations by hiring someone else to shop for you.[27]

Purchasing Situations

The **purchasing situation** includes the social and physical stimuli present in the environment where the consumer makes the purchase. Consider, for instance, the differences in the purchasing environment when buying fresh vegetables at a supermarket versus at an outdoor farmers' market. In some cases, the purchasing environment is similar to the shopping environment, but they are seldom identical. In most self-service stores, for instance, consumers pay for the products they have selected at a checkout counter at the front of the store or at various cash register locations around the store.

HIGHLIGHT 12.5

THE STORE ENVIRONMENT AS THEATER

Nike sells a lot of shoes in its hometown store in Portland, Oregon, by creating an exciting in-store environment that makes shopping fun and exciting. The entire store, Nike Town, is a fantasy experience that closely resembles theater. The center of the store is a tranquil town square, with the sounds of birds chirping. Surrounding the square, on two levels, are separate shopping areas for different types of Nike shoes. The basketball area, for instance, has a wooden truss ceiling and a wooden basketball court floor. Speakers beneath the floor subtly fill the space with the hollow bounce of basketballs and the sounds of shoes squeaking on the court. Nike Aqua Gear shoes (for water sports) are displayed surrounded by large vertical tanks containing tropical fish, and several large-screen TVs in the floor show a bed of seaweed swaying among the coral.

To keep the stock from cluttering the fantasy environment, most shoes are stored downstairs. Salespeople use computers to call down for certain models and sizes, and the shoes are sent up through clear plastic tubes via conveyor. Customer response to the store has been so strong that a much bigger store with a five-story town square is planned for Chicago.

Source: Associated Press, "Nike's Vision of the Ultimate Store Includes Fantasy," *Marketing News,* September 16, 1991, p. 9.

In some stores, the purchasing environment is designed to be quite distinct from the shopping environment. For instance, the central checkout counter at one trendy music store was designed to look like a giant piano keyboard with black and white keys. In other retail environments, such as an automobile dealership, the purchasing environment may be a separate room used exclusively for the purchase transaction. This is where the salesperson and customer(s) retire to negotiate the final details of the purchase.

Sometimes the shopping environment intrudes into the purchasing environment. For instance, checkout lines at grocery stores usually include displays of products such as magazines, gum and candy items, film, and cigarettes to stimulate impulse purchases. The information acquisition and purchase environments also may overlap. For instance, A & P, a chain of some 1,200 grocery stores, experimented with showing ads on TV monitors placed at the checkout aisle, but many consumers complained this type of information contact was too intrusive. Besides, few customers left the line to get a product that was advertised.

Marketers are particularly interested in influencing two behaviors in purchasing situations—*funds access* and the *final transaction.* For instance, many grocery stores and other retail stores have streamlined the transaction procedures in the purchasing situation by installing scanner equipment to speed up the checkout process. Sotheby's, the world-famous auction house for fine art, found that the extreme escalation of art prices in the late 1980s had created a funds access problem for customers. Buyers did not have the large sums of cash (millions, in some cases) necessary to buy fine works of art, so Sotheby's instituted a credit policy by which it would lend up to one half the cost of an artwork, using the other works of art owned by the borrower as collateral.

Consumption Situations

The **consumption situation** includes the social and physical factors present in the environments where consumers actually use or consume the products and services they have bought. Obviously, consumption behaviors (and related cognitive and affective processes such as enjoyment, satisfaction, or frustration) are most relevant in such situations.[28] Consider how clean, tidy, well lighted, and attractively decorated consumption environments in full-service and fast-food restaurants, pubs and bars, nightclubs and discos, and ice cream parlors can enhance consumers' enjoyment of the purchased products. For such businesses, the design of the consumption environment may be critically important to consumers' satisfaction with their purchase.

Consider the consumption environment in two new bars at the Minneapolis and Detroit airports.[29] Host International, a division of Marriott Corporation, re-created the Cheers bar from the famous TV show of the same name, including Sam's Red Sox jersey framed on the wall, the wooden Indian statue inside the door, and the Wurlitzer jukebox. In addition, two familiar patrons are perched at the bar – animated, robotic replicas of Norm and Cliff. Up to 46 of these Cheers bars are planned for U.S. airports.

For other products such as appliances, clothing, cars, and furniture, marketers have almost no direct control over the consumption environment. These products are taken from the retail environment and consumed elsewhere (usually in consumers' homes). Moreover, for many of these products, the consumption situation involves multiple consumption behaviors over long periods (most people own and use a car or a microwave oven for several years). In some cases, the consumption environment might change during the useful life of the product, and this could affect consumption-related cognitive and affective responses (satisfaction) and behaviors (repairs and service). Perhaps the best marketers can do is to monitor consumers' satisfaction levels and behaviors in these consumption situations over the lifetime of the product.

In other cases, however, marketers have much control over the consumption environment. For instance, many service businesses, such as hairstylists, dentists and doctors, and hotels and motels have total control over the consumption environment, since consumption of these products and services occurs on the premises of the seller. Obvious examples are golf courses, ski resorts, or

Hitachi shows how its video camera can be used in one consumption situation.

theme parks such as Euro Disneyland outside Paris or Disney World in Florida where the consumption environment is a major part of the product/service consumers buy. Disney Enterprises goes to great lengths to ensure the consumption environment is perfect. Highlight 12.5 describes another business where the consumption environment is the main attraction.

Design of the consumption environment can also be critical in the restaurant industry.[30] The Rainbow Room in New York serves halibut in gold-colored foil to enhance the theatricality of the dining experience. Highly decorated theme restaurants are popular in many U.S. cities. A restaurant in Salt Lake City replicates an 18th century French farmhouse, down to ponds with geese and swans, peacocks roaming the grounds, waitresses in period costumes, and dried herbs and flowers hanging from the beamed ceilings. An entrepreneur in Chicago created a series of offbeat restaurants where the consumption environment was as important as the food. One spot called R.J. Grunts offered a burger and health-food menu served by blue-jean-clad waitresses, with mystical, new age music playing in the background.

Not all consumption environments are successful. A singles-type restaurant called Not So Great Gritzbe's had a sign reading "Eat and Get Out." The walls were decorated with Tums and Alka-Seltzer ads, and the food critic awards were crossed out. Although the media were intrigued, consumers became worried and the restaurant closed.

Disposition Situations

For certain products, marketers may need to consider other types of environmental situations. For instance, the **disposition situation** is highly relevant for some businesses—used-car lots and used-clothing stores are obvious examples. Here the key behavior of interest is *disposal* of products. Many people simply throw away unwanted products or give them to charity. Others sell their unwanted products at flea markets, garage sales, and swap meets. These situations offer interesting environments for study.[31] Disposition situations are relevant for public policy issues, too.

In many countries, including the United States, consumers are developing stronger values of quality, cost-consiousness, and concern for the natural environment that, in turn, are fueling interest in used products and the recycling of waste. Thus, the markets for recycled goods and used products (furniture and appliances, clothing and housewares) are likely to increase, and we can expect entrepreneurs to develop strategies to serve these markets.

Marketing Implications

Marketers need to identify the key social and physical environmental features of the information, shopping, purchasing, consumption, and disposition situations for their products. Then, they need to understand consumers' affective, cognitive and behavioral responses to these environmental factors. For instance, some aspects of these environments may be blocking behaviors crucial for the marketing success of the firm's product. Marketing strategies can be developed that modify the environment to stimulate, facilitate, and reinforce the desired behaviors. For instance, if funds access is a problem for consumers, the company might introduce debit cards, accept regular credit cards, or allow charge accounts. If consumers are becoming increasingly discouraged with the shopping environment in many cities (noisy streets, difficult parking, crowded stores, etc.), clever marketers are likely to introduce alternative shopping environments, such as home-shopping opportunities through the mail or by telephone. For instance, a home delivery service for groceries has been started in San Francisco. Strong growth for such businesses is forecast for the 1990s.

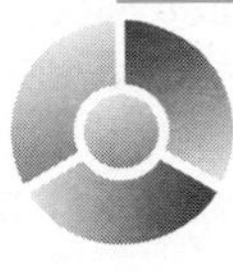

BACK TO.... CAESARS BOARDWALK REGENCY

Environmental psychology is a new area of study that cannot supply reliable data to support all the promises of DiLeonardo. However, the environmental manipulations described might affect gambling behavior. Although gambling is often a strong habit, reinforced on a powerful variable ratio schedule, the environment of a gambling casino will also have an effect. The social environment consists of friends, other gamblers, dealers, pit bosses, bartenders, and attractive waiters and waitresses—all of whom generally encourage increased gambling. Free drinks are supplied to gamblers, which helps keep them in the casino and might impair betting decisions as well as perceptions of time. Free or very inexpensive food is often available to keep gamblers from leaving a casino to eat.

A casino's interior is a closed physical environment that offers the potential for considerable behavior control. The lack of windows and clocks, the attractive colors and lighting, exciting noises, celebrities, and happy winners, plus the convenient placement of various gambling devices, tables, and bars, encourage consumers to stay in the environment and gamble.

Overall, then, while it is not clear what differential advantage Caesars has for attracting gamblers compared to other casinos, it is a safe bet that Caesars' environment will affect people's gambling behavior, as well as their cognitive and affective responses.

SUMMARY

This chapter presented an overview of environmental influences on consumer behavior. Three basic types of environments were identified: social, physical, and marketing. The social environment includes the effects on consumer behavior of culture, subculture, social class, reference group, and family. The physical environment includes the effects of both spatial and nonspatial factors. The marketing environment includes all stimuli associated with marketing strategies that influence consumers' cognitions, affect, and behaviors, either directly or indirectly.

We also discussed the important concept of situations, which involves the continuous interaction over time of consumers' affective and cognitive responses and behaviors with one or more environmental settings. We identified five broad, generic situations most relevant for consumer research — the information, shopping, purchasing, consumption, and disposition situations. And we discussed the important social and physical aspects of the environments in those situations as well as the key behaviors of interest. A basic premise of the chapter was that marketing strategies must not only be adapted to changing environmental conditions, but also play an important role in creating the environment.

Key Terms and Concepts

Complete Environment *379*

Functional (or Perceived) Environment *379*

Consensual Environment *379*

Macro Social Environment *382*

Micro Social Environment *383*

Physical Environment *386*

Marketing Environment *389*

Situation *391*

Information Acquisition Situation *393*

Shopping Situation *395*

Purchasing Situation *398*

Consumption Situation *400*

Disposition Situation *402*

Review and Discussion Questions

1. Define complete, functional, and consensual environments using examples of fast-food restaurants to illustrate your points.

2. How does the concept of marketing segmentation relate to the functional and consensual environments?

3. Consider the distinction between macro- and microenvironments for grocery shopping. Which of these are more important for marketing strategy?

4. Contrast the two approaches marketers can take to analyzing environmental effects — the "direct" effects of specific environmental factors versus considering environmental factors in the context of situations. Under what circumstances might each of these two approaches be most appropriate?

5. Use the situation of shopping for a personal cassette player to describe the relationships between the physical, social, and marketing environments.
6. What is a situation? Use examples from your own recent purchases to show how situations differ from "raw" environments.
7. Are environmental factors more important influences for new or recurring situations? Why?
8. Use the Wheel of Consumer Analysis to describe how affect and cognition and behaviors interact with environmental factors in a textbook purchase situation.
9. How can marketers use situational analysis to segment markets? Identify some product categories where the approach has been used to the advantage of the marketing organization.
10. For each of the five generic marketing situations, identify uncontrollable and controllable factors that should be considered in developing marketing strategies.

NOTES

1. Adapted for this text from Jack Block and Jeanne H. Block, "Studying Situational Dimensions: A Grand Perspective and Some Limited Empiricism," in *Toward a Psychology of Situations: An Interactional Perspective*, ed. David Magnusson (Hillsdale, N.J.: Lawrence Erlbaum, 1981), pp. 85–102.
2. C. Whan Park, Easwar S. Iyer, and Daniel C. Smith, "The Effects of Situational Factors on In-Store Grocery Shopping Behavior: The Role of Store Environment and Time Available for Shopping," *Journal of Consumer Research*, March 1989, pp. 422–33.
3. Adapted from William D. Crano and Lawrence A. Messe, *Social Psychology: Principles and Themes of Interpersonal Behavior* (Homewood, Ill.: Dorsey Press, 1982), p. 15.
4. See James A. Russell and Lawrence M. Ward, "Environmental Psychology," in *Annual Review of Psychology*, vol. 33, ed. Mark R. Rosenzweig and Lyman W. Porter (Palo Alto, Calif.: Annual Reviews, 1982), pp. 651–88; and Daniel Stokols and Irwin Altman, ed., *Handbook of Environmental Psychology* (New York: Wiley Interscience, 1987).
5. For example, see Robert J. Graham, "The Role of Perception of Time in Consumer Research," *Journal of Consumer Research*, March 1981, pp. 335–42; Lawrence P. Feldman and Jacob Hornik, "The Use of Time: An Integrated Conceptual Model," *Journal of Consumer Research*, March 1981, pp. 407–19; Jacob Hornik, "Situational Effects on the Consumption of Time," *Journal of Marketing*, Fall 1982, pp. 44–55; and Jacob Hornik, "Subjective versus Objective Time Measures: A Note on the Perception of Time in Consumer Behavior," *Journal of Consumer Research*, June 1984, pp. 615–18.
6. See Fern Schumer Chapman, "Business's Push for More Daylight Time," *Fortune*, November 12, 1984, pp. 615–18.
7. See Debra A. Michal's, "Pitching Products by the Barometer," *Business Week*, July 8, 1985, p. 45; Ronald Alsop, "Companies Look to Weather to Find Best Climate for Ads," *The Wall Street Journal*, January 19, 1985, p. 27; and

Fred Ward, "Weather, Behavior Correlated in New Market Test," *Marketing News*, June 7, 1985, p. 9.

8. See Jeff Meer, "The Light Touch," *Psychology Today*, September 1985, pp. 60–67.
9. See Mark Harris, "Evaluate Lighting Systems as a Marketing Device, Not Overhead," *Marketing News*, October 26, 1984, p. 1.
10. Carl P. Zeithaml and Valarie A. Zeithaml, "Environmental Management: Revising the Marketing Perspective," *Journal of Marketing*, Spring 1985, pp. 46–53.
11. See James H. Leigh and Claude R. Martin, "A Review of Situational Influence Paradigms and Research," in *Review of Marketing 1981*, ed. Ben M. Enis and Kenneth J. Reering (Chicago: American Marketing Association, 1981), pp. 57–74; Pradeep Kakkar and Richard J. Lutz, "Situational Influences on Consumer Behavior," in *Perspectives in Consumer Behavior*, 3rd ed., ed. Harold H. Kassarjian and Thomas S. Robertson (Glenview, Ill.: Scott, Foresman, 1981), pp. 204–15; and Joseph A. Cote, Jr., "Situational Variables in Consumer Research: A Review," Working Paper, Washington State University, 1985.
12. See Russell W. Belk, "The Objective Situation as a Determinant of Consumer Behavior," in *Advances in Consumer Research*, vol. 2, ed. Mary J. Schlinger (Chicago: Association for Consumer Research, 1975), pp. 427–38; and Richard J. Lutz and Pradeep K. Kakkar, "The Psychological Situation as a Determinant of Consumer Behavior," in *Advances in Consumer Research*, vol. 2, ed. Mary J. Schlinger (Chicago Association for Consumer Research, 1975), pp. 439–54.
13. Geraldine Fennell, "Consumers' Perceptions of the Product Use Situation," *Journal of Marketing*, April 1978, pp. 38–47.
14. Russell W. Belk, "Situational Variables and Consumer Behavior," *Journal of Consumer Research*, December 1976, pp. 157–64; and Kenneth E. Miller and James L. Ginter, "An Investigation of Situational Variation in Brand Choice Behavior and Attitude," *Journal of Marketing Research*, February 1979, pp. 111–23.
15. Kenneth E. Miller and James L. Ginter, "An Investigation of Situational Variation."
16. J. Edward Russo, Richard Staelin, Catherine A. Nolan, Gary J. Russell, and Barbara L. Metcalf, "Nutrition Information in the Supermarket," *Journal of Consumer Research*, June 1986, pp. 48–70.
17. Dennis L. McNeill and William L. Wilkie, "Public Policy and Consumer Information: Impact of the New Energy Labels," *Journal of Consumer Research*, June 1979, pp. 1–11.
18. These examples come from Skip Wollenberg, "P-O-P Campaigns Increase as Profile of Shoppers Change," *Marketing News*, April 11, 1988, p. 25.
19. Joe Agnew, "P-O-P Displays Are Becoming a Matter of Convenience," *Marketing News*, October 9, 1987, pp. 14, 16.
20. J. Davis Illingworth, "The Personal Plus," *Marketing Insights*, Winter 1991, pp. 31–33, 45.
21. Ibid.
22. Antonio Fins, "Sunglass Huts: Thriving in Nooks and Crannies," *Business Week*, July 27, 1987.
23. Jeffrey A. Trachtenberg, "When a Mall's Biggest Retailers Fall, Surviving Shops Get an Unpleasant Jolt," *The Wall Street Journal*, October 25, 1990, pp. B1, B8.
24. "Hallmark Now Marketing by Color," *Marketing News*, June 6, 1988, p. 18.
25. Meryl P. Gardner and George J. Siomkos, "Toward Methodology for Assessing Effects of In-Store Atmospherics," in *Advances in Consumer Research*, vol. 13, ed. Richard J. Lutz (Provo, Utah: Association for Consumer Research, 1986), pp. 27–31; and Robert J. Donovan and John R. Rossiter, "Store Atmosphere: An Environmental Psychology Approach," *Journal of Retailing*, Spring 1982, pp. 34–57.
26. Diane Schneidman, "Visual Aura, Kinetics Help Stabilize Store Image," *Marketing News*, October 23, 1987, p. 4.
27. Michael Solomon, "The Missing Link: Surro-

gate Consumers in the Marketing Chain," *Journal of Marketing*, October 1986, pp. 208–18.

28. Ronald E. Milliman. "The Influence of Background Music on the Behavior of Restaurant Patrons," *Journal of Consumer Research*, September 1986, pp. 286–89.

29. Patricia Strand, "Bars Tap 'Cheers' Name," *Advertising Age*, March 11, 1991, p. 16.

30. Elizabeth Ames and Geraldine Fabrikant, "Rich Melman: The Hot Dog of the Restaurant Business," *Business Week*, February 11, 1985, pp. 73–77; and Howard Riell, "Slumping Restaurant Industry Seeks New Marketing Ideas," *Marketing News*, February 18, 1991, pp. 2, 5.

31. Russell W. Belk, John Sherry, and Melanie Wallendorf, "A Naturalistic Inquiry into Buyer and Seller Behavior at a Swap Meet," *Journal of Consumer Research*, March 1988, pp. 449–70.

Additional Reading

For a readable text on environmental psychology, see:

Rappaport, Amos. *The Meaning of the Built Environment.* Bevery Hills, Calif.: Sage Publications, 1982.

For an analysis of the environments of two major U.S. theme parks, see:

Mechling, Elizabeth W., and Jay Mechling, "The Sale of Two Cities: A Semiotic Comparison of Disneyland with Marriott's Great America," *Journal of Popular Culture* 15, no. 1, 1981, pp. 166–79.

For a discussion of the meaning of "situations," see:

Cote, Joseph A., Jr. "The Person by Situation Interaction Myth: Implications for the Definition of Situations." In *Advances in Consumer Research*, vol. 13, ed. Richard J. Lutz, Provo, Utah: Association for Consumer Research, 1986, pp. 37–41.

For a discussion of the in-store environment or atmosphere, see:

Kotler, Philip. "Atmosphere as a Marketing Tool." *Journal of Retailing.* Winter 1973, pp. 48–64.

Park, C. Whan, Easwar S. Iyer, and Daniel C. Smith. "The Effects of Situational Factors on In-Store Shopping Behavior: The Role of Store Environment and Time Available for Shopping." *Journal of Consumer Research*, March 1989, pp. 422–34.

For a discussion of how marketing strategies can influence the environment and behaviors, see:

Hirshman, Elizabeth C. "Marketing as an Agent of Change in Subsistence Cultures: Some Dysfunctional Consumption Consequences." In *Advances in Consumer Research*, vol. 13, ed. Richard J. Lutz, Provo, Utah: Association for Consumer Research, 1986, pp. 99–104.

For an interesting discussion of the information/shopping/purchasing environment at a flea market, see:

Sherry, John F., Jr. "A Sociocultural Analysis of a Midwestern Flea Market." *Journal of Consumer Research*, June 1990, pp. 13–30.

For discussion of how the overall environment affects consumption behaviors, see:

O'Guinn, Thomas C., and Russell W. Belk. "Heaven on Earth: Consumption at Heritage Village, USA." *Journal of Consumer Research*, September 1989, pp. 227–38.

MARKETING STRATEGY IN ACTION

America's Movie Theaters

The price of admission to many of America's movie theaters sometimes buys an experience sensible people would pay to avoid. The blackened and musty carpet in the lobby could be a relic from the silent screen era. The $1.25 bucket of popcorn – that's the small size – holds 10 cents worth of corn covered with a strange liquid, perhaps derived from petroleum. Beneath the broken seats, sticky coats of spilled soda pop varnish the floor. The screen is tiny, the sound tinny, and the audience is rude. Oh, and one more thing – the picture stinks.

Many theater owners bought into the business at low prices after 1984, when antitrust rulings forced the major Hollywood studios, which had previously the leading theater chains, to give up their movie houses. The new owners got a great deal. They owned the only show in town (sometimes literally), and the studios promoted the movies. As the easy profits rolled in, many exhibitors lost contact with their customers. They milked the business and let their theaters deteriorate.

But the success of videocassette rentals and cable TV during the early 1980s converted many moviegoers to stay-at-homers. These changes forced exhibitors to recognize their folly. By 1985, theaters were no longer the only show in town. Attendance dropped 12 percent over 1984 figures. The $5 billion-a-year American movie theater industry was fighting for survival.

This put the theater owners in a bind. To regain the loyalty of their customers, they had to pour money into refurbishing, rebuilding, and restoring the glamour of moviegoing. But at the same time, they were being hurt by the new technologies that competed with them.

To survive during these changes, exhibitors developed a couple of temporarily successful strategies. One was to develop their lobby concession stands as a source of revenues. To keep some of their customers, theaters had kept ticket prices fairly low – the average price in 1985 was about $3.50 to $4 – prices that lagged behind inflation. Once inside, though, moviegoers were a captive market for the popcorn, soda, and candy sold at stupendous markups of 500 percent or more. A well-run concession stand generates at least $1 of sales and as much as 75 cents of profit per ticket buyer. Exhibitors found they could survive by charging even more outrageous prices for popcorn.

What brands of candy were in the typical concession stand? Usually, it was a strange mix of oversized boxes that included very few of the best-selling brands in the United States. Theaters tended to stock candy brands like Milk Duds, Sno Caps, and Jujyfruits, hardly big sellers on the outside. The exception was Snickers, the No. 1 brand in the United States, which was present in most concession stands. Do moviegoers have different tastes than the rest of the population? No, of course not. The movie house operators preferred these brands because they were more profitable. With limited space available, the operators stocked the brands with the highest profit margins.

The profits from concession sales can be considerable. For instance, in 1985 a tub of popcorn that cost 30 cents was sold for about $2 – a markup of 567 percent. A soft drink (often a Coke) that cost the theater 10 cents might have been sold for 75 cents, a 650 percent percent markup. Candy produced a much smaller profit with markups of "only" about 180 percent. On average, about 40 percent of the $850 million in annual concession sales came from popcorn, another 40 percent from soft drinks, and only about 20 percent from everything else. Critics claim that by sticking to the most profitable brands, theater owners are missing an opportunity to increase overall candy sales by stocking more popular brands. As it stands now, only about one third of moviegoers buy anything from the concession stand.

The other strategy was the multiscreen theater. During the 1970s, exhibitors began chopping up their grand old theaters into smaller ones that many moviegoers have come to hate. Individual exhibitors did great, though (as long as they owned the only theaters in town). A theater with four screens, about the national average, is four more times likely to book a hit picture; the exhibitor then shows the hit in the largest room and lesser movies in the smaller theaters.

But at a macro level, more seats were the last thing the industry needed. In 1985, the total number of tickets sold annually remained constant at about 1 billion, a number that hadn't varied much for 25 years. But when the growing population is considered, this translated into a 24 percent per capita decline in moviegoing. As a writer for *Variety* said, "Filmgoing used to be part of the social fabric. Now it is an impulse purchase." During the 1980s, the population was aging and the prime moviegoing segment of the under-30-year-olds was declining. When the damage done by VCRs and cable TV was added . . . well, you get the picture.

To survive into the 1990s, exhibitors must relearn how to woo moviegoers. There is something special about seeing a terrific film in a great theater with an appreciative audience. And by using technologies such as wide-screen 70-millimeter projection and wraparound Dolby sound, theaters can create a sense of spectacle that no TV set can match. Theater owners can make their theaters clean and comfortable again, maybe even palatial. In fact, many exhibitors have remodeled their old elegant theaters and restored them to their former grandeur. Moreover, new construction is being upgraded. One successful exhibitor coddled customers in specially designed $130 seats, costing twice the national average.

Another exhibitor says, "We have to upgrade the quality of the moviegoing experience." His newest theaters have granite-floored lobbies with painted murals, spacious auditoriums, and first-rate sound and projection. The higher construction costs paid off in more customers at higher-than-average ticket prices, and a splendid $1.35 per ticket take at the concession stand. However, such theaters are still rare.

As the drama of change pervades the movie exhibition industry, the major beneficiaries are likely to be the long-suffering moviegoers. When consumers enter the theater of the future, they may not encounter a marvel of technology, but at least they won't stick to the floor.

Discussion Questions

1. The VCR is a physical aspect of the marketing environment that has affected moviegoing behavior in the United States. Compare and contrast the consumption situations of watching a movie in a theater versus seeing the same movie at home on your VCR. Discuss the reciprocal interactions between en-

vironment, behavior, and cognitive and affective responses. What long-term effects do you think the in-home VCR environments will have on moviegoing? What can movie theaters do to improve their situation?

2. What macroenvironmental factors might affect moviegoing behaviors (both decrease and increase)? Consider their impacts on different market segments. What marketing implications does your analysis have for theater owners or movie companies?
3. Analyze the information, purchasing, and consumption environments of different movie theaters in your local area. What recommendations do you have for changing these environments to increase sales?
4. Analyze the effects of the consumption situation at movie theaters on consumers' purchase of snacks at the concession stand. What could theater owners do to change the purchasing and the consumption environment in their theaters to encourage higher levels of snack consumption and greater sales at concession stands?

Source: Alex Ben Block, "Those Peculiar Candies that Star at the Movies," *Forbes,* May 19, 1986, pp. 174–76; and Stratford P. Sherman, "Back to the Future," *Fortune,* January 20, 1986, pp. 909–14.

Cultural and Cross-Cultural Influences

CHAPTER 13

THE BIRTH OF THE CONSUMER SOCIETY

America is seen by many as the prototypic consumer society. Modern consumption cultures are a rather recent historical development. According to one analysis, the birth of the consumer society occurred in England during the 18th century when several important events occurred. For one, the new mass production technologies developed during England's Industrial Revolution allowed companies to produce large amounts of standardized goods at relatively low prices. A *cultural revolution* occurred about the same time, without which the Industrial Revolution would not have been successful.

During the 18th century, England was gradually transformed from a largely agrarian society into a more urban society. When people moved into towns, their culture changed dramatically. They developed new values, performed different types of work, and developed new lifestyles. Many people developed an increased desire for material goods, stimulated partly by new marketing strategies such as advertising. Increasingly, ordinary citizens (not just the wealthy) became concerned with the symbolic meanings of goods and felt it necessary to buy products that were fashionable and up-to-date. Owning such things helped satisfy the new cultural need

for status distinctions that had become more relevant in the relatively anonymous urban societies where few people knew each other or their family backgrounds. Thus, people began to see consumption as an acceptable way to acquire important social meanings. Finally, more people had disposable income and were willing to spend it to achieve those values.

These cultural changes, combined with the rapidly developing ability of industry to mass produce products of reasonable quality at low prices, created a dramatic increase in consumption in 18th-century England. Essentially, the same events occurred in France and the United States during the 19th century and the modern consumer society was born there, too.

Source: Adapted from Grant McCracken, "The Making of Modern Consumption," in *Culture and Consumption* (Bloomington, Ind. University of Indiana Press, 1988); and Janeen A. Costa, "Toward an Understanding of Social and World Systemtic Processes in the Spread of Consumer Culture: An Anthropological Case Study," in *Advances in Consumer Research,* vol. 17 (Provo, Utah: Association for Consumer Research, 1991), pp. 826–32.

This brief summary of the complex events at the beginning of the modern consumption society points to the importance of culture in understanding consumer behavior. To develop effective strategies, marketers need to identify important aspects of culture and understand how they affect consumers. In this chapter, we examine the topic of culture and consider its influence on consumers' affect, cognitions, and behaviors. We also describe some important characteristics of American culture and discuss the implications of cultural analysis for developing marketing strategies. Then, we present a model of the cultural process that shows how cultural meaning is transferred by marketing strategies to products and how consumers then acquire those meanings for themselves. Finally, we discuss cross-cultural (international) differences and their implications for developing global marketing strategies.

What Is Culture?

As the broadest aspect of the macro social environment, culture has a pervasive influence on consumers. Yet, despite increasing research attention, culture

The cultural meaning of the bald eagle is specific to American consumers.

remains difficult for marketers to understand. Dozens of definitions have confused researchers about what "culture" is or how culture works to influence consumers.[1] Fortunately, recent theoretical developments help clarify the concept of culture and how it affects people.[2] Basically, we can understand culture from two broad perspectives—the *content* of a culture and culture as a *process*.[3] Both approaches have useful implications for marketing strategy.

The **content of culture** includes all the beliefs, attitudes, goals, and values held by most people in a society, as well as the characteristic behaviors, rules, customs, and norms that most people follow. The content of culture also includes aspects of the social and physical environment, including the social institutions in a society (political parties, religions, chambers of commerce) and the physical objects (products, tools, buildings) used by people in a society.

The usual approach in marketing is to analyze culture in terms of its attributes or content.[4] Consumer researchers have studied the content of a culture largely in terms of the values of a society.[5] Although important, values are not the only significant component of culture. In this book, we treat **culture** more broadly as *the meanings that are shared by (most) people in a social group.* Each society establishes its own vision of the world and constitutes or constructs that cultural world by creating and using meanings to represent, organize, and

HIGHLIGHT 13.1

Holiday Buying around the World

A witch flies on a broomstick to drop Christmas gifts down Italian chimneys; a kindly old Saint Nicholas leaves gifts at the front doors of Scandinavian homes; a camel does the hauling in southern Syria; and the honorable porter's name is *Santa-san* in Japan. Although the exact method of delivery varies, shoppers around the world fill the sacks with presents every holiday season.

Each year, eager shoppers record huge purchases during the Christmas holiday season. For instance, Americans spend more than $450 billion extra during the three-month shopping season from October to New Year's. Most department stores record about one third of their annual sales during this period. Toy vendors from London to Madrid to Los Angeles expect to do about 50 percent of their yearly business in these three months.

Shopping for and giving presents at Christmastime has become a worldwide phenomenon. Even in Japan, where less than 1 percent of the population is Christian, Yuletide is widely celebrated with artfully packaged gifts and late-hour partying. West Germany's lively outdoor Christmas markets sell sausages, sweets, and holiday gifts. Shoppers in Rome's oval-shaped plaza Piazza Navona are bathed in light from stalls selling items like books, toys, records, candy, and video games while being entertained by street musicians and magicians. Even the energy shortage and sparsely stocked stores in Eastern Europe cannot extinguish Christmas cheer. Families in Warsaw, Bratislava, and Budapest surrender their bathtubs for a week to give freshwater carp, a holiday delicacy, a place to swim before dinner.

Holiday decorations, especially lights, are pop-

maintain significant cultural distinctions. For example, Highlight 13.1 presents some of the meanings of the Christmas holiday shared by people in different cultures.

Issues in Cultural Analysis

Marketers should consider several issues when analyzing culture. The first is that cultural meaning can be analyzed at different levels. Usually, cultural content is analyzed at the macro level of an entire society or country (Canada, France, Poland, Kenya, or Australia). However, because culture is the meanings shared among a group of people (of any size), marketers can also analyze the cultural meanings of subcultures (African-Americans, the elderly, people who live in New England) or social classes (middle versus working class). We discuss subcultures and social class in Chapter 14. Marketers can even analyze the ular everywhere. For instance, Christmas trees decorate plazas around the globe (and are found in 75 percent of American homes). In Scandinavia, candles glow from every window to brighten the darkness that arrives by midafternoon. The Stroget, Copenhagen's large pedestrian-only shopping district, is illuminated by thousands of colored lights and stars. The Via Condotti, Rome's pedestrian-only shopping area, is decorated with hundreds of red poinsettias, called "Christmas stars" in Italian.

For many, the winter weather in the northern hemisphere heightens the holiday mood. But cold weather and lights in the early darkness are not prerequisites for Christmas spirit. South of the equator, the holiday falls in the middle of summer. So when enthusiastic shoppers in Australia and Rio get too hot, they just head for the beach to cool off.

There are differences, of course, between the consumers in various cultures, subcultures, and social classes. Marketers need to identify these factors and understand how they are related to purchasing and consumption behavior.

However, there are also similarities between cultures. One example is the generosity and good spirit of the Christmas season. Holiday spending and gift giving seems to be fairly universal in most societies with a well-developed consumption ethic. The details, of course, often differ. The weather (cold and snowy or hot, humid, and rainy), the most desirable gifts (fur coats in Northern Europe, ice cream makers in Brazil), the particular details of the holiday rituals (who brings the gifts), and the religious symbolic meanings may vary considerably.

But the core meaning of the holiday, captured by Charles Dickens in *A Christmas Carol*, seems fairly universal. "Christmas," Dickens wrote, "is the only time I know of, in the long calendar year, when men and women seem by one consent to open their shut-up hearts freely." And, we might note, they open their pocketbooks, too.

Source: Jaclyn Fierman, "Christmas Shopping around the World," *Fortune,* December 21, 1987, pp. 92–100.

shared cultural meanings of smaller groups such as a reference group (people who live on the same dormitory floor, members of a sorority or a street gang, or a group of co-workers) or families (people in one's nuclear or extended family). We discuss reference groups and family influences in Chapter 15.

Second, the concept of shared or common meaning is critical to understanding culture. In Section 2, we examined psychological meaning—the personal, mental representations of objects, events, and behaviors stored in the memories of individual consumers. In this chapter, we consider **cultural meaning** at a more macro, social level. From that perspective, a meaning is cultural if many (most) people in a social group share the same basic meaning. We should expect these cultural meanings to be somewhat fuzzy in that all people in a social group are not likely to have exactly the same meaning for any object or activity (What is an "old" person, an "environmentally safe" product, or a "good" bargain?).[6] Meanings only have to be close enough to be treated as shared or common.

Cultural meanings are created by people. Anthropologists often say cultural meanings are constructed or negotiated by people in a group through their social interactions. We can more clearly see the *construction of meaning* at the level of smaller groups (consider the social meanings of clothing fads among college students—what look is in this semester?). At the macro societal level, cultural institutions such as government, religious and educational organizations, and business firms also are involved in constructing cultural meaning.

Cultural meanings are constantly in motion and can be subject to rapid changes. In the early days of the consumption society in 18th-century England, for instance, the cultural changes in people's values, perceptions, and behaviors were so dramatic that one observer believed a kind of madness had taken over society. Later in this chapter, we examine the processes by which cultural meanings are moved, partly through marketing strategies.

A final issue is that social groups differ in the amount of freedom people have to adopt and use certain cultural meanings. North American and European societies afford people a great deal of freedom to select cultural meanings and use them to create a desired self-identity. In most other societies, people have less freedom to do so (China, India, Saudia Arabia).

Measuring the Content of Culture

Marketers have used many procedures to measure cultural content including content analysis, ethnographic fieldwork, and measures of values. Some of these methods are different from the more traditional approaches common in consumer research (surveys, telephone interviews, focus groups).[7] Although all these techniques identify important meanings shared by people, they do not show how consumers perceive products to be related to those meanings. Means-end chains are useful for that purpose.

Content Analysis

The content of culture can often can be read from the material objects produced by the social group. For instance, consumer researchers have examined comic books to gain insights into the dominant values in a culture.[8] Other researchers have examined a historical record of print advertisements to see how American values and women's roles have changed during the past 90 years.[9]

Ethnographic Fieldwork

Marketers have begun to use ethnographic methods (adapted from anthropology) to study culture.[10] These procedures involve detailed and prolonged observation of consumers' emotional responses, cognitions, and behaviors during their ordinary daily lives. Based on this rich and detailed data, researchers infer the values and key meanings of the culture. Unlike anthropologists who might live in the studied society for months or years, consumer researchers tend to make their observations more quickly. Using a combination of direct observations, interviews, and video and audio recordings, researchers have examined consumer behavior at flea markets and swap meets.[11] During a summer-long odyssey across the United States, a team of consumer researchers tried to identify broad meaning themes concerning consumption from their observations of consumers in various behavioral settings.[12]

Measures of Values

In contrast to the inferential approach of ethnomethodology, marketers also use procedures to directly measure the dominant cultural values in a society. A popular approach is the Rokeach Value Survey in which consumers rank order 36 general values in terms of their importance. Kahle's List of Values asks consumers to rank order nine person-oriented values. Marketers can then use these data to segment consumers in terms of their dominant value orientation.[13]

Various commercial techniques regularly survey large, representative samples of consumers in the United States and Europe. For instance, the Yankelovich MONITOR tracks over 50 social trends (and value changes) and reports on their significance for consumer marketing. A commercial method called VALS (Values and Lifestyles) identifies segments of consumers with different sets of end values. VALS has been widely adapted by advertising agencies to better help them understand their target customers.

The Content of Culture

Marketers can examine the cultural content of a society by considering the shared meaning of various things in that society. The Wheel of Consumer Analysis suggests we consider the shared meanings of people's affective and cognitive responses, their behaviors, aspects of their social and physical environments, and marketing strategies. The goal is to understand the shared meanings of these concepts from the view of the consumers who experience them.[14]

Affect and Cognition

Many affective and emotional responses have distinctive cultural meanings. For instance, many Americans have similar affective or emotional responses to the raising of the American flag (patriotic feelings), a 50 percent-off sale (interest, excitement), or accidentally breaking a vase in a store (anxiety, guilt). Many Americans and northern Europeans would become angry or frustrated if kept waiting for more than 30 minutes in a checkout line, while people in other societies might not have a negative affective reaction.

Behavior

Many social behaviors have shared cultural meanings. For instance, the cultural meaning of shaking hands when greeting someone (welcome, friendliness) is shared by many peoples of the world, although some people bow or kiss instead. Protesters in the United States or other countries who burn the American flag are representing and communicating a particular meaning (disapproval or hatred). Many consumption-related behaviors also have cultural meaning that may be unique to particular societies. For instance, the cultural meaning of bargaining behaviors that are common (and expected) among shoppers in the open market bazaars of northern Africa indicate a skilled and shrewd consumer. But in the United States, such bargaining behaviors are not appropriate for shopping in K mart or Wal-Mart and might be considered naive or rude.

Environment

Many aspects of the social environment have rich cultural meanings. Consider, for instance, the cultural meanings of relative social status that are contained in the following social situations: having dinner with a group of your friends versus your parents versus your supervisor at work. Marketers are interested in the shared cultural meanings in consumption-related situations such as shopping for, purchasing, using, and disposing of products. The cultural meanings of shopping for a new sweater at a discount mall are quite different from shopping in an upscale department store such as Nordstrom's.

Many aspects of the physical or material environment — including the landscape, buildings, the weather, as well as specific objects such as products — have significant cultural meaning. Consider the cultural meanings of a wedding ring, an interview suit, or a new car or house. All societies have certain objects that symbolize key cultural meanings. Think of the shared meanings many Americans associate with the flag, the Statue of Liberty, or the bald eagle (pride, freedom, individualism). Other societies use different objects to embody important cultural meanings (the Eiffel tower in Paris, the Big Ben clock in the London Parliament building, Mt. Fuji in Japan).

Marketers need to understand the cultural meanings of their products and brands as well as of competing products. For instance, an analysis of beverage products focused on the status and age meanings carried in various beverage products — milk, for example, is weak and for younger people, while wine is sophisticated and for mature adults.[15] As we will see later, consumers seek to acquire certain cultural meanings in products and use them to create an attractive self-identity.

Marketing Strategies

Marketing strategies also have shared cultural meaning. Reactions to advertising, for instance, tend to be culturally specific.[16] In the United States, many advertising appeals are straightforward and direct, but consumers in other societies may consider such appeals blunt and offensive. Foreigners consider many U.S. ads to be overly emotional. Thus, a McDonald's ad that featured a young man with Down's syndrome who found a job and happiness at

McDonald's was a tearjerker for Americans, but it was booed and jeered at the International Advertising Film Festival in Cannes.

The British tend to be embarrassed by a direct sell; their ads are noted for self-deprecating humor. In contrast, the French rarely use humor, but prefer stylish and rather indirect appeals, which Americans may find surrealistic. For example, the best French ad in 1991 (also shown in North America) showed a lion and a tawny-haired woman crawling up opposite sides of a mountain; at the peak the woman outroars the lion for a bottle of Perrier. The Japanese like ads in which affective mood and emotional tone are emphasized over facts. Although some Japanese ads travel well to other cultures, many are not understood outside Japan.[17]

Marketing strategies such as pricing or distribution can have cultural meanings that differ across societies. Many U.S. consumers have positive reactions to frequent sales promotions such as discounting, sales, and coupons, whereas consumers in other cultures may have different meanings (Is there something wrong with this product?).

The Core Values of American Culture

Typically, an analysis of cultural content begins by identifying the core values of the social group. **Core values** are the abstract end goals people are striving to achieve. Knowing the core values held by people in a society helps marketers understand the basis for the customer-product relationship for those consumers. Figure 13.1 presents some of the basic, core values shared by most Americans. Following are some additional core values.

Individualism

Individualism is a very broad and dominant core value shared by most Americans. *Individualism* refers to relying on yourself rather than someone else and being autonomous, unique, and in control of your life. Americans tend to attribute success or failure to the personal characteristics of people and glorify individual achievement. Thus, Americans have a national fascination with determining who is best, No. 1, or in the top 10. Individualism, and the related values of self-esteem and self-fulfillment, are commonly emphasized in U.S. advertising. (Highlight 13.2 describes two ads that emphasize individualism and related cultural values.) Products such as clothing, cosmetics, and cars often are promoted as unique so that people can distinguish themselves from others. Marketers of services frequently promote the individual, specialized treatment they give the customer.

Freedom

Freedom is a strong value in the United States. Americans want to be free politically, as do many other people in the world, but the freedom value has implications for other dimensions of life. For instance, most Americans value freedom of choice — the opportunity to select from a wide variety of purchase

FIGURE 13.1
Core Cultural Values in America

Value	General Features	Relevance to Consumer Behavior
Achievement and success	Hard work is good; success flows from hard work	Acts as a justification for acquisition of goods ("You deserve it")
Activity	Keeping busy is healthy and natural	Stimulates interest in products that save time and enhance leisure activities
Efficiency and practicality	Admiration of things that solve problems (e.g., save time and effort)	Stimulates purchase of products that function well and save time
Progress	People can improve themselves; tomorrow should be better	Stimulates desire for new products that fulfill unsatisfied needs; acceptance of products that claim to be "new" or "improved"
Material comfort	"The good life"	Fosters acceptance of convenience and luxury products that make life more enjoyable
External conformity	Uniformity of observable behavior; desire to be accepted	Stimulates interest in products that are used or owned by others in the same social group
Humanitarianism	Caring for others, particularly the underdog	Stimulates patronage of firms that compete with market leaders
Youthfulness	A state of mind that stresses being young at heart or appearing young	Stimulates acceptance of products that provide the illusion of maintaining or fostering youth

Source: Leon G. Schiffman and Leslie Lazar Kanuck, *Consumer Behavior,* 3rd ed. © 1987, p. 506. Reprinted by permission of Prentice Hall, Inc., Englewood Cliffs, N.J.

alternatives. Perhaps this is why over 1,000 brands of shampoo and 200 brands of breakfast cereal are available in the United States.

Mastery and Control

Many Americans value mastery and control of their lives and the environment. The fascination with lawns (control of nature), remote controls (control over TV exposure), and time management systems (control over time) reflect this value. Perhaps this value will decrease as more people become convinced that some things (nature) cannot be closely managed and controlled.

Health and Fitness

The growth of health and fitness values in the United States over the past 20 years has created vast new markets and reduced others. These values influence people's behaviors and purchases. According to one generous estimate, 50 percent of the adult population engages in at least one athletic activity daily (versus only 25 percent a generation earlier). This has created large markets for

HIGHLIGHT 13.2

The Cultural Meaning of Beer Commercials

Marketers must select symbols and signs that signify important cultural meanings to include in their advertisements. Thus, we can examine ads to see what cultural meanings are present in them and learn something about the overall culture that produced them. Consider the following two ads for Anheuser-Busch beers that were widely shown on American television in the 1980s.

Ad 1. In the first scene, an older foreman is reading names from a clipboard and giving workers their assignments. A nervous young Polish immigrant arrives late, receives a look of disapproval from the foreman, and then sits in the back. When his name is called, the immigrant walks to the front, corrects the foreman's pronunciation of his name, and receives his assignment. Then we see a series of vignettes of the day's work in which the immigrant gradually gains the respect of his co-workers. The final scene is in a crowded tavern. The young man walks in and looks around nervously until he hears someone call his name and wave him over to the group where the foreman hands him a beer—naturally, it's a Budweiser.

Several basic meanings in American culture are represented in this ad. The themes of challenge and overcoming adversity are basic cultural meanings in America that are well illustrated in the ad. Also, comradeship and belonging are illustrated in the final scene, which is also closely tied to beer drinking and to the Budweiser brand.

Ad 2. A cowboy is herding a group of cattle over a river when a small calf is swept away by the current. The cowboy overcomes the force of the river and rescues the calf. A voice-over intones, "Sometimes a simple river crossing isn't so simple. And when you've got him back it's your turn. Head for the beer brewed natural as a mountain stream." Then we see a hand pulling a six-pack of Busch beer out of the clear water of a rushing stream.

Several cultural meanings are combined in this ad. Again we see the ubiquitous myth of overcoming challenge, a central meaning of American-style masculinity. The cowboy is perhaps the prototypic representation of the American myths of freedom, control over nature, and rugged individualism. Challenge is also represented in the actions of the cowboy who rescues a being less powerful than himself.

Also, this ad might activate (perhaps at an unconscious level) deeper meanings of moving water, in this case the river represents a force of nature that is overcome by the cowboy. The beer is actually equated to nature with the words "brewed natural as a mountain stream" and by showing the beer cans emerging dripping with water from the stream. Finally, the ad may encourage a kind of magical reasoning that allows consumers to "feel" they can acquire some of the power and purity of the mountain stream by ingesting the product.

Finally, this ad strongly communicates several basic cultural meanings that consumers can acquire by drinking Busch beer. These include the cultural myths of freedom, challenge, mastery over nature, and individual accomplishment. In addition, the ad conveys meanings of pride and accomplishment that are signified by drinking the beer as a reward for success.

Source: Lance Strate, "The Cultural Meaning of Beer Commercials," in *Advances in Consumer Research,* vol 18, eds. Rebecca H. Holman and Michael R.Solomon (Provo, UT: Association for Consumer Research, 1991), pp. 115–19.

Fitness is a strong cultural value for many American consumers.

athletic footwear and clothing. Dozens of fitness-oriented magazines clutter the newsstands, and more than 10,000 health clubs compete for members. Sales of home exercise machines, bicycles, and many other fitness products have grown steadily.

Related products have also been affected by changes in health and fitness values. Sales of diet beverages of all types are growing at a 20 percent annual rate. Many food companies have changed their formulas to reduce product attributes such as salt, sugar, and fat, which have been linked to negative health consequences.

Changing Values in America

The constant changes in American cultural values have significant effects on the success of a company's marketing strategies. Changes in values can create problems (as well as opportunities) for marketers. As consumers' values change, their means-end connections with existing products and brands also change,

HIGHLIGHT 13.3

Changing Cultural Meanings of Products

No meaning lasts forever. Consider the demise of the so-called yuppies (young urban professionals), perhaps the most prominent symbol of the consumption-oriented 1980s in the United States. By the early 1990s, many yuppie products had lost some of their status meaning, as manufacturers desperately tried to distance themselves from the dated yuppie image.

BMW, "The Ultimate Driving Machine," was probably the ultimate yuppie status symbol in the United States during the 1980s. But sales dropped for the Bayerische Motoren Werke (Bavarian Motor Works) Company in the late 1980s and early 1990s as people's perceptions and values changed and the American economy cooled. By 1989, BMW sales in the United States were more than 30 percent below their peak in 1986. In reaction, BMW developed new marketing strategies. It cut prices up to 9 percent on some models and introduced two lower-priced, "entry-level" models.

Few products gained favor faster with the yuppie crowd (and their imitators) than Corona beer, imported from Mexico. The beer developed a distinctive image, partly because it was sold in clear-glass bottles rather than brown, and partly because people added a sliver of lime before drinking it, which made the product seem more exotic. Sales surged in the mid-1980s, but then dropped precipitously at the end of the decade as yuppies and their imitators moved on to the next fashion. In 1989, Corona sold about 16 million cases of beer in the United States, a far cry from the U.S. sales of 22.5 million cases two years earlier. Although the company fought back with marketing strategies such as 12-packs, a novelty for imported beer, it seems unlikely Corona will ever again enjoy the powerful cultural meanings that fueled its early success.

When Swatch introduced its colorful (and reasonably priced) watches in the United States in about 1982, it virtually created the market for fashion timepieces. By 1990, however, many adults considered the watches a bit frivolous. So the Swiss company introduced new models to attract adults and began to advertise on network television.

Source: Kathleen Deveny, "Reality of the '90s Hits Yuppie Brands," *The Wall Street Journal*, December 10, 1990, pp. B1, B5.

which can change the important consumer-product relationship. If consumers become dissatisfied with current purchases, they may begin looking for more satisfying alternatives. One scholar eloquently described such changes at the birth of the consumer society in 18th-century England: "'Luxuries' came to be seen as mere 'decencies,' and 'decencies' came to be seen as 'necessities.' Even 'necessities' underwent a dramatic metamorphosis in style, variety, and availability."[18] Highlight 13.3 describes several cases in which value changes have changed consumers' meanings for products.

For instance, after the consumption excesses of the 1980s, many consumers became less materialistic and more concerned about social issues such as protection of the environment. The growth of environmentalism as a cultural value has affected the disposable diaper market dominated by Procter & Gamble and Kimberly-Clark Corporation, makers of Pampers and Huggies (with 25 and 32 percent market shares in the United States in1989).[19] By the late 1980s, an increasing number of consumers began to see disposable diapers as a significant contributor to the solid waste (garbage) that was filling American landfills. Essentially, disposable diapers had become a means to a negative end for some, but not all, consumers. In 1990, about half of customers did not want any restrictions or taxes on the product. In response to these cultural changes, P&G and other companies claimed that cloth (reusable) diapers had about the same environmental impact as disposables after considering the water and energy required to clean and dry them. The major companies also worked to develop a more biodegradable diaper. Highlight 13.4 presents other examples of companies' responses to changing environmental values.

Changes in consumers' values and behaviors can create new marketing opportunities, too. For instance, chicken restaurants saw significant growth as consumers turned away from burgers to products seen as more healthful. Increasing health values have led many restaurants to add "healthy or heart-conscious" items (with reduced levels of fat, sugar, and cholesterol) to their menus. Cashing in on this trend to make its products more healthy and nutritious has not been easy for Kentucky Fried Chicken.[20] For instance, early consumer reponse to a new skinless (lower fat) chicken product was weak. The company even started calling itself KFC to de-emphasize the word *fried.*

Changes in cultural values are usually accompanied by changes in behavior. For instance, the values of convenience and saving time led to increases in home shopping behaviors, including use of catalogs and TV shopping channels. Marketers often talk about behavior in terms of lifestyles—ways in which people live their lives to achieve important ends or values. Figure 13.2 lists several important lifestyle trends in American culture along with an example of how each may affect marketing strategies. Marketers should monitor these changes and adjust their marketing strategies as necessary.

Culture as a Process

Understanding the content of culture is important for developing effective marketing strategies, but it is also useful to think about *culture as a process.* Figure 13.3 presents a model of the cultural process.[21] It shows that cultural meaning can be found in three locations—in the social and physical environment, in products and services, and in individual consumers. The **cultural**

HIGHLIGHT 13.4

Environmental Concern: A Growing Cultural Value

Many companies are responding to consumers' growing environment values. Many trend watchers think the 1990s will be the decade of environmentalism, and environmental concern will become an important value for consumers all around the world. Some claim environmentalism is "absolutely the most important issue for business." Among the companies that are reacting are the following:

- Proctor & Gamble and many other marketers are trying to cast their products in an environmentally friendly light by using recycled materials for packaging and formulating some products to reduce pollution.
- Wal-Mart has asked all its suppliers for more recycled or recyclable products, which it then features prominently with in-store signs.
- Du Pont has stated a "zero pollution" goal. Among other initiatives, the company is getting out of a $750 million-per-year business in chlorofluorocarbons, which damage the earth's ozone layer, and has spent nearly $200 million developing a safe alternative.
- McDonald's is working to cut the huge waste stream produced at its 8,500 U.S. restaurants each day. For instance, it requires suppliers to use corrugated boxes containing at least 35 percent recyclable materials. In 1991, McDonald's was testing a variety of things including reusable salad lids, nonplastic utensils, pump-style containers for condiments, and refillable coffee mugs.

The growing environmental concern of consumers creates not just problems for companies, but also opportunities. Big business is forecast for companies in recycling, pollution control technology, and pollution cleanup. Consider the opportunity to design environmentally friendly packaging for compact disks. CDs now come in a plastic "jewel box" inside a long cardboard box. Originally the long box was developed to discourage shoplifting and to fit into existing record racks in stores. Besides requiring near gorilla strength to open, the discarded cardboard created 23 million pounds of garbage in 1990.

Source: Frank Edward Allen, "McDonald's Launches Plan to Cut Waste," *The Wall Street Journal,* April, 17, 1991, pp. B1, B4; Meg Cox, "Music Firms Try Out 'Green' CD Boxes," *The Wall Street Journal,* July 25, 1991, p. B1; and David Kirkpatrick, "Environmentalism: The New Crusade," *Fortune,* February 12, 1990, pp. 44–55.

process concerns *how cultural meaning is moved or transferred between these locations* by organizations (government, business, religion, education) and individuals in the society.

The model implies two driving forces for meaning transfer in a consumption-oriented society. First, consumers actively seek to acquire cultural meanings to create desirable personal identities or self-concepts. Second, marketing

FIGURE 13.2
Lifestyle Trends in America

Trends	Impact on Marketing Strategies
Control of time	Americans increasingly value their time and seek greater control of its use.
Component lifestyles	Consumer behavior is becoming more individualistic because of the wider array of available choices.
Culture of convenience	With the rising number of two-income households, consumers are spending more on services to have more free time for themselves.
Growth of home shopping	Consumers want more time for themselves and are frustrated by waiting in checkout lines.
Shopping habits of the sexes to converge	Men continue to do more of the shopping, and working women take on many male shopping habits.
Escalation of home entertainment	The VCR is the force behind the boom in home entertainment, which will bring about increased purchases of takeout food and changes in the nature of home furnishings and appliances.
Dressing for success	There has been a widespread return to fashion and concern for one's appearance.
Spread of the diversified diet	Americans are eating differently (e.g., lower beef consumption, greater fish consumption).
Self-imposed prohibition of alcohol	The trend has been toward "lighter" drinks (e.g., vodka, "lite" beer), as well as a decline in the overall consumption of alcohol.
Lightest drink of all—water	Bottled or sparkling water is considered by so-called yuppies to be chic; some individuals are concerned about the quality of their tap water.

("*continued*")

strategies are intended to transfer cultural meanings to products and services to make them attractive to consumers. In sum, this model explains the cultural process as it occurs in a highly developed consumer society.

Moving Meanings from the Cultural World into Products

Advertising has been the most closely studied method of transferring meaning from the cultural world into products.[22] From a cultural process perspective, advertising is like a funnel though which meaning from the cultural world is poured into consumer goods.[23] Advertisers must determine what cultural meanings they want their products to have and then find ways to communicate those cultural meanings in an ad, often using symbols of the desired cultural meanings.[24]

FIGURE 13.2
continued

Trends	Impact on Marketing Strategies
Bifurcation of product markets	There is a growing distance between upscale and downscale markets, and companies caught in the middle may fare poorly.
Product and service quality—more important, if not everything	Products falling below acceptance quality standards will be treated more mercilessly.
Heightened importance of visuals in advertising and marketing	With the VCR revolution, the imperative for advertisers is to make the message seen, not heard.
Fragmentation of media markets	There will be new sources of programming as loyalty to network TV fades.
Return of the family	The family will be seen as something to join, as the baby-boom generation rears its children.
New employee benefits for two-income families	Employers will offer flexible work hours, job sharing, and day-care services.
Growing appeal of work at home	Workers will want to work at home on their own computers.
Older Americans—the next entrepreneurs	Older people want to work past the traditional retirement age and have the resources to invest in their own businesses.
Young American—a new kind of conservative	Although 18 to 29 year-olds are socially liberal, they are economically and politically conservative.
Public relations—tough times ahead for business	Business does not receive the credit it deserves for the creation of new jobs, as people remain suspicious about how business operates.
Nation's mood—the new reality	The euphoric mood of the Reagan administration was divorced from economic realities; Americans are economically more sober today.

Source: Adapted from "31 Major Trends Shaping the Future of American Business," *The Public Pulse* 2, no. 1.

A symbol is something (a word, image, object) that stands for or signifies something else (the desired cultural meaning). For instance, to communicate cool, refreshing, summertime meanings, Nestle Nestea showed a person falling, fully clothed, into a cool swimming pool. The long-running "Heartbeat of America" campaign for Chevrolet showed various symbols of small-town American life to represent traditional American values such as simplicity, family, patriotism, and friendship. Some animals have distinctive symbolic meanings that marketers can associate with products (the bull in Merrill Lynch ads, the bald eagle in ads for the U.S. Postal Service's Express Mail service, the ram for Dodge "ram tough" trucks). The naked bodies shown in Calvin Klein's ads for

FIGURE 13.3
A Model of the Cultural Process

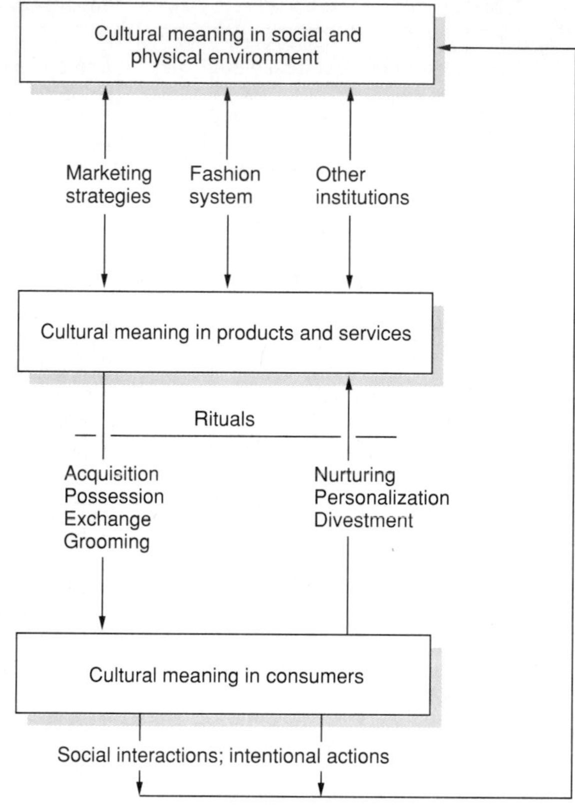

Source: Adapted from Grant McCracken, "Culture and Consumption: A Theoretical Account of the Structure and Movement of the Cultural Meaning of Consumer Goods," *Journal of Consumer Research,* June 1986, pp. 71–84.

Obsession perfume connote obvious meanings about the product. Highlight 13.5 describes another cultural symbol used in advertising.

Although advertising may be the most obvious marketing mechanism for moving meanings, virtually all aspects of marketing strategy are involved in transferring cultural meaning to products. Consider pricing strategies. Discount stores such as K mart and Wal-Mart use low prices to establish the meaning of their stores. For many consumers, high prices have desirable cultural meanings that can be transferred to certain products (Mercedes-Benz cars, Rolex watches, Chivas Regal Scotch, European clothing designers) to create a luxurious, high status, high quality image. Different price endings ($14.87 versus $14.99 versus $15.00) also may have specific cultural meanings.[25]

Japanese automobile companies intentionally design the product attributes of their cars to communicate important cultural meanings. For instance, the design of the automobile interior (leather versus cloth seats, analog versus digital gauges, wood versus plastic dash) as well as the locations of the controls and how they look and feel when one operates them can transfer cultural meaning to the product. Even distribution strategies can influence the transfer of meaning. The limited distribution of Burberry trench coats and related products in better clothing stores enhances their image.

Marketing strategies are not the only influence on meaning transfer from the cultural world to products.[26] For instance, journalists who report the results of product tests of cars, stereo systems, or ski equipment are transferring meaning into the products. The so-called fashion system, including designers, reporters, opinion leaders, and celebrities, transfers fashion-related meanings into clothing, cooking, and home furnishing products.[27] Consumer advocates such as Ralph Nader (who convinced people the Chevrolet Corvair was unsafe) or governmental agencies such as the Consumer Product Safety Commission (that required warning labels telling people not to step on the top level of a stepladder) are involved in transferring meanings to products.

Cultural Meanings in Products

It is widely recognized that products, stores, and brands contain cultural meaning.[28] For instance, certain brands have meanings concerning the sex and age groups for which they are appropriate—Virginia Slims cigarettes are for women, Camels are for men; Rollerblades and T-shirts are for young people, gardening tools and laxatives are for older people. Some products embody cultural meanings such as the Cooperstown Collection of high quality reproductions of baseball team jerseys, jackets, and hats, including defunct teams such as the Washington Senators.[29] Buying and using such products make their cultural meanings tangible and visible and communicate those meanings to others.

It is important to recognize several important points concerning the cultural meanings of products. First, product meanings are likely to vary across different societies. For instance, most societies have favorite foods that represent important meanings in that culture, but not in others—the Danes love eel, Mexicans love chilies, Irish love Guinness, French love cheese, Americans love hamburgers.

Second, all people do not always perceive a product, brand, or activity to have the same cultural meaning. For example, some teenagers might begin to smoke Marlboros to gain the positive cultural meanings they perceive to be contained in the act of smoking and in the brand. Other teens might reject smoking to avoid gaining the negative meanings they perceive in the action.

Third, while some of the cultural meanings in products are obvious to anyone who is familiar with that culture, other meanings are hidden. Nearly everyone can recognize the basic cultural meanings in different styles of

HIGHLIGHT 13.5

The Cultural Meanings in Products and Brands—"The Jolly Green Giant"

People often are unaware of the cultural origins of everyday objects in their environments, even though they may sense the fundamental meaning of these objects. Consider the Jolly Green Giant, the symbol of the Green Giant Company, canners of vegetables in Le Sueur Valley of Minnesota. In print and TV ads, the Giant stands, hands on hips, towering over the entire valley and looking down on the happy, elfin workers harvesting the succulent produce below. He is green and dressed entirely in green leaves. Perhaps you noticed the Giant doesn't move (think of the consequences for the elves) or say much beyond the obligatory "Ho, ho, ho!" at the end of each ad.

What is the cultural meaning of the Jolly Green Giant? Is the Jolly Green Giant only an easy-to-remember brand symbol or something more? From a cultural perspective, the Jolly Green Giant can be seen as a 20th-century manifestation of ancient European fertility symbols that represented the spirit of vegetation.

Figures clothed in leaves have deep cultural meanings that date back hundreds of years. Fraser described many of these symbolic figures in his masterwork, *The Golden Bough*. In many early European cultures, people celebrated the rites of spring by honoring the spirits of sacred trees or plants. By the 19th century, this ritual had become personalized in that a person from each rural community was dressed in leaves or flowers.

clothing (jeans and a sweatshirt versus a business suit), makes of automobiles (Mercedes-Benz versus Ford versus Honda), types of stores (Penny's versus Wal-Mart versus Nordstrom or Saks). But other, less obvious cultural meanings in products may not be fully recognized by consumers. For instance, you might not realize the important meanings of a stereo or a bicycle until it is broken or stolen. A research study interviewed consumers whose houses had been burglarized to learn the most significant meanings of the missing possessions.[30]

Many companies do not know much about the symbolic cultural meanings of their products. This was the case in 1985 when the Coca-Cola Company changed the taste attributes of Coca-Cola to make it slightly sweeter with less of a bite.[31] When it introduced new Coke, the company was surprised by an immediate flurry of protests from customers. Millions of consumers had consumed Coca-Cola as kids and had strong cultural meanings for (and emotional ties to) the original product. These consumers resented its removal from the marketplace, and some of them brought lawsuits against the company. In

For instance, the Gypsies of Transylvania and Romania had Green George, a boy "covered from top to toe in green leaves and blossoms." In Bavaria (southern Germany), the leaf person was Quack, in England, it was Jack in the Green, in Switzerland, it was the Whitsuntide Lout. Other popular names for the fertility symbol were the Leaf King, the Grass King, the May King, and the Queen of May.

Even as recently as 100 years ago, fertility figures representing the spirit of vegetation could be found in many parts of Eastern Europe, Germany, and England. Although the details of the costume and the ritual varied from place to place, the overall concept and the representation of the central figure were consistent. A youthful person was dressed with leaves and other vegetation. Sometimes the person was symbolically dunked into a pond or stream. Thus were the spirits of fertility and water honored, and the community was assured continued supplies of water and forage.

Clearly, these fertility figures are similar to the Jolly Green Giant. Is this just a coincidence, or does the obvious symbolism of such a figure still convey compelling meanings to the sophisticated citizens of the modern world? Did the advertising creative staff at Leo Burnett, a Chicago advertising agency, intentionally appropriate an ancient fertility symbol, or did the idea emerge from people's collective unconscious? And how did the meanings of a giant get added to the equation? Whatever these answers, the Jolly Green Giant seems to represent deep, symbolic cultural meanings that are partially responsible for the success of the product.

Can you think of other examples of ancient cultural symbols used in modern advertising. How about the Keebler elves? What about the genie-like Mr. Clean (called Mr. Proper in Germany/Austria) or Red Devil tools? Do you remember the white knight of Ajax fame who rode in with lance at the ready and blasted the dirt out of women's laundry?

Source: Tom E. Sullenberger, "Ajax Meets the Jolly Green Giant: Some Observations on the Use of Folklore and Myth in American Mass Marketing," 1974, *Journal of American Folklore* 87, pp. 53–65.

response, Coca-Cola rather quickly reintroduced the original product under the brand name Coca-Cola Classic. (The Marketing Strategy in Action in Chapter 6 deals with this situation.)

Finally, as we see later, many products contain personal meaning, in addition to cultural meanings. Personal meanings are moved into products by the actions of individual consumers. Although these meanings tend to be highly idiosyncratic and unique to each consumer, they are important as a source of intrinsic self-relevance that can affect consumers' felt involvement with the product.

Moving Meanings from Products into Consumers

The cultural process model identifies rituals as ways of moving meanings from the product to the consumer. **Rituals** are *symbolic actions performed by consumers to create, affirm, evoke, or revise certain cultural meanings.*[32] For instance, the consumption rituals performed on Thanksgiving Day by American families who feast on turkey and all the trimmings affirm their ability to provide abundantly for their needs.

Not all rituals are formal ceremonies such as a special dinner, a graduation, or a wedding. Rather, many rituals are common aspects of everyday life, although people usually do not recognize their behavior as ritualistic. Consumer researchers have begun to investigate the role of rituals in consumer behavior, but our knowledge still is limited.[33] Below, we discuss five consumption-related rituals involved in the movement of meaning between product and consumer – acquisition, possession, exchange, grooming, and divestment rituals.[34] Future research is likely to reveal other ritualistic behaviors that consumers perform to obtain the cultural meanings in products.

Acquisition Rituals

Some of the cultural meanings in products are transferred to consumers through the simple acquisition rituals of purchasing and consuming the product. For instance, buying and eating an ice cream cone is necessary to receive the meanings the product contains (fun, relaxation, a reward for hard work, a treat or pick-me-up). Other acquisition behaviors have ritualistic qualities that are important for meaning transfer. For example, collectors who are interested in possessing scarce or unique products (antiques, stamps or coins, beer cans, etc.) may perform special search rituals when they go out on the hunt, including wearing special lucky clothes. Highlight 13.6 describes some examples of search rituals performed by shoppers at a large midwestern flea market.

The bargaining rituals involved in negotiating the price of an automobile, stereo system, or some object at a garage sale can help transfer important meanings to the buyer (I got a good deal). Consider how an avid plate collector in his early 60s describes the meanings conveyed by bidding rituals at an auction or a flea market.[35]

> There's no Alcoholics Anonymous for collectors. You just get bit by the bug and that's it. The beauty and craftsmanship of some of these things is amazing. They were made by people who cared. There's nothing like getting ahold of them for yourself. Especially if you get it for a song and you sing it yourself. It's not just *getting* a great deal, it's *knowing* that you've got a great deal that makes for the thrill. It's even better if you had to bid against someone for it.

Obviously, the acquisition rituals performed in obtaining products (purchase, search, bargaining, bidding) can help move meanings to the buyer.

Possession Rituals

Possession rituals help consumers acquire the meanings in products. For instance, the new owners of a house (or apartment) might invite friends and relatives to a housewarming party to admire their dwelling and formally establish its meanings. Many consumers perform similar ritualistic displays of a new purchase (a car, clothing, stereo system) to show off their new possession, solicit

HIGHLIGHT 13.6

ACQUIRING THE MEANINGS FROM PRODUCTS—HUNTING RITUALS

Searching for appropriate products may be considered a ritual that can influence the types of meanings gained when one buys a product. Consider the rituals followed by avid collectors of antiques and other collectibles (rare coins, political buttons, beer cans, etc.) who often frequent so-called flea markets, swap meets, and arts and crafts shows where many dealers display their goods.

One large midwestern flea market is open every Saturday and Sunday throughout the year. Although the gates officially open at 7 A.M., many consumers follow the ritual of arriving several hours before to look over the merchandise and get an early deal. In the dark of winter, they hunt the grounds by flashlight. Other consumers follow the ritual of coming late on the last day in hopes of getting a good deal from dealers who do not want to pack up their merchandise for the return trip home.

Some consumers have highly developed search strategies (rituals) such as beginning with the outer row of booths and working toward the center. Some people may go around quickly until they see something interesting, while others go slowly and examine each dealer's merchandise thoroughly. Bargaining rituals may also be an important aspect of the hunt at a flea market. Some consumers feel they got a good deal only if they had a bargaining negotiation with the seller in which the price was reduced. These examples show that "consuming is an elaborate social game, as it has always been in human cultures."

Source: Adapted from John F. Sherry, Jr., "A Sociocultural Analysis of a Midwestern American Flea Market," *Journal of Consumer Research,* June, 1990, pp. 13–30.

the admiration of their friends, and gain reassurance that they made a good purchase.

Other possession rituals involve moving personal meaning from the customer into the product. For instance, product nurturing rituals put personal meaning into the product (washing your car each Saturday; organizing your record or CD collection; tuning your bicycle; working in your garden).[36] Later, these meanings can be moved back to the consumer where they are experienced and enjoyed as satisfaction or pride. These possession rituals help create strong, involving relationships between products and consumers.

Personalizing rituals serve a similar function. Many people who buy a used car or a previously owned house perform ritualistic actions to remove meanings left over from the previous owner and move new meanings of their own into the product. For instance, consumers will purchase special accessories for their new or used car to personalize it (new floor mats, a better radio, different wheels and/or tires, custom stripes). Repainting, wallpapering, or installing carpeting are rituals that personalize a house to "make it your own."

Exchange Rituals

Certain meanings can be transferred to consumers through exchange rituals such as giving gifts.[37] For instance, giving wine or flowers to your host or hostess on arriving at a formal dinner party is a ritual that transfers cultural meanings (thanks, graciousness, generosity).

People often select gifts for anniversaries, birthdays, or special holidays such as Christmas that contain special cultural meanings to be transferred to the receiver. For instance, giving a nice watch, luggage, or a new car to a college graduate might be intended to convey cultural meanings of achievement, adult status, or independence. Parents often give gifts to their children that are intended to transfer very particular cultural meanings (a puppy represents

Dining in a fine restaurant involves a number of rituals.

Opening gifts at Christmas or for a birthday is an important ritual for many families.

Auctions, in this case of fine art, involve a number of ritualistic behaviors.

HIGHLIGHT 13.7

Grooming Rituals

A recent study attempted to measure the symbolic, and perhaps largely unconscious, meanings associated with consumers' personal grooming rituals. This research found that hair-care activities dominated the grooming behavior of the young adults (18- to 25-years-old) in the sample. For instance, most of these consumers shampooed their hair nearly every day, and many felt frustrated and emotional about this activity. For instance, one 20-year-old woman said: "Fixing my hair is the most difficult. I spend hours – actually hours – doing my hair. It drives me crazy!"

Because many of the meanings associated with hair care were thought to be relatively unconscious, direct questioning could not be used to tap into these deeper, more symbolic meanings; consumers might just offer rationalizations for their behavior. So the researcher showed male and female consumers pictures of a young man using a blow dryer and a young woman in curlers applying makeup. Each consumer was asked to write a detailed story about the person in the picture. Their stories give some insights into the meanings of these grooming rituals.

For many consumers, hair grooming with the blow-dryer seemed to symbolize an active, take-charge personality who is preparing to go on the "social prowl." For example, one 20-year-old man said, "Jim is supposed to stay home and study tonight, but he's getting ready to go out, anyway. He's hoping to meet some hot chicks, and he wants his hair to look just right."

Symbolic meanings about work and success were prominent in other stories, as the following excerpt from a 21-year-old woman's story illustrates: "Susan is getting ready for her first presentation, and she's very nervous. If it goes well, maybe her boss will help with a down payment on a new car."

Uncovering consumers' deep, symbolic meanings for certain products can be quite difficult. However, the knowledge may give marketers useful insights into consumers' reactions to their strategies.

Source: Adapted with permission from "The Ritual Dimension of Consumer Behavior," by Dennis W. Rook, from the *Journal of Consumer Research,* December 1985, pp. 251–64.

responsibility; a bike represents freedom; a computer conveys the importance of learning and mastery).

Grooming Rituals

Certain cultural meanings are perishable in that they tend to fade. For instance, personal care products such as shampoo, mouthwash, and deodorants and beauty products (cosmetics, skin care) contain a variety of cultural meanings (attractive, sexy, confident, influence over others). But, when transferred to consumers, these meanings are not permanent. Such meanings must be continually renewed by drawing them out of a product each time it is used. Grooming rituals involve particular ways of using personal care and beauty products that coax these cultural meanings out of the product and transfer them to the consumer. Many people are willing to engage in rather elaborate grooming rituals to obtain these meanings (see Highlight 13.7). What types of grooming rituals do you perform when you get ready to go out?

Divestment Rituals

Consumers perform divestment rituals to remove meaning from products. Certain products (items of clothing, a house, a car or motorcycle, a favorite piece of sports equipment) can contain considerable amounts of personal meaning. These meanings may be the basis for a strong customer-product relationship. For instance, products can acquire such personal meaning through long periods of use or because they symbolize important meanings (a chair might be a family heirloom).

Often, consumers believe that some of these personal meanings must be removed before such products can be sold or even thrown away. Thus, for instance, consumers may wash or dry-clean a favorite item of clothing that they plan to give away or donate to charity to remove some of the personal meanings in the product. Consumers might remove certain highly personal parts of a house (a special chandelier), car (a special radio), or motorcycle (a custom seat) before selling it.

In certain cases, the personal meaning in the product is so great the consumer cannot part with the object. Thus, people hang onto their old cars, clothes, or furniture that have sentimental personal meaning. One study found that certain consumers had become highly attached to their Levi's jeans and kept them for years, some as much as 20 or 30 years.[38] These consumers associated many salient meanings with Levi's jeans, including the confidence they felt when wearing the product and the feeling that Levi's were appropriate in many social situations. Other consumers talked as if their Levi's were an old friend and companion who had accompanied the consumer on many adventures, and the jeans were valued for the memories they contained. If divestment rituals are unable to remove these meanings, consumers may keep such objects forever or at least until the personal meanings have faded and become less intense.

Cultural Meanings in Consumers

Consumers select and acquire cultural meanings to use in creating their self-identities. Buying goods is one way to obtain cultural meanings to be used in the ongoing process of self-construction. Consider the sports fan who buys a team hat or jacket. Major League Baseball Properties, a licensing and marketing organization, sell authentic jerseys from the New York Yankees (about $175) and the 1919 Chicago Black Sox ($245) to middle-aged fans who want to identify with their favorite teams, present and past.[39] Or consumers might buy Ben and Jerry's Rain Forest Crunch ice cream (made from nuts grown in the

Amazon rain forest) or Tide detergent sold in packages made from recycled materials to acquire the ecological values contained in these products. People buy such products to move important cultural meanings into themselves and to communicate these meanings to others.

Americans have a lot of freedom to create different selves, through their choice of lifestyles, environments, and products. Self-construction activity is especially intense during the teenage and young adult years. Young people try different social roles and self-identities and often purchase products to gain meanings related to these roles. Thus, teenage rebellions against parents' values and lifestyles usually involve the purchase and consumption of certain products. As most people become more mature with age, their self-concepts become more stable (even rigid), and their interest in self-change lessens. Of course, changes, even radical changes, in self-concept are still possible, but they are increasingly rare. Even so, consumers still use the cultural meanings in products to maintain and fine-tune their current self-identities.

Although products can transfer useful meanings to consumers, goods can not provide all the meanings that consumers need to construct a healthy self-concept.[40] People obtain self-relevant meanings from many other sources including their work, family, religious experiences, and various social activities. Often, the meanings gained through these activities are more self-relevant and more satisfying than those obtained through product consumption.

Unfortunately, especially in highly developed consumption societies, many people consume products in an attempt to acquire important life meanings. Some of these consumers may engage in almost pathological levels of consumption as they desperately purchase products seeking to acquire cultural meanings with which to construct a satisfactory self-concept. Such consumers can end up heavily in debt and very unsatisfied.

Most people have favorite possessions that are filled with very important, self-relevant meanings. People have high levels of felt involvement with such objects. Researchers have begun to study these cherished objects to understand consumer/product relationships.[41] For instance, elderly persons tend to feel strong attachments to objects such as photographs or furniture that remind them of past events,[42] while younger consumers tend to value objects that allow them to be active in self-relevant ways (sports or hobby equipment, work-related objects such as books or computers). Marketers need to understand these consumer/product relationships to develop effective strategies.

Moving Meaning to the Cultural Environment

The cultural process model in Figure 13.3 shows that the meanings in consumers can be transferred to the broad cultural environment in two ways. Because a society consists of many individuals living and working together, culture (shared meaning) is created by the people in the society. Much of the movement of meaning to the cultural environment is an automatic consequence of the daily social interactions among people. Sometimes, however, people intentionally try to create new cultural meanings in an attempt to change society. For instance, various interest groups in society (punks, greens or environmental activists, gay rights activists) try to influence others to adopt new cultural meanings. Consumer interest groups have similar goals.

In sum, Figure 13.3 portrays the cultural process as a *continuous and reciprocal movement of meanings* between the overall cultural environment, organizations, and individuals in the society. Like the Wheel of Consumer Analysis, the influences are reciprocal in that the meanings can flow in both directions.

Marketing Implications

Managing Cultural Meaning

The cultural process model suggests a basic marketing task is to manage the cultural meaning of the brand or product.[43] The shared cultural meanings of a brand are a large part of its economic value or its *brand equity*.[44] Managing brand meanings requires that marketers identify the brand meanings shared by consumers and monitor changes in those meanings. Means-end analysis would be useful for this purpose. Marketing strategies might be directed at maintaining positive brand meanings or creating new meanings. These strategies would have to select appropriate meanings from the cultural environment and move or transfer them into products and brands.

Although marketers usually think cultural meanings are fixed or static and are not affected much by a company's actions, marketing strategies do influence the overall cultural environment. A conspicuous example is the proliferation of marketing stimuli in the physical environment (signs, billboards, ads, stores, advertisements). Less obvious is how the huge volume of marketing strategies affects our social environment and the shared meanings of modern life.[45]

Using Celebrity Endorsers in Ads

A popular advertising strategy in North America and Japan for moving cultural meanings into products and brands is to use celebrities to endorse the product.[46] Among the celebrities who appear in ads in the early 1990s were the actor Michael J. Fox (Pepsi), Cher, and the ballet dancer Mikhail Baryshnikov (cologne), CEOs Lee Iacocco (Chrysler) and Victor Kiam (Remington razors), singers Whitney Houston and Michael Jackson, basketball player Michael Jordon (Nike), test pilot Chuck Yeager (car batteries), Tommy LaSorta (diet aid), and politician Tip O'Neill (a hotel chain).

From a cultural perspective, celebrities are cultural objects with specific cultural meanings. Consider, for instance, the meanings associated with James Garner, TV star and spokesperson for the Beef Council, among other products.[47] According to one analyst,

> "Garner does not play himself, the person, nor does he play a particular fictive character. Instead, he plays . . . the generalized James Garner role, the type for which James Garner is always cast—handsome, gentle, bumbling, endearing, a combination of Bret Maverick from "Maverick" and Jim Rockford from "The

> Rockford Files." The Garner celebrity is capable, but occasionally incompetent and bumbling, forthright but unassuming, and usually the master of his fate, but occasionally up against fate (usually comic situation).

For many people, Garner the celebrity offers an attractive set of self-relevant meanings.

In developing an effective celebrity endorsement strategy, marketers must be careful to select a celebrity who has appropriate meanings consistent with the overall marketing strategy (the intended meanings) for the product. For example, celebrities such as Bill Murray, Sylvester Stallone, Joanne Woodward, or Suzanne Sommers have relatively clear meanings, based largely on the types of roles they usually play. Musicians such as Elton John and Sting (for Coke) or Ray Charles (for Pepsi) have distinctive cultural images based on their records, live performances, and video appearances, which enhances their appeal as celebrity spokespersons. Some celebrities such as Madonna have shrewdly re-created their images (and their cultural meaning) over time as the appeal of one set of cultural meanings wanes.

Celebrities who have been typecast (something most actors complain about) are more likely to have shared cultural meanings that can be associated with a product. The actress Meryl Streep, for instance, may not be a desirable spokesperson because she has played such a wide variety of roles and does not have a clear set of cultural meanings.

Sometimes the cultural meanings of a celebrity spokesperson are rleated to their credibility and expertise concerning the product. For instance, Cher and Elizabeth Taylor promote their own perfume brands while Phil and Steve Mahre, the twin American ski racers, promote K2 skis. In other cases, the celebrity's cultural meanings are not logically linked to the product, but the marketer hopes the general meanings of the celebrity as a credible and trustworthy person will help transfer important meanings to the product. Apparently on this basis, Bill Cosby has been a spokesperson for Jello, E. F. Hutton, and Kodak film processing.

Marketers need to understand more about how celebrities transfer to the product. What happens to the cultural meanings of celebrities who are disgraced (Ben Johnson is caught using steroids, Pete Rose is jailed for income tax evasion), fall from public favor (an actor plays poorly in several films), retire from public life (Larry Bird stops playing basketball, Ingmar Bergman stops making films), or return again to fame and favor as their celebrity status is partially renewed (Bob Dylan or Mickey Rooney)? How can marketers use such celebrities in transferring cultural meanings to their products and brands? Do consumers gain the meanings embodied by a celebrity merely by purchasing the endorsed brand, or are ritualistic behaviors necessary?

Although it is popular to criticize the North American and European fascination with celebrities as trivial and shallow, celebrities represent important cultural meanings that many consumers find personally relevant. By purchasing and using the product endorsed by the celebrity, consumers can obtain some of those meanings and use them in constructing a satisfying self-concept.

Helping Consumers Obtain Cultural Meanings

By understanding the role of rituals in consumer behavior, marketers can create or encourage rituals that help transfer important cultural meanings from products to the customer. For instance, real estate firms might develop an elaborate purchase ritual, perhaps including an exchange of gifts on the purchase occasion, to verify the transfer of the house and its meanings to the buyer. Some upscale clothing stores have developed elaborate shopping and buying rituals for their affluent customers, including being shown to a private room, served coffee or wine, and presented with a selection of clothes. People participate in many rituals when dining in a fine restaurant that transfer special meanings to consumers including being seated by the maitre d', talking to the wine steward, using different silverware and glasses, eating each course separately, and so on.

Finally, consider the strategies used by Nissan to create rituals for American buyers that help transfer meanings about its Infinity luxury car, to consumers.[48] Dealers are supposed to gently welcome customers Japanese-style, as honored guests (not aggressively descend on the "mooches," a derogatory term for a naive customer used by some American car salespeople). Tea or coffee is to be offered, served on fine Japanese china. Each Infinity dealership should have a special shoki-screened contemplation room where consumers can sit quietly with the car, "meditating" about their purchase and the consumer/product relationship. These rituals help reinforce the low-pressure, relaxed meanings Nissan wants to develop about the Infinity approach to car selling.

Cross-Cultural Influences

Foreign markets are becoming more important for many businesses, including the U.S. film industry. Because domestic ticket sales have been flat over the past decade (about 1 billion tickets per year), film companies have looked to foreign markets for growth. In 1990, major U.S. film studios received about 35 percent of their total revenues from foreign markets, compared to 50 percent for smaller companies.[49] Thus, U.S. companies need to develop films that appeal to both U.S. and foreign consumers.

To develop strategies that are effective in different cultures, marketers have to understand the differences in cultural meanings in different societies. In this section, we examine **cross-cultural differences** in meanings and consider how these cross-cultural differences among societies affect consumers. We also discuss how marketers can treat cross-cultural differences in developing international marketing strategies.

Issues in Cross-Cultural Analysis

Cross-Cultural Boundaries

Cross-cultural differences do not always coincide with national borders. This is obvious in many countries where cultural differences among internal social groups are as great as between separate nations. Consider Yugoslavia (with several regions including Slovenia, Croatia, Serbia), the former Soviet Union (with 15 republics and many large cultural differences), Belgium (with two language cultures—Flemish and French), Canada (two language cultures—English and French), Switzerland (with German, French, Italian, and Swiss-speaking regions). Understanding the cultural influences in such regions requires an analysis of subcultures, discussed in Chapter 14.

Likewise, national borders do not always demarcate clear cross-cultural differences. For instance, many people living on either side on the long Canadian-U.S. border share similar cultural characteristics (French-speaking Quebec is an exception). Likewise, the people in southern Austria and northern Italy, or northern France and southern Belguim, share many similarities.

Differences in Consumption Culture

The level of consumption orientation in different markets is an important cross-cultural factor that companies should consider when developing international marketing strategies. The opening example pointed out that a large part of U.S. culture involves consumption activities. Many other areas of the world—including Canada, most Western European countries, and Japan—also have strong consumer cultures. Even in relatively poor countries, significant segments of society may have a developing consumer culture. For instance, India, Mexico, and many South American countries have a large middle class of consumers that can consume at significant levels. The Asian countries of the so-called Pacific Rim have a rapidly growing middle class with substantial spending power (Highlight 13.8 provides more details on this vast market).

In much of the world, however, people have less opportunity to participate in a consumption culture. For instance, the ordinary citizens of many Eastern European countries, the former Soviet Union, China, India, and most Third World countries do not have sufficient purchasing power to consume at high levels, nor are these societies able to produce goods in sufficient number and variety to meet the consumption needs of their people.

Similar Cross-Cultural Changes

It is becoming more common to find similar cultural changes occurring in many societies around the world at about the same time. For instance, the social roles for women in North American society have changed considerably over the past 20 years. As more women worked outside the home, their values, goals, beliefs, and behaviors have changed.[50] Similar changes have occurred around the world. Now, modern women in America and Europe, and increasingly in Japan and other countries, want more egalitarian marriages. They want their husbands to share in the housework and nurturing of children, and they want to establish a personal identity outside the family unit. These common cross-cultural changes have created similar marketing opportunities in many societies (for convenience products and time-saving services).

Everywhere people want more leisure and more free time. Even the world-champion workaholics, the Japanese, where up to 60 percent of workers spend

HIGHLIGHT 13.8

New Mass Markets Develop in Asia

Significant cultural changes are happening in Asia, and these changes are opening up new marketing opportunities for companies. Some of the factors fueling these massive changes in culture are listed below.

People. About 1.7 billion people live in the Asian Pacific Rim region. Although population growth is slowing, there still will be an additional 400 million people in the next 20 years. Thirty percent will be in their 30s and 40s, the prime earning and spending years.

Income. A decade of rising prosperity has spread relative affluence throughout the population. One estimate was that 72 million people in the Pacific Rim (not including Japan) had household incomes of $10,000 or more. To put it into perspective, South Korea and Taiwan, with populations of 42 million and 20 million, will have per capita incomes of $11,000 and $13,000 by 2000. These levels are slightly above current incomes in Spain and Ireland.

Cities. As has happened elsewhere, Asian people are moving off the farms and into the cities. For example, in Korea, the population went from 72 percent rural to 73 percent urban in just 30 years. In less developed countries, still largely rural, urban areas are growing rapidly. As one Asia expert puts it, "When you shift from a rural to an urban lifestyle, from spending 12 to 16 hours a day in a field or rice paddy, to working in a factory for 8 to 10 hours, suddenly things happen to you. Your values and motivations change."

Women. Almost everywhere in Asia, women are staying in school longer, marrying later, and entering the work force in greater numbers.

Families. Families are changing rapidly in Asian countries. Women are having fewer children, later in life, as in the West. The number of people in each household is decreasing, but the number of households is increasing, which creates larger markets for many types of consumer goods (appliances, home furnishings).

Communications. The incredible ability to communicate easily, quickly, and relatively cheaply around the world accelerates these cultural changes. Consumers in Taiwan and Hong Kong know what's happening in Japan and the States. Trends and fads catch on quickly everywhere. For instance, the movie "Dick Tracy" opened in Hong Kong less than one month after its U.S. opening, accompanied by the T-shirts and toys. Not long ago, the lag might have been two years.

In sum, these similarities between cultures help create global markets for many products.

Source: Ford S. Worthy, "A New Mass Market Emerges," *Fortune,* September 24, 1990, pp. 51–55.

Saturdays on the job, are beginning to loosen up and relax a bit.[51] Although the traditional Japanese values of hard work, dedication, and respect for the established order are still dominant, some Japanese, especially among the young, are starting to see certain aspects of Western culture and lifestyles as preferable to

FIGURE 13.4

A Comparison of Cultural Differences between the United States and East Asian Countries

United States	East Asian Countries
Wealth is more important than equity	Equity is more important than wealth
Consumption is highly valued	Saving and conserving resources are highly valued
Individual is the most important part of society	Group is the most important part of society
Little respect is shown for age and traditional values	Great respect is shown for age and traditional values
Emphasis is on individual motivation	Emphasis is on group motivation
Nuclear families are common	Cohesive and strong extended families are the norm—family ties are important
Protestant work ethic has declined	Work force and societies are highly disciplined and motivated
Distrust of government is pervasive	Public service is a moral responsibility
Personal conflicts are common—many lawyers	Personal conflicts are avoided—few lawyers
Society is fluid; no close social ties	Network of intricate social ties exists
Informality is important	There is a strong sense of protocol and rank
Education is an investment in individual success	Education is an investment in the prestige of the family

Source: Martin C. Schnitzer, Marilyn L. Liebrenz, and Konrad W. Kubin, *International Business* (Cincinnati: South-Western Publishing, 1985), p. 150.

their own.[52] For instance, as the Japanese become more consumption oriented and price conscious, the number of malls and discount stores is increasing rapidly.[53]

Cross-Cultural Differences

Marketers must consider cross-cultural differences when developing marketing strategies for foreign markets. Figure 13.4 presents some differences between the United States and Asian countries; we describe a few other examples below.

Self-Concept

People in different cultures may have strikingly different concepts of themselves and how they should relate to other people.[54] Consider the differences between the vision of an independent self typical in North America and Western Europe and the concept of self as highly interrelated with others that is more common in Japan, India, Africa, South America, and even some southern European cultures.

HIGHLIGHT 13.9

Cross-Cultural Analyses of Gift Giving

Gift giving is a good behavior to observe the influence of culture. Nearly all cultures have strong cultural meanings about gift giving. Flowers, for example, are an appropriate gift to bring to a Danish hostess if you have been invited to dinner; wine (or flowers) would be appropriate in the United States.

Japanese consumers are big gift givers. Especially when they return from trips abroad, the Japanese feel a rather strong social (cultural) obligation to bring souvenir gifts to the folks back home. This type of gift giving is called *omiyage.* Friends, parents, siblings, and relatives are the typical recipients. Accompanying this cultural value are environmental factors that encourage generous gifting. The Japanese are able to import up to $1,600 duty free, compared to a limit of $400 for U.S. citizens.

A quick study of *omiyage* among Japanese tourists at the Los Angeles airport revealed 83 percent had bought *omiyage*, spending an average of $566 on such items compared to $581 on personal items. The number of persons bought for was high (by American standards); 45 percent of Japanese tourists bought *omiyage* gifts for 15 or more people. The stated motivation for *omiyage* buying was reciprocity for previous gifts received. Interestingly, although nearly 80 percent of the tourists mentioned that *omiyage* was a strong social norm in Japan, only 7 percent of the respondents claimed to enjoy buying *omiyage*. Most treated it as a necessary chore.

As for marketing strategies, it is important to know that the packaging and wrapping of *omiyage* gifts has important cultural meaning, partly because gifts are seldom opened in front of the giver. The appearance of the package is highly valued by Japanese.

Source: Terrence H. Witkowski and Yoshito Yamamoto, "Omiyage Gift Purchasing by Japanese Travelers to the U.S.," in *Advances in Consumer Research,* vol. 18 (Provo, Utah: Association for Consumer Research, 1991), pp. 123–28.

Americans with their strong individualistic orientation, tend to think of self in terms of personal abilities and traits that enable people to achieve the ideals of independence from others, freedom of choice, and personal achievement. In contrast, the Japanese tend to value a self that is sensitive to the needs of others, fits into the group, and contributes positively to the harmonious interdependence of the group members. These cross-cultural differences in self-concept are likely to affect how people in those cultures interpret product meanings and use products to achieve important ends in their lives. For example, Highlight 13.9 presents an example of Japanese gift-giving behavior that is strongly affected by the socially oriented self-concept.

The meanings of the end values or goals found in means-end research are likely to be quite different in different cultures, as are the means to achieve it.

Consider the value of self-esteem or "satisfaction with self." North Americans, for instance, might satisfy self-esteem needs by acting in ways that represent their independence and autonomy from the group. But for a Japanese, cooperation with a group is an act that affirms the self. In Japan, giving in to the group is not a sign of weakness (as it might be interpreted in North America), but rather reflects tolerance, self-control, flexibility, and maturity, all aspects of a positive self-image for most Japanese. In contrast, stating one's personal position and trying to get one's way (acts valued in America as "standing up for what one believes") may be thought childish and weak by Japanese.

Materialism

Materialism has been defined as the "importance a consumer attaches to worldly possessions."[55] Consumers with this value tend to acquire many possessions, which they see as important for achieving happiness, self-esteem or social recognition (all prominent values in American culture). Although researchers disagree about its exact definition, **materialism** is a multidimensional value including *possessiveness*, *envy* (displeasure at someone else possessing something) and *nongenerosity* (unwillingness to give or share possessions).[56] Another study points to four dimensions of materialism: possessions are symbols of success or achievement (prominent American values), sources of pleasure, sources of happiness, and representations of indulgence and luxury.[57] Materialistic values underlie the development of a mass consumption society, as we saw in the opening example, and in turn are stimulated by increasing consumption opportunities.

The United States is usually considered to be the most materialistic culture in the world. But a few studies suggest Americans may not be more materialistic than other European societies. For instance, one study found that consumers in the Netherlands had about the same level of general materialism as American consumers.[58] But interestingly, the Dutch consumers were more possessive than Americans. Perhaps it is not accidental that the Dutch have no garage sales, and flea markets are rare. While U.S. consumers seem to replace old products with new ones fairly easily, the Dutch seem to form stronger relationships with their possessions.

Marketing Implications

Marketers must determine which cross-cultural differences are relevant to their situation. A sensitivity to and tolerance for cross-cultural differences in meaning is a highly desirable trait for international marketing managers. Most international companies also hire managers from the local culture because they bring an intimate knowledge of the indigenous cultural meanings to strategic decision making. The Marketing Strategy in Action at the end of this chapter describes what can happen to a company that does not pay attention to the advice of these experts concerning subtle cross-cultural factors.

Although cross-cultural differences can be large and distinctive, there are cases in which people seem to have rather similar values and consumer/product relationships. Some analysts see the entire world as moving toward an "Ameri-

Aspects of American pop culture—jeans, leather motorcycle jackets, hair styles—have been appropriated by young people in other cultures.

canized" culture, although this is a controversial idea. (Highlight 13.10 discusses some examples of the exporting of American popular culture.) To the extent that common cultural meanings are becoming similar across societies, marketers should be able to develop successful strategies that are global in scope.

Developing International Marketing Strategies

Cross-cultural differences provide difficult challenges for international marketers. Even something that seems simple, such as translating a brand or model name into another language, can cause problems. When Coca-Cola was introduced in China in the 1920s, the translated meaning of the brand name was "bite the wax tadpole!" Sales were not good, and the symbols were later changed to mean "happiness in the mouth." American Motors Matador brand had problems in Puerto Rico because matador means "killer." Ford Motor Company changed the name of the Comet to Caliente when it introduced this car in Mexico. The low sales levels were understood when it was discovered that *caliente* is slang for streetwalker. Sunbeam Corporation introduced its mist-producing hair curling iron in the German market under the name Mist-Stick, which translated meant "manure wand."[59]

HIGHLIGHT 13.10

EXPORTING AMERICAN POPULAR CULTURE

Aspects of American culture are becoming increasingly popular around the globe. One can find the icons of American popular culture nearly everywhere. Consider the worldwide presence of Coke and Pepsi, McDonald's and Pizza Hut, Mickey Mouse and Mickey Rourke, cowboys and jazz, American films and Disneyland. The spread of American culture has produced some very incongruous television scenes of Third World protesters (usually young men) burning the American flag or chanting anti-American slogans, while dressed in T-shirts, Nike shoes, and blue jeans. Although some people consider American culture to be distasteful, the general population seems to like many of its forms. Even in Anglophobic France, the uniform of young upper-middle-class Parisian women in 1990 was pure Americana—Calvin Klein jeans, a white button-down oxford shirt, a navy blazer, Bass Weejuns penny loafers, and a Marlboro cigarette.

Consumers around the world are not attracted to American products solely for their intrinsic physical qualities. People don't buy blue jeans because of some universal aesthetic for denim, nor do Coke or Marlboros or Mickey Mouse have physical attributes that are so special. Rather, these prototypically American products are attractive because they are imbued with meanings that symbolize the United States.

What are these special Americana meanings? According to a Yale professor, "It's about a dream, a utopian fantasy. Certainly it is about freedom, the freedom of people to create themselves anew, redefining themselves through the products that they buy and use, the clothes they wear, the music they listen to." Blue jeans, perhaps more than any other product, symbolize America and the individualistic meanings it represents to many. Buying jeans is a way for consumers to share in the American dream of individualism, personal freedom, and other rather mystical meanings associated with America.

It is important to recognize that American culture is popular partly because it is just that—a *popular culture*, not an elitist culture created by and for the aristocracy in a society. American culture is for the masses. Moreover, it is a highly democratic culture that everyone in the society helps to shape, not just the elite classes.

Finally, American culture lends itself to export because it is itself a combination of diverse cultural elements brought to America by the millions of immigrants who were tumbled together to create something new and desirable. Perhaps this explains why members of the elite social classes in the United States and elsewhere love to turn up their noses at the "tawdry, cheesy, popular culture" in America. Interestingly, a democratic culture can be threatening for the ruling elites in many societies.

Source: Eric Felten, "Love It or Hate It, America Is King of Pop Culture," *Insight,* March 25, 1991, pp. 14–16.

American companies are not the only ones who have difficulty translating brand names. The Chinese had to seek help to find better brand names for several products they hoped to export, including "Double Happiness" bras, "Pansy" men's underwear, and "White Elephant" batteries.[60]

The above examples illustrate how cross-cultural differences in language and related meanings can strongly affect the success of a marketing strategy. However, while differences in cultures can often be identified, marketers do not agree on how these differences should be treated. There are at least three overall approaches, which we discuss below. First, a firm can adapt its marketing strategy to the characteristics of each culture. Second, a firm can standardize its marketing strategy across a variety of cultures. Arguments over which of these is the preferred strategy have been raging for more than 20 years in the literature on marketing and consumer behavior. Third, a firm can use a marketing strategy to change the culture.

Adapting Strategy to Culture

The traditional view of international marketing is that each local culture should be carefully researched for important differences from the domestic market. Differences in consumer needs, wants, preferences, attitudes, and values, as well as in shopping, purchasing, and consumption behaviors, should be carefully examined. The marketing strategy should then be tailored to fit the specific values and behaviors of the culture.

The *adaptation* approach advocates modifying the product, the promotion mix, or any other aspect of marketing strategy to appeal to local cultures.[61] Black & Decker, for example, has to modify its hand tools because electrical outlets and voltages vary in different parts of the world. Philip Morris had to alter its ads for Marlboro cigarettes in Britain, because the government believed British children are so impressed with American cowboys they might be moved to take up smoking. Nestlé modifies the taste of its Nescafé coffee and the promotions for it in the adjoining countries of France and Switzerland to accommodate different preferences in each nation.[62]

Frames from TV commercials for WoW bras: The WoW logo is used in English-speaking countries; Armagique is the French version, and Alas is Spanish.

Standardizing Strategy across Cultures

This approach is often called **global marketing.** It argues for marketing a product in essentially the same way everywhere in the world. It is not a new idea – Coca-Cola has used this basic approach for over 40 years, called "one sight, one sound, one sell." Other companies such as Eastman Kodak, Gillette, and Timex have marketed standard products in essentially the same way for several decades.

Opinions of global marketing have varied over the past decade, but many marketers are beginning to treat the standardized approach more seriously. One of its major advocates is Professor Theodore Levitt of Harvard Business School. Levitt argues that because of increased world travel and worldwide telecommunications capabilities, consumers the world over are thinking and shopping increasingly alike. Tastes, preferences, and motivations of people in different cultures are becoming more homogeneous.[63] Thus, a common brand name, packaging, and communication strategy can be used successfully for many products. For example, given the international popularity of the "Dallas" TV show, actress Victoria Principal sells Jhirmack shampoo all over the world. Similarly, Victor Kiam sells his Remington shavers using the same pitch in 15 languages. Sales of Remington shavers have gone up 60 percent in Britain and 140 percent in Australia using this approach. Playtex markets its WoW bra in 12 countries using the same advertising appeal.

One advantage of the standardized approach is that it can be much less expensive in terms of advertising and other marketing costs.[64] Executives at Coca-Cola, for instance, estimate they save more than $8 million a year in the cost of thinking up new imagery. Texas Instruments runs the same ads throughout Europe rather than having individual ad campaigns for each country, and it estimates its savings at $30,000 per commercial. Playtex produced standardized ads for 12 countries for $250,000, whereas the average cost of producing a single Playtex ad for the United States was $100,000.[65]

For some products, a global (standardized) marketing approach can work well. However, many have severely criticized the global marketing approach.[66] We believe two issues cloud the debate between advocates of adapting versus standardizing international marketing approaches. First is the question of the nature of the product and how standardized the global approach is. For example, advocates of standardizing recognized that Black & Decker had to modify its products to suit local electrical outlets and voltages; yet they would argue the basic meaning and use of such products is becoming similar across cultures. If so, the same type of promotion campaign should work in different cultures.

Second, and perhaps more important, is the question of whether advocates of the standardizing approach are focusing on a long-term trend toward similarity across cultures or are suggesting that cultures are nearly identical today. Unlike the detractors of this approach, we believe that most advocates of global marketing have identified a long-term trend of increasing global homogeneity. We also believe advocates are suggesting this is a trend marketers should be

Benetton uses a similar image strategy across the world.

aware of and adapt to when appropriate. Thus, in essence, both sides are arguing for marketers to adapt to cultural trends; and there would seem to be little disagreement between the two positions at this level.

Change the Culture

The first approach we discussed argues for adapting marketing strategy to local cultures. The second approach argues that cross-cultural differences are decreasing and in some cases can be ignored. The third approach suggests marketing strategies can be developed to influence the culture directly to achieve organizational objectives. As the cultural process model in Figure 13.3 shows, marketing does not simply adapt to changing cultural values and behaviors of consumers; it is an active part of the cultural process.[67]

Marketing strategies both change and are changed by culture. For example, one long-run strategy may be to attempt to change cultural values and behav-

FIGURE 13.5
The (Original) European Economic Community

Nations	Population 18 and Older (000)	Households (000)
Germany	45,800	25,500
Italy	44,500	17,800
United Kingdom	42,700	21,300
France	40,300	19,500
Spain	26,800	10,600
Netherlands	11,300	5,700
Belgium	7,600	3,600
Portugal	7,200	2,800
Greece	6,600	3,000
Denmark	4,400	2,300
Ireland	2,300	1,000
Luxembourg	200	130
Total EEC	239,700	113,230

iors. Several years ago, Nestlé marketed vigorously to convince mothers in some Third World countries to change from breast-feeding to using the company's baby formula product. The campaign was very successful in persuading mothers that breast-feeding was not as healthful for their children as the company's formula, and it dramatically changed their feeding practices. Unfortunately, because of poor water sanitation and improper formula preparation, infant mortalities increased. Thus, the preference for and practice of breast-feeding had to be reinstilled in those countries, which was done successfully. This company changed cultural preferences and behaviors — and then changed them back — in a relatively short time.

Marketing Implications: The European Community

For the past several years, marketers in the United States and elsewhere have been getting ready for 1992, when 12 European countries (see Figure 13.5) become a common market of more than 325 million people (unity formally begins January 1, 1993). The **European Economic Community (EEC or EC)** is likely to grow over the next decade as other countries apply for admission (e.g., Sweden and Austria). What is the "common market" and what does it mean for international marketing? How similar are the cultural values and meanings in these 12 countries? Will the post-1992 European Community be a homogeneous society with most people acting and thinking in the same way?[68]

HIGHLIGHT 13.11

Cross-Cultural Driving Habits

Although some people still believe Europe is on the verge of becoming one culture with the arrival of economic unity January 1, 1993, the large and important cultural differences between the European countries will not go away. In fact, cross-cultural differences may intensify. Nowhere are Europe's rich cultural differences more clearly revealed than people's behaviors behind the wheel of a car or the handlebars of a motorbike.

Cultural stereotypes probably have some basis in fact. The British and Japanese will wait patiently in traffic for hours, while Germans may become upset if held up for even a few minutes. In some countries, it is an insult to be passed, while the polite drivers in the United Kingdom pull over to let speedier cars by. Many French and Italian drivers share a certain disdain for authority and the laws of the road. Germans may be somewhat aggressive and impatient, as the stereotype goes, but they follow the traffic rules. For instance, speed restrictions now found on many sections of the autobahn are rather strictly followed. But once that spot is passed, many German drivers take this to mean "go as fast as the car is capable." This can surprise the sedate British driver of an old Volkswagen who can be very quickly overtaken by a huge Mercedes-Benz traveling 130 mph.

In the safety-conscious Nordic countries, driving tests are difficult and sobriety is strictly enforced. Drivers in Norway and Finland tend to be competent and relatively placid. Enforcement of traffic laws is strict, with some fines contingent on one's income. The Swedes drive with their lights on at all times, day and night, as if anticipating the three-month winter night. In contrast, southern Europeans seem to have a more casual attitude toward the laws and driving speed, and reflect a greater propensity to take risks. In Greece, for instance, one can be surprised by a large truck traveling at high speeds down the center of a narrow mountain road. The many shrines along Greek roads give evidence of the gruesome toll.

Italian cities offer an exciting driving experience where aggressive jockeying for position in heavy traffic reminds many of a Grand Prix race. In Italy, a tiny Fiat 126 was spotted speeding recklessly down a steep mountain road. Several high-spirited teenagers were actually standing out of the tiny's car sunroof, waving wildly and laughing. Closer inspection revealed the driver was also out of the sunroof, standing on the dashboard and negotiating the mountain road with his bare feet on the steering wheel.

Will the new unified Europe create a new breed of driver with a standardized temperament? For driving, the values of the culture concerning life and death, and the macho values associated with the male ego, seem to be the key considerations. These end values seem likely to continue to vary considerably across European societies.

Source: Tony Lewin, "What Drives Machos Mad?" *The European,* June 21, 1991, p. 17 (Elan section).

Creating the EC involves many changes, including reducing the technical barriers that have separated the countries in Europe. Customs clearances and import duties will be removed so goods and people can move freely across the borders, various regulations will be standardized (size of trucks, tax levies), and legal requirements will be more similar.

Despite these changes, the considerable cross-cultural differences between the 12 EC countries will not disappear after 1992. Perhaps the vision of a single European market (in terms of common cultural meanings) is premature. Each society will retain its own language, tastes, cultural meanings, customs and rituals, and probably its own currency. In fact, some experts believe the economic union may accentuate existing cross-cultural differences. (Highlight 13.11 describes cross-cultural differences in driving habits.) More extreme forecasts predict a return to the Europe of "cultural regions" that existed before the nation states of today were created. Examples of this possibility are the 1991 hostilities in Yugoslavia, the disintegration of the Soviet Union, and the difficulties in integrating East and West Germany. Everyone agrees, though, that marketers cannot look at Europe in the same way after 1992.

Marketing to the 113 million households in these diverse markets will take agile management. It will be difficult to develop standardized marketing strategies to sell products in all countries in Europe. Although some products may lend themselves to standardized strategies, others will require careful adaptation to local cultures.

Consider the problems faced by Sara Lee Company, a $12 billion food and consumer products company based in Chicago, as it studies its various European markets.[69] Sara Lee's European operation has a best-selling herbal bath soap in Great Britain called Radox, but it has not tried to sell it in other countries because of connotations with the name. Some European consumers confuse Radox with the bug killer Raid, and others think of Radox as something with a half-life and unsuitable to put on your skin. A similar situation exists for Sanex, a Spanish soap, promoted nearly everywhere in Europe but England. To the English, Sanex comes across as "sanitary," which connotes inappropriate meanings. The company faces similar problems in transferring popular U.S. brands, such as Hanes, L'Eggs, and Sara Lee to European countries. For example, L'Eggs translates to *les oeufs* in French, which might not work very well.

But Sara Lee is developing pan-European marketing strategies for some of its products. For instance, its coffee brand, Douwe Egberts, was sold in 1989 using various brand names in seven countries. Sara Lee is standardizing the product package sizes and color to emphasize the brand name and emblem. It plans to use one standard television commercial, to be shown everywhere in Europe, that portrays the coffee as a congenial drink that binds families together. Sara Lee managers hope the brand will eventually develop a true European identity.

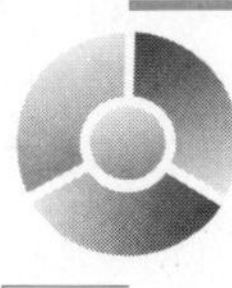

BACK TO.... THE BIRTH OF THE CONSUMER SOCIETY

The opening example described several changes in the culture of 18th-century England that led to the birth of a consumer society. One fundamental change occurred as many people moved from rural areas to larger and more anonymous urban communities. Such a cultural change can influence various cultural meanings in a continuous, reciprocal process much like that of the Wheel of Consumer Analysis. For instance, the new city dwellers were concerned about their social class status. These changes in values led to new beliefs and attitudes about products that could communicate social distinctions, which led to changes in purchase behavior. As more people bought these status products, the social environment changed for all consumers, leading to further changes in values and meanings, and so on.

Other cultural changes occurred as people's shopping and purchasing behaviors became more frequent, even daily, rather than only on the weekly market day. The shopping environment also changed in that people could buy things in various shops rather than from peddlers or street hawkers. The evolving consumption culture was also influenced by marketing strategies (especially advertising and forms of social influence such as opinion leaders).

Finally, mass consumption increased as more people had significant discretionary income. Many people who previously had been unable to buy many things (low purchasing power) or were unwilling to do so (they didn't see the need or value of making fashion-oriented purchases), now became increasingly interested in consumption. These people had developed new cultural needs, values, and goals that could be satisfied rather easily through consumption. Gradually, goods of all types became infused with symbolic mean-

ing, and people began to buy and use goods as a way to acquire these important meanings.

Many scholars who have identified social competition and peoples' need for status differentiation as largely responsible for the consumer revolution write as if they do not approve of people seeking to satisfy such "unimportant" and "trivial" values.[70] Although status distinction was (and still is) an important end state for most people, other cultural meanings also were important to people.[71] It is important to see the cultural process of meaning transfer as a natural process people use to obtain important meanings. The cultural process model is not evidence of people's inherent irrationality nor is it only applicable to "manipulative" marketing strategies. All known cultures imbue certain objects with special meaning, and people obtain and use those objects to gain those important cultural meanings. One difference is that people in modern consumer societies often *purchase* objects (products and services) to obtain cultural meaning.

Similar cultural changes occurred later in America, France, and elsewhere as those societies also developed consumption-oriented cultures. The same events are occurring right now around the world, including societies in Asia, South America, Africa, and Eastern Europe. A big difference, though, is that cultural changes spread much more rapidly today because of modern communications and more sophisticated and effective marketing strategies.

SUMMARY

In this chapter, we examined the influences of culture and cross-cultural factors on consumers' affective responses and cognitions, behaviors, and the physical and social environment. We defined culture as the meanings shared by people in a society (or in a social group), and we discussed how marketers can study the content of culture. We identified several important values and lifestyle trends in American culture, and we drew some implications for marketing strategies. We presented a model of the cultural process by which cultural meaning is moved between different locations – especially from the environment to products and on from products to consumers. Then, we examined the influences of cross-cultural differences on consumers. Finally, we discussed how marketers might use this knowledge to develop effective international marketing strategies.

Key Terms and Concepts

Content of Culture *413*
Culture *413*
Cultural Meaning *415*
Core Values *419*
Cultural Process *424*
Rituals *431*
Cross-Cultural Differences *440*
Materialism *445*
Global Marketing *449*
European Economic Community (EEC or EC) *451*

Review and Discussion Questions

1. Define culture and contrast two approaches to cultural analysis: the content of the culture versus the cultural process.
2. Identify a major change in cultural values that seems to be occurring in your society (choose one not discussed in the book). Discuss its likely effects on consumers' affect, cognitions, behaviors, and the social and physical environment.
3. Select a product of your choice and discuss two implications of your analysis in Question 2 for developing marketing strategies for that product.
4. Briefly describe one example of a price, product, and distribution strategy that moves cultural meaning into the product (do not use examples cited in the text).
5. Select a print ad and analyze it as a mechanism for moving cultural meaning into the product.
6. Choose a popular celebrity endorser and analyze the meanings being transferred to the product endorsed.
7. Select a holiday other than Christmas – for example, Thanksgiving or Independence Day. Discuss the major cultural values reflected in this holiday celebration. What rituals did your family perform for this holiday and how did they move meaning.
8. Think about what you do when getting ready to go out. Try to identify

some grooming rituals you perform that involve certain products. Try to discover how they each use some particular product (blow dryers, cologne, shampoo). What implications might this have for marketing this product?

9. Describe how possession rituals can transfer meaning from products to consumers.
10. Describe a personal experience in which you performed a divestment ritual. What personal meanings did you remove through the ritual?
11. Discuss how the three main approaches to dealing with cross-cultural factors in international marketing could be applied to the marketing of a soft drink such as Pepsi-Cola. Describe one problem with each approach. Which do you recommend?

Notes

1. Over 160 definitions of culture are reported in Frederick D. Sturdivant, "Subculture Theory: Poverty, Minorities, and Marketing," in *Consumer Behavior: Theoretical Sources*, ed. Scott Ward and Thomas S. Robertson (Englewood Cliffs, N.J.: Prentice Hall, 1973), pp. 469–520.
2. An important source is Grant McCracken, *Culture and Consumption: New Approaches to the Symbolic Character of Consumer Goods and Activities* (Bloomington, Ind.: Indiana University Press, 1988).
3. John F. Sherry, "The Cultural Perspective in Consumer Research," in *Advances in Consumer Research*, vol. 13, ed. Richard J. Lutz (Provo, Utah: Association for Consumer Research, 1986), pp. 573–75.
4. Most consumer behavior textbooks focus on the content of culture, describing the values and lifestyles of consumers in different cultures. For example, see Leon G. Shiffman and Leslie Lazar Kanuk, *Consumer Behavior*, 4th ed. (Englewood Cliffs, N.J.: Prentice Hall, 1991); William L. Wilkie, *Consumer Behavior*, 2nd ed. (New York: John Wiley & Sons, 1990).
5. Ann Swidler, "Culture in Action: Symbols and Strategies," *American Sociological Review*, April 1986, pp. 273–86.
6. McCracken, *Cuulture and Consumption*, pp. 73–74.
7. Morris B. Holbrook and John O'Shaughnessy, "On the Scientific Status of Consumer Research and the Need for an Interpretive Approach to Studying Consumption Behavior," *Journal of Consumer Research*, December 1988, pp. 398–402; and Laurel Anderson Hudson and Julie L. Ozanne, "Alternative Ways of Seeking Knowledge in Consumer Research," *Journal of Consumer Research*, March 1988, pp. 508–21.
8. Susan Spiggle, "Measuring Social Values: A Content Analysis of Sunday Comics and Underground Comix," *Journal of Consumer Research*, June 1986, pp. 100–13; and Russell W. Belk, "Material Values in the Comics: A Content Analysis of Comic Books Featuring Themes of Wealth," *Journal of Consumer Research*, June 1987, pp. 26–42.
9. Russell W. Belk and Richard W. Pollay, "Images of Ourselves: The Good Life in Twentieth-Century Advertising," *Journal of Consumer Research*, March 1985, p. 888.
10. Clifford Geertz, "Thick Description," in *The Interpretation of Cultures* (New York: Basic Books, 1973), pp. 3–30.
11. John F. Sherry, Jr., "A Sociocultural Analysis of a Midwestern American Flea Market," *Journal of Consumer Research*, June 1990, pp. 13–30; Russell W. Belk, John F. Sherry, Jr., and Melanie Wallendorf, "A Naturalistic Inquiry into Buyer

and Seller Behavior at a Swap Meet," *Journal of Consumer Research*, March 1988, pp. 449–70.

12. Russell W. Belk, Melanie Wallendorf, and John Sherry, "The Sacred and the Profane in Consumer Behavior: Theodicy on the Odyssey," *Journal of Consumer Research*, June 1989, pp. 1–38.

13. Wagner A. Kamakura and Jose Afonso Mazzon, "Value Segmentation: A Model for the Measurement of Values and Value Systems," *Journal of Consumer Research*, September 1991, pp. 208–18.

14. Craig J. Thompson, William B. Locander, and Howard R. Pollio, "Putting Consumer Experience Back into Consumer Research: The Philosophy and Method of Existential-Phenomenology," *Journal of Consumer Research*, September 1989, pp. 133–47; and Craig J. Thompson, William B. Locander, Howard R. Pollio, "The Lived Meaning of Free Choice: An Existential-Phenomenological Description of Everyday Consumer Experiences of Contemporary Married Women," *Journal of Consumer Research*, December 1990, pp. 346–61.

15. Sidney J. Levy, "Interpreting Consumer Mythology: A Structural Approach to Consumer Behavior," *Journal of Marketing*, Summer 1981, pp. 49–61.

16. Margot Hornblower, "Advertising Spoken Here," *Time*, July 15, 1991, pp. 71–72.

17. David Kilburn, "Japan's Sun Rises," *Advertising Age*, August 3, 1987, p. 42.

18. Neil McKendrick, John Brewer, and J. H. Plumb, *The Birth of a Consumer Society: The Commercialization of Eighteenth-Century England* (Bloomington, Ind.: Indiana University Press, 1982), p. 1.

19. Laurie Freeman, "Diaper Image Damaged: Poll," *Advertising Age*, June 11, 1990, pp. 1, 57.

20. Laurie M. Grossman, "Healthful Approach is Failing to Bring Sizzle to Kentucky Fried Chicken Sales," *The Wall Street Journal*, September 13, 1991, pp. B1, B8.

21. This model is an adaptation and extension of the cultural process described by Grant McCracken, *Culture and Consumption*, who focused on how cultural meanings are first transferred to products and then passed on to individuals. The following discussion elaborates McCracken's ideas and extends them into a systems model of cultural processes.

22. Grant McCracken, "Culture and Consumption: A Theoretical Account of the Structure and Movement of the Cultural Meaning of Consumer Goods," *Journal of Consumer Research*, June 1986, pp. 71–84.

23. McCracken, *Culture and Consumption*, p. 79.

24. Jeffrey F. Durgee and Robert W. Stuart, "Advertising Symbols and Brand Names that Best Represent Key Product Meanings," *Journal of Advertising*, Summer 1987, pp. 15–24.

25. Robert M. Schindler, "Symbolic Price Endings."

26. Elizabeth C. Hirschman, "The Creation of Product Symbolism," in *Advances in Consumer Research*, vol. 13, ed. R. J. Lutz (Provo, Utah: Association for Consumer Research, 1986), pp. 327–31.

27. For a brief discussion of the meaning transfer aspects of the fashion system, see McCracken, "Culture and Consumption, A Theoretical Account."

28. Mihaly Csikszentmihalyi and Eugene Rochberg-Halton, *The Meaning of Things: Domestic Symbols and the Self* (Cambridge: Cambridge University Press, 1981); Sidney J. Levy, "Interpreting Consumer Mythology"; Michael Solomon, "The Role of Products as Social Stimuli: A Symbolic Interactionism Perspective," *Journal of Consumer Research*, December 1983, pp. 319–29.

29. Seth Lubove, "Going, Going, Sold!" *Forbes*, October 14, 1991, pp. 180–81.

30. Russell W. Belk, "Possessions and the Extended Self," *Journal of Consumer Research*, September 1988, pp. 139–168.

31. Anne B. Fisher, "Coke's Brand-Loyalty Lesson," *Fortune*, August 5, 1985, pp. 44–46.

32. McCracken, *Culture and Consumption.*

33. For example, see Dennis W. Rook, "The Ritual

Dimension of Consumer Behavior," *Journal of Consumer Research*, December 1985, pp. 251–64.

34. The last four rituals are described in McCracken, "Culture and Consumption: A Theoretical Account," pp. 71–84.
35. John F. Sherry, Jr. "A Sociocultural Analysis."
36. Peter H. Bloch, "Product Enthusiasm: Many Questions, a Few Answers," in *Advances in Consumer Research*, vol. 13, ed. R. J. Lutz (Provo, Utah: Association for Consumer Research, 1986), pp. 61–65.
37. Russell W. Belk, "Gift-Giving Behavior," in *Research in Marketing*, vol. 2, ed. Jagdish Sheth (Greenwich, Conn.: JAI Press, 1979), pp. 95–126.
38. Michael R. Solomon, "Deep-Seated Materialism: The Case of Levi's 501 Jeans," in *Advances in Consumer Research*, vol. 13, ed. R. J. Lutz (Provo, Utah: Association for Consumer Research, 1986), pp. 619–22.
39. Seth Lubove, "Going, Going, Sold!"
40. Some consumer researchers have written about such topics: Belk, *Possessions and the Extended Self.*
41. Terence A. Shimp and Thomas J. Madden, "Consumer-Object Relations: A Conceptual Framework Based Analogously on Sternberg's Triangular Theory of Love," in *Advances in Consumer Research*, vol. 15 (Provo, Utah: Association for Consumer Research, 1988), pp. 163–68.
42. Edmund Sherman and Evelyn S. Newman, "The Meaning of Cherished Personal Possessions for the Elderly," *Journal of Aging and Human Development* 8, no. 2 (1977–78), pp. 181–92.
43. Thomas Reynolds and Jonathan Gutman, "Advertising Is Image Management," *Journal of Advertising Research*, 24, 1984, pp. 27–37; for a similar viewpoint, see C. Whan Park, Bernard J. Jaworski, and Deborah J. MacInnis, "Strategic Brand Concept-Image Management," *Journal of Marketing*, October 1986, pp. 135–45.
44. Peter H. Farquhar, "Managing Brand Equity," *Marketing Research*, September 1989, pp. 24–33.
45. Russell W. Belk, "ACR Presidential Address: Happy Thought," in *Advances in Consumer Research*, vol. 14, ed. M. Wallendorf and P. Anderson (Provo, Utah: Association for Consumer Research, 1986), pp. 1–4.
46. This section is adapted from Grant McCracken, "Who Is the Celebrity Endorser? Cultural Foundations of the Endorsement Process," *Journal of Consumer Research*, December 1989, pp. 310–21.
47. Michael Schudson, *Advertising, The Uneasy Persuasion* (Chicago: University of Chicago Press, 1984), p. 212.
48. Joshua Levine, "The Sound of No Dealers Selling," *Forbes*, February 19, 1990, pp. 122–24.
49. Unfortunately, many foreign markets are not growing due to competition from television and home videos (box office receipts in Finland were down about 15 percent in 1990, for example). See Kathleen A. Hughes, "You Don't Need Subtitles to Know Foreign Film Folk Have the Blues," *The Wall Street Journal*, March 5, 1991, p. B1.
50. Thompson et al., "The Lived Meaning of Free Choice."
51. Carla Rapoport, "How the Japanese Are Changing," *Fortune*, September 24, 1990, pp. 15–22.
52. Laurel Anderson and Marsha Wadkins, "Japan—A Culture of Consumption?" in *Advances in Consumer Research*, vol. 18 (Provo, Utah: Association for Consumer Research, 1991), pp. 129–34.
53. Yumiko Ono, "Japan Becomes Land of the Rising Mall," *The Wall Street Journal*, February 11, 1991, pp. B1, B6.
54. Hazel Rose Markus and Shinobu Kitayama, "Culture and Self: Implications for Cognition, Emotion, and Motivation," *Psychological Review* 98, no. 2 (1991), pp. 224–53.
55. Russell W. Belk, "Materialism: Trait Aspects of Living in the Material World," *Journal of Consumer Research*, December 1985, pp. 265–79.
56. Ibid., pp. 265–80.
57. Marsha L. Richins and Scott Dawson, "Measur-

ing Material Values: A Preliminary Report of Scale Development," in *Advances in Consumer Research*, vol. 17 (Provo, Utah: Association for Consumer Research, 1990), pp. 169–75.

58. Scott Dawson and Gary Bamossy, "Isolating the Effect of Non-Economic Factors on the Development of a Consumer Culture: A Comparison of Materialism in the Netherlands and the United States," in *Advances in Consumer Research*, vol. 17 (Provo, Utah: Association for Consumer Research, 1990), pp. 182–85.

59. For further discussion of these and many other examples, see David A. Ricks, *Big Business Blunders: Mistakes in Multinational Marketing* (Homewood, Ill.: Dow Jones-Irwin, 1983).

60. Lynne Reaves, "China's Domestic Ad Scene A Paradox," *Advertising Age*, September 16, 1985, p. 76.

61. "Global Advertisers Should Pay Heed to Contextual Variations," *Marketing News*, February 13, 1987, p. 18.

62. See Anne B. Fisher, "The Ad Biz Gloms onto 'Global'," *Fortune*, November 12, 1984, pp. 77–80. The examples in this section are taken from this article. Also see Bill Saporito, "Black & Decker's Gamble on 'Globalization'," *Fortune*, May 14, 1984, pp. 40–48.

63. For example, see "Levitt: Global Companies to Replace Dying Multinationals," *Marketing News*, March 15, 1985, p. 15; Theodore Levitt, *The Marketing Imagination* (New York: The Free Press, 1983), Chapter 2; and Theodore Levitt, "The Globalization of Markets," *Harvard Business Review*, May-June 1983, pp. 92–102.

64. Subrata N. Chakravarty, "The Croissant Comes to Harvard Square," *Forbes*, July 14, 1986, p. 69.

65. Christine Dugas and Marilyn A. Harris, "Playtex Kicks Off a One-Ad-Fits-All Campaign," *Business Week*, December 16, 1985, pp. 48–49.

66. Julie Skur Hill and Joseph M. Winski, "Goodbye Global Ads: Global Village Is Fantasy Land for Big Marketers," *Advertising Age*, November 16, 1987, pp. 22–36; and Joanne Lipman, "Marketers Turn Sour on Global Sales Pitch Harvard Guru Makes," *The Wall Street Journal*, May 12, 1988, pp. 1 & 10.

67. McCracken, "Culture and Consumption," pp. 71–84.

68. Blayne Cutler, "Reaching the Real Europe," *American Demographics*, October 1990, pp. 38–54.

69. Steve Weiner, "How Do You Say L'eggs in French?" *Forbes*, November 27, 1989, pp. 73–79.

70. McKendrick et al., *The Birth of a Consumer Society*.

71. McCracken, *Culture and Consumption* argues persuasively that status was not the only important value or meaning sought by people in 18th-century England.

Additional Reading

For a classic paper that discusses the symbolic, cultural meanings in products, see:

Levy, Sidney J. "Symbols of Sale." *Harvard Business Review*, July–August 1959, pp. 117–24.

For a well-written discussion of how consumers can use products to create a desirable self-concept, see:

Belk, Russell W. "Possessions and the Extended Self." *Journal of Consumer Research*, September 1988, pp. 139–68.

For an interesting discussion of the cultural meanings of Halloween, see:

Belk, Russell W. "Halloween, An Evolving American Consumption Ritual." In *Advances in Consumer Research*, vol. 17. Provo, Utah: Association for Consumer Research, 1990, pp. 508–17.

For three discussions of the problems (and opportunities) of developing global marketing strategies, see:

Domzal, Teresa, and Lynette Unger. "Emerging

Positioning Strategies in Global Marketing." *The Journal of Consumer Marketing*, Fall 1987, pp. 23–40.

Jain, Subhash. "Standardization of International Marketing Strategy: Some Research Hypotheses." *Journal of Marketing*, January 1989, pp. 70–79.

Jordan, Robert O. "Going Global: How to Join the Second Major Revolution in Advertising." *The Journal of Consumer Marketing*, Winter 1988, pp. 39–44.

For a discussion of the changes in American's values, see:

Kahle, Lynn, Basil Poulos, and Ajay Sukhdial. "Changes in Social Values in the United States during the Past Decade." *Journal of Advertising Research*, February–March 1988, pp. 38–39.

For interesting examples of cultural meanings sought in products that are bought by affluent Americans, see:

Hirschman, Elizabeth C. "Secular Immortality and the American Ideology of Affluence." *Journal of Consumer Research*, June 1990, pp. 31–42.

For interesting, although somewhat dated examples of cross-cultural mistakes made in creating international marketing strategies, see:

Ricks, David A. *Big Business Blunders: Mistakes in Multinational Marketing.* Homewood, Ill. Dow Jones-Irwin, 1983.

MARKETING STRATEGY IN ACTION

Procter & Gamble: Selling in Foreign Markets

The Japanese market is the second richest in the world, after the United States. But it is notoriously difficult for foreign companies to succeed in marketing their products in Japan. Yet, in the late 1980s and early 1990s, American companies have better opportunities than ever before to sell in Japan. The Japanese government has removed some trade barriers, and the powerful yen and relatively weak dollar have given U.S. firms the best price-cutting opportunity in decades. Recent cultural changes in Japan should also increase marketing opportunities. After decades of austerity, Japanese are spending more on consumer goods. Some Japanese, especially young people, have a fondness for American culture.

But it won't be easy. The Japanese market may just be the toughest on earth. The language is difficult, values and meanings are different, and customs and manners can be baffling to Westerners. In addition, attitudes toward foreign products can be frosty. For example, a 1990 survey of Japanese consumers found that 71 percent considered Japanese products to be superior to American. Only 8 percent of Japanese would even consider buying an American car (3 percent would think of buying an American TV).

Success requires an extraordinary commitment to quality, a willingness to adjust to cultural differences, a long-range perspective, and patience (lots of patience) – all qualities of the typical Japanese company. Foreign businesses intending to enter the Japanese market might analyze some earlier marketing mistakes to avoid making the same blunders. There are plenty of examples to choose from. Consider, for instance, some of the problems Procter & Gamble had doing business in Japan.

In 1973, Procter & Gamble charged into Osaka with the marketing strategies that had played so well in Ohio. The results were disastrous. By some accounts, the huge Cincinnati, Ohio, company lost about a quarter of a billion dollars over the next decade or so. Procter & Gamble started off fairly well. By the late 1970s, its Cheer brand of laundry detergent was the leading brand in Japan with a 10 percent market share, Camay bath soap had 3.5 percent of a very competitive market, and Pampers, with little competition, had 90 percent of the disposable diaper market. But P&G lost ground in all of these markets. Why it happened and what the company did to regain the lost ground provides useful lessons in the importance of understanding cultural factors and their relation to consumer behavior.

In general, the Japanese seem to have learned such lessons better than most American companies. When the Japanese enter a foreign market, they study it carefully. They do not assume that what goes in Japan also goes in the United States. P&G apparently lacked this humility and cross-cultural perspective. As one bitter ex-P&G employee summed up the problem, "They [the company] didn't listen to anybody." Cheer detergent prospered at first because of heavy price discounting. But this strategy partially backfired because it devalued the company's reputation in the eyes of many Japanese consumers. According to one expert, "Unlike Europe and the U.S., once you discount in Japan it is hard to raise prices later."

The price-cutting strategy also missed several other cultural factors. Because many Japanese housewives do not have a car, they shop in small neighborhood stores where as much as 30 percent of detergents are sold. But owners of these small stores do not like to carry discounted products because they make less money on them.

The advertising also missed the mark. In the late 1970s, Japanese housewives voted Cheer ads the least liked on TV. They were repulsed by a typical American hard-sell approach that stressed product benefits and user testimonials. Bad advertising also hurt Camay soap. In one commercial, a man meeting a woman for the first time compared her skin to that of a fine porcelain doll. Although the ad had worked well in the Philippines, South America, and Europe, the Japanese were insulted. Japanese ad executives had warned P&G that women would find the commercial offensive—"For a Japanese man to say something like that to a Japanese woman means he's either unsophisticated or rude"—but their warnings were not heeded.

The worst story was in the disposable diaper market. P&G had created the market in 1978 and invested heavily in educating Japanese consumers about the advantages of disposable diapers. By the time a small Japanese manufacturer entered the market in 1981, P&G controlled over 90 percent of a $100 million business. By 1985, it had only about 5 percent. It had underestimated both the capabilities of the Japanese company and the favorable response of Japanese consumers to a higher-quality product.

Unfortunately, there was still more. P&G also stuck too long to its policy of advertising the brand, not the company. In Japan, consumers like to know the company, and they tend to form a personal relationship with it. Most Japanese ads end with a flash of the company's name. But P&G didn't add this to its ads until 1986.

But all was not lost. P&G learned from its very expensive mistakes and is in Japan to stay. Its Ultra Pampers made inroads into the Japanese disposable diaper market, and advertising was more in tune with Japanese cultural sensibilities. P&G gained back some of its lost market share.

Dwelling on P&G's mistakes does not imply that Japanese companies are always perfect marketers. They have made some embarrassing blunders of their own in trying to market their products in foreign cultures. But often the Japanese are so determined that they succeed anyway. Their remarkable desire to please the customer is a big factor in their success, according to one P&G executive.

Consider the experience of Shiseido, a giant cosmetics company, in introducing its line of cosmetics into the United States in the mid-1960s. Only after getting products into more than 800 stores, including Bloomingdale's and Saks, did the company realize how different American women's tastes in cosmetics were from those of their Japanese counterparts. Application of Shiseido's makeup required a lengthy series of steps. Apparently Japanese women didn't mind, but American women balked. The cosmetics flopped, and the company pulled out of more than 600 stores.

But Shiseido didn't quit. Instead, it designed a new line of products to meet the needs of American women. They were beautifully packaged, easy to use, and graced with subtle scents. To promote these products the company relied less on advertising, as is the typical American approach, and more on the extraordinary personal service given customers in Japan. According to an executive of Estee Lauder, a competitor, "The service level in Japan is the highest in the world. It starts with the fact that the store manager and his executives come down to the entrance of the store every morning for 15 or 20 minutes to greet the customers." In the United States, Shiseido trains its saleswomen to treat the customer lavishly, including offering free facial massages at demonstration counters. By 1988, Shiseido's sales were growing at about 25 percent a year and its products were available in 1,000 stores.

Discussion Questions

1. Sometimes even subtle cultural factors can make a significant difference in the success of a marketing strategy. Describe several examples of this from the case. How can companies find out about these things? What factors should they consider in deciding whether or not to adapt their marketing strategies to reflect these cultural factors?
2. Using the model of the cultural process in Figure 13.3, discuss the movement of cultural meaning involved in Shiseido's marketing of cosmetics in the United States.
3. Discuss the controversy between advocates of global and local marketing strategies in the context of this case. Do you think P & G can sell its household and personal care products around the world using the same marketing strategies? Defend your answer, and then discuss your position on the debate about global marketing strategies.
4. In 1988, Kao, the $4 billion-a-year Japanese manufacturer of detergents, diapers, and toothpaste, was making plans to enter the U.S. market. Kao is a direct competitor of P&G in Japan and also in the United States. Many of its products were introduced in the United States under the Jergens name, a company Kao bought in 1988. Identify some of the more important cultural and subcultural factors Kao should consider in introducing its shampoo into the U.S. market. What implications do these cultural aspects of the social environment have for devising effective marketing strategies?

Source: Joel Dreyfuss, "How To Beat the Japanese at Home," *Fortune,* August 31, 1987, pp. 80–83: Brian Dumaine, "Japan's Next Push in U.S. Markets," *Fortune,* September 26, 1988, pp. 135–4,. Frederick Katayama, "Japan's Prodigal Young Are Dippy about Imports," *Fortune,* May 11, 1987, p. 118; Jeffrey A. Trachtenberg, "They Didn't Listen to Anybody," *Forbes,* December 15, 1986, pp. 168–69; and Carla Rapoport, "How the Japanese Are Changing," *Fortune,* September 29, 1990, pp. 15–22.

Subculture and Social Class

CHAPTER 14

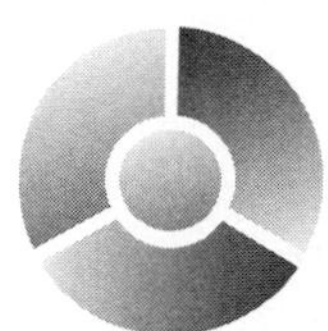

WOOING THE AGING BABY BOOMERS

The 77 million so-called baby boomers (Americans born between 1946 and 1964) are rapidly becoming middle-aged. This large group will continue to have a disproportionate effect on the culture and economy of the United States, probably even more than they did when they were teenagers and young adults. For instance, by 1997, the 35 to 44 age group will increase by 26 percent and earn an awesome $195 billion. This group will become the nation's biggest spenders. In contrast, over the next decade the number of consumers in the 25 to 34 age group will fall by 9 percent and drop $67 billion in purchasing power.

Many marketers have not understood or appreciated the middle-aged consumer. But now they are becoming too large a market for most companies to ignore. Advertisers must learn how to appeal to these older and more mature consumers and change their orientations to reflect these new realities. The old approaches of portraying baby boomers as a young and energetic bunch of jeans-wearing, granola-eating, rock music-listening kids won't work anymore.

Perhaps part of the reason Madison Avenue has been late in responding to the aging trend is that many of the people making creative advertising decisions are themselves pushing 40 and are not

too happy about it. The pervasive anxiety that many Americans have about growing older is a major impediment to creating attractive, imaginative advertising for the not-so-young. As one advertising executive put it, "Advertisers feel that youth is sexy and glamorous, old age is humorous, and middle age is dreary." This notion will have to change, and fast.

People's values and goals tend to change as they age. "Younger people like competition, showing off, looking good. Older boomers are starting to care about comfort, convenience, and financial security." Advertisers will have to overcome their obsession with youth and create acceptable mature images that fit the self-concepts, goals, and values of not-so-young consumers.

Levi Strauss is one company that has followed the baby boomers for three decades. It must continue to change with its market. To promote its new Dockers line of casual slacks, it showed a group of 40-ish men sitting around and jokingly reminiscing about the good old days. The product was not mentioned until the conclusion. According to a Levi's executive, "Real people don't sit around and talk about the brand of clothing they're wearing." The pants were already a hit, but sales accelerated after these ads were shown.

In 1992, marketing to the 35- to 44-year-old consumer was a strong trend. And, the next few years should witness an avalanche of such marketing strategies as marketers catch up to the changes in an American subculture.

Source: Faye Rice, "Wooing Aging Baby-Boomers," *Fortune,* February 1, 1988, pp. 67–77. Susan B. Garland, "Those Aging Boomers," *Business Week,* May 20, 1991, pp. 106–12.

This example illustrates the marketing importance of a major subculture in the United States (and many other countries, too) and how changing demographic characteristics can be important to marketers. In this chapter, we discuss two aspects of the macro social environment—subcultures and social class. In Chapter 12, you learned that culture, subculture, and social class are three levels of the macro social environment. The size of these social groups is a key distinction.

Culture usually is analyzed at the level of a country or an entire society; subcultures are segments of the society. Social class can be considered a special subculture defined in terms of social status. Subcultures and social classes are cultural groups in that their members share common cultural meanings; however, both are part of the larger society and thus are influenced by the overall culture. Thus, we would not expect middle-class Germans to have the same meanings, behaviors, and lifestyles as middle-class Americans. Social class and subcultures are useful for segmenting markets, understanding the shared cultural meanings of large groups of consumers, and developing targeted marketing strategies.

We begin the chapter by discussing the concept of subcultures. Next we describe several important subcultures found in the United States (and elsewhere in the world) and draw implications for marketing strategy. Then we discuss the concept of social class, illustrating it by describing the social class structure of U.S. society.

Subcultures

Subcultures are *distinctive groups of people* in a society that *share common cultural meanings* for affective and cognitive responses (emotional reactions, beliefs, values, and goals), behaviors (customs, scripts and rituals, behavioral norms), and environmental factors (living conditions, geographic location, important objects). Although most subcultures share some cultural meanings with the overall society and/or other subcultures, some of a subculture's meanings must be unique and distinctive. Highlight 14.1 describes a distinctive subculture.

Major demographic changes occurring in the United States and other countries make the analysis of subcultures more important than ever. For instance, the U.S. population is aging (in 2000, the median age will be 36, three years older than in 1990).[1] Also, many societies are becoming more culturally diverse partly through increased immigration of people from other cultures. About 20 percent of Americans were members of minority groups in the early 1980s; by 2010, this will climb to about 30 percent. The overall culture in the United States is influenced by these different subcultural groups, each with unique perspectives and cultural meanings. To understand this diversity, marketers identify subcultures and try to develop marketing strategies to address their needs.

Marketers have used a variety of mostly demographic characteristics to identify subcultures. Figure 14.1 lists several demographic characteristics used to classify people into subgroups and gives examples of subcultures. These subcultures are not mutually exclusive—a person can simultaneously be black, middle class, a male, a resident of the northwestern United States, with a

HIGHLIGHT 14.1

A Hidden Subculture

Although the gay subculture has great demographics, many companies are reluctant to target the estimated 20 million homosexuals in the United States. Gay consumers tend to be younger, more affluent, and better educated than the average American—creating a $382 billion market. A 1988 survey of readers of the eight leading gay newspapers found that the average income in gay households was $55,400 compared to the national average of $32,100. (A different survey found median incomes of $42,000 for gay households and $39,000 for lesbian households.) Nearly 60 percent of these homosexual readers were college graduates, compared to the national average of 18 percent. Some 49 percent were in professional or managerial jobs (16 percent on average), 27 percent were frequent flyers (1.9 percent of general population), and 66 percent went overseas in 1987 (14 percent of general population).

Despite their attractive demographic characteristics, companies worry about marketing directly to gays. Part of the problem is lack of information about this subculture. Identifying members of the gay subculture can be difficult, and measuring the market potential is a challenge. Marketing research can help companies learn about the gay culture, and some companies have hired research firms staffed with gay researchers to help interpret important aspects of the culture.

Another reason for reluctant marketing is the fear of having a brand labeled the "gay brand." Targeting gays involves risks for companies, including controversy and possible backlash from homophobic consumers. However, some advertisers that target gays, have done well. For instance, Remy Martin, the only cognac that advertises in the gay press, is the No. 5 brand nationally, but No. 1 in the gay community.

A final problem is the lack of media such as general-interest magazines (that do not contain classified personal ads) to effectively reach gays. One magazine begun in 1991, "Genre," won't accept such ads and has picked up several national advertisers including Atlantic Records and Prentice Hall, a publisher.

Source: Cyndee Miller, "Gays Are Affluent but Often Overlooked Market," *Marketing News,* December 24, 1990, p. 2; and Joan E. Rigdon, "Overcoming a Deep-Rooted Reluctance, More Firms Advertise to Gay Community," *The Wall Street Journal,* July 18, 1991, pp. B1, B8.

moderate income. Marketers can combine demographic distinctions to identify smaller and more narrowly defined subcultures (affluent, black consumers living in the South).

Analyzing Subcultures

As in cultural analysis, subcultures can be analyzed at different levels. Subcultural analysis is often done in stages. First, a broad subculture is identified

FIGURE 14.1
Types of Subcultures

Demographic Characteristic	Examples of Subcultures
Age	Adolescents, young adults, middle-aged, elderly
Religion	Jewish, Catholic, Morman, Buddist, Muslim
Race	Black, Caucasian, Oriental
Income level	Affluent, middle income, poor, destitute
Nationality	French, Malaysian, Australian, Canadian
Gender	Female, male
Family type	Single parent, divorced/no kids, two parents/kids
Occupation	Mechanic, accountant, priest, professor, clerk
Geographic region	New England, Southwest, Midwest
Community	Rural, small town, suburban, city

AT&T could place these two ads in English and Spanish language magazines directed at Hispanic consumers.

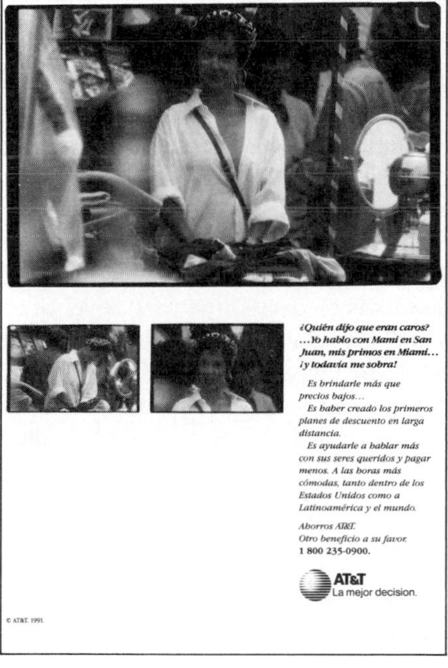

based on some broad demographic characteristic (black Americans, elderly Japanese, middle-income Italians). Then, depending on the marketing purpose, this broad group can be further segmented into sub-subcultures based on other demographic characteristics (affluent, middle-income, or poor black Americans; elderly Japanese who are healthy versus those who are ill; middle-income

Italians living in large cities or small towns). If necessary, the segmentation process could continue, creating ever smaller and more precisely defined subcultures.

Careful research and thoughtful analysis is necessary to develop a clear understanding of subcultures. Consider, for instance, the confusion about the so-called yuppies (young, urban professionals). Originally a narrow subcultural group, yuppies gradually came to mean rich, selfish youths and, due to intense media attention through 1980s, became virtually synonymous with the baby boomer generation. However, the best estimates counted only about 4 million yuppies, a mere 5 percent of the baby boomers.[2]

Subculture analysis can follow the same approach as cultural analysis discussed in Chapter 13. Typically, marketers examine the *content of the subculture* by describing the cultural meanings members of the subculture share (especially their values and lifestyles). It is much less common for marketers to examine the *cultural processes* by which cultural meanings are moved from the external world of the subculture to products and services and on to the people in the subculture.

In analyzing a subculture, marketers seek to identify the general characteristics and behavioral tendencies shared by people in those groups. However, most subcultures are diverse. The media tend to characterize members of a subculture in the same way (blacks are poor ghetto residents; elderly people are doddering and ill), but this can be a major mistake when developing marketing strategies. Members of the black or elderly subculture are likely to be quite different. For example, marketers have identified a subgroup of "young" elderly people called "Opals," who think and act younger than their years, have money to spend, and are healthy enough to do so.[3] In sum, it is difficult to identify a typical person in a subculture. (Highlight 14.2 describes some of the characteristics of the "average" American.)

The task for marketers is to determine what level of analysis is appropriate for the problem (how fine should the distinctions be?) and develop marketing strategies for that level. Consider Maybelline's strategy in developing the cosmetic line "Shades of You" for women with dark skin.[4] The company recognized that women of color (mostly blacks and darker-skinned Hispanics) have different skin tones and thus need different cosmetics. For instance, blacks have about 35 different skin colors compared to about 18 for whites. Maybelline spent considerable effort and money developing the proper formulas for 12 shades of liquid makeup and 8 blushes. Sold in drugstores and supermarkets at the lower end of the price scale, the product was almost immediately a hit with dark-skinned women.

Geographic Subcultures

Americans like to think of their country as a melting pot, but the mass American market is a myth for many product categories.[5] In different parts of the country, the physical environment (topography, climate, natural resources) and social

HIGHLIGHT 14.2

THE AVERAGE AMERICAN

The average American is a 32-year-old woman, 5 feet 4 inches, with brown hair (69 percent of all Americans have it), who weighs 143 pounds and is trying to lose weight. She wears glasses or contact lenses.

The average American drives an 8-year-old blue sedan that gets 18 miles per gallon and costs about $3,000 per year to operate. She will drive about 9,000 miles each year, and two other people will own her car before it goes to the junkyard. Some 70 percent of women wear jewelry every day, most of which they buy themselves. Although she hasn't been to church in the past week, the average American believes in God (94 percent of Americans do) and life after death (69 percent do). By age 32, the average American is married and has a child. It will cost $140,000 to raise this child to age 18.

The average American works in a technical, sales, or administrative job, and she makes less than $20,000 per year. The average American spends money as fast as she makes it. She writes 16 checks per month and charges about $2,000 per year on her 10 credit cards. The average American woman spent $339 on clothes in 1986. Working women with children bought 37 items of personal clothing, while working women without children bought 55 items. Although not rich, the average American carries $104 in her purse along with keys (97 percent of women do), a comb (80 percent), checks (76 percent), makeup (69 percent), and an address book (69 percent).

Of course, the "average" American does not really exist. She is a statistical artifact.

Source: Blayne Cutler, "Meet Jane Doe," *American Demographics,* June 1989, pp. 25–27, 62.

environment (economics, population demographics, lifestyles) are quite different and these factors affect the culture and buying behavior.[6] In reality, the United States is a polycultural nation, a mosaic of submarkets and subcultures. In some ways, Boston and Houston are as different as Hamburg (Germany) and Milan (Italy).

Marketers may find it easier to accept Europe and Latin America as separate regions than to recognize Arizona, Texas, and Louisiana as different markets. For example, product ownership varies widely across the nation. Consumers in California own a much higher percentage of foreign cars than their counterparts in the Midwest or South. Very few brands enjoy uniform sales across the country. Many national brands get 40 to 80 percent of their sales in a core region, but they are specialty brands (with lower market shares) in other areas of the country. In the mid-1980s, for instance, Ford pickups were the favorite in a number of northwestern states, while Chevy pickups dominated in many southern states.[7] Wonder Bread sells best in New York (for reasons unknown), while snack nuts sell best in Portland, Maine. Seattle leads in sales of healthy foods such as Cheerios and is also tops in Hershey's chocolate bars. Coping with this diversity requires attention to regional subcultures.

There are many ways of analyzing the United States in terms of **geographic subcultures.** In one creative approach, Joel Garreau divided the North American continent into nine geographic areas that he labeled the "nine nations" of North America.[8] U.S. marketers concentrate on the eight areas shown in Figure 14.2. Garreau argued that a variety of environmental factors – including economic, social, cultural, political, topographical, and natural resource factors – combine to form these nine areas. Figure 14.3 summarizes the "personalities" of these areas.

For some products and services, this framework may be useful in developing specific marketing strategies to appeal to consumers in each area. For example, preferences for and consumption of various beverages vary dramatically in different geographic areas of the United States, and analysis of cultural differences in these regions may help to determine which beverages can be marketed most effectively.[9]

Borderland Regions

As we emphasized in Chapter 13, cultural and subcultural differences do not always coincide with national (or other artificial) boundaries. Consider the so-called borderlands along the 2,000-mile border between Mexico and the United States.[10] About 5.2 million people (35 percent Hispanic) live in 25 borderland counties in California, New Mexico, Arizona, and Texas that have grown about 30 percent since 1980. Another 3 million people live on the Mexico side. The borderlands constitute a geographic subculture with significant marketing potential.

Consider the area called *Los Dos Laredos* (the two Laredos) – Laredo, Texas, and Nuevo Laredo, Mexico. Although separated by the Rio Grande River, residents on both sides give little thought to the border as they freely cross the bridges to shop, work, and enjoy themselves. A bank official puts it this way, "We're not the United States and we're not Mexico. We're different. We think we gather the best of both cultures." According to one citizen, "We're more like Minneapolis and Saint Paul than the U.S. and Mexico, because we are the same people."

The borderlands are an important regional market even though the overall demographics are downscale (people have lower than average incomes). The U.S. side is swelled by thousands of Mexican citizens who cross the border to work and spend their pesos. Although some shopping areas are bordertown tacky, Laredo's new retailing centers contain chain stores like Wal-Mart, Sam's, and HEB of California. Successful marketing strategies recognize the Hispanic culture as the major influence in the borderlands. For instance, many of the signs and store names are in Spanish, prices are often given in both pesos and

FIGURE 14.2

The Eight Nations of the United States

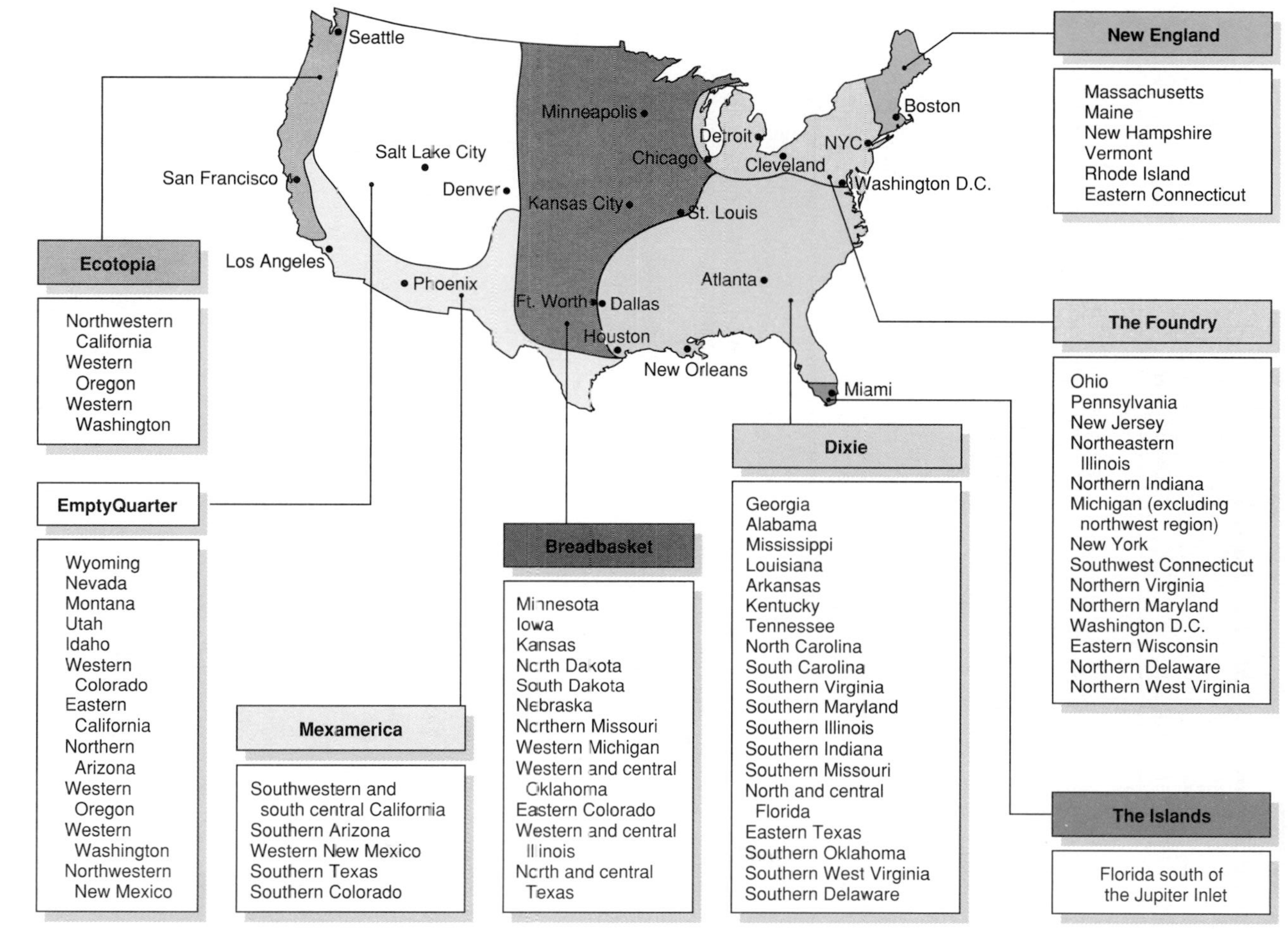

Source: Adapted from *Nine Nations of North America* by Joel Garreau. Copyright © 1981 by Joel Garreau. Adapted and reprinted by permission of Houghton Mifflin Company.

FIGURE 14.3
Capsule Summary of the Nine Nations

Nation	Description
The Foundry Capital: Detroit	Industrialized, urban, losing population, jobs; heavy unionism; old technology; work oriented. On the decline but will bounce back because of water resources; Emulators, Inner Directeds, I-Am-Me's.
Mexamerica Capital: Los Angeles	Heavy Hispanic culture; mix of well and poorly educated; hardworking, entrepreneurial spirit, growth-oriented. Becoming most influential nation; Emulators, Achievers, Societally Conscious.
The Islands Capital: Miami	Caribbean and Latin American influence, heavy illegal drug trade, young and old live here; has little in common with rest of Florida and Dixie; diverse population.
Quebec Capital: Quebec City	French-speaking Canada; steeped in history, tradition, ethnic pride; very homogeneous culture; plentiful resources; diversified economy; fiercely independent.
Dixie Capital: Atlanta	Trying to catch up; small-town way of life; undergoing rapid social and economic change; economy minded; Need-Driven, Belongers.
New England Capital: Boston	Poorest nation but "high-tech" influx bringing it back; politically diverse, cautious, brand loyal; Inner Directed, Societally Conscious, Achievers.
The Empty Quarter Capital: Denver	Wide-open spaces, energy rich, mineral rich; largest area, smallest population; frontier ethic; major economic growth foreseen; hardworking, conservative, blue-collar; Inner Directed.
Ecotopia Capital: San Francisco	"High-tech," interest-rate-based economy; quality of life important; mottos: Leave me alone, Small is beautiful; young, educated, affluent; Inner Directed, Experientials.
Breadbasket Capital: Kansas City	Agricultural economy; mainstream America; stable, at-peace-with-itself population; conservative; Conformist Belongers.

Source: Adapted from *Nine Nations of North America* by Joel Garreau. Copyright © 1981 by Joel Garreau. Adapted and reprinted by permission of Houghton Mifflin Company.

dollars, and most stores accept either currency. Because Hispanic families tend to be large, grocery stores tend to stock big sizes, including 50-pound sacks of rice.

AGE SUBCULTURES

Age groups can also be analyzed as subcultures because they often have distinctive values and behaviors. However, marketers must be cautious about segmenting consumers based on their actual age. Many adult American consumers think of themselves as 10 to 15 years younger than they really are.[11] Thus,

HIGHLIGHT 14.3

The New Elderly

For most people, age is more a state of mind than a physical state. Consider this statement from an 89-year-old woman: "I might be 89 years old. I feel good. I feel like I could fly the coop. I do. I feel younger, like I'm 45 or 50. I want to doll up, and I like to fuss. . . . I don't know I'm old. I feel like I'm going to live a long time." This suggests marketers should analyze subjective or "cognitive age" (the age one thinks of oneself as being) rather than chronological or actual age.

A new subcultural age segment may be emerging – the "new-age elderly." These people view themselves quite differently from the traditional elderly. They perceive themselves as younger and more self-confident, in control of their lives, less concerned with possessions, and more involved with new experiences, challenges, and adventures. They are a good market for concerts and plays, lectures and university courses, and vacation travel to exotic locations.

Source: Leon G. Schiffman and Elaine Sherman, "Value Orientations of New-Age Elderly: The Coming of an Ageless Market," *Journal of Business Research* 22 (1991), pp. 187–94.

their behavior, affect, and cognitions are more related to their psychological age than their chronological age (see Highlight 14.3 for an example). Many different **age subcultures** can be identified and analyzed, but we will discuss only three here: teens, baby boomers, and the mature market.

The Teen Market

The American teenage population has been gaining affluence, although it has been shrinking in size.[12] In the mid-1980s, there were about 26 million persons in the United States aged 13 to 19. This number decreased to about 23 million in the early 1990s and will increase to about 27 million by the year 2000.

This group is important not only because it has a major influence on household purchases, but also because of its own discretionary purchasing power. The annual Rand Youth Poll estimated teenagers spent over $45 billion in 1983 and put more than $9 billion into savings. Fully 16 percent of teens own a car, 66 percent own a record player, 34 percent own a television, 86 percent own a camera, 21 percent own a telephone, 12 percent own a home computer, and 14 percent own stocks and bonds.

Several studies have found that teenagers do a large portion of the grocery shopping for the family: estimates are that from 49 to 61 percent of teenage girls and 26 to 33 percent of teenage boys frequently perform this task. In addition, about 60 percent of teens help make the supermarket shopping list, and 40

Nike's visually humorous ads appeal especially to teens.

percent select some of the brands to be purchased. It is no wonder that brand-name food marketers advertise in magazines such as *Seventeen.*

Brand loyalty has also been found to form early among teenage shoppers. In a survey of women ages 20 to 34, at least 30 percent said they made a brand decision as a teenager and continued to use the brand to the present. Sixty-four percent said they looked for specific brands when they were teenagers. Thus, a final reason this market is so important for many products and services is the potential to develop brand loyalty that may last a lifetime!

Baby Boomers

Baby boomers are those persons born between 1946 and 1962. There are about 68 million people in this group—about a third of the U.S. population. This group is in its early 30s to mid-40s and entering its prime earning and spending years. The baby boomer market will be the largest and most affluent in history and will have a major economic impact for the next 45 years (see the opening example).[13] In 1982 dollars, the 35-to-44 age group will have $870 billion to spend by 1995, well over twice as much as the same age group spent in 1980. Within the next decade or so, baby boomers will account for about half of all discretionary spending.[14]

Although the baby boomer subculture is extremely diverse, some general characteristics have been identified. The group is characterized as having a blend of "me-generation" and old-fashioned family values and as strongly influencing the values of other groups.[15] A study by Cadwell Davis Partners ad

Toyota's Tercel campaign reflects the diverse values of "baby boomers."

agency found that many people who aren't baby boomers feel as if they are. Baby boomers emphasize health and exercise and have reduced their consumption of cigarettes, coffee, and strong alcoholic beverages. Forty-six percent of this market has completed college and two thirds of baby boomer wives work, compared with about half the wives in the rest of the population. In terms of products, this group emphasizes quality and is far less concerned with bargain hunting than their parents were.

Baby boomers will have a strong impact on markets for housing, cars, food, clothing and cosmetics, and financial services. For instance, nearly one fourth of boomers are single creating strong markets for vacations and convenience packaged goods. In addition, although they are having fewer children per household, the sheer size of the boomer group led to an increase in births into the early 1990s—a "baby boom echo." Boomers who are new parents are especially attractive to marketers. Given the large incomes and small family sizes of this group, spending per child is likely to be the largest in history. Markets for children's products will expand accordingly. Toy sales, for example, are expected to increase more than twice as fast as the population of children for whom they are intended. Other markets, such as child care services and computer software for tots, may double in the next few years.

The baby boomer market, then, is the most lucrative and challenging marketers have ever seen. Many firms have designed new products and redesigned and repositioned old ones for this market. Wheaties used to appeal to kids as "the breakfast of champions"; now it is promoted to adults with such slogans as "what the big boys eat." Commercials for Snickers candy bars show adults rather than children eating this candy for a snack. Crest and other brands have introduced toothpaste formulas to fight plaque, an adult problem. Levi Strauss has redesigned its jeans to give a little extra room in the seat to accommodate "booming boomer bodies" (see Highlight 14.4). Even Clearasil, traditionally an antiacne medication for teenagers, has developed Clearasil Adult Care to appeal to the growing number of baby boomer adults with skin problems.

The Mature Market

As America ages (along with other industrialized countries such as Japan and most European nations), marketers have recognized the economic importance of the mature market, defined as consumers over the age of 55.[16] The mature market is one of the most rapidly growing subcultures in American society. In 1987, the over-65 population was 30 million, up 4.5 million from 1980. In 2000, there will be 35 million consumers over 65. Nearly 80 percent of the current U.S. population is expected to live until their late 70s. At present, one in four Americans is older than 50; by 2020, over one third will be. Between now and 2020, the number of people aged 50 or older will increase by 74 percent (as baby boomers continue to age), while the number under age 50 will increase by only 1 percent.[17] In 2020, there could be as many as 58 million elderly or as few as 48 million, according to the U.S. Census Bureau. The exact number of older Americans expected in 2020 is hard to predict; it all depends on the mortality rate, especially gains made against specific diseases such as heart ailments, cancer, and stroke.

Because the mature market is quite diverse, it may be more useful to consider smaller subcultural groups based on narrower age ranges, such as older (55–64), elderly (65–74), aged (75–84), and very old (85 and over). Figure 14.4 shows how the sizes of these four age-based subgroups are changing.

HIGHLIGHT 14.4

Jeans Keep Up with the Baby Boomers

The baby boom generation created the boom market for jeans manufacturers. When the boomers were teens in the 1960s, jeans became the universal emblem of youth and rebellion (as is still the case around the world), and jeans sales increased dramatically.

As the boomers aged, manufacturers such as Levi Strauss have adapted their marketing strategies to keep pace with the changing demographics. Although Levi's key market is still 14-to-24 year-old men, this age group is shrinking, while the huge group of baby boomers is reaching middle age. Thus, Levi's and other manufacturers have developed products to appeal to the boomers and to fit their changing bodies.

The so-called jeans generation still likes jeans (partly as a symbol of youth), but the style and fit they seek has changed. As waist sizes have increased – more 36s and fewer 32s – Levi Strauss has introduced new products such as the highly successful Dockers line made to fit the middle-aged man's body. According to John Wyek, director of strategic research at Levi Strauss, "The point is to make products that are relevant. And making relevant products for the 'me' generation hasn't been easy. We have 70,000 different products – different styles, colors, silhouettes, sizes, and fabrics – so that our customers have the choice they've become accustomed to."

Levi Strauss is keeping its eye on other changes in subcultures. For instance, the key market of 18-to-24-year-olds will decline throughout the 1990s, but the number of Hispanics in this age group will increase 40 percent. Levi's has created a Spanish-language campaign targeted at Hispanics, who account for 12 percent of Levi's annual sales. Levi Strauss produced an ad campaign for 501 button-fly jeans (directed by Spike Lee) targeted at the core market of 18-to-24-year-old men that ran on MTV and late-night television programs. Yet another ad campaign was targeted at women. Print ads designed to emphasize the comfort and fit of the Levi 500 and 900 product line showed silhouettes of women in many shapes and sizes.

The trick for Levi Strauss is to market its products to all these highly diverse groups in a way that does not erode the overall value or equity of the Levi brand – the theme of "Levi-ness." The goal is for each group to feel that "Levi's are for me."

Source: Cyndee Miller, "Jeans Marketers Look for Good Fit with Older Men and Women," *Marketing News,* September 16, 1991, pp. 1, 6; and Bickly Townsend, "Beyond the Boom: An Interview with John Wyek," *American Demographics,* June 1989, pp. 40–41.

The next century will see huge increases in demand for products and services for older consumers, including adult day care, home health care, prescriptions and over-the-counter drugs, medical care of all types, and foods low in cholesterol, sugar, salt, and calories. Other nonhealth-related products include planned vacation travel, restaurants, recreational vehicles, hotels and

FIGURE 14.4
The Mature Markets: 1985 and 1995

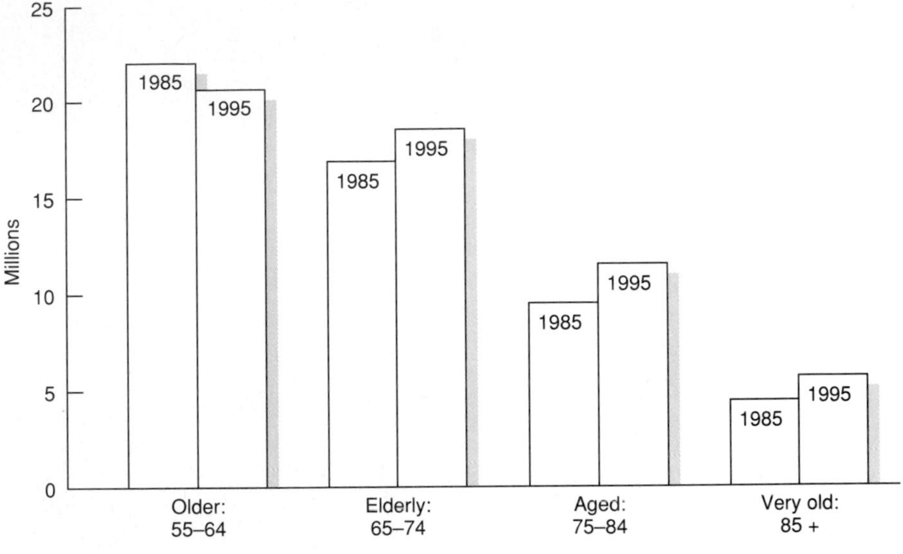

Though the "older" population (ages 55 to 64) will shrink slightly in the next decade, it will remain the largest segment of the mature market.

Source: Bureau of the Census, "Projections of the Population of the United States by Age, Sex, and Race, 1983 to 2080," *Current Population Reports,* Series P-25, No. 952, 1984, as reported in William Lazer, "Inside the Mature Market," *American Demographics,* March 1985, p. 24.

motels. In recognition that extended families will be larger, theme parks such as Six Flags—Great America have created packages for grandparents, parents, and grandkids as a group. Older people will be better educated than previous generations, which will create increased demand for educational programs, books, and news.

Traditionally, marketers have ignored the mature market, perhaps because it was assumed to have low purchasing power. However, in addition to its sheer size, the economic character of this market deserves careful consideration. While many of the members of this group no longer work, they often have considerable discretionary income. Unlike younger groups, members of mature markets are usually free of most of the financial burdens associated with child rearing, mortgages, and furnishing a household.

Given these differences, per capita discretionary income is higher for the mature group than for any other age group—about 50 percent of the nation's total.[18] In 1980, for example, for those aged 55 to 59, per capita discretionary income was \$3,500; for those aged 60 to 64, per capita discretionary income was \$3,700; for those aged 65 and over it was the highest of all—\$4,100. These

Many products are designed for consumers in the mature markets.

figures compare quite favorably with the approximately $2,000 in discretionary income available to people aged 30 to 39.

It is also important to recognize how the mature market is changing. In 1985, only 9 percent of the elderly had a college degree and only 44 percent had graduated from high school. By 1995, the share of older people with college educations will rise to more than 12 percent, and at least one fourth will have had some college. Thus, the mature market is becoming more educated and likely will have even greater incomes. Increases in income will also come about because many of those in tomorrow's mature market will benefit from pension and retirement plans.

Finally, because many people in the mature market subculture are retired, they have more time to enjoy entertainment and leisure activities. Although this market has historically spent more money on food for home consumption than away-from-home consumption, restaurants now cater to them with senior citizen discounts, early-bird dinners, and menus designed for the tastes and requirements of older people.

The elderly represent a significant market for skin care products, vitamins and minerals, health and beauty aids, and medications that ease pain and promote the performance of everyday activities. In addition, they are a significant market for condominiums in the Sunbelt states, time-share arrangements, travel and vacations, cultural activities, and luxury items given as gifts to their children and grandchildren. Overall, then, the mature market subculture represents an excellent marketing opportunity that will become even better in the future.[19]

Developing marketing strategies that appeal to consumers in the mature market is more difficult than it looks.[20] Few companies are experts at it. Many marketers have inaccurate perceptions of this large and diverse group, including persistent images of frail, stubborn, and indigent people who, if not confined to bed, are tottering around on canes. Yet only 5 percent of Americans over 65 are institutionalized. People are staying healthy and active much later into their lives than ever before.

Some ads are beginning to use themes and models that older consumers can identify with. No longer depicted as weak and dottery, older people are shown doing the things they do in real life: working, playing tennis, falling in love, and buying cars. McDonald's, for instance, was a forerunner in this style with its "Golden Years" spots that showed an elderly man and woman meeting for lunch at McDonald's and an elderly man on his first day of work at McDonald's.

Ethnic Subcultures

In the past decade, the ethnic makeup in the United States has changed dramatically.[21] In 1980, one of every five Americans was a member of a minority group. In 1990, one in four Americans claimed to have either Hispanic, Asian, African, or Native American ancestry. The increases were unequal across **ethnic subcultures,** due to different immigration and birth rates. For instance, the Asian subculture grew 80 percent during the 1980s, compared to increases of 4.4 percent in the white population, 14 percent for blacks, and 39 percent for Hispanics. Increases in these minority subcultures are expected to continue so that by 2010, more than one third of American children will be black, Hispanic, or Asian.[22]

It is important for marketers to recognize that ethnic diversity is not distributed equally across the United States.[23] The most ethnically diverse regions in the country are in the Southwest and the South; the least diverse are in the Midwest, where the proportion of whites may exceed 90 percent. The most ethnically diverse county in the nation is San Francisco with approximately equal proportions of whites, blacks, Hispanics, and Asians. New York City and Los Angeles are highly diverse cities. Following we will discuss the three major ethnic subcultures in the United States—black, Hispanic, and Asian.

The Black Subculture

The black or African-American subculture is the largest minority group in the United States, with some 31 million people and 7 million families (about 13 percent of the total population), a market worth about $170 billion annually.[24] African-Americans are a diverse group. Many black Americans are poor, but two thirds are not. More than 13 percent of black families had incomes exceeding $50,000 in 1988, up from 8 percent in 1980. However, the number of very poor

HIGHLIGHT 14.5

CLUSTER 31—BLACK ENTERPRISE

Cluster 31, or Black Enterprise, is a subcultural group created through statistical analysis by Claritas Corporation. Claritas' PRIZM system groups all of the U.S. ZIP codes and census tracts into 40 clusters or segments, based on various demographic characteristics. It ranks the clusters by size and affluence and gives each one a catchy name. Black Enterprise is made up of relatively affluent black consumers. It ranks 11th in affluence and comes closest to describing a black middle class.

In 1988, there were about 420,000 households in cluster 31 neighborhoods around the country. They were more likely to be college educated and hold white-collar jobs. They were more likely than average to sail, drink scotch, buy classical music, smoke menthol cigarettes, belong to a book club, and travel by rail. These black consumers were very unlikely to buy country music, a pickup truck, or camping equipment, or to go swimming frequently. Cluster 31 adults spend heavily on clothes, read magazines at above average rates, and watch less television than average. In many cases, these affluent blacks make choices similar to affluent white consumers, buying station wagons, using Visa cards once a month, and making three or more stock transactions per year.

Source: Brad Edmondson, "Black Enterprise," *American Demographics,* November 1989, pp. 26–27.

black families (incomes under $5,000) also grew during this period, from 10 to 12 percent. Although the 17 million relatively poor blacks concentrated in densely populated urban centers are more visible in the media, 8 million blacks live in suburban neighborhoods.

Economic conditions for blacks vary considerably in different metropolitan areas. For example, about one fourth of blacks in Washington, D.C. are affluent, compared to only 1 in 25 in Miami. In San Francisco, 1 in 10 blacks is affluent and more than half are middle class. Middle-class blacks may have more in common with middle-class whites and Asians than lower-class blacks. The diversity in the African-American subculture suggests marketers should further segment the black market based on factors such as income, social class, or geographic region. Highlight 14.5 presents an example of such a sub-subculture.

Increasingly, marketers are targeting black Americans with special products and marketing strategies. For example, Tyco, Hasbro, and Mattel are all marketing ethnically correct dolls designed for the black market (10 percent of U.S. children under 10 are black).[25] Mattel's dolls, Shani (Swahili for "marvelous") and her two friends, Asha and Nicelle, have different skin tones, hairstyles, and facial features that reflect the diversity of black women. Some marketing strategies directed at the black subculture have been highly controversial. In 1990, for instance, following intense public pressure, the R.J. Reynolds Tobacco Company withdrew plans to test market a new cigarette, "Uptown," that was targeted at black smokers.[26] In 1991, the G. Heileman Brewing Company succumbed to public pressure and canceled plans to market a high-alcohol malt beer, "PowerMaster," to low-income, inner-city black consumers.[27]

The Hispanic Subculture

According to the 1990 census, approximately 23.7 million Hispanics live in the United States (about 8 percent of the total population).[28] Hispanics are people with Spanish-speaking ancestry from such nations as Mexico (by far the largest group in the United States), Puerto Rico, Cuba, and various countries in Central and South America. When combined into a single Hispanic subculture, these people account for over $70 billion in purchasing power.

Hispanics are distributed unequally across the United States, with most living in the border states of Texas, California, Arizona, and New Mexico (each state has a Hispanic population exceeding 500,000). The top six Hispanic U.S. cities are New York (mostly Puerto Ricans and Dominicans); Miami (Cubans); Los Angeles, Houston, and San Antonio (Mexicans); and Chicago (a mix of all). In these regions, the Hispanic subculture has a very significant effect on the overall culture.

The Hispanic subculture is very diverse, and reaching Hispanic consumers efficiently and effectively can be difficult. Some Hispanics are third- or fourth-generation U.S. citizens and are well assimilated into American culture; they can be reached by traditional U.S. media (TV, radio, and magazines). Other Hispanics retain much of their original culture and may speak mostly or only Spanish. To oversimplify, marketers can identify three broad segments (subgroups) in the Hispanic subculture—only Spanish speaking; bilingual, but favoring Spanish; and bilingual, but favoring English.

Using Spanish in ads can be an effective way to reach all three groups. Recently developed Spanish-language media (special TV channels, newspapers, and magazines) make it easier than ever to reach the Hispanic market.[29] For instance, Whittle Communications launched a new magazine in late 1990, called "La Familia de Hoy," targeted at Hispanic women who speak English as a second language and have children at home. Several large companies have placed ads in Spanish in the magazine, including Procter & Gamble, American Airlines, Kraft, AT&T, and Kinney Shoes. Successful advertising campaigns tend to use large and colorful ads that combine the American dream with the traditional values of the Hispanic extended family.

In 1987, U.S. companies spent about $500 million on marketing strategies directed at the Hispanic market.[30] Yet the largest Hispanic advertiser, Philip Morris, allocated only $13.3 million to Hispanic advertising—less than 1 percent of its total ad budget. Many companies would like to develop marketing strategies targeted at the Hispanic market, but getting good information about Hispanic needs, values, and beliefs is difficult. Companies must decide whether

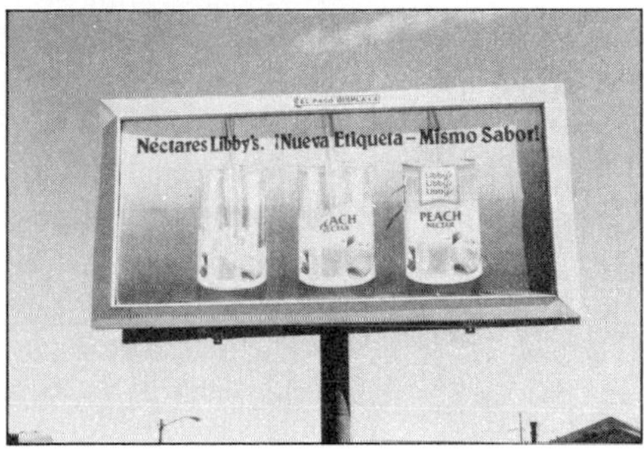

These billboards, erected in the Hispanic section of El Paso, Texas, have the same slogans that were used on English-language billboards throughout the country.

to develop one general marketing strategy for all Hispanics or adapt the strategy for each segment of the Hispanic subculture. Coors, for instance, opts for the adaptive, tailor-made approach, showing ads with a rodeo theme in Houston, but not in Miami. Goya Foods developed different products for Miami (Cubans prefer black beans) and New York (Puerto Ricans like red beans).

Marketing to domestic subcultures requires a careful analysis of consumers' affect, cognitions, and behaviors.[31] For example, a telephone company tried to target the Hispanic market by employing Puerto Rican actors. In the ad, the wife said to her husband, "Run downstairs and phone Mary. Tell her we'll be a little late." However, the commercial ignored Hispanic values and behaviors. For one thing, Hispanic wives seldom order their husbands around; for another, few Hispanics would feel it necessary to phone if they would be late, because being late is expected. Similarly, Coors ads featuring the slogan "Taste the high country" were not effective with Mexican-Americans, who could not identify with mountain life. The Spanish-language Coors ads were modified to suggest the mountains were a good source of beer, but that one did not need to live in the mountains to enjoy it. The new slogan in its English translation became "Take the beer from the high country and bring it to your high country—wherever it may be."[32]

Asian Subculture

Although less than 3 percent of the population in 1990, Asian-Americans are the most rapidly increasing ethnic group in the United States.[33] The population of people with Asian ancestry increased 80 percent in the 1980s (largely due to increased immigration), growing from 3.8 million in 1980 to about 7 million in 1989. Asian-Americans are concentrated in a few areas of the country, where they have an important influence on the overall culture. Most Asians (56 percent) live in the West, particularly in California (13 percent of Californians will be Asian in the year 2000). Asian-Americans are highly urbanized, with 93 percent living in cities (three quarters of the 3 million Californian Asians live in the Los Angeles basin or the San Francisco Bay area). The Asian subculture in these regions requires special marketing attention for many companies. Grocery stores in Koreatown in Los Angeles stock large bags of rice near the checkout counter where stores in middle America put the charcoal.

Asian-Americans are a prime market because they are more affluent than any other racial or ethnic group. In 1990, the median income of an Asian-American household was $31,500 compared to $28,700 for whites, $20,000 for Hispanics, and $16,000 for blacks. Fully 32 percent of Asian-American households had incomes greater than $50,000 (compared to 29 percent of whites). Asian income levels are high for two reasons: (1) the education level is high (35 percent of adults have completed four or more years of college, compared to 22 percent of white Americans), and (2) more Asian-Americans live in married-couple households with two wage earners.

It is tempting to think of Asian-Americans (and other minority subcultures) as a single, homogeneous market, but this subculture is highly diverse. Some Asians are well integrated in American culture, while others live in Asian communities and maintain much of their original culture, including their language.

Because Asian people come from several distinctive cultural backgrounds—Japan, China, Southeast Asia, and the Pacific Islands—many marketers further segment the Asian community into subcultures based on language or nationality.[34] MCI, for instance, developed such effective print ads targeted at recent immigrants from Hong Kong and Taiwan that the company had to hire additional Chinese-speaking operators to handle the influx of calls. Implementing such targeted marketing strategies is possible in communities where specialized media (newspapers, magazines, radio) can reach Asian subcultures.

GENDER AS A SUBCULTURE

Despite the modern tendency to downplay differences between men and women, there is ample evidence men and women differ in important respects (not only physically). For instance, women may process information differently from men and seem to be more "generous, more nurturing, and less dominating than men."[35] For some marketing purposes, gender differences may be significant enough to consider the two sexes as separate subcultures. For instance, research has found that women treat possessions differently than men do. Ownership and possession of products is seen by some men as a way to dominate and exert power over others, discriminate themselves from others (status differentiation), even engage in subtle forms of aggression over others. Women, in contrast, tend to value possessions that can enhance personal and social relationships. Compared to most men, most women seem to value caring to controlling, sharing to selfishness, cooperating to dominating. Many marketers may find it useful to develop different marketing strategies for the male and female subcultures.

Income as a Subculture

It is possible to consider level of income as a subculture, since people at different income levels tend to have different values, behaviors, and lifestyles. Typically, however, income is used to further segment a subculture defined on some other characteristic (age, ethnic group, region). Many myths and misconceptions about income distribution in the United States can confuse marketers. For instance, if you think the lower-income households are dominated by minorities, you are wrong—most poor Americans are white. Affluence doesn't necessarily increase with age, either.

Marketers often divide American households into three income categories—*downscale* (under $20,000 income per year), *upscale* (over $50,000 per year), and *middle income* ($20,000 to 50,000 per year).[36] Figure 14.5 shows some key demographic characteristics of these income groups. These data illustrate one reason to stay in college and graduate: there is a very strong relationship between college education and income level. Nearly half of the upscale adults have completed four years of college, but only 10 percent of downscale adults have done so. The Figure also shows nearly half (46 percent) of American households are downscale. Although the upscale subculture constitutes an excellent market for high quality, luxury goods, only one in five households falls into this category. The mass market is downscale, which partially accounts for the huge success of discount retailers such as Wal-Mart. American marketers have found that the downscale market can be very profitable.

Acculturation Processes

When a person from one culture moves to a different culture or subculture to live and work, acculturation processes begin. **Acculturation** refers to how people in one culture or subculture understand and adapt to the meanings (values, beliefs, behaviors, rituals, lifestyles) of another culture or subculture.[37] **Consumer acculturation** refers to how people acquire the ability and cultural knowledge to be a skilled consumer in a different culture or subculture.[38]

Acculturation processes are very important in the modern world. Many societies face the problem of assimilating large numbers of immigrants from rather different cultural backgrounds into the host culture. For instance, in the

FIGURE 14.5
Characteristics of Three Income Subcultures

Selected Characteristics of Households by Income Groups	Total	Downscale (less than $25,000)	Middle Income ($25,000 to $49,999)	Upscale ($50,000 and over)
Total households (*in thousands*)	92,830	42,569	30,927	19,332
Percent of all households	100.0%	45.9%	33.3%	20.8%
Median household income*	$27,200	$12,900	$35,500	$66,300
Family households	70.9%	56.9%	79.1%	88.7%
Married couples	56.1%	36.6%	66.9%	82.0%
Female-headed families	11.7%	17.5%	8.5%	4.1%
With children under 18	36.1%	29.2%	41.6%	42.7%
One person in household	24.5%	39.5%	15.4%	5.9%
Two or three persons in household	49.8%	44.2%	54.6%	54.6%
Four or more persons in household	25.7%	16.4%	30.0%	39.5%
Median age of householder	49	51	41	42
Percent high school graduates	75.8%	61.0%	85.1%	93.3%
Percent with four or more years of college	22.3%	9.7%	23.7%	47.5%
Black	11.4%	16.4%	8.2%	5.4%
Hispanic	7.1%	8.7%	6.6%	4.4%

* Income figures from the 1989 Current Population Survey are for 1988.
Source: *American Demographics'* tabulation of the Census Bureau's March 1989 Current Population Survey.

United States, the Hispanic and Asian subcultures grew very rapidly during the 1980s.

Acculturation is also important for people who move to different regions within the same country and must adapt to different subcultural meanings. In the United States, one of six Americans moves each year.[39] However, two thirds of these moved within the same county (the median distance moved is only 6 miles), and the subcultural changes in most of these moves are probably not great. In contrast, about 10 percent of Americans move to a different region of the country (most of these people are college graduates), and they are likely to face some acculturation problems as they learn a new regional subculture. Finally, acculturation is important for marketing managers who must try to understand the cultural meanings of consumers in different societies and subcultures than their own.

The degree to which immigrants, movers, and marketers become acculturated into a new culture or subculture depends on their level of **cultural**

interpenetration—the amount and type of social interactions they have with people in the host culture.[40] Social contact with people in other subcultures can occur through direct, personal experience at work, while shopping, or in living arrangements.

Social experiences also may be indirect or vicarious, as in observing other people from a distance or on television. Some Americans might lack a cultural understanding of people in other societies and subcultures because much of their social contact with such people has been shallow and indirect. Many Americans learn about other cultures and subcultures largely through vicarious observation of subcultural portrayals in the mass media (movies, television programs, books, news media). When people have the opportunity for deeper cultural interpenetration (through work experiences or living in proximity to other types of people), they tend to become more thoroughly acculturated.

When people come into contact with a new culture or subculture, they may go through **four stages of acculturation** corresponding to four levels of cultural interpenetration.[41] In the *honeymoon stage*, people are fascinated by the exotic foreign culture or subculture. Because cultural interpenetration is shallow and superficial, little acculturation occurs. Tourists traveling to various regions of the United States may experience this stage.

If cultural interpenetration increases, people may enter a *rejection stage*, where they recognize that many of their old behaviors and meanings may be inadequate for acting in the new subculture. Some people may develop hostile attitudes toward the new subculture and reject its key values and meanings. Cultural conflicts are maximum in this stage.

If cultural interpenetration continues and deepens, people may reach the *tolerance stage*. As people learn more cultural meanings and behaviors, they may begin to appreciate the new subculture, and cultural conflict will decrease. Finally, in the *integration stage*, adjustment to the subculture is adequate, although acculturation need not be complete or total. At this stage, people are able to function satisfactorily in the new culture or subculture, which is viewed as an alternative way of life and is valued for its good qualities.

Consider the acculturation problems faced by immigrants who come to the United States with their own cultural meanings and values and must adapt to the different cultural meanings of American society. One study of immigrants from India found that transitional objects such as Indian clothing, jewelry, special furniture, movies, photographs, and music were highly valued as reminders of their home culture.[42] Educated immigrants might tend to become more acculturated because their high education level leads to greater cultural interpenetration. Many Hispanics tend to maintain their cultural values and traditions, and full acculturation may take three or four generations. But even long-term resident Hispanic-Americans, Asian-Americans, or African-Americans may never completely incorporate all of the values, meanings, and behaviors of American culture.

An important aspect of the acculturation process is proficiency in the language of the new culture. Ability to speak English obviously influences the level of cultural interpenetration that an immigrant can achieve in the United

States. For instance, Hispanic immigrants who live and work in Spanish-speaking neighborhoods, surrounded by similar people, may penetrate little into American society and may become only partially acculturated. Immigrants with more education are more likely to speak English and can obtain better jobs, which, in turn, allows for greater cultural penetration and enables them to become more completely acculturated. Interestingly, immigrants who join families already living in the United States tend to be more passive and penetrate less deeply into American culture than the more innovative family members who were the first to come to the United States.

Social Class

An expert in social class research, Richard Coleman, has made the following observations:

> There are no two ways about it: social class is a difficult idea. Sociologists, in whose discipline the concept emerged, are not of one mind about its value and validity. Consumer researchers, to whose field its use has spread, display confusion about when and how to apply it. The American public is noticeably uncomfortable with the realities about life that it reflects. All who try to measure it have trouble. Studying it rigorously and imaginatively can be monstrously expensive. Yet, all these difficulties notwithstanding, the proposition still holds: social class is worth troubling over for the insights it offers on the marketplace behavior of the nation's consumers.[43]

We agree with these observations concerning both the problems and the value of social class analysis. For our purposes in this text, **social class** refers to a national status hierarchy by which groups and individuals are distinguished in terms of esteem and prestige. Coleman recommends that four social class groups be used for consumer analysis in the United States—*upper*, *middle*, *working*, and *lower class*. Figure 14.6 describes these groups and identifies some marketing implications for each.

Identification with each social class is influenced most strongly by one's level of education and occupation (including income as a measure of work success). But social class is also affected by social skills, status aspirations, community participation, family history, cultural level, recreational habits, physical appearance, and social acceptance by a particular class. Thus, social class is a composite of many personal and social attributes rather than a single characteristic such as income or education. The social classes can be considered as large subcultures because their members share many cultural meanings and behaviors.

Although the members of each social class share distinct values and behavior patterns to some degree, each of the four major groups can be further differentiated. While there are a number of similarities in values and behaviors within

FIGURE 14.6
Social Class Groups for Consumer Analysis

Upper Americans (14 percent of population). This group consists of the upper-upper, lower-upper, and upper-middle classes. They have common goals and are differentiated mainly by income. This group has many different lifestyles, which might be labeled postpreppy, conventional, intellectual, and political, among others. The class remains the segment of our society in which quality merchandise is most prized, special attention is paid to prestige brands, and the self-image ideal is "spending with good taste." Self-expression is more prized than in previous generations, and neighborhood remains important. Depending on income and priorities, theater, books, investment in art, European travel, household help, club memberships for tennis, golf, and swimming, and prestige schooling for children remain high consumption priorities.

Middle class (32 percent of population). These consumers definitely want to "do the right thing" and buy "what's popular." They have always been concerned with fashion and following recommendations of "experts" in print media. Increased earnings result in better living, which means a "nicer neighborhood on the better side of town with good schools." It also means spending more on "worthwhile experiences" for children, including winter ski trips, college educations, and shopping for better brands of clothes at more expensive stores. Appearance of home is important, because guests may visit and pass judgment. This group emulates upper Americans, which distinguishes it from the working class. It also enjoys trips to Las Vegas and physical activity. Deferred gratification may still be an ideal, but it is not so often practiced.

Working class (38 percent of population). Working-class Americans are "family folk" depending heavily on relatives for economic and emotional support, e.g., tips on job opportunities, advice on purchases, help in times of trouble. The emphasis on family ties is only one sign of how much more limited and different working-class horizons are socially, psychologically, and geographically compared to those of the middle class. In almost every respect, a parochial view characterizes this blue-collar world. This group has changed little in values and behaviors despite rising incomes in some cases. For them, "keeping up with the times" focuses on the mechanical and recreational, and, thus, ease of labor and leisure is what they continue to pursue.

Lower Americans (16 percent of population). The men and women of lower America are no exception to the rule that diversities and uniformities in values and consumption goals are to be found at each social level. Some members of this world, as has been publicized, are prone to every form of instant gratification known to humankind when the money is available. But others are dedicated to resisting worldly temptations as they struggle toward what some believe will be a "heavenly reward" for their earthly sacrifices.

Source: Excerpted with permission from "The Continuing Significance of Social Class to Marketing," by Richard P. Coleman in the *Journal of Consumer Research,* December 1983, pp. 265–80.

groups in a given class, there can be vast differences in family situations and income levels among subgroups.

For instance, families in each social class can be further classified as relatively overprivileged, average, or underprivileged.[44] *Overprivileged* families in each social class are those with incomes usually 25 percent to 30 percent above the median for the class, who therefore have money left over to seek forms of a better life preferred by the class. However, because these families continue to share values, behaviors, and associations with other members of the class, they typically do not move to a higher social class. The *average* families are those in the middle income range who can afford the kind of house, car, apparel, food, furniture, and appliances expected by their social class peers. Finally, the *underprivileged* families have incomes that fall at least 15 percent below the class midpoint and therefore must scrimp and sacrifice to be able to purchase the proper products for that class.

Social class and relative standing within a class are important sources of consumers' beliefs, values, and behaviors.[45] Most of the people an individual interacts with on a day-to-day basis are likely to be members of that person's social class. Family, peer groups, and friends at work, school, and in the neighborhood are all likely to be of the same social class. These people teach the individual appropriate values for the class as well as behaviors that are acceptable to it. This process can occur either through direct instruction ("You don't have a chance anymore unless you go to college") or vicariously (an individual sees neighborhood friends going to college, graduating, and purchasing new cars).

At a conceptual level, social classes are useful for investigating the process by which consumers develop different beliefs, values, and behavior patterns. For example, the upper class may well be socially secure and not find it necessary or desirable to purchase the most expensive brands to impress other people. Middle-class people, on the other hand, often engage in such conspicuous consumption. As Highlight 14.6 shows, even homeless people (perhaps the lowest social class in American society) engage in consumption behavior.

Social Class versus Income

The social class concept aids in the understanding of consumer values and behavior; it is also useful for market segmentation and prediction of consumer behavior. However, there has long been a controversy as to whether social class or income is the better variable for use in consumer analysis. Advocates of each position muster a number of arguments for the superiority of their favorite variable and point out a variety of methodological and conceptual problems with the other one.

Recently, consumer researchers have recognized that each variable has its advantages and disadvantages; and the choice between using social class, income, or a combination of the two depends on the product and the situation. For example, Shaninger offers the following tentative generalizations:[46]

1. Social class is more relevant than income for areas of consumer behavior that do not involve high dollar expenditures, but do reflect underlying differences in lifestyle, values, or homemaker roles not captured by income (e.g., using imported or domestic wines). Social class is superior for both method and place of purchase of highly visible, symbolic, and expensive objects such as living room furniture.

2. Income is generally appropriate for understanding purchases of major kitchen and laundry appliances, and products that require substantial expenditures but are not status symbols within the class.

HIGHLIGHT 14.6

THE LOWEST SOCIAL CLASS? THE HOMELESS IN AMERICA

For a variety of reasons, homeless men and women crowded many American cities during the 1980s and early 1990s. Estimates in 1987 of the homeless population ranged from over 3 million to a more likely 600,000. Without a home and seldom with a job, the homeless are at the bottom of the social class hierarchy. However, despite their very low socioeconomic status, homeless people are consumers. They exert considerable physical and cognitive effort performing various consumption behaviors—finding a place to sleep, getting food to eat, acquiring simple possessions (warm clothing), keeping their meager possessions safe. In a real sense, these consumption activities constitute a full-time job.

One intensive study of the homeless learned much about this distinctive subculture or social class. For instance, most homeless individuals do have a few possessions—a shopping cart is very desirable. Some of their possessions are scavanged from trash cans or abandoned cars and buildings, and some are purchased (hot meals are especially valued). Often individuals will exchange possessions using barter. Some homeless will earn a small income doing odd jobs or, most frequently, by recycling (selling empty bottles or scrap metals). Others may work sporadically as day laborers or washing car windows at intersections.

Maslow's Need Hierarchy identifies the basic needs of homeless people—food, water, shelter, and security.

By definition, all homeless people lack a house or apartment, but some do have housing of their own. These can range from vacant buildings or abandoned automobiles to makeshift (self-contructed) shelters on vacant lots built from abandoned building materials to partially protected areas such as bridges and tunnels that can provide useful shelter.

The consumer product most often purchased by homeless people is food. But food can also be obtained from charitable shelters, by finding "road-kill" meat, and by scavenging food from dumpsters. Some homeless become skilled at scavenging food, for instance, by checking the dumpsters of fast-food restaurants soon after closing.

Clothing is particularly important in the winter, and homeless people will try to accumulate layers of clothing to provide protection from the cold. Multiple layers of clothing also provide protection from attack (beatings and rape). Clothing is often scavenged, although charity distribution centers can be a good source.

Another need is personal hygiene and health care. Satisfying these needs is difficult for homeless people partly because of their restricted access to water. Homeless people find it difficult to wash themselves and their clothes. Shelters are useful for these purposes. Of course, virtually no homeless individuals have any health insurance. Thus, they are likely to seek medical attention from emergency rooms or free clinics. One homeless person deliberately gets arrested when he is depressed or sick to get medical attention in jail.

Finally, tools of various sorts are important possessions for many homeless people. Shopping carts are useful to carry their possessions (to keep them from being stolen). Tools that aid in scavenging parts from cars or buildings are valued (screwdrivers, flashlights, tire irons).

Source: Ronald Paul Hill and Mark Stamey, "The Homeless in America: An Examination of Possessions and Consumption Behaviors *Journal of Consumer Research,* December 1990, pp. 303–21.

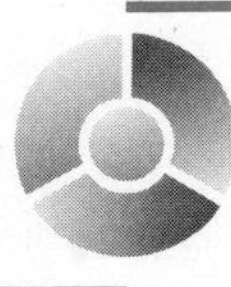

BACK TO.... WOOING THE AGING BABY BOOMERS

The baby boomer example describes an important change occurring in the subcultural social environment of America. Similar large-scale changes are occurring in the social environments of many other cultures. The example also identifies some economic reasons marketers must pay attention to this change in consumers.

Consumers in different age categories (such as 35 to 45 versus 50 to 65) are likely to have somewhat different values, cultural meanings, and behavior patterns. However, it should be recognized that these broad subcultural segments can be quite diverse. Therefore, marketers may have to use other variables to identify narrower and more precise segments. For example, the age categories could

3. The combination of social class and income is generally superior for product classes that are highly visible, serve as symbols of social class or status within class, and require either moderate or substantial expenditure (e.g., clothing, automobiles, television sets).

In sum, determining whether social class, income, a combination of these, or other variables is most useful in a particular situation requires a careful analysis of the relationships between the product and the consumer. In other words, consumer affect and cognitions, behaviors, and the environment must be analyzed to develop appropriate marketing strategies.

SUMMARY

This chapter discussed two macro social influences on consumers' behaviors, cognitions, and affective responses—subculture and social class. These social factors influence how people think, feel, and behave relative to their physical, social, and marketing environments. We discussed subcultural influences in terms of geographic area, age, ethnic groups, and other factors. Social class influences were discussed in terms of both their role in understanding consumer behavior and as a strategic tool.

be further broken down into ethnic, geographic, religious, or community subgroups. It is quite likely, for instance, that the cultural values and behavioral norms of middle-aged blacks and Hispanics are somewhat different from those of middle-aged whites. Marketers could also look at different social classes within the baby boomer group. Here, again, we would expect to see major differences in the product perceptions, values, and behavior patterns of upper-, middle-, and lower-class baby boomers.

These different social groups may require different marketing strategies. Although the opening example focused on implications for advertising, these subcultural changes also have important implications for other aspects of marketing strategy, including product development, pricing, and distribution.

Key Terms and Concepts

Subcultures *467*
Geographic Subcultures *472*
Age Subcultures *475*
Baby Boomers *476*
Ethnic Subcultures *482*
Acculturation *487*
Consumer Acculteration *487*
Cultural Interpenetration *488*
Four Stages of Acculturation *489*
Social Class *490*

Review and Discussion Questions

1. Discuss how subcultures (and social class) influence how consumers learn cultural meanings (values, behaviors, lifestyles). Give a specific example.
2. Discuss how marketing strategies can affect a subculture (or social class). Give a concrete example to illustrate your point.
3. What ethical factors should a marketer consider in developing marketing strategies targeted at particular subcultures or social classes? (What is your reaction to selling fortified wine to homeless people, cigarettes to Hispanics, or diet plans to overweight people?)

4. Are college students a subculture? Why or why not? How could a marketer use knowledge about this group to develop marketing strategy?
5. Identify the age subcultures among members of your own family (or neighborhood). How do these cultural differences affect the consumption behaviors of these people for foods, personal care products, and clothing?
6. Define the concept of social class. What are the major social class groups in the United States (or your home country)? What are the major social class groups in the immediate community where you live? How did you recognize these social class groupings?
7. Select two product classes (perhaps foods, beverages, clothing, automobiles, furniture). How might each of the social classes you have identified above respond to marketing strategies for these products.
8. Think of two subcultures not discussed in the text and briefly describe them. Discuss marketing implications for each one. What product categories would be most relevant?
9. Discuss the acculturation process by describing what might happen if you come into contact with a different subculture (say, you moved to a different area of the country or city).
10. Discuss the concept of cultural interpenetration in terms of the acculturation of immigrant populations in your country. What marketing opportunities do you see in this situation?

NOTES

1. Alecia Swasy, "Changing Times," *The Wall Street Journal*, March 22, 1991, p. B6.
2. Diane Crispell, "Guppies, Minks, and Ticks," *American Demographics*, June 1990, pp. 50–51.
3. Ibid.
4. Gretchen Morgenson, "Where Can I Buy Some," *Forbes*, June 24, 1991, pp. 82–86.
5. Thomas W. Osborne, "An American Mosaic," *Marketing Insights*, June 1989, pp. 76–83.
6. James W. Gentry, Patriya Tansuhaj, and Joby John. "Do Geographic Subcultures Vary Culturally," in *Advances in Consumer Research*, vol. 15, ed. Michael J. Houston (Provo, Utah: Association for Consumer Research, 1988), pp. 411–17.
7. Thomas Moore, "Different Folks, Different Strokes," *Fortune*, September 16, 1985, pp. 65–72.
8. Joel Garreau, *The Nine Nations of North America* (Boston: Houghton Mifflin, 1981). For a critical perspective on this approach, see Lynn R. Kahle, "The Nine Nations of North America and the Value Basis of Geographic Segmentation," *Journal of Marketing*, April 1986, pp. 37–41.
9. For a more detailed discussion, see Del I. Hawkins, Don Roupe, and Kenneth A. Coney, "The Influence of Geographic Subcultures in the United States," in *Advances in Consumer Research*, vol. 8, ed. Kent B. Monroe (Ann Arbor, Mich.: Association for Consumer Research, 1981), pp. 713–17.
10. Blayne Cutler, "Welcome to the Borderlands," *American Demographics*, February 1991, pp. 44–49, 57.

11. Associated Press, "Survey: Age Is Not Good Indicator of Consumer Need," *Marketing News*, November 21, 1988, p. 6.

12. This discussion is based on Doris L. Walsh, "Targeting Teens," *American Demographics*, February 1985, pp. 20–25.

13. This discussion is based on Geoffrey Calvin, "What the Baby-Boomers Will Buy Next," *Fortune*, October 15, 1984, pp. 28–34.

14. William Dunn, "Wheels for the Baby Boom: Detroit Discovers Demographics," *American Demographics*, May 1984, pp. 27–29.

15. Russell W. Belk, "Yuppies as Arbiters of the Emerging Consumption Style," in *Advances in Consumer Research*, vol. 13, ed. Richard J. Lutz (Provo, Utah: Association for Consumer Research, 1986), pp. 514–19.

16. This discussion is based on William Lazer, "Inside the Mature Market," *American Demographics*, March 1985, pp. 23–25.

17. Thomas Exter, "How Big Will the Older Market Be?" *American Demographics*, June 1990, pp. 30–32, 36.

18. Janet Neiman, "The Elusive Mature Market," *Ad Week*, April 6, 1987, p. 16.

19. For a complete work on this market, see Charles D. Schewe, *The Elderly Market: Selected Readings* (Chicago: American Marketing Association, 1985). Also see Eleanor Johnson Tracy, "The Gold in the Gray," *Fortune*, October 14, 1985, pp. 137–38.

20. For example, see Janice Castro, "Is That You on TV, Grandpa?" *Time*, March 6, 1989, p. 53.

21. Joe Szczesny and Richard Woodbury, "A Nation on the Move," *Time*, April 29, 1991, pp. 30–31.

22. Jon Schwartz and Thomas Exter, "All Our Children," *American Demographics*, May 1989, pp. 34–37.

23. James P. Allen and Eugene Turner, "Where Diversity Reigns," *American Demographics*, August 1990, pp. 34–38.

24. Judith Waldrop, "Shades of Black," *American Demographics*, September 1990, pp. 30–34.

25. Cyndee Miller, "Toy Companies Release 'Ethnically Correct' Dolls," *Marketing News*, September 30, 1991, pp. 1–2.

26. James R. Schiffman, "Uptown's Fall Bodes Ill for Niche Brands," *The Wall Street Journal*, January 22, 1990, pp. B1, B5.

27. Alix M. Freeman, "Heileman, Under Pressure, Scuttles PowerMaster Malt," *The Wall Street Journal*, July 5, 1991, pp. B1, B4.

28. Sigredo A. Hernandez and Carol J. Kaufman, "Marketing Research in Hispanic Barrios: A Guide to Survey Research," *Marketing Research*, March 1990, pp. 11–27.

29. Cyndee Miller, "Hispanic Media Expand; TV has Strongest Appeal," *Marketing News*, January 21, 1991, pp. 1, 10.

30. This section is derived from Ed Fitch, "Is the Red Carpet Treatment Plush Enough?" *Advertising Age*, February 8, 1988, pp. S-1, S-15, 16.

31. Rohit Deshpande, Wayne D. Hoyer, and Naveen Donthu, "The Intensity of Ethnic Affiliation: A Study of the Sociology of Hispanic Consumption," *Journal of Consumer Research*, September 1986, pp. 214–20.

32. Ricks, *Big Business Blunders: Mistakes in Multinational Marketing* (Homewood, IL: Dow Jones-Irwin, 1983), p. 70. Also see Edward C. Baig, "Buenos Dias, Consumers," *Fortune*, December 23, 1985, pp. 79–80.

33. The information in this section is from William O'Hare, "A New Look at Asian Americans," *American Demographics*, October 1990, pp. 26–31.

34. Dan Frost, "California's Asian Market," *American Demographics*, October 1990, pp. 34–37.

35. Joan Myers-Levy and Durairaj Maheswaran, "Exploring Differences in Males' and Females' Processing Strategies," *Journal of Consumer Research*, June 1991, pp. 63–70; and Floyd W. Rudmin, "German and Canadian Data on Motivations for Ownership: Was Pythagoras Right?" in *Advances in Consumer Research*, vol. 17 (Provo, Utah: Association for Consumer Research, 1990), pp. 176–81.

36. Judith Waldrop, "Up and Down the Income

Scale," *American Demographics*, July 1990, pp. 24–27, 30.

37. Ronald J. Faber, Thomas C. O'Guinn, and John A. McCarty, "Ethnicity, Acculturation, and the Importance of Product Attributes," *Psychology & Marketing*, Summer 1987, pp. 121–134.

38. Lisa N. Penaloza, "Immigrant Consumer Acculturation," in *Advances in Consumer Research*, vol. 16 (Provo, Utah: Association for Consumer Research, 1989), pp. 110–18; 121–34.

39. Larry Long, "Americans on the Move," *American Demographics*, June 1990, pp. 46–49.

40. Alan R. Andreasen, "Cultural Interpenetration: A Critical Consumer Research Issue for the 1990s," in *Advances in Consumer Research*, vol. 17 (Provo, Utah: Association for Consumer Research, 1990), pp. 847–49.

41. Kalervo Oberg, "Cultural Shock: Adjustment to New Cultural Environments," *Practical Anthropologist* 7 (1960), pp. 177–82.

42. Raj Mehta and Russell W. Belk, "Artifacts, Identity, and Transition: Favorite Possessions of Indians and Indian Immigrants to the United States," *Journal of Consumer Research*, March 1991, pp. 398–411.

43. Richard P. Coleman, "The Continuing Significance of Social Class to Marketing," *Journal of Consumer Research*, December 1983, pp. 265–80. Much of the discussion in this part of the chapter is based on Coleman's view of social class as described in this excellent article.

44. Ibid., pp. 265–80.

45. James E. Fisher, "Social Class and Consumer Behavior: The Relevance of Class and Status," in *Advances in Consumer Research*, vol. 14, ed. Melanie Wallendorf and Paul Anderson (Provo, Utah: Association for Consumer Research, 1987), pp. 492–96.

46. Adapted from Charles M. Schaninger, "Social Class versus Income Revisited: An Empirical Investigation," *Journal of Marketing Research*, May 1981, pp. 192–208.

Additional Reading

For a discussion of how age affects consumer perceptions, see:

Roedder, John, Deborah and Mita Sujan. "Age Differences in Product Categorization." *Journal of Consumer Research*, March 1990, pp. 452–60.

For a discussion of marketing to regional subcultures, see:

Carpenter, Larry. "How to Market to Regions." *American Demographics*, November 1987, pp. 44–45.

Lesser, Jack A., and Marie Adele Hughes. "The Generalization of Psychographic Market Segmentation across Geographic Locations." *Journal of Marketing*, January 1986, pp. 18–27.

For a discussion of how advertising affects consumer acculturation, see:

O'Guinn, Thomas C., and R. J. Faber. "Advertising and Subculture: The Role of Ethnicity and Acculturation in Market Segmentation." In *Current Issues and Research in Advertising*. Ann Arbor: University of Michigan, 1986.

For a discussion of a religious subculture, see:

Hirschman, Elizabeth C. "American Jewish Ethnicity: Its Relationship to Some Selected Aspects of Consumer Behavior." *Journal of Marketing*, Summer 1981, pp. 102–10.

For a discussion of Hispanic responses to a marketing strategy, see:

Kaufman, Carol J., and Sigfedo A. Hernandez. "Barriers to Coupon Use: A View from the Bodega." *Journal of Advertising Research*, October–November 1990, pp. 18–25.

For a discussion of social class differences between ethnic subcultures, see:

Ness, Thomas E., and Melvin T. Stith. "Middle-Class Values in Blacks and Whites." In *Personal*

Values and Consumer Psychology, ed R. E. Pitts and A. G. Woodside. Lexington, Mass.: D. C. Heath, 1984.

For a discussion of creating subcultural segments using statistical analysis, see:

Weiss, Michael J. *The Clustering of America.* New York: Harper & Row, 1988.

For discussions of social class and consumer behavior, see:

Gronhaug, Kjell, and Paul S. Trapp. "Perceived Social Class Appeals of Branded Goods and Services." *The Journal of Consumer Marketing*, Winter 1989, pp. 13–18.

Fisher, James E. "Social Class and Consumer Behavior: The Relevance of Class and Status." In *Advances in Consumer Research*, vol. 14. Provo, Utah: Association for Consumer Research, 1987, pp. 492–96.

MARKETING STRATEGY IN ACTION

Hyatt and Marriott Build Retirement Housing for the Elderly

As the number of older Americans increases, businesses are beginning to pay more attention to the diversity in this subculture. Many companies are trying to identify the needs of the elderly and develop products to meet those needs. For instance, both Marriott Corporation and Hyatt Hotels are developing retirement community products for the elderly market. Retirement communities combine retirement apartments, various services, and nursing care. They offer personal living quarters in apartments of varying sizes, a wide range of activities and entertainment, housekeeping services, food service options (a dining room for some meals and one's own kitchen), along with varying levels of on-site health care, including full nursing home services for some people.

The market for retirement communities is immense; more than 30 million Americans will be 65 or older by the year 2000. However, it is a fallacy to imagine that everyone over 65 is a potential customer for a retirement community. The prime customers are in their late 70s or early 80s. Also, it is wrong to think that many elderly are feeble and in need of a nursing home (only 5 percent of Americans over 65 are institutionalized). Contrary to popular belief, not all elderly live alone; many elderly are married (estimated 8.3 million in 2000). The mature market is quite diverse; only the over-85 subgroup is somewhat homogeneous. Therefore, marketers must analyze the elderly subculture carefully.

Elderly people differ considerably in how they want to live in retirement. Some want to live in a single-family home, while others want apartments or condominiums. Some want community, social interactions, and recreational amenities, while others prefer solitude and independence.

Both Hyatt and Marriott conducted detailed research using focus groups and telephone and written surveys to understand these needs. One research study identified three sub-subcultures in the elderly subcultures — the "go- go's" (65 to 75, who travel, play golf, etc.), the "slow-go's" (75 to 85, still active, but slowing down), and the "no-go's" (85 and older, somewhat active but staying closer to home). The prime target customer for retirement communities is the slow-go group.

The go-go's will be potential customers in another 10 years, while the no-go's are potential customers for the more extensive levels of nursing care.

In the past, marketing of retirement community products was simplistic—some fancy four-color brochures and corporate print ads placed in magazines and newspapers. Early research generally focused on simple demographic analyses of age, income, and competition. Thus, many marketers did not really understand the elderly market and how they perceive their own needs.

There is a big affective and cognitive problem in marketing retirement communities. Typically, a consumer's first response is "I'm not ready yet." Most elderly consumers want to stay in their own homes and remain independent until that becomes impossible. Getting consumers to buy into a retirement community requires that they think about the unthinkable (their own mortality and failing health). This is not easy for most people. In fact, many elderly, especially among the affluent subgroup, perceive themselves as younger and more fit than they actually are.

Marriott opened its first two high-rise retirement developments (350 to 400 apartments) in 1988. Its Jefferson retirement community, which opened in 1992, offers a pool, maid service, and a health club, in addition to 24-hour meals, emergency call buttons in each bathroom and bedroom, a floor with skilled nursing care, and another floor for elderly who don't require nursing care, but need other types of daily help (in dressing themselves, for example).

A well-known industry consultant suggested that direct mail is the most effective approach for marketing retirement communities. Every month a company might send something to potential customers such as postcard invitations to some event, a letter describing some service, newsletters about the people in the retirement community, even dessert recipes.

Marriott successfully used a direct-mail promotion to generate interest in its Jefferson retirement community, before it was built. It mailed brochures and information to 45,000 affluent elderly residents of the Washington, D.C., area. For a $1,000 deposit, people could reserve a $100,000 to $260,000 apartment in the not-yet-built, luxury complex. The mailing generated a phenomenal 4 percent response rate (2 or 3 percent is considered good).

Over the next several years, Marriott plans to spend more than $1 billion constructing some 150 retirement communities like the Jefferson around the country. In each, most of the apartment units are designed for independent living, but residents have the option of receiving nursing care and other types of specialized services. Marriott also intends to build another 100 developments that offer only two living opinions—assisted living and nursing care.

Hyatt developed its retirement community, Classic Residences by Hyatt, in 1990. Classic Residences are upscale apartment complexes that offer a similar set of services for people of retirement age. Hyatt's initial research also showed that elderly people had a strong initial negative reaction to retirement communities. Even people living in metropolitan areas who were exposed to a great deal of marketing information about these products thought of retirement communities as a euphemism for the dreaded "nursing home." Thus, Hyatt's marketing promotions emphasize "active lifestyle" rather than "taking care of you forever."

Hyatt also found that many elderly people thought retirement communities were extremely expensive or they had to sign away their life savings to get into a retirement community. So Hyatt salespeople compared the costs of living in one's own home to living in the retirement community. Most people did not realize how much they were spending to live in their own house, and this knowledge had some influence on their beliefs that "I'm not ready yet." Marriott, finding the same thing, is experimenting with different pricing strategies, including charging a lower initial payment, with higher monthly rent/fees, so elderly customers don't have to use so much of their accumulated savings.

Finally, both Hyatt and Marriott have developed other marketing strategies. In their sales presentations, they include seminars about retirement planning, health issues, and motivational topics. Open houses often include entertainment to attract customers. If necessary, incentives are offered to encourage prospects to take that final step, including free rent for a few months, paid moving expenses, free interior decorating advice, or expense-paid vacations.

In sum, developing successful retirement community products and marketing strategies is largely a matter of listening to the prospects and understanding their needs and interests. Many elderly consumers know what they want, and they respond to the same types of marketing strategies used to sell other services.

Discussion Questions

1. Discuss the submarkets (sub-subcultures) within the elderly subculture that are relevant for retirement communities. Discuss how social class can be combined with age subcultures to more precisely define the market segments for retirement communities. What marketing strategies would be necessary to target these different segments of the elderly market?
2. Identify the key target segments for Marriott's new health-care-oriented retirement communities (they only offer varying levels of health care). For the most attractive segment, identify and analyze the behaviors, affective responses, and cognitions most important in shopping for, purchasing, and living in such a retirement community.
3. Discuss the marketing strategies that Marriott could use to market its new health-care-oriented retirement units to the key market segments. What different promotional strategies would appeal to these subcultural groups?
4. The customer/product relationship may be a useful way to think about marketing retirement communities. What aspects of this relationship should Marriott and Hyatt consider, and why? Contrast the marketing strategies Marriott and Hyatt could use to develop the customer/product relationship *before* the purchase with the strategies they might institute *after* the sale to enhance and maintain this relationship.

Source: Sally Chapralis, "Retirement Community Marketers End Their Retirement," *Marketing News,* July 8, 1991, p. 2; Jame Gollub and Harold Javitz, "Six Ways to Age," *American Demographics,* June 1989, pp. 28–37; and Janet Novack, "Tea, Sympathy, and Direct Mail," *Forbes,* September 18, 1989, pp. 210–11.

Reference Groups and Family

CHAPTER 15

HEY, DUDE, LET'S CONSUME

Max Salvati, age 3, has a bad case of Turtlemania (that's the Teenage Mutant Ninja Turtles, the toy craze of the late 1980s and early 1990s). He sleeps on Ninja Turtle sheets, eats Ninja Turtle cereal, uses a Ninja Turtle cup and plate, wears a Ninja Turtle T- shirt, and has loads of Ninja Turtle toys. Max explains, "I love the Turtles, because they're good and they fight crime."

Spending on children is one of the fastest growing sectors of the American economy. Spending on and by kids aged 4 to 12 jumped about 25 percent in 1989 to $60 billion, compared to 2 percent growth in overall spending. In 1990, the children's market was worth about $75 billion, or nearly 2 percent of the U.S. economy.

Fueling this growth are the baby boomers who are having children later in life, creating a baby boomlet. Boomers in their 30s and 40s can afford to indulge their children because their earning power is greater than younger parents, and they already own many of the material things of life. Also, many affluent families have only one or two children, which leaves more money to spend on each child.

These demographic characteristics of American families have affected many markets. For instance, about $1 billion in children's

books were sold in 1990. The current generation of boomer parents are concerned about "building a better kid," and books are one way to do it. The growth in the children's market should continue because 4 million children were born in both 1989 and 1990, the highest level since the baby boom peak in the early 1960s.

What do kids buy for themselves? In 1989, kids under 12 spent over $10 billion on video games — $7 billion in arcades and $3 billion for games to play at home. That market is dominated by Nintendo (with about a 90 percent market share), a Japanese company that single-handedly revived the home video game market.

Sales of traditional toys are also booming. Consider that Mattel's Barbie doll brought in about $600 million in worldwide sales in 1990. To keep the interest of the 9-to-12-year-old market, Mattell has expanded the Barbie line to include girl's handbags and trading cards. Parents can even buy Barbie townhouses and mansions at up to $400. The children's toy market has also produced phenomenal growth for successful retailer Toys 'R' Us ($4.8 billion in sales in 1989).

Another popular purchase for kids are videocassettes. Eight of the 10 top video movies of all time appeal to kids — "E.T." and "Bambi" are prime examples. Parents don't mind buying videos for kids, because the children will happily watch a movie dozens of times. But adults seldom watch a movie more than once, so they rent.

Among other products for kids is Hallmark's new line of greeting cards, "To Kids with Love." These cards are intended to convey affection and encouragement from busy working parents who sometimes must leave the home before kids get up and return after the kids are in bed.

The modern American child no longer dresses in hand-me-downs from older siblings and cousins. The growing market in children's clothing is evident from the booming sales for companies such as GapKids (now with over 100 stores), Laura Ashley's Mother

and Child clothing line (accounting for 13 percent of total sales), Esprit Kids (the company's fastest growing segment with 20 percent of $780 million in annual sales). Even adult fashion designers Ralph Lauren and Christian Dior have introduced children's lines.

Source: Peter Newcomb, "Hey, Dude, Let's Consume," *Forbes,* June 11, 1990, pp. 126–31.

This example shows how changes in the American family can affect marketing strategies targeted at kids or adults who buy for kids. In making these purchasing decisions, husbands and wives (mothers and fathers) influence each other's affective responses, cognitions, and behaviors. These decisions are also influenced by other people in the social environment, including relatives, friends, and peers (both kids and adults are highly influenced by peer groups). In this chapter, we discuss two types of social influences – reference groups and family.

Reference groups and family are aspects of the micro social environment for consumers. Social interactions with reference groups and family are often direct and face to face, which can have immediate influences on consumers' cognitive, affective, and behavioral responses to marketing strategies.[1] For instance, the social environment created when two friends shop together can influence each person's shopping experience, decision processes, and overall satisfaction with a purchase. As you learned in Chapter 12 (see Figure 12.2), reference groups and family are important in transmitting (moving) cultural meanings in the overall society, subcultures, and social class to individual consumers. For all these reasons, reference groups and family have significant implications for marketing strategies.

Reference Groups

Individuals may be involved in many different types of groups. A **group** consists of *two or more people who interact with each other to accomplish some goal.* Important groups include families, close personal friends, co-workers, formal social groups (Kiwanis, professional associations), leisure or hobby groups (a bowling team), and neighbors. Some of these groups may become reference groups.

A **reference group** involves *one or more people that someone uses as a basis for comparison or point of reference in forming affective and cognitive responses and*

FIGURE 15.1
Types of Reference Groups

Type of Reference Group	Key Distinctions and Characteristics
Formal/informal	Formal reference groups have a clearly specified structure; informal groups to not.
Primary/secondary	Primary reference groups involve direct, face-to-face interactions; secondary groups do not.
Membership	People become formal members of membership reference groups.
Aspirational	People aspire to join or emulate aspirational reference groups.
Dissociative	People seek to avoid or reject dissociative reference groups.

performing behaviors. Reference groups can be of any size (from one person to hundreds of people) and may be tangible (actual people) or intangible and symbolic (successful business executives or sports heros). People's reference groups (and single referent persons) may be from the same or other social classes, subcultures, and even cultures. Figure 15.1 lists several types of reference groups and their key distinguishing characteristics. These distinctions can be combined to better describe specific groups. For example, your immediate co-workers constitute a formal, primary, membership group. While these distinctions can be useful, most consumer research has focused on two primary, informal groups—peers and family. Issues of major importance to marketing concerning reference group influence include:

1. What types of influence do reference groups exert on individuals?
2. How does reference group influence vary across products and brands?
3. How can marketers use the concept of reference groups to develop effective marketing strategies?

Analyzing Reference Groups

Reference groups are cultural groups in that members share certain common cultural meanings. For instance, peer groups of college students tend to develop specific meanings and behavior norms about appropriate clothing, and peer groups of teenage boys share certain meanings about what types of athletic shoes are hot. These reference groups can influence the affective and cognitive responses of consumers as well as their purchase and consumption behavior ("What should I wear today?").

Marketers try to determine the content of the shared meanings of various reference groups (the common values, beliefs, behavioral norms, etc.). Then they select certain reference groups to associate with or promote their products. But marketers seldom examine the social processes by which reference groups move cultural meaning to products and from products to the consumer.

Reference groups can have both positive and negative effects on consumers. Many social groups incorporate desirable, positive cultural meanings and become associative reference groups that consumers want to emulate or be affiliated with. Other social groups embody unfavorable or distasteful meanings and serve as a negative point of reference that people want to avoid; they become dissociative reference groups.

Types of Reference Group Influence

Most people are members of several primary informal groups and a few formal, membership groups (church, civic, and professional associations). In addition, people are aware of many secondary groups, both formal and informal. Why do people use some of these groups as a reference group and not others? And how do these reference groups influence consumers' affect, cognitions, and behaviors? Basically, people identify and affiliate with particular reference groups for three reasons: to gain useful knowledge, to obtain rewards or avoid punishments, and to acquire meanings for constructing, modifying, or maintaining their self-concepts. These goals reflect three types of reference group influence – informational, utilitarian, and value-expressive.

Informational reference group influence transmits useful information to consumers about themselves, other people, or aspects of the physical environment such as products, services, and stores. This information may be conveyed directly – either verbally or by direct demonstration. For instance, a consumer trying to decide on a purchase of running shoes or stereo equipment might seek the advice of friends who are knowledgeable about those categories. A person who is trying to learn to play tennis might ask friends to demonstrate how to serve or hit a backhand shot.

Consumers tend to be more influenced by reference groups if the information is perceived as reliable and relevant to the problem at hand and the information source is perceived to be trustworthy.[2] Reference sources can be a single person, as when Lee Iacocca, Dave Thomas, or Frank Perdue expound on the merits of Chrysler cars, Wendy's hamburgers, or Perdue chickens. Highly credible reference groups are more likely to have an informational influence on consumers. Thus, some marketers hire recognized experts to endorse their products and tell consumers why it is good.

Information can also be obtained indirectly through vicarious observation. For instance, an avid fisherman may carefully note the types of equipment famous bass fishermen are using in a fishing tournament or on TV fishing shows. This is common behavior; many golfers, skiers, mountain climbers, and other sports enthusiasts engage in similar vicarious observations of products used by their reference group. This is why Nike hired basketball star Michael Jordan (obviously an expert) to wear Air Jordan basketball shoes.

Information can be transmitted from reference groups to consumers in three ways. Sometimes, informational influence is intentionally sought by consumers to reduce the perceived risk of making a decision or to learn how to perform certain behaviors. Thus, most beginning sky divers listen very carefully to their new reference group of experienced skydiving instructors as they present information about how to pack a parachute or how to land correctly. Consumers who buy a new computer may seek information provided by a reference group of more experienced users who can help them learn how to use the product effectively.

In other cases, information is accidentally transmitted as when someone overhears reference group members talking about a product or observes members of a reference group using the product. A third way that information may be transferred to the consumer is when reference group members initiate the process. This can occur with enthusiastic reference group members who seek to proselytize for an activity and gain new members. For example, Rollerbladers might try to persuade others to take up the sport. Marketers might use a strategy of getting current customers to create new customers (bring along a friend for dinner and get your meal for half the price).

Utilitarian reference group influence on consumers' behaviors (and affect and cognitions) occurs when the reference group controls important rewards and punishments. Consumers usually will comply with the desires of a reference group if (*a*) they believe the group can control rewards and punishments, (*b*) the behavior is visible or known to the group, and (*c*) they are motivated to obtain rewards or avoid punishments.

In some work groups (a formal, membership reference group), people are expected to wear formal business suits, while other work groups encourage very casual dress (jeans and T-shirts in some Silicon Valley, California, companies). Rewards and punishments may be tangible (raises, bonuses, being fired), or psychological and social consequences may occur (admiring looks or snide remarks behind your back). Peer groups often administer such psychosocial rewards and punishments for adherence to and violations of the reference group code. Consider how your own peer reference group in college influences your dress behavior. Marketers use these factors by showing such sanctions in TV commercials (people recoiling from offensive body odor, bad breath, or the dandruff flakes on someone's shoulder).

Value-expressive reference group influence can affect people's self-concepts. As cultural units, reference groups both contain and create cultural meanings (beliefs, values, goals, behavioral norms, lifestyles). As you learned in Chapter 13, people are constantly seeking desirable cultural meanings to use in constructing, enhancing, or maintaining their self-concepts. By identifying and affiliating with certain reference groups that express these desired meanings, consumers can draw out some of these meanings and use them in their own self-construction project.

One group of people who buy Harley-Davidson motorcycles and associated products are middle- and upper-middle-class professional people (including doctors, dentists, lawyers, professors). Derisively called RUBS (rich urban bikers) or weekend warriors by the hard-core Harley owners (the tattooed and bearded Outlaws or pseudo Outlaws), many of these consumers treat the radical, hard-core Harley owners as an aspirational reference group (very few RUBS will ever become hard-core bikers).[3]

The hard-core Harley bikers express several desirable meanings and values for the RUBS (and probably convey negative meanings to nonbikers). By identifying to some extent with the hard-core biker as an aspirational reference group, RUBS can gain some of these important meanings, including feelings of freedom (from work and family), freedom of spirit, radical independence, patriotism (Harley's are built in the United States), and a feeling of belonging to a special, unique group. Perhaps some RUBS are also able to inspire a bit of the fear and awe among nonbikers or owners of other brands that the hard-core bikers relish.

Wearing certain types of clothing is a way of acquiring the cultural meanings associated with a reference group.

These reference group meanings can influence affect, cognitions, and behavior, including purchases of biker clothing and bike accessories. Harley-Davidson recognizes these value-expressive desires and needs, and markets (often through licensing) a variety of products to satisfy them, including black leather jackets, "colors" (clothing with insignias and biker logos), many biking accessories, and even a Harley-Davidson brand of beer.

In summary, it is important to recognize that all three types of reference group influence can be accomplished by a single reference group. For instance, as a reference group for the weekend biker, the hard-core Harley-Davidson bikers can be a source of information (through magazines and observation), rewards and punishments (waving back or haughtily ignoring the RUBS on the road), and subcultural meanings that express one's values.

Reference Group Influence on Products and Brands

Reference groups do not influence all product and brand purchases to the same degree. Based on earlier research, Bearden and Etzel proposed that reference group influence on product and brand decisions varies on at least two dimensions.[4] The first dimension concerns the degree to which the product or brand is a necessity or a luxury. A *necessity* is owned by virtually everyone (a flashlight) whereas a *luxury* is owned only by consumers in particular groups (a sailboat). The second dimension is the degree to which the object in question is conspicuous or known by other people.[5] A *public good* is one that other people are aware an individual owns and uses; one for which they can identify the brand with little or no difficulty (a car). A *private good* is used at home or in private so that other people (outside the immediate family) would be unaware of its possession or use (a hair blower).

Combining these two dimensions produces the matrix shown in Figure 15.2. This figure suggests reference group influence will vary depending on whether the products and brands are public necessities, private necessities, public luxuries, or private luxuries. Consider wristwatches, which are public necessities. Because everyone can see whether or not a person is wearing a

Primary reference groups can have a strong value-expressive influence on their members.

FIGURE 15.2

Effects of Public-Private and Luxury-Necessity Dimensions on Reference Group Influence for Product and Brand Choice

	Necessity	Luxury
Public	**Public necessities** Reference group influence Product: Weak Brand: Strong Examples: Wristwatch, automobile, man's suit	**Public luxuries** Reference group influence Product: Strong Brand: Strong Examples: Golf clubs, snow skis, sailboat
Private	**Private necessities** Reference group influence Product: Weak Brand: Weak Examples: Mattress, floor lamp, refrigerator	**Private luxuries** Reference group influence Product: Strong Brand: Weak Examples: TV game, trash compactor, ice maker

Source: Adapted from "Reference Group Influences on Product and Brand Purchase Decisions," by William O. Bearden and Michael J. Etzel, in the *Journal of Consumer Research,* September 1982, p. 185.

wristwatch, the *brand* may be susceptible to reference group influence. However, because the product class is owned and used by most people, there is likely to be little reference group influence on whether one should purchase a watch.[6]

Reference Groups and Marketing Strategy

We have seen that reference groups are an important influence on consumers. Not only do members of primary informal groups affect consumer knowledge, attitudes, and values, but they also affect the purchase of specific products and brands—and even the selection of stores in which purchases are made. In some cases, an analysis of primary informal group influences can be used to develop marketing strategies. For example, in industrial marketing, a careful analysis of the group influence dynamics among the various people who have a role in a purchase decision may be useful for determining appropriate marketing approaches.[7] Similarly, peer group influence is a major asset of firms that sell in-home to groups, as in the case of Tupperware parties. In such instances, many individuals conform to the norms of the group by purchasing a few items. Occasionally, marketers may try to stimulate reference group influence—a health club might offer you two months' service free if you get a friend to sign up for a one-year membership.

Salespeople may attempt to create a reference group influence by describing how a customer is similar to previous purchasers of the product—"There was a couple in here last week much like you. They bought the JVC speakers." Salespeople could describe themselves as a reference group—"Oh, your two children go to East High School? My kids go there, too. We bought them an IBM PC to help them with their science projects."

Finally, soliciting experts to aid in the direct sale of products can be a successful strategy for some firms. For example, a consumer's dentist is likely to be a highly influential reference individual, particularly for products related to dental care.[8] Thus, a manufacturer of the Water Pik might offer gifts to dentists for encouraging patients to use the product. The company could keep track of a dentist's sales by having consumers list their dentist on the warranty card for the product. Of course, experts can also have a negative impact on the sales of a new product if they convey negative information.[9]

For most mass-marketed products, a detailed analysis of the interactions of specific primary informal groups is impractical. Instead, marketers tend to portray both primary informal and aspirational groups in advertising:

> Reference group concepts have been used by advertisers in their efforts to persuade consumers to purchase products and brands. Portraying products being consumed in socially pleasant situations, the use of prominent/attractive people endorsing products, and the use of obvious group members as spokespersons in advertising are all evidence that marketers and advertisers make substantial use of potential reference group influence on consumer behavior in the development of their communications. Alluding to reference groups in persuasive attempts to market products and brands demonstrates the belief that reference groups expose people to behavior and lifestyles, influence self-concept development, contribute to the formation of values and attitudes, and generate pressure for conformity to group norms.[10]

There are many examples of the use of reference group concepts in advertising. Pepsi has featured popular stars such as Ray Charles and Michael Jackson and popular athletes such as Joe Montana and Dan Marino, with whom many young people may identify. Converse, Puma, Nike, and other running shoe companies for many years spent a large portion of their promotion budget in show giveaways to successful athletes, as well as to hiring these athletes to wear and recommend their brands. The very popular series of Miller Lite advertisements featuring well-known retired athletes likely appeals to baby boomers who followed the careers of these personalities and may consider some of them heroes to be emulated. Highlight 15.1 describes the aspirational reference group appeals used by American Express.

FAMILY

Most consumer behavior research takes the individual consumer as the unit of analysis. The usual goal is to describe and understand how individuals make purchase decisions so that marketing strategies can be developed to more

HIGHLIGHT 15.1

Reference Group Image Advertising

Sometimes the reference group is a single person—a referent other. Thus, movie stars such as Meryl Streep or Mickey Rourke (highly popular in France) or musicians such as Madonna or M. C. Hammer can serve as a reference group for people.

American Express has based its advertising on single-person reference group appeals since the early 1970s. It launched the classic campaign "Do You Know Me?" in 1974. Each ad featured someone who was famous for his or her achievements, but whose face was not familiar to the public. In 1987, American Express produced the highly praised "Portraits" campaign with photographs of famous people who have held American Express credit cards for varying periods of time, including Tip O'Neill, John Elway, and Willie Shoemaker/Wilt Chamberlin. The ads were intended to establish the American Express cards as *the* prestige card to own because these successful people used one. The reference group strategy worked for American Express; earnings grew at a 20 percent rate between 1970 and 1990.

But the early 1990s were a different story. Prestige and high status no longer seemed so important. Visa has been using a different advertising approach since the middle 1980s. The ads are intended to convince consumers that Visa is a more practical card because it is accepted in more places than American Express. The ads show real places like Rosalie's Restaurant or the ticket office for the Winter Olympics and have the same tag line, "If you go to (Rosalie's), be sure to bring your Visa card, because they don't take American Express." Between 1986 and 1991, Visa's worldwide share rose from 44.3 percent to 50.9, while American Express's share fell from 21.7 percent to 16.4. Calculated in dollars, these are huge changes.

In the meantime, American Express has rethought its image approach based on reference group celebrities. The 1991 campaign from American Express for its Corporate Card was still based on an aspirational reference group appeal but was not oriented toward prestige and status. Four different ads portrayed a "real-life" situation in an executive's busy life such as opening a foreign branch office or starting a small company. The ads briefly describe how the Corporate Card and the accompanying good service from American Express gave these executives an advantage in their businesses. The goal was to form a means-end chain linking the product to the customer.

Source: "American Express pulls Trigger with new Ads," *Marketing News*, March 4, 1991, p. 6; and Derrick Niederman, "Image Can Be a Fickle Thing," *Investment Vision*, October–November 1991, p. 30.

effectively influence this process. The area of family research is an exception: it views the family as the unit of analysis.[11]

Actually, marketers are interested in both families and households. The distinction between a family and a household is important.[12] The U.S. Census Bureau defines a housing unit as having its own entrance (inside or outside) and

American Express's reference group-based ads have been outperformed by Visa's appeals based on the practicality of using a widely accepted card.

basic facilities. If the housing unit has people living in it, they constitute a **household.** Except for homeless people, most Americans live in households involving many different living arrangements such as houses, townhouses, apartments, college dorm rooms, fraternity houses, military barracks, and nursing homes. Each household has a *householder*—the person who rents or owns the household. Households are categorized into types based on the relationship of the residents in the household to the householder. Marketers are concerned with two main types of households—families and nonfamilies.

Nonfamily households include unrelated people living together such as college roommates or unmarried couples of the opposite or same sex. In 1990, 3 of 10 American households were nonfamilies. In contrast, a **family** has at least two people—the householder and someone who is related to the householder by blood, marriage, or adoption. About 70 percent of American households are families. The difference between nuclear and extended families is an important distinction. The *nuclear family* includes one or more parents and one or more children living together in a household. The *extended family* is a nuclear family plus other relatives, usually grandparents, living in one household. Extended families are more common in Hispanic and Asian subcultures.

Here the Army presents itself as a valuable resource for the nuclear family.

Family Decision Making

Marketers are highly interested in **family decision making** – how family members interact and influence each other when making purchase choices for the household.[13] Research has shown that different people in the family may take on different social roles and perform different behaviors during decision making and consumption.[14] For example, the person who purchases Jif peanut butter for lunchtime sandwiches (the husband) may not be the same person who prepares the sandwiches (the mother) or eats them (the children). To fully understand family decision making, marketers need to identify which family members take on which roles. Included among these decision-making roles are the following:

Influencers provide information to other family members about a product or service (a child tells parents about a new brand of breakfast cereal).

Gatekeepers control the flow of information into the family (a mother does not tell her children about a new toy she saw at the store).

Deciders have the power to determine whether to purchase a product or service (a husband decides to buy a new snack chip at the grocery store).

Buyers actually purchase the product or service (a teenager buys milk for the family at the convenience store).

Users consume or use the product or service (the kids eat canned spaghetti bought by the parents).

Disposers dispose of a product or discontinue use of a service (a father throws out a partially eaten pizza; a mother stops a magazine subscription).

These roles clearly show that different family members may be involved in different aspects of the purchase decision process and in consumption of the product or service that is bought. From the perspective of the Wheel of Consumer Analysis, each family member and his or her roles and behaviors are part of the social environment for the other family members. Thus, studying family decision making requires that marketers study the social interactions between family members and the resulting patterns of reciprocal influence. This can be a difficult research challenge.

State Farm orients its service to the needs of the family unit.

Health and safety are two values in American culture.
Chapter 13

Courtesy Florida Orange Growers' Assoc.

Courtesy Ford Motor Co.

Courtesy Carillon Importers, Ltd.

Courtesy Carillon Importers, Ltd.

Courtesy Carillon Importers, Ltd.

This series of Absolut ads uses witty images to position the product for a middle- or upper-class clientele.
Chapter 14

These ads communicate Absolut's confident, urbane image to urban subcultures.
Chapter 14

Courtesy Carillon Importers, Ltd.

Courtesy Carillon Importers, Ltd.

Courtesy Carillon Importers, Ltd.

Courtesy Levi Strauss, Inc.

Dockers casual slacks were already a hit, but sales accelerated after Levi Strauss showed ads focusing on certain reference groups.
Chapter 15

Marketers know that in families, purchasers of products are not always the users.
Chapter 15

Courtesy Sun-Maid Growers of California

Developing successful marketing strategies for products purchased by families requires attention to questions such as these:

1. Is the product likely to be purchased for individual or joint family use?
2. Is the product likely to be purchased with individual or family funds?
3. Is the product so expensive that its purchase involves an important trade-off in purchasing other products for the family?
4. Are family members likely to disagree about the value of the product? If so, what can be done to reduce the conflict?
5. Is the product likely to be used by more than one family member? If so, are product modifications necessary to accommodate different persons?
6. Which family members will influence the purchase and what media and messages should be used to appeal to each?
7. Are particular stores preferred by various family members or by various families in the target market?

Answers to these questions influences the appropriate marketing strategy. For example, if a car is being purchased by a family for a teenager to drive to school, the type of product, method and financing, price, and appropriate promotion message and media should vary from those involved with the family's purchase of a car for use by the adult head of the household to commute to work.

Influences on Family Decision Making

Among the areas explored in research on family decision making are the following: (1) differences in product class and their relationship to family decision making, (2) the structure of husband/wife roles, and (3) the determinants of joint decision making.[15] However, relatively few generalizations for consumer analysis can be offered about family decision making. In fact, several years ago in a review of the subject, the major conclusions were:

1. Husband/wife involvement varies widely by product class.
2. Husband/wife involvement within any product class varies by specific decisions and decision stages.
3. Husband/wife involvement for any consumer decision is likely to vary considerably among families.[16]

Essentially, we should expect considerable variance both in the persons involved at each stage of the decision-making process and in the extent to which they are involved.[17] For any given marketing problem, researchers must determine the dynamics of family decision making, which family members are involved, what roles they play, and who has the major influence. This analyses will help them develop effective marketing strategies targeted at the appropriate person.

HIGHLIGHT 15.2

Bringing Up Baby

Births were at a high in the United States during the late 1980s and early 1990s; about 4 million babies were born per year or about 11,000 each day. This rate will continue into the mid-1990s. Although the numbers are lower than those of the previous period of high birthrates (when the baby boomers were born during the late 1940s, 50s, and early 60s), the expenses are much greater. Today, babies cost about twice as much as they did 30 years ago, even after adjusting for inflation. Careful estimates in 1990 suggest it costs some families about $5,800 to keep a baby for the first year. In 1958, "Life" magazine estimated that first-year baby expenses were about $800 (or about $2,900 in 1990 dollars). Why the big difference?

Day care, virtually unavailable in the 1950s, is now considered a necessity by many families, adding $2,200 to the first-year costs. Thirty years ago, kids rode in the car sitting on the seat or in someone's lap. Now many state laws mandate the use of child car seats to protect kids in case of an accident. In fact, parents need two seats during the first year—an infant seat for newborns and another for older infants (costing about $100). In the 1950s, kids drank cow's milk; now breast-feeding and formula are recommended. Breast milk is "free," but formula costs could be $500 in the first year. Cloth diapers were used 30 years ago, but many families like the convenience of disposable diapers ($570) even though they may create landfill problems. Food and feeding equipment (high chairs, utensils) cost about $850. Families spend about $350 on clothes, $1,000 on furniture (cribs, dressers, portable cribs, strollers), and another $225 on bedding and bath products.

Are these first-year expenses a sample of what is yet to come? The U.S. Department of Agriculture estimated that raising a child to age 18 costs the average American family about $100,000. Clearly, children create very large markets and many marketing opportunities.

Source: Blayne Cutler, "Rock-A-Buy Baby," *American Demographics,* January 1990, pp. 35–39.

Children and Family Decision Making

Most research on family decision making has focused on husband/wife roles and influence, while children (and other family members in extended families) have not received much attention.[18] Yet, as illustrated in the opening example, the children's market is large and important. Children—both younger kids and teenagers—can have major influences on the budget allocation decisions and purchase choices made by the family. Also, the birth of a child is a major event for a family that creates demand for a wide variety of products most couples never would have considered purchasing previously. Highlight 15.2 describes some of these purchases.

Conflict in Family Decision Making

When more than one person in a family is involved in making a purchase decision, some degree of conflict is likely.[19] **Decision conflict** arises when family members disagree about some aspect of the purchase decision. The means-end chain model provides a useful framework for analyzing decision conflict. Family members might disagree about the desired end goals of a purchase. For instance, in choosing a family vacation, the husband might want to go somewhere for lazy relaxation, the wife wants good shopping and nightlife, and the kids want adventure and excitement. Differences in end goals often create major conflict because very different choice alternatives are likely to be related to these incompatible ends. Serious negotiations may be required to resolve the conflict.

In other cases, family members might agree on the desired end goal, yet disagree about the best means to achieve it. For instance, everyone might want to go out to eat or see a movie, but the kids think a fast-food restaurant or action film is the best choice, while the parents prefer a full-service restaurant or a dramatic film. Again, some means of resolving the conflict is necessary. Often, a different alternative (a new means to the end) is purchased as a compromise (everyone goes out for pizza or to a comedy film). Finally, when either the end or the means are in conflict, family members are also likely to disagree about the choice criteria for evaluating the choice alternatives (for a new car, what is the appropriate price range, what options are necessary, what is the best color?).

Clearly, there are times when family members disagree about such factors in a purchase situation, and occasionally the conflict may be severe.[20] When this happens, family members can do several things. Some consumers might procrastinate, ignoring the problem and hoping the situation will improve by itself. Others might try to get their way in the purchase decision process by trying to influence other family members. Figure 15.3 describes several influence strategies that have been identified in family research.[21] Depending on the product being considered, the family members involved in the decision, the social class and subculture of the family, and the situational environment, a family member might use any of these strategies to influence other members of the family.

Over time, family members may learn characteristic patterns of influence behaviors that they may use repeatedly in conflict situations. In a study of furniture and appliance purchases, Spiro identified six styles of family influence used by adults.[22] These are described in Figure 15.4. Although children's influence behaviors were not considered in this study, strategies that kids use to influence their parents could also be analyzed.

Although serious conflicts can occur in family decision making, many family purchases probably do not involve major conflicts. For one thing, many family purchases are recurring, in that many products and brands are bought repeatedly over a long period. So, even though conflict might have been present in the past, it usually will have been resolved. To minimize continuous friction, families may develop choice plans to minimize or avoid potential conflict. For

FIGURE 15.3

Six Common Types of Family Influence Strategies

Expert influence is reflected by a spouse providing specific information concerning the various alternatives. For example, one spouse can try to convince the other that she/he is more knowledgeable concerning the products under consideration by presenting detailed information about various aspects of these products.

Legitimate influence deals with one spouse's attempts to draw upon the other's feelings of shared values concerning their role expectations. Therefore, the spouse's influence is based on the shared belief that she/he should make the decision because she/he is the wife/husband. For example, the husband can argue that since he is the "man of the house," he should make a particular decision.

Bargaining involves attempts by one spouse to turn the joint decision into an autonomous one in return for some favor granted to the other spouse. For example, in return for autonomy in a particular decision, one spouse may agree to give the other autonomy in another decision when she/he had previously refused to do so. "If you do this, I'll do that" may be the most common type of bargaining attempt.

Reward/referent influence is based on a combination of the reward and referent power/influence strategies. Reward influence is based on an individual's ability to reward another by doing something that the other would enjoy. Referent influence is the influence based on the identification or feeling of oneness (or desire for such an identity) of one person with another. Referent influence in marriage stems from the desire of spouses to be like their concepts of the "ideal" husband or wife.

Emotional influence attempts involve displaying some emotion-laden reaction. For example, one spouse may get angry at the other. These attempts are often nonverbal techniques. For example, one person may cry or pout, while another may use the "silent treatment."

Impression management encompasses premeditated persuasive attempts to enhance one's influence differential in a dyadic relationship. For example, one spouse may claim that the other's preferred brand was "out of stock" when, in fact, it wasn't. The objective is to convince the spouse to attribute the influence attempt to external pressures beyond the influencer's control.

Source: Reprinted with permission from "Persuasion in Family Decision Making," by Rosann L. Spiro, in the *Journal of Consumer Research,* March 1983, p. 394.

instance, a family with two children might allow one to choose the breakfast cereal or ice cream flavor one week and the other to choose the next week.

Another reason decision conflict among family members concerning purchase and consumption decisions is not often serious is that many purchases in a household are made by individuals to meet their own personal needs or those of other family members. To the degree that such purchases are reasonably consistent with family values and do not place an undue burden on family resources there is likely to be little conflict. For instance, we would expect that purchases of books, personal care items, and many food products do not involve much family conflict.

FIGURE 15.4
Patterns or Styles of Influence Behaviors

Noninfluencers. This group, which characterizes 22 percent of the individuals in the sample, is substantially lowest in reported use of all the influence types. When the people in this group do attempt to influence their spouses, they are most likely to use the expertise type of influence.

Light Influencers. This was the largest subgroup in the sample (35.9 percent). The mean scores on all the influence types are substantially higher than the scores for Noninfluencers, but relatively low compared to all the other groups. Their relative use of the various influence strategies is very similar to (although higher than) the Noninfluencers, with the exception of their use of impression management. Light influencer individuals are more likely to use some impression management as well as "expert" influence.

Subtle Influencers. This mix characterizes 18.8 percent of the sample. Relative to their use of other strategies, these people rely heavily on the reward/referent strategy and secondly on the expert strategy. Apparently, they attempt to put their partners in a favorable "mood" (by being very nice, "buttering up") before a decision is made.

Emotional Influencers. This category represents one of the two smallest groups (6.6 percent of the sample), yet its profile is quite distinctive. This profile displays the widest variations in the extent to which the different types of influence are used. These people report a high use of emotional influence and almost as high a use of reward/referent influence, a low use of legitimate and impression management, and a moderate use of both expert and bargaining strategies.

Combination Influencers. This mix (9.9 percent of the sample) is generally characterized by moderate use of all the influence strategies. In fact, there is less than one half a scale-point difference between the strategy used least—legitimate—and the strategy used most frequently—expert.

Heavy Influencers. The final group (6.6 percent of the sample) uses each of the six types of influence much more than any of the other groups. The people in this group use bargaining, reward/reference influence, and the emotional strategy more than they use expert and legitimate influence and impression management, but all of the mean scale scores are high, indicating their heavy use of all the influence strategies.

Source: Reprinted with permission from "Persuasion in Family Decision Making," by Rosann L. Spiro, in the *Journal of Consumer Research,* March 1983, p. 397.

CONSUMER SOCIALIZATION

Through socialization processes, families transmit the cultural meanings of society, subcultures, and social class to their children and thereby influence their children's affect, cognitions, and behaviors.[23] **Consumer socialization** refers to how children acquire knowledge about products and services and various consumption-related skills (how to search for bargains).[24] Younger children acquire much of their consumer knowledge from their parents, but adolescents also learn from their peers. Both younger and older children learn consumer knowledge and skills from social institutions such as the media (TV, magazines, movies) and advertising.[25]

Socialization can occur directly through intentional instruction or indirectly through observation and modeling. Indirect socialization occurs when parents talk about products and brands or take their children on shopping trips. Sometimes parents intentionally try to teach their children consumer skills such as how to search for products, find the best price, bargain with salespeople, return products to the store for a refund, and dispose of products (recycling, hold a garage sale).[26]

The consumer knowledge formed in childhood can influence people in later years. Some adults still use the same brands of products their parents purchased for them as children. Thus, some long-lived brands may be purchased and used throughout an adult's life (Campbell's soup, Crest or Colgate toothpaste, Heinz ketchup, Tide laundry detergent, among many others).

Developing early brand awareness and loyalty is an important marketing strategy for many companies. Thus, Chrysler has sponsored events during spring break at Daytona Beach (including building a 250-foot-long sand sculpture on the beach). Even though teens don't buy many cars, they can have a significant influence on their parents' choices, particularly for the second or third car in a household. As GM's basic car division, Chevrolet needs to attract today's teens, so it has advertised on MTV.[27] The strategy may be working. One third of all Camero drivers were under age 25, even though this age group accounts for only about 13 percent of car sales.

The flow of socialization is not restricted to parents influencing their young children. Children can socialize their parents, especially about new products (teens may introduce their parents to new music styles).[28] As another example, adult children can influence the consumption behavior of their aged parents, such as decisions about retirement housing (refer to the Marketing Strategy in Action in Chapter 14).[29] Finally, consumer socialization can occur throughout life as people continue to learn consumer skills and acquire product knowledge. Consider the socialization that occurs when people marry or begin cohabiting. Both partners learn from each other as they adjust to the other person's preferences and consumption behaviors.

Factors Influencing American Families

Many cultural and social changes have occurred in recent years that have influenced the structure of American families (many of these have happened in other countries, too). We briefly discuss three important changes in female employment, marriage and divorce, and childbirth and rearing practices. These changes are highly interrelated.

Changes in Female Employment

At one time in American society (say, 40 years ago), the typical role of women was as a homemaker. Today, over half of all women are in the labor force.[30] Working women are not distributed equally across all age groups, however. Over two thirds of women in their 20s, 30s, and 40s are employed outside the home, but fewer older women have outside jobs. Of the women who do work, 45 percent are employed full time the year around, compared to 65 percent of men who work full time all year. More than 50 percent of young women with preschool children are working, up from 30 percent in 1970.

The disposable income of married-couple households increases dramatically when both spouses work outside the home. The average household income for dual-earner couples with children was $49,600 in 1990, $9,600 greater than for one-earner households.[31] The total income of this segment is a staggering $890 billion, creating a vast market for many products.

Changes in Marriage and Divorce

American society has undergone major changes in people's attitudes and behaviors toward marriage and divorce.[32] Young people are delaying marriage (the median age of first marriage is 23.6 for women and 25.8 for men, a near record). Increasing numbers of Americans may never marry (in 1987, 23 percent of men

This ad targets the concerns of recently divorced or widowed, middle-aged women.

aged 30 to 35 have never married, compared to 9 percent in 1970; 15 percent versus 6 percent for women).

In the 1990s, marriage is likely to become even more of an optional lifestyle.[33] Increasing numbers of single women are remaining unmarried and raising children alone. Divorced and widowed people are waiting longer to remarry, and increasing numbers of them will never remarry. And more Americans are living together outside of marriage. Some 2.8 million households are unmarried, cohabiting couples (17 percent of unmarried people aged 25 to 29 are cohabiting and nearly half have cohabited at some time). Although some people claim cohabiting is a way to cut the chances of divorce (because people learn more about their future spouse before marriage), divorce rates actually are higher for couples who cohabited before marriage (53 percent of first marriages that begin with cohabitation end in divorce compared to 28 percent of those where the partners did not live together before marriage).

The net result is that more Americans are spending less of their lives married. These changes will have profound implications for many consumer businesses that may have assumed their market consists of traditional families. Despite these important trends, however, marketers must remember that most Americans eventually do marry (or remarry), and many of them have children. Current estimates are that 90 percent of American women will marry at some time in their lives. The point is that marketers must consider a greater variety of family types than previously was necessary.

Changes in Childbirth and Rearing Practices

As more baby boomers begin their own families, the number of births has increased to near record levels (4 million births in 1990). The number of births is up because there are more potential parents among the baby boomers, not because families are having more children. In fact, the number of children per family has been decreasing steadily since the mid-1960s. Women now bear an average of under two children, down from nearly three in 1965.[34] Despite this trend toward smaller families, there still are some large families in America. Some 6.4 million families have 3 or more children (20 percent of families with kids, down from 40 percent in the late 1960s).[35] These larger families constitute very important markets for certain family-oriented products such as breakfast cereal, milk, toothpaste, and toilet paper.

Also, because women are marrying later and having children later than their mothers did, this changes how they raise their kids and relate to them. Finally, women live many years after the children leave the home. All of these changes mean people spend less of their lives in child-oriented households than once was the case.

Demographic Changes in Household Composition

American family and nonfamily households have undergone major demographic changes during the past few decades that have significant implications for

FIGURE 15.5
Changes in American Family and Nonfamily Households

	1990		1980		1980–90	
	Households	Percent Distribution	Households	Percent Distribution	Change	Percent Change
All households	93,920	100.0%	80,467	100.0%	13,453	16.7%
Family households	66,542	70.8%	59,190	73.6%	7,352	12.4%
Married couples	52,837	56.3	48,990	60.9	3,847	7.9
Without children <18	28,315	30.1	24,210	30.1	4,105	17.0
With children <18	24,522	26.1	27,780	30.8	−258	−1.0
Other family, female head	11,130	11.9	8,205	10.2	2,925	35.6
Other family, male head	2,575	2.7	1,995	2.5	580	29.1
Nonfamily households	27,378	29.2%	21,277	26.4%	6,101	28.7%
Living alone	22,879	24.4	18,202	22.6	4,677	25.7
Men	9,119	9.7	7,075	8.8	2,044	28.9
Women	13,759	14.7	11,127	13.8	2,632	23.7
Living with nonrelatives	4,500	4.8	3,075	3.8	1,425	46.3
Male householder	2,803	3.0	1,866	2.3	937	50.2
Female householder	1,696	1.8	1,209	1.5	487	40.3

Households and change in households, in thousands.
Percent distribution and percent change by household type, 1980–90.
Source: Judith Waldrop and Thomas Exter, "What the 1990 Census Will Show," *American Demographics,* January 1990, p. 27.

marketers. Figure 15.5 summarizes some of these changes. First, the number of households grew by 17 percent in the 1980s to 93.9 million households in 1990. The number of households grew faster than the total population (now about 250 million), which means the average household size dropped to 2.6 people in 1990 from 2.8 in 1980.

American families are highly diverse, and the various types of families constitute distinctive markets for many products. Still the most common family is the *married-couple family*—householders who live with their spouse (56 percent of American households). This category grew about 8 percent over the past 10 years. Most of these households have dual earners; only 22 percent of married-couple households in 1990 contained a male breadwinner and a female homemaker, down from 61 percent in 1960.

The so-called *traditional family* has several definitions, but it usually means a married-couple family with children under 18. This category actually declined slightly during the 1980s and currently stands at 26 percent of all households. Sometimes traditional family means a working husband and a homemaker wife; only 9 percent of households are like this. Finally, if the traditional family means

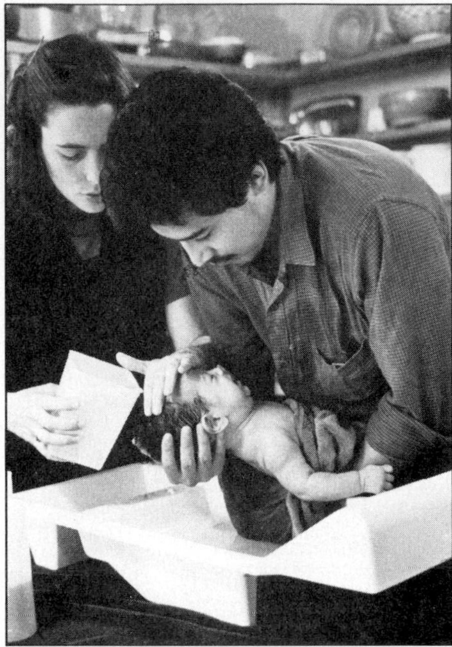

The married-couple family is still the most common family type in the United States.

a working husband, nonworking wife, and exactly two children, we are talking about only 3 percent of all American households.

So-called *nontraditional families* are also growing in number. Among this type of family, the fastest growing are households with children headed by a woman with no husband present (12 percent of American households, up 36 percent during the 1980s). Only about 3 percent of households with children are headed by single men, but this segment grew 30 percent in the 1980s. Despite this fragmentation into different types of families, the family unit is still Ameria's largest market, accounting for 71 percent of all households. The expectations are that the 1990s will be a family decade, thanks to the large numbers of baby boomers in midst of their child-rearing years. Three fourths of all boomer households will be families.

Nonfamily households make up 29 percent of all U.S. households and are growing rapidly. They are up 30 percent during the 1980s, compared to a 12 percent gain for families. For instance, households headed by a single, unmarried person constitute nearly 15 percent of all households. Unrelated people living together constitute a rapidly growing proportion (now about 5 percent) of nonfamily households. Nearly 3 million of these households are made up of unmarried couples of both sexes, sometimes called cohabiting couples. One in four nonfamily households consists of a single person living alone, up 26 percent during the 1980s. Men living alone make up 10 percent of households and women, 15 percent. Two factors are behind this surge. First,

Nontraditional families and nonfamily households are growing in number—among this segment are single-parent families and even families headed by gay couples.

HIGHLIGHT 15.3

Home Alone

The 1990 census shows that some 23 million Americans live by themselves, up 91 percent for women and 156 percent for men since 1970. Two trends are behind this surge: (1) unprecedented numbers of consumers are not marrying, and (2) an estimated 60 percent of those who do eventually divorce.

These singles, plus college students and young adults living with their parents, constitute a huge market with some $660 billion in annual earnings. It probably comes as no surprise that singles are disproportionate consumers of convenience products, fast-food and regular restaurant meals, and travel. Like any social group, there is great diversity among singles, including carefree 21-year-olds to middle-aged divorced people to elderly widows. Targeting the entire group is foolhardy. But singles are here to stay, and marketers that have traditionally treated singles as a sort of "extramarital aberration" will have to deal with them.

Consider the ad campaign "Friends and Family" from MCI Telecommunications Corporation. Because singles don't live in a nuclear family, they use the telephone to keep in touch with their families and their friends. The MCI ads showed attractive adults of varying ages in nonfamily situations making lists of friends to phone. If consumers get their friends and families to join MCI, both parties receive a 20 percent discount on calls made to each other.

Source: Laura Zinn, Heather Keets, and James B. Treece, "Home Alone—With $660 Billion," *Business Week,* July 29, 1991, pp. 76–77.

unprecedented numbers of consumers are not marrying; second, up to 60 percent of those who do will eventally divorce and become single again. These social trends toward living alone have created major opportunities for marketers, some of which are described in Highlight 15.3.

Dealing with the many demographic changes in family composition and structure can be difficult. To organize these complexities, marketers often use the concept of the family life cycle. The family life cycle is a strategic tool to identify key family segments and develop effective marketing strategies for those households.

Family Life Cycle

Thirty or forty years ago, most Americans followed the same life path and went through about the same stages of life. People got married, had children, stayed married, raised their children and sent them on their way, grew old, retired, and eventually died. The **traditional family life cycle** identifies these typical stages

FIGURE 15.6
A Traditional Family Life Cycle

Stage in Life Cycle	Buying or Behavior Pattern
1. Bachelor stage: Young single people not living at home	Few financial burdens. Fashion opinion leaders. Recreation oriented. Buy basic kitchen equipment, basic furniture, cars, equipment for the mating game, vacations.
2. Newly married couples: Young, no children	Better off financially than they will be in near future. Highest purchase rate and highest average purchase of durables. Buy cars, refrigerators, stoves, sensible and durable furniture, vacations.
3. Full nest I: Youngest child under six	Home purchasing at peak. Liquid assets low. Dissatisfied with financial position and amount of money saved. Interested in new products. Buy washers, dryers, TV, baby food, chest rubs and cough medicines, vitamins, dolls, wagons, sleds, skates.
4. Full nest II: Youngest child six or older	Financial position better. Some wives work. Less influenced by advertising. Buy larger-sized packages, multiple-unit deals. Buy many foods, cleaning materials, bicycles, music lessons, pianos.
5. Full nest III: Older couples with dependent children	Financial position still better. More wives work. Some children get jobs. Hard to influence with advertising. High average purchase of durables. Buy new, more tasteful furniture, auto travel, nonnecessary appliances, boats, dental services, magazines.
6. Empty nest I: Older couples, no children living with them, head in labor force	Home ownership at peak. Most satisfied with financial position and money saved. Interested in travel, recreation, self-education. Make gifts and contributions. Not interested in new products. Buy vacations, luxuries, home improvements.
7. Empty nest II: Older married couples, no children living at home, head retired	Drastic cut in income. Keep home. Buy medical-care products that improve health, sleep, and digestion.
8. Solitary survivor, in labor force	Income still good, but likely to sell home.
9. Solitary survivor, retired	Same medical and product needs as other retired group. Drastic cut in income. Special need for attention, affection, and security.

Source: Reprinted from William D. Wells and George Gubar, "Life Cycle Concept in Marketing Research," *Journal of Marketing Research* (November 1966), pp. 355–63. Published by the American Marketing Association.

in family life and shows how families change from one stage to another.[36] Figure 15.6 presents the family life cycle as a linear sequence of family types delineated by major life events (marriage, birth of children, aging, departure of children, retirement, death). These major life events create very different social environments (consider the birth of a baby) that influence consumers' affective reactions, cognitions, and consumption behaviors. Figure 15.6 also describes distinctive consumption-related behaviors found at each stage.

The recent cultural changes in American society such as delayed marriages, childless marriages, working women, and increased divorce rates have rendered the traditional family life cycle somewhat inadequate. Figure 15.7 presents a **modern family life cycle** that incorporates the traditional family life cycle but adds several other family types to account for the more diverse family structures of the 1990s.[37] The modern family life cycle can account for most types of families in American society, including childless couples, divorced parents, and single parents with children.

Single parents constitute 9 percent of all households. Most of these are divorced parents, but some mothers who have never married are raising children. Although income is relatively low $21,400 average, the growing numbers of such people create a sizable market.

Young singles are people under 45 who live by themselves. Currently, they are 9 million households (9 percent of all households). The tendency to delay marriage, or avoid it, is increasing this segment. Their average income level of $25,000 gives this group significant purchasing power, and their lack of responsibilities gives them considerable discretion in spending it. This rapidly increasing market is very important for companies that sell products purchased by households (appliances, kitchen utensils, TVs, basic furniture, etc.).

Older singles are people over 45 who are living alone. They are 15 million households or 16 percent of all households. Although their average income is relatively low ($17,500), their large numbers make them a significant market.

Married couples with children include two important subcategories: (1) dual-earner couples and (2) other married couples (usually a working husband and a homemaker wife). The distinction is important for two reasons: average household income is $49,600 versus $40,000, and lifestyles differ considerably in these households. Life in the dual-earner households is usually more hectic, and the parents are more harrassed for time than in other married couple households.

Television producers seem to have considered many of these stages in the family life cycle in creating television situation comedies (see Highlight 15.4).

Marketing Analysis

In this section, we discuss several considerations for using the family life cycle for marketing analysis. First, it is important to recognize that the modern family life cycle does not include nonfamily households, which currently are nearly 30 percent of all American households. This diverse category includes people who remain single and never marry, cohabiting couples, and shared households

FIGURE 15.7

A Modern Family Life Cycle

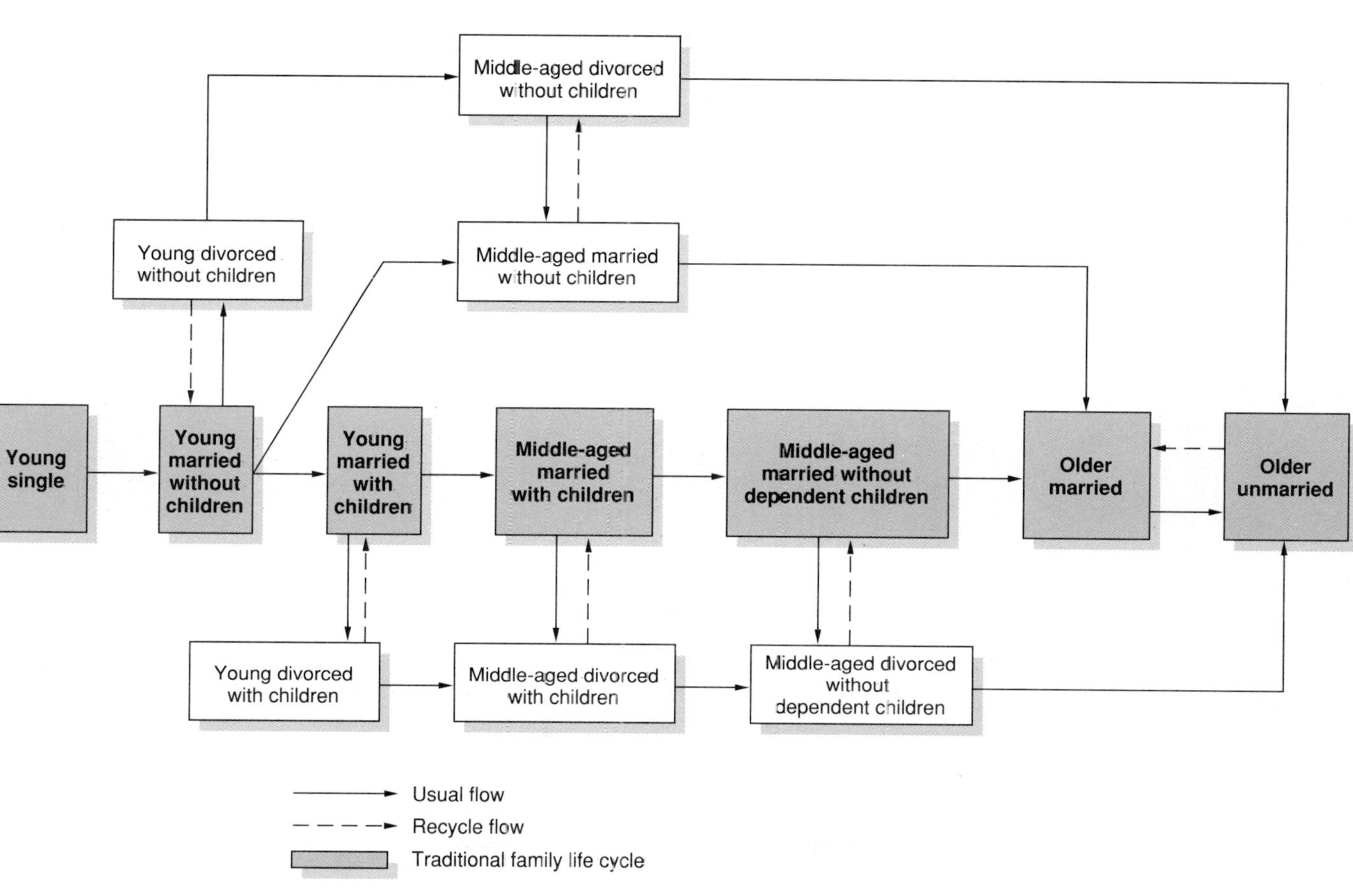

Source: Reprinted with permission from "A Modernized Family Life Cycle," by Patrick E. Murphy and William A. Staples, in the *Journal of Consumer Research*, June 1979, pp. 12–22.

HIGHLIGHT 15.4

THE FAMILY LIFE CYCLE ON TV

Several TV situation comedies in the early 1990s mirrored the diversity of the American family structure. Note how these shows fit closely with several stages of the family life cycle.

Stage in Family Life Cycle	TV Show
Married couples with children, one wage earner	"The Simpsons" "Married With Children"
Married couple with children, two wage earners	"Roseanne"
Married couple with children and related adults	"Family Matters"
Male householder with children and unrelated adults	"Full House"
Nonfamily household	"Perfect Strangers"
Married couple with children from previous marriages	"True Colors" "Step by Step"

Source: Martha Farnsworth Riche, "The Future of the Family," *American Demographics,* March 1991, pp. 44–46.

containing various combinations of unrelated residents. Although these diverse households are difficult to identify and target with marketing strategies, their numbers — 28 million — make them very attractive markets for many products.

Also, the family life cycle does not capture every possible change in family status that can occur. For instance, a new life cycle stage may be developing called the "boomerang age."[38] This group refers to the increasing number of young adults (mostly in their 20s) who left home for work or college but now are returning to live with their parents. Currently, there are more of these people than at any time since the Depression.

Actually, living with parents past high school and even college is not so unusual. Only one third of young adults (19–24) live independently of their parents (25 percent of men and 38 percent of women). Most young people begin to live independently at ages 22 to 24, but few will live alone (only about 5 percent of young adults live alone). Many will live in a nonfamily household of unrelated adults or cohabit with a potential marriage partner. And as many as 40 percent of young adults return to live in their parents' homes at least once. This "boomerang" segment of the family life cycle may offer some marketing opportunities.

Marketers use the family life cycle to segment the market, analyze market potential, identify target markets, and develop more effective marketing strategies. It is important to remember the family segments identified by the family life cycle are not entirely homogeneous. In fact, each family type is variable and contains highly diverse types of people. For instance, each family type contains people from every social class and every age, racial, ethnic, and regional subculture in the country. Consider the young single or bachelor stage of the family life cycle. In 1987, there were 29 million bachelors in the United States; 34 percent of all American men 18 and older were unmarried and many were living alone. The number of bachelors has increased 21 percent since 1980 to nearly 29 million men.

Much of this growth is due to the "new" bachelors, created by divorce. The rate of increase in divorced men (5.6 million) is increasing about twice as fast as that of never married men (21 million). For instance, 18- to 24-year-old men in the swinging years (99 percent have never married, but most will someday) are a prime market for tape decks, six-packs, and hot cars. But 35- to 45-year-old unmarried men (51 percent of whom are divorced) are more interested in toys for their kids, living room furniture, and toilet bowl cleaners. Many divorced men (19 percent of all bachelors) are only temporary bachelors; many will remarry within an average of three years. Approximately 7 percent of bachelors are widowers. With an average age of 61, their behavior resembles married men their age more closely than other bachelors. With this type of diversity, developing marketing strategies for the bachelor segment is a challenge for marketers.

Another point to recognize is that some stages in the family life cycle are more important markets than others. For instance, households headed by people aged 35 to 54 spend more on every product category (except health care) than other types of families.[39] Consider food. Middle-aged households spent about $4,700 on food in 1988, 22 percent more than average households. The youngest and oldest households spent considerably less than the average ($2,500 and $2,000, respectively). This segment of middle-aged households will become even more important through the 1990s as it grows 20 percent when all the baby boomers enter this life cycle stage. Most of these boomers will have children and will spend heavily on them.

Marketing Implications

The family life cycle can help marketers understand how important cultural trends affect family structures and consumption behavior. For example, consider the estimated 43 million "time-starved" consumers in the United States.[40] Time has become more precious to many people, as the pace of family life gets more hectic, and more families have two wage earners (two thirds of married couples with children are dual-income households) or are headed by single parents. Millions of people are stressed about time, believe they don't have enough time, and are striving to save time. They are prime candidates for convenience products of all types that can save time, which then can be used for more enjoyable or profitable purposes.

For many of these people, shopping is seen as a stressful chore that interferes with their leisure. Fully 63 percent of Americans think shopping is drudgery. According to one survey, these perceptions are strongest among married-couple families with children, especially if both parents are working. Eleven million of these people do not enjoy shopping, and half believe shopping adds to their stress level. Clearly, the thrill of shopping is gone for many (but not all) Americans.

These attitudes are reflected in various consumption-related behaviors. For instance, in 1988, the average consumer spent 90 minutes on a shopping trip to the mall; in 1990, shopping time was down to 68 minutes. Many consumers have developed shopping strategies to save time. For instance, some people shop for clothes only two or three times a year. Some shoppers follow a certain path through the store to eliminate duplication of effort. In one extreme case, a consumer followed an extremely regimented strategy by shopping for groceries each Tuesday from 4:45 to 5:15 P.M. As she sprints through the store in a virtual trance, it will be very difficult to catch her attention with a new marketing strategy. One executive bought a car at a dealer located near the airport, so he can have the car serviced during business trips.

Relatively few marketers have done much to reduce shopping time and stress, but there are many opportunities for marketers to appeal to the time-stressed shopper. These need not be highly sophisticated strategies—Dayton-Hudson changed to a central-aisle layout to make it easier for customers to find their way through the store. Following are several ideas for marketing strategies to help reduce shopping time and stress.

Provide information. Marketers that provide useful information to help consumers make the right choices will save their customers time and reduce shopping stress. For instance, Blockbuster Video has a computerized data base to help customers find films made by a certain director or starring a particular actor. Computer technology could be used to help consumers make the right choices of color, size, styles for clothing, automobiles, and home furnishings. Coordinated displays of related products such as showing entire ensembles can serve the same purpose.

Assist in planning. People often try to cope with time stress by carefully planning their shopping excursions. Marketers that help consumers form purchase plans will help them reduce stress. High quality sales assistance in the clothing store or appliance showroom can help a time-stressed customer develop a decision plan. Marketers might suggest alternatives when a product is unavailable. Blockbuster Video tries to give customers movie alternatives if their first choice film is unavailable.

Develop out-of-store selling. Although shopping once was a pleasant and desirable experience, today many consumers would rather be relaxing at home. This trend creates problems for retailers but also creates new opportunities for selling in the home or at the workplace. Avon, for example, has begun to sell its products to groups of co-workers at the work site.

Automate processes. Companies that can automate and thereby speed up transaction processes will appeal to time-stressed consumers. At Wegmen's, a supermarket chain in Rochester, New York, customers can use a computer to enter their deli orders so they don't have to wait in line to be served; they pick up their deli orders as they leave the store. A&P and Shop Rite are experimenting with automated checkout systems to reduce the waiting time in the checkout line. Some car rental companies such as Hertz and Alamo offer an automated check-in service at major airports. Hand-held computers speed the check-in process so that customers receive the invoice on the spot as they leave the car in the parking lot. Customers can speed to the airport with no waiting.

Improve delivery. Nothing upsets a time-stressed consumer more than having to wait all day at home for a service person to come to fix the washing machine. For years, GE has made precise appointments for its service calls. Sears now offers repair services six days a week and in the evening. In Pasadena, California, Vons grocery offers drive-up service for 1,400 items. How about a service court where consumers could obtain a variety of services (dry-cleaning, shoe repair, small appliance repairs, mailing) in one stop?

BACK TO....
HEY, DUDE, LET'S CONSUME

The opening example illustrates several of the concepts discussed in this chapter. First, and most obviously, it shows that "kids" are a large and growing market. Many families are willing and able to purchase high quality, high priced products and services for their children. This example of young children's purchasing behaviors is most relevant for families at certain stages of the family life cycle—

households with young children headed by a married couple or a single parent, and divorced single parents. Also, this example shows that kids often spend money on themselves. These decisions probably are influenced by their peers (friendship reference groups) and their families (parents). Marketers can use the concepts of reference group and family to analyze consumers' behaviors, segment the overall market, and develop marketing strategies to influence these segments.

Summary

This chapter concerns two aspects of the micro social environment—reference groups and family. After defining groups and reference groups, we discussed three types of reference group influence: informational, utilitarian, and value-expressive. Then, we discussed how reference groups could influence choice decisions about products and brands, and we offered ideas for using reference groups in marketing strategies. Next, we distinguished between families and households.

We discussed family decision making by families, considering the different decision-making roles taken by family members, including children. We discussed conflict in family choices and described several ways family members might try to resolve the decision conflict and influence each other. We also discussed consumer socialization—how consumers learn knowledge about products and consumer skills. Next, we described several demographic trends that have changed family households. We concluded by discussing two models of the family life cycle and showed how marketers could use the family life cycle to analyze markets and develop marketing strategies.

Key Terms and Concepts

Group *505*

Reference Group *505*

Informational Reference Group Influence *507*

Utilitarian Reference Group Influence *508*

Value-Expressive Reference Group Influence *508*

Household *514*
Nonfamily Households *514*
Family *514*
Family Decision Making *515*
Decision Conflict *519*
Consumer Socialization *521*
Traditional Family Life Cycle *528*
Modern Family Life Cycle *530*

Review and Discussion Questions

1. Identify two reference groups that influence your consumption behavior. Describe each according to the types listed in the text and tell what categories of purchases each influences.
2. From a marketing manager's viewpoint, what are some advantages and problems associated with each type of reference group influence?
3. Describe how the public visibility and the distinction between luxury and necessity goods affect reference group influence on choice at the product and brand levels.
4. What is the family life cycle? Discuss how it can be used to develop effective marketing strategies.
5. Identify three different family purchases in which you have played a role in the decision process. What role did you play? Discuss the interpersonal interactions involved in these decisions.
6. Suggest two ways in which marketing strategies could influence the decision process in your family or household. How are these different from strategies that might be used to influence individual decisions?
7. Offer examples of conflict in family household decision making that you have experienced or observed. What types of marketing strategies could help to reduce such conflict?
8. Discuss the differences between households and families. Describe how each is important to marketers.
9. How are family influence strategies similar to or different from other reference group influences? What marketing implications are related to these distinctions?
10. Identify two different household or family compositions. Assume each unit has the same level of income and discuss how the decision processes and conflicts might vary for a product such as an automobile, a vacation, or a stereo system.

Notes

1. Lakshman Krishnamurthi, "The Salience of Relevant Others and Its Effects on Individual and Joint Preferences: An Experimental Investigation," *Journal of Consumer Research*, June 1983, pp. 62–72.
2. C. Whan Park and V. Parker Lessig, "Students and Housewives: Differences in Susceptibility to Reference Group Influences," *Journal of Consumer Research*, September 1977, pp. 102–10; and William O. Bearden, Richard G. Netemeyer, and Jesse E. Teel, "Measurement of Consumer Susceptibility to Interpersonal Influence," *Journal of Consumer Research*, March 1989, pp. 473–81.
3. John W. Schouten and James H. Alexander, "Hog Heaven: The Structure, Ethos, and Market Impact of a Consumption Culture," in *Advances in Consumer Research*, vol. 19, ed. John Sherry and Brian Sternthal (Provo, Utah: Association for Consumer Research, 1992), in press.
4. William O. Bearden and Michael J. Etzel, "Reference Group Influences on Product and Brand Purchase Decision," *Journal of Consumer Research*, September 1982, pp. 183–94. The discussion in this section is based heavily on this excellent work.
5. David Brinberg and Linda Plimpton, "Self-Monitoring and Product Conspicuousness in Reference Group Influence," in *Advances in Consumer Research*, vol. 13, ed. Richard J. Lutz (Provo, Utah: Association for Consumer Research, 1986), pp. 297–300.
6. For further discussion and an alternative approach to studying reference group influences, see Peter H. Reingen, Brian L. Foster, Jacqueline Johnson Brown, and Stephen B. Seidman, "Brand Congruence in Interpersonal Relations: A Social Network Analysis," *Journal of Consumer Research*, December 1984, pp. 771–83.
7. Julia M. Bristor, "Coalitions in Organizational Purchasing: An Application of Network Analysis," in *Advances in Consumer Research*, vol. 15, ed. Michael J. Houston (Provo, Utah: Association for Consumer Research, 1988), pp. 563–68.
8. Jacqueline Johnson Brown and Peter H. Reingen, "Social Ties and Word-of-Mouth Referral Behavior," *Journal of Consumer Research*, December 1987, pp. 350–62; and Peter H. Reingen, "A Word-of-Mouth Network," in *Advances in Consumer Research*, vol. 14, ed. Melanie Wallendorf and Paul Anderson (Provo, Utah: Association for Consumer Research, 1987), pp. 213–17.
9. Dorothy Leonard-Barton, "Experts as Negative Opinion Leaders in the Diffusion of a Technological Innovation," *Journal of Consumer Research*, March 1985, pp. 914–26.
10. Bearden and Etzel, "Reference Group Influences," p. 184.
11. Joel Rudd, "The Household as a Consuming Unit," in *Advances in Consumer Research*, vol. 14, ed. Melanie Wallendorf and Paul Anderson (Provo, Utah: Association for Consumer Research, 1987), pp. 451–52.
12. This section is adapted from Diane Crispell, "How to Avoid Big Mistakes," *American Demographics*, March 1991, pp. 48–50.
13. Sunil Gupta, Michael R. Hagerty, and John G. Myers, "New Directions in Family Decision Making Research," in *Advances in Consumer Research*, vol. 10, ed. Richard P. Bagozzi and Alice M. Tybout (Ann Arbor, Mich.: Association for Consumer Research, 1983), pp. 445–50; and Jagdish N. Sheth, "A Theory of Family Buying Decision," in *Models of Buyer Behavior Conceptual, Quantitative, and Empirical*, ed. J. N. Sheth (New York: Harper and Row, 1974), pp. 17–33.
14. Dennis L. Rosen and Donald H. Granbois, "Determinants of Role Structure in Family Financial Management," *Journal of Consumer Research*, September 1983, pp. 253–85; and Irene Raj Foster and Richard W. Olshavsky, "An Exploratory Study of Family Decision Making Using a New Taxonomy of Family Role Structure," in *Advances in Consumer Research*, vol. 16,

ed. T. K. Srull (Provo, Utah: Association for Consumer Research, 1989), pp. 665–70.

15. William J. Qualls, "Household Decision Behavior: The Impact of Husbands' and Wives' Sex Role Orientation," *Journal of Consumer Research*, September 1987, pp. 264–79; Dennis L. Rosen and Donald H. Granbois, "Determinants of Role Structure in Family Financial Management," *Journal of Consumer Research*, September 1983, pp. 253–85; Charles M. Schaninger, W. Christian Buss, and Rajiv Grover, "The Effect of Sex Roles on Family Economic Handling and Decision Influence," in *Advances in Consumer Research*, vol. 9, ed. Andrew A. Mitchell (Ann Arbor, Mich.: Association for Consumer Research, 1982), pp. 43–47; and Daniel Seymour and Greg Lessne, "Spousal Conflict Arousal: Scale Development," *Journal of Consumer Research*, December 1984, pp. 810–21.

16. Harry L. Davis, "Decision Making within the Household," *Journal of Consumer Research*, March 1976, pp. 241–60.

17. George P. Moschis and Linda G. Mitchell, "Television Advertising and Interpersonal Influences on Teenagers' Participation in Family Consumer Decisions," in *Advances in Consumer Research*, vol. 13, ed. Richard J. Lutz (Provo, Utah: Association for Consumer Research, 1986), pp. 181–86.

18. George E. Belch, Michael A. Belch, and Gayle Ceresino, "Parental and Teenage Child Influences in Family Decision Making," *Journal of Business Research* 13 (1985), pp. 163–176; and Ellen R. Foxman, Patriya S. Tansuhaj, and Karin M. Ekstrom, "Family Members' Perceptions of Adolescents' Influence in Family Decision Making," *Journal of Consumer Research*, March 1989, pp. 482–91.

19. Alvin Burns and Donald Granbois, "Factors Moderating the Resolution of Preference Conflict in Family Automobile Purchasing," *Journal of Marketing Research*, February 1977, pp. 68–77; Alvin C. Burns and Jo Anne Hopper, "An Analysis of the Presence, Stability and Antecedents of Husband and Wife Purchase Decision Making Influence Assessment and Disagreement," in *Advances in Consumer Research*, vol. 13, ed. Richard J. Lutz (Provo, Utah: Association for Consumer Research, 1986), pp. 175–80; Margaret C. Nelson, "The Resolution of Conflict in Joint Purchase Decisions by Husbands and Wives: A Review and Empirical Test," in *Advances in Consumer Research*, vol. 15, ed. Michael J. Houston (Provo, Utah: Association for Consumer Research, 1988), pp. 442–48.

20. Kim P. Corfman and Donald R. Lehmann, "Models of Cooperative Group Decision-Making and Relative Influence: An Experimental Investigation of Family Purchase Decisions," *Journal of Consumer Research*, June 1987, pp. 1–13; Burns and Granbois, "Factors Moderating the Resolution of Preference Conflict," pp. 68–77; and Pierre Filiatrault and J. R. Brent Ritchie, "Joint Purchasing Decisions: A Comparison of Influence Structure in Family and Couple Decision-Making Units," *Journal of Consumer Research*, September 1980, pp. 131–40.

21. Rosann L. Spiro, "Persuasion in Family Decision Making," *Journal of Consumer Research*, March 1983, pp. 393–402.

22. Ibid; and Dennis L. Rosen and Richard W. Olshavsky, "The Dual Role of Informational Social Influence: Implications for Marketing Management," *Journal of Business Research* 15 (1987), pp. 123–44.

23. Scott Ward, Donna M. Klees, and Daniel B. Wackman, "Consumer Socialization Research: Content Analysis of Post-1980 Studies, and Some Implications for Future Work," in *Advances in Consumer Research*, vol. 17 (Provo, Utah: Association for Consumer Research, 1990), pp. 798–803.

24. George P. Moschis, "The Role of Family Communication in Consumer Socialization of Children and Adolescents," *Journal of Consumer Research*, March 1985, pp. 898–913.

25. Gilbert A. Churchill, Jr., and George P. Moschis, "Television and Interpersonal Influences on Adolescent Consumer Learning," *Journal of Consumer Research*, June 1979, pp. 23–35.

26. Sanford Grossbart, Les Carlson, and Ann Walsh, "Consumer Socialization Motives for Shopping with Children," *AMA Summer Educators' Proceedings* (Chicago: American Marketing Association, 1988); Bonnie B. Reece, Sevgin Eroglu, and Nora J. Rifon, "Parents Teaching Children to Shop: How, What, and Who?" *AMA Summer Educators' Proceedings* (Chicago: American Marketing Association, 1988), pp. 274–78; and Les Carlson and Sanford Grossbart, "Parental Style and Consumer Socialization of Children," *Journal of Consumer Research*, June 1988, pp. 77–94.

27. Ellen Graham, "Children's Hour: As Kids Gain Power of Purse, Marketing Takes Aim at Them," *The Wall Street Journal*, January 10, 1988, pp. 1, 24.

28. Karin M. Ekstrom, Patriya S. Tansuhaj, and Ellen Foxman, "Children's Influence in Family Decisions and Consumer Socialization: A Reciprocal View," in *Advances in Consumer Research*, vol. 14, ed. Melanie Wallendorf and Paul Anderson (Provo, Utah: Association for Consumer Research, 1987), pp. 283–87; Elizabeth S. Moore-Shay and Richard J. Lutz, "Intergenerational Influences in the Formation of Consumer Attitudes and Beliefs about the Marketplace: Mothers and Daughters," in *Advances in Consumer Research*, vol. 15, ed. Michael J. Houston (Provo, Utah: Association for Consumer Research, 1988), pp. 461–67; and Scott Ward, Thomas S. Robertson, Donna M. Klees, and Hubert Gatignon, "Children's Purchase Requests and Parental Yielding: A Cross-National Study," in *Advances in Consumer Research*, vol. 13, ed. Richard J. Lutz (Provo, Utah: Association for Consumer Research, 1986), pp. 629–32.

29. Susan E. Heckler, Terry L. Childers, and Ramesh Arunachalam, "Intergenerational Influences in Adult Buying Behaviors: An Examination of Moderating Factors," in *Advances in Consumer Research*, vol. 16 (Provo, Utah: Association for Consumer Research, 1990), pp. 276–84; Patricia Sorce, Lynette Loomis, and Philip R. Tyler, "Intergenerational Influence on Consumer Decision Making," in *Advances in Consumer Research*, vol. 16 (Provo, Utah: Association for Consumer Research, 1990), pp. 271–75; and George P. Moschis, "Methodological Issues in Studying Intergenerational Influences on Consumer Behavior," in *Advances in Consumer Research*, vol. 15, ed. Michael J. Houston (Provo, Utah: Association for Consumer Research, 1988), pp. 569–73.

30. For a review of these issues see Michael D. Reilly, "Working Wives and Convenience Consumption," *Journal of Consumer Research*, March 1982, pp. 407–18. Also see Charles M. Schaninger and Chris T. Allen, "Wife's Occupational Status as a Consumer Behavior Construct," *Journal of Consumer Research*, September 1981, pp. 189–96; and Charles B. Weinberg and Russell S. Winer, "Working Wives and Major Family Expenditures: Replication and Extension," *Journal of Consumer Research*, September 1983, pp. 259–63.

31. Gordon Green and Edward Welniak, "The Nine Household Markets," *American Demographics*, October 1991, pp. 36–40.

32. Martha Farnsworth Riche, "The Postmarital Society," *American Demographics*, November 1988, pp. 22–26, 60.

33. Ibid.

34. Martha Farnsworth Riche, "The Future of the Family," *American Demographics*, March 1991, pp. 44–46.

35. Diane Crispell, "Three's a Crowd," *American Demographics*, January 1989, pp. 34–38.

36. For a review of a number of these, see Patrick E. Murphy and William A. Staples, "A Modernized Family Life Cycle," *Journal of Consumer Research*, June 1979, pp. 12–22.

37. Ibid. For other approaches and discussion, see Frederick W. Derrick and Alane K. Lehfeld, "The Family Life Cycle: An Alternative Approach," *Journal of Consumer Research*, September 1980, pp. 214–17; Mary C. Gilly and Ben M. Enis, "Recycling the Family Life Cycle: A Proposal for Redefinition," in *Advances in Consumer Research*, vol. 8, ed. Andrew Mitchell

(Ann Arbor, Mich.: Association for Consumer Research, 1982), pp. 271–76; and Janet Wagner and Sherman Hanna, "The Effectiveness of Family Life Cycle Variables in Consumer Expenditure Research," *Journal of Consumer Research*, December 1983, pp. 281–91.

38. Martha Farnsworth Riche, "The Boomerang Age," *American Demographics*, May 1990, pp. 25–27, 30, 52.

39. Margaret Ambry, "The Age of Spending," *American Demographics*, November 1990, pp. 16–23, 52.

40. This section is adapted from Eugene H. Fram, "The Time Compressed Shopper," *Marketing Insights*, Summer 1991, pp. 34–39; and Eugene H. Fram and Joel Axelrod, "The Distressed Shopper," *American Demographics*, October 1990, pp. 44–45.

Additional Reading

For a discussion of how consumers make decisions in group situations, see:

Ward, James C., and Peter H. Reingen. "Sociocognitive Analysis of Group Decision Making among Consumers." *Journal of Consumer Research*, December 1990, pp. 245–62.

For a discussion of the influence of referent others, see:

Brown, Jacqueline Johnson, and Peter H. Reingen. "Social Ties and Word-of-Mouth Referral Behavior." *Journal of Consumer Research*, December 1987, pp. 350–62.

For recent research on husband-wife decision making, see:

Heslop, Louise A., and Judith Marshall. "On Golden Pond: Elderly Couples and Consumer Decision Making." In *Advances in Consumer Research*, vol. 18. Provo, Utah: Association for Consumer Research, 1991, pp. 681–87.

Menasco, Michael B., and David J. Curry. "Utility and Choice: An Empirical Study of Wife/Husband Decision Making." *Journal of Consumer Research*, March 1989, pp. 87–97.

For recent research on conflict resolution, see:

Corfman, Kim. "Models of Group Decision-Making and Relative Influence When Preferences Differ: A Conceptual Framework." In *Research in Consumer Behavior*, vol. 2, ed. Elizabeth C. Hirschman and Jagdish N. Sheth. Greenwich, Conn.: JAI Press, 1986.

Nelson, Margaret. "The Resolution of Conflict in Joint Purchase Decisions by Husbands and Wives: A Review and Empirical Test." In *Advances in Consumer Research*, vol. 15, ed. M. Houston. Provo, Utah: Association for Consumer Research, 1987, pp. 436–41.

For a discussion of spending differences in one and two earner households, see:

Rubin, Rose M., Bobye J. Riney, and David J. Molina. "Expenditure Pattern Differentials between One-Earner and Dual-Earner Households: 1972–1973 and 1984." *Journal of Consumer Research*, June 1990, pp. 43–52.

For a discussion of how women use time, see:

Anderson, W. Thomas, Jr., Linda L. Golden, William A. Weeks, and U. M. Umesh. "The Five Faces of Eve: Women's Timetable Typologies." In *Advances in Consumer Research*, vol. 16, ed. Thomas K. Srull. Provo, Utah: Association for Consumer Research, 1989, pp. 346–53.

For a discussion of group decision making in industrial buying situations, see:

Silk, Alvin J., and Manohar U. Kalwani. "Measuring Influence in Organizational Purchase Decisions." *Journal of Marketing Research*, May 1982, pp. 165–81.

MARKETING STRATEGY IN ACTION

Hotels and Resorts: Catering to Kids

For years, most of the lodging industry has merely tolerated children, and many upscale hotels and resorts have actively discouraged them. Recently, however, much of the huge travel industry, including some of America's toniest hotels and resorts, have begun to treat kids like important customers.

Major demographic changes in the makeup of American families lie behind this shift in marketing strategy. A baby boomlet occurred in the 1980s, produced when record numbers of baby boomers began having children of their own. According to one travel expert, "Baby boomers are the most widely traveled generation ever. Now as parents, they want to vacation with their kids while still having time to pursue adult activities." Because they had children at a later age and often are dual-income households, many of these families spend substantial amounts on travel and vacations.

Many hotels and resorts are now bending over backward to make children feel welcome. Even business-oriented and luxury hotels are adding elaborate day-care programs for kids. For instance, consider San Francisco's luxurious Four Seasons Clift Hotel, where average room rates are $200 per night. In 1986, the Clift realized it needed a strategy for dealing with the children who were showing up with their parents, often for extended stays. "Many people wanted to stay in a luxury hotel and still have their kids with them," said a hotel spokesperson.

Rather than discourage the trend and lose business, the hotel launched its Clift Dweller program. Now, when the hotel takes a reservation for a family, it asks for the names and ages of the children. When the family shows up, the kids are greeted at check-in with a toy or book appropriate to their age. Infants receive a first-day supply of diapers and formula or baby food at no charge. Children get their own room, connecting to the parents' room, at a discount rate. The Clift Hotel will arrange baby-sitting and escorted trips to museums or the zoo at rates of about $5 per hour. It offers bedtime snacks and 24-hour room service from a children's menu and keeps a pediatrician on call around the clock. The Clift even welcomes youngsters into its fanciest dining room, where the tuxedoed waiters have been trained to deal with small children.

Other hotels and resorts have begun to offer their own versions of programs for kids. For instance, virtually all the Sheraton hotels in Hawaii have added children's programs in recent years. Beginning in 1985 with a casual "day camp" format, they switched in 1987 to a Thursday-through-Sunday formal program for children 4 to 12 years old. For about $10 per day, parents can sign their kids up for activities ranging from tennis instruction to magic lessons.

Travel agents and vacation planners are responding to the changing market, too. Family-oriented travel agencies, like the California firm Rascals in Paradise, have been doing a good business. There's even a monthly newsletter, "Travel with Your Children," that tracks trends in the family travel market and has documented the explosion in travel services for kids. In the early 1980s, for example, only about a dozen hotels (apart from the obvious family destinations such as Disney-type theme parks) could be found that had special programs for children. By 1988, there were 50 family-friendly hotels and resorts in Hawaii alone.

Even firms that once ignored kids have learned to cater to them. Consider the marketing strategies adopted by Club Med, once the epitome of singles resorts that was geared to young, swinging baby boomers. Club Med offers fixed-price, all-inclusive vacations at its own special resorts around the world, often built on secluded beaches. But the company faced losing its clientele of young baby boomers as they got older and began to marry and have children. So beginning in the early 1980s, Club Med reshaped itself from a free-spirited camp for singles to a leader in the family-vacation market. Now more than half of Club Med's customers are married, and many bring their children. Club Med currently has six "miniclub" resorts that provide day camps and baby-sitting for kids 2 to 11 years old. In 1987, Club Med entertained almost 80,000 children (and their parents), up 10 percent from the previous year. In 1988, the company opened its first "baby club" at the Sandpiper Resort in Florida and welcomed over 1,500 kids under 2 in the first year of operation.

The author of a family travel guidebook believes these recent changes in the marketing strategies of the travel industry are only the beginning: "The catalyst is money. These are parents who have waited to have their chilren. They have money and are already used to a certain style of travel. Places will either start to accommodate them or they simply will go somewhere else."

Discussion Questions

1. Discuss how the family decision process for deciding where to go on a family vacation is likely to vary for these three types of families – families with young kids (ages under 7 or 8), families with preteens and young teens (ages 9 to 14), and families with older teens (ages 15 to 19). What implications do these differences have for the types of hotels and resorts mentioned in the case.
2. What types of conflict might occur in the three types of family situations listed above? How might that conflict be resolved? What implications does this analysis have for developing marketing strategies for the hotel and resort industry?
3. Discuss how the hotel and resort industry could use the modernized family life cycle to help identify potential market segments, and then develop targeted marketing strategies for those segments.
4. Discuss how reference groups could influence a family's vacation decisions. What implications does this analysis have for the hotel and resort industry? What types of strategies could the hotel and resort industry undertake to stimulate favorable reference group influence?

Source: Ken Wells, "Hotels and Resorts Are Catering to Kids: Day Care and Activities Programs Help Welcome Traveling Families," *The Wall Street Journal*, August 11, 1988, p. 25.

Consumer Analysis and Marketing Strategy

Section 5

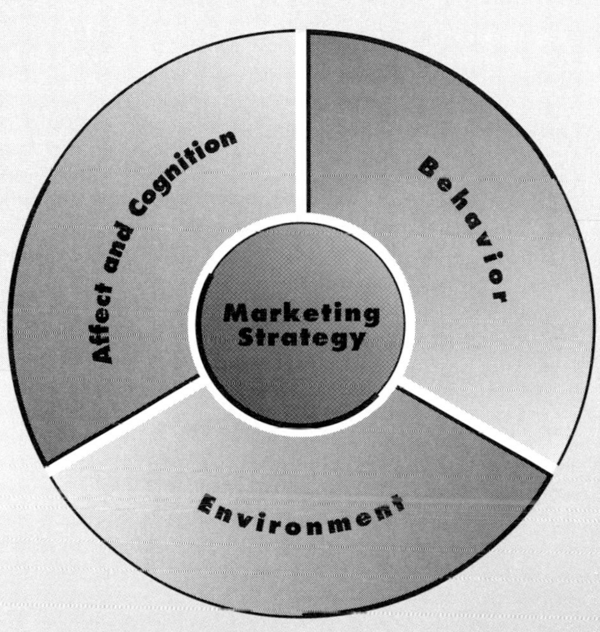

Market Segmentation and Product Positioning

CHAPTER 16

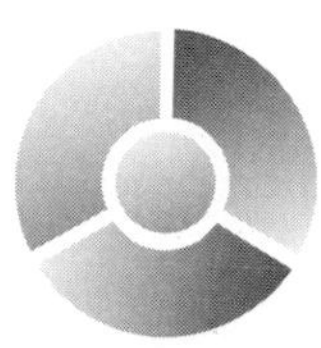

GILLETTE CO.

Gillette Co. is one of the world's best marketers of personal care products for men. In 1901, its founder, King Camp Gillette, made business history by inventing the disposable razor blade and made a fortune on sales of replacements. The company has had a long succession of product improvements involving new styles of razors and blades. In 1990, it hit the jackpot again with its Sensor blades and razors whose spring mechanism makes for what the company claims is the closest shave ever. With margins of 30 percent or more, the company can make profits of over $500 million per year on blades and razors alone. Gillette has loyal customers and dominates the market with a 63 percent share.

For all of its marketing success in the male market, Gillette has had problems marketing personal care products to women. Its personal care division, even with successful men's products Right Guard deodorant and Foamy shaving cream, has not done as well in selling personal care products for women. In one recent year, for example, the personal care division accounted for about 27 percent of Gillette's $3.8 billion in sales but only 11 percent of operating profits.

Gillette's women's products include Silkience conditioner, White

Rain shampoo, Dippity-Do hair treatment, Toni home permanent, Aapri cleanser, and Deep Magic skin cream. While these products generate about $250 million in sales and were hot brands in their day, young trendsetting consumers today view them as drugstore dinosaurs. Rejuvenating these products has been difficult. For example, a $20 million campaign was used to try to relaunch Silkience conditioner. The campaign featured model Kim Alexis holding a baby chick in her hand. The tag line was "Just hatched—new Silkience cleaner, longer conditioners." Consumers were not impressed. As one consultant put it, "The key in this industry is constant freshness, and Gillette didn't have enough news."

Source: Geoffrey Smith, "Does Gillette Know How to Treat a Lady?" *Business Week*, August 27, 1990, pp. 64–66.

Why is Gillette so successful in selling personal care products targeted to men but less so for products targeted to women? Market segmentation is one of the most important concepts in the consumer behavior and marketing literature. A primary reason for studying consumer behavior is to identify bases for effective segmentation, and a large portion of consumer research is concerned with segmentation. From a marketing strategy view, selection of the appropriate target market is paramount to developing successful marketing programs.

The logic of market segmentation is quite simple: it is based on the idea that a single product usually will not appeal to *all* consumers. Consumers' purchase goals, product knowledge, involvement, and purchase behavior vary; and successful marketers often adapt their marketing strategies to appeal to specific consumer groups. Even a simple product such as chewing gum comes in multiple flavors and package sizes, and varies in sugar content, calories, consistency (e.g., liquid centers), and colors to appeal to different consumers. While a single product will seldom appeal to all consumers, it can almost always serve more than one consumer. Thus, there are usually *groups of consumers* who can be served well by a single item. If a particular group can be served profitably by a firm, then it comprises a viable market segment. A marketer should then develop a marketing mix to serve that group.

In the past, many marketers focused on target markets in a general, nonpersonal way. While they may have had some idea of the general characteristics of their target market, they could not identify individual consumers who actually

HIGHLIGHT 16.1

HITTING TARGET MARKETS IN THE 1990S

By combining data from several sources, a company can have extensive information on its target markets and where they shop. Below are examples of the target market profiles for three products and the stores in the New York area where they are most likely to purchase them. Marketers could design special promotions in these stores to further increase the probability of purchase.

Brand	Heavy User Profile	Lifestyle and Media Profile	Top 3 Stores
Peter Pan peanut butter	Households with kids headed by 18-54 year olds, in suburban and rural areas	• Heavy video renters • Go to theme parks • Below average TV viewers • Above average radio listeners	**Foodtown Super Market** 3350 Hempstead Turnpike, Levittown, N.Y. **Pathmark Supermarket** 3535 Hempstead Turnpike, Levittown, N.Y. **King Kullen Market** 598 Stewart Ave., Bethpage, N.Y.
Stouffers Red Box frozen entrees	Households headed by people 55 and older, and upscale suburban house-holds headed by 35-54 year olds	• Go to gambling casinos • Give parties • Involved in public activities • Travel frequently • Heavy newspaper readers • Above average TV viewers	**Dan's Supreme Super Market** 69-62 188th St., Flushing, N.Y. **Food Emporium** Madison Ave. & 74th St., New York City **Waldbaum Super Market** 196-35 Horace Harding Blvd., Flushing, N.Y.
Coors Light beer	Head of household, 21-34, middle to upper income, suburban and urban	• Belong to a health club • Buy rock music • Travel by plane • Give parties, cookouts • Rent videos • Heavy TV sports viewers	**Food Emporium** 1498 York Ave., New York City **Food Emporium** First Ave. & 72nd St., New York City **Gristades Supermarket** 350 E. 86th St., New York City

Source: Michael J. McCarthy, "Marketers Zero in on Their Customers," *The Wall Street Journal,* March 18, 1991, p. B1.

purchased and used their products. However, with today's technology, including scanner and other personal data sources, improved methods of marketing research, and efficient computers for handling large data bases, marketers can have detailed, personal information on many members of its target market. For example, one tobacco company is reported to have the names, addresses, and purchasing data for over 30 million smokers. As illustrated in Highlight 16.1,

FIGURE 16.1
Tasks Involved in Market Segmentation

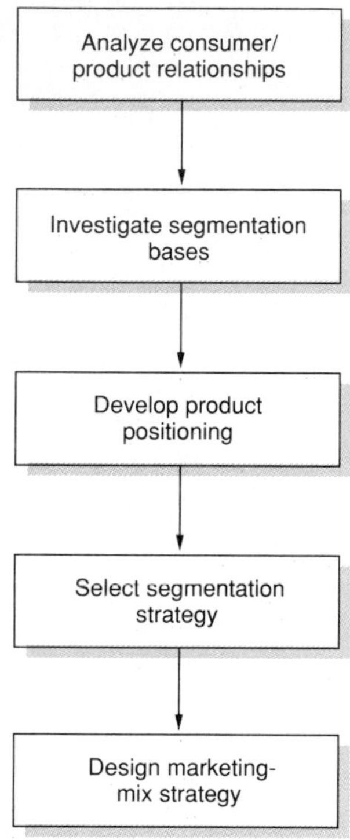

marketers can now target a product's best customers and the stores where they are most likely to shop.

In this chapter, we consider market segmentation. We define **market segmentation** as the process of dividing a market into groups of similar consumers and selecting the most appropriate group(s) and individuals for the firm to serve. We can break down the process of market segmentation into five tasks, as shown in Figure 16.1. In the remainder of this chapter, we discuss each of the market segmentation tasks shown in the figure. While we recognize that these tasks are strongly interrelated and their order may vary (depending on the firm and the situation), market segmentation analysis can seldom (if ever) be ignored. Even if the final decision is to mass market and not to segment at all, this decision should be reached only *after* a market segmentation analysis has been conducted. Thus, market segmentation analysis is critical for sound marketing strategy development.

Analyze Consumer/Product Relationships

The first task involved in segmenting markets is analyzing consumer/product relationships. This entails analysis of the affect and cognitions, behaviors, and environments involved in the purchase/consumption process for the particular product. There are three general approaches to this task. First, marketing managers may brainstorm the product concept and consider what types of consumers are likely to purchase and use the product and how they differ from those less likely to buy. Second, focus group and other types of primary research can be useful for identifying differences in attributes, benefits, and values of various potential markets. Third, secondary research may be used to further investigate differences in potential target markets, determine the relative sizes of these markets, and develop a better understanding of consumers of this or similar products.

For many established product categories, considerable information is available for analyzing various markets. For product categories like automobiles, toothpaste, and many food products, various target markets are well established. For example, the category of automobile buyers includes luxury, sports, midsize, compact, and subcompact markets.

Within each of these markets further analysis may offer insights into market opportunities. One market of great concern to General Motors is the group that purchases foreign automobiles. Only one in five of these buyers even considers a General Motors car. GM executives believe that if they produce an American car that is comparable to cars like Honda and Toyota make, they can recapture up to 80 percent of this market. In fact, GM has invested $3.5 billion to produce the Saturn automobile to appeal to this market. Given the high satisfaction of owners of many Japanese cars, this would appear to be a very risky strategy unless GM has thoroughly analyzed the affect and cognitions, behaviors, and environments of foreign car buyers and can build an American car that these consumers will purchase instead of foreign brands.[1]

For many products, the initial breakdown in markets is between the prestige and mass market. The prestige market seeks the highest quality (and often the highest priced) product available. Often, particular products for consumers in this market have very important meanings, such as expressions of good taste, expertise, and status. Brands such as Rolex watches, Mercedes-Benz automobiles, Hartmann luggage, and Gucci handbags are targeted to these consumers.

The marketing strategies for these products generally involve selling them in exclusive stores at high prices and promoting them in prestige media. For consumers in this market, affect and cognitions (feelings about and meaning of the product), behaviors (shopping activities), and environments (information and store contact) differ from those of consumers in the mass market. Thus, the initial analysis of consumer/product relationship has important implications for all of the tasks involved in market segmentation and strategy development.

HIGHLIGHT 16.2

Targeting the College Market

It starts with a box of free samples left in college dorm rooms. The free magazines soon follow. Concerts beamed into the student lounge include commercials. Wallboards feature ads next to the campus calendar.

Madison Avenue has invaded the Ivory Tower, and advertisers are making increased use of targeted media to stay there. In one recent year, advertisers spent about $100 million trying to sway the shopping choices of 12 million collegians.

The group has considerable economic potential. College students have an estimated $20 billion to spend after paying for books, board, and tuition, according to a recent Simmons Market Research study. Other studies estimate the average student has about $200 a month to spend after paying for school-related expenses.

The college segment is a delight for consumer product marketers. Many of its members are away from home for the first time, now making their own decisions on what brands of soap, deodorant, and hair mousse to buy.

But shaping brand loyalties isn't easy. This is a hip, educated audience that grew up in front of the television set and learned to spot even the most casual commercial plug. Even without skepticism about sales pitches, getting a sales message to college students can be difficult. They tend to watch television less frequently, listen to radio less often, and read metropolitan newspapers more rarely than their peers who didn't go to college. Traditional advertising vehicles often don't do the job.

As a result, marketers try to latch onto things students seem to pay attention to – college newspapers, college-oriented magazines, programs carried on college television systems, and billboards listing campus events. Market Source Corp. developed a backlit electronic billboard and has placed 1,250 of them on 550 campuses. They have room for an ad, a campus calendar, and an electronic message space. Minimum annual charges for advertising on the billboards run about $200,000.

Both Market Source and Whittle Communication distribute a variety of products and coupons in about 1.2 million sampler boxes each fall. The sampling programs "are the best vehicle we have" to reach college students, said Carole Johnson, a marketing manager for Gillette Co., which spent about $105,000 to include Soft 'N Dri deodorant in 700,000 kits one fall. Thus, while it may be a hard market to reach, many marketers feel it is worth the effort.

Source: Excerpted from "Advertisers Target College Market," *Marketing News* 21, no. 22 (October 23, 1987), p. 5. Published by the American Marketing Association.

The analysis of these differences in consumers is also important when companies seek new target markets. For example, Holiday Inns has saturated the midprice lodging market with over 265,000 motel rooms. Based on a survey of Holiday Inn guests that found over one third wanted to pay less for a room, management decided to test a smaller facility that didn't offer lounge or food services. Holiday Inn opened its first Hampton Inn in 1984 and now has over 165 nationwide. Hampton Inns charge an average price of $39 per room compared with an average of $52 at a Holiday Inn. Here, a difference in consumers' cognitions about lodging prices led to a change in marketing strategy (resegmenting the midprice market) and the lodging environment (addition of Hampton Inns), which led to a change in consumer behavior (staying at Hampton Inns instead of Holiday Inns). Marriott Corporation is also targeting this market with its Fairfield Inns.[2]

The above example demonstrates how the analysis of consumer/product relationships led to a successful marketing strategy for Holiday Inns. However, a number of other tasks occur after the initial analysis of consumer/product relationships and before marketing strategies are finalized. A logical next step is to investigate various bases on which markets could be segmented. Highlight 16.2 discusses an example of a marketing strategy to reach the college market.

Investigate Segmentation Bases

Unfortunately, there is no simple way to determine the relevant bases for segmenting markets. In most cases, however, at least some initial dimensions can be determined from previous, purchase trends, and managerial judgment. For example, suppose we wish to segment the market for all-terrain vehicles. Several dimensions come to mind for initial consideration: sex (male); age (18 to 35); lifestyle (outdoorsman); and income level (perhaps $25,000 to $40,000). At a minimum, these variables should be included in subsequent segmentation research.

A number of bases for segmenting consumer markets are presented in Figure 16.2. This is by no means a complete list of possible segmentation variables, but it represents some useful categories. Two general approaches to segmenting markets are benefit segmentation and psychographic segmentation. A third general approach is called person/situation segmentation. These three approaches will be discussed in some detail below.

Benefit Segmentation

The belief underlying the **benefit segmentation** approach is that the *benefits* people are seeking in consuming a given product are the basic reasons for the existence of true market segments.[3] This approach thus attempts to measure consumer value systems and consumers' perceptions of various brands in a product class. The classic example of a benefit segmentation, provided by Russell Haley, concerned the toothpaste market. Haley identified four basic segments—Sensory, Sociable, Worrier, and Independent—as presented in Figure 16.3. Haley argued this segmentation could be very useful for selecting

FIGURE 16.2
Useful Segmentation Bases for Consumer Markets

Segmentation Bases/Descriptors	Illustrative Categories
Geographic	
Region	Pacific; Mountain; West North Central; West South Central; East North Central; East South Central; South Atlantic; Middle Atlantic; New England
Size of city, county, or standard metropolitan statistical area (SMSA)	Under 5,000; 5,000–19,999; 20,000–49,999; 50,000–99,999; 100,000–249,999; 250,000–499,000; 500,000–999,999; 1,000,000–3,999,999; 4,000,000 or over
Population density	Urban; suburban; rural
Climate	Warm; cold
Demographic	
Age	Under 6; 6–12; 13–19; 20-29; 30–39; 40–49; 50–59; 60+
Sex	Male; female
Family size	1-2; 3–4; 5+ persons
Family life cycle	Young, single; Young, married, no children; young, married, youngest child under 6; young, married, youngest child 6 or over; older, married with children; older, married, no children under 18; older, single; other
Income	Under $10,000; $10,000–$14,999; $15,000–$24,999; $25,000–$34,999; $35,000 to $49,999; $50,000 or over
Occupation	Professional and technical; managers, officials, and proprietors; clerical, sales; craftsmen, foremen; operatives; farmers; retired; students; housewives; unemployed
Education	Grade school or less; some high school; graduated from high school; some college; graduated from college; some graduate work; graduate degree
Religion	Catholic; Protestant; Jewish; other
Race	White; black; Oriental; other
Nationality	American; British; French; German; Italian; Japanese
Psychosocial	
Social class	Upper Americans; middle class; working class; lower Americans
Lifestyle	Traditionalist; sophisticate; swinger
Personality	Compliant; aggressive; detached

(continued)

FIGURE 16.2
continued

Cognitive, Affective, and Behavioral	
Attitudes	Positive; neutral; negative
Benefits sought	Convenience; economy; prestige
Readiness stage	Unaware; aware; informed; interested; desirous; intention to purchase
Perceived risk	High; moderate; low
Innovativeness	Innovator; Early Adopter; Early Majority; Late Majority; Laggard; Nonadopter
Involvement	Low; high
Loyalty status	None; some; total
Usage rate	None; light; medium; heavy
User status	Nonuser; ex-user; potential user; current user
Usage situation	Home; work; commuting; vacation

FIGURE 16.3
Toothpaste Market Benefit Segments

	Sensory Segment	**Sociable Segment**	**Worrier Segment**	**Independent Segment**
Principal benefit sought	Flavor, product appearance	Brightness of teeth	Decay prevention	Price
Demographic strengths	Children	Teens, young people	Large families	Men
Special behavioral characteristics	Uses of spearmint-flavored tooth-paste	Smokers	Heavy users	Heavy users
Brands disproportionately favored	Colgate	Ultra Brite	Crest	Cheapest brand
Lifestyle characteristics	Hedonistic	Active	Conservative	Value oriented

Source: Adapted from Russell I. Haley, "Benefit Segmentation: A Decision-Oriented Research Tool," *Journal of Marketing* 32 (July 1968), pp. 30–35. Published by the American Marketing Association.

There are many bases for segmenting markets. How would you describe these segments?

advertising copy, media, commercial length, packaging, and new-product design. For example, colorful packages might be appropriate for the Sensory segment, perhaps aqua packages (to indicate fluoride) for the Worrier group, and gleaming white packages for the Sociable segment because of their interest in white teeth.[4]

Psychographic Segmentation

Psychographic segmentation divides markets on differences in consumer lifestyles. Generally, psychographic segmentation follows a post hoc model. That is, consumers are first asked a variety of questions about their lifestyles and then are grouped on the basis of the similarity of their responses. Lifestyles are measured by asking consumers about their activities (work, hobbies, vacations), interests (family, job, community) and opinions (about social issues, politics, business). The activity, interest, and opinion **(AIO)** questions in some studies are very general. In others, at least some of the questions are related to specific products. However, as illustrated in Highlight 16.3, psychographic information can be obtained from sources other than company-sponsored research projects.

Psychographic segmentation studies often include hundreds of questions and provide a tremendous amount of information about consumers. Thus, psychographic segmentation is based on the idea that "the more you know and

HIGHLIGHT 16.3

AN INTERESTING SOURCE OF LIFESTYLE INFORMATION

Many consumers use 800 and 900 telephone numbers. Here's how marketers get lifestyle information about consumers who do so. Do you think marketers have a right to this information?

1. **Make a phone call:** You call an 800 or 900 number to buy a product, get information, or express an opinion.
2. **Connect to computer:** In many cases, the call goes to a computer in Omaha, Nebraska, owned by AT&T and American Express. It has 10,000 continuously operating phone lines.
3. **Computer identifies you:** Using your phone number, the computer connects with a marketing service to get your name and address and display it on a salesperson's computer screen. Tens of millions of names can be searched in a second or two.
4. **Do your business:** The salesperson can greet you by name, then takes your order, answers questions, or asks you for more information.
5. **Instant check on your credit:** If you order something by credit card, the computer checks an electronic credit authorization bureau to make sure your credit is good.
6. **Your call is recorded:** Your name, address, phone number, and the subject of your call are provided electronically to the sponsoring company or organization, which then can use it for targeted mailing lists or marketing campaigns.
7. **Marketers analyze your lifestyle:** The sponsoring company can match this data with information in other data bases – voter lists, magazine subscriptions – to find out even more about your lifestyle.

Source: Robert S. Boyd, "How Big Brother Sees Consumers," *Wisconsin State Journal,* July 8, 1990, p. 4B.

understand about consumers, the more effectively you can communicate and market to them."[5]

To date, no consensus has been reached concerning how many different lifestyle segments there are in the United States – or in other countries. Psychographic studies frequently reach different conclusions about the number and nature of lifestyle categories. For this reason, the validity of psychographic segmentation is sometimes questioned.[6]

A well-known psychographic segmentation was developed at SRI International in California. The original segmentation divided consumers in the United States into nine groups and was called **VALS**,™ which stands for "values and lifestyles." However, while this segmentation was commercially successful, it tended to place the majority of consumers into only one or two groups and SRI thought it needed to be updated to reflect changes in society. Thus, SRI developed a new typology called VALS 2(TM).[7]

VALS 2 is based on two national surveys of 2,500 consumers who responded to 43 lifestyle questions. The first survey developed the segmentation, and the second validated it and linked it to buying and media behavior. The questionnaire asked consumers to respond to whether they agreed or disagreed with statements such as "My idea of fun at a national park would be to stay at an expensive lodge and dress up for dinner" and "I could stand to skin a dead animal." Consumers were then clustered into the eight groups shown and described in Figure 16.4.

The VALS 2 groups are arranged in a rectangle and are based on two dimensions. The vertical dimension represents resources, which include income, education, self-confidence, health, eagerness to buy, intelligence, and energy level. The horizontal dimension represents self-orientations and includes three different types. *Principle-oriented consumers* are guided by their views of how the world is or should be; *status-oriented consumers* by the actions and opinions of others; and *action-oriented consumers* by a desire for social or physical activity, variety, and risk taking.

Each of the VALS 2 groups represents from 9 to 17 percent of the United States adult population. Marketers can buy VALS 2 information for a variety of products and can have it tied to a number of other consumer data bases.

PERSON/SITUATION SEGMENTATION

Markets can often be divided on the basis of the usage situation in conjunction with individual differences of consumers. This is known as **person/situation segmentation.** For example, clothing and footwear markets are divided not only on the basis of the consumer's sex and size, but also on usage situation dimensions such as weather conditions, physical activities, and social events.[8] As another example, expensive china is designed for special occasions; Corelle dinnerware is designed for everyday family use. Dickson argues, "In practice the product whose unique selling propositions (quality, features, image, packaging, or merchandising) is not targeted for particular people in particular usage situations is probably the exception rather than the rule."[9] Thus, Dickson suggests the approach to segmentation outlined in Figure 16.5. This approach not only combines the person and the situation, but also other important segmentation bases: benefits sought, product and attribute perceptions, and marketplace behavior.

Operationally, Dickson suggests this segmentation approach involves the following steps:

> Step 1: Use observational studies, focus group discussions, and secondary data to discover whether different usage situations exist and whether they are determinant, in the sense that they appear to affect the importance of various product characteristics.

FIGURE 16.4
VALS 2™ Eight American Lifestyles

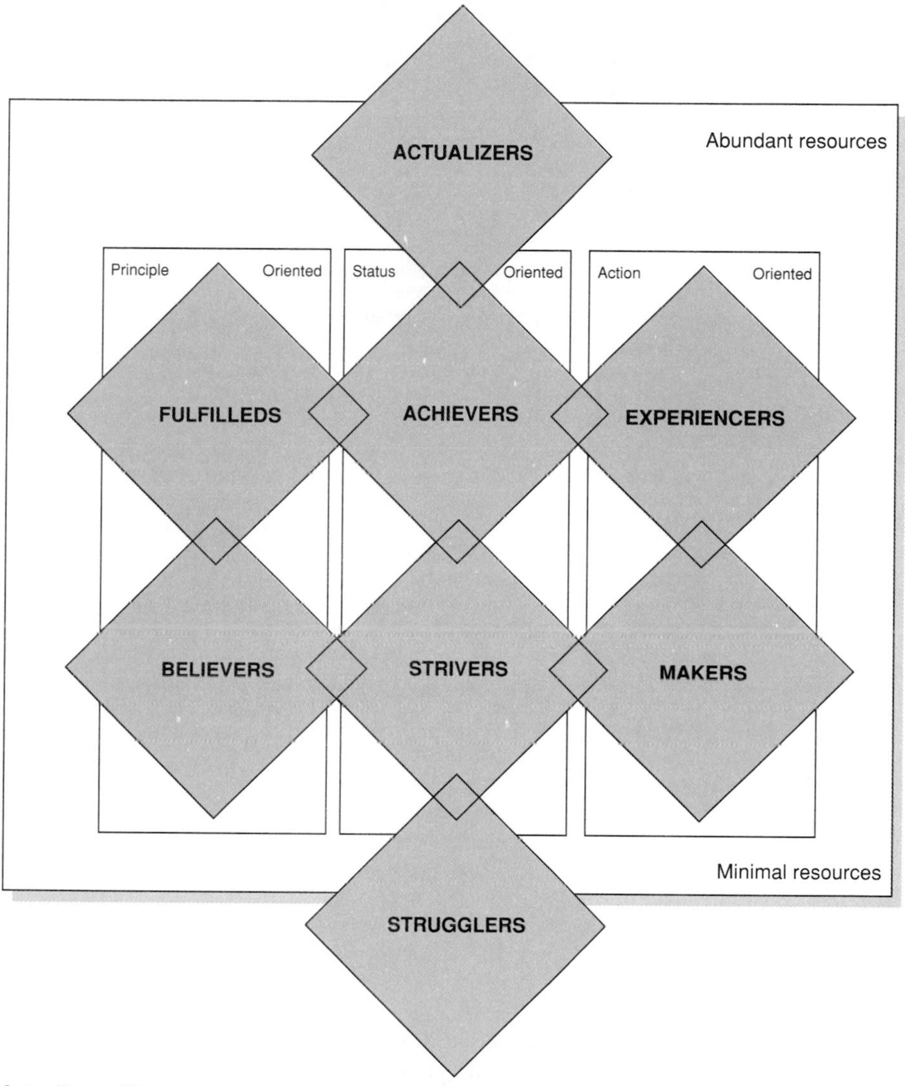

Actualizers. These consumers have the highest incomes and such high self-esteem and abundant resources that they can indulge in any or all self-orientations. They are located above the rectangle. Image is important to them as an expression of their taste, independence, and character. Their consumer choices are directed toward the finer things in life.

(continued)

FIGURE 16.4
continued

Fulfilleds. These consumers are the high resource group of those who are principle-oriented. They are mature, responsible, well-educated professionals. Their leisure activities center on their homes, but they are well-informed about what goes on in the world and they are open to new ideas and social change. They have high incomes but are practical consumers.

Believers. These consumers are the low resource group of those who are principle-oriented. They are conservative and predictable consumers who favor American products and established brands. Their lives are centered on family, church, community, and the nation. They have modest incomes.

Achievers. These consumers are the high resource group of those who are status-oriented. They are successful, work-oriented people who get their satisfaction from their jobs and families. They are politically conservative and respect authority and the status quo. They favor established products and services that show off their success to their peers.

Strivers. These consumers are the low resource group of those who are status-oriented. They have values very similar to Achievers but have fewer economic, social, and psychological resources. Style is extremely important to them as they strive to emulate people they admire and wish to be like.

Experiencers. These consumers are the high resource group of those who are action-oriented. They are the youngest of all the segments with a median age of 25. They have a lot of energy, which they pour into physical exercise and social activities. They are avid consumers, spending heavily on clothing, fast foods, music, and other youthful favorites—with particular emphasis on new products and services.

Makers. These consumers are the low resource group of those who are action-oriented. They are practical people who value self-sufficiency. They are focused on the familiar—family, work, and physical recreation—and have little interest in the broader world. As consumers, they appreciate practical and functional products.

Strugglers. These consumers have the lowest incomes. They have too few resources to be included in any consumer self-orientation and are thus located below the rectangle. They are the oldest of all the segments with a median age of 61. Within their limited means, they tend to be brand-loyal consumers.

Source: Martha Farnsworth Riche, "Psychographics for the 1990s," *American Demographics,* July 1989, pp. 24–26ff.

Step 2: If step 1 produces promising results, undertake a benefit, product perception, and reported market behavior segmentation survey of consumers. Measure benefits and perceptions by usage-situation as well as by individual difference characteristics. Assess situation usage frequency by recall estimates or usage-situation diaries.

Step 3: Construct a person/situation segmentation matrix. The rows are the major usage situations and the columns are groups of users identified by a single characteristic or combination of characteristics.

Step 4: Rank the cells in the matrix in terms of their submarket sales volume. The person/situation combination that results in the greatest consumption of the generic product would be ranked first.

Step 5: State the major benefits sought, important product dimensions, and unique market behavior for each nonempty cell of the matrix. (Some types of people will never consume the product in certain usage situations.)

FIGURE 16.5
Person/Situation Benefit Segmentation

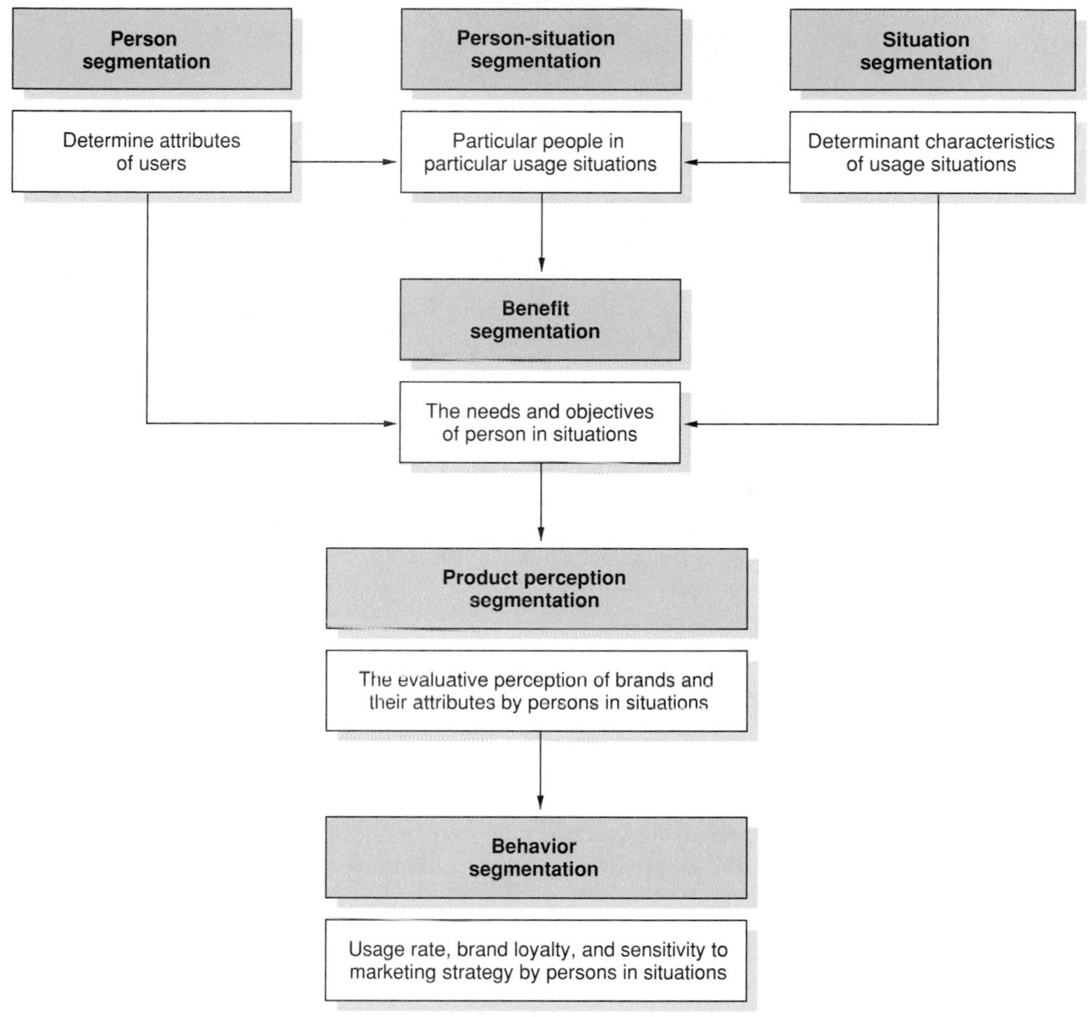

Source: Adapted from Peter R. Dickson, "Person-Situation: Segmentation's Missing Link," *Journal of Marketing* 46 (Fall 1982), pp. 55–64. Published by the American Marketing Association.

Step 6: Position your competitors' offerings within the matrix. The person/situation segments they currently serve can be determined by the product feature they promote and other marketing strategies.

Step 7: Position your offering within the matrix on the same criteria.

A product designed for a person/situation segment: apartment dwellers.

Step 8: Assess how well your current offering and marketing strategy meet the needs of the submarket compared to the competition's offering.

Step 9: Identify market opportunities based on submarket size, needs, and competitive advantage.[10]

This approach incorporates all four of the major factors discussed in our text—affect and cognition, behavior, environment, and marketing strategy. It thus offers a more comprehensive analysis than many other approaches.

Develop Product Positioning

By this time, the firm should have a good idea of the basic segments of the market that potentially could be satisfied with its product. The next step involves **product positioning:** positioning the product relative to competing products in the minds of consumers.[11] A classic example of positioning is the 7UP "Uncola" campaign. Before this campaign, Seven-Up had difficulty convincing consumers the product could be enjoyed as a soft drink and not just as a mixer. Consumers believed colas were soft drinks, but they apparently did not think of 7UP in this way. By promoting 7UP as the Uncola, the company

HIGHLIGHT 16.4

An Operational Approach to Product Positioning

1. **Identify the competitors.** This step involves defining the relevant market for the firm's offering. For example, Diet Coke might define its competition as (*a*) other diet cola drinks, (*b*) other cola drinks, (*c*) other soft drinks, (*d*) other nonalcoholic beverages, or (*e*) other beverages. Usually there will be a primary group of competitors (other diet colas) and a secondary group (other colas and soft drinks). Research identifying consumer product use situations is useful here.
2. **Determine how competitors are perceived and evaluated.** This step involves identifying product attributes and associations made by consumers so that competitive brand images can be defined.
3. **Determine the competitor's position.** This step involves determining how competitors (including the firm's own entry) are positioned with respect to the relevant product associations. Multidimensional scaling and other multivariate approaches are useful at this stage.
4. **Analyze the customers.** This step involves developing a thorough knowledge of the behavior of various market segments, including the role of the product class in the customers' lifestyle, and consumer motivations, habits, and behavior patterns.
5. **Select the position.** While there is no cookbook solution for selecting an optimal position, key decision criteria include (*a*) the nature of the market segments, (*b*) economic criteria, especially market potential and penetration probability, (*c*) a consistent image across time, and (*d*) not positioning the product to be better than it is.
6. **Monitoring the position.** A positioning strategy should be monitored across time to evaluate it and to generate diagnostic information about future positioning strategies. This involves ongoing research and may include one or more techniques such as multidimensional scaling.

Source: Condensed from David A. Aaker and Gary Shandy, "Positioning Your Product," *Business Horizons*, May–June 1982, pp. 56–62.

positioned it both as a soft drink that could be consumed in the same situations as colas and as an alternative to colas. This positioning was very successful.[12]

The key objective of positioning strategy is to form a particular brand image in consumers' minds. This is accomplished by developing a coherent strategy that may involve all of the marketing mix elements. There are at least five approaches to positioning strategy, including positioning by attribute, by use or application, by product user, by product class, and by competitor.[13] We discuss these approaches below. Highlight 16.4 offers an operational approach to product positioning.

Positioning by Attribute

Probably the most frequently used positioning strategy is **positioning by attribute** — associating a product with an attribute, a product feature, or a customer benefit. Consider imported automobiles. Hyundai and Yugo have emphasized low price. Volvo has stressed safety and durability, showing commercials of crash tests and citing statistics on the average long life of its cars. Fiat, in contrast, has made a distinct effort to position itself as a European car with European craftsmanship. BMW has emphasized handling and engineering efficiency, using the tag line "the ultimate driving machine" and showing BMW performance capabilities at a racetrack.

A new product can also be positioned with respect to an attribute that competitors have ignored. Paper towels had emphasized absorbency until Viva stressed durability, using demonstrations supporting the claim that Viva "keeps

Positioning by safety attributes.

on working." Bounty paper towels are positioned as being "microwave safe" with dyes that do not come off in microwave ovens.

Sometimes a product can be positioned in terms of two or more attributes simultaneously. In the toothpaste market, Crest became a dominant brand with positioning as a cavity fighter, a claim supported by a medical group endorsement. Aim, however, achieved its 10 percent market share by positioning in terms of two attributes, good taste and cavity prevention. More recently, Aquafresh was introduced by Beecham as a gel/paste that offers both cavity-fighting and breath-freshening benefits.

The price/quality attribute dimension is commonly used for positioning products as well as stores. In many product categories, some brands offer more in terms of service, features, or performance — and a higher price is one signal to the customer of this higher quality. For example, Curtis-Mathes TVs are positioned as high priced, high quality products. Conversely, other brands emphasize low price and good quality. The Yugo automobile, for example, is so positioned.

In general-merchandise stores, Neiman-Marcus, Bloomingdale's, and Saks Fifth Avenue are near the top of the price/quality scale. Below them are Macy's, Robinson's, Bullock's, Rich's, Filene's, Dayton's, Hudson's, and so on. Stores such as Montgomery Ward and J. C. Penney are positioned below these but above discount stores like K mart or Shopko. Interestingly, J. C. Penney and K mart have both attempted to upgrade their positions to avoid competing directly with successful discount and warehouse stores such as Wal-Mart. Recently, Sears has attempted to lower its prices to compete more directly with discount stores.

Positioning by Use or Application

Another strategy is **positioning by use** or application. Campbell's soup for many years was positioned for use at lunchtime and advertised extensively over noontime radio. Now, many Campbell's soups are positioned for use in sauces and dips, or as an ingredient in main dishes. AT&T has positioned long-distance calling by particular uses. For example, the "reach out and touch someone" campaign positions long-distance calls as a method of communicating with loved ones.

Products can have multiple positioning strategies, although increasing the number involves difficulties and risks. Often a positioning-by-use strategy represents a second or third position designed to expand the market. Thus, Gatorade, introduced as a summer beverage for athletes who need to replace body fluids, attempted to develop a winter positioning strategy as the beverage to drink when one is ill and the doctor recommends drinking plenty of fluids. Similarly, Quaker Oats attempted to position a breakfast food as a natural whole-grain ingredient for recipes. Arm & Hammer baking soda has successfully positioned its product as an odor-destroying agent in refrigerators.

Positioning by Product User

Another approach is **positioning by product user** or a class of users. Revlon's Charlie cosmetic line has been positioned by associating it with a specific lifestyle profile. Johnson & Johnson increased its market share from 3 to 14 percent when it repositioned its shampoo from a product used for babies to one used by people who wash their hair frequently and therefore need a mild shampoo. A similar strategy was used to get adults to use Johnson's Baby Lotion.

Miller High Life, once the "champagne of bottled beers," was purchased by the upper class and had an image of being a woman's beer. Philip Morris repositioned it as a beer for the heavy beer-drinking, blue-collar working man. Miller's Lite beer used convincing beer-drinking personalities to position it as a beer for the heavy beer drinker who dislikes that "filled up feeling." In contrast, earlier efforts to introduce low-calorie beers positioned with respect to the low-calorie attribute were dismal failures. Miller's positioning strategies are in part why it moved up to the No. 2 brewing company in the United States.

Positioning by Product Class

Some critical positioning decisions involve **positioning by product class.** For example, Maxim freeze-dried coffee was positioned with respect to regular and

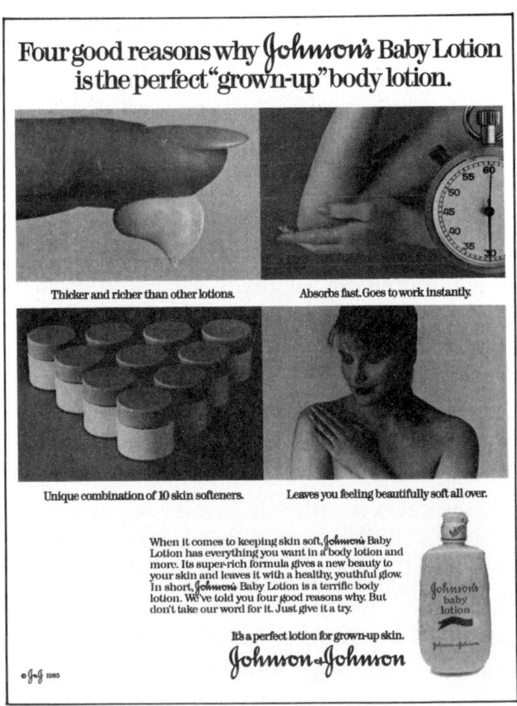

Positioning by product user.

instant coffee. Some margarines are positioned with respect to butter. A maker of dried milk introduced an instant breakfast drink positioned as a breakfast substitute and a virtually identical product positioned as a meal substitute for those on diets. The soap Caress, made by Lever Brothers, was positioned as a bath-oil product rather than a soap. The 7UP example we discussed earlier is also an example of positioning by product class. Recently, dates have been positioned as the "wholesomely sweet alternative to raisins" in television commercials.

Positioning by Competitors

In most positioning strategies, an explicit or implicit frame of reference is the competition (**positioning by competitor**). Often, the major purpose of this type of positioning is to convince consumers that a brand is better than the market leader (or another well-accepted brand) on important attributes. Positioning with respect to a competitor is commonly done in advertisements in which a competitor is named and compared. For example, Burger King ads argued that McDonald's burgers had less beef and did not taste as good as Burger King's because McDonald's product was not flame broiled. Both Pepsi and Coke have run comparative ads claiming their brand tastes better than the other one.

A classical example of this type of positioning was the Avis "We're No. 2, so we try harder" ad campaign. The strategy was to position Avis with Hertz as a major car-rental agency and away from National, which at the time was at least as large as Avis. This strategy was quite successful.

Select Segmentation Strategy

Having completed the analysis in the previous stages, the appropriate **segmentation strategy** can now be considered. There are four basic alternatives. First, the firm may decide not to enter the market. Analysis to this stage may reveal there is no viable market niche for the product, brand, or model. Second, the firm may decide not to segment but to be a mass marketer. This may be the appropriate strategy in at least three situations:

1. When the market is so small that marketing to a portion of it is not profitable.
2. When heavy users make up such a large proportion of the sales volume that they are the only relevant target.
3. When the brand is dominant in the market and targeting to a few segments would not benefit sales and profits.[14]

Third, the firm may decide to market to only one segment. Fourth, the firm may decide to market to more than one segment and design a separate marketing mix for each. In any case, marketers must have some criteria on which to base segmentation strategy decisions. Three important criteria are that a viable segment must be measurable, meaningful, and marketable:

1. *Measurable.* For a segment to be selected, marketers must be able to measure its size and characteristics. For example, one of the difficulties with segmenting on the basis of social class is that the concept and its divisions are not clearly defined and measured. Alternatively, income is much easier to measure.
2. *Meaningful.* A meaningful segment is one that is large enough to have sufficient sales and growth potentials to offer long-run profits.
3. *Marketable.* A marketable segment is one that can be reached and served profitably.

Segments that meet these criteria are variable markets for the product. The marketer must now give further attention to the marketing mix.

BACK TO.... GILLETTE CO.

This chapter suggested the first step in segmenting markets is to analyze consumer/product relationships. Gillette apparently has done this well for its personal care products targeted to men. In general, it seems likely that products such as razors, blades, deodorant, and shaving cream are judged primarily by how easy they are to use and how well they work at a functional level. It may be easy for men to judge the relative effectiveness of these products, and the Gillette name may connote quality to this market.

However, it appears Gillette has not done as good a job analyzing consumer/product relationships for its women's products. For example, according to the consultant, Gillette did not recognize the importance of having fresh new products for today's women to try. It also seems likely that while shaving products for men have developed to a stage where the market is satisfied with current offerings, some personal care products for women have not reached this stage.

Design Marketing Mix Strategy

The firm is now in a position to complete its marketing strategy by finalizing the marketing mix for each segment. Selecting the target market and designing the marketing mix go hand in hand, and thus many marketing mix decisions should have already been carefully considered. For example, if the target market selected is price sensitive, some consideration has already been given to price levels. Product positioning also has many implications for selecting appropriate promotions and channels. Thus, many marketing mix decisions are made *in conjunction with* (rather than after) target market selection. In the remaining chapters of this section, consumer behavior and marketing mix strategies will be discussed in more detail.

Many women may still be searching for a shampoo that meets their specific needs. In fact, the market for shampoos and skin creams is dominated by teenage girls and young women, many of whom have little brand loyalty to existing products.

Finally, the appearance of a person's hair in our culture is important to many people. Given the many colors, textures, thicknesses, styles, and tinting options for hair, one shampoo is not likely to meet everyone's needs nearly as well as one type of razor blade could. For both men and women, hair care products may have greater social significance than shaving products.

In sum, it would appear that Gillette may understand consumer/product relationships for its men's products, such as razors and blades, but less so for its women's products, hair care, and skin treatments. Perhaps because its marketing strategy has been so successful in the men's market for so long, it has not analyzed today's personal care market for women carefully enough and has not properly adapted its strategy for these consumer/product relationships.

Summary

This chapter provided an overview of market segmentation analysis. Market segmentation was defined as the process of dividing a market into groups of similar consumers and selecting the most appropriate group(s) for the firm to serve. Market segmentation was analyzed in terms of five interrelated tasks: (1) analyze consumer/product relationships; (2) investigate segmentation bases; (3) develop product positioning; (4) select segmentation strategy; and (5) design marketing mix strategy. Market segmentation analysis is a major cornerstone of sound marketing strategy development and is one of the major bridges between the literature dealing with consumer behavior and that dealing with marketing strategy.

Key Terms and Concepts

Market Segmentation *550*
Benefit Segmentation *553*
Psychographic Segmentation *556*
AIO *556*
VALS *557*
Person/Situation Segmentation *558*
Product Positioning *562*
Positioning by Attribute *564*
Positioning by Use *565*
Positioning by Product User *566*
Positioning by Product Class *566*
Positioning by Competitor *567*
Segmentation Strategy *567*

Review and Discussion Questions

1. Define market segmentation and describe the management tasks involved in applying the concept.
2. Select a product (other than toothpaste) with which you are fairly knowledgeable and develop a preliminary description of possible benefit segments following the structure presented in Figure 16.3.
3. Identify potential advantages and problems associated with marketing to benefit segments.
4. Use the VALS 2 categories to suggest marketing strategies for psychographic segments of buyers for hotel/motel services.
5. Consider person/situation segmentation as a way of viewing the snack food market. State the needs and objectives of persons in situations for at least three segments that you identify.

6. Explain each of the five approaches to product positioning and offer an example (not in the text) for each approach.
7. How does the concept of segmentation relate to positioning strategies?
8. What options are available to the organization after identifying segments in the market? When would each of these options represent a reasonable choice?
9. How would segmentation and positioning decisions be different for a small business entrepreneur than for a large corporation?

NOTES

1. See Alex Taylor III, "Back to the Future at Saturn," *Fortune*, August 1, 1988, pp. 63–72.
2. See "When Cheap Gets Chic," *Forbes*, June 13, 1988, pp. 108–9.
3. Russell I. Haley, "Benefit Segmentation: A Decision-Oriented Research Tool," *Journal of Marketing*, July 1968, pp. 30–35; also see Russell I. Haley, "Beyond Benefit Segmentation," *Journal of Advertising Research*, August 1971, pp. 3–8; and Russell I. Haley, "Benefit Segmentation—20 Years Later," *Journal of Consumer Marketing* 2 (1983), pp. 5–13.
4. Haley, "Benefit Segmentation: A Decision-Oriented Research Tool."
5. Joseph T. Plummer, "The Concept and Application of Life Style Segmentation," *Journal of Marketing*, January 1974, p. 33.
6. See W. D. Wells, "Psychographics: A Critical Review," *Journal of Marketing Research*, May 1975, pp. 196–213; and John L. Lastovicka, "On the Validation of Lifestyle Traits: A Review and Illustration," *Journal of Marketing Research*, February 1982, pp. 126–38.
7. This discussion of VALS 2™ is abstracted from Martha Farnsworth Riche, "Psychographics for the 1990s," *American Demographics*, July 1989, pp. 24–26ff.
8. Russell W. Belk, "A Free Response Approach to Developing Product Specific Consumption Situation Taxonomies," in *Analytic Approaches to Product and Marketing Planning*, ed. Allan D. Shocker (Cambridge, Mass.: Marketing Science Institute, 1979).
9. Peter R. Dickson, "Person-Situation: Segmentation's Missing Link," *Journal of Marketing*, Fall 1982, p. 57.
10. Ibid., p. 61.
11. It should be noted that the concept of "positioning" is somewhat ambiguous in the marketing literature and is used in a number of different ways. See John P. Maggard, "Positioning Revisited," *Journal of Marketing*, January 1976, pp. 63–73.
12. See Jack Trout and Al Ries, "The Positioning Era Cometh," in *Readings in Marketing Strategy*, ed. Jean-Claude Larreche and Edward L. Strong (Palo Alto, Calif.: The Scientific Press, 1982), pp. 141–51. Also see Al Ries and Jack Trout, *Positioning: The Battle for Your Mind* (New York: McGraw-Hill, 1981); and Al Ries and Jack Trout, *Marketing Warfare* (New York: McGraw-Hill, 1986).
13. David A. Aaker and J. Gary Shansby, "Positioning Your Product," *Business Horizons*, May–June 1982, pp. 36–62. The discussion that follows is based on this work.
14. Shirley Young, Leland Ott, and Barbara Feigin, "Some Practical Considerations in Market Segmentation," *Journal of Marketing Research*, August 1978, p. 405.

MARKETING STRATEGY IN ACTION

Hershey Foods

U.S. consumers spend about $8 billion a year on candy. Throughout the 1970s, Mars Candy Company was the candy king and by the end of that decade had pushed its market share to 14 percentage points ahead of competitors. However, in the 1980s, Hershey Foods caught up with Mars, and the two companies now share market leadership. The two companies together control 70 percent of the candy bar market and make all 10 of the best-selling candy bars (five for Hershey's and five for Mars). Peter Paul Cadbury, maker of Mounds and Almond Joy, sells about 9 percent of the U.S. candy bars. Nestlé, maker of Nestlé Crunch, sells about 6 percent.

One reason for Hershey's success in the 1980s is that it has been very active in introducing new products. In fact, almost 20 percent of its candy sales came from new products in 1984 versus 7 percent in 1979. Hershey's research shows that most people who walk up to the candy counter will choose from 6, maybe as many as 12, items that are acceptable. Hershey's has 17 of the 60 best-selling candy bars; Mars has only 9 in this group.

Many of Hershey's brands are targeted to adults – the baby boom grown-ups. While children under 12 are still a very important market, people over 18 eat 55 percent of all candy sold. Hershey's strategy is to carefully target to mothers, because it reasons that mothers determine children's early taste in candy. This strategy has made Hershey's the top seller in food stores, where half of candy dollars are spent. Because Mars' single bars sell faster than Hershey's, however, Mars is No. 1 at newsstands and vending machines. Mars' Snickers bar is the No. 1 U.S. candy, with 1984 sales of about $400 million.

Targeting to adults led to several successful changes in marketing strategy. Two candy bars, Take Five and Skor, were introduced with less

Additional Reading

For conceptual discussions on the nature of marketing segmentation, see:

Burr, Robert L. "Market Segments and Other Revelations." *Journal of Consumer Marketing*, Winter 1987, pp. 51–59.

Dickson, Peter R., and James L. Ginter. "Market Segmentation, Product Differentiation, and Marketing Strategy." *Journal of Marketing*, April 1987, pp. 1–10.

For discussions and reviews of types of consumer groups, see:

Bawa, Kapil, and Robert W. Shoemaker. "The Coupon-Prone Consumer: Some Findings Based on Purchase Behavior across Product Classes." *Journal of Marketing*, October 1987, pp. 99–110.

Szymanski, David M., and Paul S. Busch. "Identifying the Generics-Prone Consumer: A Meta-Analysis." *Journal of Marketing Research*, November 1987, pp. 425–31.

For developments of empirical procedures for use in segmentation, see:

Grover, Rajiv, and V. Srinivasan. "A Simultaneous Approach to Market Segmentation and Market Structuring." *Journal of Marketing Research*, May 1987, pp. 139–53.

Kamakura, Wagner A. "A Least Squares Procedure

chocolate and less sugar than in children's candies. Skor, a chocolate-covered toffee bar, now sells more than the traditional Heath bar. In December 1983, Hershey raised wholesale prices enough to push up the retail price of a standard candy bar to 35 cents. While this was very profitable for Hershey's (particularly because adults are likely to be less price sensitive than children), it could hurt competitive brands aimed at kids. Hershey also introduced the Big Block line—larger, 2.2-ounce candy bars selling for 50 cents that appeal to adult males. Golden Almond and Golden Pecan bars weigh 3.2 ounces, sell for $1.19 at retail, and contain a smoother blend of chocolate and whole (rather than chopped) nuts. These bars are designed to appeal to adult consumers as a higher quality product. These products, along with New Trail granola bars, bring in about $100 million in annual sales.

In addition, traditional brand sales have done very well. A national ad campaign led to Hershey's Kisses tripling its sales between 1977 and 1984; and a contest on the package led to double-digit increases in sales of Reese's Peanut Butter Cups for both 1983 and 1984.

Finally, Hershey's chocolate milk is widely admired as a marketing coup: the familiar brown and silver labels on the milk cartons double as small advertising billboards for chocolate bars in almost every supermarket in the country.

Discussion Questions

1. What are the advantages of targeting candy bars to adults rather than to children?
2. Does targeting to adults require a change in image for candy products?
3. Describe your most recent purchase of a candy bar in terms of relevant affect and cognitions, behaviors, and environments.
4. What means-end chains might different consumers have for candy bars?

Source: Excerpted from Steve Lawrence, "Bar Wars: Hershey Bites Mars," *Fortune,* July 8, 1985, pp. 52–57.

for Benefit Segmentation with Conjoint Experiments." *Journal of Marketing Research*, May 1988, pp. 157–67.

For empirical approaches to developing product positioning, see:

Keon, John W. "Product Positioning: TRINODAL Mapping of Brand Images, Ad Images, and Consumer Preferences." *Journal of Marketing Research*, November 1983, pp. 380–92.

Shugan, Steven M. "Estimating Brand Positioning Maps Using Supermarket Scanning Data." *Journal of Marketing Research*, February 1987, pp. 1–18.

For a psychographic study concerned with an important social issue, see:

Lastovicka, John L.; John P. Murry, Jr.; Erich A. Joachimsthaler; Gaurav Bhalla; and Jim Scheurich. "A Lifestyle Typology to Model Young Male Drinking and Driving." *Journal of Consumer Research*, September 1987, pp. 257–63.

For further research evaluating various aspects of the validity of lifestyle segmentation, see:

Lastovicka, John L.; John P. Murry, Jr.; and Erich A. Joachimsthaler. "Evaluating the Measurement Validity of Lifestyle Typologies with Qualitative Measures and Multiplicative Factoring." *Journal of Marketing Research*, February 1990, pp. 11–23.

Novak, Thomas P., and Bruce MacEvoy. "On Comparing Alternative Segmentation Schemes: The List of Values (LOV) and Values and Life Styles (VALS)." *Journal of Consumer Research*, June 1990, pp. 105–9.

Consumer Behavior and Product Strategy

CHAPTER 17

ADMIRAL HOME APPLIANCES

It has been a long time since product innovation played much of a role in the refrigerator business. The first frost-free units were introduced in 1954 and automatic ice makers in 1956. But in the years since, the "only thing else that's changed much is the colors," says John Green, president of Admiral Home Appliance, a division of Magic Chef, Inc. "The industry has pretty much operated on the theory that all consumers want is a reliable and economic box to keep their food fresh."

Green is trying to change that. Operating under what he calls his Marketing Manifesto, Admiral has embarked on an ambitious plan to introduce at least one new product each year. Begun with a refrigerator called the Entertainer (featuring a built-in wine rack and microwave storage trays), the strategy seems to be successful. In fact, it has increased Admiral's fourth-place share of the refrigerator and freezer market by 50 percent and has turned annual losses into profits.

Admiral's gains in an industry dominated by much larger and richer companies has also given a boost to Magic Chef, which bought the then-floundering Admiral business from Rockwell International in 1979. At the time, Admiral was posting annual deficits

of close to $40 million a year, and some appliance experts believed Magic Chef was making a mistake. "They practically bet the whole company on Admiral," said Eugene Mondry, president of Highland Appliance, a Detroit retail chain.

Admiral brought out an even more expensive model in 1983. It was priced at $1,299 and could make ice cream, soup, and chilled drinks. "The idea was to turn a refrigerator partly into a food processor," said Green. Sales of the model, called the A la Mode, exceeded $22 million in the first 12 months, sharply higher than even Admiral's ambitious forecast. Almost all of the sales represented new business.

Combined with a new blast freezer that, among other things, can make ice cubes in 45 minutes, Admiral's new products have given it an estimated 15 percent of the more than $4.5 billion-a-year refrigerator and freezer market, up from about 10 percent in 1980.

To some extent, Green attributes Admiral's success to the chance to stick to a long-term marketing plan. "At Rockwell, the Admiral division had virtually a new management and a new operating team every year. A lot of those plans probably would have worked just as well as ours, but they never had a chance. We haven't altered our strategy once in the last five years."

Source: Excerpted from John Koten, "Innovative, Upscale Iceboxes Mark a Sales Coup for Admiral," *The Wall Street Journal,* April 19, 1984, p. 29.

Why do you think Admiral's upscale refrigerators have been so successful? The product area is considered by many experts to be the most important element of the marketing mix. For example, Booz, Allen & Hamilton, a business consulting company, noted a number of years ago, "If it is accepted that products are the medium of business conduct, then business strategy is fundamentally product planning."

Of course, a key element in product planning is the matching of products with consumer markets. While products may be the medium of business conduct from the producer's viewpoint, the exchange of consumer assets for products is the acid test that determines whether products will succeed or fail.

FIGURE 17.1
The Wheel of Consumer Analysis: Product Strategy Issues

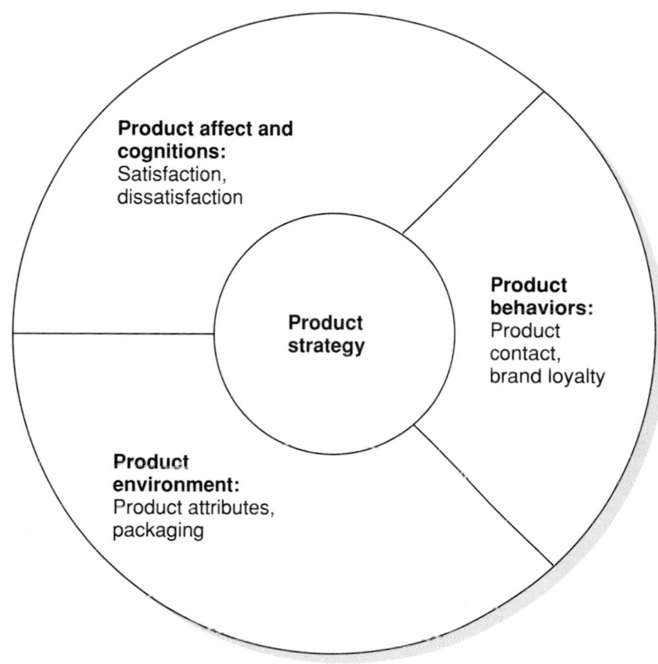

In this chapter, we focus on product strategy and some consumers' product-related affect and cognitions, behaviors, and environmental factors. Figure 17.1 provides the framework for this chapter and lists the topics to be discussed. Although many of the topics previously discussed in our text concern consumer/product relationships, the topics in this chapter have special relevance for product strategy. We begin by investigating product affect and cognitions, behaviors, and environmental element and then discuss product strategy in terms of a number of characteristics that influence product success.

Product Affect and Cognitions

Much of our discussion of affect and cognition in Section 2 of this text focused on products and how consumers feel about and interpret and intregrate information about them. One area of research that deserves special consideration in product strategy concerns *satisfaction* and *dissatisfaction.*

SATISFACTION

Consumer satisfaction is a critical concept in marketing thought and consumer research. It is generally argued that if consumers are satisfied with a product or brand, they will be more likely to continue to purchase and use it and to tell others of their favorable experiences with it. If they are dissatisfied, they will be more likely to switch brands and complain to manufacturers, retailers, and other consumers.

Given its importance to marketing, satisfaction has been the subject of considerable consumer research. While there are a variety of approaches, the most heavily researched is called the *disconfirmation paradigm*, advocated by Oliver.[1] This approach views satisfaction with products and brands as a result of two other cognitive variables, prepurchase expectations and disconfirmation. **Prepurchase expectations** are beliefs about anticipated performance of the product; **disconfirmation** refers to the difference between prepurchase expectations and postpurchase perceptions. Prepurchase expectations are confirmed when the product performs as expected and are disconfirmed when it does not. There are two types of disconfirmation: **negative disconfirmation** occurs when product performance is less than expected, and **positive disconfirmation** occurs when product performance is better than expected. Satisfaction occurs when performance is at least as good as expected; dissatisfaction occurs when performance is worse than expected.

Based on these ideas, Oliver defines satisfaction as follows:

> Satisfaction may best be understood as an evaluation of the surprise inherent in a product acquisition and/or consumption experience. In essence, it is the summary psychological state resulting when the emotion surrounding disconfirmed expectations is coupled with the consumer's prior feelings about the consumption experience. Moreover, the suprise or excitement of this evaluation is thought to be of finite duration, so that satisfaction soon decays into (but nevertheless greatly affects) one's overall attitude toward purchasing products, particularly with regard to specific retail environments.[2]

One advantage of Oliver's approach is that it integrates the concept of satisfaction with consumers' attitudes and purchase intentions. As shown in Figure 17.2, prepurchase intentions are a function of prepurchase attitudes, which, in turn, are a function of prepurchase expectations. After the product is purchased and experienced, it is hypothesized that prepurchase expectations, if positively disconfirmed or confirmed, will lead to satisfaction; if they are negatively disconfirmed, this will lead to dissatisfaction. Postpurchase attitudes and intentions are then influenced by the degree of satisfaction/dissatisfaction as well as the prepurchase levels of these cognitions.

Most research on consumer satisfaction using this approach has supported the model.[3] One exception is the work by Churchill and Surprenant, which found support for the model with a nondurable good but not with a durable good.[4] Bearden and Teel found support for the model and also extended it to the study of dissatisfaction and complaining behavior.[5]

Marketers sometimes conduct surveys to gauge consumer satisfaction.

NO POSTAGE NECESSARY IF MAILED IN THE UNITED STATES

BUSINESS REPLY MAIL

FIRST CLASS PERMIT NO. 3488, MADISON, WI 53791

POSTAGE WILL BE PAID BY ADDRESSEE

Carriage House
An Ethan Allen Gallery
5302 Verona Road
Madison, WI 53711

On behalf of our Ethan Allen Gallery we would like to thank you for your purchase of the merchandise our drivers have just delivered to you.

We would very much appreciate your being kind enough to give us your opinions of our service by checking off the questions on the other half of this card and mailing it back to us. No postage is necessary.

George F. Heine Jr.

Carriage House
An Ethan Allen Gallery
5302 Verona Road
Madison, WI 53711

	Yes	No
Has our Designer who assisted you been helpful and courteous?	☐	☐
Has the merchandise you have just received been prepared as you expected would be?	☐	☐
Have the drivers making your delivery been courteous and considerate?	☐	☐

COMMENTS: ______________________________

____

____

____

____

Date ______________ Signed: ______________________________ (optional)

Please fold and staple or tape edge.

CH50918

FIGURE 17.2

Cognitive Antecedents and Consequences of Satisfaction

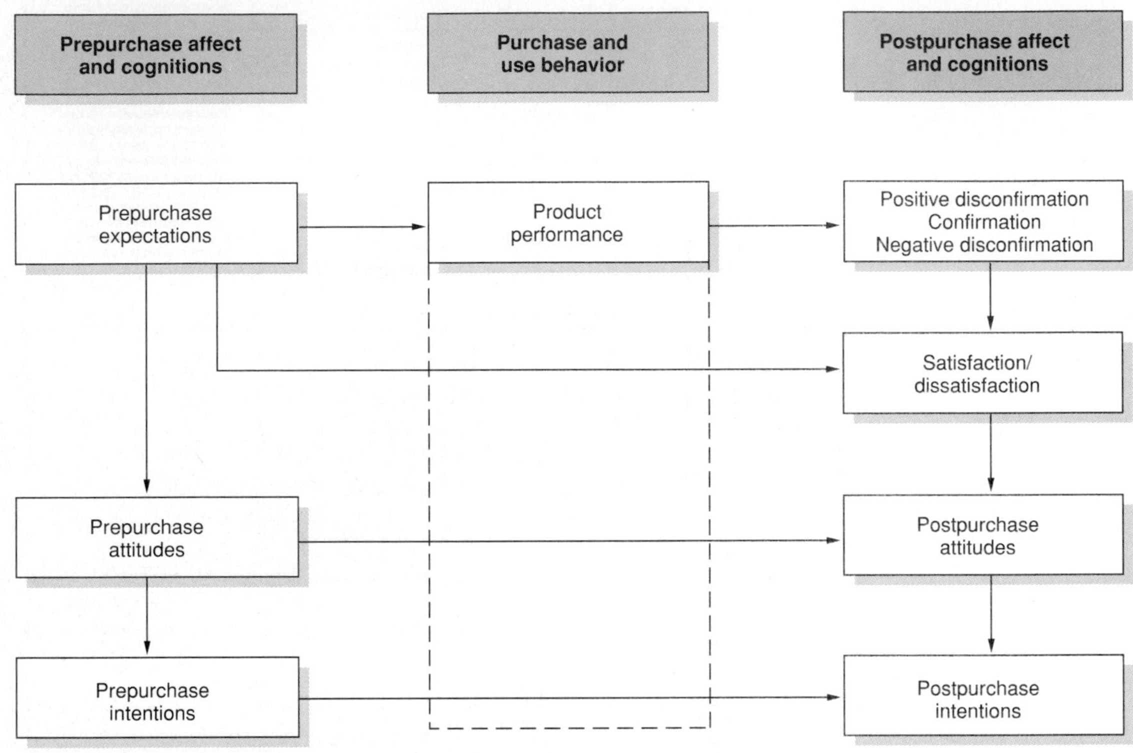

Source: Adapted from Richard L. Oliver, "A Cognitive Model of the Antecedents and Consequences of Satisfaction Decisions," *Journal of Marketing Research* 17 (November 1980), p. 462. Published by the American Marketing Association.

DISSATISFACTION

As we have noted, **dissatisfaction** occurs when prepurchase expectations are negatively disconfirmed. That is, the product performs worse than expected. Consumers who are dissatisfied with products are not likely to purchase them again and may complain to manufacturers, retailers, and other consumers. Several generalizations have been offered about consumer dissatisfaction and complaint behavior:

1. Those who complain when dissatisfied tend to be members of more upscale socioeconomic groups than those who do not complain.

HIGHLIGHT 17.1

HANDLING CONSUMER COMPLAINTS AT P&G

Since it first instituted an 800 telephone number in 1974, Procter & Gamble has been a leader in "consumer services" (its term for the system that allows customers easy access to the company). By 1979, P&G had printed the 800 number on every consumer product it sold in the United States.

In 1983, P&G received 670,000 mail and telephone contacts about its products, and this amount increases nearly every year. P&G employs 75 people in the consumer service department, 30 to answer calls, and the rest to answer letters and anlayze the data.

According to Gibson Carey, P&G manager for general advertising, the calls fall into three broad categories – requests for information, complaints, and testimonials (praise). P&G uses these data to spot problems and correct them early. Because most consumers call with the package in their hand, and because each package has a code printed on it that identifies the plant, the manufacturing date, and sometimes even the shift and line that made it, P&G can trace a problem to the source and correct it. Based on calls received about various products, P&G has:

- Included instructions for baking at high altitudes on Duncan Hines brownies packages.
- Added a recipe for making a wedding cake to its white cake mix package.
- Told users what to do if Downy liquid fabric softener accidentally freezes. (Numerous customers had that problem during a cold spell.)

Carey notes, "We don't look at [consumer service] as a source for new product ideas." Instead, P&G considers the 800-number system as "a distant, early warning signal" of product problems. Without it, "we wouldn't find out about them for weeks or months."

Source: Reprinted from "Customers: P&G's Pipeline to Product Problems," July 11, 1984, issue of *Business Week*, by special permission, copyright © 1984 by McGraw-Hill, Inc.

2. Personality characteristics, including dogmatism, locus of control, and self-confidence, are only weakly related to complaint behavior, if at all.
3. The severity of dissatisfaction or problems caused by the dissatisfaction are positively related to complaint behavior.
4. The greater the blame for the dissatisfaction placed on someone other than the one dissatisfied, the greater the likelihood of a complaint.
5. The more positive the perception of retailer responsiveness to consumer complaints, the greater the likelihood of a complaint.[6]

Highlight 17.1 discusses Procter & Gamble's system for handling consumer complaints.

Product Behaviors

From a strategic viewpoint, a major objective of marketing is to increase the probability and frequency of consumers coming into contact with products, purchasing and using them, and repurchasing them. We will discuss this objective in terms of two classes of consumer behavior—product contact and brand loyalty.

Product Contact

When we introduced the idea of **product contact** in this text, we discussed it in terms of a common retail purchase sequence. We argued that in the context of a retail store purchase, product contact involved behaviors such as locating the product in the store, examining it, and taking it to the checkout counter. In addition, a number of marketing tactics designed to increase product contacts were mentioned.

Product contacts can occur in other ways besides visits to retail stores. For example, many students may become familiar with personal computers from courses taken while in school. When the time comes to purchase a personal computer, the product contact at school may strongly influence the brand purchased. Computer firms seem aware of this possibility, for they frequently donate their products to universities or offer them at reduced costs.

Consumers may come in contact with products and experience them in a variety of other ways. They may receive a free sample in the mail or on their doorstep, or be given a sample in a store; they may borrow a product from a friend and use it; they may receive a product as a gift; or they may simply see someone else using the product and experience it vicariously.

Brand Loyalty

From a marketing strategy viewpoint, **brand loyalty** is a very important concept. Particularly in today's low-growth and highly competitve marketplace, retaining brand-loyal customers is critical for survival; and it is often a more efficient strategy than attracting new customers. It is estimated that it costs the average company six times more to attract a new customer than to hold a current one.[7]

Unfortunately, little research has been reported on brand loyalty in recent years. Much research was conducted on this topic in the 1950s and 1960s, but a comprehensive review of the literature by Jacoby and Chestnut found few generalizations to offer.[8] In fact, few conclusions could be drawn despite the fact that over 300 articles had been published on the topic.

The study of brand loyalty has been plagued by whether it is better to conceptualize this variable as a cognitive or a behavior phenomenon. As a cognitive phenomenon, brand loyalty is often thought of as an internal commit-

FIGURE 17.3
Examples of Purchase Pattern Categories and Brand Purchase Sequences

Purchase Pattern Category	Brand Purchase Sequence
Undivided brand loyalty	A A A A A A A A A A
Brand loyalty/occasional switch	A A A B A A C A A D
Brand loyalty/switch	A A A A A B B B B B
Divided brand loyalty	A A B A B B A A B B
Brand indifference	A B C D E F G H I J

ment to purchase and repurchase a particular brand. As a behavior phenomenon, brand loyalty is simply repeat purchase behavior.

Consistent with the theme of our book, we believe both cognitive and behavior approaches to studying brand loyalty have value. We define brand loyalty as repeat purchase intentions and behaviors. While the major focus of our discussion is on brand loyalty as a behavior, we want to emphasize that cognitive processes strongly influence the development and maintenance of this behavior.

In some cases, brand loyalty may be the result of extensive cognitive activity and decision making. A consumer may seriously compare and evaluate many brands of automobiles, conclude that a Honda Accord is the perfect car, and purchase a new one every few years. In other cases, brand-loyal behavior may occur without the consumer ever comparing alternative brands. A consumer may drink Ovaltine as a child and purchase and use the product throughout life without ever considering other brands. Yet even in this case, cognitive activity must occur. Decisions have to be made about where and when to purchase the product; some knowledge of the product and its availability must be activated from memory; intentions to purchase it and satisfaction influence the purchase behaviors.

As shown in Figure 17.3, brand loyalty can be viewed on a continuum from undivided brand loyalty to brand indifference. The market for a particular brand could be analyzed in terms of the number of consumers in each category, and strategies could be developed to enhance the brand loyalty of particular groups.

Undivided brand loyalty is an ideal. In some cases, consumers may purchase only a single brand and forgo purchase if it is not available. *Brand loyalty with an occasional switch* is likely to be more common, though. Consumers may switch occasionally for a variety of reasons: their usual brand may be out of stock, a new brand may come on the market and be tried once, a competitive brand is offered at a special low price, or a different brand is purchased for a special occasion.

Purchase of generics indicates brand indifference.

Brand-loyalty switches are a competitive goal in low-growth or declining markets. As an example, competitors in the blue jean market or the distilled spirits industry must obtain brand switches for long-run growth. However, switching loyalty from one to another of the brands of the same firm can be advantageous. For example, Procter & Gamble sells both Pampers and Luvs disposable diapers. A switch from Pampers to Luvs might be advantageous to P&G in that Luvs are more expensive and may have a higher profit margin.

Divided brand loyalty refers to consistent purchase of two or more brands. For example, the shampoo market has a low level of brand loyalty. One reason for this might be that households purchase a variety of shampoos for different family members or for different purposes. Johnson's Baby Shampoo may be used by both youngsters and frequent shampoo users. Other household members may have dandruff problems and use Head and Shoulders. Thus, this household would have loyalty divided between the two brands.

Brand indifference refers to purchases with no apparent repurchase pattern. This is the opposite extreme from undivided brand loyalty. While we suspect total brand indifference is not common, some consumers of some products may exhibit this pattern. For example, a consumer may make weekly purchases of whatever bread is on sale, regardless of the brand.

In many ways, these loyalty categories are somewhat arbitrary. The point is that there are various degrees of brand loyalty. The degree of brand loyalty can be viewed as a continuum, and various quantitative indexes can be developed to categorize individuals or households in terms of particular products.[9]

FIGURE 17.4
Brand Loyalty and Usage Rate

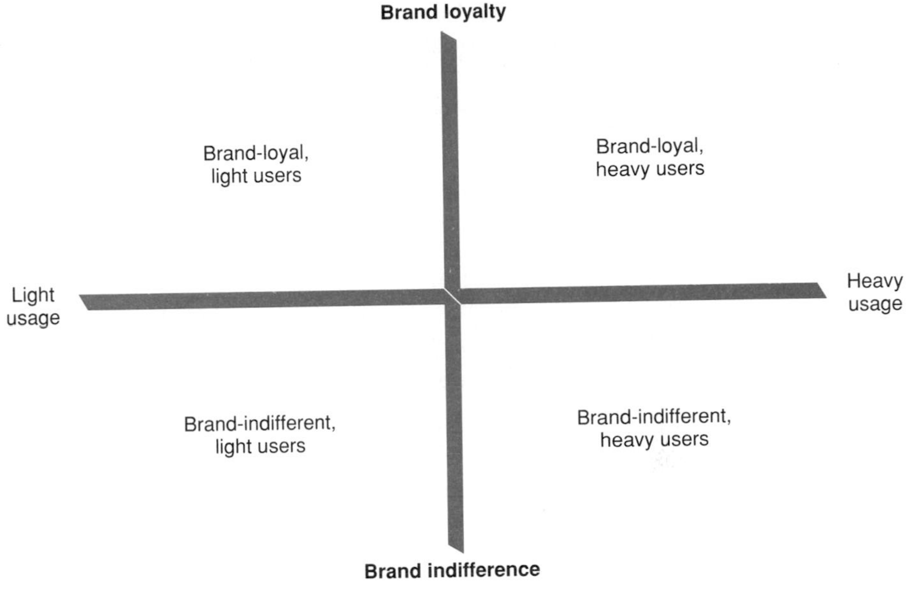

Developing a high degree of brand loyalty among consumers is an important goal of marketing strategy. Yet the **rate of usage** by various consumers cannot be ignored. For example, the 18-to-24-year-old age group uses almost twice as much shampoo as the average user, and families of three or more people make up 78 percent of the heavy users of shampoo. Clearly, obtaining brand loyalty among these consumers is preferable to attracting consumers who purchase and use shampoo less frequently, other things being equal.

The relationship between brand loyalty and usage rate is shown in Figure 17.4. For simplicity, we have divided the dimensions into four categories of consumers rather than consider each dimension as a continuum.

Figure 17.4 shows that achieving brand-loyal consumers is most valuable when the consumers are also heavy users. This figure could also be used as a strategic tool by plotting consumers of both the firm's brands and competitive brands on the basis of brand loyalty and usage rates. Depending on the location of consumers and whether they are loyal to the firm's brand or a competitive one, several strategies might be useful:

1. If the only profitable segment is the brand-loyal heavy user, focus on switching consumer loyalty to the firm's brands. For example, comparative advertising such as that used by Avis in the car-rental industry or by Burger

King in the fast-food industry may have been appropriate strategies for switching heavy users.

2. If there is a sufficient number of brand-loyal light users, focus on increasing their usage of the firm's brand. For example, the baking soda market might have been characterized as being composed of brand-loyal light users of Arm & Hammer baking soda. This brand then demonstrated new uses of the product, such as for freshening refrigerators. It is reported that half the refrigerators in America now contain a box of baking soda.

3. If there is a sufficient number of brand-indifferent heavy users, attempt to make the firm's brand name a salient attribute and/or develop a new relative advantage. For example, no firm in the hot dog market has more than a 12 percent market share. Firms such as Oscar Mayer stress the brand name in advertising in an attempt to increase the importance of brand name to the consumer. In addition, Oscar Mayer successfully developed the market for hot dogs with cheese in them to increase sales.

4. If there is a sufficient number of brand-indifferent light users, attempt to make the firm's brand name a salient attribute and increase usage of the firm's brand among consumers, perhaps by finding a sustainable relative advantage. For example, a portion of the market that shops at Wal-Mart are brand-indifferent consumers attracted by lower prices.

As we noted, it is also important to plot consumers of competitive brands to develop appropriate strategies. For example, if a single competitor dominates the brand-loyal heavy-user market and has too much market power to be overcome, then strategies may have to be focused on other markets.

The Product Environment

The *product environment* refers to product-related stimuli that are attended to and comprehended by consumers. In general, the majority of these stimuli are received through the sense of sight, although there are many exceptions. For example, the way a stereo sounds or how a silk shirt feels also influence consumer affect and cognitions and behaviors. In this section, we will focus on two types of environmental stimuli: product attributes and packaging.

Product Attributes

Products and product attributes are major stimuli that influence consumer affect, cognitions and behaviors. These attributes may be evaluated by consumers in terms of their own values, beliefs, and past experiences. Marketing and other information also influence whether purchase and use of the product is likely to be rewarding or not. For example, the product attributes of a new shirt might include color, material, sleeve length, type and number of buttons, and type of collar. By investigating these attributes and by trying the shirt on, a consumer might conclude, "This shirt is well made and I look good in it," "This shirt is for nerds," or "This shirt is well made but just isn't for me."

It is unlikely that many consumers would purchase a shirt based on these product attributes alone, however. The price of the shirt would likely be important; the store selling the shirt (and the store's image) might be considered. In addition, the packaging, brand name, and brand identification would likely be factors. In fact, for many purchases, the image of the brand created through the nonproduct variables of price, promotion, and channels of distribution may be the most critical determinant of purchase.

PACKAGING

Packaging is an element of the product environment for which marketers spend over $50 billion annually. Traditionally, four packaging objectives are considered. First, packaging should *protect* the product as it moves through the channel to the consumer. Second, packaging should be *economical* and not add undue cost to the product. Third, packaging should allow *convenient* storage and use of the product by the consumer. Fourth, packaging can be used effectively to *promote* the product to the consumer.

In some cases, packaging can obtain a relative advantage for a product. For example, Oscar Mayer's use of zip-lock packages for its hot dogs, bacon, and lunch meats made these products easier for consumers to keep fresh after opening. Procter & Gamble introduced the Crest Neat Squeeze dispenser, which draws unused toothpaste back into the container to make it neater and more economical for consumers. Duracell uses a package with a built-in tester to allow consumers to assure the batteries they buy are fresh. Glad's zip-lock bags use of blue and yellow channels, which turn green when they are sealed, allows consumers to be sure the bags are sealed properly. In these examples, mature products were differentiated on the basis of packaging alone.[10] Highlight 17.2 discusses other examples and lists some of the positive affects of good packaging.

Package Colors

In addition to the nature of the package itself, it has been argued that package colors have an important impact on consumers' affect, cognitions and behaviors. This impact is more than just attracting attention by using eye-catching colors (like Tide's orange). Rather, it has been argued that package colors connote meanings to consumers and can be used strategically.[11]

For instance, the color of the Ritz cracker box was changed to a deeper red trimmed with a thin gold band. This change was made to appeal to young, affluent consumers. Microsoft Corporation changed its software packages from green to red and royal blue, because consultants argued that green was not eye-catching and connoted frozen vegetables and gum to consumers rather than

HIGHLIGHT 17.2

Packaging for Profits

Many companies have learned that spending time and money on packaging can be a good investment. The Kroger stores enjoyed a 200 percent increase in first-year sales of a private-label cheese product after the package was redesigned. After Memorex redesigned its audio- and videocassette tape packages, profits increased more than $1 million during the first year—the new package allowed the company to enter previously closed distribution channels. Since McCormick/Schilling redesigned its gourmet spice line in 1985, it has generated a double-digit increase in sales.

An effective package is never a substitute for a quality product offered at a competitive price. However, effective packaging can:

- Enhance the ways consumers think of the product.
- Increase the visibility of the product and company.
- Reinforce the brand image in the store and at home.
- Retain current customers and attract new ones.
- Enhance the cost effectiveness of the marketing budget.
- Increase the product's competitive edge and profits.

Source: Reprinted from Davis L. Masten, "Packaging's Proper Role Is to Sell the Product," *Marketing News* 22, no. 2 (January 18, 1988), p. 16. Published by the American Marketing Association.

high-tech software. Swanson dropped the turquoise triangle from its frozen dinners, because that color was thought to give the product a dated, 1950s look. Canada Dry changed the color of its cans and bottles of suger-free ginger ale from red to green and white when consultants argued that red sent a misleading cola message to consumers. Canada Dry sales were reported to increase 25 percent after this color change.

It has also been reported that consumer perceptions of products may change with a change in package color. For example, when designers at Berni Corporation changed the background hue on Barrelhead sugar-free root beer cans from blue to beige, consumers reported that the product tasted more like old-fashioned root beer—even though the beverage remained the same. Similarly, consumers ascribed a sweeter taste to orange drinks when a darker shade of orange was used on the can or bottle.

Brand Identification and Label Information

The brand identification and label information on the package (as well as on the product) provide additional stimuli for consideration by the consumer. Brand identification in many cases simplifies purchase for the consumer and makes the

Packaging can give a product a relative advantage.

Label information can influence purchase behavior.

loyalty development process possible. As we noted previously, brand names such as Gloria Vanderbilt, Cadillac, or Florsheim may well be discriminative stimuli for consumers.

Label information includes use instructions, contents, lists of ingredients or raw materials, warnings for use and care of the product, and the like. For some products, this information can strongly influence purchase. For example, consumers often carefully examine label information on over-the-counter drugs such as cough medicines. Health-conscious consumers often consult package information to determine the nutritional value, sugar content, and calories in a serving of products such as cereal.

Product Strategy

Product strategies are designed to influence consumers in both the short and the long run. In the short run, new-product strategies are designed to influence consumers to try the product; in the long run, product strategies are designed to develop brand loyalty and obtain large market shares.

A critical aspect of designing product strategies involves analyzing consumer/product relationships. This means consumers' product-related affect, cognitions, behaviors, and environments should be carefully considered in introducing new products and should be monitored throughout a product's life cycle. In this section, we first examine some personal characteristics of consumers that affect product adoptions. Then, we examine some characteristics of products that influence the adoption process.

Characteristics of Consumers

In analyzing consumer/product relationships, it is important to recognize that consumers vary in their willingness to try new products. Different types of consumers may adopt a new product at different times in the product's life cycle. Figure 17.5 presents the classic **adoption curve** and five categories of adopters. The adoption curve represents the cumulative percentage of purchasers of a product across time.

Traditionally, the five adopter groups are characterized as follows: **innovators** are venturesome and willing to take risks; **early adopters** are respectable and often influence the early majority; the **early majority** avoid risks and are deliberate in their purchases; the **late majority** are skeptical and cautious about new ideas; **laggards** are very traditional and set in their ways.

Designers of product strategies find innovators particularly important because they may influence early adopters, who in turn may influence the early majority to purchase. Thus, a new product's chances of success are increased once innovators purchase the product and tell others about it. Also, early adopters and others can learn vicariously about the product by seeing innovators using it.

A major focus of consumer research has been to identify the characteristics of innovators and their differences from other consumers. A review of this research found that innovators tend to be more highly educated and younger, and to have greater social mobility, more favorable attitudes toward risk (more venturesome), greater social participation, and higher opinion leadership than other consumers.[12]

FIGURE 17.5
The Adoption Curve

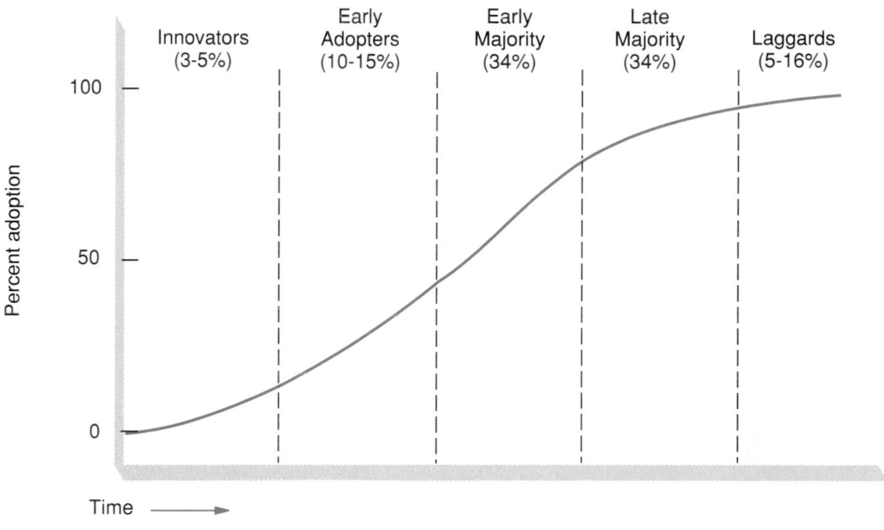

Innovators also tend to be heavy users of other products within a product class. For example, Dickerson and Gentry found that adopters of home computers had greater experience with other technical products – such as programmable pocket calculators and video television games – than did nonadopters.[13] Innovators may have better developed knowledge structures for particular product categories. This may enable them to understand and evaluate new products more rapidly and thus adopt earlier than other consumers.[14]

Finally, it should be noted that the five adopter categories and the percentages in Figure 17.5 are somewhat arbitrary. These categories were developed in research in rural sociology that dealt with major farming innovations. Their validity has not been fully supported in consumer research, particularly for low-involvement products.[15]

However, the idea that different types of consumers purchase products in different stages of the products' life cycles does have important implications for product strategy. Namely, product strategy (and other elements of marketing strategy) must change across time to appeal to different types of consumers.

Characteristics of Products

In analyzing consumer/product relationships, it is also important to consider the product characteristics listed in Figure 17.6. A number of these characteristics have been found to influence the success of new products and brands.[16] There is

FIGURE 17.6

Some Important Questions in Analyzing Consumer/Product Relationships

Compatibility—How well does this product fit consumers' current affect, cognitions, and behaviors?

Trialability—Can consumers try the product on a limited basis with little risk?

Observability—Do consumers frequently see or otherwise sense this product?

Speed—How soon do consumers experience the benefits of the product?

Simplicity—How easy is it for consumers to understand and use the product?

Relative advantage—What makes this product better than competitive offerings?

Product symbolism—What does this product mean to consumers?

Marketing strategy—What is the role of other marketing mix elements in creating a functional or image-related relative advantage?

no absolute demarcation, but some of the dimensions are more directly involved with facilitating trial while others both facilitate trial and encourage brand loyalty. We will discuss each of these characteristics below.

Compatibility

Compatibility refers to the degree to which a product is consistent with consumers' current affect, cognitions, and behaviors. Other things being equal, a product that does not require an important change in consumer values and beliefs or purchase and use behaviors is more likely to be tried by consumers. For example, Chewels chewing gum – the gum with a liquid center – required little change on the part of consumers to try the product.

Trialability

Trialability refers to the degree to which a product can be tried on a limited basis or divided into small quantities for an inexpensive trial. Other things being equal, a product that facilitates a nonpurchase trial or a limited-purchase trial is more likely to influence the consumer to try the product. Test driving a car, trying on a sweater, tasting bite-sized pieces of a new frozen pizza, accepting a free trial of a new encyclopedia, or buying a sample-size bottle of a new shampoo are ways consumers can try products on a limited basis and reduce risk.

Observability

Observability refers to the degree to which products or their effects can be sensed by other consumers. New products that are public and frequently discussed are more likely to be adopted rapidly. For example, many clothing styles become popular after consumers see movie and recording stars wearing them. Satellite disks are highly observable, and this feature likely influences their purchase.

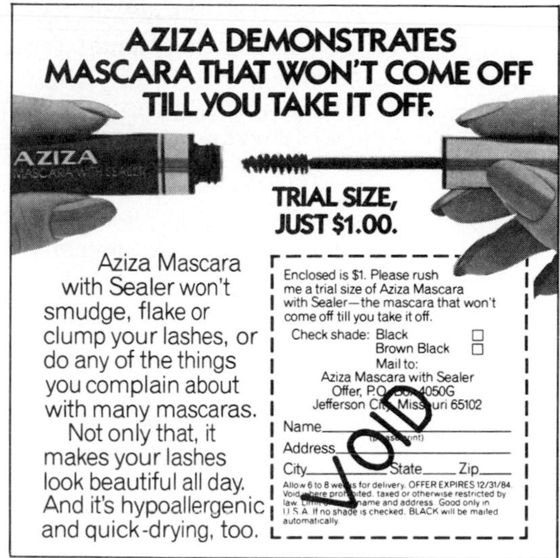

A marketing strategy to increase trialability.

Speed

Speed refers to how fast the benefits of the product are experienced by the consumer. Because many consumers are oriented toward immediate rather than delayed gratification, products that can deliver benefits sooner rather than later have a higher probability of at least being tried. For example, weight-loss programs that promise results within the first week are more likely to attract consumers than those that promise results in six months.

Simplicity

Simplicity refers to the degree to which a product is easy for a consumer to understand and use. Other things being equal, a product that does not require complicated assembly and extensive training for the consumer to use it has a higher chance of trial. For example, many computer products, such as those made by Apple, are promoted as being user-friendly to encourage purchase.

Relative Advantage

Relative advantage refers to the degree to which an item has a *sustainable, competitive differential advantage* over other product classes, product forms, and brands. There is no question that relative advantage is a most important product characteristic not only for obtaining trial, but also for continued purchase and development of brand loyalty.

In some cases, a relative advantage may be obtained through technological developments. For example, at the product-class level, RCA introduced the videodisc player, which showed programs on any TV set. The disc player cost half as much as cassette machines, and the discs were cheaper than videocassettes. However, videocassette players had a relative advantage over disc players: they could record programs, and the disc players could not. RCA thought recording ability was not an important factor to consumers – and lost more than $500 million finding out otherwise.

At the brand level, however, it is often difficult to maintain a technological relative advantage. This is because new or improved technology is often quickly copied by competitors. In addition, many brands within product groups are relatively homogeneous in terms of their functional benefits for consumers. For these reasons we believe one of the most important sources of a sustainable relative advantage comes from product symbolism rather than technological changes or functional differences in products.

Product Symbolism

Product symbolism refers to what the product or brand means to the consumer and what the consumer experiences in purchasing and using it. Consumer researchers recognize that some products possess symbolic features, and that consumption of them may depend more on their social and psychological meaning than on their functional utility.[17] For example, the blue jean market is dominated by major brands such as Levi's, Wrangler, and Lee, and it is difficult to determine clear differences in these jeans except in pocket design and brand labeling. If these brand names meant nothing to consumers and were purchased only on the basis of product attributes such as materials and styles, it would be difficult to explain differences in market shares, given the similarity among brands. Similarly, it would be difficult to describe how a brand such as Guess? jeans obtained $200 million in sales in its first three years.

It seems clear that jeans brand names have meanings and symbolize different values for consumers. For example, teenagers make up a large portion of the market for Guess? jeans. These consumers may be seeking to present an identity different from that of wearer of traditional brands, such as their parents. Highlight 17.3 offers an example of the importance of product symbolism in the car market.

Marketing Strategy

To this point, we have suggested that a variety of product characteristics partially account for the success or failure of products and brands. Though not strictly a product characteristic, the quality of the *marketing strategy* employed also has an important bearing on whether a product is successful and profitable.

We have also argued that at the brand level, the image or symbolism a brand carries is often the only relative advantage a firm has to offer. This frequently happens because in many product classes, the brands offered are relatively homogeneous in their functional utility to the consumer.

In many cases, a favorable image is created through the other elements of the marketing mix. *Promotion* is commonly used to create a favorable image for the brand by pairing it with positively evaluated stimuli, such as attractive models. In addition, promotion informs consumers as to what attributes they

HIGHLIGHT 17.3

Product Symbolism and Larger Cadillacs

In 1984, General Motors reduced the size of its Cadillac automobile by two feet and sales dropped dramatically, forcing the company to rethink the way it designs cars. Traditionally, GM interviewed car buyers only at the start of product development. However, to deal with this new problem, the company decided to meet with five consumer groups over a three-year period. Each group consisted of 500 owners of Cadillacs and other models. GM planners placed these people behind the wheel of prototype cars, letting them fiddle with switches and knobs on the instrument panel, door handles, and seat belts while engineers sat in back and took notes.

What was the result? The new Cadillac De Villes and Fleetwoods that cruised into showrooms for 1988 were nine inches longer and sported subtle tail fins and fender skirts – all reminiscent of the opulent automobiles of the 1950s. In the fourth quarter of 1988, Cadillac sold 36 percent more De Villes and Fleetwoods than they had a year earlier and overall Cadillac volume grew for the first time in five years.

Why weren't the smaller Cadillacs successful? It seems clear that Cadillac buyers want a distinctive-looking car, and the smaller-sized versions probably looked too much like other GM cars. Also, the larger versions, with features similar to those from the 1950s, may have special meanings to some consumers. For example, the 1950s were a relatively worry-free, secure period in history. For some Cadillac owners, the larger car may represent physical, social, and financial security, something they did not feel with the smaller models. In other words, the large Cadillacs may be symbolic of important consumer values.

Source: Based on Patricia Sellers, "Getting Customers to Love You," *Fortune,* March 13, 1989, pp. 38–49.

should be looking for in the product class and emphasizes the superiority of the brand in terms of those attributes. Few consumers can tell the difference in the taste of various brands of beer – and, in fact, many consumers do not initially like the taste of beer. Thus, many commercials try to teach consumers that a particular brand tastes great, or at least as good as more expensive beers. We suspect brand image is a key determinant of beer brand choice, although many consumers would likely disavow image and insist that taste is the most important consideration.

Price can also create brand images as well as provide a functional relative advantage. In terms of brand images, high prices can connote high quality for some products; and it is often stated that consumers perceive a relationship between price and quality. Price can also be used to position a brand as a good value for the money; e.g., Suave hair-care products are as good as the expensive

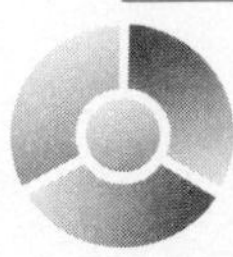

BACK TO....
ADMIRAL HOME APPLIANCES

Admiral was clearly successful in introducing its new upscale refrigerators, which included several product-design modifications. Admiral designed the Entertainer model based on consumer surveys that showed a trend toward increased entertaining at home. Although it introduced the premium-priced refrigerator during a recession, and at a time when most other manufacturers were pushing economical, stripped-down models, the new refrigerator almost instantly became the company's best-selling unit, with deliveries equaling $10 million in the first year. The success of the A la Mode model has already been noted.

However, one must question whether the addition of product attributes such as a built-in wine rack and microwave storage trays is a sufficient explanation for the success of this product. We suspect the higher price of these models may have been important in generating a favorable quality image—a mature product generally considered a dull necessity may have been converted into a status symbol by the higher price. In other words, perhaps the relative advantage was created partly through product symbolism, as well as a few relatively inexpensive product modifications.

The fact that many of the purchases were made by consumers

brands but much cheaper. As a functional relative advantage, through vast economies of scale and large market shares, a firm can sometimes sustain a price advantage that no competitor can meet. Campbell's soups have long enjoyed such an advantage.

Finally, a variety of *distribution* tactics can be used to gain a relative advantage. Good site locations and a large number of outlets are important advantages in the fast-food market and in the markets for other products and services. Also, a variety of in-store stimuli, such as displays, can offer products at least a temporary relative advantage.

who enjoyed entertaining at home suggests these purchasers may have an "audience" of guests (a reference group) to whom they can show the new appliance. The product-design modifications offer an entree for showing off the product and a justification for the high price paid. In addition, during a recession, many consumers may have forgone purchasing a new home and stayed in an apartment or remodeled their current home. It is possible that remodeling and adding high-quality appliances may have been substituted for such new home purchases. In essence, then, the purchase and display of an expensive refrigerator with convenience-oriented design features and psychosocial consequences may have been a way for consumers to tell themselves and others that they were doing well, even if they weren't buying a new home.

The new premium refrigerators did enhance the overall quality image of the company's entire product line—with both consumers and retailers. In fact, the number of outlets selling Admiral refrigerators rose 33 percent, to more than 6,000. Thus, while consumer demand may have pulled the refrigerators to the retail level, the increase in the number of outlets also helped to increase product contacts.

Overall, then, whether it was the result of product-design modifications or changes in other marketing mix variables (price and distribution), the success of Admiral's long-term marketing strategy is noteworthy.

Summary

This chapter investigated some product-related affect, cognitions, behaviors, and environmental factors as well as several aspects of product strategy. Initially, product affect and cognitions were discussed in terms of consumer satisfaction and dissatisfaction. Developing satisfied consumers is clearly a key to successful marketing. The analysis of behavior looked at product contact and brand loyalty and emphasized several strategies based on the relationships between brand loyalty and usage rates. Product attributes and packaging were among the environmental factors examined. Finally, the product strategy discussion focused on a number of characteristics of consumers and products that influence whether or not products are adopted and become successful.

Key Terms and Concepts

Consumer Satisfaction *578*
Prepurchase Expectations *578*
Disconfirmation *578*
Negative Disconfirmation *578*
Positive Disconfirmation *578*
Dissatisfaction *580*
Product Contact *582*
Brand Loyalty *582*
Rate of Usage *585*
Adoption Curve *590*
Innovators *590*
Early Adopters *590*
Early Majority *590*
Late Majority *590*
Laggards *590*
Compatibility *592*
Trialability *592*
Observability *592*
Speed *593*
Simplicity *593*
Relative Advantage *593*
Product Symbolism *594*

Review and Discussion Questions

1. Describe the process by which the consumer comes to experience satisfaction or dissatisfaction. Illustrate each result with an experience of your own.
2. Gather several consumer complaints from friends or classmates and make recommendations for marketing strategies to prevent similar problems.
3. Define brand loyalty as a cognitive phenomenon and as a behavioral phenomenon. Extend each of these definitions to the purchase pattern categories illustrated in Figure 17.3.
4. Recommend a marketing strategy for a brand that competes with one for which you are a brand-loyal heavy user. How successful do you believe the strategy would be and why?
5. Identify the key stimuli in the product environment that influence your purchasing behavior for: (*a*) soft drinks, (*b*) frozen pizza, (*c*) shampoo, and (*d*) jeans.
6. To which adopter category do you belong in general? Explain.
7. Explain characteristics of new products that would be useful for predicting success and for prescribing effective marketing strategies.

8. Discuss the problem and advantages that could be associated with appealing to innovators when marketing a new consumer packaged good.
9. Analyze the consumer/product relationships for a new presweetened cereal product. Include both product and consumer characteristics.

NOTES

1. For example, see Richard L. Oliver, "A Cognitive Model of the Antecedents and Consequences of Satisfaction Decisions," *Journal of Marketing Research*, November 1980, pp. 460–69. Also see Richard L. Oliver and Wayne S. DeSarbo, "Response Determinants in Satisfaction Judgments," *Journal of Consumer Research*, March 1988, pp. 495–507; Richard L. Oliver and John E. Swan, "Equity and Disconfirmation Perceptions as Influences on Merchant and Product Satisfaction," *Journal of Consumer Research*, December 1989, pp. 372–83; and Robert A. Westbrook and Richard L. Oliver, "The Dimensionality of Consumption Emotion Patterns and Consumer Satisfaction," *Journal of Consumer Research*, June 1991, pp. 84–91.
2. Richard L. Oliver, "Measurement and Evaluation of Satisfaction Processes in Retail Settings," *Journal of Retailing*, Fall 1981, p. 27.
3. For example, see P. A. LaBarbera and D. Mazursky, "A Longitudinal Assessment of Consumer Satisfaction/Dissatisfaction: The Dynamic Aspect of the Cognitive Process," *Journal of Marketing Research*, November 1983, pp. 393–404.
4. Gilbert A. Churchill, Jr., and Carol Suprenant, "An Investigation into the Determinants of Customer Satisfaction," *Journal of Marketing Research*, November 1982, pp. 491–504. Also see David K. Tse and Peter C. Wilton, "Models of Consumer Satisfaction Formation: An Extension," *Journal of Marketing Research*, May 1988, pp. 204–12.
5. William O. Bearden and Jesse E. Teel, "Selected Determinants of Consumer Satisfaction and Complaint Reports," *Journal of Marketing Research*, February 1983, pp. 21–28. Also see Robert A. Westbrook, "Product/Consumption-Based Affective Responses and Postpurchase Processes," *Journal of Marketing Research*, August 1987, pp. 258–70.
6. Marsha L. Richens, "Negative Word-of-Mouth by Dissatisfied Consumers: A Pilot Study," *Journal of Marketing*, Winter 1983, p. 69. Also see Jagdip Singh, "Consumer Complaint Intentions and Behavior: Definitional and Taxonomical Issues," *Journal of Marketing*, January 1988, pp. 93–107; and Jagdip Singh, "A Typology of Consumer Dissatisfaction Response Styles," *Journal of Retailing*, Spring 1990, pp. 57–98.
7. See Larry J. Rosenberg and John A. Czepiel, "A Marketing Approach to Customer Retention," *Journal of Consumer Marketing* 2 (1983), pp. 45–51.
8. Jacob Jacoby and Robert W. Chestnut, *Brand Loyalty: Measurement and Management* (New York: John Wiley & Sons, 1978). Also see Terry Elrod, "A Management Science Assessment of a Behavioral Measure of Brand Loyalty," in *Advances in Consumer Research*, vol. 15, ed. Michael J. Houston (Provo, Utah: Association for Consumer Research, 1987), pp. 481–86; and Richard E. DuWors, Jr., and George H. Haines, Jr., "Event History Analysis Measures of Brand Loyalty," *Journal of Marketing Research*, November 1990, pp. 485–93.
9. For example, see John W. Keon and Judy Bayer, "Analyzing Scanner Panel Households to Determine the Demographic Characteristics of Brand Loyal and Variety Seeking Households Using a New Brand Switching Measure," in *AMA Educator's Proceedings*, ed. Russell W. Belk et al. (Chicago: American Marketing Association, 1984), pp. 416–20.

10. For additional discussion of packaging issues, see Howard Schlossberg, "Effective Packaging 'Talks' to Consumers," *Marketing News*, August 6, 1990, p. 6; and Cyndee Miller, "Right Package Sets Mood for Image-Driven Brands," *Marketing News*, August 5, 1991, p. 2.
11. These examples are taken from Ronald Alsop, "Color Grows More Important in Catching Consumers' Eyes," *The Wall Street Journal*, November 29, 1984, p. 37
12. Hubert Gatignon and Thomas S. Robertson, "A Propositional Inventory for New Diffusion Research," *Journal of Consumer Research*, March 1985, pp. 849–67; and Vijay Mahajan, Eitan Muller, and Frank M. Bass, "New Product Diffusion Models in Marketing: A Review and Directions for Research," *Journal of Marketing*, January 1990, pp. 1–26.
13. Mary Dee Dickerson and James W. Gentry, "Characteristics of Adopters and Non-Adopters of Home Computers," *Journal of Consumer Research*, September 1983, pp. 225–35. Also see William E. Warren, C. L. Abercrombie, and Robert L. Berl, "Characteristics of Adopters and Nonadopters of Alternative Residential Long-Distance Telephone Services," in *Advances in Consumer Research*, vol. 15, ed. Michael J. Houston (Provo, Utah: Association for Consumer Research, 1987), pp. 292–98.
14. Elizabeth C. Hirschman, "Innovativeness, Novelty Seeking, and Consumer Creativity," *Journal of Consumer Research*, December 1980, pp. 283–95.
15. Gatignon and Robertson, "A Propositional Inventory," p. 861.
16. See Everett M. Rogers, *Diffusion of Innovations* (New York: Free Press, 1983).
17. Michael R. Solomon, "The Role of Products as Social Stimuli: A Symbolic Interactionism Perspective," *Journal of Consumer Research*, December 1983, pp. 319–29. Also see Morris B. Hollbrook and Elizabeth C. Hirschman, "The Experiential Aspects of Consumption: Consumer Fantasies, Feeling, and Fun," *Journal of Consumer Research*, September 1982, pp. 132–40; and Morris B. Hollbrook, Robert B. Chestnut, Terence A. Oliva, and Eric A. Greenleaf, "Play as a Consumption Experience: The Roles of Emotions, Performance, and Personality in the Enjoyment of Games," *Journal of Consumer Research*, September 1984, pp. 728–39.

Additional Reading

For discussions of the effects of product purchase timing on consumer behavior, see:

Bayus, Barry L. "The Consumer Durable Replacement Buyer." *Journal of Marketing*, January 1991, pp. 42–51.

Simonson, Itamar. "The Effect of Purchase Quantity and Timing on Variety-Seeking Behavior." *Journal of Marketing Research*, May 1990, pp. 150–62.

For research on consumer satisfaction/dissatisfaction with services, see:

Bitner, Mary Jo; Bernard H. Booms; and Mary Stanfield Tetreault. "The Service Encounter: Diagnosing Favorable and Unfavorable Incidents." *Journal of Marketing*, January 1990, pp. 71–84.

For research on consumer evaluations of brand extensions, see:

Aaker, David A., and Kevin Lane Keller. "Consumer Evaluations of Brand Extensions." *Journal of Marketing*, January 1990, pp. 27–41.

For suggested changes in the traditional view of adoption processes, see:

Antil, John H. "New Product or Service Adoption: When Does It Happen?" *Journal of Consumer Marketing*, Spring 1988, pp. 5–16.

For a complete discussion of new-product planning and development, see:

Crawford, C. Merle. *New Products Management*, 3rd ed. Homewood, Ill.: Richard D. Irwin, Inc., 1991.

For a discussion of consumer complaint management, see:

Fornell, Claes, and Birger Wernerfelt. "Defensive Marketing Strategy by Customer Complaint Management: A Theoretical Analysis." *Journal of Marketing Research*, November 1987, pp. 337–46.

For discussions of product perceptions and quality, see:

Bloch, Peter H., and Marsha L. Richens. "A Theoretical Model for the Study of Product Important Perceptions." *Journal of Marketing*, Summer 1983, pp. 69–81.

Curry, David J., and David J. Faulds. "Indexing Product Quality: Issues, Theory, and Results." *Journal of Consumer Research*, June 1986, pp. 134–45.

Jacobson, Robert, and David A. Aaker. "The Strategic Role of Product Quality." *Journal of Marketing*, October 1987, pp. 31–44.

Tellis, Gerald J., and Claes Fornell. "The Relationship between Advertising and Product Quality over the Product Life Cycle." *Journal of Marketing Research*, February 1988, pp. 64–71.

MARKETING STRATEGY IN ACTION

Harley-Davidson, Inc.—Motorcycle Division

Harley-Davidson, Inc., a diversified company founded in 1903, is the only remaining American motorcycle manufacturer, although there have been over 140 U.S. motorcycle manufacturers. During the 1950s and 1960s, Harley-Davidson had a virtual monopoly on the heavyweight motorcycle market. Japanese manufacturers entered the market in the 1960s with lightweight motorcycles backed by huge marketing programs that increased demand for motorcycles. These manufacturers, which included Honda, Kawasaki, Suzuki, and Yamaha, eventually began building larger bikes that competed directly with Harley-Davidson.

Recognizing the potential for profitability in the motorcycle market, American Machine and Foundry (AMF, Inc.) purchased Harley-Davidson in 1969. AMF almost tripled production to 75,000 units annually over a four-year period to meet increased demand. Unfortunately, product quality deteriorated significantly. More than half the cycles came off the assembly line missing parts, and dealers had to fix them to make sales. Little money was invested in improving design or engineering. The motorcycles leaked oil, vibrated badly, and could not match the excellent performance of the Japanese products. While hard-core motorcycle enthusiasts were willing to fix their Harleys and modify them for better performance, new motorcycle buyers had neither the devotion nor skill to do so.

In late 1975, AMF put Vaughn Beals in charge of Harley-Davidson. Beals set up a quality control and inspection program that began to eliminate the worst of the production problems. However, Beals and the other senior managers recognized it would take years to upgrade the quality and performance of their products to compete with the faster, high-performance Japanese bikes.

To stay in business while the necessary changes in design and product were being accomplished, the executives turned to William G. Davidson,

Harley's styling vice president. Known as "Willie G." and a grandson of one of the company founders, he frequently mingled with bikers and with his beard, black leather, and jeans was accepted by them. Willie G. understood Harley customers and noted:

> They really know what they want on their bikes: the kind of instrumentation, the style of bars, the cosmetics of the engine, the look of the exhaust pipes and so on. Every little piece on a Harley is exposed, and it has to look just right. A tube curve or the shape of a timing case can generate enthusiasm or be a total turnoff. It's almost like being in the fashion business.

Willie G. designed a number of new models by combining components from existing models. These included the Super Glide, the Electra Glide, the Wide Glide, and the Low Rider. While these were successful, Harley-Davidson was still losing market share to Japanese competitors that continued to pour new bikes into the heavyweight market.

By 1980, AMF was losing interest in investing in the recreational market and sold the company to 13 senior Harley executives in a leveraged buyout June 16, 1981. Although the company was starting to make money in the early 1980s, its creditors wanted payment, and Harley-Davidson nearly had to file for bankruptcy at the end of 1985. However, through some intense negotiations, it stayed in business and rebounded to a highly profitable company.

By 1990, Harley-Davidson controlled over 62 percent of the superheavyweight (850cc and larger) motorcycle market, far more than its all-time low of 23 percent just seven years earlier. Its products are considered to have "bulletproof reliability" due to manufacturing and management changes that resulted in products of excellent quality.

Although its machines are not generally as fast as Japanese bikes, owners of Harleys are highly brand loyal and over 94 percent of them state they would buy another Harley. The company sponsors the Harley Owner Group (HOG), which has over 650 chapters and 134,000 members. Executives of the company frequently meet with chapters to obtain suggestions for product improvements.

Harley's 1991 product line includes 21 models with price ranges from $4,359 for an 883cc Sportster to over $18,000 for the top of the line 1340cc Ultra Classic Electra Glide with a sidecar attached.

The company has over 600 domestic dealers with average sales of 75 to 100 units each annually. Harley has instituted a Designer Store program to improve the appearance, image, and merchandising of its products at the retail level. The stores sell not only motorcycles but also a variety of Harley-Davidson parts, clothing, and accessories. In 1990, overall motorcycle division sales were $595.3 million, of which $110 million was parts and accessories. The company could not produce motorcycles fast enough to meet demand in 1991.

Discussion Questions

1. What kind of consumer owns a Harley?
2. What accounts for Harley owners' satisfaction and brand loyalty?
3. What role do you think the Harley Owner Group plays in the success of the company?
4. What threats do you think Harley-Davidson faces in the 1990s?

Source: Thomas Gelb, "Overhauling Corporate Engine Drives Winning Strategy," *The Journal of Business Strategy,* November–December 1989, pp. 8–12; "How Harley Beat Back the Japanese," *Fortune,* September 25, 1989, pp. 155–64; Bob Wiedrich, "Harley Zooms Crest of Cycle Comeback," *Wisconsin State Journal,* January 7, 1990, p. 1F; and John Kekis, "Business Rev Charges Harley after Long Slump," *Wisconsin State Journal,* June 17, 1991, p. 6B.

Consumer Behavior and Promotion Strategy

CHAPTER 18

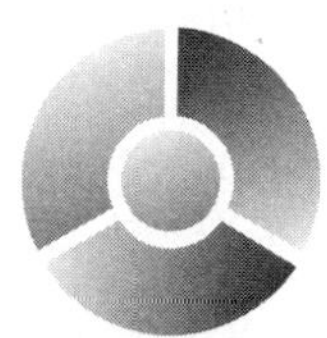

THREE WINNING PROMOTION STRATEGIES

Each year the Promotion Marketing Association of America honors the most effective consumer promotions in the country with Reggie Awards, in the form of small golden cash registers. In 1984, McDonald's won the Super Reggie Award for its successful sales promotion strategy called "When the USA Wins, You Win." That year, McDonald's was a major sponsor of the Los Angeles Summer Olympic Games. To capitalize on its investment, the restaurant chain developed a sales promotion game with the objectives of increasing store contacts by 8 percent and sales by 5 percent. Customers were given a game card with a rub-off spot that revealed the name of an Olympic event. If a U.S. athlete won a gold medal in that event, the card bearer received a free sandwich. French fries and soft drinks were given for silver and bronze medals. As recognized by the Reggie award, McDonald's promotion was quite successful. Store contacts increased by 11.2 percent, and sales at the average franchise increased $10,000. As an extra benefit, the promotion also encouraged TV viewership of the Olympics, thus increasing the impact of McDonald's heavy advertising investment.

General Foods won a Gold Reggie for its sales promotion intended to wean consumers away from their dependency on coffee

coupons. During December for several years, GF offered a free holiday ornament attached to Maxwell House Instant coffee containers. In 1984, three different ornaments were used to encourage multiple purchases, and each was dated to encourage collectibility. On a national basis, the promotion increased brand market share by 3.8 percent, and GF rated the program 40 percent more effective than typical consumer promotions.

Beatrice/Hunt-Wesson also won a Gold Reggie. Although the company had a winning product in its Orville Redenbacher popcorn, it wanted a promotion strategy to further increase consumer awareness, trial, and consumption. With the help of a promotion consulting company, it conceived the "Watch My Bow Tie" contest that offered a trip for five to Hollywood to dine with Orville Redenbacher himself. It distributed freestanding newspaper inserts that contained two coupons for the product plus details on the contest. To enter, consumers had to watch Redenbacher's TV ads to determine the color of his bow tie. The promotion strategy was supported with TV and print ads and in-store displays depicting Orville without the tie, as well as price reductions on the product. Not only did the three-month promotion increase advertising awareness and impact, but it also helped boost brand sales 38 percent over the previous year.

Source: "McDonald's Olympic Promotion Gets the Gold," *Marketing News,* June 7, 1985, pp. 12–13.

This example describes three highly successful sales promotion strategies. Marketers develop **promotions** to communicate information about their products and to persuade consumers to buy them. There are four major types of promotions—*advertising*, *sales promotions*, *personal selling*, and *publicity*. Like all marketing strategies, promotions are experienced by consumers as social and physical aspects of the environment, which may influence consumers' affective and cognitive responses as well as their overt behaviors. From the view of marketing management, the importance of promotion cannot be overstated.

Most successful products and brands require promotions such as those described in the opening example to create and maintain a *differential advantage* over their competitors.

Because they are so highly visible, promotion strategies are often the target of marketing critics. Some critics claim promotions are expenses that add nothing to the value of products, but increase their cost to the consumer. Supporters, on the other hand, argue that marketing promotions inform consumers about product attributes and consequences, prices, and places where products are available. This information may save consumers both time and money by reducing the costs of search. Moreover, advocates of promotion point out that some promotion strategies save consumers money directly. The A. C. Nielsen Company estimated manufacturers' coupons, a prime sales promotion strategy, saved American consumers an estimated $3 billion in 1989, up from $2 billion in 1985, and compared to a $502 million savings in 1978.[1]

In this chapter, we discuss how promotion strategies affect consumers' affective and cognitive responses and their overt behaviors. We begin by briefly describing the four types of promotion strategies. Then we discuss the communication process. Next we examine selected aspects of the promotion environment, consumers' affective and cognitive responses to promotions, and promotion-related behaviors. These topics are shown in the Wheel of Consumer Analysis in Figure 18.1. We conclude by detailing how marketing managers can use their understanding of consumers to manage promotion strategies.

Types of Promotions

The four types of promotion strategy — advertising, sales promotions, personal selling, and publicity — together constitute a promotion mix that marketers try to manage to achieve organizational objectives. Perhaps the most obvious promotion strategy is advertising.

Advertising

Advertising is any paid, nonpersonal presentation of information about a product, brand, company, or store. It usually has an identified sponsor. Advertising is intended to influence consumers' affect and cognitions — their evaluations, feelings, knowledge, meanings, beliefs, attitudes, and images concerning products and brands. In fact, advertising has been characterized as *image management* — creating and maintaining images and meanings in consumers' minds.[2] Advertisements may be conveyed via a variety of media — TV, radio, print (magazines, newspapers), billboards, signs, and miscellaneous media such as hot-air balloons or T-shirt decals.

Although the typical consumer is exposed to hundreds of ads daily, the vast majority of these messages receive low levels of attention and comprehension.

FIGURE 18.1
The Wheel of Consumer Analysis: Promotion Strategy Issues

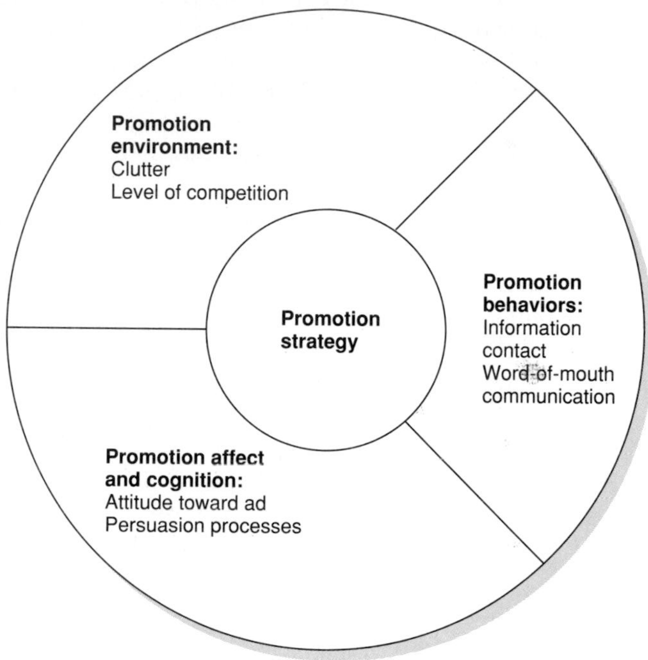

Thus, it is a major challenge for marketers to develop ad messages and select media that expose consumers, capture their attention, and generate appropriate comprehension.

In the mid-1980s, Nike Corporation made a big splash with a series of billboard ads featuring strong visual images of athletes – Carl Lewis long jumping or Michael Jordan leaping for the basket – and little else. The outdoor ads contained only the Nike "swoosh" logo in the corner and the athletes wearing Nike shoes and clothes. At first, consumers probably had to look twice to comprehend what product was being advertised. But once the association was made, Nike-related meanings were easily activated when consumers encountered other ads in the series. In markets where the ads were run, Nike sales increased an average of 30 percent.[3]

Sales Promotions

Sales promotions are direct inducements to the consumer to make a purchase.[4] TV advertising may be more glamorous, but more money is spent on sales promotions in the United States. In 1985, about 65 percent of promotion budgets was spent on all types of sales promotions, compared to 35 percent on advertising.[5]

The many types of sales promotions—including temporary price reductions through coupons, rebates, and multi-pack sales; contests and sweepstakes; trading stamps; trade shows and exhibitions; point-of-purchase displays; free samples; and premiums and gifts—make defining them difficult. According to Parker Lindberg, president of the Promotion Marketing Association of America, the key aspect of sales promotions is to "move the product today, not tomorrow. A sales promotion gets people to pick the product up at retail and try it by offering something concrete—a premium, cents off, or whatever."[6] In sum, most sales promotions are oriented at changing consumers' immediate purchase behaviors.

Consider a back-to-school promotion Dow offered on its Ziploc sandwich bags. The promotion included a 15-cent coupon plus a mail-in offer for free bread with two proofs of purchase. A premium was also included in the package—a set of stickers of the beasties from the movie *Gremlins*. As Ziploc was the no. 2 brand with a 28 percent share, this promotion was intended to get consumers to stock up on the brand, thereby preempting purchases of competitive brands. Sales volume increased 42 percent, and Ziploc became the top brand in the category for the first time.[7]

Personal Selling

Personal selling involves direct personal interactions between a potential buyer and a salesperson. Personal selling can be a powerful promotion method, for at least two reasons. First, the personal communication with the salesperson may increase consumers' felt involvement with the product and/or the decision process. Thus, consumers may be more motivated to attend to and comprehend the information the salesperson presents about the product. Second, the interactive communication situation allows salespeople to adapt their sales presentations to fit the informational needs of each potential buyer.

Certain consumer products are traditionally promoted through personal selling, such as life insurance, automobiles, and houses. In retailing, personal selling has decreased over the past 20 years as self-service has become more popular. Recently, however, some retailers like Nordstrom (the highly successful, West coast department store) have established a differential advantage by emphasizing personal selling and customer service. Besides lots of personal attention from a courteous sales staff, customers are coddled by pianos softly playing and champagne bars in the store.

For other businesses, a form of personal selling by telephone—called *telemarketing*—has become increasingly popular as the costs of a direct sales call increased to between $100 and $200 in 1985.[8] Telemarketing selling differs considerably from face-to-face selling. The telemarketer usually follows a prepared script, never travels, makes 20 to 50 calls per day that last from one to two minutes, works about four to six hours per day, and is closely supervised. In contrast, a conventional salesperson often travels, usually must improvise the sales presentation to fit the buyers' needs, makes only 2 to 10 sales calls per day that last about 1 hour each, works about 8 to 12 hours per day, and is loosely supervised.[9]

Both Avon and Mary Kay Cosmetics, among the largest U.S. marketers of skin-care products, were built on personal selling. In their earlier days, neither company spent much on advertising or customer sales promotions. Mary Kay, for instance, spent a minuscule $1 million on advertising in 1980 (out of $167 million in sales). Instead, most of the Mary Kay promotion budget was spent on sales incentives directed at salespeople. In addition to symbolic prizes such as medals, ribbons, and commemorative certificates, Mary Kay gives jewelry, calculators, briefcases, and furs as rewards to salespeople. Top sellers receive the use of pink Cadillacs or Buick Regals. Mary Kay also spends heavily on motivational and training programs for sales personnel, which in 1980 numbered some 150,000 women (Mary Kay has virtually no salesmen).[10]

Publicity

Publicity is any unpaid form of communication about the marketers' company, products, or brands. For instance, an article in *PC World* comparing various brands of word-processing software provides useful product information to consumers at no cost to the marketers of the sofware. Similarly, descriptions of new products or brands; brand comparisons in trade journals, newspapers, or news magazines; or discussions on radio and TV talk shows provide product information to consumers.

Publicity can be either positive or negative. Nike received a bonanza of free publicity in the form of favorable news stories about its billboard campaign. One TV news segment in Los Angeles concluded with the reporter urging viewers to "give a honk for Nike, which has raised the billboard from visual blight to at least camp art."[11] Tylenol, on the other hand, twice received unfavorable publicity when people were poisoned by Tylenol capsules that had been tampered with.

Sometimes publicity can be more effective than advertising, for consumers may not screen out the messages so readily. In addition, publicity communications may be considered more credible because they are not being presented by the marketing organization. Publicity is difficult to manage, however. Marketers sometimes stage "media events" in hopes of garnering free publicity. Procter & Gamble, for example, held a glitzy news conference at a New York City disco to introduce new Liquid Tide – complete with a 20-foot-high inflatable model of the product![12] P&G hoped the media would report the event and perhaps show a picture of the product, but the company had little control over what type of publicity (if any) would result.

The Promotion Mix

Ideally, marketing managers should develop a coherent overall promotion strategy that combines the four types of promotions into an effective promotion mix.

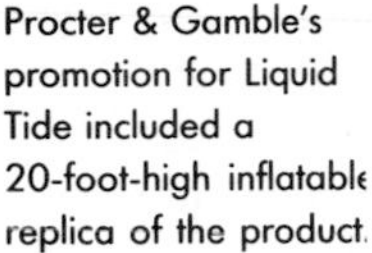
Procter & Gamble's promotion for Liquid Tide included a 20-foot-high inflatable replica of the product.

Major environmental forces in the United States over the past two decades have changed the balance of marketing effort devoted to the various types of promotions. In particular, sales promotion expenditures have increased much more rapidly than those for advertising. From 1976 to 1986, spending on sales promotions increased from $30 billion to $107 billion, while ad spending increased from $22 billion to $58 billion.[13]

During the recession of the early 1990s, sales promotion gained additional ground, while advertising, especially on network TV, decreased (down about 7 percent in 1991). Moreover, new forms of promotion communications were developed, such as direct marketing and magazines dedicated to a single advertiser, which allow highly accurate targeting of the desired consumer audience. Despite the attention on advertising and sales promotions, publicity and personal selling remain important promotion strategies for certain products. For instance, Mary Kay Cosmetics did very well in the early 1990s using its personal selling strategy.

A controversy is raging in marketing about the relative importance of advertising versus personal selling. As you might expect, most advertising agencies argue that advertising is the best (only?) way to create a strong consumer/

brand relationship.[14] Other marketers believe sales promotion can also enhance the consumer/brand relationship and has more powerful effects on immediate buying behaviors and eventual brand success.[15] Some analysts believe a longer range trend is occurring in which advertising will no longer be the centerpiece of a company's promotion mix.[16] There is evidence that advertising is having a decreasing influence on consumers' behaviors, due partly to people's increasingly hectic lifestyles and growing pressures on their time. The promotion mix of the future is likely to be more eclectic with many more options, including event sponsoring (Pepsi sponsoring rock concerts), sports marketing (Volvo sponsors tennis matches), direct marketing (sending coupons to purchasers of your competitor's brand), and public relations. These promotion types are being developed partly because of the high costs of advertising and partly because of the need to target customers more precisely. Highlight 18.1 describes an event sponsorship promotion.

Another factor in advertising's decline is the documented decrease in consumers' ability to remember ads they have seen. In 1986, 64 percent could remember, unaided, an ad campaign seen in the previous month. This figure plunged to 48 percent in 1990.[17] Attention to individual ads has decreased due to remote controls, the clutter of 30- and 15-second ads during commercial breaks, and consumers' dropping loyalty to favorite brands. Simultaneously, price has become more important as a choice criterion, further increasing the effectiveness of sales promotions, which are often based on price reduction.

A Communication Perspective

All promotions are experienced by consumers as information in the environment. Thus, the cognitive processing model of decision making (see Figure 3.5 or 7.1) is relevant for understanding their effects on consumers. First, consumers must be exposed to the promotion information. Then, they must attend to the promotion communication and comprehend its meaning. Finally, the resulting knowledge, meanings, and beliefs about the promotion may be integrated with other knowledge to create brand attitudes and make purchase decisions (form purchase intentions).

The Communication Process

A cognitive processing perspective suggests that developing successful promotion strategies is largely a communication problem.[18] Figure 18.2 presents a simple model that identifies the key factors in the **communication process.** The process begins when the *source* of the promotion communication determines what information is to be communicated and *encodes* the message in the form of appropriate symbols (using words, pictures, actions). Then the message is *transmitted* to a receiver over some medium such as a television show, direct

HIGHLIGHT 18.1

Promotion through Event Sponsorship

More companies have been seeking alternatives to advertising to promote their brands, including sponsoring various events (rock concerts and tours, bicycle races, and tennis tournaments). Since 1986, the number of companies sponsoring events has doubled to 4,200 and spending has tripled to $2.94 billion. One reason for this change is the spiraling cost of television advertising.

Consider the John Hancock Bowl (once called the Sun Bowl) held in December in El Paso, Texas. Most people remember the score of the 1990 game as Michigan State, 17, Southern California, 6. But for John Hancock Financial Services, the sponsor of the event, the score was $5.1 million to $1.6 million. The company spent about $1.6 million in direct expenditures, but garnered about $5.1 million in equivalent advertising value.

Hancock is serious about documenting the effectiveness of its sponsorship promotions. For instance, it clipped 7,800 newspaper and magazine articles about the John Hancock Bowl. The reach of each story was estimated and converted to equivalent advertising value. Hancock computed the stories had a total value of over $1 million in advertising equivalency.

The major value of the sponsorship, however, came from the CBS broadcast of the game, which Hancock estimated to be worth about $3.1 million in advertising equivalence based on the repeated references to the company, shots of the scoreboard, and the company logo at midfield and on the uniforms.

Tracing the effects of the bowl sponsorship to actual sales of Hancock products was more difficult. One indirect indicator of behavioral impact was that the proportion of consumers who claimed they would consider buying from Hancock rose from 41 percent to 54 percent. Also, consumer awareness of the Hancock advertising campaign rose to 96 percent from 90 percent.

Of course, some companies find the payoffs of event sponsorship to be less impressive. For instance, Sunkist, one of the originating sponsors of football bowl games, paid $1.6 million to sponsor the 1991 Fiesta Bowl on New Year's Day. Sunkist decided not to be a sponsor in 1992 because it believed the number of other companies sponsoring other games had diluted their impact.

Source: Michael J. McCarthy, "Keeping Careful Score on Sports Tie-Ins," *The Wall Street Journal,* April 24, 1991, pp. B1, B5.

mail, signs, or a magazine. The *receiver* or consumer, if exposed to the promotion, must *decode* it or interpret its meaning. Then, the consumer might take *action*, which could include going to a store or making a purchase. Marketing managers are usually the sources of promotion communications, and managing the promotion mix is their responsibility. As the target of promotion communications, consumers may be influenced by them.

FIGURE 18.2

A General Model of the Communication Process for Promotions

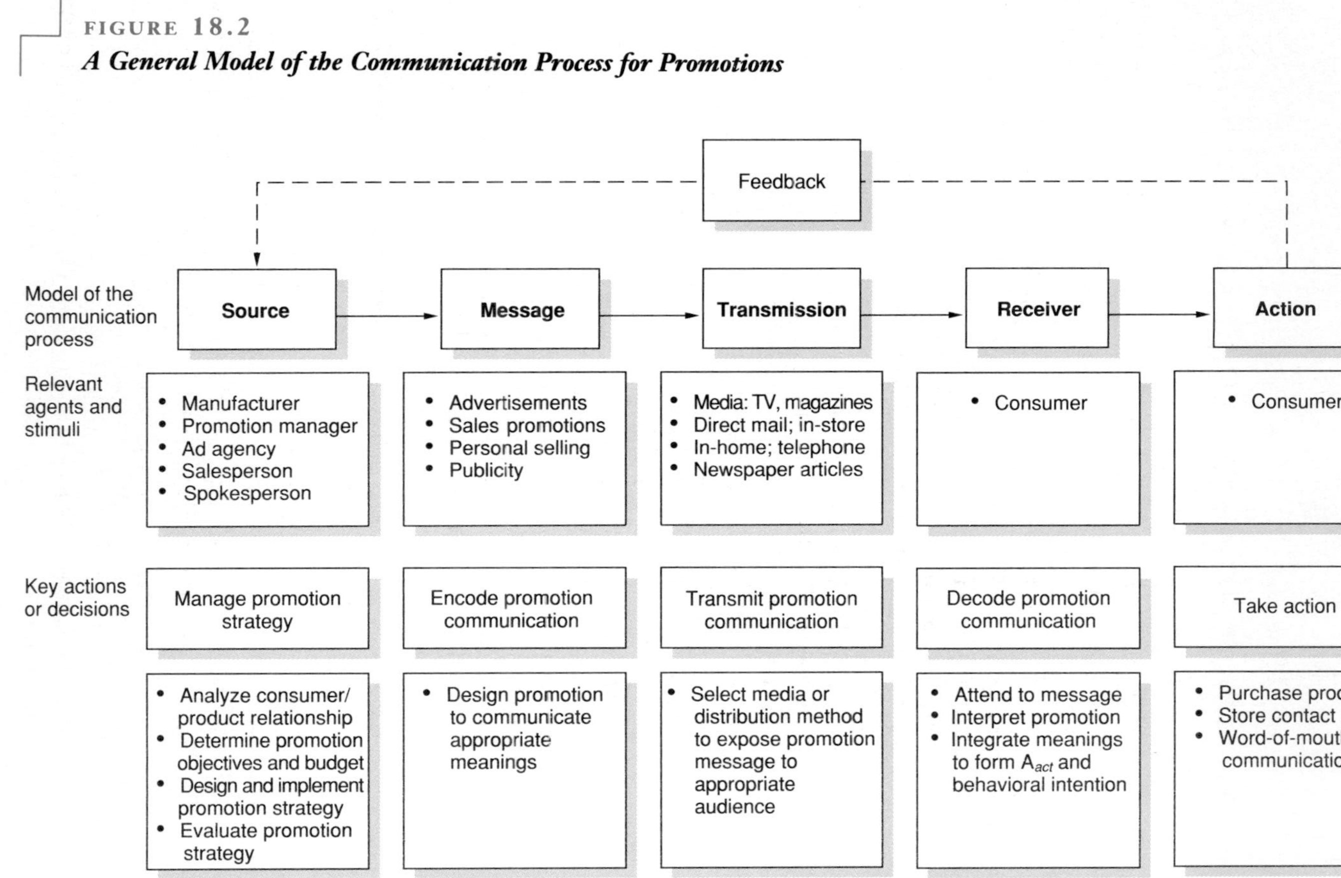

Source: Adapted from Figure 8.1 in Henry Assael, *Consumer Behavior and Marketing Action,* 3rd ed. (Boston: PSW-KENT Publishing Company, 1987), p. 210. © by Wadsworth, Inc. Used by permission of PSW-KENT Publishing Company, a division of Wadsworth, Inc.

Two stages of the communication model are particularly important to the success of promotion strategies. The first occurs when the marketer creates the promotion communication to encode a particular meaning. As you learned in Chapter 13, the marketer selects cultural meanings from the environment to create a message that will convey the intended meaning about the brand to the consumer.[19] The other critical stage is *decoding*, when consumers attend to and comprehend the information in the promotion communication and construct their personal interpretation of its meaning.

Goals of Promotion Communications

Researchers have identified five types of communication effects that promotion information may have on consumers.[20] They can be ordered in a hierarchical sequence of effects that are necessary before consumers can/will purchase a brand. From the marketing manager's perspective, these effects can be treated as a sequence of goals or objectives for promotion communications.

- Consumers must have a *recognized need* for the product category or product form.
- Consumers must be *aware* of the brand.
- Consumers must have a *favorable brand attitude.*
- Consumers must have an *intention to purchase* the brand.
- Consumers must *perform various behaviors* to purchase the brand (e.g., travel to store, find the brand in the store, talk to salespeople).

In this section, we discuss each communication goal, identify the types of promotion strategies best suited for each goal, and briefly describe how these communication effects can be created. Several concepts discussed earlier in the text will be relevant for our analysis.

Stimulate Category Need

Before they make any brand purchase, consumers must recognize (feel) a need for the product category or the product form. Only those consumers who have recognized the self-relevance of the product and have formed a general intention to purchase it are "in the market" for the product. As you learned in Chapters 6 and 7, consumers' intentions to buy a brand are based on their attitudes toward buying and social beliefs about what others want them to buy. A_{act} in turn is based on consumers' beliefs about the consequences of buying the brand. Thus, to stimulate a category need, marketers need to create beliefs about the positive consequences of buying and using the product category or form.

When consumers in the target market already recognize a category need, marketers can concentrate promotion strategies on other goals. However, at any given time, relatively few consumers are likely to have a general intention to buy a product. For instance, perhaps 20 percent of consumers might intend to buy laundry detergent at any time, compared to 1 percent who intend to buy a new car. Moreover, it can be difficult to distinguish the consumers who have formed such an intention from those not in the market.

Marketers usually use advertising to stimulate category need among additional consumers, although publicity and personal selling also can influence category need to some extent. These strategies should be designed to convince consumers that the product category or form is associated with important end goals and values. Essentially, stimulating product need involves creating positive means-end chains at the level of the product category or product form.

Brand Awareness

Because consumers cannot buy a brand unless they are aware of it, brand awareness is a general communication goal for all promotion strategies. By creating brand awareness, the marketer hopes that whenever the category need arises, the brand will be activated from memory for inclusion in the consideration set of choice alternatives for the decision. Advertising probably has the greatest influences on brand awareness,[21] although publicity, personal selling, and sales promotion also can have an effect.

Sales personnel in the store can generate brand awareness by bringing certain brands to consumers' attention. Various sales promotion strategies such as colorful price discount signs and end-of-aisle displays (a large stack of brand packages at the end of the supermarket aisle) draw consumers' attention to brands. Also, shelf position and brand placement within the store can influence brand awareness. Finally, prominent brand-name signs (buses and billboards) also remind consumers of the brand name and maintain brand awareness.

The level of consumers' brand awareness necessary for purchase varies depending on how and where they make their purchase decisions for that product category or form. Many brand choice decisions about grocery and personal care products, clothing items, appliances, and electronic products are made in the store. Consumers do not need to remember a brand name; they need only be able to quickly recognize familiar brands (often based on package cues), which then activates their relevant brand knowledge in memory. Thus, one strategic implication is to show the brand package in the advertising so consumers can more easily recognize the brand in the store.[22]

In other decision situations, a higher level of brand awareness is necessary to influence brand choice. If the purchase decision is made at home or in another environment where few brand-related cues are available, the brand must be recalled from memory for it to enter the consideration set. Restaurant choices tend to be like this. In such cases, knowledge in memory may be more important than environmental factors. Unless consumers are able to recall the brand name (activate it from memory), the brand is not likely to be considered or purchased.

The level of consumers' brand awareness can be measured by asking them to state the brand names they can remember (with no hints – unaided recall) or by seeing which brands consumers recognize as familiar. Whether brand recall or recognition is suitable depends on where and when the purchase decision is made.[23]

Appropriate brand awareness strategies depend on how well known the brands are. Sometimes the marketing goal is to maintain already high levels of brand awareness. Much of the advertising for well-known brands such as Coca-Cola, IBM, and Anacin serves a reminder function that keeps the brand name at a high level of awareness.[24] This makes brand activation more likely in a decision situation. Publicity and sales promotions can also have reminder effects. Managers of less familiar brands have a more difficult task of creating brand awareness and may have to spend heavily to do so.

Brand Attitude

As you learned in Chapter 6, consumers are likely to have an attitude toward every brand they purchase. Each promotion strategy can influence consumers' brand attitudes, but the specific communication objective depends on consumers' current attitudes toward the brand. More specifically, for a new or unfamiliar brand, the goal might be to *create* a brand attitude. For an already popular brand, marketers may be content to *maintain* existing favorable brand attitudes. For brands with neutral or slightly unfavorable attitudes, marketers

Promotion for new products often strives to create an attitude about the brand in consumers.

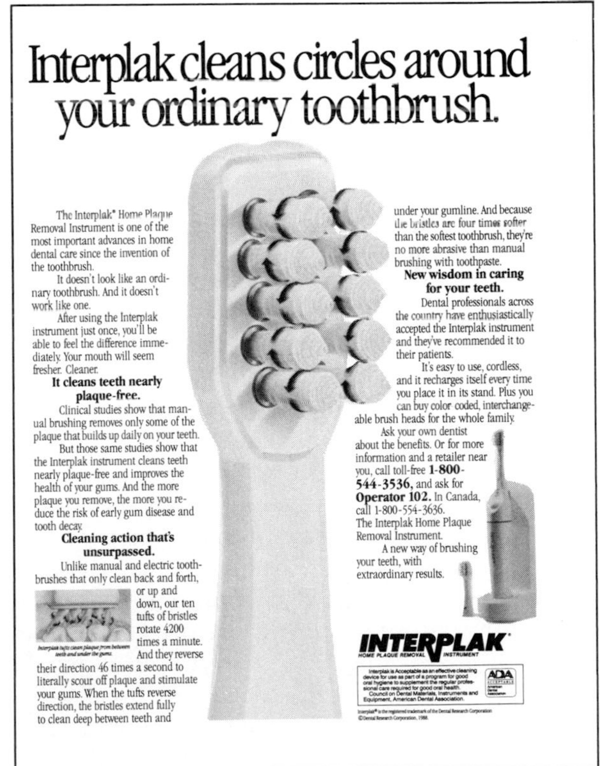

may wish to *increase* the existing attitude. In each case, the general promotion strategy will be to create more favorable beliefs about the consequences of salient brand attributes.[25]

Marketers make a big mistake if they analyze consumers' brand attitudes in an absolute or very general sense, without specifying the situational context. Usually the salient beliefs about important attributes, consequences, and end goals will vary across situations and contexts. Therefore, brand attitudes are likely to vary from one decision context to another. As you learned in Chapter 4, the meanings of beliefs about brand consequences depend on the ends to which they are related. For instance, a functional consequence for toothpaste such as "makes my mouth feel fresh" can lead to several different ends, including "sensory enjoyment, eliminate bad breath, avoid offending others, feel more alive." In general, the overall communication goal is to create means-end knowledge structures that link the brand to important consequences and values.

Brand Purchase Intention

Most promotion strategies are intended by marketers to increase (or maintain) the probability that consumers will buy the brand (increase *BI*). As you learned in Chapters 6 and 7, all voluntary behaviors are based on intentions to behave ("I will buy Pert shampoo this afternoon"). Behavioral intentions (*BI*) may be activated from memory as stored decision plans ("When I run low on mouthwash, I will buy Scope"). Alternatively, *BI* can be constructed through integration processes at the time of the decision choice, usually in the store ("I'll buy this red Hanes T-shirt"). An intention to buy a brand is based on a consumer's attitude toward buying the brand (A_{act}) as well as the influence of social norms (*SN*) about what other people want him/her to do. A_{act} is based on means-end chains of beliefs about the consequences and values associated with the acts of buying or using the brand.

To develop effective promotion strategies directed at brand purchase intentions, marketers must know when *BI* are formed by most of the target consumers. Consumers do not necessarily form an intention to buy immediately on exposure to advertising information about the brand. Only consumers who recognize the category need and are actively in the market for the product (they have a general intention to buy the product) are likely to form a brand purchase intention at the time of exposure to an ad.[26]

More typically, formation of a brand *BI* is delayed until well after exposure to advertising, when the consumer is in a purchase context such as a store. This situation is more likely for brands that are not high in intrinsic self-relevance (candy bars), which are more likely to be purchased on impulse (i.e., environmental cues tend to trigger purchase). About 85 percent of candy purchases, 83 percent of snack purchases, and 45 percent of soft drinks are based on impulse where the *BI* to purchase is formed in the store.[27]

In contrast, personal selling and sales promotions usually are designed to influence purchase intentions at the time of exposure to the promotion information.[28] The goal is for consumers to immediately form a connection between the brand and important consequences and values. For example, a lower price due to a 25-percent-off price promotion might be seen as leading to "saving money" and "having more money to use for other things," which in turn is linked to the values of "being a careful consumer" and "self-esteem." Thus, consumers might form a positive A_{act} and *BI* on the spot.

Facilitate Other Behaviors

Finally, some promotion strategies are designed to facilitate behaviors other than purchase. As you learned in Chapter 11, consumers often must perform several other behaviors to make a brand purchase. For instance, buying certain brands of clothing requires consumers to enter the stores that carry such brands. Sales promotions and publicity are not likely to have much influence on these other behaviors. Some advertising and personal selling strategies are intended to increase the probability of these other behaviors. For instance, an ad might be directed at encouraging consumers to come to the dealership to test-drive a new

Some promotion is used to facilitate behaviors other than purchase—such as making a call to an insurance agent.

car. Salespeople might encourage consumers to operate the controls of an appliance or audio equipment, which increases the probability of making a purchase. Other advertising strategies might encourage consumers to engage in positive word-of-mouth communications by telling other people about a brand.

The Promotion Environment

The *promotion environment* includes all the stimuli associated with the physical and social environment in which consumers experience promotions strategies. Many of these factors can affect the success of a promotion. In this section, we discuss two environmental factors that can influence advertising and sales promotion strategies—promotion clutter and level of competition.

Promotion Clutter

A key promotion objective is to increase the probability that consumers come into contact with, attend to, and comprehend the promotion message. In recent years, however, the amount of marketing promotion has so increased that the effectiveness of any given promotion strategy may be impaired by **promotion clutter**—the growing number of competitive strategies in the environment. For instance, over 320,000 television commercials were shown in 1989, up 20 percent over 1985.[29]

Advertisers have long been worried that the clutter created by multiple ads during commercial breaks and between TV programs will reduce the communication effectiveness of each ad (see Highlight 18.2).[30] There is good reason for alarm: Fewer consumers can remember ads they have seen. The average proportion of consumers able to recall an ad seen 24 hours earlier fell from 24 percent in 1979 to 21 percent in 1984. Clutter also affects other types of promotion strategies, especially sales promotions. Over the past decade, marketers have dramatically increased their spending on sales promotions. Traditionally, *couponing* has been the most popular form of sales promotion, and its use has grown every year. Approximately 95 percent of major U.S. consumer-goods companies used coupon promotions in 1984. The sheer number of coupons is staggering: 267 billion were distributed in 1989, nearly 3,000 coupons per household.[31] Coupon redemption rates have not kept pace, though. Across all methods of distribution, less than 3 percent of coupons were redeemed. Some marketers wonder whether this promotion clutter will cause couponing to become a victim of its own success.

Level of Competition

The *level of competition* for a product category is a key aspect of the promotion environment. As competition heats up, marketers' use of promotions usually

HIGHLIGHT 18.2

Clutter and the 15-Second Commercial

At one time, the 60-second commercial was the most common ad on TV. Over the years, marketers had collected a body of research data that established benchmarks of effectiveness for these longer ads. Then, in the late 1960s, a crisis came along. All of this research was jeopardized by the introduction of 30-second commercials. At the time, it was thought the shorter ads, and the extra "clutter" they would create, would cause havoc with advertising effectiveness and measurement. It didn't happen, and the 30-second ad became the standard.

But a new crisis loomed in the mid-1980s: 15-second ads. What will their effect be?

Preliminary evidence provided by a large-scale comparison of 30 15-second and 5,221 30-second ads suggested the new ads won't wreak havoc, either. When the average 30-second commercial scored 100 for communication performance, the average 15-second ad scored 78. The 15-second ads also scored well on a measure of the number of ideas in the ad played back later by the viewer – 2.6 versus 2.9 for the 30-second ads. Finally, both ad lengths scored about the same in terms of the sense of importance of the main idea created by the commercial. Yet the 15-second ad costs only slightly more than half as much money to run.

So, will the 15-second ads be a problem? Probably not. It is not the length per se that makes an ad effective or ineffective. If an ad establishes a reason – a reward – for viewing it in the first few seconds, consumers are likely to pay attention and comprehend its meaning, no matter how long it is.

Certain communication goals are more difficult to achieve with 15-second ads: a feeling of newness, a multistep process, a sense of variety, creating a mood or emotion, and humor. But the very same problems were mentioned for the 30-second ads, and we know how that turned out.

Source: Adapted from Robert Parcher, "15-Second TV Commercials Appear to Work 'Quite Well.'" *Marketing News* 20 (January 3, 1986), pp. 1 and 60. Published by the American Marketing Association.

increases. We saw this in the large number of promotions tried by the airlines and telephone companies when deregulation created a more competitive environment. Moreover, the types of promotion strategies change as competitive pressures increase.

Comparative advertising, featuring direct comparisons with competitive brands, has become more common.[32] Sometimes miniature "wars" are fought through TV commercials. In one notable example, Pepsi "challenge" ads claimed taste preference superiority over Coke, and Coca-Cola retaliated with taste tests that showed consumers preferring Coke. A new battle erupted in 1989 when Coke claimed Pepsi drinkers were switching to Diet Coke.

In fiercely competitive environments, promotion often becomes the key element in the marketers' competitive arsenal.[33] Marketers of breakfast cereals, for instance, have developed complex promotion mixes that include couponing, in-pack prizes, premiums, advertisements, price reductions, contests, games, and publicity. Rental car companies such as Hertz, Avis, and Budget promote continuously, mostly on price, by offering various deals and discounts, but they also mount extensive advertising campaigns and offer frequent traveler programs along with occasional contests and prizes.

Promotion Affect and Cognition

Promotion affect and cognition include all of the affective and cognitive responses we discussed in Section 2. Interpretation of promotion communications (attention and comprehension) and integration processes (forming attitudes and intentions) are extremely important. But some researchers claim ad information can influence consumers without any affective or cognitive responses—(see Highlight 18.3).

As we discussed in Chapter 5, consumers' comprehension processes vary in depth and elaboration, depending on their levels of knowledge and felt involvement.[34] Thus, exposure to a promotion communication—whether an ad, a coupon, or a sales presentation—may produce meanings that vary in number (elaboration), level (deep versus shallow), and interconnectedness. Consumers also may form inferences about product attributes or consequences, or the marketer's motivation.[35] In this section, we will examine two other concepts relevant to understanding the effects of advertising—consumers' attitudes toward ads and persuasion processes.

Attitude toward the Ad

Advertisers have long been interested in measuring consumers' evaluations of advertisements.[36] Recently, researchers have become interested in consumers' **attitude toward the ad**—their affective evaluations of the ad itself. Research suggests consumers' attitudes toward the ad can influence their attitudes toward the advertised product or brand.[37] That is, ads that consumers like seem to create more positive brand attitudes and purchase intentions than ads they don't like. The "mechanism" that accounts for the liking effect on brand attitude is not known. It may be that liking for ads influences attention (people pay more attention to ads they like)[38] and comprehension (consumers devote more effort to elaborating the information in likable ads).

Currently, a number of other issues remain to be resolved, including what aspects of the ads (perhaps the visual material in print ads) have the greatest influence on ad attitudes and whether consumers' evaluative reactions to the

HIGHLIGHT 18.3

Subliminal Advertising

Although most advertisers pay little or no attention to the topic, *subliminal persuasion* in advertising just won't go away. Writers like Wilson Key keep turning out widely read books that claim subliminal advertising is all around us. Key claims marketers intentionally embed subliminal stimuli — usually sexual objects, symbols, or words — in advertisements. Moreover, he claims these hidden, subliminal stimuli affect us in powerful ways of which we are unaware.

What do we know about the effects of subliminal stimulation? First, it is clear that stimulation below the level of a person's conscious awareness *can* be shown to have measurable effects upon some aspects of that person's behavior. That is, people can respond to stimuli without being consciously aware of the stimuli. But these stimuli are not necessarily subliminal — that is, they are not necessarily presented at intensities below our perceptual threshold. They just tend not to be consciously noticed as consumers go about their business. As we have seen throughout this text, a great deal of cognitive activity occurs automatically. Thus, consumers often are not able to report the existence of a stimulus or an awareness that some cognitive process has occurred.

With regard to Key's claims about sexual embedding, two issues are in question. First, are subliminal embeddings being made in advertisements as a matter of course, as Key claims? Virtually no evidence exists that this is so. Certainly, overtly sexual stimuli are found in a great many advertisements, but these are not subliminal embeds. Second, could subliminal stimuli affect goal-directed behaviors like purchase choices?

Most stimuli have little or no influence on our cognitions or behaviors when presented at a recognizable level. Why, then, should they suddenly have a strong impact when presented subliminally? Key claims that humans have two processing systems, one of which operates on a completely unconscious level and immediately picks up on the alleged subliminal embeds. However, no psychological theories or data support such a system of cognition.

A key finding in cognitive psychology that we have emphasized throughout this text is that the meaning of a stimulus is not inherent in the stimulus itself. Rather, meanings are constructed by consumers in active and sometimes complex ways as they come into contact with the stimulus.

None of this is to say that ads may not have effects on consumers' meanings at a subconscious level — but the stimuli don't have to be subliminal for that to occur.

Source: Jack Haberstroh, "Can't Ignore Subliminal Ad Charges," *Advertising Age,* September 17, 1984, pp. 3, 42; and Timothy E. Moore, "Subliminal Advertising: What You See Is What You Get," *Journal of Marketing,* Spring, 1982, pp. 38–47.

advertising influence their brand attitudes through classical conditioning processes or cognitive integration processes.[39]

Persuasion Processes

Persuasion refers to the cognitive and affective processes by which consumers' beliefs and attitudes are changed by promotion communications – usually advertisements. A currently popular model of the persuasion process, called the Elaboration Likelihood Model, identifies two "routes" or types of cognitive processes by which advertising persuades – central and peripheral.[40]

In the **central route to persuasion,** consumers pay attention to the key product claims communicated explicitly or implicitly in the ad. This type of processing tends to occur when consumers feel more involved with the product information. The resulting motivation to process produces deeper, more elaborate comprehension processes in which consumers think actively about the product's attributes and consequences and its ability to satisfy their needs and desired ends.[41] In sum, during central route processes consumers (1) attend to and interpret product-related aspects of the advertisement to form beliefs about product attributes and consequences, (2) integrate those meanings to form brand attitudes and possibly purchase intentions.[42]

The **peripheral route to persuasion** is quite different. Here, consumers tend to have low levels of felt involvement with the product information and are not motivated to process the ad message about the brand. However, consumers still might pay some attention to the ad, perhaps for its interest or entertainment value. Pepsi's ads featuring pop singers such as Michael Jackson seem to encourage this type of peripheral processing.

Consumers devote most attention in peripheral processing to nonproduct features of the ad such as the pictures in a print ad or the scenery or actors in a TV commercial. Although consumers do not form a brand attitude at the time of exposure, they may form evaluations of the ad as a whole or form beliefs about peripheral aspects of the ad. Later, consumers may retrieve these meanings from memory and integrate them to construct a brand attitude. As we saw above, evidence is mounting that these peripheral beliefs and attitudes (attitude toward the ad) can influence brand attitudes, thus causing indirect persuasion.

Marketers can try to stimulate either central, product-related processing or peripheral processing by varying the information content of the ads, including visual images,[43] explicit comparisons between competitive brands,[44] or type of product attribute information.[45]

Whether consumers engage in central or peripheral processing depends on their goals (what end states are activated?) and their felt involvement with the brand (how relevant is the advertised product to those goals?).[46] For instance, if consumers are exposed to an ad for a product they are actively considering buying, they are likely to engage in central processing of the ad message. However, we suspect that much of the advertising consumers come into contact with on a daily basis is not very relevant to their current goal states. Relatively few consumers in the audience are in the market for the product category. Therefore, it seems likely that a great deal of mass advertising receives only peripheral processing or perhaps very little attention at all. Certainly, the low current recall rates suggest this is the case.

PROMOTION BEHAVIORS

Ultimately, promotion strategies must affect not only consumers' cognitions, but also their behaviors. A firm's sales, profits, and market-share objectives can be accomplished only if consumers perform a variety of behaviors, including purchase of its product. Different types of promotions can be used to influence the various behaviors in the purchase/consumption sequence. Because we have already discussed purchase behavior in this chapter and throughout the book, we focus here on two other behaviors that are critical to the success of promotion strategies: information contact and word-of-mouth communication with other consumers.

INFORMATION CONTACT

Consumers must come in contact with promotion information for it to be successful. *Information contact* with promotions may be *intentional* (as when consumers search the newspapers for food coupons), but probably is most often *incidental* (the consumer just happens to come into contact with a promotion when engaging in some other behavior). Sometimes promotion contact can even trigger the purchase decision process, as might occur when accidentally coming across a sale or other incentive promotion. As a practical matter, the marketer must place the promotion message in the target consumers' physical environment to maximize chances for exposure and must design the promotion so it will be noticed (attended to). For advertising promotions, this requires knowledge of the media habits of the target market—what TV shows do they watch, what radio shows do they listen to, what magazines do they listen to?

Placing information in consumers' environments may be easy when target consumers can be identified accurately. For example, catalog marketers can buy lists of consumers who have made mail-order purchases in the past year. Then they can send promotion materials directly to these target consumers. Of course, sending coupons or a sweepstakes promotion through the mail does not guarantee consumers will open the envelop and read its contents. See Highlight 18.4 for a new form of information contact.

Contact for personal selling promotions can be achieved through "cold calls" on consumers. But referrals and leads (or consumers who initiate contact with salespeople during the search process) are likely to be more successful. Marketers sometimes encourage referrals by offering gifts in return for the names of potential customers.

HIGHLIGHT 18.4

A New Form of Information Contact

Sixty-second ads are almost a thing of the past, and keeping viewers' attention on 30- or even 15-second commercials is difficult. In this context, the information contact strategy used by Toyota to promote its new minivan, Previa, might be considered a bit risky.

Toyota's ad agency, Saatchi and Saatchi, created an eight-minute videotape commercial for the Previa and mailed it to some 200,000 potential customers. (Toyota assumed nearly all these people owned a VCR.) The video had a fragile story line about a woman ad writer assigned to push the new Previa. It portrayed her family (husband and fresh-faced kids) driving around in the car, while she explained its special features. In the background, an orchestra played the Toyota theme song, "I love what you do for me."

The costs of this promotion were high, estimated at about $1.5 million, including buying the mailing list, producing the video, and mailing the $4 plastic cassettes. Future promotions might use cardboard cassettes which work for about five plays and cost only about $2. The effectiveness of the Previa tape was hard to determine, but about 2 percent of those who received it visited a Toyota showroom within three months.

The big information contact issue is would people actually watch such videos? If they did, the video surely communicated the Previa name and its special attributes better than any television commercial or print ad.

Source: Philip Glouchevitch, "Cruel and Unusual Punishment?" *Forbes,* October 15, 1990, p. 182

Telemarketing is an increasingly popular method of information contact. State Farm Insurance, for example, has used a telemarketing approach in which consumers are called and asked what time of the year they pay their homeowners' and automobile insurance premiums. Then, just before that time, rate information is sent to these consumers to encourage a switch to State Farm's insurance products.

Exposure to promotion messages is not enough, however. Consumers must also attend to the promotion messages. Big promotions (large discounts, expensive prizes) tend to be situational sources of felt involvement and thus are more likely to be noticed and receive higher levels of attention. How well the promotion interacts with such consumer characteristics as intrinsic self-relevance and existing knowledge also affects the level of attention. For instance, the effectiveness of price-reduction promotions depends largely on consumers' price sensitivity.

WORD-OF-MOUTH COMMUNICATION

Marketers may want to encourage consumers' **word-of-mouth communication** about a promotion. This helps to spread awareness beyond those consumers who come into direct contact with the promotion.[47] Consumers may share information with friends about good deals on particular products, a valuable coupon in the newspaper, or a sale at a retail store. For example, a consumer may phone a friend who is looking for tires to say Sears is having a great sale. Consumers sometimes recommend that their friends see a particular salesperson who is especially pleasant or well informed, or who offers good deals on merchandise. Consumers often pass on impressions of a new restaurant, retail store, or movie to their friends.

As these examples illustrate, by simply placing promotion information in consumers' environment, marketers can increase the probability that the information will be communicated to other consumers. And because personal com-

This ad reflects the power of word-of-mouth influence on consumers' behavior.

munication from friends and relevant others is a powerful form of communication, marketers may try to design promotions that encourage word-of-mouth communication (get a friend to join the health club and you will get two months' membership free).

Managing Promotion Strategies

Developing and implementing effective promotion strategies is a complex, difficult task. No single approach or "magic formula" can guarantee an effective promotion. The model presented in Figure 18.3 identifies the key activities in managing promotion strategies.

Analyze Consumer/Product Relationships

Developing effective promotion strategies begins with an analysis of the relationships between consumers and the products or brands of interest. This requires identifying the appropriate target markets for the product. Then marketers must identify consumers' needs, goals and values, their levels of product and brand knowledge and involvement, and their current attitudes and

FIGURE 18.3
Managing Promotion Strategies

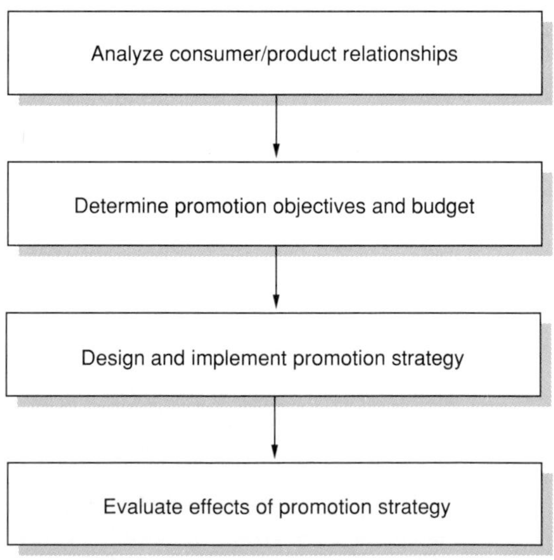

behavior patterns. In short, marketers must strive to understand the *relationship* between their target consumers and the product or brand of interest.

When dealing with a new product or brand, marketers may have to conduct considerable marketing research to learn about the *consumer/product relationship*. This research could include interviews to identify the dominant means-end chains that reveal how consumers perceive the relationships between the product or brand and their own self-concepts.[48] Other methods might include focus group interviews, concept tests, attitude and use surveys, and even test marketing. For existing products and brands, marketers may already know a great deal about consumer/product relationships. Perhaps only follow-up research would be necessary.

The FCB Grid

Figure 18.4 presents a simple grid model used by Foote, Cone & Belding, a major advertising agency, to analyze consumer/product relationships.[49] The figure also shows the typical locations of several different products, based on extensive consumer research conducted around the world. The **Foote, Cone &**

FIGURE 18.4

The Foote, Cone & Belding Grid for Analyzing Consumer/Product Relationships

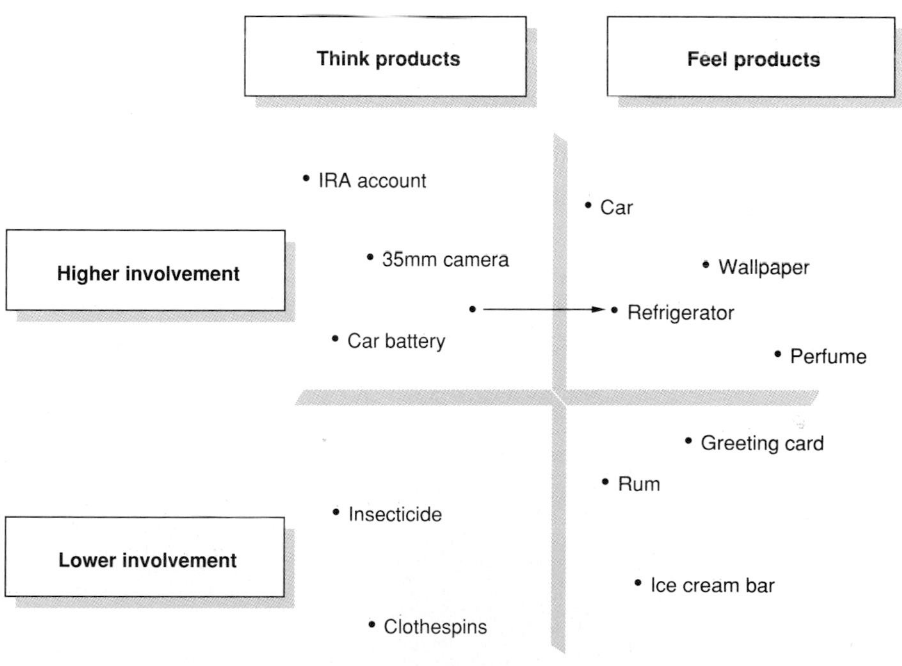

Source: David Berger, "Theory into Practice: The FCB Grid," *European Research,* January 1986, p. 35.

Belding (FCB) grid is based on two concepts you studied in earlier chapters: consumers' involvement and their salient knowledge, meanings, and beliefs about the product.

Consumers have varying degrees of felt involvement with a product or brand, due to intrinsic and situational sources of self-relevance. Moreover, various types of knowledge, meanings, and beliefs may be activated when consumers evaluate and choose among alternative products or brands. Some products are considered primarily in terms of rational meanings, such as the functional consequences of using the product.[50] These are termed *think products* in the grid model. Included in this category are such products as investments, cameras, and car batteries — all products purchased primarily for their functional consequences.

In contrast, *feel products* are considered by consumers primarily in terms of nonverbal images (visual or other types of sensory images) and emotional factors, such as psychosocial consequences and values.[51] For instance, products purchased primarily for their sensory qualities — ice cream, soft drinks, cologne — as well as products for which emotional consequences are dominant — flowers or jewelry — are feel products in the FCB grid.

Because the consumer/product relationships are quite different in the four quadrants of the grid, the FCB grid also has implications for developing creative advertising strategies, measuring advertising effects, and selecting media in which to place ads.

The appropriate promotion strategy depends on the product's position in the grid. Sometimes, a product can be "moved" within the grid, like the refrigerator in Figure 18.4, which was shifted from a think to a feel product by the following strategy. A South American client of FCB once had a problem: 5,000 ugly green refrigerators in inventory were not selling while competing brands offered desirable product features such as ice makers. High-involvement products such as refrigerators tend to be sold in terms of functional conse-

Scent strips allow consumers to experience "feel" products.

quences, but in this case there was no rational benefit to promote. So FCB designed a promotion strategy to move refrigerators from the think quadrant to the feel quadrant. The agency created ads that featured Venezuelan international beauty queens and termed the refrigerators "another Venezuelan beauty." The 5,000 refrigerators sold out in 90 days. In general, FCB has found that traditional *think* products often can be marketed successfully using *feel* advertising promotion strategies. In sum, the FCB grid model helps marketers analyze consumer/product relationships to develop more effective promotions.

Determine Promotion Objectives and Budget

Promotions can affect consumers' affect, cognitions, and behaviors.[52] Thus, promotion strategies may be designed to meet one or more of the following objectives:

- *To influence behaviors:* Change or maintain consumers' specific behaviors concerning the product or brand—usually purchase behaviors.
- *To inform:* Create new knowledge, meanings, or beliefs about the product or brand in consumers' memories.
- *To persuade:* Change consumers' beliefs, attitudes, and intentions toward the product or brand.
- *To transform affective responses:* Modify the images, feelings, and emotions that are activated when consumers consider the product or brand.
- *To remind:* Increase the activation potential of the brand name or some other product meaning in consumers' memories.

Before designing a promotion strategy, marketers should determine their specific promotion objectives and the budget available to support it. The long-run objective of most promotion strategies is to influence consumer behaviors, especially store patronage and brand purchase. Shopping malls sponsor auto, boat, or home-builder shows to build consumer traffic. Many sales promotions are designed to directly and quickly affect consumer purchases of a particular brand. The rebate programs and low-interest financing offered by automakers are intended to stimulate short-run sales of certain brands and models.

Finally, some promotions have multiple objectives. Frito-Lay frequently uses a sales promotion strategy of placing coupons on the package. This promotion is designed to stimulate immediate sales and to encourage repeat sales, with the long-run goal of creating more brand-loyal consumers.

Some promotions are designed to first influence consumers' cognitions in anticipation of a later influence on their overt behaviors. When a new product or brand is introduced, a primary objective for advertising promotions may be to create awareness of the product and some simple beliefs about it. Marketers also try to generate publicity for new products for these reasons, as well as to create a favorable brand attitude. These cognitions are intended to influence purchase intentions and sales behaviors later.

Design and Implement Promotion Strategy

Designing alternative promotion strategies and selecting one to meet the promotion objectives are based largely on the *consumer/product relationships* that have been identified through marketing research. Implementing the promotion strategy may include creating ads and placing them in various media, designing and distributing coupons, putting salespeople to work, and developing publicity events. Many of these tasks may be done with the aid of an advertising agency or a promotion consultant.

Designing Promotion Strategies

The design of effective promotion strategies must be sensitive to the consumer/product relationships represented in different market segments. Consider the various consumer segments portrayed in Figure 18.5. These groups are defined by consumers' past purchase behavior and current attitudes toward a brand. Consumers who dislike the brand and never buy it are not likely to be influenced by any promotions and can be ignored. But consumers who never buy the brand but have a favorable (or at least neutral) attitude toward it are vulnerable to the company's promotions. Free samples, premiums, contests, or coupons might create an intention to try the brand and move consumers to an occasional user segment.

Occasional purchasers of the brand are vulnerable to the promotion strategies for competing brands. In that situation, marketers might have a promotion objective to encourage repeat purchases of the brand. A purchase plan such as offering a free donut after the consumer has bought 12 or a premium for saving proofs of purchase may be effective strategies. Or a firm might try to demonstrate the superiority of its brand over competing brands. For example, Burger King and Pepsi-Cola have used comparative advertising to "prove" their brand is better than McDonald's and Coca-Cola, respectively.[53]

Finally, brand-loyal consumers who like a company's brand and purchase it consistently can be influenced by promotions designed to keep them happy customers. The airlines have used a phenomenally successful promotion, frequent flyer programs, to reinforce the attitudes and purchase behavior of their frequent customers. Consumers rack up mileage on flights taken with the airline and receive free trips when sufficient mileage has been accumulated. The programs are supposed to be limited to frequent flyers, usually defined as those taking 12 or more plane trips per year. However, by 1984 an estimated 7 million Americans had enrolled in frequent-flyer programs, many more than the estimated 1 million frequent flyers. Currently, more than a third of air travelers are enrolled in four such programs — not exactly what the airlines had in mind when the promotion was begun.[54] In any case, these incentive programs have seemed so successful that they are being copied by hotels, car rental firms, restaurants, and other types of companies (see Highlight 18.5).

Phone calls by salespeople to "check on how things are going" may reinforce past customers' attitudes and intentions to rebuy when the need arises.

FIGURE 18.5
An Analysis of Consumer Vulnerability

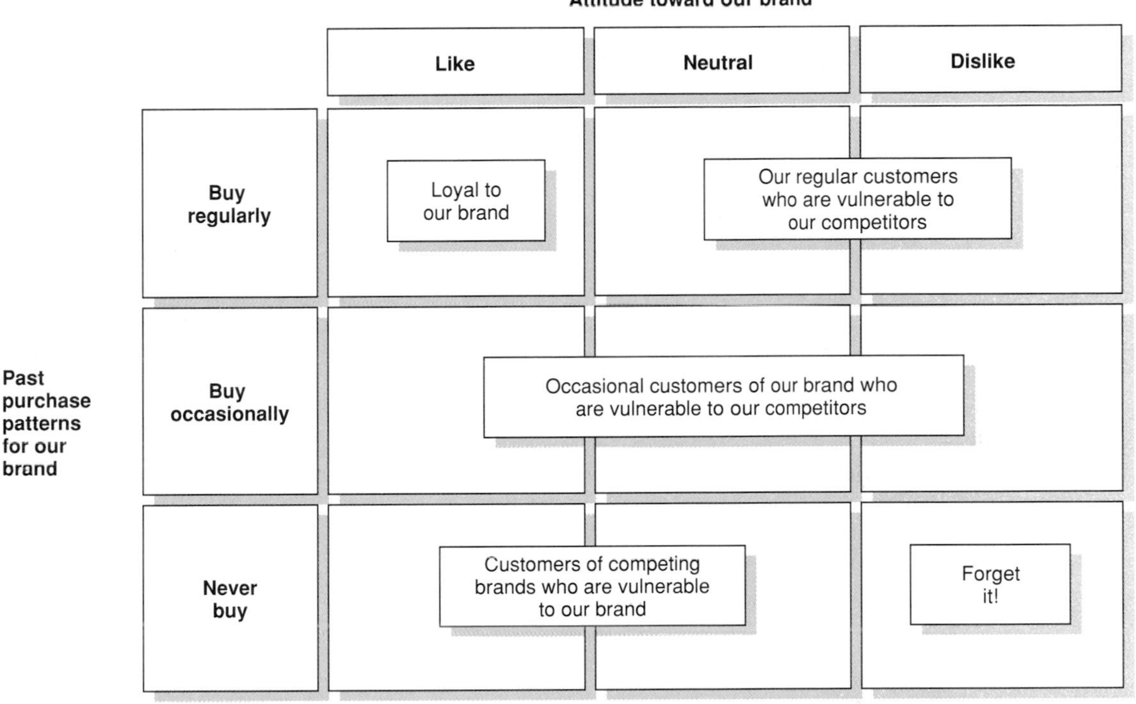

Source: Adapted from Yoram Wind, "Brand Loyalty and Vulnerability," in *Consumer and Industrial Buying Behavior:* ed. A. G. Woodside, J. N. Sheth, and P. D. Bennett (New York: North Holland Publishing, 1977), pp. 313–20.

When Joe Girard was the top car salesperson in the United States for 11 years in a row, he sent out over 13,000 cards to his customers each month, wishing them Happy New Year from Joe Girard, Happy St. Patrick's Day, and so on.[55] Finally, promotions can inform current consumers of new uses for existing products. Advertising campaigns promoted Saran Wrap for use in microwave cooking and Static Guard to eliminate static electricity from carpets around computers.

These brief examples illustrate three important points. First, appropriate promotions depend on the type of relationship consumers have with the product or brand, especially their intrinsic self-relevance.[56] Second, promotion methods vary in their effectiveness for achieving certain objectives. Personal selling, for example, is usually more effective for closing sales, while advertising is more effective for increasing brand awareness among large groups of consumers.

HIGHLIGHT 18.5

Promoting Customer Purchase Loyalty

For airlines, the concept of rewarding loyal customers with free flights has worked like a dream. American Airlines considers its frequent-flyer program "the single most successful marketing tool we've ever had." Now an increasing number of companies from banks to retailers to car rental agencies are trying to mimic the airline's success with frequent-buyer programs of their own. Under these plans, customers accumulate points, usually based on dollars spent, that can be cashed in for prizes or discounts.

Lester Wunderman, chairman of Young & Rubicam's direct marketing group, finds the trend refreshing. "The history of American marketing has been to breed disloyalty to get someone to try something new," he says. "These frequent-purchase programs are just the opposite. American business is beginning to understand the enormous profit leverage in loyalty."

But these clone programs may not be as successful as the frequent-flyer programs. Airlines can award free flights at minimal expense because planes often fly with vacant seats. Companies in other industries must devise rewards that tantalize consumers and figure ways of handling the record keeping without breaking the bank.

Neiman-Marcus, the upscale Dallas-based retailer, started its InCircle program in 1984 to differentiate itself from competitors such as Saks Fifth Avenue. Neiman offers relatively modest rewards. For $3,000 in annual purchases, customers receive periodic deliveries of chocolates. They get caviar for spending $12,000. The costs for administering the program are modest, too, because almost all participants use the Neiman charge card and thus are on its computer system. The program seemed to work—more InCircle customers remained high spenders than before the program was instituted.

Source: John Paul Newport, Jr., "Frequent-Flyer Clones," *Fortune,* April 29, 1985, p. 201.

Third, promotion objectives will change over a product's life cycle as changes occur in consumers' relationships with the product and the competitive environment.[57] The promotion strategy that worked well when the product was introduced is not likely to be effective at the growth, maturity, or decline stages.

Developing Advertising Strategy

An advertising strategy defines how a product or brand is meaningfully linked to the consumer.[58] Means-end chains provide a useful perspective for thinking about advertising strategy. The **MECCAS model** (*means-end chain conceptual-*

Promoting a new use for an existing product.

ization of advertising strategy) shown in Figure 18.6 defines four elements of advertising strategy and provides a brief description of each.[59] These four aspects of advertising strategy—the driving force, the leverage point, consumer benefits, and message elements—are based on analyses of consumers' means-end knowledge structures. The fifth component of the MECCAS model, the executional framework, refers to the details of the actual advertisement developed by the creative staff to communicate the four aspects of the ad strategy.

As you have learned, the first step in creating any marketing strategy is to understand the consumer/product relationship. Measuring consumers' means-end knowledge structures for the category or product form is useful for this purpose. The key attributes, consequences, and values important to a consumer in purchase may be identified in laddering studies (refer to Figure 4.6). Any means-end chain can be "translated" into a possible advertising strategy using the MECCAS model, but not all such strategies would be equally desirable.

Knowing which product attributes are salient for consumers helps marketers decide which information to include as *message elements* in the ad strategy. (Should the ads for Ruffles potato chips emphasize their flavor, their crunchiness, or their ridges?) Knowing which functional consequences are important to consumers helps marketers identify the key *consumer benefits* to be empha-

FIGURE 18.6
The MECCAS Model

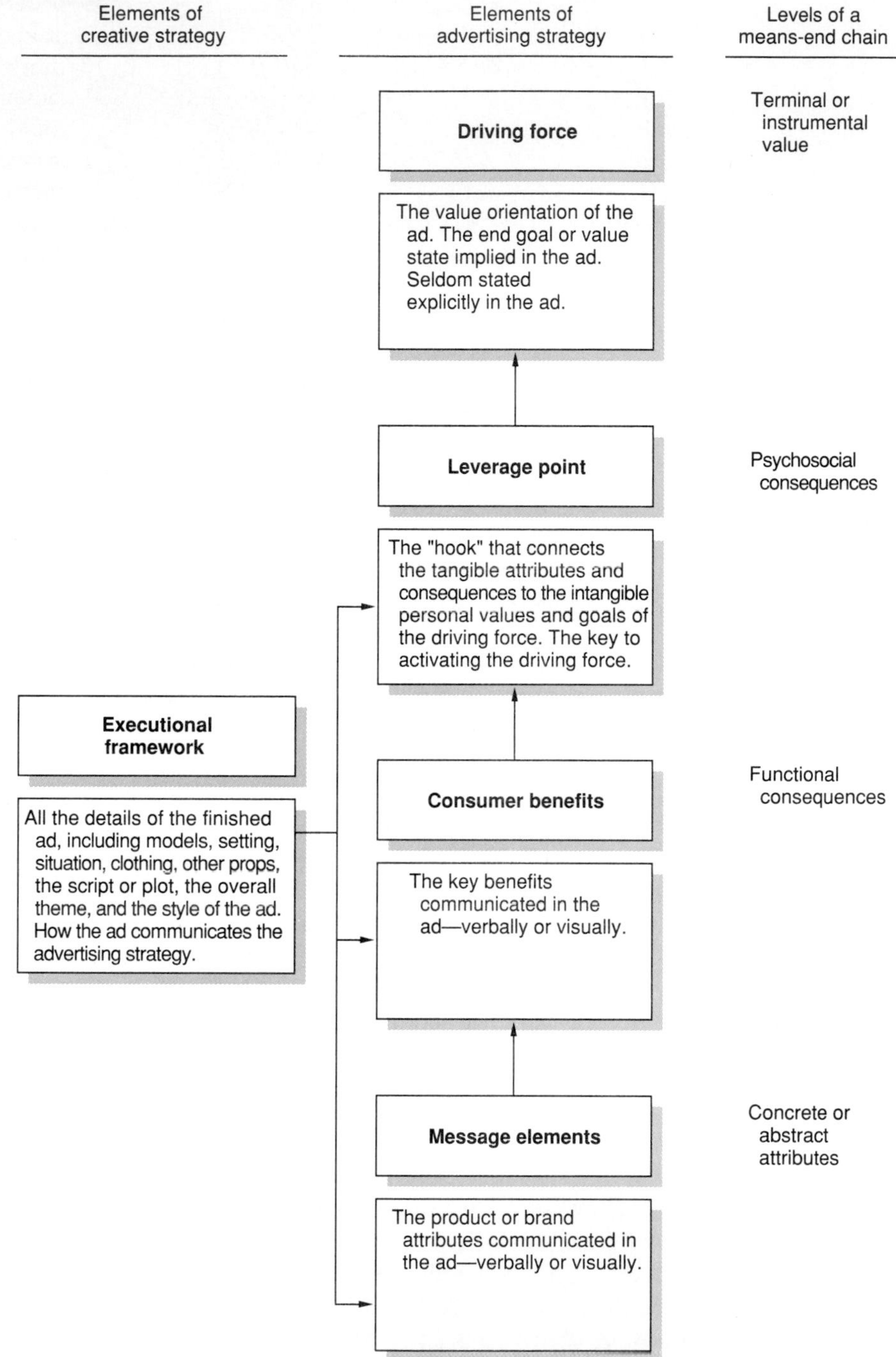

Source: Adapted from Jerry C. Olson and Thomas J. Reynolds, "Understanding Consumers' Cognitive Structures Implications for Advertising Strategies," in *Advertising and Consumer Psychology,* ed. Larry Percy and Arch Woodside (Lexington, Mass.: Lexington Books, 1983), pp. 77–90.

sized. (Are Ruffles chips for dipping or an accompaniment for sandwiches?) Ideally, these benefits should be linked by the ad to the salient attributes.

The *driving force* is the basic end goal or value communicated by the ad. However, this communication is usually indirect and somewhat subtle. End values are seldom mentioned explicitly in ads. That would be perceived as heavy-handed by most consumers, who might react negatively to being told what value they should be thinking of. Because values are in the consumer, they must be activated and "connected" to the more tangible attributes and consequences of the advertised brand. Once activated and linked to the brand, the emotional and motivational power of these desirable end goals or values create a self-relevant consumer/product relationship and provide a driving force for action, including purchase of the brand.

The fourth component of ad strategy is the important *leverage point* that links the relatively tangible message elements and consumer benefits of the product to the rather abstract driving force of values in the consumer. The leverage point is like a hook that reaches into the consumer and connects the product to the implied value orientation of the ad strategy. Often the leverage point is a representation or portrayal of an important psychosocial consequence of the advertised brand. Because consumers tend to automatically perceive the value states associated with psychosocial consequences, the ad does not have to explicitly mention the value state.

In sum, the advertising strategy defines how the ad will connect the brand to the important ends desired by the consumer to create a meaningful consumer/product relationship. The creative advertising team must then devise an ad that will communicate these meanings and the linkages between them in a persuasive manner. The *executional framework* refers to the various details of the ad execution (how it will be produced) that will effectively communicate the ad strategy. These decisions about the executional details (what type of models, how should they be dressed, what is the setting?) require creative imagination.

The MECCAS model does not make developing advertising strategies or creating specific ads easy or foolproof. Neither does the MECCAS model claim that all effective ads must contain all elements of the model. Rather, MECCAS is a convenient framework that organizes the aspects of ad strategy and provides a guide for the many decisions that must be made.[60]

The broad goal of advertising promotions is to create a meaningful consumer/product relationship. The MECCAS model can be quite useful in developing, analyzing, and evaluating advertising strategies. Marketers can use the MECCAS model to translate means-end chain data into possible ad strategies, which then can be evaluated for their competitive advantages. The MECCAS model can be used as a framework for evaluating one's current advertising to see what is being communicated and how the ads could be changed to be more persuasive. Competitor's ads can also be evaluated.[61] Finally, the MECCAS model could be used as a guide to measure how effectively an ad execution communicates the basic ad strategy.[62] The execution should communicate both the means-end chain levels of the ad strategy and the links between the levels. In sum, the MECCAS model is a useful framework for developing and evaluating potential advertising strategies.

Developing Personal Selling Strategies

The process of developing a personal selling promotion strategy is illustrated in Figure 18.7.[63] This is the **ISTEA model,** which stands for impression, strategy, transmission, evaluation, and adjustment. This model suggests salespeople's influence depends on their skills at performing five basic activities: (1) developing useful *impressions* of the customer, (2) formulating selling *strategies* based on these impressions, (3) *transmitting* appropriate messages, (4) *evaluating* customer reactions to the messages, and (5) making appropriate *adjustments* in presentation should the initial approach fail.

According to this model, the personal selling process works as follows:

> In the first activity, the salesperson combines information gained through past experience with information relevant to the specific interaction to develop an impression of the customer. Salespersons can derive information about their target customers by examining past experiences with this and other customers, by observing the target customer during an interaction, and by projecting themselves into the target customer's decision-making situation.
>
> In the second activity, the salesperson analyzes his/her impression of the customer and develops a communication strategy which includes an objective

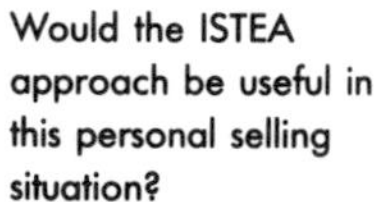
Would the ISTEA approach be useful in this personal selling situation?

FIGURE 18.7

A Model of the Personal Selling Process

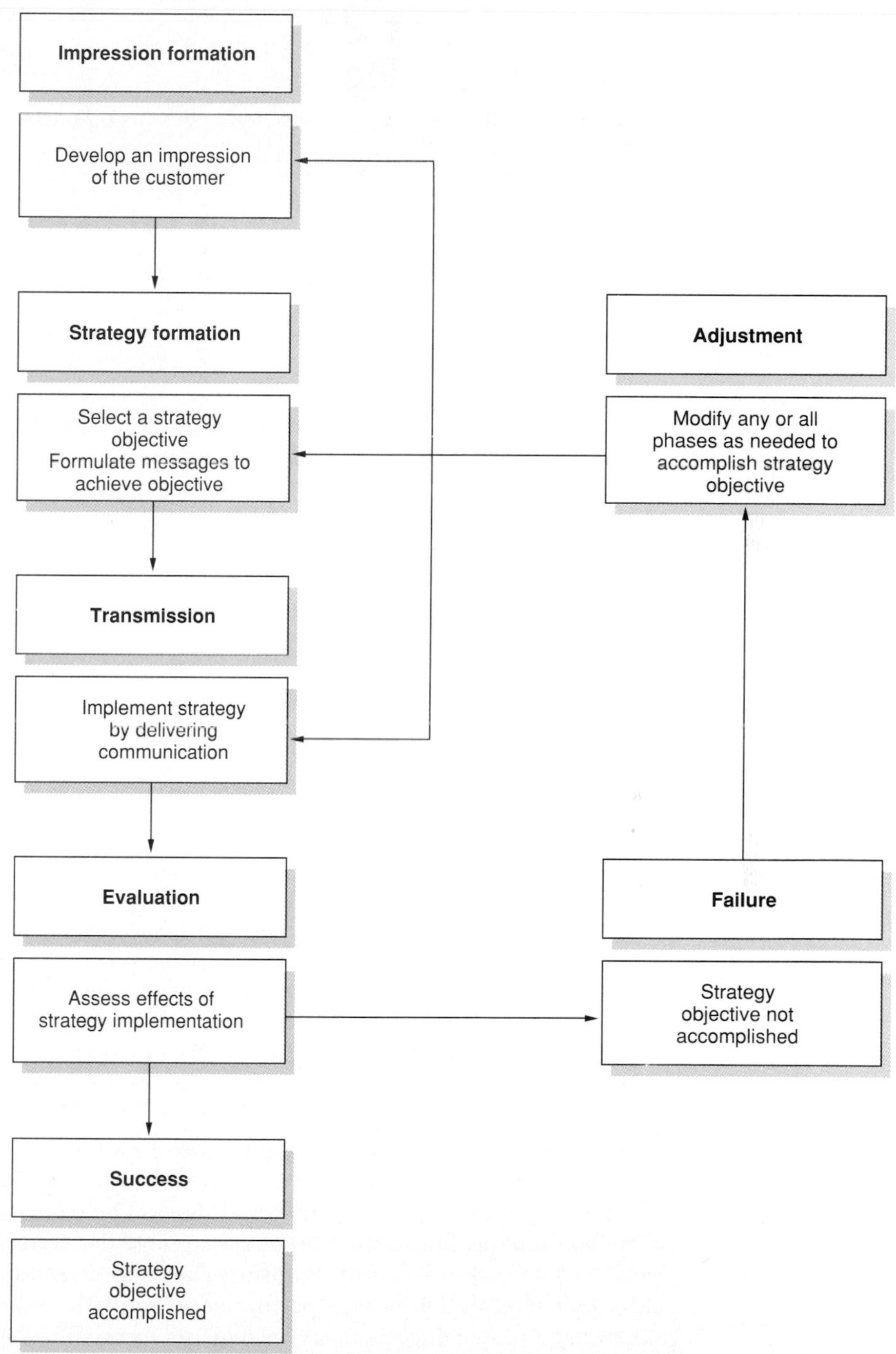

Source: Adapted from Barton A. Weitz, "Relationship between Salesperson Performance and Understanding Customer Decision Making," *Journal of Marketing Research* 15 (November 1978), p. 502. Published by the American Marketing Association.

HIGHLIGHT 18.6

Single-Source Advertising Research

Information Resources, Inc., knows what Paxton Blackwell of Williamsport, Pennsylvania, eats for breakfast, what television shows he watches, the coupons he uses, where he shops, the products and brands he buys, and which newspapers he reads. He says he doesn't mind the meters on his TV or the frequent surveys he fills out. Mr. Blackwell is a part of an evolving methodology called *single-source research*. This methodology could revolutionize the advertising research business and may be able to show how – or perhaps whether – advertising works to affect brand purchase choices.

Many companies are developing single-source research systems. As they become perfected, marketers will have powerful new methods for determining the effectiveness of advertising. For example, IRI, the pioneer of the methodology, monitors more than 3,000 households in eight small U.S. towns with cable TV service. Microcomputers record when the TV is on and what station it is tuned to. Thus, IRI knows which ads each household receives.

IRI is also able to send special test commercials over the cable channels in place of the regularly scheduled ads. When a member of the household checks out at the supermarket counter, he/she presents an ID card. As the selected items go through the scanner, the brand purchases (including package size, sale price, and number of units bought) are automatically recorded. IRI can then compare what products are bought against the ads

for the strategy; a method for implementing the strategy, and specific message formats.

Having formulated the strategy, the salesperson transmits the messages to the customer. As the salesperson delivers the messages, she/he evaluates their effects by observing the customer's reactions and soliciting opinions. On the basis of these evaluations, the salesperson can make adjustments by either reformulating the impression of the customer, selecting a new strategic objective, or changing the method for achieving the strategic objective, or the salesperson can continue to implement the same strategy.[64]

Although the ISTEA model was developed for industrial (business-to-business) marketing situations, it is consistent with the communication approach to consumer promotion discussed above. The model emphasizes analysis of the customer as the starting point for strategy development. Research confirms that impression formation (consumer analysis) and strategy formulation by salespeople improved their sales performance. Similarly, research on sales transactions in retail sporting goods stores suggests successful salespeople adapt their communication style to interact appropriately with customers.[65]

the consumer presumably saw. This is the basis for the name "single-source" – one method of tracking consumer behavior from ad exposure to brand purchase.

Of course, there are problems with the single-source system, not the least of which is figuring out how to analyze and summarize the mountains of data the system generates. In addition, single-source research can't tell who, if anyone, in the household actually saw each commercial. Moreover, there are so many other possible influences on purchase besides the advertisement that concluding an ad is solely responsible for a sale usually is not possible. Finally, and most important of all, single-source research does not answer the all-important question of *why* consumers purchase a particular brand.

Despite these drawbacks, however, the single-source systems can be very useful. Consider a demonstration study conducted in Denver by Arbitron Ratings Co., another supplier of single-source research data. Arbitron found that 18 percent of 200 test households had bought General Foods' Post Grape-Nuts cereal in the previous six-month period, placing the product fourth behind General Mills' Cheerios and Kellogg's Raisin Bran and Corn Flakes. But a closer look revealed these purchasers had bought only 40 ounces of Grape-Nuts out of an average total of 250 ounces during the period, well below average. This suggested a new ad strategy. General Foods could try to find current Grape-Nuts buyers and persuade them to buy and use more of the product. To make that possible, Arbitron discovered which television shows Grape-Nuts buyers tended to watch. Then it showed General Foods how to place ads on selected shows to reach many more of the target consumers with no increase in ad budget. With this kind of single-source data, General Foods was able to spend its promotional budget more effectively and precisely to communicate with the target audience.

Source: Felix Kessler, "High-Tech Shocks in Ad Research," *Fortune,* July 7, 1986, pp. 58–62; Joanne Lipman, "Learning about Grape-Nuts in Denver," *The Wall Street Journal,* February 16, 1988, p. 36; and Joanne Lipman, "Single-Source Ad Research Heralds Detailed Look at Household Habits," *The Wall Street Journal,* February 16, 1988, p. 36.

Evaluate Effects of Promotion Strategy

Evaluating the effects of a promotion strategy involves comparing its results with the objectives. While this might seem simple, determining promotion effects can be difficult. For example, even clearly stated cognitive objectives, such as "increase brand awareness by 25 percent," are not easily evaluated, since different methods of measuring awareness may give different results. Moreover, it is often difficult to determine whether a change in brand awareness resulted from the promotion strategy or from something else, such as word-of-mouth communications.

Similarly, promotion objectives stated in behavior terms – "increase sales by 10 percent" – can be hard to evaluate. It is often difficult to determine what factors caused a sales increase. Increases in competitors' prices, opening new territories and outlets, changes in consumers' attitudes, and various other factors may be responsible for the increase in sales. Likewise, if sales decrease or remain the same during the promotion period, it is difficult to determine whether the promotion strategy was ineffective or whether other factors were responsible.[66]

In other cases, however, evaluation of promotion effects can be relatively straightforward. Sales promotion tools such as coupons are used to stimulate short-term sales, and coupon redemption rates can give a good idea of effectiveness.[67] The dollar amounts sold by different salespeople can also be compared to determine their relative effectiveness. In sum, while measuring the effectiveness of promotion strategies may be difficult, marketers do have methods for estimating these effects.

Measuring Advertising Effects

Because the main immediate impact of advertising is on consumers' affective responses and cognitions, measuring the effects of advertising is difficult. However, because the costs of advertising are very high (an estimated $110 billion was spent in the United States in 1987), marketers are very interested in determining the communication effectiveness of their ads so they can be improved. A wide variety of approaches have been taken to measuring advertising effects, including *pretesting* (testing the effects of ads that are in rough, unfinished form before the ad is run in the natural environment) and *copy testing* (determining the meanings consumers derive from ads).[68]

Three broad criteria have been used as indicators of advertising effectiveness – sales, recall, and persuasion. Many researchers have tried to relate advertising to *sales* by measuring the aggregate purchase behavior of large groups of consumers who supposedly were exposed to the ads. Linking sales to advertising has proven quite difficult given the number of factors in addition to advertising that influence purchase behavior. However, current technology is moving marketers closer to the day when they may be able to relate advertising exposure to purchase of the product. Highlight 18.6 describes this technology.

Another common measure of ad effectiveness is consumers' *recall* of the ad, or some aspect of the ad. For example, in day-after recall studies, researchers telephone consumers the day after a TV commercial has run and ask them if they watched the TV program the previous evening. If so, consumers are asked if they remember any ads, and what they specifically recall about the ad in question. Only viewers who can remember a visual element or a sales message are counted as having recalled the ad. In 1988, the average ad received a recall rating of about 21 percent, down from about 24 percent in the late 1970s.[69] Of course, many ads score both lower and higher than that. Recall has been attacked for not really measuring the most important impacts of ads (such as creating product meanings or affective responses), but it can be an important objective in certain cases.[70] For ads that are intended primarily to enhance consumers' awareness of the brand, recall may be quite appropriate as a measure of effectiveness.

The third major criteria for advertising effectiveness is *persuasion.*[71] Most studies of persuasion measure whether consumers' comprehension of the ad produced changes (positive ones, preferably) in beliefs about the attributes or consequences of the product, brand attitudes *(A_o)*, attitudes toward buying the brand *(A_{act})*, or purchase intentions *(BI)*.[72] Another useful approach is to see if the ad created the desired means-end chains of product knowledge — that is, find out whether consumers formed an appropriate association between the brand and self-relevant ends.[73]

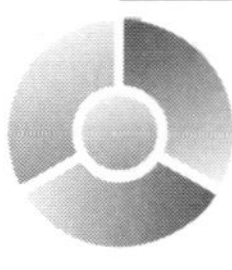

BACK TO.... THREE WINNING PROMOTION STRATEGIES

The opening example described three successful sales promotion strategies to change consumers' short-term behaviors. More recently, each of these companies has undertaken other sales promotion strategies. For instance, McDonald's ran a successful promotion during the 1988 Olympics, and its long-running sales promotion based on the game Monopoly was also successful in increasing store contacts and overall sales.

Although not mentioned in this example, these companies use other types of promotion strategies besides sales promotions, including advertising, personal selling, and publicity. All of these promotions create information in consumers' environments that may influence their behaviors (store visits or brand purchase) and affective and cognitive responses. Each type of promotion has unique advantages and disadvantages that must be considered in developing an overall mix of promotion strategies. In designing effective promotion strategies, marketers may make use of all the concepts that we discussed in the first four sections of this book.

Summary

This chapter discussed how knowledge about consumers' affect and cognitions, behaviors, and environments can be used by marketers to develop more effective promotion strategies. We began by describing four types of promotions—advertising, sales promotions, personal selling, and publicity. Then we detailed how the basic communication model can be used for thinking about promotions as marketing communications. Next we discussed some important aspects of the promotion environment (clutter and level of competition), affective and cognitive responses to promotions (attitudes toward the ad and persuasion processes), and promotion-related behaviors (information contact and word-of-mouth communication). Finally, we examined a managerial model for designing and executing promotion strategies. We described the various goals and objectives marketers may have for promotion strategies, and looked at two special models for developing advertising strategies and personal selling strategies. We concluded with a discussion of how to evaluate the effectiveness of promotion strategies.

Key Terms and Concepts

Promotions *604*
Advertising *605*
Sales Promotions *606*
Personal Selling *607*
Publicity *608*
Communication Process *610*
Promotion Clutter *618*
Attitude toward the Ad *620*
Central Route to Persuasion *622*
Peripheral Route to Persuasion *622*
Word-of-Mouth Communication *625*
Foote, Cone & Belding (FCB) Grid *627*
MECCAS Model *632*
ISTEA Model *636*

Review and Discussion Questions

1. As a consumer of fast-food products, evaluate the usefulness of promotion strategies to your decision processes. Do you side with the critics or the advocates?
2. Using the soft-drink industry as an example, define and illustrate each of the four major types of promotion strategies.

3. Are the major promotion methods equally effective in influencing high- and low-involvement decisions? Explain.

4. Select a specific advertisement or sales promotion strategy and evaluate it in terms of the elements of the communication model.

5. Describe how the two routes to persuasion differ and discuss their implications for developing effective advertising strategies.

6. Use the FCB grid model to illustrate consumer/product relationships for four products you have purchased in the last six months. Would this information be helpful to the promotion managers for these products?

7. Describe the MECCAS model for developing an effective advertising strategy. Illustrate the use of the model by suggesting a strategy for an athletic shoes promotion.

8. Do you agree with the suggestion that personal selling tends to create higher levels of felt involvement than other promotion strategies? How would your conclusion affect your use of the ISTEA model of personal selling (Figure 18.7)?

9. Identify a specific promotional strategy. Use the Wheel of Consumer Analysis model to analyze its effects on target consumers. Then suggest specific criteria that could be used to measure the effects of the promotion.

10. Suggest reasons for the increasing emphasis on sales promotion and publicity in the promotion mix of many marketing organizations.

NOTES

1. Felix Kessler, "The Costly Coupon Craze," *Fortune*, June 9, 1986, pp. 83–84; and Richard Gibson, "Recession Feeds the Coupon Habit," *The Wall Street Journal*, February 20, 1991, p. B1.

2. C. Whan Park, Bernard J. Jaworski, and Deborah J. MacInnis, "Strategic Brand Concept Image Management," *Journal of Marketing*, October 1986, pp. 135–45; and Thomas J. Reynolds and Jonathan Gutman, "Advertising Is Image Management," *Journal of Advertising Research*, February–March 1984, pp. 27–37.

3. Kevin Higgins, "Billboards Put Nike Back in the Running," *Marketing News*, June 7, 1985, p. 7.

4. For example, see Katherine E. Jocz, ed., *Research on Sales Promotion: Collected Papers* (Cambridge, Mass.: Marketing Science Institute, 1984); and James Cross, Steven W. Hartley, and Richard Rexeisen, "Sales Promotion: A Review of Theoretical and Managerial Issues," in *Marketing Communications—Theory and Research*, ed. Michael J. Houston and Richard J. Lutz (Chicago: American Marketing Association, 1985), pp. 60–64.

5. Kessler, "The Costly Coupon Craze," pp. 83–84.

6. "McDonald's Olympic Promotion Gets the Gold," *Marketing News*, June 7, 1984, pp. 12–13.

7. Ibid.

8. Mary Ann Falzone, "Survey Highlights Lower

Costs, Higher Productivity of Telemarketing," *Telemarketing Insider's Report* (Special Report, 1985), pp. 1–2.

9. Stewart W. Cross, "Can You Turn a 1985 Salesperson into a TSR?" *Telemarketing Insider's Report*, April 1985, p. 2.
10. David Einhorn, "Dynamo of Direct Sales," *Marketing Communications*, February 1982, pp. 12–14.
11. Higgins, "Billboards Put Nike Back in the Running," p. 7.
12. Bill Saporito, "Procter & Gamble's Comeback Plan," *Fortune*, February 4, 1985, pp. 30–37.
13. Michael Wahl, "Eye POPping Persuasion," *Marketing Insights*, 1989, pp. 130–34.
14. W. E. Philips, "Continuous Sales (Price) Promotion Destroys Brands: Yes," *Marketing News*, January 16, 1989, pp. 4, 8.
15. Bill Robinson, "Continuous Sales (Price) Promotion Destroys Brands: No," *Marketing News*, January 16, 1989, pp. 4, 8; and Chris Sutherland, "Promoting Sales Out of a Slump," *Marketing Insights*, Winter 1990, pp. 41–43.
16. Wahl, "Eye POPping Persuasion."
17. Joanne Lipman, "Ads on TV: Out of Sight, Out of Mind," *The Wall Street Journal*, 1991, pp. B1, B8.
18. Deborah J. MacInnis and Bernard J. Jaworski, "Information Processing from Advertisements: Toward an Integrative Framework," *Journal of Marketing*, October 1989, pp. 1–24.
19. Alan J. Bush and Gregory W. Boller, "Rethinking the Role of Television Advertising during Health Crises: A Rhetorical Analysis of the Federal AIDS Campaigns," *Journal of Advertising*, 20, no. 1 (1991), pp. 28–37.
20. This section is adapted from John R. Rossiter and Larry Percy, *Advertising and Promotion Management* (New York: McGraw-Hill, 1987), pp. 129–64.
21. Rao Unnava and Robert E. Burnkrant, "Effects of Repeating Varied Ad Executions on Brand Name Memory," *Journal of Marketing Research*, November 1991, pp. 406–16.
22. Kevin Lane Keller, "Memory and Evaluation Effects in Competitive Advertising Environments," *Journal of Consumer Research*, March 1991, pp. 463–76.
23. James R. Bettman, *An Information Processing Model of Consumer Choice* (Reading, Mass.: Addison Wesley, 1979).
24. Punam Anand and Brian Sternthal, "Ease of Message Processing as a Moderator of Repetition Effects in Advertising," *Journal of Marketing Research*, August 1990, pp. 345–53.
25. Banwari Mittal, "The Relative Roles of Brand Beliefs and Attitude toward the Ad as Mediators of Brand Attitude: A Second Look," *Journal of Marketing Research*, May 1990, pp. 209–19.
26. Cornelia Pechmann and David W. Stewart, "The Effects of Comparative Advertising on Attention, Memory, and Purchase Intentions," *Journal of Consumer Research*, September 1990, pp. 180–91.
27. Wahl, "Eye POPping Persuasion."
28. Aradhna Krishna, "Effect of Dealing Patterns on Consumer Perceptions of Deal Frequency and Willingness to Pay," *Journal of Marketing Research*, November 1991, pp. 441–51.
29. Wahl, "Eye POPping Persuasion."
30. See Peter H. Webb and Michael L. Ray, "Effects of TV Clutter," *Journal of Advertising Research*, June 1979, pp. 7–12.
31. Gibson, "Recession Feeds the Coupon Habit."
32. George E. Belch, "An Examination of Comparative and Noncomparative Television Commercials: The Effects of Claim Variation and Repetition on Cognitive Response and Message Acceptance," *Journal of Marketing Research*, August 1981, pp. 333–49; and Cornelia Droge and Rene Y. Darmon, "Associative Positioning Strategies through Comparative Advertising: Attribute versus Overall Similarity Approaches," *Journal of Marketing Research*, November 1987, pp. 377–88.
33. Cornelia Pechmann and S. Ratneshwar, "The Use of Comparative Advertising for Brand Positioning: Association versus Differentiation,"

Journal of Consumer Research, September 1991, pp. 145–60.

34. Richard L. Celsi and Jerry C. Olson, "The Role of Involvement in Attention and Comprehension Processes," *Journal of Consumer Research*, September 1988, pp. 210–24; Michael J. Houston, Terry L. Childers, and Susan E. Heckler, "Picture-Word Consistency and the Elaborative Processing of Advertisements," *Journal of Marketing Research*, November 1987, pp. 359–69; and Deborah J. MacInnis, Christine Moorman, and Bernard J. Jaworski, "Enhancing and Measuring Consumers' Motivation, Opportunity, and Ability to Process Brand Information from ads," *Journal of Marketing*, October 1991, pp. 32–53.

35. Alan G. Sawyer and Daniel J. Howard, "Effects of Omitting Conclusions in Advertisements to Involved and Uninvolved Audiences," *Journal of Marketing Research*, November 1991, pp. 467–74.

36. Mary Jane Schlinger, "A Profile of Responses to Commercials," *Journal of Advertising Research*, April 1979, pp. 37–46; and David A. Aaker and Douglas M. Stayman, "Measuring Audience Perceptions of Commercials and Relating Them to Ad Impact," *Journal of Advertising Research*, August–September 1990, pp. 7–18.

37. See Andrew A. Mitchell and Jerry C. Olson, "Are Product Attribute Beliefs the Only Mediator of Advertising Effects on Brand Attitude?" *Journal of Marketing Research*, August 1981, pp. 318–32; and Meryl Paula Gardner, "Does Attitude toward the Ad Affect Brand Attitude under a Brand Evaluation Set?" *Journal of Marketing Research*, May 1985, pp. 192–98.

38. Thomas J. Olney, Morris B. Holbrook, Rajeev Batra, "Consumer Responses to Advertising: The Effects of Ad Content, Emotions, and Attitude toward the Ad on Viewing Time," *Journal of Consumer Research*, March 1991, pp. 440–53.

39. Scott B. MacKenzie, Richard J. Lutz and George E. Belch, "The Role of Attitude toward the Ad as a Mediator of Advertising Effectiveness: A Test of Competing Explanations," *Journal of Marketing Research*, May 1986, pp. 130–43; Andrew A. Mitchell, "The Effect of Verbal and Visual Components of Advertisements on Brand Attitudes and Attitude toward the Advertisement," *Journal of Consumer Research*, June 1986, pp. 12–24; Pamela M. Homer, "The Mediating Role of Attitude toward the Ad: Some Additional Evidence," *Journal of Marketing Research*, February 1990, pp. 78–86; and Douglas M. Stayman and Rajeev Batra, "Encoding and Retrieval of Ad Affect in Memory," *Journal of Consumer Research*, May 1991, pp. 232–39.

40. Richard E. Petty, John T. Cacioppo, and David Schumann, "Central and Peripheral Routes to Advertising Effectiveness: The Moderating Role of Involvement," *Journal of Consumer Research*, September 1983, pp. 135–46.

41. Celsi and Olson, "The Role of Involvement; and Deborah J. MacInnis and C. Whan Park, "The Differential Role of Characteristics of Music on High- and Low-Involvement Consumers' Processing of Ads," *Journal of Consumer Research*, September 1991, pp. 161–73.

42. John L. Swasy and James M. Munch, "Examining the Target of Receiver Elaborations: Rhetorical Question Effects on Source Processing and Persuasion," *Journal of Consumer Research*, March 11, 1985, pp. 877–86.

43. H. Rao Unnava and Robert E. Burnkrant, "An Imagery-Processing View of the Role of Pictures in Print Advertisements," *Journal of Marketing Research*, May 1991, pp. 226–31.

44. Cornelia Droge, "Shaping the Route to Attitude Change: Central versus Peripheral Processing through Comparative versus Noncomparative Advertising," *Journal of Marketing Research*, May 1989, pp. 193–204.

45. David W. Schumann, Richard E. Petty, and D. Scott Clemons, "Predicting the Effectiveness of Different Strategies of Advertising Variation: A Test of the Repetition-Variation Hypotheses," *Journal of Consumer Research*, September 1990, pp. 192–202.

46. See Manoj Hastak and Jerry C. Olson, "Assessing the Role of Brand-Related Cognitive Responses as Mediators of Communication Effects on Cognitive Structure," *Journal of Consumer Research*, March 1989, pp. 444–56.

47. Barry L. Bayus, "Word of Mouth: The Indirect Effects of Marketing Efforts," *Journal of Advertising Research*, June–July 1985, pp. 31–39.

48. Jon Gutman, "Analyzing Consumer Orientations towards Beverages through Means-End Chain Analysis," *Psychology and Marketing*, 3/4 (1984), pp. 23–43.

49. See David Berger, "Theory into Practice: The FCB Grid," *European Research*, January 1986, pp. 35–46; Richard Vaughn, "How Advertising Works: A Planning Model," *Journal of Advertising Research*, October 1980, pp. 27–33; and Richard Vaughn, "How Advertising Works: A Planning Model Revisited," *Journal of Advertising Research*, February–March 1986, pp. 57–66.

50. Roberto Friedman and V. Parker Lessig, "A Framework of Psychological Meaning of Products," in *Advances in Consumer Research*, vol. 13, ed. Richard J. Lutz (Provo, Utah: Association for Consumer Research, 1986), pp. 338–42.

51. Julie A. Edell, "Nonverbal Effects in Ads: A Review and Synthesis," in *Nonverbal Communication in Advertising*, ed. David Stewart and Sidney Hecker (Lexington, Mass.: Lexington Books, 1988); Werner Kroeber-Riel, "Emotional Product Differentiation by Classical Conditioning," in *Advances in Consumer Research*, vol. 11, ed. Thomas C. Kinnear (Ann Arbor, Mich.: Association for Consumer Research, 1984), pp. 538–43; and Marian Chapman Burke and Julie A. Edell, "The Impact of Feelings on Ad-Based Affect and Cognition," *Journal of Marketing Research*, February 1989, pp. 69–83.

52. Meryl P. Gardner and Roger A. Strang, "Consumer Response to Promotions: Some New Perspectives," in *Advances in Consumer Research*, vol. 11, ed. Thomas C. Kinnear (Ann Arbor, Mich.: Association for Consumer Research, 1984), pp. 420–25.

53. Belch, "An Examination of Comparative and Noncomparative Television Commercials," pp. 333–49; and William L. Wilkie and Paul W. Farris, "Comparison Advertising: Problems and Potential," *Journal of Marketing*, October 1975, pp. 7–15.

54. Coleman Lollar, "From Sales Gimmick to Global Reality," *Frequent Flyer*, November 1984, pp. 75–85.

55. Thomas J. Peters and Robert H. Waterman, Jr., *In Search of Excellence: Lessons from America's Best-Run Companies* (New York: Warner Books, 1982), p. 158.

56. Celsi and Olson, "The Role of Involvement," pp. 210–24; and C. Whan Park and S. Mark Young, "Consumer Response to Television Commercials: The Impact of Involvement and Background Music on Brand Attitude Formation," *Journal of Marketing Research*, February 1986, pp. 11–24.

57. Marian C. Burke and Julie A. Edell, "Ad Reactions over Time: Capturing Changes in the Real World," *Journal of Consumer Research*, June 1986, pp. 114–18.

58. Thomas J. Reynolds and John P. Rochon, "Means-End Based Advertising Research: Copy Testing Is Not Strategy Assessment," *Journal of Business Research* 22 (1991), pp. 131–42.

59. Material for this section is derived from Jerry C. Olson and Thomas J. Reynolds, "Understanding Consumers' Cognitive Structures: Implications for Advertising Strategies," in *Advertising and Consumer Psychology*, ed. Larry Percy and Arch Woodside (Lexington, Mass.: Lexington Books, 1983), pp. 77–90.

60. Martin R. Lautman and Larry Percy, "Cognitive and Affective Responses in Attribute-Based versus End-Benefit Oriented Advertising," in *Advances in Consumer Research*, vol. 11, ed. Thomas C. Kinnear (Ann Arbor, Mich.: Association for Consumer Research, 1984), pp. 11–17; and Jerry C. Olson, "Meaning Analysis in Advertising Research," in *Advertising and Consumer Psychology*, vol. 3, ed. Jerry Olson and Keith Sentis (New York: Praeger, 1986), pp. 275–83.

61. For instance, see Thomas J. Reynolds and Alyce Byrd Craddock, "The Application of the MECCAS Model to the Development and Assessment of Advertising Strategy: A Case Study," *Journal of Advertising Research*, April–May 1988, pp. 43–54.

62. For example, see Thomas J. Reynolds and

Charles Gengler, "A Strategic Framework for Assessing Advertising: The Animatic vs. Finished Issue," *Journal of Advertising Research*, June–July 1991.

63. Barton W. Weitz, "Relationship between Salesperson Performance and Understanding of Customer Decision Making," *Journal of Marketing Research*, November 1978, p. 502. Also see Barton W. Weitz, "Effectiveness in Sales Interactions: A Contingency Framework," *Journal of Marketing*, Winter 1981, pp. 85–103. For other views on salesperson effectiveness, see David M. Szymanski, "Determinants of Selling Effectiveness: The Importance to the Personal Selling Concept," *Journal of Marketing*, January 1988, pp. 64–77; and Gilbert A. Churchill, Neil M. Ford, Steven W. Hartley, Jr., and Orville C. Walker, Jr., "The Determinants of Salesperson Performance: A Meta-Analysis," *Journal of Marketing Research*, May 1985, pp. 103–18.

64. Barton A. Weitz, Harish Sujan, and Mita Sujan, "Knowledge, Motivation and Adaptive Behavior: A Framework for Improving Selling Effectiveness," *Journal of Marketing Research*, October 1986, pp. 174–91.

65. Harish Sujan, "Smarter versus Harder: An Exploratory Attributional Analysis of Salespeople's Motivations," *Journal of Marketing Research*, February 1986, pp. 41–49; Kaylene C. Williams and Rosann L. Spiro, "Communication Style in the Salesperson-Customer Dyad," *Journal of Marketing Research*, November 1985, pp. 434–42; and Rosann L. Spiro and Barton A. Weitz, "Adaptive Selling: Conceptualization, Measurement and Nomological Validity," *Journal of Marketing Research*, February 1990, pp. 61–69.

66. Albert C. Bemmaor and Dominique Mouchoux, "Measuring the Short-term Effect of In-Store Promotion and Retail Advertising on Brand Sales: A Factorial Experiment," *Journal of Marketing Research*, May 1991, pp. 202–14.

67. Kapil Bawa and Robert W. Shoemaker, "The Effects of a Direct Mail Coupon on Brand Choice Behavior," *Journal of Marketing Research*, November 1987, pp. 370–76; P. S. Raju and Manoj Hastak, "Consumer Response to Deals: A Discussion of Theoretical Perspective," in *Advances in Consumer Research*, vol. 7, ed. Jerry C. Olson (Ann Arbor, Mich.: Association for Consumer Research, 1980), pp. 296–301; and Robert Blattberg, Thomas Biesing, Peter Peacock, and Subrata Sen, "Identifying the Deal Prone Segment," *Journal of Marketing Research*, August 1978, pp. 369–97.

68. For a review of various measures of advertising effectiveness, see David W. Stewart, Connie Pechmann, Srinivasan Ratneshwar, John Stroud, and Beverly Bryant, "Advertising Evaluation: A Review of Measures," in *Marketing Communications—Theory and Research*, ed. Michael J. Houston and Richard J. Lutz (Chicago: American Marketing Association, 1985), pp. 3–6. For a discussion of copy testing, see Benjamin Lipstein and James P. Neelankavil, "Television Advertising Copy Research: A Critical Review of the State of the Art," *Journal of Advertising Research*, April–May 1984, pp. 19–25; Joseph T. Plummer, "The Role of Copy Research in Multinational Advertising," *Journal of Advertising Research*, October–November 1986, pp. 11–15; and Harold M. Spielman, "Copy Research: Facts and Fictions," *European Research*, November 1987, pp. 226–31.

69. Jeffrey A. Trachtenberg, "Viewer Fatigue?" *Forbes*, December 26, 1988, pp. 120, 122.

70. Lawrence D. Gibson, "Not Recall," *Journal of Advertising Research*, February–March 1983, pp. 39–46; Herbert E. Krugman, "Low Recall and High Recognition of Advertising," *Journal of Advertising Research*, February–March 1986, pp. 79–86; and Jan Stapel, "Viva Recall: Viva Persuasion," *European Research*, November 1987, pp. 222–25.

71. Marvin E. Goldberg and Jon Hartwick, "The Effects of Advertiser Reputation and Extremity of Advertising Claim on Advertising Effectiveness," *Journal of Consumer Research*, September 1990, pp. 172–79.

72. Jerry C. Olson, Daniel R. Toy, and Phillip A. Dover, "Do Cognitive Responses Mediate the Effects of Advertising Content on Cognitive Structure?" *Journal of Consumer Research*, December 1982, pp. 245–62; Arno J. Rethans, John L. Swasy, and Lawrence J. Marks, "Effects of Television Commercial Repetition, Receiver

Knowledge, and Commercial Length: A Test of the Two-Factor Model," *Journal of Marketing Research*, February 1986, pp. 50–61; and Daniel R. Toy, "Monitoring Communication Effects: A Cognitive Structure/Cognitive Response Approach," *Journal of Consumer Research*, June 1982, pp. 66–76.

73. Jon Gutman and Thomas J. Reynolds, "Coordinating Assessment to Strategy Development: An Advertising Assessment Paradigm Based on the MECCAS Approach," in *Advertising and Consumer Psychology*, vol. 3, ed. Jerry Olson and Keith Sentis (New York: Praeger, 1987).

Additional Reading

For a discussion of how advertising works to affect consumers, see:

Batra, Rajeev, and Michael L. Ray. "How Advertising Works at Contact." In *Psychological Processes and Advertising Effects: Theory, Research, and Application*, ed. Linda Alwitt and Andrew A. Mitchell, Hillsdale, N.J.: Lawrence Erlbaum, 1985, pp. 129–55.

Mitchell, Andrew A. "Theoretical and Methodological Issues in Developing an Individual-Level Model of Advertising Effects." In *Psychology and Marketing*, vol. 3, ed. Jerry Olson and Keith Sentis. New York: Praeger, 1986, pp. 172–96.

For a discussion of how advertising interacts with direct personal experiences, see:

Deighton, John. "The Interaction of Advertising and Evidence." *Journal of Consumer Research*, December 1984, pp. 763–70.

For a discussion of how ads influence the product meanings consumers form, see:

Friedmann, Roberto, and Mary R. Zimmer. "The Role of Psychological Meaning in Advertising." *Journal of Advertising* 1 (1988), pp. 31–40.

For a discussion of the role of affective factors in consumers' responses to advertising, see:

Holbrook, Morris B., and John O'Shaughnessy. "The Role of Emotion in Advertising." *Psychology and Marketing*, Summer 1984, pp. 45–64.

For a discussion of subliminal advertising, see:

Saegert, Joel. "Why Marketing Should Quit Giving Subliminal Advertising the Benefit of the Doubt." *Psychology and Marketing* 2 (1987), pp. 107–20.

For a discussion of how sales promotions can be used by marketers of consumer products and services, see:

Hardy, Kenneth G. "Key Success Factors for Manufacturers' Sales Promotions in Package Goods." *Journal of Marketing*, July 1986, pp. 13–23.

For a discussion of the importance of brand awareness, see:

Moran, William T. "Brand Presence and the Perceptual Frame." *Journal of Advertising Research*, October–November 1990, pp. 9–16.

For a discussion of how advertising portrays women, see:

Richins, Marsha L. "Social Comparison and the Idealized Images of Advertising." *Journal of Consumer Research*, 1991, pp. 71–83.

For a discussion of how salespeople's knowledge influences their effectiveness, see:

Leong, Siew Meng, Paul S. Busch, and Deborah Roedder John. "Knowledge Bases and Salesperson Effectiveness: A Script-Theoretic Analysis." *Journal of Marketing Research*, May 1989, pp. 164–78.

Sujan, Harish, Mita Sujan, and James R. Bettman. "Knowledge Structure Differences between More Effective and Less Effective Salespeople." *Journal of Marketing Research*, February 1988, pp. 81–86.

For a discussion of how ads in the form of a drama (a play) can persuade consumers, see:

Deighton, John, Daniel Romer, and Josh McQueen. "Using Drama to Persuade." *Journal of Consumer Research*, December 1989, pp. 335–43.

For a discussion of how marketers might evaluate an entire advertising campaign, see:

Edell, Julie A., and Kevin Lane Keller. "The Information Processing of Coordinated Media Campaigns," *Journal of Marketing Research*, May 1989, pp. 149–63.

For a discussion of the role of humor in advertising, see:

Weinberger, Marc G., and Leland Campbell. "The Use and Impact of Humor in Radio Advertising." *Journal of Advertising Research*, December–January 1990/1991, pp. 44–51.

MARKETING STRATEGY IN ACTION

Promotional Battles in the Breakfast Cereal Market

The breakfast cereal market is one of the most fiercely competitive in the United States. Four companies control about 75 percent of this market—Kellogg, General Mills, General Foods (Post cereals), and Quaker Oats. Competition between these firms is characterized by new-product development and huge expenditures on various types of promotions, especially advertising. More so than most products, breakfast cereal is "marketing sensitive." That is, dollars spent on mediocre promotions simply fall into the void—they have no noticeable effect on consumers. But the same amount of money spent on a well-designed promotion strategy can dramatically increase sales and produce significant shifts in market shares.

In the early 1980s, Kellogg, the market leader, began to turn up the competitive heat by introducing a stream of new cereal products and substantially increasing promotion expenditures, especially on advertising. This resulted in a 4.5 percent increase in Kellogg's market share from its low of 36.7 percent in 1983 to 41.2 percent in 1988. During this period, the no. 2 company, General Mills, gradually increased its market share from 20 to 21 percent. In contrast, General Food's Post cereal division fared badly in this promotion competition—market share dropped from 16 percent in 1983 to 13.2 percent in 1988. These changes were not small. By 1988, the ready-to-eat cereal market in the United States was over $5 billion, so each share point was worth about $50 million in sales.

Post/General Foods. In 1983–1984, Post focused most of its advertising promotions on two brands. Fruit & Fiber was successful in attracting adult consumers, but Smurfberry Crunch, a kids' cereal, fizzled despite very heavy advertising spending. So when Kellogg began to step up its advertising expenditures (in 1984, for instance, Kellogg outspent Post by a 3-to-1 margin—$160 million to $52 million), Post had limited funds to counter. In addition, Post wasn't able to develop good advertising strategies, so it decided not to spend money to show ineffective ads. Instead, Post focused promotion strategies on cents-off coupons and discounts to grocers. This promotion mix strategy encouraged one-time sales, but did not build brand loyalty the way good advertising can.

In the mid-1980s, Post changed its promotion mix strategy by stepping up advertising promotions of five core brands—Raisin Bran, Grape Nuts, Fruit & Fiber, Super Golden Crisp, and

Pebbles – by over 40 percent. It also developed stronger advertising appeals. For instance, the Grape Nuts campaign, with its tag line "Are you right for Grape Nuts?" increased sales by 10 percent, compared to industry growth of only 3 percent. In addition, Post introduced a new cereal, Horizon, based on a trail mix concept of peanuts and grains clumped together (not in flakes). And Post reformulated Raisin Bran by removing preservatives, increasing the fiber, and taking the sugar off the raisins. To promote this "new" product in ads, Post hired singer John Denver, who represents to some people the essence of all that is wholesome.

The odds that these promotion strategies would be successful were not good. Of the dozens of product entries in recent years, only a few brands such as General Mills' Honey Nut Cheerios and Post's Fruit & Fiber have gained a sustainable 1 percent market share. In fact, despite these strong efforts, Post's share of the cereal market continued to decline. Its problems in part were due to the strong promotion strategies of General Mills, Quaker Oats, and Kellogg's, the primary competitors.

General Mills. From 1985 to 1987, General Mills introduced 6 new cereal products, giving it 28 brands in 1987. Although none were big hits, only one, Rocky Road, was an outright failure. In contrast, the usual failure rate for new grocery products is about 9 out of 10. In 1987, General Mills introduced a seventh new cereal brand. Total Oatmeal. This product was targeted directly at Quaker Oats, the leading company in the $500 million hot breakfast cereal market with a 68 percent share. General Mills promoted Total Oatmeal with a large budget, including a $12 million, six-month advertising campaign that claimed Total had "more nutrition than any other hot cereal." General Mills also distributed 175 million coupons for the product.

Quaker Oats. Quaker Oats (the fourth-largest cereal company in 1987 with an overall market share of 7.7 percent) countered with its own stepped-up advertising campaign communicating a "sensible nutrition" theme. Ads featured grandfatherly spokesperson Wilford Brimley, who claimed Quaker Oats is "the right thing to do." Quaker Oats' promotional strategy also included placing 12.5 million free samples of its instant oatmeal in boxes of its ready-to-eat cold cereal and a game promotion that gave away 1,500 Amana microwave ovens and 5,000 microwave cookbooks.

Kellogg. As the industry leader, Kellogg kept up the competitive pressure during the 1980s. Kellogg's marketing promotions were heavily oriented toward television advertising, although it supplemented the ads with standard sales promotion devices such as coupons and free samples. Most of Kellogg's new products were aimed at the 80 million health-oriented baby boomers (ages 25 to 49, the fastest-growing age segment in the United States). By encouraging these consumers to eat more breakfast cereal, Kellogg upped total consumption by 26 percent over 1983 levels. In fact, Kellogg's successful new adult-oriented products and very heavy promotion expenditures had increased the overall market for breakfast cereal to $5 billion by 1988. Do you remember Kellogg's 1984 campaign for Frosted Flakes—"Frosted Flakes have the taste adults have grown to love?" Previously a children's cereal, Frosted Flakes had become the No. 1 U.S. brand in 1988; Cheerios, a General Mills brand, was second.

Consider Kellogg's introduction of Müeslix in 1986. The product consisted of flakes, fruit, and nuts adapted from European-style cereals to appeal to American tastes. Kellogg's introduced Müeslix with a $33 million promotion budget, an industry record. Most of the money was spent on TV advertising, which featured misty morning scenes of rural Europe and Swedish actor Max Von Sydow touting "the centuries-old balance" of healthy ingredients as "what breakfast was meant to be." The product was an immediate success, garnering about $100 million in sales the first year, even though it cost considerably more (per ounce) than Corn Flakes.

Further growth in breakfast cereal is likely to come mainly from international markets. Curiously, in terms of breakfast cereal consumption, the United States comes in fourth at 9.6 pounds per person per year (in 1988), after the Irish, British, and Australians. The average breakfaster in the rest of the world eats less than two pounds of cereal per year. To change the cognitions and behaviors of these people, you can be sure U.S. breakfast cereal companies like Kellogg's, General Mills, Quaker Oats, and Post will be spending heavily on promotion strategies.

Discussion Questions

1. Present your intuitions about the consumer/product relationship for two key segments of the breakfast cereal market—kids (ages 8 to 16) and maturing baby boomers (ages 25 to 49). If accurate, what implications would your analyses have for designing effective marketing promotions?
2. Find a current print ad for an adult-oriented breakfast cereal. Identify the means-end chains of product knowledge it is trying to communicate. Analyze the advertisement using the MECCAS model described in the text (identify the driving force, message elements, leverage point, etc.), and critique this promotion strategy.
3. Discuss how the goals and objectives of brand-oriented advertising differ from sales promotion strategies (such as coupons, price reductions, prizes, and premiums) when promoting new brands of breakfast cereal. Under what marketing circumstances would each be appropriate?
4. Use the Wheel of Consumer Analysis to discuss the long-run implications of using the different approaches to promotion. What are relative long-term advantages and disadvantages of weighting advertising or sales promotions more heavily in the promotion mix?
5. Why do you think the breakfast cereal market is so "marketing sensitive?" Why does the market respond to good marketing promotions and not at all to poor promotions?

Sources: Patricia Sellers, "How King Kellog Beat the Blahs," *Fortune,* August 9, 1988, pp. 54–64; Pamela Sherrid, "Fighting Back at Breakfast," *Forbes,* October 7, 1985, pp. 126–30; and Steve Weiner, "Food Fight," *Forbes,* July 27, 1987, pp. 86–87.

Consumer Behavior and Pricing Strategy

CHAPTER 19

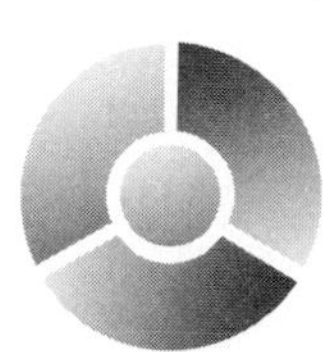

VINNIE BOMBATZ

Vinnie Bombatz is a construction worker who makes $12 per hour. While he could work overtime on Saturday at $18 per hour, he takes off two consecutive Saturdays to go fishing.

Vinnie is a heavy drinker . . . of Diet Pepsi. On the morning of his first Saturday off, he walks two blocks to a convenience food store to purchase a 12-pack for his fishing trip. The price is $5 plus 5 percent sales tax. Vinnie complains about the high price and is told by the clerk: "I don't set the prices. Take it or leave it, Jack!" Vinnie is more than a little upset, but he pays the money because he's in a rush to get to the lake. He vows to himself never to get ripped off like this again. He walks home. The whole trip has taken 10 minutes.

On the next Saturday, Vinnie again needs a 12-pack of Diet Pepsi for his fishing trip. Remembering his previous experience at the convenience store, he decides to get in his car and drive six miles to the discount supermarket. He is pleasantly surprised that Diet Pepsi is on sale for $2.99 a dozen plus tax. Although the store is a bit crowded and it takes him a while to get through the checkout, he drives home feeling good about the purchase and the money he saved. This shopping trip takes 45 minutes.

On which Saturday did Vinnie get a better price? In several ways, *price* is the most unusual element of the marketing mix. For one thing, it is the only one that involves revenues; all of the other elements, as well as marketing research, involve expenditures of funds by organizations. Another difference is that although price may seem tangible and concrete, it is perhaps more intangible and abstract than other elements of the marketing mix.

For example, in the product area, consumers often have a tangible product to examine, or at least information about a service to evaluate. In the promotion area, consumers have magazine and newspaper ads and information from salespeople to see, listen to, and evaluate. In the distribution area, consumers have malls and stores to experience. However, the price variable is a rather abstract concept that, while represented as a sign or tag, has relatively little direct sensory experience connected with it. Perhaps because of this, basic research on pricing issues in marketing has been relatively modest compared to work done on the other marketing mix elements.

These differences should not lead you to underestimate the importance of price to marketing and consumer behavior, however. For example, Rao states:

> The effects of price changes are more immediate and direct, and appeals based on price are the easiest to communicate to prospective buyers. However, competitors can react more easily to appeals based on price than to those based on product benefits and imagery. It can be argued that the price decision is perhaps the most significant among the decisions of the marketing mix (strategy) for a branded product.[1]

In this chapter, we focus on some important relationships among consumer affect, cognitions, behaviors, and the environment as they relate to the price variable of the marketing mix. These variables and relationships are shown in Figure 19.1, which provides an overview of the topics to be discussed. We begin our discussion by offering a conceptual view of the role of price in marketing exchanges. We then discuss price affect and cognitions, behaviors, the environment, and, finally, pricing strategy.

Conceptual Issues in Pricing

From a consumer's point of view, *price* is usually defined as what the consumer must give up to purchase a product or service. Research typically views price only in terms of dollar amount asked or paid for an item or service. Because we believe price is a pivotal element in the exchange process, we offer a conceptual view of price that encompasses more than dollar amount or financial cost to the consumer. Our discussion is intended to help you better understand the role of price in marketing strategy development.

Figure 19.2 offers a general model of the nature of marketing exchanges and highlights the role of price in this process. Although we will focus on for-profit

FIGURE 19.1
The Wheel of Consumer Analysis: Pricing Strategy Issues

organizations, the model could be developed and discussed in terms of nonprofit marketing. The major differences in nonprofit exchanges are that (1) while nonprofit organizations may seek money from consumers, they (at least in theory) do not seek surplus funds beyond costs, and (2) the value derived by consumers in nonprofit exchanges is often less tangible.

Figure 19.2 identifies four basic types of consumer costs: money, time, cognitive activity, and behavior effort. These costs, when paired with whatever value or utility the product offers, are a convenient way to consider the meaning of price to the consumer. While we do not argue that consumers finely calculate each of these costs for every purchase, we do believe they are frequently considered in the purchase of some products.

In Figure 19.2 we have also divided marketing costs into the four categories of production, promotion, distribution, and marketing research. Most business costs and investments could be attributed to one or another of these categories. These costs, when paired with the desired level of profit a firm seeks, offer a convenient way to consider the marketing side of the exchange equation. Basically, the model implies products must usually cover at least variable costs

FIGURE 19.2
The Pivotal Role of Price in Marketing Exchanges

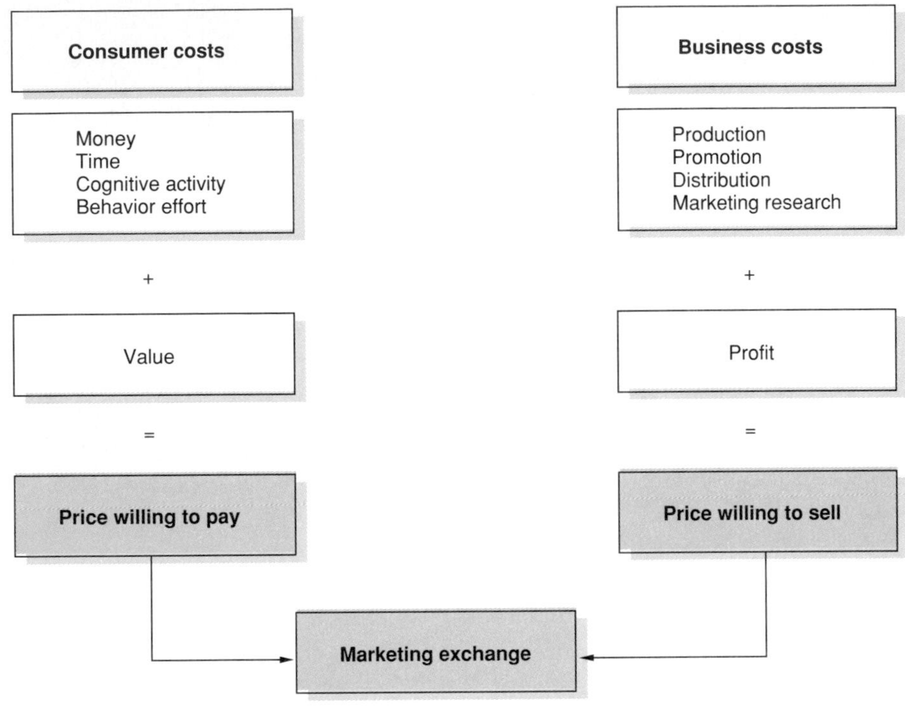

and make some contribution to overhead or profits for the offering to be made to the marketplace.

For marketing exchanges to occur, the price consumers are willing to pay must be greater than or equal to the price at which marketers are willing to sell. However, while this may seem simple enough, a number of complex relationships need to be considered when pricing is viewed from this perspective. Of major importance is the nature of consumer costs and the relationships between them. What should become clear is that the dollar price of an item may often be only a part of the total price of an exchange for the consumer.

MONEY

As we have noted, most pricing research has focused only on *money*—the dollar amount a consumer must spend to purchase a product or service. This research has recognized that the same dollar amount may be perceived differently by different individuals and market segments, depending on income levels and

A marketing strategy to reduce several consumer costs.

other variables. However, several important aspects of the dollar cost of offerings are not always considered. One of these concerns the *source* of funds for a particular purchase. We suspect that money received as a tax rebate, gift, interest, or as gambling winnings has a different value to many consumers than money earned through work. Consequently, the dollar price of a particular item may be perceived differently by the same individual, depending on what sources of funds are used to pay for it.

Similarly, the actual price of a credit-card purchase that will be financed at 22 percent for an extended period is much different from the price if cash is used. To consumers who are accustomed to carrying large credit-card balances, this difference may be irrelevant; to others, the difference may forestall or eliminate a purchase. In addition, the type of work consumers do may affect how valuable a particular amount of money is to them—as well as affecting their willingness to spend that money on particular products and services.

A number of methods can reduce the dollar amount spent for a particular item, although they often involve increasing other costs. For example, time, cognitive activity, and behavior effort are required to clip and use coupons or mail in for rebates. Shopping at different stores seeking the lowest price involves not only time, cognitive activity, and behavior effort, but also increases other dollar costs such as transportation or parking. Highlight 19.1 lists tactics marketers use to lower prices.

HIGHLIGHT 19.1

Some Short-Term Price Reduction Tactics

1. Cents-off deals: "Package price is 20¢ off."
2. Special offers: "Buy one, get one free"; "Buy three tires and get the fourth free."
3. Coupons: Store or manufacturer coupons in newspaper, magazines, flyers, and packages.
4. Rebates: Mail in proof-of-purchase seals for cash or merchandise.
5. Increase quantity for same price: "2 extra ounces of coffee free."
6. Free installation or service for a limited time.
7. Reduce or eliminate interest charges for a limited time: "90 days same as cash."
8. Special sales: "25 percent off all merchandise marked with a red tag."

Time

The *time* necessary to learn about a product or service and to travel to purchase it, as well as time spent in a store, can be important costs to the consumer. Most consumers are well aware that convenience food stores usually charge higher prices than supermarkets. Many convenience food stores are very profitable, for most consumers purchase from them at least occasionally. Clearly, these consumers often make a trade-off of paying more money to save time, particularly if only a few items are to be purchased. Time savings may result because the convenience outlets are located closer to home and thus require less travel time or because less time is required in the store to locate the product and wait in line to pay for it. Given the high cost of operating an automobile, it might even be cheaper in dollar terms to shop at stores that are closer to home, even if they have higher prices! Thus, bargain hunters who travel all over town to save 25 cents here and 50 cents there may be fooling themselves if they think they are saving money.

However, we should not treat time only as a cost of purchasing. In some situations, the process of seeking product information and purchasing products is a very enjoyable experience—rather than a cost—for consumers. Many consumers enjoy Christmas shopping and spend hours at it, for instance. Some consumers enjoy window-shopping and purchasing on occasion, particularly if the opportunity cost of their time is low. In areas that offer shopping on Sunday, some consumers prefer going to the mall rather than sitting at home watching football games. Similarly, some consumers enjoy spending hours looking through catalogs of their favorite merchandise. Thus, while in an absolute sense consumers must spend time to shop and make purchases, in some cases this may be perceived as a benefit rather than a cost.

Cognitive Activity

One frequently overlooked cost of making purchases is the *cognitive activity* involved. Thinking and deciding what to buy can be very hard work. For example, when all of the styles, sizes, colors, and component options are considered, one Japanese manufacturer offers over 11 million variations of custom-made bicycles. Consumers would never evaluate all 11 million options, but consider the cognitive activity required to evaluate even a small fraction of them. Clearly, it would not only take a lot of time, but it would also be very taxing in terms of cognitive work.[2] Yet, if even a few comparisons are made, some cognitive effort must be expended.

In addition to all of the cognitive work involved in comparing purchase alternatives, the process can also be stressful. Some consumers find it very difficult and dislike making purchase (or other types of) decisions. To some, finding parking spaces, shopping in crowded malls and stores, waiting in long checkout lines, and viewing anxiety-producing ads can be a very unpleasant experience emotionally. Thus, the cognitive activity involved in purchasing can be a very important cost.

The cost involved in decision making is often the easiest one for consumers to reduce or eliminate. Simple decision rules or heuristics can reduce this cost considerably. By repeatedly purchasing the same brand, consumers can practically eliminate any decision making within a product class, for example. Other heuristics might be to purchase the most expensive brand, the brand on sale or display, the brand mom or dad used to buy, the brand a knowledgeable friend recommends, or the brand a selected dealer carries or recommends.

On the other hand, there are some situations in which consumers actively seek some form of cognitive involvement. Fishing enthusiasts frequently enjoy comparing the attributes of various types of equipment, judging their relative merits, and assessing the ability of different equipment to catch fish. We suspect that while consumers may enjoy periods in which they are not challenged to use much cognitive energy or ability, they may also seek purchasing problems to solve as a form of entertainment.

Behavior Effort

Anyone who has spent several hours walking around in malls can attest to the fact that purchasing involves *behavior effort*. When large shopping malls were first developed, one of the problems they faced was that consumers had long walks from the parking lot and considerable distance to cover within the mall itself. Many consumers were not physically comfortable with this much effort, and some avoided malls or shopped in only a small number of the stores available. Benches and chairs were placed in malls primarily to overcome this problem by giving consumers places to rest while shopping.

As with time and cognitive activity, behavior effort can also be a benefit rather than a cost. For example, walking in malls and stores is good exercise and is sometimes done as a source of relaxation. Some malls have started early-morning mall-walking programs for senior citizens. These programs may create a positive image for malls and bring in potential buyers.

Perhaps the most interesting aspects of behavior effort is the willingness of consumers to take on some marketing costs to reduce the dollar amount they spend and to make trade-offs among various types of costs. In some cases, consumers will perform part of the production process to get a lower dollar price. For example, consumers may forgo the cost of product assembly for bicycles and toys and do it themselves to save money. Heathkits produces a large line of electronic gadgets that are cheaper but must be assembled by the consumer.

There are also cases in which consumers will take on at least part of the cost of distribution to lower the dollar price. At one time, for example, it was common for milk to be delivered to the home; now most consumers purchase it at stores. Consumers with access to a pickup truck frequently bring home their own furniture and appliances rather than pay a store for delivery. Catalog purchases require the consumer to pay the cost of shipping directly, yet may be less expensive than store purchases. If they are not, the consumer at least saves shopping time and effort to have the product delivered to the home. As we noted earlier in the text, consumers will also perform promotion and marketing research for firms to receive lower prices or other merchandise "free."

A final trade-off of interest in terms of pricing concerns the degree to which consumers participate in purchase/ownership. Consumers have several options with regard to purchase: (1) they can buy the product and enjoy its benefits as well as incur other costs such as inventory and maintenance; (2) they can rent or lease the product and enjoy its benefits but forgo ownership and often reduce some of the other costs, such as maintenance; (3) they can hire someone else to perform whatever service the product is designed to perform and forgo ownership and other postpurchase costs; or (4) they can purchase the product and hire someone else to use and maintain it for them. For many durable goods, such as automobiles, appliances, power tools, furniture, and lawn mowers, at least several of these options are available. Clearly, as we stated at the beginning of the chapter, price is a lot more than just dollars and cents!

VALUE

We have discussed four aspects of price from the consumer's point of view. We have suggested that consumers can sometimes reduce one or more of these costs, but this usually requires an increase in at least one of the other costs. Purchases can be viewed in terms of which of the elements is considered a cost or a benefit and which is considered most critical for particular purchases. However, regardless of what cost trade-offs are made, it seems that whatever is being purchased must be perceived to be of greater *value* to the consumer than merely the sum of the costs. In other words, the consumer perceives that the purchase offers benefits greater than the costs and is willing to exchange to receive these benefits.

Creating perceptions of value.

First QUALITY... then PRICE, and only then VALUE!

Our now-famous $21.50 Oxford: An incredible value! Quality is expressed here in the 100% cotton Oxford cloth, given a neat, soft, button-down collar. Long tails stay put, generous cut comforts. 4 no-nonsense colors, plus blend version that needs no ironing.

The Squall™ jacket, family-priced from $39.50. From tot-hood to adult-hood, the same quality fabric and tailoring. 3-ply (not 2-ply) Supplex® shell. Polartec® lining. Thinsulate® in sleeves staves off wince. No finer quality anywhere. Believe it!

The Original Attache: half-a million now tour the world! $39.50 a copy. Its 18-oz. quality canvas bends and stretches to hold more than it's meant to. Makes no pretentious statements. Just does the job superbly.

From the very first, we at Lands' End have been obsessed with a first-come, first-serve commitment to quality, in every piece of merchandise we offer. Once that is in hand, we can consider price, meaningfully. If the price we must ask to enjoy a fair profit truly reflects that quality and still represents an attractive buy, we have a Lands' End value which we GUARANTEE. PERIOD.®

Elsewhere on this page, each in its own way, typical Lands' End products proclaim their quality. Perhaps in the fabric they're made of, the tailoring of that fabric, or sometimes even the range of colors and the fastness of a dye. Whatever. Please examine these offerings, if you will. Hopefully, they may prompt you to send for our latest catalog, crammed with hundreds of additional items, all subjected to our rigid quality standards and – because we're Direct Merchants, with no middlemen to answer to–blessed with a realistic pricing policy hard to match elsewhere. Just fill out the coupon.

Hopefully, even as we speak.

Just $18 buys you a genuine mesh knit classic! Shop around–comparable shirts run $40 and up. Yet this one is pre-treated against shrinkage. Collar won't rip out, or curl. Buttons cross-stitched on for keeps. "Cool" in every meaning of the word.

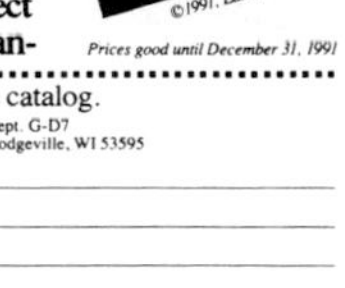

©1991, Lands' End, Inc.

Prices good until December 31, 1991

Write for free catalog.
Lands' End Dept. G-D7
1 Lands' End Lane, Dodgeville, WI 53595

Name ______
Address ______
City ______
State ______ Zip ______

While this view of price is useful, we want to restate that consumers seldom (if ever) finely calculate each of these costs and benefits in making brand level decisions. Rather, for many types and brands of consumer packaged goods, the amounts of money, time, cognitive activity, and behavior effort required for a purchase are very similar. For these goods, choices between brands may be made on the basis of particular benefits or imagery, although price deals may be important.

For some purchases, all of the costs and trade-offs may be considered by consumers. Yet, the major importance of our view of price is not the degree to which consumers actively analyze and compare each of the costs of a particular exchange. Instead, this view is important because it has direct implications for the design of marketing strategy, as discussed later in the chapter.

Price Affect and Cognitions

As we noted, typically little sensory experience is connected with the price variable. Yet information about prices is often attended to and comprehended,

HIGHLIGHT 19.2

Some Different Terms for Dollar Price

Alternative Terms	What Is Given in Return
Price	Most physical merchandise
Tuition	College courses, education
Rent	A place to live or the use of equipment for a specific period
Interest	Use of money
Fee	Professional services (lawyers, doctors, consultants, etc.)
Fare	Transportation (air, taxi, bus, etc.)
Toll	Use of road or bridge, or long-distance phone rate
Salary	Work of managers
Wage	Work of hourly workers
Bribe	Illegal actions
Commission	Sales effort

Source: From page 576, *Principles of Marketing,* 3rd ed. by Thomas C. Kinnear and Kenneth L. Bernhardt. Copyright © 1990 by Scott, Foresman and Company. Reprinted by permission.

and the resulting meanings may influence consumer behavior. For some purchases, consumers may make a variety of price comparisons among brands and evaluate trade-offs among the various types of consumer costs and values. At a minimum, consumers must learn and understand the many different terms used to designate price, such as those shown in Highlight 19.2.

There have been several attempts to summarize the research on the effects of price on consumer affect and cognitions and behavior, but these reviews have found few generalizations.[3] For example, it has long been believed that consumers perceive a strong relationship between price and the quality of products and services. Experiments typically find this relationship when consumers are given no other information about the product except dollar price. However, when consumers are given additional information about products (which is more consistent with marketplace situations), the price/quality relationship is diminished.

In general, all of these reviews conclude that research on the behavioral effects of pricing has not been based on sound theory, and that most of the studies are seriously flawed methodologically. Thus, it should not be surprising that there is little consensus on basic issues of how price affects consumer choice processes and behavior.

PRICE PERCEPTIONS AND ATTITUDES

Price perceptions are concerned with how price information is comprehended by consumers and made meaningful to them. One approach to understanding price perceptions is information processing, which has been advocated by Jacoby and Olson.[4] An adaptation of this approach is outlined in Figure 19.3.

This model illustrates an approach to describing price effects for a high-involvement product or purchase situation. Basically, it suggests price information is received through the senses of sight and hearing. The information is then comprehended, which means it is interpreted and made meaningful (i.e., consumers understand the meaning of price symbols through previous learning and experience).

In the cognitive processing of price information, consumers may make comparisons between the stated price and a price or price range they have in mind for the product. The price they have in mind for making these comparisons is called the **internal reference price.** The internal reference price may be what consumers think is a fair price, what the price has been historically, or what consumers think is a low market price or a high market price. Basically, an internal reference price serves as a guide for evaluating whether the stated price is acceptable to the consumer or not.[5] For example, a consumer may think 50 cents is about the right price to pay for a candy bar. When a vending machine offers candy bars for 75 cents, the internal reference price may inhibit purchase because the asking price is too high.

The stated price for a particular brand may be considered a product attribute. This knowledge may then be compared with the dollar prices of other brands in a product class, other attributes of the brand and other brands, and other consumer costs. Finally, an attitude is formed toward the various brand alternatives.

For a low-involvement product or purchase situation, dollar price may have little or no impact on consumer affect and cognitions or behaviors. For many products, consumers may have an implicit price range, and as long as prices fall within it, price is not even evaluated as a purchase criterion. Similarly, some products are simply purchased without ever inquiring as to the price but simply paying whatever is asked for at the point of purchase. Impulse items located in the checkout area of supermarkets and drugstores may frequently be purchased this way, as might other products for which the consumer is highly brand loyal. In the latter cases, consumers may make purchases on the single attribute of brand name without comparing dollar price, other consumer costs, or other factors.

In other cases, price information may not be carefully analyzed because consumers have a particular price image for the store they are shopping in.

FIGURE 19.3

Conceptual Model of Cognitive Processing of Price Information

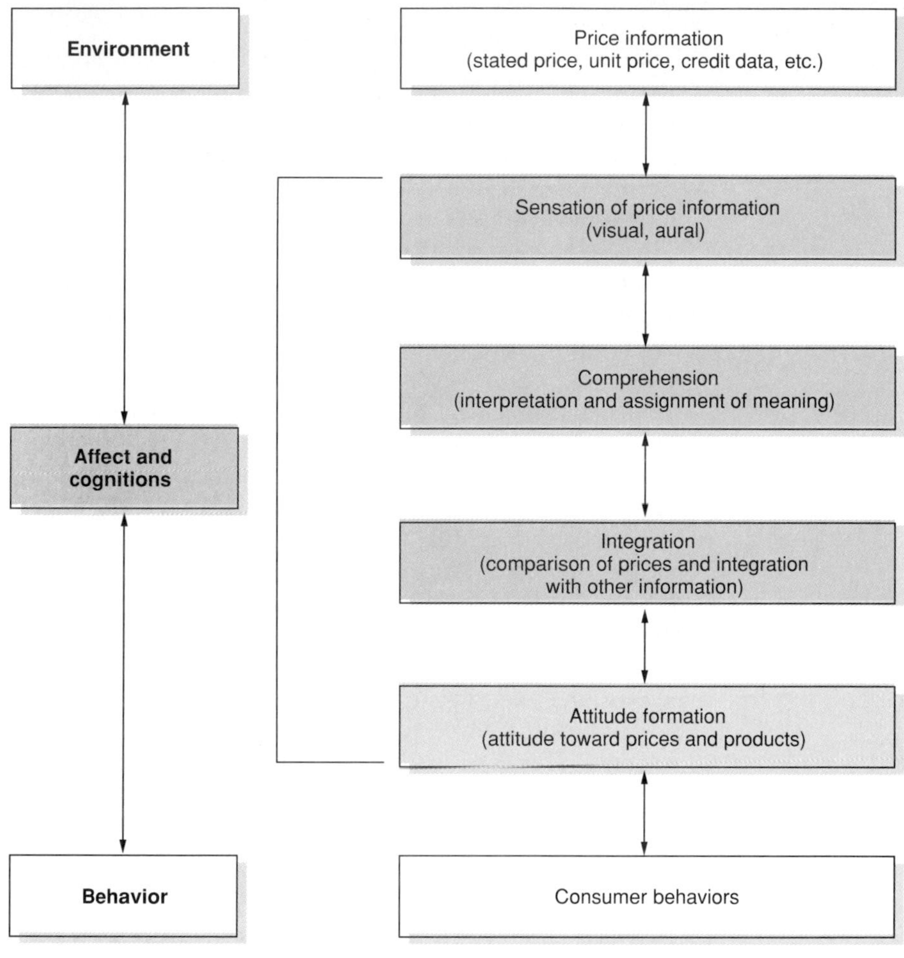

Discount stores such as Wal-Mart or Shopko may be generally considered low-priced outlets, and consumers may forgo comparing prices at these outlets with those at other stores.

Consumers often do not carefully store detailed price information in memory, even for products they purchase. For example, in a study of grocery shoppers, the researchers concluded:

> What is surprising is just how imperfect [price] information attention and retention are at the very point of purchase. The fact is that less than half of the shoppers could recall the price of the item they had just placed in their shopping basket, and less than half were aware they had selected an item that was selling at a reduced price. Only a small minority of those who bought a special knew both its price and the amount of the price reduction.[6]

There are good reasons many consumers do not carefully store in memory the prices of individual products. Consumers probably do not want to exert the considerable effort necessary to obtain, store, and revise prices for the many products they buy. For many purchases, other than using coupons or haggling, consumers must pay the stated price or forgo purchase. Thus, if they choose to purchase, the price is uncontrollable by them and it may make little sense to carefully store price information when it has little impact on saving money. In sum, the cognitive activity costs, behavior effort costs, and time costs involved in storing price information and shopping carefully are often not worth expending to save a few dollars.

Price Behaviors

Depending on the consumer, the product and its availability in various stores and other channels, and other elements of the situation, price could affect a variety of consumer behaviors. Two types of behaviors are of particular relevance to the price variable: funds access and transaction.

Funds Access

One source of embarrassment for most of us as consumers is to arrive at the point in the purchase process where we have to produce funds for an exchange and realize we do not have sufficient funds available. Not having enough money at the grocery checkout counter and having to replace several items can be embarrassing, particularly when the total amount of money needed is quite small! Similarly, it is embarrassing to bounce a check, to have a credit-card purchase refused because we have exceeded our limit, or to be refused a purchase because of a poor credit rating. For these reasons, most of us are likely to plan for funds access to ensure sufficient funds are available when we go shopping.

As we have noted previously, there are many ways consumers can access funds. First, many consumers carry a certain amount of cash to pay for small purchases. This cash supply may be replenished as needed for day-to-day activities. Second, many consumers also may carry checkbooks (or at least a few blank checks) in case a need arises for a larger amount of money. Third, millions of Americans carry credit cards to handle purchases. Although the interest rates on credit cards may be high, this method of accessing funds is very popular.

We suspect credit-card purchases and payments are not only convenient for the consumer but also may make the purchase seem less expensive. This is because consumers do not see any cash flowing from their pockets or a reduction in their checkbook balances, but merely need to sign their names and not even think about payment until the end of the month. In one sense, if no balance is carried over on the credit card, the purchase is "free" for the time between the exchange and the payment. We suspect that while many consumers may keep tabs on their checkbook balance, they may be less concerned throughout the month with their credit-card balances—unless, they are close to their credit limits.

Credit cards also facilitate purchasing because little effort is required to access funds. Even going to a bank to cash a check before shopping requires more effort than using a credit card. Thus, overall, the use of credit cards may reduce consumers' time, cognitive activity, and behavior effort costs.

Transaction

The exchange of funds for products and services is typically a relatively simple transaction. It usually involves handing over cash, filling out a check, signing a credit slip, or signing a credit contract and following up by making regular payments.

However, as we have emphasized throughout this chapter, consumers exchange much more than simply money for goods and services. They also exchange their time, cognitive activity, and behavior effort—not only to earn money, but also to shop and make purchases. Thus, analysis of these elements, and of the value consumers receive in purchase and consumption, may provide better insights into the effects of price on consumer behavior.

Price Environment

As we stated at the beginning of the chapter, price is perhaps the most intangible element of the marketing mix. From an environmental perspective, this means the price variable typically offers very little for the consumer to experience at the sensory level, although it may generate considerable cognitive activity and behavior effort. In the environment, price is usually a sign, a tag, a few symbols on a package, or a few words spoken on TV, on radio, or by a salesperson in a store or on the phone. The price variable also includes purchase contracts and credit-term information.

The price variable may also include an external reference price. An **external reference price** is an explicit comparison of the stated price with another price in advertising, catalog listings, price guides, on shopping tags and store displays, or in sales presentations. For example, the stated price may be compared with the seller's former price ("$11.95, marked down from $15.00"), with the manufacturer's suggested retail price ("Manufacturer's suggested retail price – $50, on sale today for $39.95"), or with prices at competing stores ("$54.95, lowest price in town"). External reference prices are used to enhance the attractiveness of the stated price.[7]

One area that has been the subject of consumer research on price information in the environment is **unit pricing.** Unit pricing is common for grocery products and involves a shelf tag that indicates the price per unit for a specific good. For example, a 13-ounce can of Hills Brothers electric perk coffee that sells for $3.69 might include a shelf tag that indicates it costs $.284 per ounce. This information is designed to help shoppers make more informed purchases in comparing various brands and package sizes.

One interesting study of unit pricing replicated a previous study conducted 10 years earlier in two Safeway stores in the Washington, D.C., area.[8] This study found an increase in the use of unit-pricing information by consumers over the 10-year period, in both a city and a suburban store. In the city store, usage of unit prices increased from 24.8 percent of consumers to 33.1 percent; in the suburban store, usage increased from 37.6 to 59.9 percent. Thus, while usage of unit-price information increased over the 10-year period, considerably more suburban shoppers used unit prices than did city shoppers.

Differences were also found between awareness and comprehension of unit pricing in the suburban versus the city store, as well as the use of that information to compare and switch between package sizes and brands. This study demonstrates there are differences in the effects on consumer affect, cognitions, and behaviors of various types of price information in the environment.

How price information is communicated also has an effect. For example, the advent of scanner checkout systems has reduced price information in the environment for many grocery products, because prices are no longer stamped on each package or can. A study by Zeithaml found that having each item marked increased consumers' certainty of price recall and decreased errors in both exact price and unit-price recall.[9] The study also found some differences in the impacts of shelf price tags, supporting the idea that not only the price itself but also the method by which price information is communicated influences consumer affect, cognitions, and behaviors.

Pricing Strategy

Pricing strategy is of concern in three general situations: (1) when a price is being set for a new product, (2) when a long-term change is being considered for an established product, and (3) when a short-term price change is being consid-

FIGURE 19.4
A Strategic Approach to Pricing

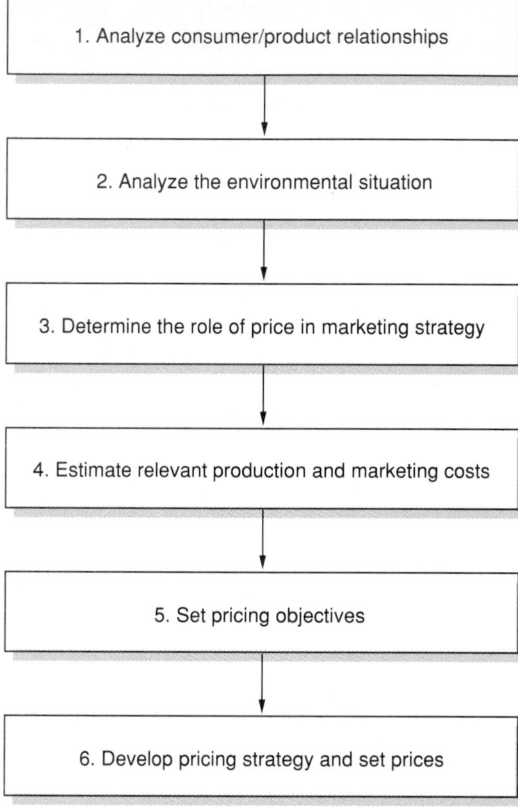

ered. Marketers may change prices for a variety of reasons, such as an increase in costs, a change in the price of competitive products, or a change in distribution channels.

Many models have been offered to guide marketers in designing pricing strategies.[10] Most of these models contain very similar recommendations and differ primarily in terms of how detailed the assumptions are, how many steps the pricing process is divided into, and in what sequence pricing tasks are recommended. For our purposes, we have developed a six-stage model, which is shown in Figure 19.4. Our model differs from traditional approaches primarily in that greater emphasis is placed on consumer analysis and greater attention is given to the four types of consumer costs in developing pricing and marketing strategies.

FIGURE 19.5
Relative Consumer Costs for Various Pizza Product Forms

Cost	Pizza Mix	Frozen Pizza	Pizzeria Pizza Home Delivery
Money	Low	Middle	High
Time	High	Middle	Low
Cognitive activity	High	Middle	Low
Behavior effort	High	Middle	Low
Value: Taste	Worst	Middle	Best

The six stages in our strategic approach to pricing are discussed below. Although consumer analysis is not the major focus in all of them, our discussion is intended to clarify the role of consumer analysis in pricing and to offer a useful overview of the pricing process.

Analyze Consumer/Product Relationships

Pricing strategy for a new product generally starts with at least one given: the firm has a product concept or several variations of a product concept in mind. When a price change for an existing product is being considered, typically much more information is available, including sales and cost data.

Whether the pricing strategy is being developed for a new or existing product, a useful first stage in the process is to analyze the consumer/product relationships. Answers must be found for questions such as: How does the product benefit consumers? What does it mean to them? In what situations do they use it? Does it have any special psychological or social significance to them? Of course, the answers to these questions depend on which current or potential target market are under consideration.

A key question that must be answered honestly is whether the product itself has a clear differential advantage that consumers would be willing to pay for, or whether a differential advantage must be created on the basis of other marketing mix variables. This question has important implications for determining which of the four areas of consumer costs (time, money, cognitive activity, or behavior effort) can be appealed to most effectively.

Suppose a firm is considering marketing pizza for home consumption and is analyzing consumer/product relationships. The firm is considering three forms of pizza and, after considerable research, has developed the data presented in Figure 19.5. This type of analysis illustrates several important concepts. First, it is clear that consumers of the three types of pizza make trade-offs in the costs they are willing to incur. Consumers of pizza made from a mix are willing to spend a greater amount of time, cognitive activity, and behavior effort to save money, and may get a poorer-tasting pizza. Consumers of pizzeria pizza, on the other hand, are willing to pay a higher dollar price to reduce these other costs and may get a better-tasting pizza.

Second, this analysis has clear implications for segmentation. It is important to determine the size of the markets for the different forms, their demographic profiles, and the degree of market overlap. That is, are these different consumer groups or are they the same consumers who eat different types of pizza in different situations?

Third, while this analysis has a number of implications for all facets of marketing strategy, our focus is on the implications for pricing. The question of what pizza means to consumers is critical for determining appropriate pricing strategies. For example, the pizza-mix market is apparently very price sensitive. Thus, while a reduction of the other types of consumer costs or an increase in value (taste) may offer market opportunities, the dollar price of the mix would likely have to remain low. Perhaps the consumer/product relationship could be summarized as "Pizza is a low-dollar-cost, filling meal."

The frozen-pizza consumer apparently values having the product on hand—and while willing to make some trade-offs, wants a better-tasting pizza. This market is not as price sensitive as the pizza-mix market and likely considers preparation effort an important cost. Thus, within the frozen-pizza market, consumers may pay a higher dollar cost for better-tasting pizza or pizza that can be prepared more quickly and easily (e.g., microwave pizza). Perhaps the consumer/product relationship could be summarized as "Pizza is a quick meal or relatively tasty snack."

The consumer of home-delivered pizzeria pizza likely focuses strongly on taste and convenience and is not highly price sensitive. Thus, taste, ingredients, and fast delivery are worth a higher price. Note, however, that even a price of $10 or $15 is inexpensive for a family meal when compared to the price of going to a nice restaurant. Perhaps the consumer/product relationship could be summarized as "Pizza is a delicious meal, and it sure beats cooking."

This brief example illustrates an approach to evaluating the relationships between consumers and products. One of the important outcomes of this analysis is an estimate of how sensitive consumers are to various dollar prices, other costs being relatively the same. In economics, this is called **price elasticity,** which is a measure of the relative change in demand for a product for a given change in dollar price. Once the firm has a clear idea of these relationships and opportunities, it can then focus attention on other aspects of the environment.

Analyze the Environmental Situation

There is no question that a firm must consider elements of the environment—economic trends, political views, social changes, and legal constraints—when developing pricing strategies. These elements should be considered early in the process of formulating any part of marketing strategy and should be monitored continually. By the time a firm is making pricing decisions, many of these issues have already been considered. While this may also be true for competitive analysis, consideration of competition at this point is critical for developing pricing strategies.

In setting or changing prices, the firm must consider its competition and how that competition will react to the price of the product. Initially, consideration should be given to such factors as:

1. Number of competitors.
2. Market share of competitors.
3. Location of competitors.
4. Conditions of entry into the industry.
5. Degree of vertical integration of competitors.
6. Financial strength of competitors.
7. Number of products and brands sold by each competitor.
8. Cost structure of competitors.
9. Historical reaction of competitors to price changes.

Analysis of these factors helps determine whether the dollar price should be at, below, or above competitors' prices. However, this analysis should also consider other consumer costs relative to competitive offerings. Consumers often pay higher dollar prices to save time and effort.

Determine the Role of Price in Marketing Strategy

This step is concerned with determining whether the dollar price is to be a key aspect of positioning the product or whether it is to play a different role. If a firm is attempting to position a brand as a bargain product, then setting a lower dollar price is clearly an important part of this strategy. Barbasol shaving cream positions itself as just as good as but half the price of the other brands, for example. Similarly, if a firm is attempting to position a brand as a prestige, top-of-the-line item, then a higher dollar price is a common cue to indicate this position. Chivas Regal scotch has long used this approach, for example. The success of these types of strategies also depends on analyzing the trade-offs with other elements of consumer costs.

In many situations, dollar price may not play a particularly important positioning role other than in terms of pricing competitively. If consumers enjoy greater convenience in purchasing (e.g., free delivery), or if the product has a clear differential advantage, the price may be set at or above those of the competition but not highlighted in positioning strategy. In other cases, when the price of a product is higher than that of the competition but there is no clear differential advantage, the price may not be explicitly used in positioning. For

A pricing strategy for positioning a prestige product.

example, premium-priced beers do not highlight price as part of their appeal. Highlight 19.3 discusses several other marketing strategy dimensions of pricing.

Estimate Relevant Production and Marketing Costs

The costs of producing and marketing a product effectively provide a very useful benchmark for making pricing decisions. The variable costs of production and marketing usually provide the lowest dollar price a firm must charge to make an offering in the market. However, there are some exceptions to this rule. These exceptions typically involve interrelationships among products. For example, a firm may sell its cameras below cost to sell a greater volume of film, or a grocery store may sell an item below cost (i.e., a loss leader) to build traffic and increase sales of other items.

Set Pricing Objectives

Pricing objectives should be derived from overall marketing objectives, which, in turn, should be derived from corporate objectives. In practice, the most common objective is to achieve a target return on investment. This objective has the advantage of being quantifiable, and it also offers a useful basis for making not only pricing decisions but also decisions on whether to enter or remain in

HIGHLIGHT 19.3

Some Things to Know for Pricing Decisions . . .

Know your customers and markets.

Know your product and competitive products.

Know your costs and objectives.

Know your environment and situation.

. . . And Some Pricing No-Nos

Price fixing – conspiring with competitors to fix prices.

Deceptive pricing – pricing practices that mislead consumers, such as marketing items with a fictitious price, crossing this price out, and then putting on the normal price as though it were a bargain.

Predatory pricing – setting prices low to drive out competitors and then raising the prices.

Price discrimination – charging similar, competing channel members different prices, which lessens competition or tends to create a monopoly.

FIGURE 19.6
Some Potential Pricing Objectives

1. Increase sales.
2. Target market share.
3. Maximum long-run profits.
4. Maximum short-run profits.
5. Growth.
6. Stabilize market.
7. Desensitize customers to price.
8. Maintain price-leadership arrangement.
9. Discourage entrants.
10. Speed exit of marginal firms.

specific markets. For example, if a firm demands a 20 percent return on investment, and the best estimates of sales at various prices indicate a product would have to be priced too high to generate demand, then the decision may be to forgo market entry. Other types of pricing objectives are listed in Figure 19.6.

Develop Pricing Strategy and Set Prices

A thorough analysis in the preceding stages should provide the information necessary to develop pricing strategies and set prices. Basically, the meaning of the product to the consumer and consumer costs have been analyzed. The environment has been analyzed, particularly competition. The role of pricing marketing strategy has been determined. Production and marketing costs have been estimated. Pricing objectives have been set. The pricing task now is to determine a pricing strategy and specific prices that are (1) sufficiently above costs to generate the desired level of profit and achieve stated objectives, (2) related to competitive prices in a manner consistent with the overall marketing and positioning strategy, and (3) designed to generate consumer demand based on consumer cost trade-offs and values.

In some cases, prices may be developed with a long-run strategy in mind. For example, a **penetration price policy** may include a long-run plan to sequentially raise prices after introduction at a relatively low price, or a **skimming price policy** may include a long-run plan to systematically lower prices after a high-price introduction.

However, most price changes occur as a result of a change in consumers, the environment, competition, costs, strategies, and objectives. A dramatic example of the relationships among these variables can be found in the pricing of airfares.

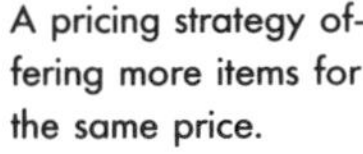
A pricing strategy offering more items for the same price.

HIGHLIGHT 19.4

Increasing Consumer Prices

The price consumers pay for products can be increased in a number of ways. Prices can be increased for the same quantity and quality or maintained for less quantity, less quality, or fewer auxiliary services. Price deals could be reduced or eliminated or interest rates and charges could be increased. Recently, a number of marketers have focused their pricing strategies on the second option, maintaining the same price but offering less quantity. Below are several examples of the use of this strategy.

Brand	Product	It Looks Like . . .	You Pay . . .	But You Get . . .
Knorr	Leek soup and recipe mix	More: Box is 1/2" deeper	The same	Less: Makes three 8-oz. servings, reduced from four
StarKist	Canned tuna	A bit less: Can is 1/16" less tall	The same	Less: Weight of tuna reduced by 3/8 oz., or 5.8%
Lipton	Instant lemon-flavored tea	The same	The same	Less: Weight reduced by 7.5%; company claims it contains same number of servings as before
Brim	Decaffeinated coffee	The same	The same	Less: Weight reduced by 4.2%; company claims it contains same number of servings as before

Source: David E. Kalish, "Prices Stable, but Products Are Less Filling," *Wisconsin State Journal*, January 6, 1991, p. 1D.

Before deregulation, prices were set by the Civil Aeronautics Board. Price increases were the result of petitions to this agency based on evidence of increased costs of operation. Thus, price was not a very important competitive weapon, as all carriers charged the same fare for the same route. Shortly after deregulation, however, price became a most critical competitive tool—and, in fact, in some periods up to 5,000 price changes were made in a single day! Major carriers attempted to compete with low-price "no-frills" airlines by lowering the price on competitive routes and raising the price on routes the low-price airlines did not serve. In addition, the major carriers engaged in efforts to cut costs to try to be more competitive with the no-frills airlines. Consumers had a basic choice between attempting to minimize dollar cost by spending more time shopping for low prices, forgoing some flexibility in departure times and dates, and giving up some additional services versus paying full fare and receiving these benefits. Business travelers often paid the higher full-fare price, while leisure travelers spent the time and effort necessary to get cheaper fares.

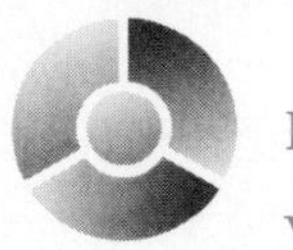

BACK TO.... VINNIE BOMBATZ

When considering only the money cost of the Diet Pepsi, at first glance it may appear that the supermarket price is better: $2.99 plus $.15 tax, which equals $3.14, versus the convenience store price of $5 plus $.25 tax, which equals $5.25.

Now let's consider the cost of operating Vinnie's car. Assume it costs $.20 per mile; driving 12 miles thus equals $2.40. The supermarket purchase now costs Vinnie $3.14 plus $2.40, which equals $5.54—more than the convenience store price of $5.25.

Next, it seems reasonable to estimate the cost of Vinnie's time. Several rates could be considered. While his market value for this time is $18 per hour, when considering taxes and other deductions Vinnie does not take home the full amount. Let's assume he takes home $9 per hour and agree this is the value of the time to Vinnie.

The convenience-store trip had a time cost of 10 minutes (at $9 per hour, which equals $1.50, for a total of $5.25 plus $1.50, which equals $6.75. The supermarket trip has a time cost of 45 minutes at $9 per hour, which equals $6.75, for a total of $5.54 plus $6.75, which equals $12.29. The convenience store trip now appears to be a real bargain!

Finally, let's consider how Vinnie felt about the two trips and what he experienced. In terms of cognitive activity, the convenience

This example illustrates how a change in the environment (deregulation) led to a change in competitors (entrance of no-frills airlines), which led to a change in pricing strategies (price cuts for some seats but overall attempts to maximize revenues per flight) and cost-cutting efforts. Many consumers also changed as they became more involved in the purchase of airline tickets and perhaps even traveled more by plane as dollar prices fell, at least in the short run. Highlight 19.4 lists some methods of increasing consumer prices.

store trip was clearly stressful and unpleasant and likely required more behavior effort than the trip to the supermarket. However, the exercise may have been good for him physically. On the other hand, the supermarket trip was pleasant, and Vinnie felt very good about the purchase.

So which was the better trip? To Vinnie, it was the price paid at the supermarket, for he ignored other costs. However, if one accepts the economic assumptions involved in valuing Vinnie's automobile operating costs and time, an outside observer might conclude the convenience store price was a better buy. Depending on how the cognitive activity and behavior effort are evaluated, either of the two may be considered to be the better purchase.

Finally, consider the fact that Diet Pepsi was on sale at the convenience store for $2.79 plus tax on the same day that Vinnie went to the supermarket and paid $2.99 plus tax. Had he known this, Vinnie could have walked to the convenience store and saved both money and time.

Which was the better price? It depends on whether we consider the question from Vinnie's point of view or from that of an outside observer with perfect information. In addition, it depends on whether we analyze only the dollar price of the item or also consider the other dollar costs, time, cognitive activity, and behavior effort involved.

SUMMARY

This chapter presented an overview of pricing decisions and consumer behavior. Initially, the chapter focused on developing a conceptual framework for considering pricing decisions that included discussion of four types of consumer costs—money, time, cognitive activity, and behavior effort. These elements, when coupled with value, provide a framework for examining price from the consumer's point of view. Next, affect and cognitions, behaviors, and environmental factors relative to price were discussed. The cognitive factors examined included price perceptions and attitudes, and the behaviors described included funds access and transactions. The discussion of the environment focused on price information. Finally, a pricing strategy model was developed for use in pricing new products or for making price-change decisions.

Key Terms and Concepts

Price Perceptions *663*
Internal Reference Price *663*
External Reference Price *666*
Unit Pricing *667*
Price Elasticity *670*
Penetration Price Policy *674*
Skimming Price Policy *674*

Review and Discussion Questions

1. Define price and explain the differences between price strategy and other elements of the marketing mix.
2. In what situations are consumers willing to pay a higher dollar cost to save time, cognitive activity, and behavior effort?
3. Use the Wheel of Consumer Analysis to identify the interactions associated with consumer response to a credit-card pricing strategy. You could consider the Sears Discover Card or select your own example.
4. How can price be used to position a product like basketball shoes or luggage?
5. Explain how consumers determine that a particular price is too high. Use the conceptual model of cognitive processing (Figure 19.3) to structure your answer.
6. Offer alternate behavior views of consumer response that could explain the response to price in Question 5 above.
7. Could the marketing manager change price perceptions with strategies aimed at funds access and transaction behaviors? Explain and give examples.
8. The text suggests little research has examined the price environment. Use your experiences to suggest some areas for research on the price environment.
9. Analyze consumer costs associated with the purchase of automobile insurance or airline tickets. What are some of the strategy implications suggested by your analysis?
10. How would changing environmental factors influence price setting or price changes for hamburgers in your community?

Notes

1. Vithala R. Rao, "Pricing Research in Marketing: The State of the Art," *Journal of Business*, January 1984, p. S39.
2. For a model and approach to measuring this cost, see Steven M. Shugan, "The Cost of Thinking," *Journal of Consumer Research*, September 1980, pp. 99–111.
3. Rao, "Pricing Research," p. S39; Jerry C. Olson, "Price as an Informational Cue: Effects on Product Evaluations," in *Consumer and Industrial Buyer Behavior*, ed. Arch G. Woodside, Jagdish N. Sheth, and Peter D. Bennett (New York: Elsevier-North Holland Publishing, 1977), pp. 267–86; Valarie A. Zeithaml, "Issues in Conceptualizing and Measuring Consumer Response to Price," in *Advances in Consumer Research*, vol. 11, ed. Thomas C. Kinnear (Provo, Utah: Association for Consumer Research, 1984), pp. 612–16; and Kent B. Monroe and R. Krishman, "A Procedure for Integrating Outcomes across Studies," in *Advances in Consumer Research*, vol. 10, ed. Richard P. Bagozzi and Alice M. Tybout (Ann Arbor, Mich.: Association for Consumer Research, 1983), pp. 503–8.
4. Jacob Jacoby and Jerry C. Olson, "Consumer Response to Price: An Attitudinal, Information Processing Perspective," in *Moving Ahead with Attitude Research*, ed. Yoram Wind and Marshall Green (Chicago: American Marketing Association, 1977), pp. 73–86. Also see Jerry C. Olson, "Implications of an Information Processing Approach to Pricing Research," in *Theoretical Developments in Marketing*, ed. Charles W. Lamb, Jr., and Patrick M. Dunne (Chicago: American Marketing Association, 1980), pp. 13–16.
5. Abhijit Biswas and Edward A. Blair, "Contextual Effects of Reference Prices in Retail Advertisements," *Journal of Marketing*, July 1991, pp. 1–12.
6. Peter R. Dickson and Alan G. Sawyer, "The Price Knowledge and Search of Supermarket Shoppers," *Journal of Marketing*, July 1990, p. 49.
7. Biswas and Blair, "Contextual Effects of Reference Prices."
8. David A. Aaker and Gary Ford, "Unit Pricing Ten Years Later: A Replication," *Journal of Marketing*, Winter 1983, pp. 118–22.
9. Valarie A. Zeithaml, "Consumer Response to In-Store Price Information Environments," *Journal of Consumer Research*, March 1982, pp. 357–68.
10. For a complete work on pricing strategy, see Kent B. Monroe, *Pricing: Making Profitable Decisions*, 2nd ed. (New York: McGraw-Hill, 1990).

Additional Reading

For research on price elasticity, see:

Bemmaor, Albert C., and Dominique Mouchoux. "Measuring the Short-Term Effect of In-Store Promotion and Retail Advertising on Brand Sales: A Factorial Experiment." *Journal of Marketing Research*, May 1991, pp. 202–14.

Sethuraman, Raj, and Gerard J. Tellis. "An Analysis of the Tradeoff between Advertising and Price Discounting." *Journal of Marketing Research*, May 1991, pp. 160–74.

For additional discussion and research on reference prices, see:

Kalwani, Manohar U., Chi Kin Yim, Heikki J. Rinne, and Yoshi Sugita. "A Price Expectations Model of Customer Brand Choice." *Journal of Marketing Research*, August 1990, pp. 251–62.

Lichtenstein, Donald R., and William O. Bearden. "Contextual Influences on Perceptions of Merchant-Supplied Reference Prices." *Journal of Consumer Research*, June 1989, pp. 55–66.

MARKETING STRATEGY IN ACTION

Timex Corporation

Timex Corporation was one of the first companies to offer low-cost, durable mechanical watches. These watches were completely mass-produced with hard-alloy bearings that were less costly than jeweled bearings but much longer lasting than nonjeweled watches had been before. Timex attempted to sell these watches in jewelry stores, offering a 30 percent markup. However, jewelers commonly received 50 percent markup on merchandise, and many refused to stock the Timex watches. Timex then began selling direct to drugstores, hardware stores, and even cigar stands—and at one point had a distribution system of nearly a quarter of a million outlets.

This mass-distribution strategy was coupled with heavy TV advertising demonstrating the durability of the watches. For example, one ad showed a Timex watch being strapped to an outboard motor propeller and continuing to work after the engine had been run for several minutes. Such ads were used to support the contention that Timex watches could "take a licking and keep on ticking." To keep dealers and prices firmly in line, Timex limited production to about 85 percent of anticipated demand, making the watches somewhat scarce.

This strategy was extremely successful. By the late 1960s, Timex had a 50 percent market share in the United States and as much as 20 percent of worldwide sales. In 1970, Timex had aftertax profits of $27 million on sales of $200 million.

After a quarter of a century of dominance in the low-price watch market, Timex began to face serious competition in the mid-1970s. A major technological advance, which Timex executives initially judged to be unimportant, was the development of electronic watches. By the time Timex recognized the importance of this change and introduced an electronic watch, competitors had already developed and marketed much-improved models. In fact, the Timex electronic watches were so big and clumsy that employees nicknamed them "quarter pounders," and prices ended up 50 percent above competitive, much more attractive watches.

By 1983, Timex's U.S. market share had plummeted to about 17 percent, and operating losses approached $100 million. Distribution had

Urbay, Joel E., and Peter R. Dickson. "Consumer Normal Price Estimation: Market versus Personal Standards." *Journal of Consumer Research*, June 1991, pp. 45–51.

For research and discussion of price/quality relationships, see:

Lichtenstein, Donald R., and Scot Burton. "The Relationship between Perceived and Objective Price-Quality." *Journal of Marketing Research*, November 1989, pp. 429–43.

Rao, Akshay R., and Kent B. Monroe. "The Effect of Price, Brand Name, and Store Name on Buyer's Perceptions of Product Quality: An Integrative Review." *Journal of Marketing Research*, August 1989, pp. 351–57.

Tellis, Gerard J., and Gary J. Gaeth. "Best Value,

declined to 100,000 outlets. Timex ranked fifth in volume behind Japan's Seiko, Citizen, and Casio, and a Swiss combine, ASUAG-SSIH Ltd. Digital and quartz analog watches dominated the market, and even the successful Japanese companies faced increased price competition from manufacturers in Hong Kong. In fact, when the export price of the average digital watch dropped in 1981 from $5 to less than $2, many companies were forced out of business with margins of only a few cents per watch.

Timex at this point decided to attempt to rebuild its watch market and make itself less vulnerable by diversifying into home health-care products and home computers. To rebuild its timekeeping business, the company invested over $100 million to retool and redesign its watch and clock lines. Timex's marketing vice president supported this investment by stating, "We were thick, fat, ugly, overpriced, and behind in technology."

The strategy then became to produce watches that were just as attractive as higher priced brands and to keep the major portion of the line priced under $50. Of course, this forced Timex to compete in a world already overloaded with too many inexpensive watch brands. In addition to watches from Japan and Hong Kong, Swiss manufacturers scored a big hit with a trendy timepiece called Swatch, which was made of brightly colored plastic and sold for $30. Sales of Swatches soared to 100,000 units per month, and the watches could not be produced fast enough.

Timex also attempted to compete in the over-$100 price range with its super-thin quartz analog Elite collection that sold in department and jewelry stores for up to $120. However, as one competitor summed up the market potential of the Timex Elite collection, "It's got one disadvantage; it's got a $12.95 name on it."

Discussion Questions

1. In what situations do consumers shop for and purchase new watches?
2. What problems and opportunities does Timex have in the low priced watch market, and what strategy recommendations would you offer?
3. What problems and opportunities does Timex have in the high priced watch market, and what strategy recommendations would you offer?

Source: Adapted for purposes of this text from J. Paul Peter and James H. Donnelly, Jr., *Marketing Management: Knowledge and Skills* (Homewood, Il.: BPI/Irwin, 1989), pp. 281–83.

Price-Seeking, and Price Aversion: The Impact of Information and Learning on Consumer Choices." *Journal of Marketing*, April 1990, pp. 34–45.

For further discussions of pricing strategy, see:

Nagle, Thomas T. *The Strategy and Tactics of Pricing.* Englewood Cliffs, N.J.: Prentice Hall, 1987.

Tellis, Gerard J. "Beyond the Many Faces of Price: An Integration of Pricing Strategies." *Journal of Marketing.* October 1986, pp. 146–60.

Consumer Behavior and Channel Strategy

CHAPTER 20

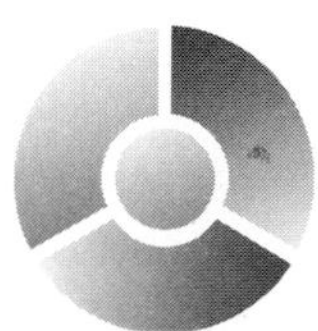

IBM

A bear when it sells big computers to corporations, IBM is a Bambi of a storefront retailer. In the early 1980s, the company began opening grandly decorated computer stores called IBM Product Centers in high-rent business districts all over America. While the first 81 stores had sales estimated at $100 million in 1983, IBM shelved plans to expand the chain to 100 stores.

The centers sell IBM's Personal Computer (PC) and typewriters, along with add-on gear and software made by IBM and others. Burdened with start-up costs and high overhead, the stores made far less than the 20 percent per year IBM is accustomed to earning on invested capital.

Glimpsing the chance to sell typewriters to small businesses and branch offices of big companies without costly door-to-door calls, IBM had opened three Product Centers by mid-1981. Then, when the PC burst on the scene, the company decided to plunk stores down in every metropolitan area. However, most of the 1,600-odd independent stores that carry the firm's PC and competing makes have done a better job of selling the target clientele. The rival stores belong mostly to big chains such as ComputerLand, Entré Computer Centers, and Sears Business Systems Centers.

IBM made mistakes right off the bat. Although it is a major producer of sophisticated point-of-sale computer systems to centralize billing, inventory, and sales audits, the company forced its own salespeople to record transactions on Stone Age carbon-paper invoices. At the end of each day, clerks typed the information into a computer in the back room. Result: mistakes galore in record-keeping and billing.

In choosing the Product Centers' decor, IBM revealed retailing naiveté. Anxious not to appear cold and remote, it abandoned its traditional icy blue and decorated the centers in bright red. "Red doesn't just irritate bulls," remarked Warren Winger, chairman of CompuShop, a Dallas-based chain, "it makes salesmen hostile and alarms customers." To keep its stores classy, IBM eschewed the usual tacky trappings of computer retailing—flashy in-store displays, brochures, and racks of impulse items near the cash registers. "The in-store merchandising—we never realized how important it was," confessed Jim Turner, the IBM vice president in charge of the centers. IBM also staffed the stores entirely with its own career salespeople, few of whom had retailing experience. Consumer research by a large New York ad agency showed the staff intimidated first-time customers. In interviews the customers revealed they expected more of IBM Product Centers than of other computer stores, but came away disillusioned.

Source: Excerpted from Peter Petre, "IBM's Misadventures in the Retail Jungle," *Fortune*, July 23, 1984, p. 80.

What mistakes did IBM make in operating its own retail stores? From an economic perspective, channels of distribution are thought of as providing form, time, place, and possession utilities for consumers. **Form utility** means channels convert raw materials into finished goods and services in forms the consumer seeks to purchase. **Time utility** means channels make goods and services available *when* the consumer wants to purchase them. **Place utility** means goods

An example of form utility.

and services are made available *where* the consumer wants to purchase them. **Possession utility** means channels facilitate the transfer of ownership of goods to the consumer.

While this view of channels is useful, it perhaps understates their role in our society. Channels of distribution have a very important impact on consumer affect, cognitions, and behavior. The locations of malls, shopping centers, and stores, as well as specific products and other stimuli within these environments strongly influence what consumers think and feel and what behaviors they perform, such as store contacts, product contacts, and transactions. In return, consumer actions at the retail level determine the success or failure of marketing strategies and have an important impact on the selection of future strategies.

In this chapter, we focus on the relationships among consumer affect, cognitions, behaviors, and environments at the retail level. Our primary focus is on these interactions for store retailing rather than for nonstore retailing, because some form of store is involved in about 95 percent of product sales to

FIGURE 20.1
The Wheel of Consumer Analysis: Channel Strategy Issues

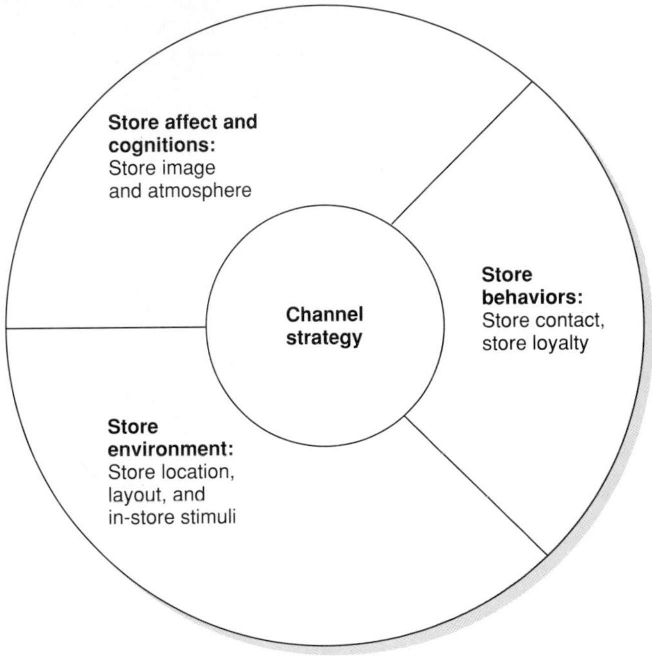

the consumer and in the majority of service sales. Some noteworthy areas of nonstore retailing, such as mail-order sales and direct-to-home retailing, will not be treated in detail in this text.[1]

Figure 20.1 provides a model of the issues addressed in this chapter. We begin by discussing store-related affect and cognitions, behaviors, and environmental factors and then turn to issues in channel strategy development.

Store-Related Affect and Cognitions

A variety of affective and cognitive processes could be discussed in relation to retail stores. However, two major variables of managerial concern at the retail level are *store image* and *store atmosphere*. While the marketing literature is not clear on the exact differences between these two variables, it is clear that both deal with the influence of store attributes on consumers' affect and cognitions, rather than how marketing managers perceive the stores.

Dressing salespeople as referees helps to create a sports image for this store.

STORE IMAGE

For our purposes, we will treat **store image** as what consumers *think* about a particular store. This includes perceptions and attitudes based on sensations of store-related stimuli received through the five senses. Operationally, store image is commonly assessed by asking consumers how good or how important various aspects of a retail store's operation are. Commonly studied dimensions of store image are such things as merchandise, service, clientele, physical facilities, promotion, and convenience. Store atmosphere is also often included as part of store image.

Store image research involves polling consumers concerning their perceptions of and attitudes about particular store dimensions. Typically, these dimensions are broken into a number of store attributes. For example, the merchandise dimension might be studied in terms of quality, assortment, fashion, guarantees, and pricing. The service dimension might be studied in terms of

HIGHLIGHT 20.1

Models of Store Image Development

Market-based store-image model	Internally based store-image model	Trade-based store-image model
Retailer selects target-market segment	Store image created or evolves based on internalized values and traditions held by the store's founders and successive managements	Retailer observes store-images of similar retailers in its line of trade
↓	↓	↓
Retailer determines needs of market segments and identifies relevant store-choice evaluation criteria	Image projected into the market in the belief that there will be sufficient numbers of customers attracted by this store image	Retailer develops or alters store-image to mirror peer reference group of similar retailers
↓	↓	↓
Retailer creates or alters store-image dimensions to conform to consumer store-choice evaluation criteria	As long as sales and/or profits are satisfactory, no conscious effort is made to alter the store image	Retailer expects to attract patronage with this image because it seems to be "What everybody is doing and it seems to be working for everybody else."
↓	↓	↓
Retailer monitors changes in consumer store-choice evaluation criteria	When sales and/or profits decline, retailers may evaluate and attempt to change store image	Retailer monitors and follows peer reference group and makes changes in its image based on changes made by reference group
↓	↓	↓
	Directions for change come from internally held values from which the retailer believes it has strayed: "We must return to our original time-honored values."	
↓	↓	↓
Outcome	**Outcome**	**Outcome**
Congruence achieved between store-image dimensions and consumers' store-choice evaluation criteria	Congruence achieved between store-image dimensions and traditional values held by the store's founders	Congruence achieved between retailer's store image and typical image projected by peer reference group

Source: Bert Rosenbloom, "Congruence of Consumer Store Choice Evaluative Criteria and Store Image Dimensions" in *Patronage Behavior and Retail Management,* ed. William R. Darden and Robert F. Lusch (New York: Elsevier-North, Holland Publishing, 1983), pp. 83–84.

general service, salesclerk service, degree of self-service, ease of merchandise return, and delivery and credit services.

Often the same attributes will be studied for competitive stores to compare the strengths and weaknesses of a particular store's image with that of its closest competitors. Based on this research, store management may then change certain attributes of the store to develop a more favorable image.

Developing a consistent store image is a common goal of retailers. This involves coordinating the various aspects of store image to appeal to specific market segments. However, store images sometimes have to be changed to adapt to changes in consumers shopping habits and in competitive position.

For example, in the early 1980s, J. C. Penney was a traditional general merchandiser. As discount chains began to dominate the general merchandise market, Penney's began repositioning its stores to create the image of a moderately priced fashion specialist. The company quit selling hard goods, such as sporting goods and photography products, and focused its efforts on clothing and home and leisure products. Recently, it changed its apparel strategy from selling designer names such as Halston and Mary McFadden to improving its private-label fashions and adding more national brands such as Levi's and Bugle Boy. Nearly half of its sales today are women's wear, and its gross margins have improved dramatically. Apparently, the company successfully changed its store image in the minds of consumers.[2] Highlight 20.1 presents three models for developing appropriate store images.

Store Atmosphere

Donovan and Rossiter argue that **store atmosphere** primarily involves affect in the form of in-store *emotional states* that consumers may not be fully conscious of when shopping.[3] Thus, many controlled studies fail to find that store atmosphere has significant effects on behavior, because these emotional states are difficult for consumers to verbalize, are rather transient, and influence in-store behavior in ways consumers may not be aware of.

The basic model underlying the Donovan and Rossiter research, shown in Figure 20.2, is taken from the environmental-psychology literature. Basically, the model posits that environmental stimuli affect consumers' emotional states, which, in turn, affect approach or avoidance behaviors. *Approach behaviors* refer to moving toward and *avoidance behaviors* refer to moving away from various environments and stimuli. Four types of approach or avoidance behaviors are related to retail stores:

1. *Physical* approach and avoidance, which can be related to store patronage intentions at a basic level.
2. *Exploratory* approach and avoidance, which can be related to in-store search and exposure to a broad or narrow range of offerings.
3. *Communication* approach and avoidance, which can be related to interactions with sales personnel and floor staff.

4. *Performance and satisfaction* approach and avoidance, which can be related to frequency of repeat-shopping as well as reinforcement of time and money expenditures in the store.

These authors investigated the relationships between the three types of emotional states shown in Figure 20.2 (pleasure, arousal, and dominance) and stated intentions to perform certain store-related behaviors. *Pleasure* refers to the degree to which the consumer feels good, joyful, happy, or satisfied in the store; *arousal* refers to the degree to which the consumer feels excited, stimulated, alert, or active in the store; and *dominance* refers to the extent to which the consumer feels in control of or free to act in the store. The study was conducted in 11 different types of retail outlets, including department, clothing, shoe, hardware, and sporting goods stores.

The Donovan and Rossiter research found that simple *affect*, or store-induced pleasure, is a very powerful determinant of approach-avoidance behaviors within the store, including spending behavior. Further, their research suggests *arousal*, or store-induced feelings of alertness or excitement, can increase time spent in the store as well as willingness to interact with sales personnel. They suggest that in-store stimuli that induce arousal include bright lighting and upbeat music. However, the inducement of arousal works positively only in store environments that are already pleasant; arousal may have no influence, or even a negative influence, in unpleasant store environments.

Overall, then, pleasure and arousal influenced consumers' stated (1) enjoyment of shopping in the store, (2) time spent browsing and exploring the store's offerings, (3) willingness to talk to sales personnel, (4) tendency to spend more money than originally planned, and (5) likelihood of returning to the store. The third emotional dimension, *dominance*, or the extent to which consumers feel in control of or free to act in the store, was found to have little effect on consumer behaviors in the retail environment.

FIGURE 20.2
A Model of Store Atmosphere Effects

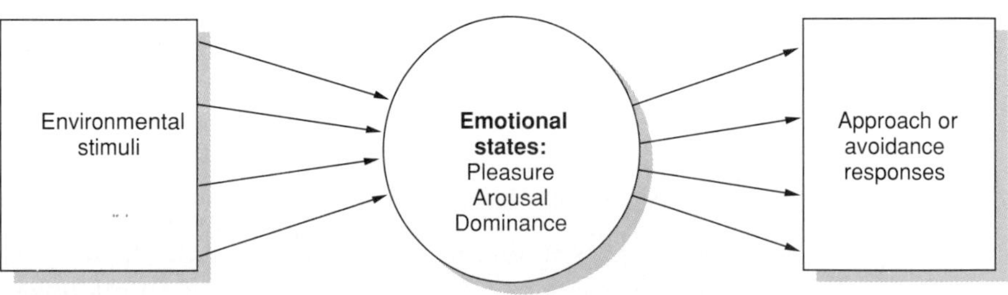

Source: Robert J. Donovan and John R. Rossiter, "Store Atmosphere: An Environmental Psychology Approach," *Journal of Retailing,* Spring 1982, p. 42.

Store-Related Behaviors

Marketing managers want to encourage many behaviors in the retail environment. Two basic types of behavior are discussed here: store contact and store loyalty. Highlight 20.2 lists several tactics designed to influence consumer behavior in retail stores.

Store Contact

As we mentioned in Chapter 11, *store contact* involves the consumer locating, traveling to, and entering a store. We also noted that putting carnivals in parking lots, having style shows in department stores, and printing maps and location instructions in the Yellow Pages are common tactics to increase these behaviors. In addition, other commonly used tactics include store coupons, rebates, and local advertising.

A number of the variables discussed in this chapter are also concerned with obtaining store contacts. For example, store location decisions are strongly influenced by heavy traffic and pedestrian patterns, which facilitate store contact.

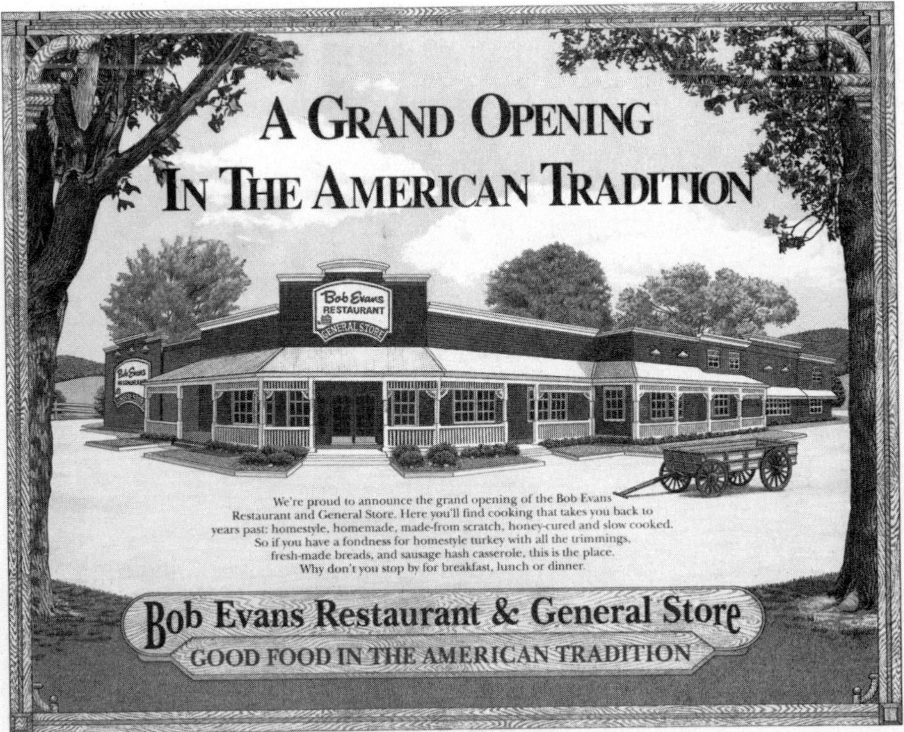

A strategy to initiate store contact.

HIGHLIGHT 20.2

Examples of Retail Tactics Used to Influence Consumer Behavior

Retail Design Element	Specific Example	Intermediate Behavior	Final Desired Behavior
Store layout	End of escalator, end of aisle, other displays	Bring customer into visual contact with product	Product purchase
Purchase locations	Purchase possible from home, store location	Product or store contact	Product purchase
In-store mobility	In-store product directories, information booths	Bring consumer into visual contact with product	Product purchase
Noises, odors, lights	Flashing lights in window	Bring consumer into visual or other sensory contact with store or product	Product purchase

Source: Reprinted from Walter R. Nord and J. Paul Peter, "A Behavior Modification Perspective on Marketing," *Journal of Marketing,* 44 (Spring 1980), p. 43. Published by the American Marketing Association.

Also, the visibility of the store and its distance from consumers are variables used to select locations that can increase store contact. For many small retail chains and stores, selecting locations in the vicinity of major retail stores such as Sears, J. C. Penney, K mart, or a major grocery store may greatly increase the probability of consumers coming into contact with them. In fact, one of the major advantages of locating in a successful shopping center or mall is the store contact available from pedestrians passing by on their way to another store. From the consumers' viewpoint, such locations can reduce shopping time and effort by allowing a form of one-stop shopping.

Store Loyalty

Most retailers do not want consumers to come to their stores once and never return: rather, repeat patronage is usually desired. **Store loyalty** (repeat patronage intentions and behavior) can be strongly influenced by the arrangement of the environment, particularly the reinforcing properties of the retail store. For example, the in-store stimuli and the attributes discussed in this chapter in terms of store image are the primary variables used to influence store loyalty.

Consider one further example of a tactic that may be used to develop store loyalty—in-store unadvertised specials. These specials are often marked with an attention-getting orange sign. Typically, consumers go to a store shopping for a particular product or just to go shopping. While going through the store, a favorite brand or long-sought-after product the consumer could not afford is found to be an unadvertised special. This could be quite reinforcing and strongly influence the probability of the consumer returning to the same store, perhaps seeking other unadvertised specials. Quite likely, the consumer would not have to find a suitable unadvertised special on every trip to the store; a variable ratio schedule might well be powerful enough to generate a high degree of store loyalty.

These additional trips to the store allow the consumer to experience other reinforcing properties, such as fast checkout, a pleasant and arousing store atmosphere, or high quality merchandise at competitive prices. In sum, reinforcing tactics and positive attributes of the store are used to develop store loyalty.

Store loyalty is a major objective of retail channel strategy, and it has an important financial impact. For example, it has been estimated that the loss of a single customer to a supermarket can cost the store about $3,100 per year in sales. Thus, the analysis of the store environment, and consumers' store-related affect and cognitions and behaviors, are critical for successful marketing.[4]

Store Environment

As we noted previously, retail stores are relatively closed environments that can exert a significant impact on consumer affect, cognitions, and behavior. In this section, we will consider three major decision areas in designing effective store environments: store location, store layout, and in-store stimuli.

Store Location

Although not part of the internal environment of a store, **store location** is a critical aspect of channel strategy. Good locations allow ready access, can attract large numbers of consumers, and can significantly alter consumer shopping and purchasing patterns. As retail outlets with very similar product offerings proliferate, even slight differences in location can have a significant impact on market share and profitability. In addition, store location decisions represent long-term financial commitments, and changing poor locations can be difficult and costly.

Research on retail location has been dominated by a regional urban economics approach rather than a behavioral approach. Thus, many of the assumptions on which the models are based offer poor descriptions of consumer behavior. For example, these approaches generally assume consumers make single-purpose shopping trips from a fixed origin. Considerable behavioral

Locating in a mall is often a wise channel strategy.

research suggests, however, that 50 to 60 percent of all shopping trips are multipurpose. The regional models also assume consumers have equal levels of knowledge about different stores, and they often ignore the impact of store advertising and promotion on consumers.

Although recent work has begun to integrate behavioral variables such as store image into location models, the models still place primary emphasis on economic variables and assumptions and on *predicting* rather than *describing* consumer behavior. Consumers are considered primarily in terms of demographic and socioeconomic variables and in terms of traffic patterns and distances to various locations.

Despite these criticisms, many retail location models are quite sophisticated and can deal with a variety of criteria. While we will not review all of the approaches available for selecting trading areas, business districts, shopping centers, and optimal store sites,[5] we briefly discuss four general approaches to store location. These include the checklist method, the analog approach, regression models, and location allocation models.[6]

Checklist Method

The checklist method attempts to systematically evaluate the relative value of a site compared to other potential sites in the area. Essentially, it involves an evaluation of various factors likely to affect sales and costs at a site. Marketing managers then make decisions about the desirability of the site based on these comparisons. Checklists commonly include information about socioeconomic and demographic composition of consumers in the area, level of consumption, and consumer expenditure patterns. Site-specific factors, such as traffic count, parking facilities, ease of entry and exit, and visibility are also often considered.

Analog Approach

The analog approach first identifies an existing store or stores similar to the one that is to be located. Surveys are used to observe the power of these analog stores to draw consumers from different distance zones. The ability of the analog stores to attract consumers is then used to estimate the trading area and the expected sales at alternative sites. The site with the best expected performance is then chosen for the new store.

Regression Models

Regression models are commonly used to investigate the factors that affect the profitability of retail outlets at particular sites. Retail performance has frequently been studied in regression models as a function of store location, store attributes, market attributes, price, and competition. In most of the studies, performance has been found to be affected by population size and socioeconomic characteristics of consumers in the store's market area, as well as by service factors such as local promotion and advertising.

Location Allocation Models

While the above approaches are most commonly used to evaluate store location sites, location allocation models typically have been used to assess an entire market or trading area. Location allocation models generally involve the simultaneous selection of *several* locations and the estimation of demand at those locations to optimize some specified criteria. These models allow the investigation of the effects on profitability of one store in a chain if another store is added in the same trading area, and they can be used to systematically consider the impacts of possible changes in the future marketing environment, such as competitive reactions.

STORE LAYOUT

Store layout can have important effects on consumers. At a basic level, the layout influences such factors as how long the consumer stays in the store, how many products the consumer comes into visual contact with, and what routes the consumer travels within the store. Such factors may affect what and how many purchases are made. There are many types and variations of store layouts; two basic types are grid and free-flow.

Grid Layout

Figure 20.3 presents an example of a **grid layout** common in many grocery stores.[7] In a grid, all counters and fixtures are at right angles to each other and resemble a maze, with merchandise counters acting as barriers to traffic flow.

FIGURE 20.3

Basic Store Layout

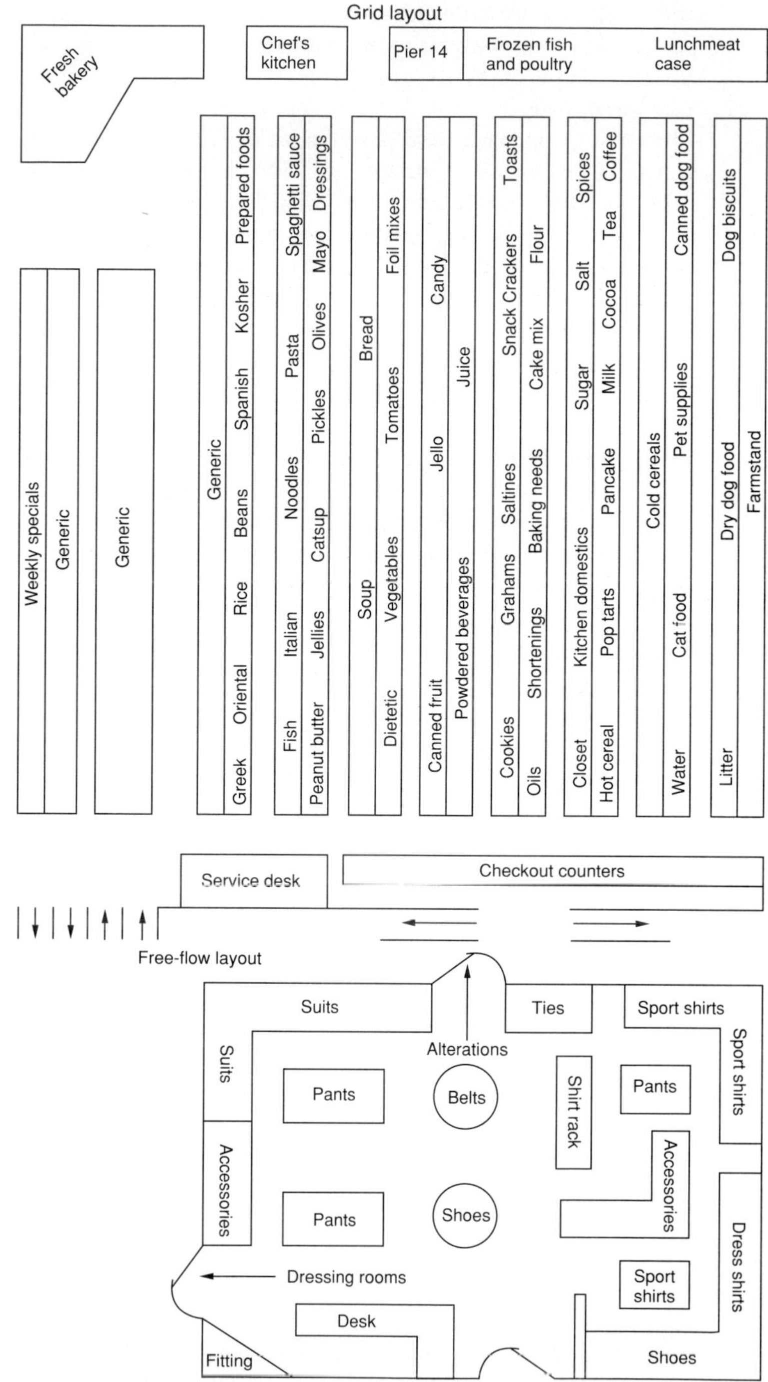

Source: J. Barry Mason and Morris L. Mayer, *Retailing,* 3rd ed. (Plano, Texas: Business Publications, Inc., 1988, pp. 416–17.

The grid layout in a supermarket forces customers to the sides and back of the store where items such as produce, meat, and dairy products are located. In fact, 80 to 90 percent of all consumers shopping in supermarkets pass these three counters.

In a supermarket, such a layout is designed to increase the number of products a consumer comes into visual contact with, thus increasing the probability of purchase. In addition, because produce, meat, and dairy products are typically high-margin items, the grid design can help channel consumers toward these more profitable products. Similarly, the location of frequently purchased items toward the back of the store requires consumers, who may be shopping only for these items, to pass many other items. Because the probability of purchasing other items is increased once the consumer is in visual contact with them, the grid layout can be very effective in increasing the number of items purchased.

The grid layout is more likely to be used in department and specialty stores to direct customer traffic down the main aisles. Typically, these retailers put highly sought merchandise along the walls to pull customers past other merchandise to slow-moving merchandise areas. For example, sale merchandise may be placed along the walls not only to draw consumers to these areas, but also to reward consumers for spending more time in the store and shopping carefully. This may increase the probability of consumers returning to the store and following similar traffic patterns on repeat visits. Expensive items can be placed along the main aisles to facilitate purchases by less price-sensitive consumers. The grid layout is commonly found on the main floors of multilevel department and specialty stores and at mass merchandisers.

Free-Flow Layout

Figure 20.3 also presents an example of a **free-flow layout.** The merchandise and fixtures are grouped into patterns that allow unstructured flow of customer traffic. Merchandise is divided on the basis of fixtures and signs, and customers can come into visual contact with all departments from any point in the store. A free-flow arrangement is often used in specialty stores, boutiques, and apparel stores. This arrangement is particularly useful for encouraging relaxed shopping and impulse purchases.

It may also be useful for aiding store salespeople to move consumers to several different types of merchandise. For example, it may aid in selling a collection of different items, such as a suit, shirt, tie, and shoes in a clothing store, thus increasing the total sale. Figure 20.4 presents a summary of the major advantages and disadvantages of the grid and free-flow layouts.

In-Store Stimuli

In most environments, there is an endless number of stimuli that could influence affect, cognitions, and behavior. A retail store is no exception. Stores have many stimuli that influence consumers: the characteristics of other shoppers and

FIGURE 20.4
Advantages and Disadvantages of Grid and Free-Flow Layouts

Advantages	Disadvantages
Grid	
Low cost	Plain and uninteresting
Customer familiarity	Limited browsing
Merchandise exposure	Stimulator of rushed shopping behavior
Ease of cleaning	Limited creativity in decor
Simplified security	
Possibility of self-service	
Free-flow	
Allowance for browsing and wandering freely	Loitering encouraged
Increased impulse purchases	Possible confusion
Visual apeal	Waste of floor space
Flexibility	Cost
	Difficulty of cleaning

Source: From Robert F. Lusch, *Management of Retail Enterprises* (Boston: Kent Publishing Company, 1982), p. 471. © by Wadsworth Inc. Reprinted by permission of PWS-KENT Publishing Company, a division of Wadsworth, Inc.

salespeople, lighting, noises, smells, temperature, shelf space and displays, signs, colors, and merchandise, to name a few.

Although the effects of some in-store stimuli have been studied extensively, much of this research is proprietary. (It is not available in the marketing or consumer research literature, because it has been conducted by firms seeking a differential advantage over competitors.) Much of the research available in the literature is dated and of questionable validity in today's marketplace. In addition, of the research that is available, the results are seldom consistent, in that some studies find large effects of in-store stimuli, some find small effects, and some find no effects. Differences in findings are often attributable to methodological issues, but we believe effects are highly situation specific and no single in-store tactic should be expected to be effective in all cases.

With these caveats, we turn to some of the research findings concerning the effects of in-store stimuli on consumer affect, cognitions, and behavior. Four areas are discussed: the effects of signs and price information, color, shelf space and displays, and music.

Signs and Price Information

In-store signs are useful for directing consumers to particular merchandise and for offering product benefit and price information. McKinnon, Kelly, and

FIGURE 20.5
Sales Results for Six Types of Signs

	Average Daily Sales Results (Units)
Regular Price	
No sign	7.66
Price sign	6.11
Benefit sign	7.81
Sale Price	
No sign	15.35
Price sign	19.07
Benefit sign	22.96

Source: Gary F. McKinnon, J. Patrick Kelly, and E. Doyle Robison, "Sales Effects of Point-of-Purchase In-Store Signing," *Journal of Retailing,* Summer 1981, p. 57.

Robison conducted an experiment that investigated the use of signs, the type of message included on the sign (price-only or product-benefit statements), and the effects of a regular versus a sale price being included on the sign.[8] The six products studied were bath towels, panty hose, ladies' slacks, men's dress slacks, men's jeans, and men's shirts. All six products were studied in varying conditions over a three-week period in three department stores.

Figure 20.5 presents a summary of the sales results obtained in the study. Based on the statistical analysis of these sales differences, the following conclusions were drawn:

1. Price influences sales more than sign type.
2. At regular prices, the addition of a price sign will not increase sales; but when the item is on sale, a price sign will increase sales.
3. Benefit signs increase sales at both regular and sale prices, but at a greater rate when the item is on sale.
4. A benefit sign is more effective than a price-only sign at both a regular and a sale price.

Overall, these results suggest that at regular prices, a benefit sign should be the only type of sign used, while at a sale price, both a price-only and a benefit sign will increase sales over a no-sign condition, with a benefit sign being the most effective. Thus, these results support the idea that signs affect consumer cognitions (consumers apparently processed different sign information) and consumer behavior (sales increased with the use of certain types of signs).

FIGURE 20.6

Percentage Increase in Unit Sales for Expanded Shelf Space and Special Display

Product	Expanded Shelf Space	Special Display
Camay soap—bath	39%	234%
Piggly Wiggly pie shells—2 per pkg.	30	185
White House apple juice—32 oz.	16	77
Mahatma rice—1 lb.	27	103

Source: Reprinted from J. B. Wilkinson, J. Barry Mason, and Christine H. Paksoy, "Assessing the Impact of Short-Term Supermarket Strategy Variables," *Journal of Marketing Research* 19 (February 1982), p. 79. Published by the American Marketing Association.

Color

Color has been shown to have a variety of physical and psychological effects on both humans and animals. Bellizzi, Crowley, and Hasty examined the effects of color on consumer perceptions of retail store environments in a laboratory experiment.[9] While noting the limitations of their study, the authors concluded color can have customer drawing power as well as image-creating potential. An interesting finding was that consumers were drawn to warm colors (red and yellow) but felt that warm-color environments were generally unpleasant; cool colors (blue and green) did not draw consumers but were rated as pleasant. The authors offered the following summary of the implications of their work for store design:

> Warm-color environments are appropriate for store windows and entrances, as well as for buying situations associated with unplanned impulse purchases. Cool colors may be appropriate where customer deliberations over the purchase decision are necessary. Warm, tense colors in situations where deliberations are common may make shopping unpleasant for consumers and may result in premature termination of the shopping trip. On the other hand, warm colors may produce a quick decision to purchase in cases where lengthy deliberations are not necessary and impulse purchases are common.[10]

Shelf Space and Displays

Research generally supports the idea that more shelf space and in-store displays increase sales. In a portion of a larger study, Wilkinson, Mason, and Paksoy examined the impact of these two variables on sales of four grocery products in an in-store experiment.[11] Comparisons were made between normal display (regular shelf space), expanded display (double the regular shelf space allocation), and special display (regular shelf space plus special end-of-aisle or within-aisle product arrangement).

Figure 20.6 presents the products studied and the percentage increases in unit sales using expanded shelf spaces and special displays. While the percentage

HIGHLIGHT 20.3

Stick by Checkouts, Gum Firms Find

It pays to have your product near the checkout in supermarkets, a chewing gum company has discovered.

A survey of 279 stores in 22 states that do $2 billion of business yearly found that the profit per square foot for the checkout-displayed products was nearly four times that of the regular shelf-displayed products.

The survey was commissioned by American Chicle, which produces gums and breath mints.

The survey results showed that checkout items take up 0.26 percent of the store's selling space, but contribute to 1 percent of a store's gross profit.

Since the survey was commissioned by a gum and mint company, it is perhaps not surprising to note that one of the results pointed out in a press release was that "the stores that allocate additional space to confectionary at the checkouts generated disproportionately higher sales and profits."

In other words, "put our stuff near the checkout and we'll both make more money."

Source: *The Wall Street Journal,* January 24, 1982, p. 3.

increases varied by product, as would be expected, both tactics consistently increased sales for all of the products. Further, special displays consistently outperformed expanded shelf spaces. These results support the idea that the presentation of merchandise in the store has an important impact on consumer behavior. See Highlight 20.3 for additional evidence of the effects of display placements on consumer behavior.

The study also found that in-store price reductions affected sales, but newspaper advertising was not a strong short-term strategy variable for three of the four products. This supports the idea that in-store stimuli have very important effects on consumer behavior — and in this case, are more important than out-of-store advertising.

Music

Considerable research supports the idea that music played in the background while other activities are being performed affects attitudes and behavior. Music is played in many retail stores, but relatively little basic research has been conducted on its effects on consumer behavior. Milliman examined the effects of one aspect of music — tempo — on the behavior of supermarket shoppers.[12] Three treatments were used: no music, slow music, and fast music. The basic hypotheses investigated were that these treatments would differentially affect

(1) the pace of in-store traffic flow of supermarket shoppers, (2) the daily gross volume of customer purchases, and (3) the number of supermarket shoppers expressing an awareness of the background music after they left the store.

The findings supported the idea that the tempo of background music affects consumer behavior. The pace of in-store traffic flow was slowest under the slow-tempo treatment and fastest under the fast-tempo treatment. Further, the slow-tempo musical selections led to higher sales volumes, as consumers spent more time and money under this condition. On average, sales were 38.2 percent greater under the slow-tempo condition than under the fast-tempo condition. Interestingly, when questioned after shopping, consumers showed little awareness of the music that had been playing in the supermarket. Thus, it seems likely that music affected behavior without consumers being totally conscious of it. In terms of marketing strategy, the author suggests:

> It is possible to influence behavior with music, but this influence can either contribute to the process of achieving business objectives or interfere with it. . . . Certainly, in some retailing situations, the objective may be to slow customer movement, keeping people in the store for as long as possible in an attempt to encourage them to purchase more. However, in other situations, the objective may be the opposite, that is, to move customers along as a way of increasing sales volume. A restaurant, for instance, will most likely want to speed people up, especially during lunch, when the objective is to maximize the "number of seats turned" in a very short period of time, normally about two hours or less. Playing slow-tempo music in a restaurant might result in fewer seats turned and lower profit, although it could encourage return visits if customers preferred a relaxed luncheon atmosphere. Again, the point is that the music chosen must match the objectives of the business and the specific market situation.[13]

Channel Strategy Issues

Marketing managers have many decisions to make in designing effective channels of distribution. For example, decisions must be made as to whether to market directly to the consumer through company-owned or franchised stores or indirectly through combinations of middlemen, such as independent retailers, wholesalers, and agents. Decisions must be made as to whether to use store retailing or nonstore retailing or some combination of the two. Decisions must be made about plant and warehouse locations, how products will be delivered to consumers, and who will perform what marketing functions within the channel.

In some cases, manufacturers market products in their own stores. For example, Sherwin-Williams paint company owns and operates its own retail outlets, and Hart, Shaffner & Marx, a clothing manufacturer, operates its own specialty clothing stores. The majority of manufacturers sell through independent retailers and retail chains, however.

Selling through independent retailers can lead to a conflict in objectives for the two types of marketing institutions. That is, while *manufacturers* are concerned with developing consumer brand loyalty (repeated purchase of their brand), *retailers* are concerned with developing consumer store loyalty (repeated patronage of their stores). For instance, retailers may not be highly concerned with which brand of coffee the consumer buys, as long as it is purchased in their particular stores. This situation has led many manufacturers to put a large portion of their marketing budgets into trade promotions directed at retailers (e.g., 1 case free for every 10 purchased by the retailer). Trade promotions may influence retailers to put up special displays, give more shelf space to a brand, lower prices to consumers, and sponsor local advertising of the brand for the manufacturer.

Our discussion highlights the fact that different members of a distribution channel may be primarily concerned with influencing different consumer behaviors. This is an important point; the role of retail management is often overlooked in discussions of marketing and consumer behavior. Retailers affect consumers most directly, and perhaps most influentially, for many types of products and most services. As a result, in this part of the chapter, we view channel strategy from the manufacturer's perspective and consider criteria for selecting channel members, particularly retailers.

As with the other elements of the marketing mix, the starting point for designing effective channels is an analysis of consumer/product relationships. At least six basic questions must be considered:

1. What is the potential annual market demand? That is, given a particular marketing strategy, how many consumers are likely to purchase the product and how often?
2. What is the long-run growth potential of the market?
3. What is the geographic dispersion of the market?
4. What are the most promising geographic markets to enter?
5. Where and how do consumers purchase this and similar types of products?
6. What is the likely impact of a particular channel system on consumers? That is, will the system influence consumer affect, cognitions, and behaviors sufficiently to achieve marketing objectives?

While these questions emphasize that consumers are the focal point in channel design, the answers require an analysis of a variety of other factors. As suggested in Figure 20.7, these factors must be analyzed both in terms of their relationships with and impact on the consumer, and in terms of their relationships with the other variables. We briefly discuss each of these factors, starting with commodity.

FIGURE 20.7
Channel Design Criteria

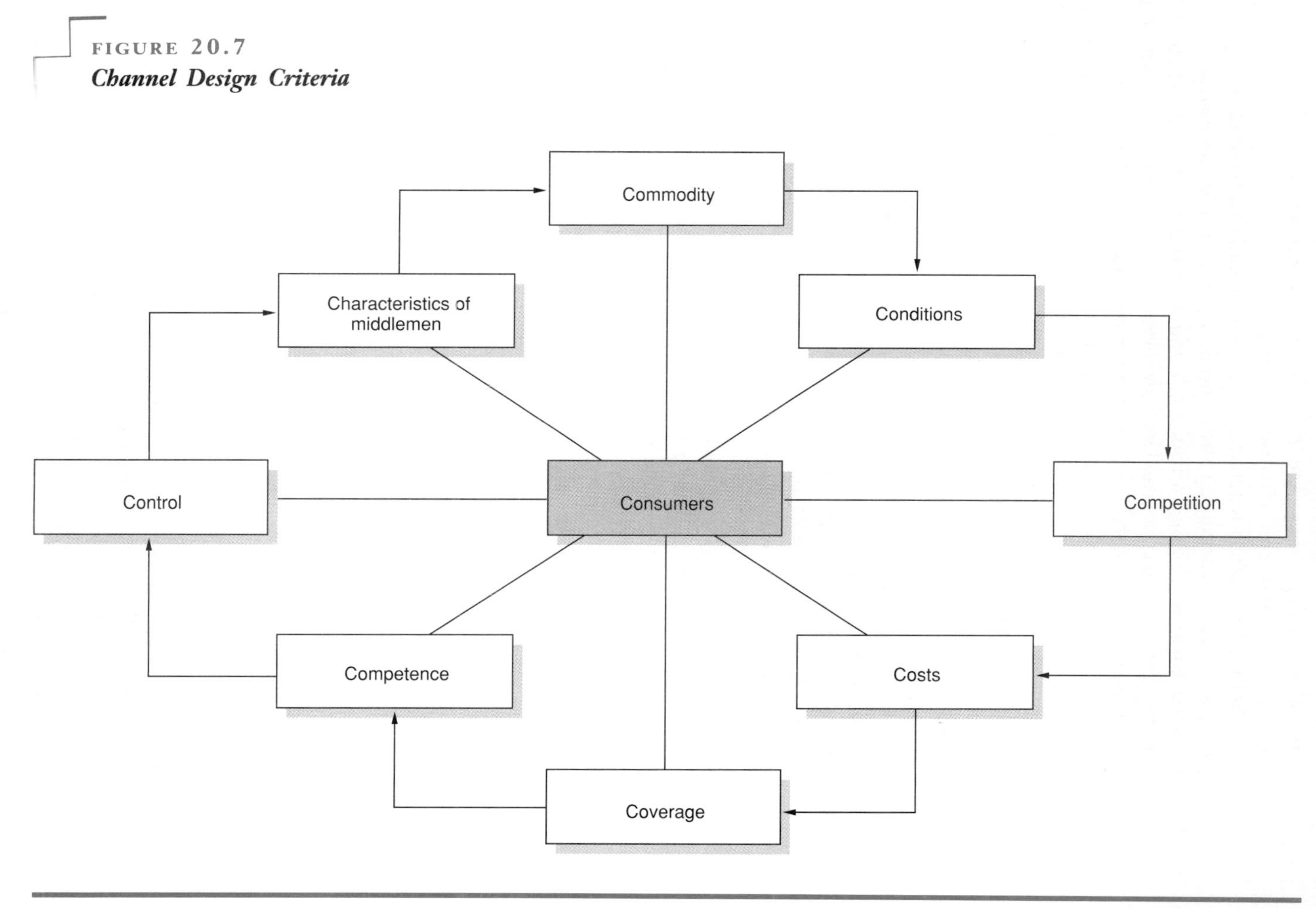

Commodity

By *commodity*, we mean the nature of the product or service offered to the consumer. Different products and services vary in their tangibility, perishability, bulkiness, degree of standardization, amount of service required, and unit value. These factors influence whether it is effective to market the commodity directly to consumers (as with hairstyling services) or indirectly through a number of middlemen (as with designer jeans).

Key consumer-related questions in considering the nature of the product or service are (1) what consequences or values does the product or service provide the target market, (2) how much time and effort are target market consumers willing to expend to shop for, locate, and purchase the product, and (3) how often do target-market consumers purchase the product. Thus, it is the *relationships* among consumers, the commodity, and the channel that are critical, rather than the analysis of these factors in isolation.

Conditions

Conditions refer to the current state of and expected changes in the economic, social, political, and legal environments in which the firm operates. This information is critical in channel design, because channels typically involve long-term commitments by the firm that may be difficult to change. For example, one of the major problems that led to the dramatic loss of market share and consolidation of A&P supermarkets was that A&P had long-term leases for many small stores in inner cities. Consumers were moving to the suburbs and purchasing in the larger, well-stocked, conveniently located suburban stores of competitors. Thus, situational analysis of the macroenvironment is critical in channel design to respond to potential problems and to exploit opportunities.

Competition

The size, financial and marketing strengths, and market share of a firm's competitors are major concerns in designing effective marketing strategies. For channel decisions, a key issue concerns how major competitors distribute products and how their distribution system affects consumers. In some cases, emulating the channels of major competitors in the industry is the only feasible alternative. For example, many convenience goods require intensive distribution to all available retailers.

In other cases, a differential advantage can be obtained by selecting nontraditional channels. For example, one reason for the success of companies such as Mary Kay Cosmetics and Tupperware is that they sell their products in homes rather than in traditional retail outlets.

Costs

While channel strategies seek to provide form, time, place, and possession utilities to influence consumer affect, cognitions, and behavior, these strategies

HIGHLIGHT 20.4

What Intermediaries Add to the Cost of a Compact Disc

Production of disc	.74	
Packaging (tuck box, etc.)	1.72	
American Federation of Musicians dues	.27	
Songwriters' royalities	.39	
Recording artists' royalties	1.01	
Freight to wholesaler	.36	
Manufacturer's advertising and selling expenses	1.74	
Manufacturer's administrative expenses	1.76	
Manufacturer's cost	$7.99	
Manufacturer's profit margin	1.10	
Manufacturer's price to wholesaler	$9.09	
Freight to retailer	.38	
Wholesaler's advertising, selling, and administrative expense	.47	
Wholesaler's cost	$9.94	
Wholsaler's profit margin	.80	
Wholesaler's price to retailer	$10.74	$6.90
Retailer's advertising, selling, and administrative expenses	1.76	
Retailer's profit margin	3.49	
Retailer's price to consumer	$15.99	

Source: From *Principles of Marketing,* 3rd. ed., p. 339, by Thomas C. Kinnear and Kenneth L. Bernhardt. Copyright © 1990, 1986 by Scott, Foresman and Company. Reprinted by permission of Harper Collins, Publishers.

are constrained by the cost of distribution. In general, a basic goal is to design a distribution system that facilitates exchanges between the firm and consumers but does so in a cost-efficient manner. Distribution costs include transportation, order processing, cost of lost business, inventory carrying costs, and materials handling. Thus, costs can be viewed as a constraint on the firm's ability to distribute products and services and to serve and influence consumers. In general, firms seek distribution systems that minimize total distribution costs at a particular level of customer service. Highlight 20.4 shows the cost breakdown across middlemen in the distribution of compact discs.

Coverage

The term *coverage* has two separate meanings in channel strategy. First, there is the idea that seldom can every member of a selected target market receive

FIGURE 20.8

Exclusive, Selective, and Intensive Distribution: Market Coverage

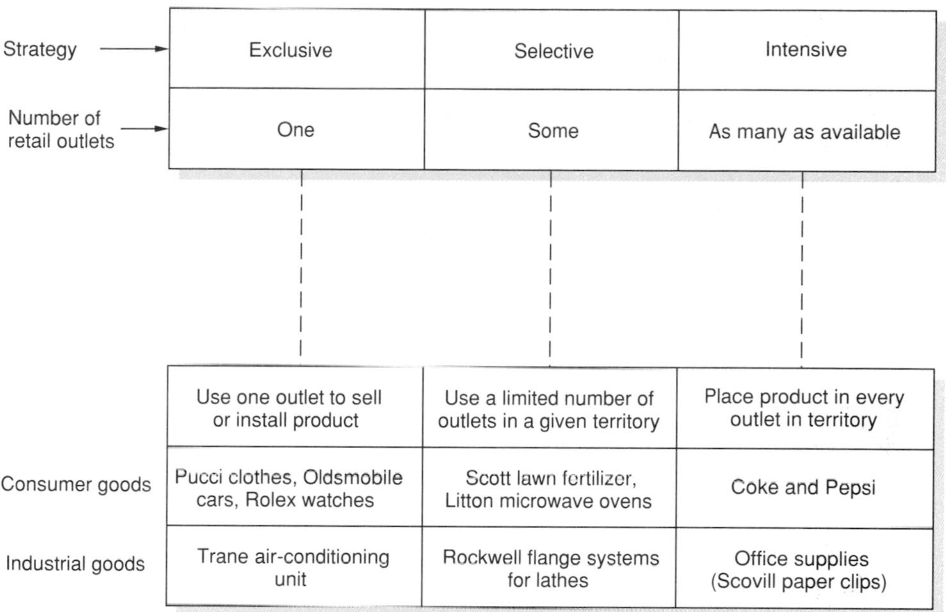

Source: From page 355, *Principles of Marketing,* 3rd ed., by Thomas C. Kinnear and Kenneth L. Bernhardt. Copyright © 1990 by Scott, Foresman and Company. Reprinted by permission.

sufficient marketing coverage to bring about an exchange. Because of cost considerations, even major consumer-goods companies often cannot afford to distribute their products in outlets that do not serve a relatively large population.

Second, coverage also refers to the number of outlets in a particular geographic area in which the product or service will be sold. Distribution coverage can be viewed along a continuum ranging from intensive through selective to exclusive distribution. Figure 20.8 explains the basic differences in these three alternatives.

Competence

A frequently overlooked criterion in designing channels is the firm's *competence* to administer the channels and to perform channel tasks at all levels to ensure effective distribution to the consumer. Both financial strength and marketing skills are crucial, but many production-oriented firms seriously underestimate the importance of marketing and overestimate their marketing abilities. Further, many manufacturers do not have a sufficiently large product line to develop their own retail stores. These firms opt for intermediaries, such as Sears, which sells 75 percent of its merchandise under its own label. Finally, marketing skills for one market are not always transferable to other markets. For example, many of the failures in international marketing have resulted from firms not adapting their products and marketing strategies to foreign markets.

Critics of marketing frequently point out that marketing intermediaries increase the cost of products, because the profits these wholesalers and retailers make add to the cost of the product to the consumer. These critics generally do not understand that intermediaries are used because they can perform some marketing functions more efficiently and cheaply than the manufacturer can.

Control

An important managerial criterion in designing channels is the *degree of control* desired for effective marketing of the product to the consumer. In general, there is greater control in direct channels, because no intermediaries are involved. Franchised channels also involve greater control than indirect channels, because the franchiser typically places strong contractual constraints on the operations of the franchisee. This control is quite important in delivering the major benefit of franchises to the consumer (i.e., standardized products and services).

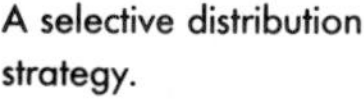

A selective distribution strategy.

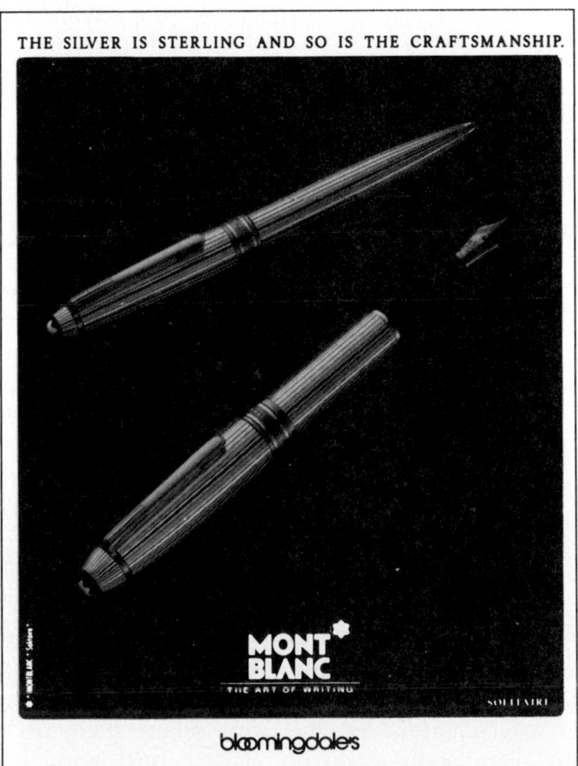

THERE'S AIR IN OUR WALKING SHOES BECAUSE THERE'S NONE IN SIDEWALKS.

Patented Nike-AIR® cushioning. Washable. Breathable. Widths. The Nike Air Healthwalker Max and Air Healthwalker Plus. Because it's a sidewalk out there.

Courtesy Nike, Inc.

The athletic shoe market has become highly segmented as consumers' product knowledge and involvement have increased.
Chapter 4

The True Test Of A Woman Runner.

Check "T" following the statement that's most true for you. Then look below to see which New Balance shoe best fits your running style.

1. You have unstable feet. You either over-pronate—feet roll inward—or over-supinate—feet roll outward. You may experience "runner's knee."
T☐ F☐

2. You love hitting the road, but not "feeling" it. You want to minimize the effect of jarring. Since you may have rigid, high-arched feet, you need substantial cushioning.
T☐ F☐

3. You're a mid- to high-mileage runner who requires generous, but not excessive, cushioning. You may over-pronate or over-supinate, but not excessively.
T☐ F☐

4. You like to train at a faster pace. While you want superior cushioning and flexibility, your motto is basically this: Less is more.
T☐ F☐

1. The 676 2. The 495 3. The 595 4. The 650

Courtesy New Balance Athletic Shoe, Inc.

Courtesy Hallmark Cards

Hallmark has more than 30,000 card types — selling sentiment to American consumers is big business!
Chapter 7

The A.C. Nielsen People Meter is one attempt to measure consumer attention to television programs and to advertisers' commercials.
Chapter 5

Courtesy A.C. Nielsen Co.

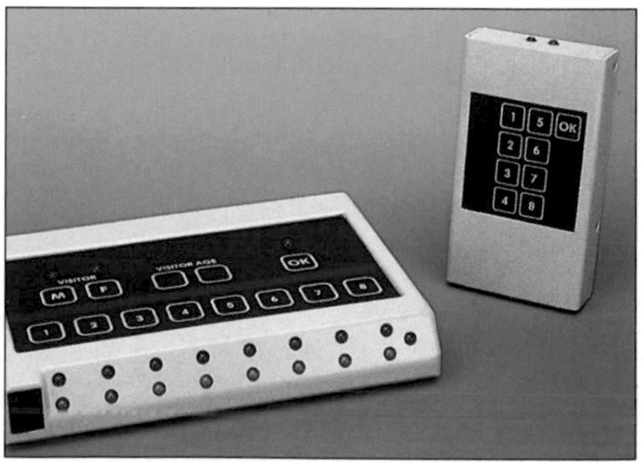

Courtesy A.C. Nielsen Co.

Twist and Shoot.

The engineers at Hitachi have just come up with a remarkable new twist in video technology. It's called the Twist and Shoot and it's the only camcorder that twists open for instant shooting.

Closed, its super-thin, 2⅜" profile makes it the world's thinnest video camcorder. It'll fit easily into a purse or a coat pocket.

Open, it's fully automatic. Revolutionary twin beam auto focus produces a precise, clear, stable picture. At the same time, shutter speed, lens opening and white balance are adjusted automatically for the best possible exposure.

In addition to all its convenience, the Twist and Shoot produces sharp, true-to-life pictures everytime.

To appreciate this revolutionary new kind of camcorder, call 1-800-HITACHI for your nearest dealer. Then shoot on down and twist one for yourself.

HITACHI

Courtesy Hitachi Home Electronics (America), Inc.

One way to get consumers' attention is to communicate a sense of value, or of features resulting in positive benefits.
Chapter 5

TWO ROOMS. TWO BUSINESS DEALS. TWICE THE PRODUCTIVITY.

EMBASSY SUITES. TWICE THE HOTEL.

Free, cooked-to-order breakfast.

For people who travel a lot on business, there is no better partner than Embassy Suites hotels.

TWICE THE ROOM. A large private bedroom. A separate spacious living room with a well-lit work area perfect for small meetings. Each suite also has two telephones, two TVs, a wet bar with refrigerator, coffee maker and microwave. Computer modem hookup available in most suites.

TWICE THE VALUE. A free, cooked-to-order breakfast is served each morning. Two hours of complimentary beverages+ each evening. Both sure to help keep your expense report in line.

Next time you need a hotel room, Think Twice. Then call your travel agent or Twice The Hotel. 1-800-EMBASSY.

EMBASSY SUITES

Courtesy Embassy Suites

Marketers try to influence consumers' brand attitudes and decision making by developing new product attributes that provide important consumer benefits.
Chapter 7

Reproduced with permission of Kimberly-Clark Corporation

Consumers' attitudes toward product attributes depend on what benefits they provide.
Chapter 6

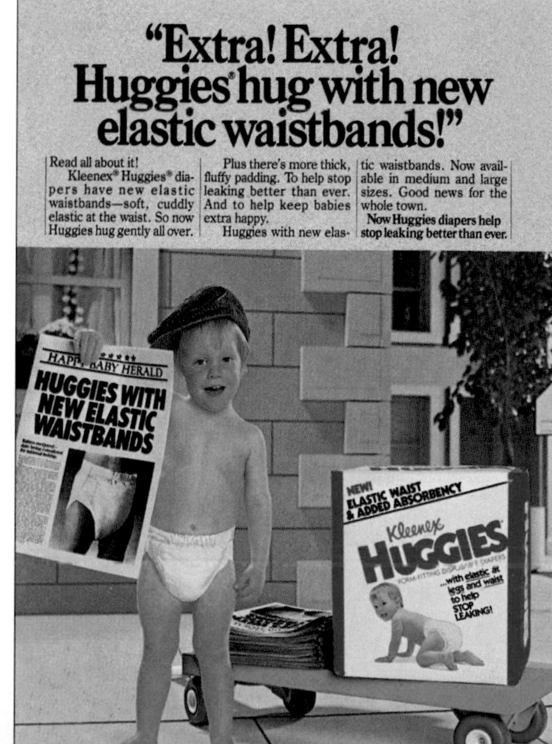

Reproduced with permission of Kimberly-Clark Corporation

HIGHLIGHT 20.5

Merry-Go-Round Enterprises

In the 1980s, a number of retailers recognized that the teenage population was shrinking and decided to switch to other markets. In 1975, there were 30 milllion teenagers in the United States, but by 1990, there were only 22.7 million. However, according to one poll, teenage spending doubled in this period to a whopping $57 billion. Merry-Go-Round Enterprises thought there was still a lot of money to be made in selling reasonably priced funky fashions to young adults, especially men. In 1990, sales from the company's three divisions—Merry-Go-Round, Cignal, and Menz (which runs stores under the names DJ's, Dejaiz, and Attivo)—were up 30 percent and earnings rose 69 percent to $37.5 million.

Few other retailers understand the teenage and young-adult market as well as Merry-Go-Round. The company recognizes that over half the men who shop in its stores still live at home and spend the majority of their income on cars, stereos, and clothes. Because there are so few teens, it's easier for them to get jobs, even in a recession. Buyers who select styles and colors for Merry-Go-Round stores keep a careful eye on what's happening in the teenage world and know what musical groups and fashions are hot.

Step inside any of the company's rap- and rock-music-filled stores and you'll be greeted with "How are you?" rather than "Can I help you?" (You can't answer no to the first question.) New salespeople are shown how to select outfits, the proper way to escort a customer to the dressing room, and how to close the sale in a nonoffensive manner. The stores carry brands such as Skidz, Get Used, and Major Damage and quickly discount new items that its computerized merchandise tracking system shows are selling poorly. Apparently, Merry-Go-Round Enterprises understands consumer/store relationships and responds quickly to changes in the teenage and young-adult market.

Source: Susan Caminiti, "If It's Hot, They've Got It," *Fortune,* June 3, 1991, p. 103.

Characteristics of Middlemen

A final but extremely important consideration in designing channels concerns the characteristics of the intermediaries that are available and willing to handle the manufacturer's product. If no acceptable middlemen are available, then the firm must either market direct, encourage the development of intermediaries, or forgo entering a particular market.

In addition to such factors as the size, financial strength, and marketing skills of intermediaries, *consumer perceptions* of intermediaries can be crucial in channel strategy. For example, many consumers view discount stores as places to purchase good-quality merchandise, but not necessarily prestige items. Manufacturers of prestige products (such as Polo shirts by Ralph Lauren) may lower

This case demonstrates a number of points raised in this chapter and provides evidence for some of them. To start with, IBM is an effective producer and marketer of computers when selling door to door in the industrial market, as well as when selling through independent retailers. However, these marketing skills clearly did not transfer when the firm began selling in its own retail stores. Consider IBM's store image. Consumers initially had a very positive image, but this image changed—in the wrong direction for IBM. Also, consider IBM's mistakes in the selection of a red decor, in-store merchandising, and salespeople inexperienced in retail sales.

This case is also a good example of management changing an environment based on consumer affect, cognitions, and behavior.

the image of their products by selling them in discount stores. Thus, manufacturers (and retailers) must consider the consumer/store relationships; that is, the relationships among the store environment, consumer affect and cognitions, and consumer behaviors. Highlight 20.5 discusses one company that has developed an understanding of consumer/store relationships for those teenagers who like to wear funky clothes.

Summary

This chapter presented an overview of consumer behavior and channel strategy. Initially, consumer store-related affect and cognitions, behaviors, and environmental factors were emphasized. The two most critical store-related affect and cognitions for channel strategy are store image and store atmosphere. The store-related behaviors discussed in this chapter included store contact and store loyalty, both of which are primary objectives of retail channel strategy. The examination of store environment emphasized store location, store layout, and

Because the original strategy resulted in a poor store image and store atmosphere, and with store contact, product contact, and transactions at unsatisfactory levels, IBM changed the store environment.

For one thing, salespeople started to receive formal training to be more effective in dealing with customers. A point-of-sales computer system was installed, and less-forbidding store design with cozier colors, point-of-sale gimmicks, and the look of a place where you can "get a deal" was implemented.

However, the stores still avoided price cutting and "bundling"—mixing and matching computer components to make up specially priced packages. IBM's emphasis on service rather than on price and bundling led one retail competitor to remark that the Product Centers were "a delight to compete with."

in-store stimuli. The final part of this chapter delineated several criteria relevant for designing effective channels. This part of the chapter emphasized it is the consumer and the relationships the consumer has with the other criteria that determine appropriate channel strategy.

Key Terms and Concepts

Form Utility *684*
Time Utility *684*
Place Utility *684*
Possession Utility *685*
Store Image *687*
Store Atmosphere *689*
Store Loyalty *692*
Store Location *693*
Store Layout *695*
Grid Layout *695*
Free-Flow Layout *697*

Review and Discussion Questions

1. Consider situations in which each of the models of store image development shown in Highlight 20.1 would be appropriate strategies. Which one would you generally advocate?

2. Offer examples of situations in which you have experienced each of the four types of approach or avoidance responses to retail store environments.

3. Relate the concept of shaping to the store contact and store loyalty concerns in this chapter. Make a series of strategy recommendations to achieve the desired ends.

4. Why do many retailers put impulse goods near the front of the store?

5. Research suggests many consumers make over 80 percent of their grocery purchase decisions while in the store. What do you think are the most important in-store influences on these purchases? (Examples such as cookies, chips, apples, or frozen entrees could be used to focus your answer.)

6. What specific environmental factors account for the difference in atmosphere between eating at McDonald's versus eating at an expensive restaurant?

7. What are the advantages and disadvantages to the consumer in purchasing from a mail-order catalog rather than from a retail store?

8. From a retailer's point of view, what would be the advantages and disadvantages of mail-order selling?

9. If you were recommending a store location site for a clothing specialty store, which methods or models of store location would you use and why?

10. Identify some of the circumstances in which the desired consumer response guiding channel strategy development would be different for the retailer than for the manufacturer.

NOTES

1. For a discussion of the essentials of nonstore retailing, see Barry Berman and Joel R. Evans, *Retail Management: A Strategic Approach*, 4th ed. (New York: Macmillan, 1989), pp. 115–18. For a discussion of consumer resistance to catalog shopping, see Maggie McComas, "Catalogue Fallout," *Fortune*, January 20, 1986, pp. 63–64.

2. Amy Dunkin and Brian Bremner, "The Newly Minted Penney: Where Fashion Rules," *Business Week*, April 17, 1989, pp. 88–90.

3. Robert J. Donovan and John R. Rossiter, "Store Atmosphere: An Environmental Psychology Approach," *Journal of Retailing*, Spring 1982, pp. 34–57.

4. For further discussion of store loyalty, see Kau Ah Keng and A. S. C. Ehrenberg, "Patterns of Store Choice," *Journal of Marketing Research*, November 1984, pp. 399–409. Also see Susan Spiggle and Murphy A. Sewell, "A Choice Sets Model of Retail Selection," *Journal of Marketing*, April 1987, pp. 97–111.

5. For excellent discussions of these topics, see C. Samuel Craig, Avijit Ghosh, and Sara McLafferty, "Models of the Retail Location

Process: A Review," *Journal of Retailing*, Spring 1984, pp. 5–36; and J. Barry Mason, Morris L. Mayer, and Hazel F. Ezell, *Retailing*, 3rd ed. (Plano, Texas: Business Publications, Inc. 1988), pp. 244–77.

6. The information in this section on store location is based heavily on the discussion in Craig, Ghosh, and McLafferty, "Models of Retail Location," pp. 20–27.
7. The figures and part of the discussion of store layout are based on Mason, Mayer, and Ezell, *Retailing*, pp. 414–16.
8. Gary F. McKinnon, J. Patrick Kelly, and E. Doyle Robison, "Sales Effects of Point-of-Purchase In-Store Signing," *Journal of Retailing*, Summer 1981, pp. 49–63.
9. Joseph A. Bellizzi, Ayn E. Crowley, and Ronald W. Hasty, "The Effects of Color in Store Design," *Journal of Retailing*, Spring 1983, pp. 21–45. Also see J. Edward Russo, Richard Staelin, Catherine A. Nolan, Gary J. Russell, and Barbara L. Metcalf, "Nutrition Information in the Supermarket," *Journal of Consumer Research*, June 1986, pp. 48–70.
10. Ibid., p. 43.
11. J. B. Wilkinson, J. Barry Mason, and Christie H. Paksoy, "Accessing the Impact of Short-Term Supermarket Strategy Variables," *Journal of Marketing Research*, February 1982, pp. 72–86. Also see Rockney G. Walters and Scott B. MacKenzie, "A Structural Equations Analysis of the Impact of Price Promotions on Store Performance," *Journal of Marketing Research*, February 1988, pp. 51–63; and V. Kumar and Robert P. Leone, "Measuring the Effect of Retail Store Promotions on Brand and Store Substitution," *Journal of Marketing Research*, May 1988, pp. 178–85.
12. Ronald E. Milliman, "Using Background Music to Affect the Behavior of Supermarket Shoppers," *Journal of Marketing*, Summer 1982, pp. 86–91.
13. Ibid., p. 91. For additional support for these ideas, see Ronald E. Milliman, "The Influence of Background Music on the Behavior of Restaurant Patrons," *Journal of Consumer Research*, September 1986, pp. 286–89. Also see Richard Yalch and Eric Spangenberg, "Effects of Store Music on Shopping Behavior," *Journal of Consumer Marketing*, Spring 1990, pp. 55–63; and Gordon C. Bruner II, "Music, Mood, and Marketing," *Journal of Marketing*, October 1990, pp. 94–104.

Additional Reading

For research and further discussion of the effects of in-store factors on consumer affect and cognitions and behaviors, see:

Achabal, Dale D., Shelby H. McIntyre, Cherryl H. Bell, and Nancy Tucker. "The Effects of Nutrition P-O-P Signs on Consumer Attitudes and Behavior." *Journal of Retailing*, Spring 1987, pp. 9–24.

Quelch, John A., and Kristina Cannon-Bonventre. "Better Marketing at the Point of Purchase." *Harvard Business Review*, November–December 1983, pp. 162–69.

Tellis, Gerald J. "Consumer Purchasing Strategies and the Information in Retail Price." *Journal of Retailing*, Fall 1987, pp. 279–97.

For further discussion of retail location strategy, see:

Ghosh, Avijit, and C. Samuel Craig. "Formulating Retail Location Strategy in a Changing Environment." *Journal of Marketing*, Summer 1983, pp. 56–68.

For complete works on retailing strategy and management, see:

Davidson, William R., Daniel J. Sweeney, and Ronald W. Stampfl. *Retailing Management*, 6th ed. New York: John Wiley & Sons, 1988.

Mason, J. Barry, Morris L. Mayer, and Hazel F. Ezell. *Retailing*. Plano, Texas: Business Publications, 1988.

MARKETING STRATEGY IN ACTION

WAL-MART STORES INC.

For many years, Americans bought more goods from Sears, Roebuck and Co. than from any other retailer. However, in fiscal 1991, Wal-Mart became the No. 1 retailer and Sears slipped to third behind second-place K mart. Although 1991 witnesed one of the worst recessions in recent years, Wal-Mart sales rose 26 percent to $32.6 billion. The phenomenal success and growth of Wal-Mart are shown below.

Wal-Mart sells a variety of standard consumer goods ranging from laundry detergent to sporting goods. What accounts for its success? For one thing, consumers are willing to travel much farther to go to a Wal-Mart than to buy the same products at nearby stores. Priscilla Patterson, for instance, drove 25 minutes from her Mount Prospect, Illinois, home to a Wal-Mart outlet in Lake Zurich to buy a portable radio for her son. "I thought I could get the best price," she said, remembering a previous purchase she had made at Wal-Mart.

A trip down the aisles of the Lake Zurich Wal-Mart offers some clues to its marketing strategy. Apart from a once-a-month, full-color advertising circular, in-store signs are virtually all the advertising Wal-Mart does. Brightly colored signs hang from the ceiling and steer shoppers toward tables offering tantalizing bargains on summer shoes, garden supplies, diapers, and toothpaste.

Signs under a hair-care display boast an everday low price of 97 cents for a 16-ounce bottle of shampoo. A nearby discount health and beauty aids store sells the same bottle for $1.46, or 49 cents more. A popular outdoor barbecue grill sells for $54.94 at Wal-Mart. A leading competitor in a nearby mall sells it for $64.97, a $10.03 difference.

If consumers bring in an ad for a product sold by a competitor at a lower price, Wal-Mart lowers its price to match. Department managers and other price checkers routinely shop other stores to make price comparisons and log the prices that beat theirs into a store computer.

Wal-Mart's expansion strategy was to build stores in trading areas that could support one but not two large discount stores. In this way, it avoided direct competition with other discounters such as K mart or Target. As it grew and became more profitable, it eventually expanded into larger trading areas. However, it avoided locations in major shopping malls, preferring to locate on the edges of cities where property was less expensive.

Wal-Mart is an expert at holding down over-

Mason, J. Barry, and Morris L. Mayer, *Modern Retailing*, 5th ed. Homewood, Ill.: BPI/Irwin, 1990.

For further discussion of the effects of environmental factors on consumer shopping, see:

Iyer, Easwar S. "Unplanned Purchasing: Knowledge of Shopping Environment and Time Pressure," *Journal of Retailing*, Spring 1989, pp. 40–57.

Park, C. Whan, Easwar S. Iyer, and Daniel C. Smith. "The Effects of Situational Factors on In-Store Grocery Shopping Behavior: The Role of Store Environment and Time Available for Shopping," *Journal of Consumer Research*, March 1989, pp. 422–33,

Wal-Mart's Rise to the Top

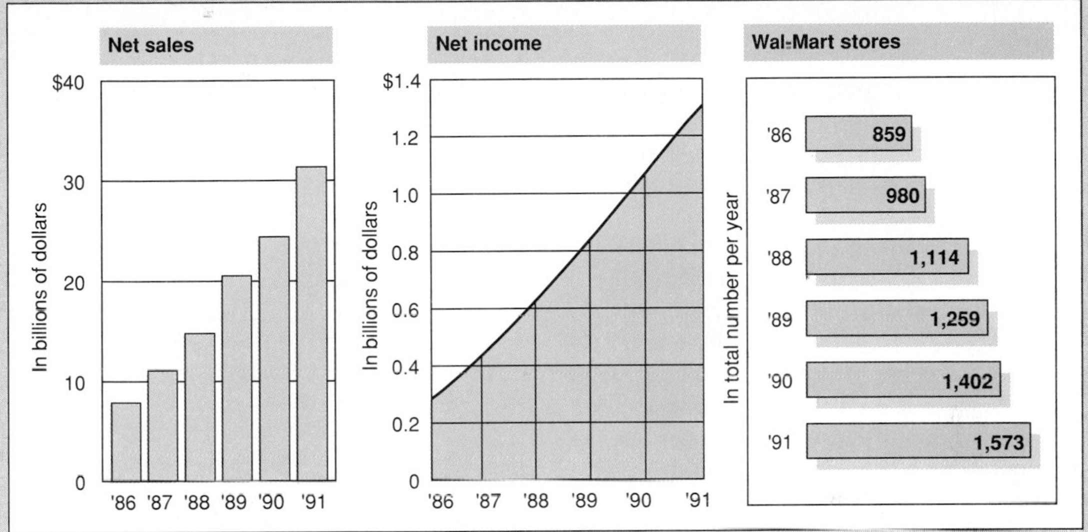

head costs. It has sophisticated warehouse and information systems that enable it to keep operating costs down to an enviable 16 percent, the lowest in the industry. Wal-Mart sends checkout-line information on sales of some Procter & Gamble products, such as diapers, directly to P&G at the same time it records the sale in its own computer records. This means P&G has immediate information on sales and can adjust production and shipping schedules to allow efficient replenishment of Wal-Mart's stock. Given that Wal-Mart sells such huge volumes of merchandise, it can demand the best prices from manufacturers such as P&G.

The company has also developed a number of employee programs to promote sales and friendly service for consumers. For example, each in-store sales associate selects one piece of merchandise to sponsor for a year. The sales associate builds a display for it and keeps it clean and full of stock.

In a store with 200 employees, this means someone is watching 200 of the store's products extra carefully.

Individual rewards for sponsoring a product are not monetary; workers simply seek recognition for their efforts from fellow employees and bosses—all of whom are on a first-name basis. The best of the merchandising ideas make their way to headquarters, allowing small but good-selling concepts to be adopted nationwide.

About the only venture Wal-Mart has tried that has not succeeded is the development of hypermarts. Wal-Mart built four of these that sold groceries and everything else in huge stores (225,000 square feet), as big as five football fields. While the hypermarket concept was successful in Europe, apparently Americans did not like searching through such large stores for convenience products.

Also, hypermarts often did not have as deep a selection of products as more specialized stores. For example, the hypermart in Arlington, Texas, carries only three brands of videocassette recorders while electronics stores in the area carry seven brands. Wal-Mart announced it had no plans to build any more hypermarts but would instead focus on stores no larger than 150,000 square feet.

Discussion Questions

1. Compare your perceptions of the store images and store atmospheres of Wal-Mart and K mart. Which of these stores do you prefer? Why do you prefer it?
2. What are the advantages and disadvantages of Wal-Mart's store locations to consumers?
3. List all of the reasons you can think of why Wal-Mart is so successful at satisfying consumers and building store loyalty.

Source: Kevin Kelly and Amy Dunkin, "Wal-Mart Gets Lost in the Vegetable Aisle," *Business Week,* May 28, 1990, p. 48; and Marianne Taylor, "Wal-Mart Prices Its Way to Top of Retail Mountain," *Wisconsin State Journal,* May 5, 1991, pp. 1c, 2c.

Social and Ethical Considerations

CHAPTER 21

McDONALD'S CORPORATION–EARLY 1990s

Founded in San Bernardino, California, in 1947, McDonald's Corporation has grown to become the largest food-service operation in the world. It has 11,000 restaurants in 54 countries, 8,500 of them in the United States, where more than 18 million people visit a McDonald's each day. One in every 15 working Americans gets his or her first job at McDonald's.

In the early 1990s, McDonald's recognized it faced two major problems. First, environmentalists had long criticized the company for the amount of garbage its packaging and leftovers put in the environment. In the United States alone, McDonald's outlets sent 2 million pounds of garbage per day to incinerators and landfills, much of which was polystyrene burger containers and other plastic implements that did not readily decompose. Second, nutritionists had long been critical of McDonald's menu for the high levels of fat and sodium in it. For example, millionaire health activist Phil Sokolof bought full-page national newspaper ads headlined: "McDonald's, your hamburgers have too much fat."

To help clean up the environment, McDonald's instituted a 42-point plan to eliminate 80 percent of the waste from its restaurants. The plan included such things as replacing polystyrene sand-

wich boxes with a thin-layered wrap, using new napkins with 21 percent less paper, using brown paper bags made of recycled paper, recycling behind-the-counter cardboard boxes, eliminating plastic cutlery wrappers where allowed by local laws, and trying reusable coffee mugs, reusable coffee filters, and pump-style bulk condiment dispensers instead of individual-serving packages. The Environmental Defense Fund praised McDonald's for these changes.

To improve the nutritional value of its menu, McDonald's made several changes. It concocted a new burger, the McLean Deluxe, which is 9 percent fat by weight, compared with 20 to 30 percent in most hamburgers. It phased out ice cream and replaced it with frozen yogurt. It replaced animal fat in its french-fry grease with vegetable oil. It test marketed more healthy foods such as catfish, pasta, and sliced carrots and celery.

Source: "McBurger Goes Low Fat," *Wisconsin State Journal,* March 14, 1991, p. 6B; "Brown Bagging It: McDonald's to Cut Garbage 80%," *Wisconsin State Journal,* April 17, 1991, p. 1; and "Some Feel McDonald's Image Could Be Leaner and Greener," *Wisconsin State Journal,* June 3, 1991, p. 6B.

Why did McDonald's make these changes? In this text, we have presented what we believe to be a useful description of some important relationships between consumer affect and cognitions, consumer behaviors, the environment, and marketing strategy development. One of the major underlying premises of the text is that marketing is an important and powerful force in society; properly designed and executed marketing strategies are often effective in changing consumer affect, cognitions, and behaviors to achieve organizational objectives.

We have also argued that attempts to modify and control affect, cognitions, and behaviors are part of the fabric of society. We believe the majority of social exchanges involve such attempts. Thus, even though marketing may attempt to do so in a systematic and effective manner, the majority of marketing practices are not unethical per se.

Further, we believe marketing and free enterprise offer the best and most effective system of exchange that has been developed. For example, we believe survival of the human species is a primary objective of any society. Given the development and marketing of a variety of products and services, life expectancies and the quality of life have been dramatically improved for many people.

There is also no question that marketing can be used to encourage a variety of socially desirable behaviors, such as reductions in littering, smoking, pollution, and other such negative behaviors.

This is not to say marketers always perform in a manner that is good for society, however. There are clear examples where marketers have misused their power to influence consumer affect, cognitions, and behaviors. Thus, the purpose of this final chapter is to discuss the responsibility of marketing to consumers and society at large.

The Rights of Marketers and Consumers

Both marketers and consumers are granted certain rights by society, and both have a degree of power. Overall, many people believe marketers have considerably more power than consumers. Several years ago, Professor Philip Kotler provided the following list of rights granted to marketers (sellers):

1. Sellers have the right to introduce any product in any size, style, color, etc., so long as it meets minimum health and safety requirements.
2. Sellers have the right to price the product as they please so long as they avoid discrimination that is harmful to competition.
3. Sellers have the right to promote the product using any resources, media, or message, in any amount, so long as no deception or fraud is involved.
4. Sellers have the right to introduce any buying schemes they wish, so long as they are not discriminatory.
5. Sellers have the right to alter the product offering at any time.
6. Sellers have the right to distribute the product in any reasonable manner.
7. Sellers have the right to limit the product guarantee or postsale services.[1]

While this list is not exhaustive, it illustrates that marketers have a good deal of power and latitude in their actions.

Since the Consumer Bill of Rights was issued in the early 1960s, consumers have been granted at least four basic rights. First, consumers are granted the *right to safety*, which means the right to be protected against products and services that are hazardous to health and life. Second, consumers are granted the *right to be informed*, which is the right to be protected against fraudulent, deceitful, or misleading advertising or other information that could interfere with making an informed choice. Third, consumers are granted the *right to choose*—the right to have access to a variety of competitive products that are priced fairly and are of satisfactory quality. Finally, consumers are granted the *right to be heard* or the right to be ensured that their interests will be fully and fairly considered in the formulation and administration of government policy.

While this list may appear to grant the consumer considerable rights and protection, it has an important weakness: most of these rights depend on the assumption that consumers are both capable of being and willing to be highly involved in purchase and consumption. In fact, however, many consumers are neither. Young children, many elderly people, and the uneducated poor often do not have the cognitive abilities to process information well enough to be protected.[2] Further, even those consumers who do have the capacity often are not willing to invest the time, money, cognitive energy, and behavior effort to ensure their rights.

The right to choose is also predicated on the assumption that consumers are rational, autonomous, knowledgeable cognitive processors and decision makers. While we believe most consumers are capable of being so, evidence suggests consumers often do not behave this way.[3] Further, the right to choose ignores the power of marketing to influence attitudes, intentions, and behaviors. Consumers' needs, wants, and satisfaction can be developed through conditioning and modeling processes used by marketers, for instance. Thus, the assumption of consumer autonomy is not easily supported.

Finally, no matter how much effort consumers exert to ensure they are choosing a good product, they cannot process information that is not available. For example, consumers cannot be aware of hidden product safety risks.

Overall, then, if there were no other forces in society, marketers might well have more rights and power than consumers do. This is not to say consumers cannot exert countercontrol on marketers or consumers do not vary in the degree to which they are influenced by marketers. However, as our society and system of government and exchange evolved, a number of constraints or societal influences on marketing activities have also developed. As shown in Figure 21.1, these include legal, political, competitive, and ethical influences.

Before discussing each of these societal influences, three points should be noted. First, as we stated earlier, we believe marketing and the free enterprise system offer the best and most effective system of exchange that has ever been developed. This does not mean the system could not be improved. For example, there are still many poor, uneducated, hungry people in our society who have little chance of improving their lot.

Second, while marketing usually receives the brunt of society's criticism of business, marketing managers are no more or less guilty of wrongdoing than other business executives. Corporate responsibility to society is a shared responsibility of all business executives, regardless of functional field. In addition, marketing executives are no more or less ethical than most other groups in society.[4] Similarly, while business, particularly big business, is commonly singled out for criticism, there is no question that other fields—including medicine, engineering, and law—also have their share of societal problems. Some consumers could also be criticized for the billions of dollars of merchandise that is shoplifted annually, as well as for other crimes against businesses and society.

Third, while some critics of marketing focus on the field in general, many of the problems are confined to a relatively small percentage of firms and practices. Figure 21.2 lists some of the most commonly cited areas of concern, divided into

FIGURE 21.1
Major Sources of Consumer Protection

FIGURE 21.2
Some Problem Areas in Marketing

Product Issues	Promotion Issues
Unsafe products	Deceptive advertising
Poor quality products	Advertising to children
Poor service/repair/maintenance after sale	Bait-and-switch advertising
Deceptive packaging and labeling practices	Anxiety-inducing advertising
Environmental impact of packaging and products	Deceptive personal selling tactics
Pricing Issues	**Distribution Issues**
Deceptive pricing	Sale of counterfeit products and brands
Fraudulent or misleading credit practices	Pyramid selling
Warranty refund problems	Deceptive in-store selling influences

FIGURE 21.3
Examples of Recent Consumer-Oriented Legislation

Year	Legislation	Major Provision of Law
1985	Saccharin Study and Labeling Act Amendment	Extends for two years the moratorium on FDA actions under the Food, Drug and Cosmetic Act to ban or restrict distribution of saccharin as a possible carcinogen.
1986	Recreational Boating Safety Act Amendment	Enhances boating safety by requiring a report relating to informational displays on gasoline pumps.
1986	Truth in Mileage Act	Amends the Motor Vehicle Information and Cost Savings Act to strengthen, for the protection of consumers, the provisions respecting disclosure of mileage when motor vehicles are transferred.
1986	Petroleum Overcharge Distribution and Restitution Act	Provides for distribution to injured consumers of escrow funds remaining from oil company settlements of alleged price allocation violations under the Emergency Petroleum Allocation Act of 1973.
1986	Superfund Amendments and Reauthorization Act	Extends and amends the Comprehensive Environmental Response Compensation and Liability Act of 1980. Authorizes appropriations for and revises the EPA Hazardous Substance Response Trust Fund program for financing cleanup of uncontrolled hazardous waste sites.
1986	Anti-Drug Abuse Act	Amends the Food, Drug and Cosmetic Act to revise provisions on regulation of infant formula manufacture.
1986	Processed Products Inspection Improvement Act	Amends the Meat Inspection Act to eliminate USDA continuous inspection requirements for meats, poultry, and egg processing plants for a six-year trial period.
1986	Emergency Response Act	Amends the Toxic Substances Control Act to require the EPA to promulgate regulations pertaining to inspections, development of asbestos management plans and response actions.
1986	Safe Drinking Water Act Amendments	Amends the Safe Drinking Water Act. Authorizes appropriations for and revises EPA safe drinking water programs, including grants to states for drinking water standards enforcement and groundwater protection programs.
1986	Drug Export Amendments Act	Amends the Food, Drug and Cosmetic Act to remove restrictions on export of human and veterinary drugs not yet approved by FDA or USDA for use in the United States and establishes conditions governing export of such drugs.
1986	Comprehensive Smokeless Tobacco Health Education Act	Provides for public education concerning the health consequences of using smokeless tobacco products. Prohibits radio and television advertising of smokeless tobacco.
1988	Toxic Substance Control Act Amendment	Provides adequate time for planning and implementation of school asbestos management plans.
1988	Federal Food, Drug, and Cosmetic Act Amendment	Bans reimportation of drugs produced in the United States. Places restrictions on distribution of drug samples, bans certain resales of drugs by health-care facilities.

Source: John R. Nevin, "Consumer Protection Legislation: Evolution, Structure and Prognosis," Working paper, University of Wisconsin-Madison, Madison, Wis., August 1989.

FIGURE 21.4
Some Important Federal Regulatory Agencies

Agency	Responsibilities
Federal Trade Commission (FTC)	Enforces laws and develops guidelines regarding unfair business practices
Food and Drug Administration (FDA)	Enforces laws and develops regulations to prevent distribution and sale of adulterated or misbranded foods, drugs, cosmetics, and hazardous consumer products
Consumer Product Safety Commission (CPSC)	Enforces the Consumer Product Safety Act, which covers any consumer product not assigned to other regulatory agencies.
Interstate Commerce Commission (ICC)	Regulates interstate rail, bus, truck, and water carriers
Federal Communications Commission (FCC)	Regulates interstate wire, radio, and television
Environmental Protection Agency (EPA)	Develops and enforces environmental protection standards
Office of Consumer Affairs (OCA)	Handles consumer complaints

Source: E. Jerome McCarthy and William D. Perreault, Jr. *Basic Marketing,* 10th ed. (Homewood, Ill.: Richard D. Irwin, 1990), p. 113.

product, promotion, pricing, and distribution issues. Many of these practices are subject to legal influences or constraints.

Legal Influences

Legal influences are federal, state, and local legislation and the agencies and processes by which these laws are upheld. Figure 21.3 presents examples of federal legislation designed to protect consumers. Some federal legislation is designed to control practices in specific industries (such as food); others are aimed at controlling functional areas (such as product safety).

A variety of government agencies are involved in enforcing these laws and investigating business practices. In addition to state and local agencies, this includes a number of federal agencies, such as those listed in Figure 21.4.

One marketing practice of major interest to the Federal Trade Commission is deceptive advertising—advertising that misleads consumers. One FTC approach to dealing with this problem is **corrective advertising.** Corrective advertising requires that firms that have misled consumers must rectify the deception in future ads.[5] Profile bread advertising led consumers to believe it was effective in weight reduction; Domino sugar advertising led consumers to

FIGURE 21.5
Examples of Corrective Ads

Profile Bread

"Hi, (celebrity's name) for Profile bread. Like all mothers, I'm concerned about nutrition and balanced meals. So, I'd like to clear up any misunderstanding you may have about Profile bread from its advertising or even its name.

"Does Profile have fewer calories than any other breads? No, Profile has about the same per ounce as other breads. To be exact, Profile has seven fewer calories per slice. That's because Profile is sliced thinner. But eating Profile will not cause you to lose weight. A reduction of seven calories is insiginficant. It's total calories and balanced nutrition that count. And Profile can help you achieve a balanced meal because it provides protein and B vitamins as well as other nutrients.

"How does my family feel about Profile? Well, my husband likes Profile toast, the children love Profile sandwiches, and I prefer Profile to any other bread. So you see, at our house, delicious taste makes Profile a family affair."

(To be run in 25% of brand's advertising, for one year.)

Amstar

"Do you recall some of our past messages saying that Domino Sugar gives you stength, energy, and stamina? Actually, Domino is not a special or unique source of strength, energy, and stamina. No sugar is, because what you need is a balanced diet and plenty of rest and exercise."

(To be run in one of every four ads for one year.)

Ocean Spray

"If you've wondered what some of our earlier advertising meant when we said Ocean Spray Cranberry Juice Cocktail has more food energy than orange juice or tomato juice, let us make it clear: we didn't mean vitamins and minerals. Food energy means calories. Nothing more.

"Food energy is important at breakfast since many of us may not get enough calories, or food energy, to get off to a good start. Ocean Spray Cranberry Juice Cocktail helps because it contains more food energy than most other breakfast drinks.

"And Ocean Spray Cranberry Juice Cocktail gives you and your family Vitamin C plus a great wake-up-taste. It's . . . the other breakfast drink."

(To be run in one of every four ads for one year.)

Sugar Information, Inc.

"Do you recall the messages we brought you in the past about sugar? How something with sugar in it before meals could help you curb your appetite? We hope you didn't get the idea that our little diet tip was any magic formula for losing weight. Because there are no tricks or shortcuts; the whole diet subject is very complicated. Research hasn't established that consuming sugar before meals will contribute to weight reduction or even keep you from gaining weight."

(To be run for one insertion in each of seven magazines.)

Source: Reprinted from William L. Wilkie, Dennis L. McNeill, and Michael B. Mazis, "Marketing's 'Scarlet Letter': The Theory and Practice of Corrective Advertising," *Journal of Marketing* 48 (Spring 1984), p. 13. Published by the American Marketing Association.

believe it was a special source of strength, energy, and stamina; Ocean Spray Cranberry Juice Cocktail misled consumers about food energy; and Sugar Information, Inc., misled consumers about sugar benefits. Figure 21.5 presents the text and number of ads required for correcting these deceptions.

Legal influences and the power of government agencies to regulate business and marketing practices grew dramatically in the 1970s; but the 1980s witnessed a decrease in many areas of regulation. In fact, deregulation of business was the major thrust in that period and government agencies considerably reduced their involvement in controlling business practices.[6] However, it seems likely the 1990s will witness a resurgence of legal influences at the federal level aimed at consumer and environmental protection.

FIGURE 21.6
Some Political Groups Concerned with Consumerism

Broad-Based National Groups
Consumer Federation of America
National Wildlife Federation
Common Cause
Environmental Defense Fund

Smaller Multi-issue Organizations
National Consumer's League
Ralph Nader's Public Citizen

Special-Interest Groups
American Association of Retired Persons
Group against Smoking and Pollution

Local Groups
Public-interest research groups
Local consumer protection offices
Local broadcast and newspaper consumer "action lines"

Source: Adapted from Paul N. Bloom and Stephen A. Greyser, "The Maturing of Consumerism," *Harvard Business Review*, November—December 1981, pp. 130–39.

Political Influences

By **political influences** we mean the pressure exerted to control marketing practices by various consumer groups. These groups use a variety of methods to influence marketing practice, such as lobbying with various government agencies to enact legislation or working directly with consumers in redress assistance and education. Figure 21.6 lists some organizations designed to serve consumer interests. These are but a few examples; one tally found over 100 national organizations and over 600 state and local groups concerned with consumerism.[7]

Bloom and Greyser argue that consumerism has reached the mature stage of its life cycle and its impact has been fragmented.[8] Yet they believe consumerism will continue to have some impact on business, and they offer three strategies for coping with it. First, businesses can try to accelerate the decline of consumerism by *reducing demand* for it. This could be done by improving product quality, expanding services, lowering prices, and toning down advertising claims. Highlight 21.1 describes one industry's attempt to reduce demand for consumerism.

Second, businesses can *compete* with consumer groups by having active consumer affairs departments that offer redress assistance and consumer education. Alternatively, a business could fund and coordinate activities designed to "sell" deregulation and other probusiness causes.

Third, businesses can *cooperate* with consumer groups by providing financial and other support. Overall, most of these strategies would likely further reduce the impact and importance of political influences. However, to the degree that following these strategies leads business firms to increase their social responsibility activities in the long run, the consumer could benefit.

HIGHLIGHT 21.1

Political Influences: TV Network Guidelines for Advertising to Children

Each of the major television networks has its own set of guidelines for children's advertising, although the basics are very similar. A few rules, such as the requirement of a static "island" shot at the end, are written in stone; others, however, occasionally can be negotiated.

Many of the rules below apply specifically to toys. The networks also have special guidelines for kid's food commercials and for kid's commercials that offer premiums.

	ABC	CBS	NBC
Must not overglamorize product	✓	✓	✓
No exhortative language, such as "Ask Mom to buy . . ."	✓	✓	✓
No realistic war settings	✓		✓
Generally no celebrity endorsements	✓	Case-by-case	✓
Can't use "only" or "just" in regard to price	✓	✓	✓
Show only two toys per child or maximum of six per commercial	✓		✓
Five-second "island" showing product against plain background at end of spot	✓	✓	✓ (4 to 5)
Animation restricted to one third of a commercial	✓		✓
Generally no comparative or superiority claims	Case-by-case	Handle w/care	✓
No costumes or props not available with the toy	✓		✓
No child or toy can appear in animated segments	✓		✓
Three-second establishing shot of toy in relation to child	✓	✓ (2.5 to 3)	
No shots under one second in length		✓	
Must show distance a toy can travel before stopping on its own		✓	

Source: Joanne Lipman, "Double Standard for Kids' TV Ads," *The Wall Street Journal*, June 10, 1988, p. 21.

Competitive Influences

Competitive influences refer to actions of competing firms intended to affect each other and consumers. These actions can be taken in many ways. For example, one firm might sue another firm or point out its alleged fraudulent activities to consumers. Johnson & Johnson frequently took competitors to court to protect its Tylenol brand of pain reliever from being shown in com-

Obtaining shelf space is a competitive struggle.

petitive ads. Burger King publicly accused McDonald's of overstating the weight of its hamburgers.

Perhaps the most important consumer protection generated by competition is that it reduces the impact of information from any single firm. In other words, in a marketing environment where there are many active competitors, no single firm can dominate the information flow to consumers. In this sense, conflicting competitive claims, images, information, and offers may help consumers from being unduly influenced by a single firm or brand. Conversely, it may also lead to information overload.

Consumers may also benefit from the development and marketing of better products and services brought about by competitive pressure. Current merger trends and the concentration of various industries may lessen these competitive constraints and societal advantages, however.

Ethical Influences

Perhaps the most important constraints on marketing practices are **ethical influences** and involve **self-regulation** by marketers. Many professions have codes of ethics (see Highlight 21.2), and many firms have their own consumer affairs offices that seek to ensure the consumer is treated fairly. In addition, some companies have developed a more positive image with consumers by emphasizing consumer-oriented marketing tactics such as offering toll-free hot lines for information and complaints, promoting unit pricing, and supporting social causes.

HIGHLIGHT 21.1

CODE OF ETHICS OF THE AMERICAN MARKETING ASSOCIATION

Members of the American Marketing Association (AMA) are committed to ethical professional conduct. They have joined in subscribing to this Code of Ethics embracing the following topics:

Responsibilities of the Marketer

Marketers must accept responsibility for the consequence of their activities and make every effort to ensure that their decisions, recommendations, and actions function to identify, serve, and satisfy all relevant publics: customers, organizations, and society.

Marketers' professional conduct must be guided by:

1. The basic rule of professional ethics: not knowingly to do harm;
2. The adherence to all applicable laws and regulations;
3. The accurate representation of their education, training, and experience; and
4. The active support, practice, and promotion of this Code of Ethics.

Honesty and Fairness

Marketers shall uphold and advance the integrity, honor, and dignity of the marketing profession by:

1. Being honest in serving consumers, clients, employees, suppliers, distributors, and the public;
2. Not knowingly participating in conflict of interest without prior notice to all parties involved; and
3. Establishing equitable fee schedules including the payment or receipt of usual, customary, and/or legal compensation or marketing exchanges.

Rights and Duties of Parties in the marketing exchange process

Participants in the marketing exchange process should be able to expect that:

1. Products and services offered are safe and fit for their intended uses;
2. Communications about offered products and services are not deceptive;
3. All parties intend to discharge their obligations, financial and otherwise, in good faith; and
4. Appropriate internal methods exist for equitable adjustment and/or redress of grievances concerning purchases.

It is understood that the above would include, *but is not limited to*, the following responsibilities of the marketer:

A difficult problem in discussing ethical constraints is that there is no single standard by which actions can be judged. Laczniak summarizes five ethical standards proposed by various marketing writers:

In the area of product development and management,

- Disclosure of all substantial risks associated with product or service usage;
- Identification of any product component substitution that might materially change the product or impact on the buyer's purchase decision;
- Identification of extra-cost added features.

In the area of promotions,

- Avoidance of false and misleading advertising;
- Rejection of high pressure manipulation, or misleading sales tactics;
- Avoidance of sales promotions that use deception or manipulation.

In the area of distribution,

- Not manipulating the availability of a product for purpose of exploitation;
- Not using coercion in the marketing channel;
- Not exerting undue influence over the resellers choice to handle the product.

In the area of pricing,

- Not engaging in price fixing;
- Not practicing predatory pricing;
- Disclosing the full price associated with any purchase.

In the area of marketing research,

- Prohibiting selling or fund raising under the guise of conducting research;
- Maintaining research integrity by avoiding misrepresentation and omission of pertinent research data;
- Treating outside clients and suppliers fairly.

Organizational Relationships

Marketers should be aware of how their behavior may influence or impact on the behavior of others in organizational relationships. They should not demand, encourage, or apply coercion to obtain unethical behavior in their relationships with others, such as employees, suppliers, or customers.

1. Apply confidentiality and anonymity in professional relationships with regard to privileged information;
2. Meet their obligations and responsibilities in contracts and mutual agreements in a timely manner;
3. Avoid taking the work of others, in whole, or in part, and represent this work as their own or directly benefit from it without compensation or consent of the orginator or owner;
4. Avoid manipulation to take advantage of situations to maximize personal welfare in a way that unfairly deprives or damages the organization or others.

Any AMA members found to be in violation of any provision of this Code of Ethics may have his or her Association membership suspended or revoked.

Source: The American Marketing Association, Chicago.

1. *The Golden Rule:* Act in the way you would expect others to act toward you.
2. *The Utilitarian Principle:* Act in a way that results in the greatest good for the greatest number.

FIGURE 21.7
Marketing Scenarios that Raise Ethical Questions

Scenario 1

The Thrifty Supermarket Chain has 12 stores in the city of Gotham, U.S.A. The company's policy is to maintain the same prices for all items at all stores. However, the distribution manager knowingly sends the poorest cuts of meat and the lowest quality produce to the store located in the low-income section of town. He justifies this action based on the fact that this store has the highest overhead due to factors such as employee turnover, pilferage, and vandalism. *Is the distribution manager's economic rationale sufficient justification for his allocation method?*

Scenario 2

The independent Chevy Dealers of Metropolis, U.S.A., have undertaken an advertising campaign headlined by the slogan: "Is your family's life worth 45 MPG?" The ads admit that while Chevy subcompacts are *not* as fuel efficient as foreign imports and cost more to maintain, they are safer according to government-sponsored crash tests. The ads implicitly ask if responsible parents, when purchasing a car, should trade off fuel efficiency for safety. *Is it ethical for the dealers association to use a fear appeal to offset an economic disadvantage?*

Scenario 3

A few recent studies have linked the presence of the artificial sweetener subsugural to cancer in laboratory rats. While the validity of these findings has been hotly debated by medical experts, the Food and Drug Administration has ordered products containing the ingredient banned from sale in United States. The Jones Company sends all of its sugar-free J. C. Cola (which contains subsugural) to European supermarkets because the sweetener has not been banned there. *Is it acceptable for the Jones Company to send an arguably unsafe product to another market without waiting for further evidence?*

Scenario 4

The Acme Company sells industrial supplies through its own sales force, which calls on company purchasing agents. Acme has found that providing the purchasing agent with small gifts helps cement a cordial relationship and creates goodwill. Acme follows the policy that the bigger the order, the bigger the gift to the purchasing agent. The gifts range from a pair of tickets to a sports event to outboard motors and snowmobiles. Acme does not give gifts to personnel at companies that it knows have an explicit policy prohibiting the acceptance of such gifts. *Assuming no laws have been violated, is Acme's policy of providing gifts to purchasing agents morally proper?*

Scenario 5

The Buy American Electronics Company has been selling its highly rated System X Color TV sets (21, 19, and 12 inches) for $700, $500, and $300, respectively. These prices have been relatively uncompetitive in the market. After some study, Buy American substitutes several cheaper components (which engineering says may slightly reduce the quality of performance) and passes on the savings to the consumer in the form of a $100 price reduction on each model. Buy American institutes a price-oriented promotional campaign that neglects to mention that the second-generation System X sets are different from the first. *Is the company's competitive strategy ethical?*

Scenario 6

The Smith & Smith Advertising Agency has been struggling financially. Mr. Smith is approached by the representative of a small South American country on good terms with the U.S. Department of State. He wants S & S to create a multimillion-dollar advertising and public relations campaign that will bolster the image of the country and increase the likelihood it will receive U.S. foreign aid assistance and attract investment capital. Smith knows the country is a dictatorship that has been accused of numerous human rights violations. *Is it ethical for the Smith & Smith Agency to undertake the proposed campaign?*

Source: Gene R. Laczniak, "Framework for Analyzing Marketing Ethics," *Journal of Macromarketing,* Spring 1983, p. 8.

3. *Kant's Categorical Imperative:* Act in such a way that the action taken under the circumstances could be a universal law or rule of behavior.

4. *The Professional Ethic:* Take actions that would be viewed as proper by a disinterested panel of professional colleagues.

A classic example of corporate social responsibility.

The party begins.

I can drive when I drink.

2 drinks later.

I can drive when I drink

After 4 drinks.

After 5 drinks.

7 drinks in all.

The more you drink, the more coordination you lose. That's a fact, plain and simple.

Still, people drink too much and then go out and expect to handle a car.

When you drink too much you can't handle a car.

You can't even handle a pen.

The House of Seagram

For reprints please write Advertising Dept. PL 782, The House of Seagram, 375 Park Ave., N.Y., N.Y. 10152. © 1973 The House of Seagram

5. *The TV Test:* A manager should always ask: "Would I feel comfortable explaining to a national TV audience why I took this action?"[9]

Following these standards could result in many different interpretations of an ethical marketing practice. If you doubt this, try applying them to the scenarios in Figure 21.7 and then comparing your answers with those of other readers.

Overall, then, what constitutes ethical marketing behavior is a matter of social judgment. Even in areas such as product safety, what constitutes ethical marketing practices is not always clear. While at first blush it might be argued that all products should either be completely safe or not be allowed on the market, deeper inspection reveals questions such as "How safe?" and "For whom?" For example, bicycles often head the list of the most hazardous products, yet few consumers or marketers would argue that bicycles should be banned from the market. Much of the problem in determining product safety concerns the question of whether the harm done results from an inherent lack of product safety or unsafe use by the consumer.

BACK TO.... McDONALD'S CORPORATION—EARLY 1990s

McDonald's has traditionally followed the marketing concept and has given consumers what they wanted: tasty food at clean restaurants with good service at affordable prices. The company has been able to deal with competitors effectively and was not required by law to change its practices. However, political influences led the company to make changes, and the Environmental Defense Fund helped McDonald's draft the plan to reduce garbage. Changes made to improve the environment are consistent with current values and could lead to a differential advantage for the company since consumers may believe McDonald's is socially responsible for doing so.

The changes in McDonald's food are also influenced by political pressures by consumer activists. However, many nutritionists are still unhappy with McDonald's menu. For example, Bonnie Liebman, nutritional director for the Center for Science in the Public Interest in Washington, stated, "What the company has done is made a few modest improvements in a few foods and made a few more dramatic changes in a few foods. If McDonald's really wanted to improve the public's health, it would remove 80 percent of the foods from its menu board and introduce fresh fruit salad, fresh vegetables, and whole-grain buns." To these suggestions, the president of McDonald's U.S. operations responded, "What the hell sense does it make to have that stuff on the menu if nobody's going to buy it?"

In this case, political influences helped to change the environmental practices and nutrition levels of McDonald's food in directions consistent with the overall welfare of consumers. However, whether consumers want to purchase nutritional food and pay for more enviromentally sensitive packaging are important issues to consider.

SUMMARY

In the final chapter of the text, we have discussed some of the important relationships among marketing, consumer behavior, and social responsibility. Overall, while society offers marketers considerable power and latitude in performing marketing tasks, marketers also have a variety of constraints placed on their behavior. In addition to consumer countercontrol and individual differences in consumers, these include legal, political, competitive, and ethical influences.

KEY TERMS AND CONCEPTS

Legal Influences *723*	Competitive Influences *726*
Corrective Advertising *723*	Ethical Influences *727*
Political Influences *725*	Self-Regulation *727*

REVIEW AND DISCUSSION QUESTIONS

1. Compare the rights of marketers and rights of consumers discussed in the beginning of the chapter. Which group do you think has more power?
2. Which of the buyer and seller rights become a problem if we assume consumers are not highly involved in most purchases?
3. Define each of the four major sources of consumer protection. In which of these sources can the consumer participate?
4. Evaluate the actions in each of the scenarios in Figure 21.7.
5. Which of the ethical standards proposed in the text do you think would be most useful to you as a marketing manager? Why?
6. In a bait and switch advertisement, the retailer advertises a low price on an item, but either doesn't stock the item or pressures consumers into buying a more expensive item when they come into the store. Evaluate the ethics of this practice.
7. Select three newspaper ads you consider to be misleading. Tell what elements of the communication are deceptive and which groups of consumers might be harmed.
8. Discuss with other members of the class the ethics of tobacco or liquor marketing. Could you develop a code of personal ethics to guide you as a promotion manager in these industries?
9. Prepare lists of obligations to complement the lists of rights of marketers and consumers.

Notes

1. Phillip Kotler, "What Consumerism Means for Marketers," *Harvard Business Review*, May–June 1972, pp. 48–57. Also see Joseph V. Anderson, "Power Marketing: Its Past, Present, and Future," *Journal of Consumer Marketing*, Summer 1987, pp. 5–13.
2. See, for example, Deborah Roedder John and Catherine A. Cole, "Age Differences in Information Processing: Understanding Deficits in Young and Elderly Consumers," *Journal of Consumer Research*, December 1986, pp. 297–315; and Gary J. Gaeth and Timothy B. Heath, "The Cognitive Processing of Misleading Advertising in Young and Old Adults; Assessment and Training," *Journal of Consumer Research*, March 1988, pp. 471–82.
3. For example, see Richard W. Olshavsky and Donald H. Granbois, "Consumer Decision Making: Fact or Fiction?" *Journal of Consumer Research*, September 1979, pp. 93–100.
4. For empirical support of this statement, see Shelby D. Hunt and Lawrence B. Chonko, "Marketing and Machiavellianism," *Journal of Marketing*, Summer 1984, pp. 30–42.
5. For an excellent, comprehensive discussion of corrective advertising, see William L. Wilkie, Dennis L. McNeill, and Michael B. Mazis, "Marketing's 'Scarlet Letter': The Theory and Practice of Corrective Advertising," *Journal of Marketing*, Spring 1984, pp. 11–31.
6. See Christine Dugas and Paula Dwyer, "Deceptive Ads: The FTC's Laissez-Faire Approach Is Backfiring," *Business Week*, December 2, 1985, pp. 136–40; and John Wilke, Mark N. Vamos, and Mark Maremont, "Has the FCC Gone Too Far?" *Business Week*, August 5, 1985, pp. 48–54.
7. Ann P. Harvey, *Contacts in Consumerism: 1980–1981* (Washington, D. C.; Fraiser/Associates, 1980).
8. Paul N. Bloom and Stephen A. Greyser, "The Maturing of Consumerism," *Harvard Business Review*, November–December 1981, pp. 130–39.
9. Gene R. Laczniak, "Framework for Analyzing Marketing Ethics," *Journal of Macromarketing*, Spring 1983, pp. 7–18.

Additional Reading

For additional discussion of marketing power, see:

Anderson, Joseph V. "Power Marketing: Its Past, Present, and Future." *Journal of Consumer Marketing*, Summer 1987, pp. 5–13.

For further discussions of ethical dimensions in marketing, see:

Ferrell, O. C., and Steven J. Skinner. "Ethical Behavior and Bureaucratic Structure in Marketing Research Organizations." *Journal of Marketing Research*, February 1988, pp. 103–9.

Laczniak, Gene R., and Patrick Murphy, eds. *Marketing Ethics: Guidelines for Managers.* Lexington, Mass.: Lexington Books, 1986.

Lantos, Geoffrey P. "An Ethical Base for Marketing Decision Making." *Journal of Consumer Marketing*, Fall 1986, pp. 5–10.

Robin, Donald P., and R. Eric Reidenbach. "Social Responsibility, Ethics, and Marketing Strategy: Closing the Gap between Concept and Application." *Journal of Marketing*, January 1987, pp. 44–58.

For further discussion of legal influences on specific marketing practices, see:

Boedecker, Karl A., Fred W. Morgan, and Jeffrey J. Stoltman. "Legal Dimensions of Salespersons' Statements: A Review and Managerial Suggestions." *Journal of Marketing*, January 1991, pp. 70–80.

Murphy, Patrick E., and William L. Wilkie, eds. *Marketing and Advertising Regulation: The Federal Trade Commission in the 1990s.* Notre Dame, IN: University of Notre Dame Press, 1990.

MARKETING STRATEGY IN ACTION

The Tylenol Crisis

Pain relievers are a lucrative, $1.2 billion-a-year industry. Until recently, there were no chemical or medicinal differences among brands of non-aspirin pain relievers, so aggressive marketing was the key to gain market share. For example, in a recent year, $130 million was spent on advertising for pain relievers. Johnson & Johnson, producer of Tylenol analgesic, developed very successful marketing strategies and obtained the largest share of the pain reliever market, 37 percent, in a few years. Then a tragedy threatened its strong position.

In 1959, Johnson & Johnson acquired McNeil Laboratories, which had introduced the Tylenol brand in 1955 in the form of an elixir for children as an alternative to aspirin and its irritating side effects. Traditionally, Tylenol was sold "ethically" through physicians and pharmacists and not directly to end-use consumers. Specifically, it was sold only as a prescription drug until 1960 and then as a nonprescription drug advertised only to doctors and pharmacists, who, in turn, recommended it to patients.

In 1975, Bristol-Meyers introduced Datril, a

EXHIBIT 1

Market Shares: Pain Reliever Industry

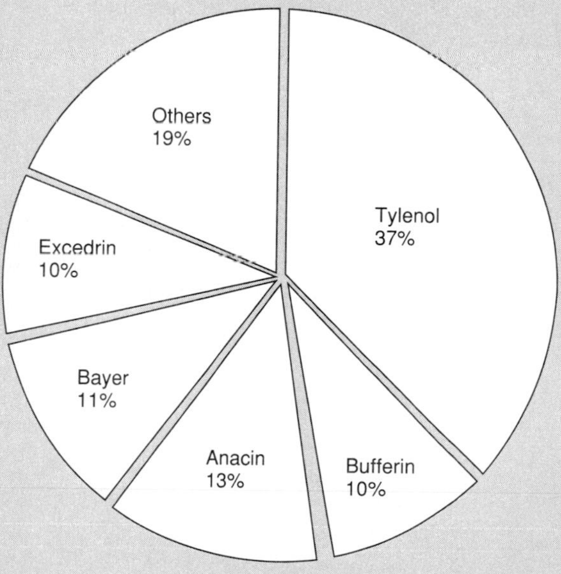

nonaspirin pain reliever, and successfully marketed it directly to end users. Datril's success forced Johnson & Johnson to expand its marketing effort to end users. The company cut prices, formed a sales force, and spent $8 million on advertising in which Tylenol was represented as an alternative to aspirin. Tylenol's solid reputation among pharmacists and physicians gave it a definite competitive advantage with end-use consumers as it was perceived to be a safe product endorsed by health professionals. In fact, two of every three Tylenol customers started using the product because it was recommended by their doctors.

In 1976, Extra-Strength Tylenol was introduced and was the first product to contain 500 milligrams of painkiller per tablet. Market research had indicated that many consumers believed Tylenol was too gentle to be effective. Extra-Strength Tylenol was advertised as the most "potent pain reliever available without a prescription." Tylenol's market share rose from 4 percent to 25 percent in 1979, due largely to the extra-strength version of the brand. In 1982, Tylenol had 37 percent market share, as shown in Exhibit 1.

Competitors frantically tried to defend their brands against Tylenol. Excedrin, Anacin, and Bayer each introduced extra-strength versions of their brands, with little success. Datril turned out to be a noncontender in the fight for market share because of failure to build a favorable reputation among physicians and pharmacists. Tylenol seemed unbeatable. The product became the largest selling health and beauty aid, breaking the 18-year dominance of Procter & Gamble's Crest toothpaste.

Tylenol employed very aggressive competitive tactics to dominate the industry. For example, court litigation was a very important competitive strategy, since Johnson & Johnson took several competitors to court with claims of infringement on Tylenol's trademark and name. Tylenol found that through the use of litigation, competitors could be barred from active competition for up to two years. After that time, the competition was in a weakened market position and seldom recovered. This strategy was especially effective against Anacin. Tylenol sued Anacin four times, once for trademark infringement and three times for false advertising, and won each suit. One marketing expert went so far as to credit Johnson & Johnson with inventing the fifth "P" of marketing – plaintiff.

In the early fall of 1982, eight Chicago-area consumers of Extra-Strength Tylenol died tragically. These consumers had taken Tylenol capsules that had been tampered with and laced with cyanide. The coupling of the Tylenol name with the eight deaths caused Tylenol's market share to drop from 37 percent to 7 percent overnight.

Research indicated many consumers had misconceptions about the poisoning incidents. For example, many consumers were not aware (1) the company was absolved of all responsibility by the investigating authorities, (2) Tylenol's production process conformed to all safety standards, (3) only Tylenol capsules were involved, not tablets, and (4) the tragic deaths were confined to the Chicago area.

Tylenol's competitors benefited greatly from the tragedy. Anacin won about 25 percent of Tylenol's lost business, mainly by aggressively advertising Anacin-3, and Bufferin and Bayer each took 20 percent of Tylenol's business. Most experts predicted the Tylenol brand would never recover. The situation was described as a consumer-goods marketer's darkest nightmare.

Very soon after the crisis, Johnson & Johnson made a strategic decision to attempt to save the brand that had been so successful and profitable. The company had built up a reservoir of consumer trust and loyalty that management felt would play a key role in the Tylenol brand's recovery. The company had always tried to live up to the credo set for it in 1940s by its leader, General Robert Wood Johnson: "We believe our first responsibility is to the doctors, nurses, and patients, to mothers and all others who use our products and services. In meeting their needs, everything we do must be of high quality." Company management interpreted the crisis as a monumental challenge to live up to this credo against overwhelming odds.

Discussion Questions

1. What tactics should Johnson & Johnson use to rebuild consumer trust in Tylenol?
2. What lessons are there for marketers of drug products in Tylenol's response to the crisis that resulted in the recovery of 90 percent of the lost market share in less than one year?
3. Should Johnson & Johnson have abandoned Tylenol and marketed a new brand?

Source: This case was prepared by Maragaret L. Friedman, Assistant Professor, School of Business, University of Wisconsin-Whitewater. Used by permission. Based on "Tylenol, the Painkiller, Gives Rivals Headache in Stores and in Court," *The Wall Street Journal,* September 2, 1982; "A Death Blows for Tylenol?" *Business Week,* October 18, 1982, p. 151; "The Fight to Save Tylenol," *Fortune,* November 29, 1982, pp. 44–49; "Rivals Go after Tylenol's Market, but Gains May Be Only Temporary," *The Wall Street Journal,* December 2, 1982, pp. 25ff; and taken from J. Paul Peter and James H. Donnelly, *Marketing Management: Knowledge and Skills,* 3d ed. (Homewood, Ill.: Richard D. Irwin, 1992), pp. 619–22.

GLOSSARY OF CONSUMER BEHAVIOR TERMS

abstract attributes Intangible, subjective characteristics of the product, such as the quality of a blanket or the stylishness of a car.

accessibility The probability that a meaning concept will be (or can be) activated from memory. Highly related to top-of-mind awareness and salience.

accidental exposure Occurs when consumers come in contact with marketing information in the environment that they haven't deliberately sought out. Compare with **intentional exposure.**

accretion The most common type of cognitive learning. Adding new knowledge, meanings, and beliefs to an associative network.

acculturation The process by which people in one culture or subculture learn to understand and adapt to the meanings, values, life styles, and behaviors of another culture or subculture.

activation The essentially automatic process by which knowledge, meanings, and beliefs are retrieved from memory and made available for use in cognitive processing.

adopter categories A classification of consumers based on the time of initial purchase of a new product. Typically, five groups are considered including Innovators, Early Adopters, Early Majority, Late Majority, and Laggards.

adoption curve A visual representation of the cumulative percentage of persons who adopt a new product across time.

adoption process An ambiguous term sometimes used to refer to a model of stages in the purchase process ranging from awareness to knowledge, evaluation, trial, and adoption. In other cases, it is used as a synonym for the diffusion process.

advertising Any paid, nonpersonal presentation of information about a product, brand, company, or store.

affect A basic mode of psychological response that involves a general positive/negative feeling and varying levels of activation or arousal of the physiological system that consumers experience in their bodies. Compare with **cognition.** See also **affective responses.**

affective responses Consumers can experience four types of affective responses—emotions, specific feelings, moods, and evaluations—that vary in level of intensity and arousal.

age subcultures Groups of people defined in terms of age categories (teens, elderly) with distinctive behaviors, values, beliefs, and life styles.

AIO An acronym standing for activities, interest, and opinions. AIO measures are the primary method for investigating consumer lifestyles and forming psychographic segments.

aspirational group A reference group an individual consumer wants to join or be similar to.

associative network An organized structure of knowledge, meanings, and beliefs about some concept such as a brand. Each meaning concept is linked to other concepts to form a network of associations.

attention The process by which consumers select information in the environment to interpret. Also the point at which consumers become conscious or aware of certain stimuli.

attitude A person's overall evaluation of a concept. An attitude is an affective response at a low level of intensity and arousal. General feelings of favorability or liking.

attitude models See **multiattribute attitude models.**

attitude toward objects (A_o) Consumers' overall evaluation (like/dislike) of an object such as a product or store. May be formed in two quite different ways: a cognitive process that involves relatively controlled and conscious integration of information about the object, and a largely automatic and unconscious response of the affective system.

attitude toward the ad (A_{ad}) Consumers' affective evaluations of advertisements themselves, not the product or brand being promoted.

attitude toward the behavior or action (A_{act}) The consumer's overall evaluation of a specific behavior.

automatic processing Cognitive processes tend to become more automatic—to require less conscious control and less cognitive capacity—as they become more practiced and familiar.

baseline The frequency of the problem behavior before an intervention strategy.

behavior Overt acts or actions that can be directly observed.

behavior approach An approach to studying consumer behavior that focuses on the relationship between overt behavior and the environment.

behavior change strategy A strategy developed to change the frequency or quality of a problem behavior.

behavior effort The effort consumers expend when making a purchase.

behavioral intention *(BI)* A plan to perform an action—"I intend to go shopping this afternoon." Intentions are produced when beliefs about the behavioral consequences of the action and social normative beliefs are considered and integrated to evaluate alternative behaviors and select among them.

behaviors Specific overt actions directed at some target object.

belief evaluation (e_i) Reflects how favorably the consumer perceives an attribute or consequence associated with a product.

belief strength (b_i) The perceived strength of association between an object and its relevant attributes or consequences.

beliefs The perceived association between two concepts. May be represented cognitively as a proposition. Beliefs about products often concern their attributes or functional consequences. For example, after trying a new brand of toothpaste, a consumer may form a belief that it has a minty taste. Beliefs are synonymous with knowledge and meaning in that each term refers to consumers' cognitive representations of important concepts.

benefits Desirable consequences or outcomes that consumers seek when purchasing and using products and services.

benefit segmentation The process of grouping consumers on the basis of the benefits they seek from the product. For example, the toothpaste market may include one segment seeking cosmetic benefits such as white teeth and another seeking health benefits such as decay prevention.

brand choice The selection of one brand from a consideration set of alternative brands.

brand equity The value of a brand. From the consumer's perspective, brand equity is reflected by the brand attitude based on beliefs about positive product attributes and favorable consequences of brand use.

brand indifference A purchasing pattern characterized by a low degree of brand loyalty.

brand loyalty The degree to which a consumer consistently purchases the same brand within a product class.

brand switching A purchasing pattern characterized by a change from one brand to another.

categorization A cognitive process by which objects, events, and persons are grouped together and responded to in terms of their class membership rather than their unique characteristics.

category accessibility The degree to which a consumer can activate a category of meaning from memory. A cognitive approach to describing modeling effects, where the process of viewing a model's behavior involves the activation of an interpretive schema.

central route to persuasion One of two types of cognitive processes by which persuasion occurs. In the central route, consumers focus on the product messages in the ad, interpret them, form beliefs about product attributes and consequences, and integrate these meanings to form brand attitudes and intentions. See **peripheral route to persuasion.**

choice Choice among alternative actions or behaviors is the outcome of the integration processes involved in consumer decision making. See also **behavioral intention.**

choice alternatives The different product classes, product forms, brands, or models available for purchase.

choice criteria The specific product attributes or consequences used by consumers to evaluate and choose from a set of alternatives.

classical conditioning A process through which a previously neutral stimulus, by being paired with an unconditioned stimulus, comes to elicit a response very similar to the response originally elicited by the unconditioned stimulus.

cognition The mental processes of interpretation and integration, and the thoughts and meanings they produce.

cognitive activity The mental thought and effort involved in interpreting and integrating information, as in a purchase decision. Often considered as a cost.

cognitive dissonance A psychologically uncomfortable condition brought about by an imbalance in thoughts, beliefs, attitudes, or behavior. For example, behaving in a way that is inconsistent with one's beliefs creates cognitive dissonance and a motivation to reduce the inconsistency.

cognitive learning The processes by which knowledge structures are formed and changed as consumers interpret new information and acquire new meanings and beliefs.

cognitive processing The mental activities (both conscious and unconscious) by which external information in the environment is transformed into meanings and combined to form evaluations of objects and choices about behavior.

cognitive representations The subjective meanings that reflect each person's personal interpretation of stimuli in the environment and of behavior.

cognitive response The thoughts one has in response to a persuasive message such as support arguments or acceptance thoughts, counterarguments, and curiosity thoughts.

communication A type of behavior that marketers attempt to increase, involving two basic audiences: consumers who can provide the company with marketing information and consumers who can tell other potential consumers about the product and encourage them to buy it.

communication model A simple representation of human communication processes that focuses on characteristics of the source, message, medium, and receiver.

compatibility The degree to which a product is consistent with consumers' current cognitions and behaviors.

compensatory integration processes In decision making, the combination of all the salient beliefs about the consequences of the choice alternatives to form an overall evaluation or attitude (A_{act}) toward each behavioral alternative. See also **noncompensatory integration strategies.**

compensatory rule In evaluating alternatives, the

compensatory rule suggests a consumer will select the alternative with the highest overall evaluation on a set of criteria. Criteria evaluations are done separately and combined such that positive evaluations can offset (or compensate for) negative evaluations. This term is also called compensatory process, compensatory integration procedure, and compensatory model. See also **noncompensatory rules.**

competitive influences Actions of competing firms intended to affect each other and consumers.

complete environment The total complex of physical and social stimuli in the external world that is potentially available to the consumer.

comprehension The cognitive processes involved in interpreting and understanding concepts, events, objects, and persons in the environment.

concrete attributes Tangible, physical characteristics of a product such as the type of fiber in a blanket or the front-seat legroom in a car.

confirmation In consumer satisfaction theory, confirmation refers to a situation in which a product performs exactly as it was expected to, i.e., prepurchase expectations are confirmed.

conjunctive rule See **noncompensatory rules.**

consensual environment Those parts of the environment that are attended to and similarly interpreted by a group of people with relatively similar cultural and social backgrounds.

consideration set A set of alternatives that the consumer evaluates in making a decision. Compare with **evoked set.**

consumer acculteration The process by which people acquire the ability and cultural knowledge to be a skilled consumer in a different culture or subculture.

consumer behavior (1) The dynamic interaction of cognition, behavior, and environmental events by which human beings conduct the exchange aspects of their lives; (2) a field of study concerned with (1) above; (3) a college course concerned with (1) above; and (4) the overt actions of consumers.

consumer behavior management (CBM) models Based on ideas in applied behavior analysis, this model is concerned with the development and maintenance of consumer behavior.

consumer decision making The cognitive processes by which consumers interpret product information and integrate that knowledge to make choices among alternatives.

consumer information processing The cognitive processes by which consumers interpret and integrate information from the environment.

consumer/product relationship The relationship between target consumers and the product or brand of interest. How consumers perceive the product as relating to their goals and values. Important to consider in developing all phases of a marketing strategy. See also **means-end chains.**

consumer promotion Marketing tactics, such as coupons and free samples, designed to have a direct impact on consumer purchase behavior.

consumer satisfaction The degree to which a consumer's prepurchase expectations are fulfilled or surpassed by a product.

consumer socialization How children acquire knowledge about products and services and various consumption-related skills.

consumption Use of a product.

consumption situation The social and physical factors present in the environments where consumers actually use and consume the products and services they have obtained.

content of culture All the beliefs, attitudes, goals, and values shared by most people in a society, as well as the typical behaviors, rules, customs, and norms that most people follow, plus characteristic aspects of the physical and social environment.

continuous reinforcement schedule A schedule of reinforcement that provides a reward after every occurrence of the desired behavior.

core values The abstract, broad, general end goals that people are trying to achieve in their lives.

corrective advertising Ads that are mandated to correct the false beliefs created by previous misleading or deceptive advertising.

covert modeling In this type of modeling, no actual behaviors or consequences are demonstrated; instead, subjects are told to imagine observing a model behaving in various situations and receiving particular consequences.

cross-cultural differences How the content of culture (meanings, values, norms) differs between different cultures.

cross-cultural research Studies in which marketers seek to identify the differences and similarities in the cultural meaning systems of consumers living in different societies.

cultural interpenetration The amount and type of social interaction between newcomers to a culture (immigrants) and people in the host culture. Influences the degree of acculturation the newcomers can attain.

cultural meanings The shared or similar knowledge, meanings, and beliefs by which people in a social system represent significant aspects of their environments.

cultural process The process by which cultural meaning is moved or transferred between three locations in a society—the social and physical environment, products and services, and individual consumers.

culture The complex of learned meanings, values, and behavioral patterns that are shared by a society.

deal proneness A consumer's general inclination to use promotional deals such as buying on sale or using coupons.

decision A choice between two or more alternative actions or behaviors. See also **choice** and **behavioral intention.**

decision conflict Arises when family members disagree about various aspects of the purchase decision such as goals and appropriate choice criteria.

decision making See **consumer decision making.**

decision plan The sequence of behavioral intentions produced when consumers engage in problem solving during the decision-making process. See also **behavioral intention.**

declarative knowledge The meanings that consumers construct to represent important informational stimuli they encounter in the environment. Compare with **procedural knowledge.**

diffusion process The process by which new ideas and products become accepted by a society. See also **adopter categories.**

disconfirmation In consumer satisfaction theory, disconfirmation refers to a situation in which a product performs differently than expected. See also **negative disconfirmation** and **positive disconfirmation.**

discriminant consequences Consequences that differ across a set of alternatives that may be used as choice criteria.

discriminative stimulus A stimulus that by its mere presence or absence changes the probability of a behavior. For example, a "50 percent off" sign in a store window could be a discriminative stimulus.

disjunctive rule See **noncompensatory rules.**

disposition situation The physical and social aspects of the environments in which consumers dispose of products, as well as consumers' goals, values, beliefs, feelings, and behaviors while in those environments.

dissatisfaction Occurs when prepurchase expectations are negatively confirmed; i.e., when the product performs worse than expected.

dissociative group A reference group that an individual does not want to join or be similar to.

early adopters The second group of adopters of a new product.

early majority The third group of adopters of a new product.

elaboration The extensiveness of comprehension processes; the degree of elaboration determines the amount of knowledge or the number of meanings produced during comprehension as well as the richness of the interconnections between those meanings.

end goal The most abstract or most basic consequence, need, or value a consumer wants to achieve or satisfy in a given problem-solving situation.

enduring involvement The personal relevance of a product or activity. See also **intrinsic self-relevance.** Compare with **situational involvement.**

environment The complex set of physical and social stimuli in consumers' external world.

environmental prominence The marketing strategy of making certain stimuli obvious or prominent in the environment.

episodic knowledge Cognitive representations of specific events in a person's life. Compare with **semantic knowledge.**

ethical influences Basic values concerning right and wrong that constrain marketing practices.

ethnic subcultures Large social groups based on consumers' ethnic background. In the United States the important ethnic subcultures include African-American or blacks, Hispanics, Asians, and Native Americans.

European Economic Community (EEC or EC)

evaluation An overall judgment of favorable/unfavorable, pro/con, or like/dislike. An attitude toward an object such as a brand, an ad, or a behavioral act.

evoked set The set of choice alternatives activated directly from memory.

expectancy theory A possible explanation for modeling, this cognitive theory suggests models influence observer behavior by influencing their expectations.

expertise Occurs when consumers are quite familiar with a product category and specific brands, possessing substantial amounts of declarative and procedural knowledge organized in schemas and scripts.

exposure Occurs when consumers come into contact with information in the environment, sometimes through their own intentional behaviors and sometimes by accident.

extensive decision making A choice involving substantial cognitive and behavioral effort, as compared to limited decision making and routine choice behavior.

external reference price Explicit comparison of the stated price with another price in advertising, catalogs, and so on.

extinction The process of arranging the environment so that a particular response results in neutral consequences, thus diminishing the frequency of the response over time.

family A group of at least two people formed on the basis of marriage, cohabitation, blood relationships, or adoption. Families often serve as a basis for various types of consumer analysis.

family decision making The processes, interactions, and roles of family members involved in making decisions as a group.

family life cycle A sociological concept that describes changes in families across time. Emphasis is placed on the effects of marriage, births, aging, and deaths on families and the changes in income and consumption through various family stages.

felt involvement Consumers' subjective perception of the personal relevance of an object, activity, or situation. Experienced as feelings of arousal or activation and interest or importance. Determined by **intrinsic and situational self-relevance.**

Fishbein Behavioral Intentions Model An earlier name for the Theory of Reasoned Action.

fixed ratio schedule A type of reinforcement schedule where evey second, third, tenth, etc., response is reinforced.

focal attention A controlled, conscious level of attention that focuses cognitive processes on relevant or prominent stimuli in the environment. Compare with **preconscious attention.**

Foote, Cone & Belding (FCB) grid A two-by-two grid developed by the Foote, Cone & Belding advertising agency for analyzing consumers and products. The FCB grid categorizes products based on consumers' level of involvement (high or low) and on whether consumers' dominant response to the product is cognitive or affective (think or feel).

form utility What occurs when channels convert raw materials into finished goods and services in forms the consumer seeks to purchase.

four stages of acculturation Four levels of acculturation a newcomer to a culture could achieve, depending on the level of cultural interpenetration: honeymoon, rejection, tolerance, and integration stages.

free-flow layout A store layout that permits consumers to move freely rather than being constrained to movement up and down specific aisles.

functional consequences The immediate outcomes of product use that can be directly experienced by consumers. For instance, a toothpaste may get your teeth white.

functional (or perceived) environment Those parts of the complete environment that are attended to and interpreted by a particular consumer on a particular occasion.

funds access The ways consumers obtain money for their purchases. Primary marketing issues include the methods consumers use to pay for particular purchases and the marketing strategies used to increase the probability that consumers are able to access their funds for purchase.

geographic subculture Large social groups defined in geographic terms. For instance, people living in different parts of a country may exhibit cultural differences.

global marketing An approach that argues for marketing a product in essentially the same way everywhere in the world.

goal hierarchy The end goal and the subgoals that are involved in achieving it.

grid layout A store layout where all counters and fixtures are at right angles to each other, with merchandise counters acting as barriers to traffic flow.

group Two or more people who interact with each other to accomplish some goal. Examples include families, co-workers, bowling teams, and church members.

heuristics Propositions connecting an event with an action. Heuristics simplify problem solving. For example, "buy the cheapest brand" could be a choice heuristic that would simplify purchase choice.

hierarchy of effects model An early model that depicted consumer response to advertising as a series of stages including awareness, knowledge, liking, preference, conviction, and purchase.

hierarchy of needs See **Maslow's need hierarchy.**

high involvement See **involvement.**

household The people living in a housing unit—a dwelling with its own entrance and basic facilities.

ideal self-concept The ideas, attitudes, and meanings people have about themselves concerning what they would be like if they were perfect or ideal. Compare with **self-concept.**

impulse purchase A purchase choice typically made quickly in-store with little decision making effort.

inferences Meanings or beliefs that consumers construct to represent the relationships between concepts that are not based on explicit environmental information.

information acquisition situation Includes physical and social aspects of environments where consumers acquire information relevant to a problem-solving goal, such as a store choice or a decision to buy a particular brand.

information contact A common early stage in the purchase sequence that occurs when consumers come into contact with information about the product or brand. This often occurs in promotions, where such contact can be intentional (consumers search newspapers for coupons) or accidental (a consumer just happens to come into contact with a promotion while engaging in some other behavior). See also **exposure.**

information processing See **consumer information processing.**

information-processing model Used to divide complex cognitive processes into a series of simpler subprocesses that are more easily measured and understood.

information search Consumers' deliberate search for relevant information in the external environment.

informational reference group influence Information from a group that is accepted if the consumer believes it will help achieve a goal.

innovativeness A personality trait to account for the degree to which a consumer accepts and purchases new products and services.

innovators The first group of consumers to adopt a new product.

instrumental conditioning See **operant conditioning.**

instrumental values One of two major types of values proposed by Milton Rokeach. Instrumental values represent preferred modes of conduct or preferred patterns of behavior. See **terminal values.**

integration process The process by which consumers combine knowledge to make two types of judgments. Attitude formation concerns how different types of knowledge are combined to form overall evaluations of products or brands. Decision making concerns how knowledge is combined to make choices about what behaviors to perform.

intentional exposure Occurs when consumers are exposed to marketing information due to their own intentional, goal-directed behavior. Compare with **accidental exposure.**

internal reference price Price consumers have in mind for a product.

interpretation processes The processes by which consumers make sense of or determine the meaning of important aspects of the physical and social environment as well as their own behaviors and internal affective states.

interrupts Stimuli that interrupt or stop the problem-solving process, such as unexpected information encountered in the environment.

intrinsic self-relevance A consumer's personal level of self-relevance for a product. Cognitively represented by the general means-end chains of product/self relationships that consumers have learned and stored in memory. Compare with **situational self-relevance.**

involvement The degree of personal relevance a product, brand, object, or behavior has for a consumer. *A high-involvement* product is one a consumer believes has important personal consequences or will help achieve important personal goals. A *low-involvement* product is one that is not strongly linked to important consequences or goals. See also **felt involvement.**

ISTEA model A model for the process of developing a personal selling promotion strategy; stands for impression, strategy, transmission, evaluation, and adjustment.

knowledge Cognitive representation of products, brands, and other aspects of the environment that are stored in memory. Also called meanings or beliefs.

laggards The last group to adopt a new product.

late majority The next-to-last group to adopt a new product.

legal influences Federal, state, and local legislation and the agencies and processes by which these laws are upheld.

level of competition A key aspect of the promotion environment for a product category—as competition heats up, marketers' use of promotions usually increases.

level of comprehension Refers to the different types of meanings that consumers construct during interpretation processes.

levels of abstraction Consumers' product knowledge is at different levels of abstraction from concrete attributes to more abstract functional consequences to very abstract value outcomes.

lexicographic rule See **noncompensatory rules.**

lifestyle The manner in which people conduct their lives, including their activities, interests, and opinions.

limited capacity The notion that the amount of knowledge that can be activated and thought about at one time is limited and quite small.

limited decision making A choice process involving a moderate degree of cognitive and behavioral effort. See also **extensive decision making.**

macro social environment The broad, pervasive aspects of the social environment that affect the entire society or at least large portions of it; including culture, subculture, and social class.

market segmentation The process of dividing a market into groups of similar consumers and selecting the most appropriate group(s) for the firm to serve.

marketing concept A business philosophy that argues organizations should satisfy consumer needs and wants to make profits.

marketing environment All of the social and physical stimuli in consumers' environments that are under the control of the marketing manager.

marketing strategy A plan designed to influence exchanges to achieve organizational objectives; a part of the environment consisting of a variety of physical and social stimuli.

Maslow's need hierarchy A popular theory of human needs developed by Abraham Maslow. The theory suggests humans satisfy their needs in a sequential order starting with physiological needs (food, water, sex), and ranging through safety needs (protection from harm), belongingness and love needs (companionship), esteem needs (prestige, respect of others), and, finally, self-actualization needs (self-fulfillment).

materialism A multidimensional value held by many consumers in developed countries. Materialism includes possessiveness, envy of other people's possessions, and nongenerosity.

meanings People's personal interpretations (cognitive representations, knowledge, or beliefs) of stimuli in the environment.

means-end chain A simple knowledge structure that links product attributes to more functional and social consequences and perhaps to high-level consumer values. Means-end chains organize consumers' product knowledge in terms of its self relevance.

MECCAS model Attempts to simplify the difficult task of developing effective advertising strategies by identifying five key factors; stands for means-end chain conceptualization of advertising strategy.

micro social environment Important aspects of consumers' immediate social environment, especially reference groups and family.

modeling See **vicarious learning.**

modern family life cycle The various life stages for modern American families, including the stages of the traditional family life cycle, plus other stages found in modern culture such as divorce, single (never married), and single parents.

multiattribute attitude models Models designed to predict consumers' attitudes toward objects (such as brands) or behaviors (such as buying a brand) based on their beliefs about and evaluations of associated attributes or expected consequences.

multiple-baseline design Commonly used in applied behavior analysis, these designs demonstrate the effect of an intervention across several different behaviors, individuals, or situations at different times.

negative disconfirmation In consumer satisfaction theory, negative disconfirmation refers to a situation in which a product performs worse than expected.

negative reinforcement Occurs when the frequency of a given behavior is increased by removing an aversive stimulus. See also **reinforcement.**

noncompensatory integration processes Choice strategies in which the positive and negative consequences of the choice alternatives do not balance or compensate for each other. See also **compensatory integration strategies.** In evaluating alternatives using noncompensatory rules, positive and negative consequences of alternatives do not compensate for each other. Included among the types of noncompensatory integration processes are conjunctive, disjunctive, and lexicographics. The *conjunctive rule* suggests consumers establish a minimum acceptable level for each choice criterion and accept an alternative only if it equals or exceeds the minimum cutoff level for every criteria. The *disjunctive rule* suggests consumers establish acceptable standards for each criterion and accept an alternative if it exceeds the standard on at least one criterion. The *lexicographic rule* suggests consumers rank choice criteria from most to least important and choose the best alternative on the most important criterion.

nonfamily households Unrelated people living together in same household—about 30 percent of American households.

observability The degree to which products or their effects can be sensed by other consumers.

operant conditioning The process of altering the probability of a behavior being emitted by changing the consequences of the behavior.

opportunity to process The extent to which consumers have the chance to attend to and comprehend marketing information; can be affected by factors such as time pressure, consumers' affective states, and distractions.

overt modeling The most common form of vicarious learning, this requires the consumers actually observe the model performing the behavior.

penetration price policy A pricing strategy that includes a plan to sequentially raise prices after introduction at a relatively low price.

perceived risk The expected negative consequences of performing an action such as purchasing a product.

peripheral route to persuasion One of two types of cognitive processes by which persuasion occurs. In the peripheral route, the consumer does not focus on the product message in an ad but on "peripheral" stimuli such as an attractive, well-known celebrity or popular music. Consumers' feelings about these other stimuli may influence beliefs and attitude about the product. Compare with **central route to persuasion.**

person/situation segmentation Occurs when markets are divided on the basis of the usage situation in conjunction with individual differences of consumers.

personal selling Direct personal interactions between a salesperson and a potential buyer.

personality The general, relatively consistent pattern of responses to the environment exhibited by an individual.

persuasion Refers to the cognitive and affective processes by which consumers' beliefs and attitudes are changed by promotion communications.

physical environment The collection of nonhuman, physical, tangible elements that comprises the field in which consumer behavior occurs. Compare with **social environment.**

place utility Occurs when goods and services are made available where the consumer wants to purchase them.

political influences The pressure exerted to control marketing practices by various consumer groups.

positioning See **product positioning.**

positioning by attribute Probably the most frequently used positioning strategy, this associates a product with an attribute, a product feature, or a customer benefit.

positioning by competitor A positioning strategy where the explicit or implicit frame of reference is the competition.

positioning by product class A positioning strategy involving product-class associations (for example, positioning a margarine with respect to butter).

positioning by product user A positioning approach where a product is associated with a user or class of users.

positioning by use A positioning strategy where the product is associated with its use or application.

positive disconfirmation In consumer satisfaction theory, positive disconfirmation refers to a situation in which a product performs better than expected.

positive reinforcement Occurs when rewards are given to increase the frequency with which a given behavior is likely to occur. See also **reinforcement.**

possession utility Occurs when channels facilitate the transfer of ownership of goods to the consumer.

preconscious attention The highly automatic, largely unconscious selection of certain stimuli for simple cognitive processing. More likely for familiar concepts of low importance. Further processing tends to lead to **focal attention.**

prepurchase expectations Beliefs about anticipated performance of a product.

price elasticity A measure of the relative change in demand for a product for a given change in dollar price.

price perceptions Concerned with how price information is comprehended by consumers and made meaningful to them.

problem representation Consumers' cognitive representations of the various aspects of the decision problem. Includes an end goal, a set of subgoals, relevant product knowledge, and a set of choice rules or simple heuristics by which consumers search for, evaluate, and integrate this knowledge to reach a choice.

problem solving A general approach to understanding consumer decision making. Focuses on consumers' cognitive representation of the decision as a problem. Important aspects of the problem representation include end goals, subgoals, and relevant knowledge. Consumers construct a decision plan by integrating knowledge within the constraints of the problem representation.

procedural knowledge Consumers' cognitive representations of how to perform behaviors. See also **scripts.**

product contact Occurs when a consumer comes into physical contact with a product.

product positioning Designing and executing a marketing strategy to form a particular mental representation of a product or brand in consumers' minds. Typically, the goal is to position the product in some favorable way relative to competitive offerings.

product symbolism The various meanings of a product to a consumer and what the consumer experiences in purchasing and using it.

promotion clutter The growing number of competitive promotion strategies in the environment.

promotion strategies Used by marketers to help achieve their promotion objectives, these include advertising, sales promotions, personal selling, and publicity.

promotions Information that marketers develop to communicate meanings about their products and persuade consumers to buy them.

psychographic segmentation Dividing markets into segments on the basis of consumer lifestyles.

psychosocial consequences This term refers to two types of outcomes or consequences of product use: psychological consequences (I feel good about myself) and social consequences (Other people are making fun of me).

publicity Any unpaid form of communication about the marketer's company, products, or brand.

pull strategies Ways to encourage the consumer to purchase the manufacturer's brand, such as cents-off coupons.

punishment A term used to describe the process of a response being followed by a noxious or aversive event, thus decreasing the frequency of the response.

purchase intentions A decision plan or intention to buy a particular product or brand. See also **behavioral intention.**

purchasing situation Includes the physical and social stimuli that are present in the environment where the consumer actually makes the purchase.

push strategies Ways to enhance the selling efforts of retailers, such as trade discounts.

rate of usage The rate at which a consumer uses or uses up a product.

reciprocal determinism The idea that affect and cognition, behavior, and the environment cause and are caused by each other continuously over time.

reference group People who influence an individual's affect, cognitions, and behaviors.

reinforcement A consequence that occurs after a behavior that increases the probability of future behavior of the same type.

reinforcement schedules The rate at which rewards are offered in attempts to operantly condition behavior.

relative advantage Refers to the degree to which an item has a sustainable, competitive differential advantage over other product classes, product forms, and brands.

relevant knowledge Appropriate or useful knowledge activated from memory in the context of a decision or interpretation situation.

respondent conditioning See **classical conditioning.**

response hierarchy The total list of behaviors a consumer could perform at any given time arranged from most probable to least probable.

restructuring A rare type of cognitive learning that occurs when an entire associative network of knowledge is revised, reorganizing old knowledge and creating entirely new meanings. Very complex and infrequent compared with **accretion** and **tuning.**

reversal design In this approach, the problem behavior of a subject or group of subjects is first assessed to determine baseline performance. After a stable rate of behavior is determined, the intervention is introduced until behavior changes. The intervention is then withdrawn and then reintroduced to determine if it is influencing the behavior.

rituals Actions or behaviors performed by consumers to create, affirm, evoke, revise, or obtain desired symbolic cultural meanings.

routinized choice behavior A purchase involving little cognitive and behavioral effort and perhaps no decision. Purchase could be merely carrying out an existing decision plan. Compare with limited and extensive decision making.

sales promotions Direct inducements to the consumer to make a purchase, such as coupons or cents-off deals.

salient beliefs The set of beliefs activated in a particular situation; may be represented as an associative network of linked meanings.

scanner cable method A method of monitoring a number of stages in a purchase sequence. One such system, BehaviorScan, is designed to predict which products will be successful and which ads will work best to sell them.

schema An associative network of interrelated meanings that represents a person's declarative knowledge about some concept. Compare with **script.**

script A sequence of productions or mental representations of the appropriate actions associated with particular events. Consumers often form scripts to organize their knowledge about behaviors to perform in familiar situations. Compare with **schema.**

segmentation See **market segmentation.**

segmentation strategy The general approach marketers use to approach markets such as mass marketing, or marketing to one or more segments.

selective exposure A process by which people selectively come into contact with information in their environment. For instance, consumers may avoid marketing information by leaving the room while commercials are on TV.

self-concept The ideas, meanings, attitudes, and knowledge people have about themselves. See also **self-schema.**

self-regulation A form of ethical influence employed by marketers; many professions have codes of ethics and many firms have their own consumer affairs offices that seek to ensure the consumer is treated fairly.

self-schema An associative network of interrelated knowledge, meanings and beliefs about one's self. See also **self-concept.**

semantic knowledge The general meanings and beliefs people have acquired about their world. Compare with **episodic knowledge.**

shaping A process of reinforcing successive approximations of a desired behavior, or of other required behaviors, to increase the probability of the desired response.

shopping situation The physical and spacial characteristics of the environments where consumers shop for products and services.

simplicity The degree to which a product is easy for a consumer to understand and use.

situation The ongoing stream of reciprocal interactions between goal-directed behaviors, affective and cognitive responses, and environmental factors that occur over a defined period of time. Situations have a purpose and a beginning, middle, and end.

situational involvement Temporary interest or concern with a product or a behavior brought about by the situational context. For example, consumers may become situationally involved with buying a hot water heater if their old one breaks. See also **situational self- relevance.** Compare with **enduring involvement.**

situational self-relevance Temporary feelings of self-relevance due to specific external physical and social stimuli in the environment. Compare with **intrinsic self-relevance.**

skimming price policy A pricing strategy that includes a plan to systematically lower prices after a high-price introduction.

social class A status hierarchy by which groups and individuals are categorized on the basis of esteem and prestige. For example, one classification divides American society into upper class (14 percent of the population), middle class (32 percent of the population), working class (38 percent of the population), and lower class (16 percent of the population).

social environment Includes all human activities in social interactions.

socialization The processes by which an individual learns the values and appropriate behavior patterns of a group, institution, or culture. Socialization is strongly influenced by family, reference groups, and social class.

social learning theory One of a number of theories of human behavior.

social marketing Programs and strategies designed to change behavior in ways that are deemed good for consumers and for society.

social stratification See **social class.**

speed Refers to how fast the benefits of the product are experienced by the consumer.

spreading activation Through this usually unconscious process, interrelated parts of a knowledge structure may be activated during interpretation and integration processes (or even daydreaming).

store atmosphere Affective and cognitive states that consumers experience in a store but may not be fully conscious of while shopping.

store contact An important aspect of most consumer-goods purchases, this includes locating the outlet, traveling to the outlet, and entering the outlet.

store image The set of meanings consumers associate with a particular store.

store layout The basic floor plan and display of merchandise within a store. At a basic level, this influences such factors as how long the consumer stays in the store, how many products the consumer comes into visual contact with, and what routes the consumer travels within the store. Two basic types are *grid* and *free-flow layouts.*

store location Where a store is situated in a specific geographic area.

store loyalty The degree to which a consumer consistently patronizes the same store when shopping for particular types of products.

store patronage The degree to which a consumer shops at a particular store relative to competitive outlets.

subcultures Segments within a culture that share a set of distinguishing meanings, values, and patterns of behavior that differ from those of the overall culture.

subjective or social norm *(SN)* Consumers' perceptions of what other people want them to do.

subliminal perception A psychological view that suggests attitudes and behaviors can be changed by stimuli that are not consciously perceived.

symbolic meaning The set of psychological and social meanings products have for consumers. More abstract meanings than physical attributes and functional consequences.

target behavior The earliest behavior in the purchase sequence not being performed, or not being performed appropriately or frequently enough to lead to the next behavior. Also known as *problem behavior.*

terminal values One of two major types of values proposed by Milton Rokeach. Terminal values represent preferred end states of being or abstract, global goals that consumers are trying to achieve in their lives. Compare with **instrumental values.**

Theory of Reasoned Action A theory developed by Martin Fishbein that assumes consumers consciously consider the consequences of alternative behaviors and choose the one that leads to the most desirable outcomes. The theory states behavior is strongly influenced by behavioral intentions, which in turn are determined by attitudes toward performing the behavior and social normative beliefs about the behavior.

time utility Occurs when channels make goods and services available to consumers when the consumer wants to purchase them.

trade promotion marketing tactics, such as advertising or display allowances, designed to get channel members to provide special support for products or services.

traditional family life cycle The typical stages of life followed by most American families some 30 to 40 years ago. Each stage is distinguished by a major life event: marriage, birth of children, aging, retirement, and death.

transactions The exchanges of funds, time, cognitive activity, and behavior effort for products and services. In a micro sense, the primary objective of marketing, where consumers' funds are exchanged for products and services.

trialability The degree to which a product can be tried on a limited basis or divided into small quantities for an inexpensive trial.

tuning A type of cognitive learning that occurs when parts of a knowledge structure are combined and given a new, more abstract meaning. More complex and less frequent than **accretion.**

unit pricing Common for grocery products, this involves a shelf tag that indicates the price per unit for a specific good.

utilitarian reference group influence Compliance of an individual with perceived expectations of others to obtain rewards or avoid punishments.

VALS An acronym standing for Values And Life-Styles. VALS and VALS 2 are well-known psychographic segmentations marketed by SRI International.

value-expressive reference group influence An individual's use of groups to enhance or support his or her self-concept.

values The cognitive representations of important, abstract life goals that consumers are trying to achieve.

variable ratio schedule Occurs when a reinforcer follows a desired consequence on an average of one half, one third, one fourth, etc., of the time the behavior occurs, but not necessarily every second or third time, etc.

verbal modeling In this type of modeling, behaviors are not demonstrated and people are not asked to imagine a model performing a behavior; instead, people are told how others similar to themselves behaved in a particular situation.

vicarious learning Changes in an individual's behavior brought about by observing the actions of others and the consequences of those actions.

WOM An acronym standing for Word-of-Mouth communication.

word-of-mouth communication Occurs when consumers share information with friends about products and/or promotions; e.g., good deals on particular products, a valuable coupon in the newspaper, or a sale at a retail store.

NAME INDEX

C

D

E

F

G

H

I

J

K

L

M

N

O

P

Q

R

S

T

U

V

W

Y

Z

SUBJECT INDEX

A

B

M

N

O

P

Q

R

S

T

U

V

W

Y

Photo Credits

p. 10 Courtesy Boys Club of America
p. 12 Courtesy Toyota Motor Sales, U.S.A., Inc.
p. 15 Courtesy Pepsi-Cola Company
p. 24 Courtesy New Balance Athletic Shoe, Inc.
p. 26 Laimute Druskis/Stock, Boston
p. 27 Peter Menzel/Stock, Boston
p. 33 Courtesy Life Fitness Inc.
p. 35 Courtesy Swift-Eckrich, Inc.
p. 46 top left: Bob Daemmrich/The Image Works; top right: Spencer Grant/Photo Researchers; bottom: John A. Coletti/Stock, Boston
p. 51 Courtesy U.S. Armed Forces
p. 55 Courtesy Calvin Klein
p. 66 Courtesy Nordic Track
p. 94 Courtesy Colgate-Palmolive Co.
p. 96 Courtesy Volvo Cars of North America
p. 97 Courtesy Bertolli
p. 107 Courtesy The Procter & Gamble Company
p. 112 Toni Michaels/The Image Works
p. 117 top: Susan M. Klemens/Stock, Boston; bottom: Bob Daemmrich/Stock, Boston
p. 119 © Mars, Incorporated 1989
p. 138 top: Thelma Shumsky/The Image Works; bottom: Alan Carey/The Image Works
p. 145 © Churchill & Klehr
p. 146 Courtesy Kemper Financial Services, Inc.
p. 149 Courtesy of Avis, Inc.
p. 151 Courtesy Hershey Foods Corporation. HERSHEY'S is a registered trademark of Hershey Foods Corporation.
p. 152 Don Smetzer, TSW/Click, Chicago, Ltd.
p. 153 Courtesy and Copyright © The Paddington Corporation, Reprinted with permission
p. 155 Courtesy Nike, Inc.
p. 164 Courtesy R. J. Corr Naturals, Inc.
p. 177 Courtesy Jaguar, Inc.
p. 184 Courtesy Sony Corporation of America
p. 188 Courtesy Buick Motor Division, General Motors Corporation
p. 195 Courtesy Champion Products
p. 196 © Gerber Products Company
p. 197 Courtesy Beef Industry Council
p. 227 Courtesy Southwest Airlines
p. 230 Courtesy General Motors Corporation
p. 231 Courtesy H. J. Heinz Co.
p. 234 Courtesy Alfa-Romeo, Inc.
p. 237 Courtesy Cotter & Company
p. 243 Courtesy The Marriott Corporation
p. 245 Spencer Grant/Stock, Boston
p. 251 Dion Ogust/The Image Works
p. 275 left: Courtesy Hyundai; right: Mark Antman/The Image Works
p. 277 Courtesy Mars, Incorporated, 1992
p. 280 Courtesy The Russell Corporation
p. 295 Courtesy Liz Claiborne Cosmetics. Photo: Pam Hanson
p. 298 Courtesy Pepperidge Farm, Inc.
p. 300 Owen Franken/Stock, Boston
p. 304 David S. Strickler, TSW/Click, Chicago, Ltd.
p. 321 Alan Carey/The Image Works
p. 323 Courtesy Carnation Co.
p. 325 Charles Gupton/Stock, Boston
p. 329 Courtesy of Lever Brothers Company
p. 334 Courtesy Nintendo of America, Inc.
p. 352 Mark Antman/The Image Works
p. 353 top: Day Williams/Photo Researchers; bottom: Cary Wolinsky/Stock, Boston

p. 355 top left: Mike Mazzaschi/Stock, Boston: top right: Bob Daemmrich/Stock, Boston; bottom left: David S. Strickler, TSW/Click, Chicago, Ltd.; bottom right: George W. Gardner

p. 356 ©1992 Joseph H. Jacobson/O.G.S., Inc. All rights reserved

p. 359 Ulrike Welsch/Photo Researchers

p. 363 Courtesy Information Resources, Inc.

p. 384 Courtesy of the Wm. Wrigley Jr. Company

p. 386 Courtesy Pfizer, Inc. Photo: David Langley

p. 387 Courtesy Nestle Beverage Company

p. 396 left: Thelma Shumsky/The Image Works; right: Mike Mazzaschi/Stock, Boston

p. 401 Courtesy Hitachi Home Electronics (America), Inc.

p. 413 Courtesy United States Postal Service

p. 422 Reprinted by permission of Reebok International, Ltd.

p. 434 top left: Chester Higgins, Jr./Photo Researchers; bottom left: Elizabeth Crews/The Image Works; right: © Topham-PA/The Image Works

p. 446 Peter Menzel/Stock, Boston

p. 448 Courtesy International Playtex, Inc.

p. 450 Courtesy Benetton Cosmetics

p. 469 Courtesy AT&T

p. 476 Courtesy Nike, Inc.

p. 477 Courtesy Toyota Motor Sales, U.S.A., Inc.

p. 481 Courtesy Playtex Jhirmack, Inc.

p. 485 Durrett Wagner/The Bookworks, Inc.

p. 509 Courtesy The Ad-Sert Group, Inc.

p. 510 Hubert Schreibel, Graphic Productions

p. 514 © Visa U.S.A. Inc. 1990. All rights reserved. Reproduced with the permission of Visa U.S.A. Inc.

p. 515 Army photographs courtesy U.S. Government, as represented by the Secretary of the Army

p. 516 Courtesy State Farm Insurance Companies

p. 523 Courtesy Colgate-Palmolive Company

p. 526 Elizabeth Crews/Stock, Boston

p. 527 top: Katherine McGlynn/The Image Works; bottom left: Katherine McGlynn/The Image Works; bottom right: S. Gazin/The Image Works

p. 556 left: Courtesy AkPharma Inc.; right: Courtesy Vassarette

p. 562 Courtesy Speed Queen, a Raytheon Company

p. 564 Courtesy Volvo Cars of North America

p. 566 Courtesy Johnson & Johnson

p. 579 Courtesy Ethan Allen Gallery

p. 584 Cathy Melloan, TSW/Click, Chicago, Ltd.

p. 589 top: Courtesy The Procter & Gamble Company; bottom: Robert Ferck, TSW/Click, Chicago, Ltd.

p. 593 Courtesy Cheesebrough-Pond's, Inc.

p. 609 Jeff Jacobson/Archive Pictures, Inc.

p. 615 Reprinted by permission of Bausch & Lomb. INTERPLAK is the registered trademark of Bausch & Lomb Oral Care Division. Copyright © Bausch & Lomb Oral Care Division, 1988

p. 617 Courtesy Metropolitan Life Insurance Co., N.Y. Snoopy: © 1958, United Feature Syndicate, Inc.

p. 625 Courtesy Toyota Motor Sales, U.S.A., Inc.

p. 628 Courtesy Parfums Stern Inc.

p. 633 Courtesy The Dow Chemical Company

p. 636 Jeffry Myers/Stock, Boston

p. 657 Courtesy Avis Rent A Car System, Inc.

p. 661 Lands' End, Inc. Reprinted courtesy of Lands' End, Inc.

p. 672 Courtesy 375 Spirits Company

p. 674 Courtesy Tyco

p. 685 Courtesy Kohler Co.

p. 687 Monika Franzen

p. 691 Courtesy Bob Evans Restaurants

p. 694 Ulrike Welsch/Photo Researchers

p. 708 Courtesy Mont Blanc

p. 727 Barbara Alper/Stock, Boston